RUSSIAN FOREIGN POLICY IN THE TWENTY-FIRST
CENTURY AND THE SHADOW OF THE PAST

RUSSIAN FOREIGN POLICY IN THE TWENTY-FIRST CENTURY AND THE SHADOW OF THE PAST

Edited by Robert Legvold

COLUMBIA UNIVERSITY PRESS   NEW YORK

COLUMBIA UNIVERSITY PRESS

Publishers Since 1893

NEW YORK   CHICHESTER, WEST SUSSEX

Library of Congress Cataloging-in-Publication Data

Russian foreign policy in the twenty-first century and the
shadow of the past / edited by Robert Legvold

p. cm.

Includes bibliographical references and index.

ISBN-13: 978-0-231-14122-2 (alk. paper)

ISBN-10: 0-231-14122-x

1. Russia (Federation)—Foreign relations.   2. Russia
(Federation)—Politics and government—1991.   3. Soviet
Union—Foreign relations.

DK510.764.R866 2007

327.47—dc22   2006033152

Columbia University Press books are printed on
permanent and durable acid-free paper.

This book is printed on paper with recycled content.

Printed in the United States of America

c 10 9 8 7 6 5 4 3 2 1

We dedicate this book to
Marshall D. Shulman
and the model he has been

CONTENTS

ACKNOWLEDGMENTS   IX

INTRODUCTION   3

1. Living in the Hood: Russia, Empire, and Old and New Neighbors
Ronald Grigor Suny   35

2. Russian Foreign Policy During Periods of Great State Transformation
Robert Legvold   77

3. Domestic Conjunctures, the Russian State, and
the World Outside, 1700–2006
David McDonald   145

4. How Persistent Are Persistent Factors?
Alfred J. Rieber   205

5. Russian Concepts of National Security
Lawrence T. Caldwell   279

6. Russia in Northeast Asia: In Search of a Strategy
Gilbert Rozman   343

7. Reluctant Europeans: Three Centuries of Russian Ambivalence
Toward the West
Angela Stent   393

8. Global Challenges and Russian Foreign Policy
Celeste A. Wallander   443

CONTRIBUTORS   499

INDEX   503

ACKNOWLEDGMENTS

THIS IS A LONG book, and so too its path to print. Hence, my first and greatest debt is to my co-authors who tolerated gracefully and with something approximating good cheer the importuning to do a second draft and then a third. Part of the blame for the misery I inflicted I pass to two anonymous outside readers whose conscientious, constructive, and highly informed criticisms of the manuscript pushed all of us to do better. Paul Schroeder, no stranger to the enterprise of melding history and the study of international relations, gave the manuscript a particularly thorough reading and then offered suggestions as blunt as they were intelligent. He did not read the introduction and so has not had a chance to rescue ideas of his own that I put to my particular use. My colleague at Columbia, Volker Berghahn, did read the introduction, and in his soft, gentle way made plain the shortcomings in my treatment—or, more accurately, missing treatment—of the debates among contemporary historians. I turned to him too late to take real advantage of his prodding, but it does explain my pleading at the beginning of the introduction's discussion of history and the study of foreign policy. Fritz Stern, too, read the introduction and chapter 2, and apart from pertinent specific suggestions offered assurance that history has not been too badly misused in them.

Then I want to thank those who aided at various stages in the book's preparation. First, Graeme Robertson, who drafted the excellent report from our initial authors' meeting at Belmont House. Second, two superb copy editors: Diane McCree, who did the most to shape the prose, and Eileen Chetti, who put the manuscript in final form for publication. Peter Dimock and Kabir Dandona were the editors who shepherded the book within the Columbia University Press. Anne McCoy and Debbie Masi oversaw the book's production. Frank Bohan, the Harriman Institute's financial manager, served as the overseer for the not-always-easy tracking and reporting of the project's finances. And Celeste Newbrough brought her highly-regarded professional services to the task of preparing the index.

There would have been no book and none of these people to thank, however, had it not been for the Carnegie Corporation of New York. Again, as so many times in the past, this foundation has made possible what we hope will be a useful and reasonably original contribution to an enhanced understanding of Russia. Within the Foundation Deana Arsenian was the moving spirit for the project.

Finally, and most importantly, all of us who have been part of this project owe a very large collective debt to someone whose career and example serves as the inspiration for our efforts. His unyielding determination to stand aloof from the passions generated by the ebb and flow of U.S.-Soviet relations, to bring to the Soviet subject a cool and constructive objectivity, and to offer to all who would listen the exhortation to make of Russia a complex, not a cardboard object stands as the model we, with whatever measure of success, have sought to emulate. For that reason we dedicate this book to Marshall Shulman.

RUSSIAN FOREIGN POLICY IN THE TWENTY-FIRST
CENTURY AND THE SHADOW OF THE PAST

INTRODUCTION
Robert Legvold

W HEN A NATION'S WHOLE being is undone, as Russia's has been over
the last two decades, conventional analysis alone cannot capture the
effect on Russian thinking and behavior, including the ache felt by its leaders
and elite when dealing with the world outside. Because the turbulence surrounding Russia's actions at home and abroad goes so much beyond the normal buffeting most countries endure, the straightforward questions usually
asked about a country's foreign policy attitudes, aims, and conduct come up
short. They imply an ordinariness that is not there, a settled inner core that
does not exist. They count on the prosaic choices that states make when im-
mersed in the everyday give-and-take of international politics, choices shaped
by outlooks taken for granted and in domestic settings more or less settled.
And they shy away from the slippery, shapeless issues of a country's emotional
state, or shaken identity, or, still more elusive, stage in its historical evolution.

Since the collapse of the Soviet Union, however, the standard frameworks
fail or, at a minimum, leave too much unconsidered, too much pressed into
narrow channels of thought. Like it or not, the slippery, shapeless issues in-
trude constantly and imperiously, urging larger and more remote perspectives from which to judge them. History is one of those, because it allows one
to stand back from the cluttered, confusing twists and turns of the moment
and pick out the more substantial, the more defining features of contemporary Russian foreign policy, features that link the past to the future—albeit
not in predetermined ways. History, when not a prism too crudely fashioned,
helps to separate the transitory from the enduring, to distinguish the
truly different from the unchanging, and to see policy's deeper substructure.
In any case, exploiting history for this purpose is what we try to do in this
book.

By any measure, Russian foreign policy during the decade and half of the country's independence has lurched through many different—often radically different—phases. Initially, although it now seems long ago, Boris Yeltsin and his foreign minister, Andrei Kozyrev, embraced the foreign policy revolution of Mikhail Gorbachev with its liberal internationalist thrust, even taking it several steps beyond. Where Gorbachev had raised universal values and the interdependence of states above class struggle and the notion of two social systems locked in mortal conflict, Yeltsin and Kozyrev turned their backs sharply and disdainfully on any trace of Marxist-Leninist theology. Where Gorbachev had sought to soften the East-West divide by speaking of a "Common European Home" and touting a new level of cooperation between the two superpowers, Yeltsin and his foreign minister declared a readiness to integrate Russia into the democratic West, sketching in those early years the image of a "democratic zone of trust, cooperation and security" spanning the Northern Hemisphere from "Vancouver to Vladivostok." Where Gorbachev spoke of "freedom of choice" as the path to the revitalization of socialism in Eastern Europe, Yeltsin and Kozyrev, as part of the Charter for American-Russian Friendship and Cooperation signed in June 1992, undertook to safeguard the "sovereignty and independence" of a new set of neighbors risen from the ruins of socialism. And, where Gorbachev signed a series of treaties constraining intermediate-range and strategic nuclear missiles and shrinking conventional forces in Central Europe in the name of increased international stability (and a reduced defense burden), Yeltsin and Kozyrev, at the outset, embraced dramatic cuts in nuclear arms and overall defense spending on the grounds that neither the United States nor NATO any longer posed a threat.

Scarcely two years later, however, talk of joining the West and of an indivisible security sphere uniting Eurasia and the Euro-Atlantic had begun to fade, and instead Yeltsin stressed Russia's "need to strike a balance in our foreign policy relations with the West and the East," as he would tell the Indian Parliament in January 1993. The April 1993 "foreign policy concept" placed the accent on Russia as "a great power," on the need to protect the sovereignty and unity of the state and the rights of Russians in countries where they were now a minority, and on the importance of promoting the integration of the Commonwealth of Independent States (CIS). At about the same time, Kozyrev and the Russian president began stressing Russia's responsibility as the chief enforcer of stability in the post-Soviet space and exhorting the United Nations to say so. By 1994 their dyspeptic reaction to NATO's planned enlargement into

Central Europe signaled a further drift from the amiable expectations of the initial years.

Yeltsin and his increasingly besieged foreign minister had no intention of turning against the United States or the Europeans, and, indeed, during the years 1993–1996 they continued to emphasize the constructive side of their mutual relations—the common interest they had in controlling the proliferation of weapons of mass destruction; in managing regional conflicts; in stemming the flow of drugs, arms, and human trafficking; in fighting terrorism; and, above all, in mobilizing the West's economic resources to speed Russia's economic transformation. But Russian policy had lost the simple positive dynamism inherited from the Gorbachev years. More and more it was taking on a mixed character, with dark and agitated swipes at U.S. policy and fewer moments of camaraderie and common cause.

By 1999, a mere seven years after the collapse of the Soviet Union and the early roseate hopes of Russian leaders, policy had hardened into a harsh and bitter skepticism over Russia's relations with the West and particularly with the United States. Much of this was driven to a near frenzy by the 1999 war over Kosovo, but relations had been sliding downward or, at best, had been unsteady since 1997, when a reluctant Russia, pretty much without alternatives, signed the Final Act, accepting Poland's, the Czech Republic's, and Hungary's entry into NATO in return for a makeshift arrangement intended to imply Moscow's own special relationship with NATO. The Russians never took the Permanent Joint Council, the institutional face of the arrangement, seriously, and, during the war in Kosovo, cut off all contact with it.

During these years, Yeltsin and by now his new foreign minister, Yevgeny Primakov, stopped short of a wholesale rift with the United States and its European allies. The dialogue continued, but in a dilatory, half-hearted fashion. Little progress was achieved on the issues roiling U.S.-Russian relations. Moscow did next to nothing to ease the Clinton administration's concern over the Russian-sponsored nuclear project at Bushehr in Iran (in sharp contrast with its swift retreat on the sale of cryogenic technology to India, when in the early 1990s the Americans objected). For lack of initiative, it left the sputtering negotiations over national missile defense, a modification of the conventional forces in Europe agreement, and other arms control measures to languish. Talk of partnership with the United States disappeared, and in its place Yeltsin and especially Primakov railed against the idea of a unipolar world and the notion that any nation, no matter how powerful, should have a special say in international affairs. With the Chinese and the Indians, they took every occasion to praise the virtues of multipolarity and pledge their determination to bring it about.

It was not that Russia enjoyed the option of an anti-U.S. alliance with China or, even had Beijing been willing, that its leaders would have wished one. Despite their similar outlook on international trends and parallel policies on a host of issues, neither Russia nor China could afford to rupture its ties with the United States. Yet, the fact that Yeltsin's Russia now shared more common views and harmonized more policies with China than with the United States and its Western partners spoke volumes about how much Russian policy had changed since 1992. Russia was not choosing China over the West, but Yeltsin and many of those around him were cutting free of any commitment to make their country a part of the Western democratic camp. The effects were twofold: First, on the larger issues in the direct bilateral relationship with the United States, Russia simply disengaged. True, the Clinton administration, distracted by its own internal woes and thrown into doubt over Russia's future course following the August 1998 financial and governmental crisis, did the same.

Second, closer to home, where the U.S.-Russian interaction was more indirect, the Russians grew more agitated over the U.S. and NATO role within the post-Soviet space. A sense of strategic rivalry, incipient in the middle years 1993–1996, now flared, as Russia's leadership and political elite treated every Western initiative, from NATO "partnership for peace" exercises in the region to the development of ties with states such as Georgia, Azerbaijan, and Uzbekistan, as aimed at rolling back Russian influence or driving Russia into a corner. This too stood in sharp contrast to the early years, when Yeltsin and Kozyrev cared far more about relations with the Western democracies than with their struggling new neighbors, and even seemed to invite a larger Western role in helping to douse the flames of violent conflict erupting from Moldova to Tajikistan.

Such was the situation when the unknown Vladimir Putin arrived as Yeltsin's successor in fall 1999. Initially little changed. If anything, Putin added to the inertia of the U.S.-Russian relationship by conspicuously dismissing a now lame-duck U.S. president. On the other fronts, he invigorated Russian policy in the post-Soviet space, actively courting those states most suspicious of his country and most open to Western blandishments. And he pushed forward relations with China, arranging in summer 2001 a new Treaty of Goodneighborliness, Friendship, and Cooperation; he also reached out to North Korea, a regime Yeltsin had earlier shunned when wooing its southern neighbor.

At a deeper level, however, during this period Putin's approach to foreign policy betrayed a lack of both clear priorities and conceptual depth. Even as he raced about the world, traveling from Seoul to Havana, twenty-nine trips to more than twenty countries in fifteen months, and brought greater coherence to policy at the tactical level, substituting economic for cruder military instruments, his assumptions about the world Russia faced seemed muddled. He appeared torn between, on the one hand, adjusting policy to deal with a world dominated by economic globalism, a phenomenon punishing those who could not keep pace, and, on the other, a lingering uneasiness over how much of the old world endured, one dominated by traditional security threats, where an expanding NATO, U.S. nuclear ambitions, and the maneuvering of Euro-Atlantic allies in regions such as the Balkans still mattered. He, it seemed, incorporated in his own person the debate bubbling within the Russian foreign policy elite over the need to get beyond past habits of thought and to get on with addressing the challenges of globalization or instead somehow to secure a weakened Russia against familiar threats that refused to go away.

Then suddenly on September 11 all this changed. Scarcely had the rolling tidal wave of debris from the collapsed World Trade towers settled, then Putin, who in foreign policy as in politics at home had labored to be all things to all people, sharply and emphatically rallied to the American cause. For the next year his identification with the Bush administration's fury implied far more than a handy way to appeal to the Americans or to vindicate his own prior warnings about the dangers of "global terrorism" (linked in no small way to his new war in Chechnya). At last he seemed to have made a fundamental strategic choice. At last he seemed to be aligning his country with the United States, indisputably the key actor, if the struggle against terrorism was to be the first priority.

More than concern over terrorism, however, guided Putin's dramatic embrace of U.S. policy—or so it seemed. When, contrary to the natural instincts of his own entourage, he blessed the deployment of U.S. forces to Central Asia as part of the war effort in Afghanistan, he appeared to be saying that other things mattered more than checkmating the arrival of U.S. military power in this or that part of the world, even one close to Russia's border. Indeed, over the next nine months, he meekly yielded when the Bush administration backed out of the ABM treaty, notwithstanding the considerable huffing and puffing of a year earlier. In May 2002 he treated as a minor triumph the signing of a strategic arms treaty that did little more than codify the decline of Russia's nuclear forces and sanction U.S. modernization plans. And a few weeks later in

Rome he joined NATO members in celebrating the creation of a new NATO-Russia Council, viewed as a fresh start in place of the discredited Permanent Joint Council (PJC).

Four months earlier, in a *Wall Street Journal* interview, he also began stressing Russia's potential role as a reliable energy partner of the West.[1] The new theme fit with Russia's mounting interest in more serious negotiations over entry into the World Trade Organization, its readiness to engage the European Union as an essential bridge to European-Russian economic cooperation, and its emphasis on building relations within the post-Soviet space around economic interests and the use of its sizable economic leverage. By all indications, Putin's earlier ambivalence appeared to have ended. It looked as though he had decided that economic imperatives would take precedence over traditional security concerns. From this followed a logical sequence: If accelerating the modernization of the Russian economy trumped all other issues, then easing Russia into the flow of the global economy became the first order of business, which meant joining the World Trade Organization, creating a partnership with the European Union, and enhancing Russia's standing in the Group of Eight. And this, in turn, required the blessing of the industrial democracies, at the head of which stood the United States.

Perhaps Putin had come to see things more clearly after the drama of September 2001; perhaps he had made up his mind to put the U.S.-Russian relationship on a different footing, not least because this would aid a Russian agenda attuned to the world of globalization. But, if so, it was a fair-weather choice. Because he had neither developed a strategy by which to give substance to his strategic choice and to overcome skeptics at home, a good number of whom were in his own immediate circle, nor prepared himself for moments when the seas grew rough, as they would by early 2003 when the United States marched toward war in Iraq, any clarifying thrust that Putin had given to Russian foreign policy dissolved by the end of his first term in office.

Again the pendulum swung in the other direction, or, since the path traced by Russian policy more resembled a gyroscope, it settled in a position not seen before. The Russians continued to emphasize the economic dimension of foreign policy, but no longer with deference to the Europeans or Americans. Putin and his colleagues wanted Russia in the World Trade Organization; wanted progress on what came to be known as the "four common spaces" supposedly uniting Russia with the European Union; and certainly wanted the imprimatur attending the chairmanship of the 2006 Group of Eight summit. They, however, no longer felt a need to concede anything beyond what they wished to get these things. They, notably Putin himself, no longer trusted that U.S. actions to which Russia objected could be sidestepped, while focusing on the U.S. role in facilitating Russia's entry into the global economic arena or, for that matter, on their two governments' partnership against "global terrorism." And no longer was Putin ready to look the other way when it came to uncongenial developments in the post-Soviet space and the West's perceived role in them, a change vividly evident in his enraged reaction to the color revolutions in Georgia (2003) and Ukraine (2004).

Three powerful trends had converged to produce the new state of affairs: disaffection over the Bush administration's foreign policy, the course of events within Russia, and high oil prices. The damage done by the discord over U.S. policy did not stem from the Bush administration's policies toward Russia—at least not until well into 2006—but rather its handling of the nuclear truants— Iraq, Iran, and North Korea. In Moscow's eyes the Iraq war was reckless, the Iran policy, counterproductive and dangerous, and the treatment of North Korea, rigid and obstructionist. Layer was added on layer, persuading the Russians to keep their distance from the United States, and, when necessary, to oppose it.

Second, trends within Russia did their part. As the Putin leadership tightened its grip over political institutions, independent voices, and the public discourse, Western governments sounded off. As they did, Putin and those around him stiffened, offended by the criticism, determined to follow their own course, and, alas, readier than before to treat Europe and the United States as an alien model. The effect on Russian foreign policy, however, would have been less had it not been for the upheaval in Ukraine during the 2004 presidential election. What Washington, Brussels, and Warsaw saw as popular outrage over a manipulated vote, Moscow viewed as the result of Western meddling. Coming a year after a similar uprising produced Georgia's Rose Revolution, which, too, was seen as the work of Western nongovernmental organizations and intelligence agencies, the Ukrainian events not only underscored the deep rift between Russia's and the West's definition of legitimate democratic change, but also dripped poison into the relationship by convincing Putin's conspiracy-minded advisers that very influential players in the West were bent on using democratic chicanery to undo Russian influence in neighboring countries, and perhaps weaken Russia itself.

Third, between 2004 and 2006, oil prices went from $35 per barrel to $72 per barrel, a steep ascent that filled Russian coffers, freeing it from any need of the

International Monetary Fund, World Bank, or European Bank for Reconstruction and Development and dramatically easing the burden of debt repayment. Equally significant, the new uncertainties agitating global energy markets drove home Russia's importance as the major alternative source of oil and gas to that from a turbulent Middle East. This notable shift in fortunes, more than anything, corrected the great deficit in prior Russian foreign policy: a lack of self-confidence. By 2005, shortly into Putin's second term in office, the Russians developed a distinctly more assertive approach to the outside world. With the Europeans they relished the attention a new preoccupation with "energy security" gave them; with immediate neighbors, such as Ukraine, Moldova, and Georgia, they put their energy prowess to ungentle use; and with the Chinese and Japanese they were not slow to recognize how energy wealth had transformed their country from a weak and disregarded bystander in East Asia into a player that mattered.

Energy as a source of power and standing filled a void and gave the Putin leadership the confidence that Russia was no longer a "taker" in international politics. It did not, however, lessen their insecurities—their nervous sense that politics in neighboring countries could easily go awry, turning them against Russia, and, worse, infecting politics in Russia, complicating their efforts to carefully manage the 2008 political succession. Nor did it diminish their tendency to see the West's criticism of their heavy-handed use of the energy instrument as disingenuous, a shroud for the Western leaders' real unwillingness to accept a self-assured Russia once more attentive to its national interests and insisting on being taken seriously.

Thus, in scarcely more than a decade, Russian foreign policy had gone from the naively optimistic expectation that Russia's future lay with the West, a comfortable refuge while the country built democracy and a market economy in a world increasingly shaped by Wilsonian values, to a hard-bitten, touchy, power-seeking enterprise, at arm's length from the United States and Europe, committed to rebuilding the country's military power, determined to maximize Russian influence in the post-Soviet space, an arena regarded as Russia's natural sphere of influence, and driven by a Hobbesian view of the world. Along the way, it had passed through a series of unsettled, tumultuous stages, each marked by powerful, often contrasting undercurrents. Each reflected deep uncertainties about Russia's place in the world. Each left Russia wavering among the challenges that it thought most important to address. Swings of this magnitude and velocity are not a normal feature of a country's foreign policy, and they cannot easily be understood by operating only within normal analytical frameworks. Maybe history can help.

History and the Study of Russian Foreign Policy[2]

One need not go as far as Jules Michelet's admonition—"those who confine themselves to present times will not understand present reality"—to justify consulting history for aid in assessing contemporary affairs. Still, because, as E. H. Carr put it, "there is a two-way traffic between past and present, the present being molded out of the past, yet constantly recreating the past," history does offer insights missed when events of the moment are left to stand by themselves.[3] The helping hand comes from the patterns present over time. Understand the factors producing these patterns and three prospects open up. First, the deeper forces, impulses, and constraints operating on a country's foreign policy emerge more clearly. Second, sturdier criteria for distinguishing the enduring from the ephemeral offer themselves. Third, and most important, understanding when and whether these factors have lost their grip provides the most profound basis for judging how fundamentally different a country's foreign policy will henceforth be.

History possesses no capacity to predict the future, and nothing says that characteristics or behavior often repeated in the past must continue today or tomorrow. Indeed, a critical school of historiography argues that history's real meaning derives from "the multiplicity of individual manifestations at different ages and in different cultures. All of them are unique and equally significant strands in the tapestry of history: All of them, in Ranke's famous phrase, are 'immediate to God,'" and to pretend that they form part of a "universal structure, whether deterministic or teleological," is to profane or, at least, to suborn the enterprise.[4] Not that the historian's craft any longer fully embraces nineteenth-century "historicism's" passion for, as Johann Gottfried von Herder urged, "feeling" oneself into the historical moment in order to do justice to the "infinite variety of historical forms."[5] Yet, without accepting either the historicist's naive desire to study things only as they were or the "interpretivist's" determination to construct reality only by viewing it through the subject's eyes, many contemporary historians are still in pursuit of what Paul Schroeder calls the "pure particular"—still striving to understand events "by thinking one's way into them and seeing them from inside through a process of empathetic understanding."[6] For them the regularities and neat patterns that stir the political scientist's curiosity and fire his ambitions are, if not a chimera, then often a warping of reality.

This does not mean that history for them is inaccessible to theory or too concrete and distinctive to tolerate abstraction. As Carr wrote in *What Is History?* "The world of the historian, like the world of the scientist, is not a photographic copy of the real world, but rather a working model which enables him more or less effectively to understand it and to master it."[7] But it does mean that the world of the historian is only *like* the world of the scientist, not in fact his world. Other historians, it is true, would disagree, arguing, as they have since Henry Thomas Buckle, that the study of history is or should be as scientific an enterprise as the study of natural phenomena. He and they insist not only that history contains the same regularities as nature but also that these are "caused" in law-like fashion, a process that in turn can be unearthed by bringing to bear the methods of science, including careful statistical analysis.[8]

Deciding just how scientific historical scholarship can be or just how objective (the sister concern that has stirred even more passion) is not, however, a task we have given ourselves in this book. Rather, we care not so much about reconstructing as about using history. Our stake is less in history as such than in the light history may shed on the course of contemporary Russian foreign policy. Hence, if self-conscious reflection is in order at the outset, what matters is not the intrahistorical debate as much as the interhistorical–social science dialogue.

Here, however, the tendency to create false contrasts frequently obscures the conversation. Wrongly it is assumed that historiography privileges the unique, while political science (or sociology) cares only about the general; that history goes about its business by telling stories, while political science does so by discovering "causal mechanisms"; that the study of history is of necessity unsystematic because its subject is sprawling and conditioned by many influences, while political science chooses to study things that can be cut, shaped, and compressed into a like, but narrow universe; and that a "historical work seems to resemble a literary work much more than a scientific treatise," while the product of the only discipline that, perhaps partially out of insecurity, has the word "science" in its name must aspire to something more.[9]

In fact, the historian feels as compelled as the political scientist, in Carr's phrase, "to simplify the multiplicity of his answers, to subordinate one answer to another, and to introduce some order and unity into the chaos of happenings and the chaos of specific causes."[10] Or, to go a step further, "Even histories that are narrative-descriptive in form . . . are clearly nomothetic in the sense that they develop hypotheses, assign particular causes for events and developments, and establish general patterns."[11] Too much can be made of the notion that historiography "aims to understand the unique and the nonrecurrent," leaving the establishment "of abstract general laws for indefinitely repeatable processes" to the sciences.[12] This misses the more essential ways in which historical insight differs from formal, theoretically driven accounts, differences that are directly relevant to what the reader will find in the chapters that follow.

First, much of contemporary political science, like economics, from which it increasingly draws, thrives on attacking a specific puzzle (Why do some democracies redistribute income more than others? When and why do political elites at times block economic development? Why is international cooperation possible when pervasive uncertainty should induce states to avoid meaningful commitments?); privileges deductive theory; and requires that the canons of the scientific method be honored, including the falsifiability of explicit hypotheses.[13] Historians, too, attack puzzles, but they are often large and ungainly: Why did the Chinese revolution of 1912 occur? When and why did the nineteenth-century Concert of Europe expire? Why did the Enlightenment arise in Europe and why in the eighteenth century? Even more often, however, historians are interested in exploring the nature of an era, the impact of a leader or a set of key actors, the interaction among diverse social, cultural, and political phenomena, or an extended chain of events. In this case, not one, but many "why" questions need answers. In either case, carefully specified hypotheses, each with a limited number of candidate "causes" or influences, and all capable of being isolated and measured or "tested" statistically, leaving a trail others can duplicate, would be either too unwieldy or hopelessly undoable.[14]

Second, while the study of history, lest it be the artist's fiction, must be empirical, and, therefore, "founded on evidence, bounded by it, and challengeable and corrigible on the basis of it," political science at some stage need not be.[15] It can be purely theoretical, far more attentive to the mathematically verifiable consistency of an argument's internal logic than to its fit with any given real-world instance. Partially this explains why political scientists often begin with theory—usually deductive theory—and then locate their cases in point, preferably "useful" cases, while historians come to theory, maybe even subconsciously, only after their worldly inquiry requires it. Partially it also explains why political scientists invest a good deal in "testing alternative theories, whereas diplomatic historians often amass evidence in support of a specific thesis,"[16] and why political scientists sort through and tighten theory in order to reduce the number of causal influences until a primary cause is found, while historians tolerate theory only to the degree that it does not do an injustice to the multicausal explanations they see as corresponding to reality.

Third, in the contrast between "storytelling" (recounting how it might have happened) and discovering "causal mechanisms" (demonstrating how it did happen), historians by nature settle for the former, while political scientists, although much of what they do remains storytelling, would like to think they can achieve the latter—at least a growing portion of them does.[17] Historical narrative, of course, is in essence storytelling, and it bears a quality that goes to the heart of the difference between the disciplines. To be convincing, a historical account not only must enfold enough of the factors at work to capture the complexity of events—and they usually are plural—but also must start far enough back to encompass the course of events. Historical explanations therefore tend to be, as Paul Schroeder says, "synoptic," that is, characterized by comprehensiveness and breadth. Political science explanations tend to be more selectively focused, prizing rigor over richness.

The chapters in this book, including those written by political scientists, are distinctly on the historian's side of these differences. The authors may in varying degree be theoretically informed, but none, with the exception of Ronald Suny, a historian among us, is theoretically explicit. None pretends to have exposed the inner workings of the mechanisms causing Putin's Russia to behave as it does. None organizes her or his chapter around a hierarchically ordered set of hypotheses that are then systematically tested. And none joined the enterprise in hopes of using Russian foreign policy and its historical antecedents to vindicate or discredit a theory or set of theories, or to fashion a brand new theory.

They, however, including the historians, do have something more in common with political scientists than with a venerable bias that has long marked an important segment of the history profession. They believe that history can enlarge perspectives on the present and therefore that its insights should be mobilized to this effect. On this historians have long been divided. One school, represented by scholars such as Arthur O. Lovejoy and Herbert Butterfield, rejects the notion that "the function of history is to solve 'problems of our present'" and believes that one's interest in the past should be "for its own sake";[18] that the stake in history is intrinsic, not pragmatic. Others believe that the "notion that historical inquiry simply reinstates the events that once happened 'as they actually happened' is incredibly naïve."[19] True, for John Dewey this led to a related proposition but one separate from the idea that history should be used to illuminate or instruct the present. Instead Dewey argued that the present instructs history or, more precisely, "that the conceptual material employed in writing history is that of the period in which a history is written."[20] He meant that the ideas and conceptions prevalent at any given moment are the only basis on which we are capable of fashioning explanations and selecting evidence for judging the past. Since history cannot be written *in toto* and "lived over again," we choose a facet that interests us, and in the process "an act of judgment has loosened it from the total complex of which it was a part, and has given it a place in a new context, the context and the place both being determinations made in inquiry, not native properties of original existence."

My co-authors in this book would not, I think, disagree with Dewey or with his ultimate claim that "in using what has come to them as an inheritance from the past, ["men"] are compelled to modify it to meet their own needs, and this process creates a new present in which the process continues. History cannot escape its own process."[21] But they are going further; they are, by the nature of their work, saying that history has explanatory power, that any existential reality has a biography, that it is a momentary sum in the course, cycle, or story of change, and that by retrieving salient parts from this biography, reality reveals itself more fully. They would not for a moment deny that theoretical generalizations, assembled from similar and self-contained phenomena without regard to time and place, can offer insights—indeed, more disciplined insights—into the same reality. They do not so much see the two as alternative paths to understanding, with one capable of being judged better than the other. Rather they are, in their minds, separate and independent paths, serving different analytical and practical purposes. Granted each approach has things to teach the other, but, in the end, they reflect a basically different sense of what is knowable and how to know it.

PATTERNS

Precisely what, however, can usefully be taken from history? What in the historian's enterprise helps to shed light on current events? If history has utility in coping with contemporary realities, it is less in uncovering their causes or predicting their future than in putting them in perspective. History in this sense offers not a law-like account of why something is happening as it is, drawn from a wider universe of similar happenings, but a tailored tracing of the path traveled to get here. When the processes and people that intervened along the way are revisited, outcomes acquire a broader context and, in the process, more nuanced meaning. Take a fatal automobile accident caused by a driver who failed to yield at a red traffic light. Maybe the direct cause was alcohol, or slow reflexes, or the distraction of a cell phone conversation, but the full significance of the tragedy emerges from circumstances that put a drunk behind the wheel, or the age and health factors that slowed the reflexes, or the earlier emotional contretemps that occasioned the distracting call.[22] One knows more about the event and can judge it better, perhaps even respond more effectively, even if the immediate causes remain as before.

In this book, however, not historical reconstruction, but another use of history occupies the authors. They are interested in patterns, that is, ideas, behaviors, and effects that repeat themselves or, as they evolve, that retain a core embodying their antecedents. Unlike the patterns for which social scientists look across space and time, here the patterns are only over time, but patterns they are. Our assumption is that, if aspects of contemporary Russian foreign policy conform to patterns evident in the past, we will know more about them—more about their origins, their strength, their durability, and their inter-relationships. Patterns teach us about the deeper underpinnings of Russia's response to its international environment, about the biases, aspirations, and fears that endure over time, and about the influences that cannot be easily reduced or escaped. They also create benchmarks for distinguishing continuity from discontinuity and provide a basis for identifying what in contemporary Russian foreign policy is fundamentally new.

Hunting for patterns of this sort is not a new enterprise. Nearly any historical text does it, and a lot of current analysis does as well. But systematic efforts whose whole purpose resides in locating these patterns are fewer and farther between. One of the more noteworthy examples appeared long ago, in the early 1960s, when Russia was Soviet, and the task was to decide how much of the imperial past survived in the actions, if not the mind-set, of the tsars' communist successors.[23] In that book Cyril Black contributed an essay called "The Pattern of Russian Objectives."

First, however, he started with a fundamental proposition about Russia's place in the world that has even more dramatic significance today. Russia, he said, "within a period of three centuries" has moved "from the periphery to the center of international affairs."[24] So, one asks, is the most primal fact about the international circumstance of contemporary Russia that for the first time in four centuries the country has been moving in the other direction? If so, the patterns of the past are subject to a very different momentum, with important implications—perhaps altering or even ending them, or, on the contrary, intensifying them. True, given the uncertain shape of the international order a decade or two from now, coupled with Russia's uncertain evolution between now and then, the country could conceivably re-emerge in a more pivotal role as part of a changing constellation of great powers. Or, short of that, it is still more likely that Russian leaders for the foreseeable future will cling to this prospect, acting on it rather than the other more painful reality. Either way, these overarching uncertainties do nothing to diminish the value of learning as much as one can from past patterns.

Black pointed to four. First, ahead of all other impulses, through the centuries Russian foreign policy has been shaped by the struggle to stabilize the empire's borders. Because geography for the most part was of little assistance, this meant dueling with more powerful neighbors to the west and south, usually in contests that came down to a test of arms. Where the space to the east was relatively empty, Russia had preemptively imposed its political control. Weak or strong, the aggrieved or the aggressor, Russia, decade after decade, had fought, probed, retreated, and ultimately expanded all along its frontiers in a great sweep from the Baltic, through Eastern Europe, to the Caucasus, across Central Asia, and into the Far East. Throughout, the ebb and flow created a defining dynamic: Russia's insecurity led to the insecurity of its neighbors; Russia's effort to defend against European powers, perennially perceived as a potential threat, or against the memory of past depredations left its neighbors constantly on guard and quick to unite against Russia; and Russia's conquest, loss, and regathering of territory along its periphery drew it ever more deeply into the quarrels of a European-dominated international system.

Second, through the ages, Russia's way of linking its economic fortunes and national security has echoed in foreign policy, often complicating its relations with neighbors and other major powers. Black argued that economic growth built on commerce impelled the Russians, from Muscovy forward, to master the Baltic Sea region, to guarantee egress from the Black Sea, and to harvest from widening spaces first furs and later mineral resources. Whether it was the struggle to block rivals in the Baltic after 1721, or the enduring contest with the Ottoman Empire and other outside powers from 1774 on over its newly won commercial rights to the outlets to the Mediterranean, or its broadening quests in Central Asia and to the Far East, Russia's imperious solutions dictated the reception it received in the wider world.

Third, tracing back to Ivan III in the fifteenth century, Russians have coveted what they regard as the natural writ of Russia—territories at some point under its sway or simply the home of fellow Slavs. From the original fourteenth- and fifteenth-century forced melding of the scattered principalities under the rule of the prince of Moscow, through the incorporation of Polotsk, Chernigov, Kyiv, and Smolensk, the eighteenth-century partition of Poland, and the nineteenth-century ventures on behalf of Orthodox Slavs, to Stalin's postwar aggrandizement, Russians have treated their advance not as expansion but as unification, the unification or "gathering" of Russian lands. Seen from this perspective, the results of World War II meant that "for the first time since the thirteenth century all of the eastern Slavs were united under one government."[25] The impulse, deeply ingrained over four centuries of imperial exertion, constitutes the pattern most in need of revision—and almost certainly the one Russians have had the most difficulty revising.

Black's fourth pattern focused on Russia's approach to international relations; its view of alliances; its attitude toward the international order of the day; and its use of international institutions and regimes. Rarely, he argued, has Russia sought long-term alliances with other major powers, the nineteenth-century collaboration with the Habsburgs and Hohenzollerns and the twentieth-century Sino-Soviet partnership (which he mistakenly included when writing in 1960) being the exceptions. Historically it has settled for short-term marriages of convenience, either as an expedient in wartime or for momentary relief from isolation in peacetime. For the most part, over the longest periods of time, including much of the eighteenth and all of the nineteenth centuries, it has backed the international status quo as a bulwark against disruptive change, such as the threat to conservative monarchy posed by revolutionary France. And, despite the Soviet defection, it has generally embraced international institutions, including international law, particularly the maritime rights of neutrals.

Others see the patterns differently. John LeDonne, for example, peels away the layers of historical detail to get at what he believes is the deep, underlying pattern at the root of imperial Russian foreign policy (1700–1917). Borrowing from Halford Mackinder and Alfred Mahan, he argues that Russian behavior over four hundred years reflected, without deviation, the drive of a "core area" to expand to the edges of the Eurasian "Heartland." Mackinder's heartland extended from the Elbe River to beyond Lake Baikal. It was bounded by other core areas (the Swedish, Polish, Hapsburg, Ottoman, and Persian empires and China) and the great "coastlands" (Great Britain and Japan). Russia pressed to these outer edges and against the other core powers, not according to any preconceived plan of its rulers, but as the natural "product of an accumulation of energy seeking release after the completion of a preliminary stage of 'state' building."[26] The story of Russian foreign policy over the centuries, LeDonne believes, is the outward thrust of Russia, which brought it into continual conflict with the other core areas, each straining to gain the upper hand in the heartland's "frontier" zones.

Following the Time of Troubles in the sixteenth century, Russia gathered strength as rival centers of power—Sweden, Poland, Turkey, and Persia—began their decline. LeDonne sees this as the reason Russia was able to advance steadily toward the full occupation of the heartland, then only to be checked by the Germanic powers in the west and the British "coastland" to the south, creating a permanent frustration that the empire's natural contours remained incomplete. Throughout, however, Russian behavior had a settled and solid core: Russia regularly sought the "destabilization of the frontier by exploiting local opposition," regularly worked to incorporate the elites in the contested "zones" into "an Imperial ruling elite," and regularly strove to weaken the other core areas from within. He finishes, not surprisingly, by asking "whether today's Russia, reduced to its 1650 borders in much of the three frontiers, will not seek once again to restore in the Heartland a hegemony to which it had become accustomed in the heyday of Imperial and Soviet Russia."[27]

Nothing, of course, says that everyone examining the history of Russian foreign policy will detect the same shapes and patterns. Thus, it is impressive how much overlap there is in the judgments of the authors in this book. Even where their views diverge, as in some important respects they do, it is less over premises than over the significance attached to them. Although they approach their various topics from different angles, the building blocks are often made of the same material, and their working assumptions represent variations on a common theme. But before turning to the patterns they feature, a word should be said about those they do not.

The reader will not find in the following chapters an argument on behalf of the patterns long commonplace in popular thinking about Russia. None of the contributors defends the notion that Russia century after century sought to commandeer the warm-water ports nature had denied it. Nor do any lend credence to the simple syllogism linking expansionism to autocracy by way of the vulnerability of a regime standing over, rather than arising from, the people, a vulnerability eased by deflecting attention to the ardors and rewards of conquest abroad. Nor is there support in this book for the notion that a messianic mission radiates throughout all of Russian foreign policy, from the sixteenth-century idea of Russia as "the Third Rome" to the Pan-Slavism of the nineteenth century to the Marxist-Leninist slogan of world revolution.

These my co-authors would regard as myths rather than identifiable patterns. But like most myths, they have, beyond their utility for those who hold them, a basis in reality. They simply misappropriate features that have been a prominent part of Russia's encounter with the outside world. If Russia has not persistently plotted a path to the seizure of warm-water ports, its stake in the Baltic region, its need to export grain from its southern regions, and its security requirements as its borders were pushed deeper into the Far East have made the fate of waterways intimately a part of a complex nexus of influences shaping Russia's relations with the European powers, the Ottoman Empire, and Japan. Similarly, while autocracy did not necessarily dictate imperialism, it can be fairly argued that imperialism—that is, the burden of managing an increasingly multiethnic, multiconfessional empire—did sanctify autocracy in the eyes of Russia's power holders. And, while, with the exception of the Bolsheviks' pretensions, the impulse to remake the world for some higher purpose has not been at the heart of Russian foreign policy, a sometimes arrogant, sometimes injured sense of exceptionalism regularly has been. When it surfaces, as it has in sputtering fashion in Putin's Russia, it either adds to Russia's remoteness or contributes to its arrogated claims to a status apart.

Historical patterns marking the long haul of Russian foreign policy, however, need to be explained. Most of the book's authors try to do that. For, while identifying the patterns and describing their consequences give the greatest insight into what is new and not so new in contemporary Russian policy, tracing their roots provides the only basis for determining when and to what degree a pattern can be expected to lose its hold. The roots traced in the chapters that follow weave together a series of themes: the powerful but often perverse impact of absolutism, the impulse and burden of shapeless borders, the effect of perennial economic backwardness, the consequences of empire in lieu of more modern national forms, and the allied and ultimately most poignant influence, Russia's permanent and sometimes agonizing quest for identity.

Alfred Rieber's chapter (chapter 4) deals most directly with what he calls the "persistent factors" shaping Russian foreign policy. He chooses to call them persistent, rather than permanent, precisely because, in his view, they are not immutable, not always of the same force or with the same effect, and they are very much subject to an evolving international setting as well as to the procession of Russian leaders. If the four factors he singles out have something in common, it is that they constitute vulnerabilities, but paradoxically with opportunities built into them. As one Russia after another, one Russian leadership after another, has defended against the first and seized the second, it has often weakened Russia by strengthening it—or, more precisely, by the way it has gone about strengthening it. The reason, Rieber says, is that the four persistent factors are often antinomies, that is, solutions selected to deal with one problem often worsen another. Viewed from this perspective, the historic question is whether contemporary Russia can transcend these factors, can resist the pressures to resolve problems in ways that heighten the country's vulnerabilities, and can free itself from challenges eased only by raising others.

Like Cyril Black, Rieber stresses the role that Russia's soft, mobile frontier has played in forming Russian foreign policy over time. However, where Le-Donne treats geography as destiny, creating a single primal urge for Russia to expand to the outer limits of the heartland, Rieber sees it as a curse. Fate gave to Russia "ill-defined, unstable, underpopulated" borders contested in every century by powerful rivals. Neither conquest nor colonization relieved the problem. The more Russia pushed its strategic perimeter outward, the more it encountered still stronger competitors deployed along an ever-longer border. Ultimately, as Gilbert Rozman notes in his chapter (chapter 6), Russia's nineteenth-century expansion into the Far East added to the country's vulnerability by leaving it with "isolated outposts distant from [the] main population and production centers" and within the reach of "culturally distinct" peoples, soon themselves the victim of Europe's encroaching powers. Ronald Suny (chapter 1) regards the "lack of clearly defined borders" as one of several factors endowing Russian foreign policy with a permanent sense of "weakness and insecurity." Indeed, argues Rieber, conquest and colonization simply brought under Russian sway larger numbers of ethnically and religiously separate communities, borderlands that formed the "shatter zone" of empire.

David McDonald (chapter 3) and Lawrence Caldwell (chapter 5) do not quarrel with the notion that geography has dealt Russia a difficult hand, but, in their view, the burden is neither unmitigated nor beyond mastery. McDonald makes the point that in war Russia has been helped, often decisively, by "General Winter"; that historically the encirclement it feared did not compare with the encirclement Germany faced; and that at key junctures, such as for much of the nineteenth century, Russia benefited from relatively pacific relations with major European powers and from powers in decline on its other borders.

Caldwell argues that, for the most part, Russian leaders have eased Russia's physical disadvantages by maintaining an acute sense of "strategic distance." He means that they have thought about their surroundings as a set of concentric circles and have normally saved their deepest entanglements for regions nearest their strengths. They get into trouble when this sense fails them, as he maintains it did with the gambits under Nicholas II leading to the Russo-Japanese War and, again, under Nikita Khrushchev, when the Soviet Union went adventuring far afield in Africa and the Middle East.

For Rieber, however, "porous frontiers" have produced patterned behavior that is more constant and more concrete. From the start four centuries ago, Russia's most instinctive response has been to seal its borders, whether exemplified by the tyrannical blessing required of Ivan IV for even the most privileged to travel abroad, or Nicholas I's suffocating regulations governing foreign education and travel, or the Soviets' attempts to build a hermetic barrier against alien goods, ideas, and radio waves, no less. But so has the response been more fundamentally aggressive. From Ivan's efforts to absorb Livonia as his "ancestral land" in the sixteenth century to Brezhnev's war in Afghanistan in 1979, Russia has dealt with anxiety over the sturdiness of its borders by invading the territory adjacent. Often it has acted on the assumption that, unless secured, these borderlands will become staging areas for foreign aggression against Russia. In the process, however, it has brought within its realm lands soon viewed, to cite Stalin's specter, as "zones of foreign intervention and occupation." Russian rulers have responded in moments of greatest distress by ruthless Russification or, worse, by making these lands less non-Russian, the extreme version of which was Stalin's mass deportations during World War II.

It is true that, at times, as Rieber notes, the Russians have tried to turn their conquered borderlands into a double-edged sword, hoping, as Stalin apparently did, that the union republics arrayed along the Soviet Union's borders would have a subversive effect on fellow ethnics in neighboring countries. But far more often the threat posed by the borderlands has been from within—the threat of violent resistance or rebellion. Whether Hungary in 1849, Poland in 1863, East Germany in 1953, Hungary and Poland in 1956, or Czechoslovakia in 1968, an uprising in one borderland has stirred Russian fears of the contagion spreading, producing a consistent Russian reaction. The threat, of course, stemmed from Russia's most voracious moves to enlarge the glacis, such as the Polish partitions at the end of the eighteenth century and the "fourth Polish partition" engineered under the 1939 Nazi-Soviet nonaggression pact.

Nearly all of my co-authors identify a second seminal Russian weakness—the country's perpetual economic backwardness. It is the first of Rieber's persistent factors and since the fifteenth century has led Russian leaders to push outward in quest of the arable land, stone, and natural resources missing in the original Muscovite core, but at the price of permanent military mobilization and frequent war, which further retarded the country's economic modernization. Backwardness is a relative concept, and from the earliest times to the present, Russian leaders have measured it by comparison with the West, first and longest Europe; then, after World War II, the United States. Today's Russia, because others in Asia and elsewhere have passed it by, has an unwelcome wider range of comparative options. Still, since the yardstick remains, as it always has been, sociocultural as well as economic, the West continues to be the vexing shadow against which Russia judges itself. "Catching up and surpassing the United States," the watchword of Khrushchev's Soviet Union, has a long ancestry tracing back at least to Peter's time. And, while this has regularly inspired Russia's rulers to borrow technique, technology, and capital from Europe and later the industrial democracies, this, as Angela Stent stresses in chapter 7, has always been from "Europe as a model," not "Europe as an idea."

Economic backwardness, however, has affected Russian foreign policy in still more complex ways, not least because it is intertwined with the effects of autocracy. As McDonald argues, at every turn Russia's leaders chose absolutism over economic progress whenever progress required tolerating social forms and market forces that endangered their grasp on power. The very essence of the Russian experience to our own day, he says, is the contrast between an "absolutist" and a *"doux commerce"* tradition. The first insists on an autonomous, self-contained state, standing above society, mobilizing its resources, managing its economic development, and dictating who can enter the field of play. The second, resting on the institution of private property, leaves it to markets and the rule of law to produce economic efficiency and constructive mutual dependency.

Suny contends that the empire's economic inferiority and autocratic political structure went hand in hand. In the nineteenth century, particularly, Russia's political system impeded the reforms needed to overcome economic backwardness, and once started, following Russia's crushing defeat in the Crimean War, "only exacerbated the contradictions between the practices of autocracy and the requirements for capitalist industrialization." Moreover, the "hierarchies and distinctions" integral to the autocracy, he adds, continually hindered the country's ability to mobilize for war.

Celeste Wallander, in looking at the impact of different eras of globalization on Russian foreign policy, reaches a similar conclusion in chapter 8. When changing phenomena in the outside world lanced Russia's protective barriers and impinged on the domestic order, Russia's rulers hastened to contain the effect, usually by tightening their political control. But by reinforcing autocracy, Russian leaders invariably depreciated the value to be had from globalization. As a result, she says, Russia tended to "fall back on a foreign policy strategy of catching up, of managing weakness and second-class status among the great powers." When the failure to get from globalization adequate economic, scientific, and technological benefits risked creating an impression of weakness, its leaders then sought to right the balance by "military and political means."

Caldwell cautions that the durable image of Russia's economy lagging behind those of the other great powers should not obscure the fact that at many points Russia has more than matched the military technology of its potential adversaries. More than once, from Ivan's *streltsy* (musketeers under the tsar's direct command) to Khrushchev's nuclear weapons program, the Russians have shown the way with tactical innovations and technological advances, scarcely justifying the inferiority complex outsiders assign to them. Still, these exceptions do not gainsay the constraints imposed by Russia's more basic economic deficits. In fact, they underscore how unbalanced Russia's modernization generally has been, with military prowess nearly always taking precedence over broad-based economic development. Even in the military sphere, as Caldwell notes, the tendency of the Red Army to favor quantity over quality, to invest first in massive arms and large armies and then in technology, has a very long tradition.

Rieber's third persistent factor is the burden of a multinational society, but this is the heritage of empire and treated as such by most of the authors in this book. Suny, whose chapter deals directly with the topic, starts from the assumption that Russia's history as a multinational empire produced a fragile, fragmented national identity, which in turn contributed to both a lack of social and economic dynamism and a resistance to reform. Over the three hundred years of their rule, the Romanovs failed to make of the empire a nation or even to make the Russians within the empire a nation. Even the Bolsheviks, who came to power professing to be neither an empire nor a nation-state, but "an anti-imperialist state, a federation of sovereign states, a voluntary union, and a prefiguration of a future nonstate," ended by becoming an empire and "replicat[ing] the imperialist relations" of its predecessor. Ultimately, having made no effort to create a "Soviet nation" in its futile effort to create the "new Soviet Man," and having modernized ethnically coherent peoples within national shells, when the regime exhausted its capacity to continue modernizing, it spelled the Soviet empire's demise. Not the flames of nationalism, he says, but the erosion of central authority destroyed the Soviet Union.

Russia's imperial identity and accompanying ideology did not preclude Russia's leaders from practicing realpolitik, indeed, Machtpolitik, but they did infuse policy with a particular notion of national interest, allies and enemies, and which aspects of international politics deserved pride of place. In the Soviet period the infusion grew extreme, and only at the end, with the arrival of Mikhail Gorbachev, did those at the top attempt to rethink the link between empire and foreign policy, struggle to give the country a new identity, and work to free themselves from the dead weight of encrusted ideas. The correction came late, however, and never had a chance to penetrate very deeply into the system or society. Hence, argues Suny, a fair portion of the Soviet way of viewing the world survived into the new era, even after the empire had crumbled.

It is not, however, just that Russia's identity as an empire matters, but the tortured way that it has mattered. Nearly every chapter in this book addresses the issue. Rieber's fourth persistent factor is what he calls "cultural alienation," the long-standing perception among Europeans (and Asians) that Russia does not belong or is, at best, a semi-alien entity, and the sense among Russians that Russia's European identity is either unrequited or, alternatively, nonexistent and unsuitable. It goes to the heart of Stent's analysis of Russia's relations with Europe. From Peter's day forward Russia's rulers have been pulled and torn by their country's physical and political presence in Europe, by the centrality of Europe in its foreign policy, and by Europe's attraction as a practical model, matched at the same time by their aversion to Europe's political institutions and values. Soviet leaders, Stent contends, at least until the Gorbachev era, suspended the tension by delegitimizing the idea of the capitalist West, and in the process brought both Russia's role in and divorce from Europe to their pinnacles. When the Soviet Union collapsed, the historical ambivalence resumed from where it had left off early in the century.

Wallander, for her part, argues that Stalin differed from Peter only in the degree to which he rendered Russia in but not of a Western-dominated international system. "Where Peter and his successors sought to selectively import European methods and resources to modernize the economy while limiting political change, Stalin expropriated large portions of East European industry and human capital and raised an Iron Curtain to keep out influences the Soviet system could not control." Rozman suggests that the deeper Russia thrust itself into Asia after 1860, the more trouble it had deciding whether it came as the "vanguard of a Western civilizing mission" or the "champion . . . of Asiatic resistance to it." Even in the Soviet period the leadership and elite could not resolve whether communism united the Soviet Union with China, North Korea, and North Vietnam or Asia's alien culture created an unbridgeable gap—until the Sino-Soviet conflict settled the matter.

In chapter 2 I assign a special importance to the ambiguity of Russian identity and its hold over the country's foreign policy because this becomes especially influential in those periods that I call "great state transformation," when the upheaval unleashed from above, as during the times of Ivan IV, Peter the Great, Alexander II, Lenin and Stalin, and Gorbachev and Yeltsin, crosses a qualitative threshold and turns all of society upside down. In those moments, Russia, conflicted at the most existential level, finds it particularly difficult to make clear strategic choices, and acts of two minds, frustrating potential partners, disconcerting the remaining major powers, and leaving the question of its role in the outside world muddied and dubious. When weak, as during the last three cases, its natural and sensible response is to retrench foreign policy, but often in ways replete with bile and aggressiveness.

Continuity, Discontinuity, and the Future of Russian Foreign Policy

Viewed from this distance, the imprint of the past on contemporary Russian foreign policy is clearly visible, but in important respects, Russia has begun to trace new and different paths. The unanswered question, however, is whether these new paths lead far enough to free Russia from the burdens of the historical patterns discussed in this book. History, of course, has no fatal authority over Russia's choices. Were Russian leaders determined to seize the moment to liberate their country from the most baleful traditions of imperial and Soviet Russia, and were they to use wisely the opportunities a fluid, albeit turbulent international environment presents, they could write a very different future.

This, however, will not happen easily. If transforming Russia into a modern liberal democracy is a matter not merely of grafting onto Russian society institutions and best practices from the West, but of breaking with a deeply engrained "absolutist tradition," then it should be no surprise that elements of that tradition reappear in the new Russia. Today's Russia, McDonald suggests, honors a well-established precedent, when it makes "domestic renewal" the handmaiden of renewed great-power status and sets about the task by reconstituting a "powerful, managerial state, acting with relative autonomy at home and abroad." Indeed, to cite Wallander, the seeming departure represented by a foreign policy of economic growth appears less so, if understood not as economic growth for the sake of economic growth, but "for the sake of power, autonomy, and global position." Stent adds the insight that contemporary Russians accept the idea of partnership with the West, "but only on the basis of [Russia's] own unique model," a model that entrusts modernization to a reascendant state. As she says, the notion of Russia as a European player above or outside European norms is hardly new, and the goal of making Russia a market economy by privileging a "strong, centralized state" becomes simply the latest version of Russia's long-assumed exceptionalism.

Nor has the new Russia moved from under the shadow of Rieber's persistent factors. Its borders, rolled back to those of 1650, are more porous than ever, permeable to all manner of contraband, terror, and violence from neighboring conflicts, and more difficult to police, because they "were not originally designed to be international." Worse, Russia is again without what might be called "strategic frontiers," since its new de jure borders offer weak parapets from behind which to plan a forward defense. Economic backwardness overwhelms virtually every other policy consideration, except that of the country's political stability, with which it is intimately connected. So, Russian leaders bend the nation's efforts to doubling annual economic growth in the name of reaching the level of Portugal in ten years' time, and in the meantime seize what economic instruments they have, such as oil and gas, to compensate for the economic wherewithal they lack. To economic backwardness must be added the country's dramatic demographic decline, which is a foreign policy issue because Putin has openly underscored its threat to national security.

Russia's multinational character also continues to weigh on the country. The traces are there in the nervousness with which the Russian elite contemplates its Muslim populations; in the frictions with non-Russian neighbors over Russians now living in foreign countries; and to agonizing degree in the Chechen war and a tension-ridden North Caucasus. The fourth of the persistent factors, "cultural alienation," survives in contemporary Russia's testy response to the West's upbraiding over its democratic failings and its on-again, off-again entertainment of the idea that Russia remains a country apart—uniquely Eurasian or, if not that, then special in some other way. And it echoes in the West's tendency, when trouble arises, to fall back on the negative version of the idea that Russia is, indeed, a country apart.

In some combination the lingering effects of these factors sustain what Rozman regards as the single, central weakness of Russia's policy in East Asia: its inability to turn away from a traditional geopolitical approach focused on what divides the area, preoccupied with security over economic opportunity, unwilling (or unable) to adapt Russian institutions to attract Asian investment, and insensitive to Asia's "Confucian civilizational heritage." In short, historical continuities still plague Russia's ability to meet the imperatives of globalization when it comes to actual policy, despite Putin's talk of its importance.

Cyril Black argued that Russia has often been the protagonist of the international status quo, and Caldwell notes the strong strain of conservatism in Russian policy, not least because of its rulers' conservatism when confronting change at home. Contemporary Russian foreign policy preserves both characteristics, and in one respect perversely so. Historically and particularly when Russia is weak, Russians have clung to what exists, both at home and abroad, for fear of the alternative. Today, discomforted and worried about the transformations a headstrong, preponderant United States seeks to impose on the world, Russia frequently accepts the status quo as the lesser evil. And in the modern version of its commitment to international institutions, also Black's point, Russia insists on a central role for the UN Security Council as a fetter on U.S. unilateralism. More perilously and closer to home, however, it also defends neighborhood authoritarians, no matter how reactionary or repressive, lest their departure open the door to U.S. or NATO penetration.

Continuity resonates as well in the agitation that swirls around the issue of Russian identity. To employ Suny's construction, Russians more than ever lack a consensus on what, where, and with whom Russia is. Is it complete within its present borders or within borders yet to be determined? Is it democratic and capitalist or "statist" and social democratic? Is it a genuine federation or a strong unitary state with federal features? Is it a Russia that includes Belarus but no longer the North Caucasus, or neither, or both? The leadership since 2000, he says, has set about "reintegrating the Soviet past into the 'democratic' capitalist present," but how this may turn out perplexes Russians as much as the outside world. And in foreign policy, the upset is equally great: Is Russia with the West? With China or India or both? If it is with the West, is it with Europe or with the United States? Or is it with none of the above, and is Russia on its own or bolstered only by deferential post-Soviet neighbors?

All this said, none of the authors in this book believes that the story ends here—that Russia is fated to repeat its history or that the patterns of the past cannot weaken or even expire. On the contrary, most of us recognize that Russia has arrived at a historic fork in the road, as fateful and filled with potential as any in its history. Already the change is far-reaching. Russia has made of itself something different from any Russia before, and it has introduced into its foreign policy features never before present.

McDonald goes farthest among the contributors in asserting that Russia under Putin may have at last transcended the chasm separating domestic from foreign policy—may have at last managed to reconcile Russia's great-power aspirations and traditional concept of statehood with a nod to Russian society and a recognition of the marriage needed if Russia is to function well in a changing international environment. Putin, he writes, seems to know that the "state's power as an international actor derives from a domestic sphere conceived in terms of economic development and 'managed' popular support." If so, it "represents an almost unprecedented acknowledgment of the interrelation between both spheres as a basis for the conduct of the state's foreign policy."

Suny, too, concludes that Russia as an actor in the outside world is becoming something different, although in more mixed ways. While it covets as much as ever an identity as a great power, it practices a pragmatism in greatpower relations that is purer and less contaminated by ideology than ever in the past. It well appreciates that great powers "seldom operate under the same rules and constraints as lesser powers" and expects this dispensation when defending its interests among the lesser powers on its borders. But it also knows the limits of its power. It remains a multinational state with "imperial pretensions in Chechnya" and "dreams of hegemony in the near abroad," but it also senses that events and its unresolved quest for identity have "left it without a clear justification for hegemony."

Rozman, while critical of the lingering habits of thought and practice in Russia's East Asian policy, entertains the possibility that enough has changed to make plausible a dramatically different approach. In a region with multiple rising powers, Russia needs to abandon crude geostrategic maneuvering and find ways to create balanced relations with the most important of them. To the extent that multilateralism grows in response to the region's problems, such as that of North Korea, Russia needs to be fully engaged. It needs not merely to declare Asia's importance to the development of the Russian Far East, but to make it possible by permitting the integration of the region's local economies into the larger Asian economy, even if inevitably this means diluting the region's ethnic Russian character amid an influx of Asian workers and businesspeople. And Russia needs to set aside its cultural aloofness and make a serious effort to engage Asia's Confucian traditions. That Rozman would treat these recommendations as realistic testifies to the change under way.

It is change that Caldwell finds reflected in the new Russia's national security strategy. No longer is Russia unmindful of the many sides to security and the shortsightedness, even danger, of entrusting too much of it to military force. No longer does it insist on overmatching or undercutting potential military adversaries, which is impossible in the case of the United States and eventually will be with China. And no longer does it embrace quantity over quality as it struggles to fashion a new military better suited to the imminent threats that it faces, rather than the traditional enemy that it once feared. As a consequence its leaders show far greater flexibility in navigating among the major powers and a far greater capacity to use other than military means to further their foreign policy agenda.

Does this mean that contemporary Russia has passed from the disorientation of the last twenty years to a firmer frame of mind, blessed by a foreign policy whose outlines now have definition and a chance of lasting? Some of my co-authors think so. McDonald, for example, portrays Russia as having righted government and society after being tossed about by the chaos and economic tempest of the transition, placed the political order back on the continuum of its historical traditions, but with innovations fitting it to modern circumstances, and marked an independent foreign policy course designed to match the country's aims with its resources. Stent cites the Russian analyst Dmitri Trenin, who contends that Russia has ceased to worry about whether or how it will integrate with the West, and has resolved to stand by itself, or rather to put itself at the center of its own "solar system" of sympathetic post-Soviet states.[28] He suggests that Russia has found an equilibrium point in its foreign policy. Confident that U.S. power has reached its natural limits and is ebbing, that the European Union will remain an economic entity without great political or military weight, and that China is for the moment a useful but remote economic and foreign policy partner, Russian leaders mean to set their own course, cooperating with whomever they choose whenever its suits their purposes, making Russia no one's enemy but neither anyone's ally among the major powers, insulating themselves from the West's importuning, concentrating on their interests in the post-Soviet space and restoring their rights as a player of note in the wider world.

Most of those contributing to this book, however, see a less fully formed Russia, pursuing an inchoate foreign policy distinguished more by its time-biding quality than its clear commitments. For Wallander, Russia under Putin and his successors is likely to be "active but not expansionist"; eager to keep "challenges at a distance rather than addressing them"; open to the United States, Europe, and China, but not "deeply engage[d]" with any; and unwilling to deal with "global threats," if it entails "entangling alliances." I put the point somewhat more strongly in my chapter: If periods of great state transformation have a peculiarly unsettling impact on Russian foreign policy, then when they end has a particular significance, and little suggests that this one has ended. Because Russia's internal evolution remains still so incomplete, its basic strategic choices abroad are yet to be made, and the outside world should expect a Russia that does not have its mind made up; that is jealous of its power before its time; that uses the leverage that chance and high oil prices give it calmly but ruthlessly when circumstances permit, more impetuously when things go wrong; that wavers between meeting the challenge of globalization and indulging concerns over national security; and, most important, that fashions its relations with the United States, Europe, China, Japan, and India issue by issue, not according to some deeper and more coherent strategic design.

History's insights suggest that before Russia assumes a convincing and fuller identity in international politics, it must first complete its historic passage from one chapter of its existence to another. If and when this fuller identity emerges, if it is to differ fundamentally from earlier Russias, the factors that have generated past patterns will have to fade or be surmounted. Porous borders will have to lose their terror, either because an efficient and well-governed Russia guards against their effects or because they are made safe by friendly and cooperative neighbors who themselves are not menaced by instability and internal deterioration. Economic backwardness will have to cease to shape foreign policy, either because Russia has recovered its economic vibrancy in a sustainable form, even if it continues to lag behind other more advanced economies, or because Russia has, at a minimum, found a way to profit from economic globalization without, as Wallander stresses, squandering its benefits by zealously micromanaging its effects.

It will have to prove that "sovereign democracy," the phrase popular within Putin's circle, is not simply "bureaucratic authoritarianism," as Russian critics claim; or if they are one and the same, that it works—that it can tap the country's energies and resources in ways sustaining balanced economic growth; cleanse the system and society of its pathologies (corruption, deteriorating mortality, bloated bureaucracy, and public alienation); shepherd society's sharply separated social groupings and rising middle class safely into a workable amalgam; and effect the structural reforms necessary to move the economy toward genuine modernity. But that is not all. "Sovereign democracy" is a euphemism (unlike its predecessor, "managed democracy," which was a contradiction in terms), and it remains to be proved that it is compatible with a constructive or even an unembittered relationship with Europe and the United States. For the emphasis is on the adjective "sovereign," meaning do not interfere in Russia's domestic affairs, and "democracy" is to be what Russia's leaders say it is.

Were it simply that Russia's return to "statist" or "dirigiste" practice, to use McDonald's characterization, introduced an awkward element into Russia's relations with the West, this need not create great wreckage, provided it does not give way to untrammeled repression. The real risk is elsewhere. As already shown by the frictions between Moscow on the one side and Washington and Brussels on the other over the color revolutions in Georgia, Ukraine, and Kyrgyzstan and the authoritarian turn in Belarus and Uzbekistan, an illiberal Russia fosters political outcomes in the surrounding area to which the Europeans and Americans do have deep and genuine objection, not the least because in the case of Georgia, Ukraine, and Belarus, these outcomes impinge directly on Europe's welfare and security.

It would, of course, be fantasy to assume that all these hazards, particularly the echo of ancient disadvantages, can easily be overcome or will soon disappear. But the possibilities open to Russian foreign policy and the direction that it ultimately takes will depend on the degree to which they are mitigated, transcended, or isolated. If Russia can generate a self-confidence based on a renewed sense of security and knowledge that the country is prospering and well governed—not merely that it has escaped the worst, re-enthroned the state, and acquired an energy lever—it will be able to sort out its strategic options, choose with the longer run in view, and give a steadiness to foreign policy that was conspicuously missing during the last two turbulent decades. Alternatively, the more it reinforces the effects of these hazards and disadvantages by yielding to narrow-minded concerns, duplicates old patterns of behavior, and chooses badly at home, the longer it will take Russia to escape its past and the heavier will be history's weight. To understand what this means and what will be needed to move beyond, the reader is invited to turn to the chapters that follow.

NOTES

1. Karen Elliott and Andrew Higgins, "Putin Says Bush Shouldn't Go It Alone When Deciding How to Deal with Iraq but the Russian President Reaffirms Global Importance of His Nation's Close Ties to Its Former Cold War Foe," *Wall Street Journal*, February 11, 2002.

2. In what follows I make no attempt to deal with contemporary debates over the historian's craft. My purpose is to use classic arguments to establish a basis for judging the usefulness of history in foreign policy studies.

3. E. H. Carr, "Victorian History," *Times Literary Supplement*, June 19, 1953, cited by Richard J. Evans in "Introduction" to E. H. Carr, *What Is History?* rev. ed. (London: Palgrave, 2001), p. xiii.

4. Hans Meyerhoff, "History and Philosophy," in *The Philosophy of History in Our Time*, ed. Hans Meyerhoff (New York: Doubleday, 1959), p. 10.

5. Ibid., pp. 10–11.

6. Paul W. Schroeder, "History and International Relations Theory," *International Security* 22, no. 1 (Summer 1997): 65.

7. Carr, *What Is History?* p. 98.

8. Buckle published his two-volume *History of Civilization in England* between 1856 and 1861, and in the introduction, he wrote, "It will be observed, that the preceding proofs of our actions [the "actions" of the English] being regulated by law, have been derived from statistics; a branch of knowledge which, though still in its infancy has already thrown more light on the study of human nature than all the sciences put together." Quoted in Fritz Stern, ed., *The Varieties of History: From Voltaire to the Present* (New York: Vintage, 1973), p. 127.

9. The quoted phrase is from Meyerhoff, *The Philosophy of History*, p. 19.

10. Carr, *What Is History?* p. 84.

11. Schroeder, "History and International Relations Theory," p. 66.

12. Ernest Nagel, the philosopher of science, quarrels with this notion and explores the degree to which history is both nomothetic and idiographic in "Some Issues in the Logic of Historical Analysis," *Scientific Monthly* 74, no. 3 (March 1952): 162–169. (The quoted phrase is from page 162.)

13. It would be misleading to leave the impression that the discipline's scientific aspirations and eagerness to emulate the rigor and techniques of economics are only of late. For an interesting account of G. E. G. Catlin, whose *Science and the Method of Politics* (New York: Knopf, 1927) laid out the case for "abstract hypotheses and . . . a scientific method" applied to the study of politics long before the behavioralists of the 1950s and who said that "to pass from political to economic theory is like passing from sea-fog to mountain air," see John G. Gunnell, "Political Science on the Cusp: Recovering a Discipline's Past," *American Political Science Review* 99, no. 4 (November 2005): 600, 601.

14. Not that political scientists and economists have not tried to explain large-scale historical phenomena by working from "rational-choice" assumptions and

employing a formal game-theoretic approach. See, for example, Robert H. Bates, Jean-Laurent Rosenthal, Margaret Levi, Barry R. Weingast, Avner Greif, *Analytic Narratives* (Princeton: Princeton University Press, 1998). Impressive and imaginative as this work is in displaying the craft in its advanced form, whether it provides a better, or even an adequate, explanation for the history it features has generated far less agreement. Indeed the sharpest criticism on this score came not from the historian's guild but from a fellow political scientist. See Jon Elster, "Rational Choice History: A Case of Excessive Ambition," *American Political Science Review* 94, no. 3 (September 2000): 685–695. A more favorable reviewer nonetheless finished by suggesting that "history, even analytical history, remains art more than science. Like an advocate in court, it combines evidence, analysis, and rhetorical manipulation, all in order to stifle doubt," a "demanding standard" that only "one or two chapters here satisfy." See Avner Offer, "Analytic Narratives," *Journal of Economic History* 60, no. 1 (March 2000): 312–314.

15. The quoted phrasing is Schroeder's in "History and International Relations Theory," p. 69.

16. Stephen H. Haber, David M. Kennedy, and Stephen D. Krasner, "Brothers Under the Skin: Diplomatic History and International Relations," *International Security* 22, no. 1 (Summer 1997): 42–43.

17. The categories and their implications are explored by Jon Elster, *Nuts and Bolts for the Social Sciences* (New York: Cambridge University Press, 1989), pp. 3–21.

18. Meyerhoff, *The Philosophy of History*, p. 173.

19. John Dewey, *Logic: The Theory of Inquiry* (New York: Holt, 1938), p. 236.

20. Ibid., p. 234.

21. Ibid., p. 239. Or, as William Faulkner wrote in *Requiem for a Nun*, "The past is never dead. It's not even past."

22. John Lewis Gaddis sees a similarity between the historian piecing together the course of events surrounding a set of phenomena and the political scientist, recognizing "that insurmountable difficulties arise when one tries to apply the methods of replicable science to the nonreplicable realm of human affairs," resorting to the method of "process-tracing." Gaddis, "History, Theory, and Common Ground," *International Security* 22, no. 1 (Summer 1997): 83.

23. Ivo J. Lederer, ed., *Russian Foreign Policy: Essays in Historical Perspective* (New Haven: Yale University Press, 1962).

24. Cyril E. Black, "The Pattern of Russian Objectives," in Lederer, *Russian Foreign Policy*, p. 5.

25. Black, "The Pattern of Russian Objectives," p. 18.

26. John P. LeDonne, *The Russian Empire and the World 1700–1917* (New York: Oxford University Press, 1997), p. xiii.

27. LeDonne, *The Russian Empire*, p. xvii.

28. Dmitri Trenin, "Russia Leaves the West," *Foreign Affairs* 85, no. 4 (July/August 2006): 87–96.

CHAPTER 1

Living in the Hood: Russia, Empire, and Old and New Neighbors

Ronald Grigor Suny

IRONICALLY, WITH THE DEMISE of the great overseas empires and the collapse of the largest land empire in the world, scholars have begun to re-engage the problematic of imperialism. "Empire" has become the intellectual flavor of the month as the United States confidently proclaims the right to global hegemony, preventive war, and preemption, raising the specter of new forms of empire that confound conventional definitions. Its great adversary during the Cold War, the Soviet Union, no longer constrains U.S. international ambitions, and the successor states—Russia included—now live in a much more vulnerable world dominated by a single hyperpower. Where have the past and present practices of empire left Russia? Has the Russian Federation made the transition not only from authoritarianism to democracy but also from empire to some form of nation-state? What does empire, both as a political structure and as an identity, say about the past, present, and future foreign policies of post-Soviet Russia?

Beginning with a constructivist approach to international relations, this chapter argues that foreign policy is not merely a product of geographical and historically determined imperatives or opportunities, or the differential in power among states, but is determined by perceptions, ideas, and identities articulated as "national interests" to be defended and promoted in the international arena. Identification as an empire has effects on perceived interests that differ from those associated with identification as a nation-state. States act on the basis of their perceived interests, but conceptions of the kind of state, its historical purposes, and its operative belief systems, as well as the discursive universe in which it operates, are all fundamental to construction of those interests.

Six factors help to explain the foreign policy of Russia and the Soviet Union in light of their historical experience. First, Russian foreign policy over many centuries, with a few brief exceptions, has been guided principally by its leaders' perception of weakness and insecurity vis-à-vis Russia's international and nearby competitors. Second, among the most fundamental sources of weakness are Russia's size and place within the international order, a lack of clearly defined borders, low population density, and a relatively underarticulated social and communications infrastructure. Third, Russia is a multinational state whose imperial history has produced a fragile, fragmented national identity that has consequences for its generation of interests. The structure and ideology of empire, as well as the costs and constraints of an imperial system, contributed to a lack of social and economic dynamism and resistance to reform. Fourth, although Russia's leaders have often thought in realist terms, their self-conceptions (identities), ideas of history, and narratives about the past and future have influenced their perceptions of Russian interests. Ideology (in the broad sense of a discourse of politics), rather than simple realpolitik (itself an ideology), has played a motivating, sometimes debilitating, role in determining policy. Fifth, Russia's internal composition, deriving from its historical formation and geopolitical location, is key to defining its identities and interests. Sixth, Russia today, as in much of the past, lives in a dangerous neighborhood. Both real and perceived dangers have historically contributed to its sense of weakness and insecurity. Today these include threats from (1) the peripheries within the country (e.g., Chechnya), (2) the near abroad (e.g., the spread of Islam), (3) the expansion of NATO, and (4) the other great powers.

International relations theorists have long contested the relationship of interests and identities. In the case of Russia and the Soviet Union, authors have alternately treated them like other states that act in their national interest or as ideologically driven states that operate from a particular identity (e.g., the Third Rome or the Vanguard of the Proletariat). The most ubiquitous approach to national interest has invoked it as an objective, unavoidable, permanent fact of life that must be a feature of a country's foreign policy if disaster is to be avoided. Lord Palmerston provided the most famous and succinct statement of this view: "England has neither permanent friends nor permanent enemies; she has permanent interests."[1] But the pedigree of this idea goes back at least to Niccolò Machiavelli and Carl von Clausewitz and has been further developed by international relations theorists such as Hans Morgenthau, George Kennan, Kenneth Waltz, and John Mearsheimer. Summing up the concept, Ernest Haas wrote, "Usually it is contended that the national interest includes all those features of state aspirations which bear a relation to the permanent and enduring needs of the state. . . . Thus stated, the national interest concept acquires the sanctity of a fixed historical law for each state, immutable over long periods and always properly understood by intelligent and imaginative statesmen, misunderstood and bungled by those who did not really appreciate the position and interests of their country in world affairs."[2]

A second approach argues that national interest is a subjective understanding of the way the world works; it is a cognitive and emotional calculation of what is desirable. Rather than the state having given, fixed, and permanent interests, in this view individuals and groups in society have interests that influence and shape what is understood to be the national interest. Haas sums up this view: "National interest to one may well be national lack of interest to another. In fact, it may be concluded that the conception of national interest which prevails at any one time is no more than an amalgam of varying policy motivations which tend to pass for a 'national' interest as long as the groups holding these opinions continue to rule."[3]

In earlier incarnations, "national interest" was distinguished from the "interest of the Prince" and implied that the interests of the monarch or the ruling elite were different from those of the people. Ruling nobilities, for example, might identify national interest with the preservation of the existing order when it benefits them more than anyone else. In contrast, the people's national interest might be to overthrow the existing order because it does not benefit them. In democratic states, where governors are elected by the population, the national interest is understood to reflect the interests of the polity as a whole and is identified with the preservation and promotion of the democratic order. But even though the interests expressed by elected leaders are said to be equivalent to those of the nation, in contemporary democracies, power and material differences of class, ethnicity, and gender compromise any notion of congruence between elite and more general interests. What becomes an operative national interest is the result of the actual politics in a given country.

The language of national interest has fallen out of international relations theories in recent decades, while enjoying an afterlife in everyday language and government communiqués. Defensive realist theorists, such as Waltz, and offensive realists, such Mearsheimer, hold that the fundamental, irreducible interest of states in an anarchic international arena is survival. Other interests, such as increasing power vis-à-vis other states or becoming more prosperous, are in the end explained by the underlying interest of survival. A supreme pessimist, Mearsheimer elaborates a simple but powerful theory about the way the world works, an ontology of interstate behavior. Taking an uncompromising structuralist approach, he argues that the nature of the international system causes states to think and act aggressively and seek hegemony. The desire to survive leads to aggressive behavior. Each state fears the others and seeks the largest share of world power to become the hegemon.[4]

Offensive realists reject the argument of liberal theorists that the internal characteristics of states must be considered, that democracies are less aggressive than dictatorships, and that international institutions enhance the capacity for cooperation among states, thus reducing the probability of war. Not only do they largely ignore the internal composition of states; they are also unconvinced about the power of international institutions to restrain states in most cases. As for defensive realists, who assume that states simply seek to preserve the balance of power, Mearsheimer claims that they underestimate how much power states want. While liberals have often asserted that one could have expected that Soviet totalitarianism would produce an aggressive, expansionist Soviet foreign policy, defensive realists have argued that the Soviet state would act like other states to preserve its power. Mearsheimer, on the other hand, sees both Russia and the Soviet Union as rational actors that are suspicious of other states, that anticipate danger, and that seek to increase their power whenever possible. It does not matter who the leader is—Nicholas I, Joseph Stalin, or Vladimir Putin—Russia will be Russia, that is, a state acting as a great power, seeking to become a hegemon, at least in its own region, if not globally. Russia, like all other great states, is a power maximizer, concerned about relative, not absolute, power.[5]

At the other pole of international relations theory, social constructivists, such as Alexander Wendt and Ted Hopf, consider the formulations of the realists better applied to epistemology than to ontology. That is, while they believe that they are describing the way the world actually is, they are in fact explaining how people in power (and many international relations theorists) think the world is. As Mearsheimer has famously argued, many leaders of great states act as if the international arena is made up of aggressive billiard balls and that his theory provides insights into the mentalities of such actors. But at the same time, other leaders (e.g., presidents Woodrow Wilson and Bill Clinton) act as liberals and consider the kinds of states with which they are dealing. Many leaders, particularly of smaller powers, believe that international institutions are a serious constraint on great and small states alike. Different leaders imagine the world in ways different from those of the realists and act accordingly.

In realist international relations theory, the world comprises bounded, coherent, territorialized sovereign states that aim to increase their security and independence of action in an anarchical international system. These states have but one identity: that of self-interested security seekers. Yet, say critics of realism, when making life-and-death calculations about the behavior of rival states, state leaders consider not only questions of physical and material might but also the probability of threatening behavior from other states. Leaders make such calculations on the basis of their perceptions of how other states might act; they are concerned about other actors' preferences and intentions. In other words, they consider their own and the other states' identities. Constructivists argue that identity and interest cannot be taken for granted or deduced from an abstract model of international relations. Rather, they are dependent variables to be explained.[6]

Unlike realism, constructivism "assumes that the selves, or identities, of states are a variable; they likely depend on historical, cultural, political, and social context."[7] These identities are the product of the social practices among agents and between agents and structures. "No one denies," writes Wendt, "that states act on the basis of perceived interests, and few would deny that those interests are often egoistic." Moreover, constructivists differ with the realists' view that national interests "have a material rather than social basis, being rooted to some combination of human nature, anarchy, and/or brute material capabilities."[8] For constructivists, power is both material and discursive; that is, it is also about the generation of meanings that are shared intersubjectively by different actors. Ideas constitute interests, indeed, "in some sense interests *are* ideas."[9] Action gains legitimacy, even motivating force, only in the context of specific discourses. Subjects who fight for their king in one discursive universe may fight against him and for the nation in another. Identities, which to some degree are fluid, multiple, and overlapping, can be thought of as a "congealed reputation" or a "provisional stabilization" of who one is or is thought to be.[10] Depicting an international arena of ordered contingency, understandable only through a contextualized, historicized investigation of identities, constructivists hold that conflict and cooperation are intimately tied to perceptions of threats embedded in historical experiences.

Not all interests are constructed, according to Wendt, who takes a more moderate position than radical constructivists, who argue for "constructivism all the way down." He argues that even though many interests are socially constructed, states as states do have universal national interests. Among these, he lists survival, autonomy, economic well-being, and collective self-esteem.[11] States, he writes, "are homeostatic structures that are relatively enduring over time. Like other cultural forms states are self-fulfilling prophecies; . . . once up and running they acquire interests in reproducing themselves that create resistance to disappearing of their own accord. This creates substantial path-dependency and 'stickiness' in international politics."[12] For Wendt, states operate on the basis of perceived interests, which are often egoistic because objective (state) interests to survive and prosper produce a bias in the international system toward interpreting and thinking about interests in an egoistic, realist way.[13] But there is more flexibility in Wendt's theory than in Mearsheimer's. States operate on the basis of perceived interests; interests are often egoistic; but interests are constituted essentially by ideas and perceptions, and there is no a priori reason that states cannot cooperate or identify with one another. State actors "always have an element of choice in defining their identities and interests."[14]

In this chapter I have adopted a somewhat eclectic theory of state behavior that leans toward social constructivism but maintains some elements of structural realism.[15] It contains eight propositions. First, state leaders wish to preserve territorial integrity and, to the extent possible, the sovereignty of their states.[16] Second, the international system is in general anarchic (i.e., there is no uncontested, universally recognized supranational authority to settle disputes or enforce agreements among states). Therefore state leaders usually believe that they must rely on their country's resources (self-help) and those of their allies (and in some cases the "international community") to protect against foreign threats. Third, state leaders generally wish to stay in power, to increase their domestic base of support by appealing to different constituencies, and to preserve that part of the existing political order that secures the leaders' position of power and privilege. Fourth, foreign policy defeats, like domestic defeats, weaken state leaders, who therefore seek to avoid them. Fifth, military force is a constant possibility in international disputes. Sixth, social groups influence domestic and foreign policy ends and means that coincide with their particular interests, most effectively in democracies but in other systems as well. Seventh, regime types constrain some leadership choices and promote others. Empires act differently from nation-states, dictatorships from democracies, given the constellation of individuals and groups that can influence policy and express their interests. Different kinds of states have different self-conceptions and ambitions, even though certain factors (e.g., geopolitical position and the anarchic international environment) stay relatively constant. Eighth, for the reasons discussed above, both structures and identities matter. No structure, however, exists outside a discursive construction that imparts meaning and value to that structure. Structures do not determine actions in an unmediated way. State behavior is affected not only by certain objective factors (e.g., geopolitical location, level of economic development, and physical power) but also by a state's reputation, whether its actions are predictable or not (e.g., the behavior of revolutionary regimes or collapsing empires tends to be less predictable than that of more stable regimes), and the forms of knowledge that the regime can generate.

Three final points should be made about interests and identities. First, interests are ultimate ends—that is, preferences of individuals, groups, or states—and they should not be conflated with the strategies to achieve those ends. Preserving one's state and keeping one's homeland intact may be a universal interest of leaders and their constituents, but how to achieve them—for example, invading a weaker country, making the world safe for democracy, creating lebensraum, or promoting socialist revolution—are strategic choices that may or may not be rational or effective as regards national interest. Second, identities and the ways actors construct the world have profound effects on the choices of both ends and means. Identities generate an array of permissible and appropriate behaviors and norms of how one should and should not act, and a repertoire of justifications for actions taken. Finally, interests and identities are at times confused and contradictory. The choices that leaders make to preserve or enhance their domestic power or promote their worldview may in fact be destructive to the interests of the nation or the state. Russian leaders from Nicholas II to Mikhail Gorbachev offer many illustrations of such contradictions and confusion.[17]

EMPIRE AND NATION-STATE AS REGIME TYPES

Russian regimes have undergone a series of momentous changes, some revolutionary, others more evolutionary, that have influenced both their identities and related interests. Over the last three centuries, Russia has given rise to six regime types: the Petrine empire (1700–1825); the modernizing empire (1825–1917); the internationalist state of nations (1917–1932); the nationalizing empire (1932–1985); the transitory empire (1985–1991); and the weakened multinational state with ambitions of hegemony (1991–2006).

Of these, four are understood as forms of empire. "Empire" has become the preferred word to describe the Soviet Union since its collapse. A highly normative term, it was most notably applied in the 1980s to "the evil empire" and only later, less pejoratively, to the "affirmative action empire" or the "empire of nations" in which "imperialism [w]as the highest stage of socialism."[18] Even though the Soviet Union was imperial in its relationships with Mongolia and the bordering states in East Central Europe, to consider it as a contiguous empire requires something more than just a typological distinction. What does "empire" say about the workings of the Soviet Union and why it succeeded for so long in maintaining relative ethnic peace within its borders? What utility does empire offer in efforts to understand the Soviet disintegration?

Like other contested words, such as "revolution" or "modernity," "empire" is essentially a comparative term. It gains in conviction insofar as it robustly links shared characteristics and dynamics of a set of polities and sharply distinguishes that set from other political structures. Much comes down to how one defines "empire." Too broad and inclusive a definition—such as that employed by Francine Hirsch ("a state characterized by having a great extent of territories and variety of peoples under one rule")—or avoidance of a definition altogether leads to conceptual confusion.[19] I define "empire" as a particular form of domination or control between two units set apart in a hierarchical, inequitable relationship, or more precisely a composite state in which a metropole dominates a periphery to the disadvantage of the periphery.[20] Like Michael Doyle, I emphasize that an imperial state differs from the broader category of multinational states, confederations, or federations because it "is not organized on the basis of political equality among societies or individuals. The domain of empire is a people subject to unequal rule."[21] Inequitable treatment might involve cultural or linguistic discrimination or disadvantageous redistributive practices from the periphery to the metropole (but not necessarily, as, for example, in the Soviet empire). This ideal type of empire, then, is fundamentally different from that of the nation-state. Whereas empire is inequitable rule over a people that is in some way distinct and different, nation-state rule is, at least in theory if not always in practice, the same for all members of the nation. Empires rule over subjects; nation-states govern citizens.

Besides inequality and subordination, the relationship of the metropole to the periphery is marked by difference—for example, by ethnicity, geographic separation, or administrative distinction.[22] If peripheries are fully integrated into the metropole (as various appanage principalities were into Muscovy), and if they are treated as well or as badly as the metropolitan provinces, then the relationship is not imperial. The westward expansion of the United States in the eighteenth and nineteenth centuries was carried out through conquest and annexation and, as such, was an imperial effort. But once the conquered territories were integrated into the federation of states on an equal basis with the original core states, the arrangement was no longer imperial—except, arguably, toward the original indigenous peoples, who were treated as distinct "nations," inferior to the white settlers and dominated by their federal government.

The metropole need not be defined ethnically or geographically. It is the ruling institution. In several empires, the ruling institution had a status or class character, an endowed nobility or political class (e.g., the Osmanli in the Ottoman Empire, the imperial family and upper layers of the landed gentry and bureaucracy in the Russian Empire, and, analogously, the communist nomenklatura in the Soviet Union). In my understanding, neither tsarist Russia nor the Soviet Union was an ethnically Russian empire with the metropole completely identified with a ruling Russian nationality. Rather, the ruling institution—nobility in one case, the Communist Party elite in the other—was multinational, though primarily Russian, and ruled imperially over Russian and non-Russian subjects alike. In empires, the distance and difference of the rulers were part of the ideological justification for the superordination of the ruling institution. The right to rule an empire resides with the ruling institution, not in the consent of the governed.

Empire, then, is a fundamentally different kind of polity from a nation-state. Whereas empires are hierarchical, inequitable, and about subordination and institutional differentiation between those ruling and those ruled, nation-states are about horizontal equivalence among citizens. I define a "nation" as a group of people that imagines itself to be a political community distinct from the rest of humankind; its members believe that they share characteristics—for example, origins, values, historical experiences, language, or territory. And on the basis of their defined culture, they are entitled to self-determination, which usually entails control of their own territory (the "homeland") and state.[23]

From roughly the late eighteenth century to the present, the "state" (the territorially bounded authority that increasingly held the monopoly of legitimate violence) has merged with the nation. Almost all modern states claim to be nation-states, either in an ethnic or a civic sense, with governments deriving power from and exercising it in the interest of the nation.[24] Modern states legitimize themselves in reference to both the nation and the claims to popular sovereignty implicit in the discourse of the nation.[25] Borrowing a term from Hugh Seton-Watson, Benedict Anderson discusses "official nationalism" as the response of modern empires in the age of nationalism to the threats presented by the emerging discourse of the nation. By the nineteenth century, the "lexicographic revolution in Europe . . . created, and gradually spread, the conviction that languages (in Europe at least) were, so to speak, the personal property of quite specific groups—their daily speakers and readers—and moreover that these groups, imagined as communities, were entitled to their autonomous place in a fraternity of equals."[26] The adoption of vernacular into state languages in the Habsburg, Romanov, and Ottoman realms, like the choice of certain print languages with print capitalism, had nothing to do with nationalism, but rather had to do with a policy of unifying and universalizing dynastic or imperial rule. But given the "rapidly rising prestige all over Europe of the national idea, there was a discernible tendency among the Euro-Mediterranean monarchies to sidle towards a beckoning national identification."[27] The danger, of course, to dynastic monarchies and empires was that with nationalism came the idea that the nation was a distinct community that, by virtue of its culture and historical or ethnographic constitution, ought to rule itself or, at the very least, be ruled by representatives of its community. The appeals to divine right, conquest, or inheritance that kings and emperors used in past centuries to justify their rule seemed increasingly artificial. Instead of emphasizing their difference from and superiority to the peoples they ruled, monarchs sought to naturalize their dynastic right to govern by "stretching the short, tight, skin of the nation over the gigantic body of the empire."[28] Official nationalism, then, was the "willed merger of nation and dynastic empire" adopted *after*, and *in reaction to*, the popular national movements proliferating in Europe since the 1820s.[29]

THE DILEMMA OF A NATIONALIZING EMPIRE

Russia was the classic case of an empire that tried "to appear attractive in national drag."[30] A latecomer to nationalism as state policy, only in the reign of Alexander III (1881–1894) did the tsarist government attempt to Russify many of its subject peoples, and then only tentatively and intermittently. As Anderson's model of official nationalism shows, the Russian monarchy sought to identify an authoritarian monarchy ruling over a multiethnic population with a purported nation. But tsarist Russia succeeded only too well in building an empire, though it failed to create a "Russian nation" within that empire. Muscovy and imperial Russia were successful in integrating the core regions of Russia's empire (often referred to as the *vnutrennie guberniia*) into a single nationality. But diverse administrative practices, as well as the compactness of the local ethnicities and the effects of settlement policies, maintained and intensified differences between the Russian core and the non-Russian peripheries.[31] In many peripheries, such as Transcaucasia and Central Asia, integration succeeded only with the elites (and only partially), not with the peasant or nomadic populations, who retained their tribal, ethnic, and religious identities. Some elites, such as the Tatar and Ukrainian nobles, dissolved into the Russian *dvoriantsvo* (nobility). But others, such as the German barons of the Baltic or the Swedish aristocrats of Finland, retained privileges and separate identities. In some areas the tsarist regime managed to create loyal subjects through the transformation of cultural identities, but its policies were inconsistent and varied enormously. Its efforts to Russify non-Russians began too late, decades after popular national identification had begun for many peoples, and the state did little to push an ethnic nation-making project even among Russians. There was no program, as in France, to educate and affiliate millions of people around an idea of the nation or turn peasants into Russians.

The problem of empire versus nation in the nineteenth century most acutely disturbed Russia's military leadership. Just as the Germans in the period of the French Revolution had to confront the French *levée-en-masse* (mass recruitment), and realized the potential in rallying around the nation, so the Russian military in the late nineteenth century concluded that the future defense of the empire required "drafting the nation."[32] Convinced by his senior advisers to embark on a military reform that would conscript Russians without consideration of social rank, Emperor Alexander II stated in an 1874 decree that Germany's recent military successes over Austria and France had demonstrated that a state's strength is enhanced "when the business of defending the fatherland becomes the general affair of the people [*narod*], when all, without distinction of title or status, unite for that holy cause."[33] In the next four decades, however, wide recruitment did not end ethnic or class discrimination in the military. Those in the army who "preached (and believed in) the long-term goal of the multiethnic nation" in the short term practiced "imperial policies of discrimination" (e.g., forming special Muslim units that were ordered to serve outside Muslim areas).[34] More was at stake than simply broadening recruitment, for in an empire divided by social class and legal estate (*soslovie*) and fragmented among dozens of ethnicities, the consolidation of a coherent national identity was a monumental undertaking. The signifier "nation" was hardly a neutral political term, but indeed a claim to a new form of state legitimation based on popular sovereignty and identification of the ruler with the ruled.

The very structure and ideology of empire, then, presented Russia's rulers with liabilities in the fierce international competition with the powerful nation-states of Europe and, by the late nineteenth century, with Japan, a far more coherent, "nationalized" empire. The hierarchies and distinctions prevalent in the Russian Empire frequently hindered its ability to mobilize for war; time and again—in 1809, 1853–1856, 1904–1905, and finally 1914–1917—it failed this ultimate test. In 1878, after victories over the Ottoman Empire, Russia was forced to bow to the will of the other European powers and withdraw its forces from Turkish territory. Certainly, the empire's economic inferiority and autocratic political structure played a role in Russia's relative weakness. A convincing argument can be made, however, that Russia's political structure hindered the kinds of reforms necessary for economic development and, once the reforms were begun, only exacerbated the contradictions between the practices of autocracy and the requirements for capitalist industrialization.[35] Notably, the three states that fared the worst in military confrontations in the nineteenth century—and that ultimately collapsed in World War I—were the most ethnically diverse, with the most archaic political structures and the least developed cohesive "national" identity. Over time absolutist empires became anomalous polities in the age of nation-states, far less effective in connecting ruling elites with the population below that was undergoing the modernizing effects of industrialization, urbanization, the spread of education, and increased social mobility.

Scholars differ on the question of Russian "nationness" during tsarist times. In his study of patriotism during World War I, Hubertus Jahn writes, "Patriotic imagery reveals that Russians had a pretty clear idea against whom they were fighting in the war, but not for whom and for what. If a nation is a community imagined by its members as Benedict Anderson convincingly argues, then Russia was not a nation during World War I."[36] Joshua Sanborn, on the other hand, concludes that imperial Russia and eventually the Soviet Union did form nation-states, at least to the extent that military leaders and others had a clearly national project in mind as they carried out reforms from above.[37] Sanborn argues that there were three responses to Russia's entry into World War I—individual private responses, public support, and public opposition (draft riots). He also argues that national identity should not be confused with national unity. In a reply to Sanborn, S. A. Smith contends that "the war strengthened rather than weakened national identity"; however, one should not "underestimate the extent to which nation, empire, and class pulled in different directions. . . . By the summer of 1917, politics had become polarized between an imperial language of nation, used mainly by the privileged and educated strata, an anti-imperial language, used mainly by the elites of the non-Russian nationalities, and a language of class, used mainly by the subaltern classes."[38] Later the equation shifted again, ultimately with national identity proving to be much more robust than class identity.[39] Geoffrey Hosking has most consistently maintained that only in Soviet times, most dramatically in the resistance to the Nazi invasion, were the state and party able to link "civilian and military, empire and local community" in ways that the tsars had failed to accomplish. In Hosking's words, "The Second World War did more than any other event to crystallize Russian nationhood."[40]

In my view, tsarist Russia remained to the end a composite state with unequal relations between a Russian metropole and non-Russian populations that ultimately failed to create either a nation within the whole empire or even a sense of nation among the core Russian population. As a great state on the edge of other great states, it was inevitably drawn into conflict with the ambitions of other economically and politically expanding states, most notably Germany and Austro-Hungary. Tsarist Russia collapsed not primarily because of nationalism from the peripheries but, like its Soviet successor, because of the progressive weakening and disunity of the center. The tearing of the seams was along both class and estate lines, as well as along political-ideological lines. Elites withdrew support from the monarchy, and, more broadly, the regime became increasingly alienated from the intelligentsia and workers, strategically located in the largest cities. Policies of industrialization and the limited reforms after 1905 had created new constituencies that demanded representation in the political order that the tsar, who harbored hopes of a return to full autocracy, refused to grant. In the new world in which discourses of civilization centered on the nation, constitutionalism, economic development (which tsarism was seen to be hindering), and (in some quarters) socialism and revolution, imperial Russia's autocratic political structure was ever more widely considered a fetter on further advances. When the monarchy failed the test of the Great War, its last sources of popular affection and legitimacy withered away.

THE CONTRADICTIONS OF THE SOVIET EMPIRE STATE

By the early twentieth century, a transnational critique of empires and imperialism undermined much of the support for the great multinational contiguous empires of Europe. The idea of national self-determination, popular among liberals and social democrats, became a principal justification for the massive killing that occurred during World War I, as the Wilsonian ideal of states that matched the nations within was adopted as one of the war aims of the victorious Entente Cordiale. Empires persisted for several more generations, but the establishment of nation-states on the ruins of Austro-Hungary, Germany, and the Ottoman Empire suggested to many a macrohistorical progression from the lower form of empire to the higher form of nation-state as the unavoidable end of history. The great paradox of Russia's twentieth-century evolution was that a self-proclaimed empire fell in 1917 to be replaced by what became a neo-imperial state that not only refused to see itself as an empire, not only considered itself to be the major anti-imperialist power on the globe, but became the unwitting incubator of new nations within it.

The original Soviet state was ideologically conceived as temporary, provisional, and transitory from the era of capitalism, nationalism, and imperialism to the moment of successful international socialist revolution. That "state," which in one sense was to be the negation of states as they had hitherto existed, was at the same time the carapace of the first socialist government, the vehicle for the Bolshevik Party to carry out its program of disempowering the bourgeoisie and the old ruling classes, ending an imperialist war, and spreading the international civil war beyond the bounds of Russia. In the understanding of its paramount leaders, the Soviet Union was neither a nation-state nor an empire. It was simultaneously an anti-imperialist state, a federation of sovereign states, a voluntary union, and a prefiguration of a future nonstate, designed (initially, at least in Lenin's view) to be an example of equitable, nonexploitative relations among nations, a model for further integration of the other countries and the fragments of the European empires. All these were claims that the Soviet state's opponents could easily dismiss as self-serving and disingenuous. Yet, for the Bolshevik leaders, anti-imperialism was both a model for the internal structure of the USSR and a posture to attract supporters from abroad. Lenin, along with Woodrow Wilson, was the principal contributor to the delegitimizing of imperialism and empires, and anti-imperialism remained until the end of the USSR a powerful trope in Soviet rhetoric.

The Soviet Union became an empire despite the intentions of its founders. Yet, almost from its inception, the Soviet Union replicated imperialist relations familiar in other empires. The regathering of "Russian" lands, carried out in conditions of civil war, foreign intervention, and state collapse by a relatively centralized party and the Red Army, created an inequitable relationship between center and periphery that was enforced by Russia's greater material power and the Bolsheviks' willingness to use violence. The power of the metropole, as well as the large number of ethnic Russians, exceeded that of any of the other units of the new state or, indeed, of all of them combined. This unevenness prejudiced the new state's distribution of power, even though Soviet leaders made convoluted plans to offset the imbalance. One of Lenin's last designs was to have the Central Executive Committee of the soviets *"presided over* in turn by a Russian, Ukrainian, Georgian, etc."[41] Concessions were made to the perceived power of nationalism, which the Bolsheviks believed was the product of and contingent on imperialist oppression. However appropriate nationalism might be for a certain stage of history, it was, in the Bolsheviks' view, soon to be superseded. Lenin assumed that political and cultural rights for non-Russians, the systematic constraint of Russian nationalism, and the development of a socialist economy would be sufficient to solve the "national question."

There is no agreement among scholars on the genuineness of the Bolsheviks' anti-imperial, pro-national intentions. An earlier historiography treated Lenin's gestures toward the non-Russian peoples as cynical maneuvers disguised as noble principles; others argued that the Bolshevik leader risked his own health to struggle for equality among Russia's nationalities.[42] Terry Martin argues a middle position, viewing the formation of the "affirmative action empire" as "a strategy aimed at disarming nationalism by granting what were called the 'forms of nationhood'" and, later, as "a strategy designed to avoid the perception of empire."[43] For Martin the affirmative action empire that eventually emerged was "never an independent Bolshevik goal. It was instead a strategy to prevent the emergence of a potentially dangerous obstacle, non-Russian nationalism, to the accomplishment of other core Bolshevik goals: industrialization, nationalization of the means of production, abolition of the market, collectivization of agriculture, and the creation of socialism and its export abroad."[44]

The Bolshevik program of "national self-determination" within a "socialist federation" provided ideological cover for something like the tsarist program of "official nationality." In this sense, it resembled an essentially imperial state in an age in which consent of the "nation" was universally recognized as the principal form of state legitimation. From their first days in power, the Bolsheviks made tactical choices to deal with the simultaneous problems of fissiparous nationalisms and the territorial integrity, defense, and security of their new state. But the choices they made for pragmatic or principled reasons created a state structure that constrained further choices and led to outcomes unanticipated by its own founders. The Soviet empire, even in its earliest phase, was like other empires a state based on institutionalized distinctions replicated in hierarchies of power. Despite official rhetoric of equality and liberation and a bounded range of decision making left to the non-Russians, sovereignty steadily moved from the periphery to the center. Relations between the metropole and the periphery differed on the political, economic, and cultural levels. Politically, power, certainly most pronouncedly in the first decade of Soviet rule, was somewhat defused, with bargaining taking place between the center and the republics and autonomies. As the regime became ever more centralized and bureaucratized in Moscow, the inequitable, imperial relations between the center and the peripheries became the norm until actual sovereignty existed only in the center.

In the economic sphere, the emphasis on efficiency often resulted in disregard for ethnocultural factors. While creating national territorial units with broad cultural privileges, the new government's overwhelming concern was that the new multinational federal state be a single integrated economy. On this point, there was to be no compromise. Economic policy was statewide, and each federal unit was bound to others and to the center by economic ties and dependencies. In the 1920s, communists intensely debated whether economics should take priority over national culture, with the more economically oriented, such as Avel Enukidze, promoting administrative division of the country according to an economic rationale (*raionirovanie*), and officials in the People's Commissariat of Nationality Affairs (Narkomnats) and representatives of various non-Russian peoples favoring boundaries that corresponded to ethnicity.[45] Although much attention was paid to regional and cultural particularities, at least in the 1920s, over time economic regionalization became an extra-ethnic practice; party members were regularly encouraged to consider specialization, education, and training over ethnic qualifications in cadre policy.[46] The very repetition of this call, however, indicates that ethnic favoritism as underlined by the *korenizatsiia* (indigenization) policy constantly pulled against purely economic decision making.

In the cultural sphere, *korenizatsiia* stressed promotion of the "native" culture and local elites. The new state attempted to incorporate elites that were not hostile to Soviet power and to allow the development of "nations" within the Soviet federation. Nevertheless, the political order, in which a single party monopolized all decision making everywhere, constrained from the beginning and ultimately undermined local centers of power. In the first decade and a half of the Soviet experience, the smallest ethnicities were given political recognition, schools in their own languages, and, in some cases, even alphabets and literatures, while the Great Russians were denied specifically ethnic Russian institutions. For more than a decade, "great power chauvinism" was considered a larger danger to Soviet internationalism than small-nation nationalism, even as real power to make binding decisions steadily accrued to the central authorities.

Beginning roughly in 1932, Soviet nationality policy began a gradual shift away from this Russophobic program toward a growing identification of the Russian nation with the Soviet project. *Korenizatsiia* was scaled back; many national Communist Party leaders who had promoted their own peoples were purged, jailed, or executed; Russian heroes and history were celebrated as the models for a new state patriotism.[47] Russians became the state-bearing nation in the full sense as the country approached and then emerged victorious from World War II. As defense of the motherland became paramount in the mind of Stalin, the USSR became a nationalizing empire intent on founding its identity and security on a new "imagined community": the Soviet people. But this new people, made up of dozens of nations and nationalities, was to be identified primarily with the practices and values stemming from the imperial Russian past.

Although there was an attempt to create a "Soviet people," shockingly little effort was made to create a "Soviet nation." Eventually everyone in the USSR carried a passport inscribed with a nationality, but no one was permitted to declare himself or herself a Soviet by nationality. The various nationalities over time were thought of as primordial, based on birth and heredity, the nationality of one's parents. With its almost racial finality, nationality was rooted in the national republics and regions below the all-union federation. The nations of the Soviet Union were based on what were conceived as preexisting ethnic, religious, or linguistic communities, and in some cases on earlier polities. Nevertheless, whatever the degree of national cohesion and consciousness in 1917 (generally fairly low), for both ideological and politically expedient reasons, Soviet leaders promoted national construction among the non-Russian peoples.[48] The effect of this dualistic policy—which, on the one hand, stressed a kind of ethnically blind modernization and a Soviet patriotism, and, on the other, encouraged ethnocultural particularism and local political power within bounds—was to create a hybrid "empire of nations." Increasingly coherent, compact, and conscious national populations within the republics were supposed to live together under the umbrella of a Russified Soviet identity.

Building on earlier touchstones of loyalty, such as the October Revolution, victory in the civil war, the cult of Lenin, and the sense that history was on the

side of socialism, Stalin accelerated the construction of a cohesive identification of the people with the socialist state in the 1930s through a nationalizing
ideology based on the Russian (and to a degree the nationalities') past. The
prehistory of the Soviet Union was no longer told as a parade of defunct social
classes (as described by the Bolshevik historian Mikhail Pokrovsky) or revolutionary heroes from Spartacus through Karl Marx (as in the earliest Soviet
monuments). Rather, it became a largely Russian narrative, stretching back to
Ivan the Terrible and Peter the Great, with a generous sprinkling of military
leaders and sanctioned poets. Soviet socialist identity was heavily Soviet Russian.[49] With the tragic and heroic experience of the Great Fatherland War,
Soviet and national (Russian and other) identities melded into a synthetic,
integrated identification with the USSR, its victory, and its resplendent future.
The Soviet Union emerged from World War II with a fairly complete political
integration between traditional national affiliations and loyalty to the Soviet
socialist project. Given the effectiveness of mass education, the restriction of
alternative views, and the limited knowledge of the West, as well as the power
of the party/state and the system of material and psychic rewards, the Soviet
imperial state enjoyed the kind of connection with and support (or at least acquiescence) of the population that was generally uncharacteristic of traditional
empires and more familiar in democratic nation-states.

Of the many ironies in Soviet history, certainly a principal one must be that
a radical socialist elite that proclaimed an internationalist agenda that was to
transcend the bourgeois nationalist stage of history in fact ended up making
nations within its own political body. Another irony is that the very successes
of the Soviet system, not least this making of nations, but also the industrialization, urbanization, and mass education of the country, made the political
system that had revolutionized society largely irrelevant. Instead of legitimizing
the system, as it had done earlier, modernization undermined it at the end by
creating the conditions and the actors that were able to act without the direction
of the Communist Party. This dialectic of empire took on a revolutionary color-
ation in the Soviet case. Whatever the intentions of the Bolsheviks, they succeeded only too well in creating the conditions for their ultimate demise. Like
other great empires in the modern world, the Soviet Union was a transfor-
mative state. It was interested not in preserving, but in shaking up, social and
cultural relations. The communists built and then petrified a hierarchical, inequitable, nondemocratic political structure that progressively became an obstacle to further political—and to a large extent, social, economic, and cultural—
development.[50] This state structure became increasingly irrelevant, setting the

stage for decay and ultimately a crisis of legitimacy. The time arrived when the political structure of the Soviet state had to change or society and the economy would simply continue to stagnate and decline.

With the agenda ultimately set in Moscow, the relationship between the center and the republics was one of subordination of the non-Russian periphery to the Russian (more accurately, Soviet) metropole. In some periods local elites had considerable influence, but their effective participation in the political, economic, or cultural life of the country required a cultural competence in Russian and a loyalty to the entire Soviet project that superseded local identities and loyalties. Through generous rewards of power, prestige, and influence, along with severe punishments, the Soviet center attracted "the best and the brightest" among the national elites, many of which were created during Soviet times, to collaborate with the all-Soviet rulers. The costs of refusing to work in this way or of displaying "local nationalism" were extraordinarily severe. But the Soviet recruitment of native elites had different effects on different members of the non-Russian elites. Those who were particularly competent in Russian and Soviet cultural practices (and were of certain nationalities—such as the peoples of the Baltic states, Ukrainians, and Armenians—and Jews in the early Soviet years) became part of a cosmopolitan Soviet elite, highly mobile, largely interchangeable, and dedicated to the greater Soviet (imperial and developmental) project. These men (and they were usually men) were the carriers of Soviet culture, enforcers of party policy, and agents of the center in the peripheries. Leonid Brezhnev was such a figure. Born in Ukraine of Russian parents, he served in several republics, rising to become first secretary of Soviet Moldavia and later first secretary of Soviet Kazakhstan. But in Moldavia, Kazakhstan, and other republics, there existed a local elite skilled in the language, culture, and native practices of the people of that republic. Among them were Armenian poets, Georgian musicians, Estonian politicians whose Estonian was far better than their Russian, and others whose skills and interests aided them in making national rather than all-union careers.

In the early Soviet period, these "national Communists" were frequently the targets of antinationalist campaigns. In the great purges of the late 1930s, Stalin exterminated a whole generation of these initial builders of the national republics. But later, after Stalin's death in 1953, as the hold of the center loosened on the peripheries and a policy of indirect rule replaced the hypercentralization of Stalinism, native cadres with local ties and constituencies solidified their power. Content to pay lip service to the ideology of Sovietism, long-tenured party chieftains sponsored both local nationalisms and economic practices that basically enriched the locals and thwarted the goals of the central authorities. As the center abdicated much of its control over the country during the Gorbachev years, non-Russian (and Russian) communists were torn between those who wanted to preserve the larger state (without its imperial aspects) and those ready to move off into separate sovereignty.[51]

Reform ultimately led to revolution; renewal and restructuring, to collapse and disintegration. When the center weakened, the non-Russian elites (and in some cases the people as well) acted to free themselves of the metropole's grip. As in the fall of tsarism, so in the Soviet demise: nationalism was not the primary cause of the collapse of the Soviet system. The erosion of central power— the evaporation of political will and confidence—precipitated the centrifugal forces that tore the USSR into new states. Until the attempted August 1991 coup, centripetal forces remained strong. But in its aftermath a scramble ensued to abandon the sinking ship that seemed unable to steer a new course away from imperial practices. The Soviet empire collapsed in the context of (and because of) a failed attempt by a few top Soviet leaders to transform the USSR into a more "modern," "Western-style," "civilized" multinational state and system. This involved economic reform and eventually marketization; political reform leading ultimately to democratization; and the end of empire and the creation of a new form of multinational state. The problems were formidable, perhaps insurmountable, yet the centripetal pull of the center remained competitive until the August coup. By the late 1980s, Gorbachev and his closest comrades were convinced that the empire, which they believed had many of the cohesive characteristics of a nation, had to be transformed. Gorbachev's sincere hope, however, that the end of the empire did not also mean the end of the Soviet state was shared by few of those about to make history. The ultimate failure of the Soviet empire came with its disintegration into fifteen states, all claiming effectively to be nation-states.

Unlike in the tsarist period, when the hierarchies and divisions between classes, estates, and nationalities weakened the possibility of mobilization and the synthesis of a national identity, in the Soviet period the state authorities were far more successful in linking the population with the state. This was accomplished through institutions such as the Communist Party and the system of soviets; practices such as surveillance, censorship, and terror; and, more positively, the creation of overlapping identities—identification with the Soviet project of "building socialism," the creation of "Soviet Man" (and Woman), and the USSR as *otechestvo* (fatherland) or *rodina* (motherland), as well as identification with one's nationality and national republic. There was always potential and actual competition between the universal Soviet and the local nationality identities, but these identities began to undermine each other most fatally only as central state authority eroded in the last decades of Soviet power.

FOREIGN POLICIES OF AN EMPIRE IN DENIAL

The story of the Soviet empire as told here has so far been largely concerned with the internal composition of the Soviet state, the problem of managing a huge multinational state, and the consequences for political stability of the contradiction between imperial practices and nation-making endeavors by state and nonstate actors. The argument is that the Soviet state became an empire despite its intentions. It would seem, then, that an identity as empire for a state that was an empire in denial could not have any foreign policy implications. But "actually existing imperialism" as a practice of state formation and maintenance is connected not only to social facts and differentials in material power between the metropole and the peripheries of the Soviet Union, but also to underlying values and beliefs that legitimize making an empire. Just as Western imperialism had affinities with liberal humanist ideas of civilization and the liberating promise of development, so Soviet imperialism was connected to the original Bolshevik idea of using material power and the state to improve the lot of the less fortunate.

For all its cruelty and abuse, colonialism has been justified by its practitioners around the world as a necessary means to enlightenment and a better life. Soviet ideology proclaimed a global evolution from lower stages of development to higher ones, culminating in communism. Bolsheviks everywhere as the vanguard of the international proletariat were tasked with raising the downtrodden, breaking the shackles of the great imperialist powers, and setting the peoples of the colonial and semicolonial world on the road to socialism. When this liberation was not accomplished by the workers of other lands, or when the required proletariat did not yet exist, Soviet arms might accelerate the wheel of history. In the interwar period, this happened rarely (Lenin's enthusiasm for the 1920 invasion of Poland being a singular example). There were few real successes. No country followed the Soviet Union into socialism in the interwar period, and those that did after World War II did so at the behest of Soviet occupiers. Once established, the Soviet empire in East Central Europe was justified by communists as a higher stage of history and an alternative road to modernity.

Soviet self-identification as a historically unique social and ideological formation, the leader of the "camp of peace and socialism," rejected the West's identification of the USSR as an expansionist and destabilizing renegade in the international arena. For Lenin and Leon Trotsky, security for the Soviet Union was consonant with world revolution. For a realist such as Stalin, territorial expansion of the Kremlin's reach was more dependable than either alliances with the capitalist West or revolutionary adventures. For Nikita Khrushchev and Leonid Brezhnev, negotiation, agreements, and military parity with the West were essential for security in the nuclear age. Only with Mikhail Gorbachev was a new Soviet identity adopted, one that reversed the orthodoxies of the Cold War, abandoned the two-camp image of a world divided, and divested the Soviet Union of its foreign empire. Soviet national interest no longer was opposed to that of the non-Soviet world in a zero-sum game, but was seen as commensurate with cooperation and the end of the arms race.

By the mid-1920s, Soviet foreign policy had swung from its initial revolutionary phase to a more conventional approach. The USSR acted as a state among states, and given its weakness vis-à-vis the European powers (even Józef Piłsudski's Poland, which had defeated the Soviet Union in 1920, was considered a major threat), the Soviets were generally cautious and defensive until the late 1930s. Comintern policy at times was more adventurous, and Commissar of Foreign Affairs Georgy Chicherin was often at odds with the plots and plans of the International. But the Comintern was generally ineffective, unable to overturn a single government or sponsor a single successful revolt in the interwar years, though it caused enough consternation that relations with the victors in World War I remained tense. The USSR, as a revisionist state like its ally Weimar Germany, opposed the Versailles settlement until the mid-1930s. Then, confronted by the Nazi danger, the Soviet Union reversed its policy, adopted the strategy of collective security (complemented by the Popular Front strategy of the Comintern), and joined the League of Nations. Ideology appears to have played a secondary role to the imperatives of finding reliable allies. Therefore, when Stalin became convinced that there was no chance of support from the British and French, who had appeased Adolf Hitler at the 1938 Munich conference and failed to defend Czechoslovakia, he abruptly signed a pact with Germany. Opportunity and practicality seemingly trumped Marxism, for the primary incentive in signing the pact was Stalin's realist notion of survival in a dangerous neighborhood. The dangers presented by that neighborhood, however, stemmed from how the Soviet (and the fascist) leaders constructed who they were and who their enemies were. Marxism as a frame that divided the world into allies and enemies based on notions of class and fierce zero-sum conflict between capitalists and communists meshed effortlessly with Stalin's suspicion of foes (and even apparent friends) at home and abroad.

In its rhetoric and public posture, the USSR spoke in the idiom of Marxism-Leninism, and though the official ideology was hardly a recipe for specific policies, it certainly framed the way leaders and followers understood reality. Like liberals who see democracies as better prospects for alliance and as more likely to avoid war with other democracies, Soviet Marxists took class analysis very seriously and considered the mode of production (capitalist or socialist) as a reliable predictor of the value of an ally. Within this frame Lenin, Stalin, and their successors saw the world through a realist lens, calculating how to preserve their power and the system they ruled, how to weaken their opponents, and how to win friends and influence people around the world. But their realism depended on an evaluation of threat that was tied to their own and others' socialist, capitalist, or imperialist identities.

Identities are related to ideology but not reducible to it. Like ideology, they give a person or a state a "social cognitive structure" (or in Clifford Geertz's term, a "web of significance") that allows it to distinguish between threats and opportunities, enemies and potential allies.[52] Identity as the leading socialist state, which was heavily influenced by ideology and ideological education, led to construction of the capitalist West as an opponent. After Stalin's death, however, new leaders and new ideas reconstructed the West as not necessarily an immediate threat and, three decades later, as a potential ally. From Stalin to Gorbachev, Soviet socialist identity created an affinity with the nationalist anticolonialist movements in the third world, with the Cuban Revolution, and with other leftist regimes, which were seen as a zone of peace opposed to Western imperialism.[53] None of this construction of identity is one-sided. How Soviet leaders conceived of the world, its threats and opportunities, was shaped in part by its adversaries and allies.

The tension within the Soviet leadership between two competing ideological constructions of international affairs—their Marxist-Leninist framing and realism—was on full display in its tortured decision to intervene in Afghanistan in 1979. The USSR had had largely untroubled relations with Afghanistan from its earliest days, when it backed the reformist efforts of Amanullah Khan and supported successive royalist regimes. The Soviet leadership, disturbed by the coming to power of the leftist People's Democratic

Party of Afghanistan in April 1978, resisted the repeated calls of its leader, Nur Mohammad Taraki, for Soviet military aid. But, as Hopf writes, "Soviet leaders found themselves in a quagmire made of their own identity relations, institutional biases, deterrence fears, and allied manipulation."[54] The Soviets were fearful both of the costs of intervening and of allowing the Afghan government to fall to its enemies. Only after the more radical Hafizullah Amin had Taraki murdered and appeared to be moving away from the Soviets did the Kremlin send in troops, kill Amin, and replace him with Babrak Karmal. The aging Soviet leadership felt compelled for both strategic and ideological reasons to back the Afghans and to prevent the revolution from spinning out of control. Their aims were embedded in their identities as socialists, their perceptions of the world, and their fears of the American "other."[55] Not surprisingly, the West and many Islamic countries saw the Soviet incursion as expansionist and imperialist.

With the coming to power of Gorbachev, a fundamental—indeed revolutionary—change occurred in the Soviet leadership's conception of the socialist project, the USSR's primary identity and, consequently, both in the way the country was ruled internally and how it would behave internationally. No longer was the Soviet Communist Party considered the vanguard of an international socialist movement that was obligated to follow the orders of the Soviet leadership and emulate the Soviet model. No longer was the USSR moving in a direction different from the mainstream of civilization. As the country embarked on perestroika, glasnost, and *demokratizatsiya*, the Soviet government eschewed the use of force in maintaining control over East Central Europe, lessened its imperial grasp over the constituent republics of the Soviet federation, withdrew its troops from Afghanistan, and brought the Cold War to an end. New identities adopted by Gorbachev and his foreign minister, Eduard Shevardnadze, required a reconceptualization of Soviet interests that in a short time led to the reunification of Germany, the end of Communist Party rule in most of the former Soviet bloc, and a frustrated effort to convince the Western powers that the USSR was a worthy partner in a new world order. But the rapidity with which superficial new identities were handed down from above did not permit their institutionalization or widespread acceptance. The failed coup by conservative communists in August 1991 was a desperate reaction by those who subscribed to older identities and ways of doing business. Although their efforts at restoration of the old failed miserably, the powerful identities associated with the Soviet period continued to influence events in the post-Soviet states.[56]

In the minds of many analysts, the collapse of the USSR is the final proof that the Soviet project was an impossible, utopian effort at social transformation. For them, the final "crisis of empire" of the Gorbachev years demonstrates the inevitability of nationalism overcoming empire. The flaw in this view stems less from the fatalism of its teleology from empire to nation than from an overestimation of the resistance of the periphery and an underappreciation of the top-down, Gorbachev-initiated disintegration of metropolitan power. In addition, the collapse reveals the limits of leaders' relying on identities and understandings that diverge too far from actual structures and social dynamics. While some Soviet party bosses, such as Gorbachev and Shevardnadze, were sensitive to the pathologies in the system, they failed to find an effective path from imperial rule to a more horizontally equivalent, less hierarchical multinational state. Trying to "rebuild the ship of state while at sea" sank the whole enterprise.[57]

The Soviet Union's imperial structure at home, as well as its East European empire abroad, came with great costs and were kept intact only through the authoritarian structures of Communist Party rule and the threat, and occasional use, of coercion. Gorbachev may have believed his own rhetoric and the ideological notions of a fraternal socialist bloc and "friendship of the (Soviet) peoples." But once he refused to practice empire—without a viable alternative to offer the various elites and publics in the republics—the opening appeared for nationalist movements (in Armenia, Estonia, Georgia, Latvia, Lithuania, and Moldova) and opportunistic party bosses (in Belarus, Russia, and Ukraine) to pull the weakened state down—and Gorbachev along with it. Once the dust cleared, it was evident that instead of a great global power, Russia had been reduced to a vulnerable fragment of its former self.

CONFLICTED IDENTITIES

Since 1990 Russia's strategic weakness and its shifting, contested self-identification have influenced its foreign policy. Both authoritarian nationalist writers and more democratically oriented authors have interpreted Russia's post-Soviet "identity crisis" as a product of the radical, imposed turn from the "natural" course of history by the Bolsheviks. For the self-styled "democrats" around Boris Yeltsin, the seventy years of Soviet power were imagined as a deviation, a distortion that had to be undone if Russia was to return to the path to civilization. This interpretation contributed to, and was shaped by, the revolutionary shift from the Soviet regime, with its clearly articulated ideology, to one that eschewed official imposition of ideological conformity. The nature of that shift, limply labeled a "transition," was extraordinarily abrupt, with a sharp rejection of the norms and values of Soviet society, its view of history and the political world, and, in the name of reform, the establishment of a systemless system with which the majority of people were completely unfamiliar. A world that had been experienced, even with all its repression, mundane imperfections, and corruption, as one of order, progress, and purpose (at least up through the mid-1970s) was abandoned by Russia's new leaders and many intellectuals. In its place emerged a world of unpredictability, embedded corruption and criminality, economic hardship, military weakness, and the precipitous decline of Russia from great-power status to a wounded, humiliated, truncated state. As the liberal professor of philosophy Igor Chubais put it, "The euphemism 'reform' . . . is used in reality to explain the abolition of the old rules—often unacceptable but sometimes fair—and the failure to accept any new norms at all. In the current situation, the term 'reform' has become a synonym of the concept 'chaos.' "[58]

Post-Soviet Russian attitudes toward the Soviet past have been ambivalent, if not downright contradictory. People on both the Left and the Right have become more aware of the excesses of Stalinism—terror, repression, and censorship—as well as the corruption of the Soviet elite and the passivity of the population before the all-powerful state. But at the same time, experiencing the insecurities of the unpredictable present, they express a nostalgia for the stability and security of the past. "Russia in 1999," writes Hopf, "did not reject its Soviet past altogether. In five ways, Russians valued the Soviet experience: they appreciated the Soviet Union's status as a great power in world affairs; they recognized that democracy was already emergent under Soviet rule; they fondly recalled the high quality of Soviet mass culture; they acknowledged the superior conditions the Soviet government created for young people; and last, but touted only [by] the Left, they acknowledged Soviet economic performance, especially in agriculture."[59]

No general consensus on national or state identity emerged in Russia after the erosion of the Soviet value system. Although many democratic and Western values gained greater acceptance among Russians throughout the 1990s, the country remained deeply divided between those who supported the general direction of the economic and political changes initiated by Gorbachev and Yeltsin and those for whom the rejection of the Soviet past as an authentic part of Russia's history and tradition meant their ejection from the rebuilding of the nation. People who had fought for and suffered for that system were overnight rendered disgruntled, disoriented, red-flag-waving marginals. The turn back to symbols and institutions of the pre-Soviet past—the double-headed eagle, the imperial flag, the Orthodox Church, the reburial of the last tsar's family (though not yet the revival of the Romanov anthem, "God Save the Tsar")—met with resistance among many former *sovki*, not to mention the 20 percent of Russia's population that was neither Orthodox nor ethnically Russian.[60] Yeltsin's successor, Vladimir Putin, has moderated some of Yeltsin's hostility to the Soviet past, perhaps best symbolized in Putin's resurrection of the old Soviet national anthem with new post-Soviet words. Since January 2000 the Russian government has steadily been reintegrating the Soviet past into the "democratic" capitalist present.

Throughout the 1990s and into the early twenty-first century, Russian political elites as well as public opinion were deeply divided on the question of what constitutes the Russian nation and state. Russians remain uncertain about their state's boundaries, where its border guards ought to patrol (at the edge of the federation or the Confederation of Independent States), what its ultimate shape will be (is Chechnya in or out?), its relations with neighboring states (is Belarus in or out?), and even its internal structure as an asymmetrical federation.[61] Many analysts of post-Soviet Russia have noted the deep divisions in discourses about domestic and foreign policy. Vera Tolz argues that three groups with incompatible views of legitimate Russian statehood have been vying for acceptance. The first comprises conservative nationalists, the most militant communists, and the so-called Eurasianists, who believe that "the Russian Federation should initiate the restoration of a union, which should be joined by as many of the former Soviet republics as possible."[62] The second group has adopted an idea of the Russian nation that was prevalent in the prerevolutionary period—Russia as the union of Great Russians, White Russians (Belarusians), and Little Russians (Ukrainians). This conception of Slavic unity, closely identified with Alexander Solzhenitsyn, extends to inclusion of other areas with Russian populations, such as northern Kazakhstan, within the new Russian state. The third group seeks the formation of a republic of Russian speakers, integrating the Russian-speaking diaspora into the federation, and, perhaps, the allowance of some non-Russian autonomies to separate from the Russian state.

To Tolz's list of "homeland myths," a fourth might be added: the generally operative one that Russia is a multinational state in which "Russian" is understood both as ethnic Russian (*russky*) and as citizen of the republic (*rossiisky*). During the Yeltsin years, government policy gradually shifted from "a vision of Russia as a kin state of all Russian speakers," dominant from 1992 to 1994, to "policies facilitating the re-creation of some form of union on the territory of the USSR," becoming more important from late 1994.[63] Polling data reveal that "the idea that the new Russia should be primarily the state of Russian speakers who enjoy a legally defined dominant status, as well as the idea that the Slavic nucleus of the USSR should reunite, attracts the largest support within the Russian Federation."[64] Tolz ominously concludes that "the view that the borders of the Russian Federation are in urgent need of revision is more widespread among Russian intellectuals, politicians, and the public at large than is usually assumed in western scholarly literature."[65]

Looking at foreign policy, Hopf distinguishes three principal discourses on Soviet identity in the 1990s: a liberal, pro-European discourse opposed to the Soviet past; a conservative pro-Soviet discourse that wanted to restore Russia as a great power; and a centrist discourse that looked outward to European social democracy and backward to an idealized Soviet past. During the early Yeltsin years, as liberals and conservatives fought to a standstill that ultimately led to a bloody showdown in October 1993 and the defeat of the conservatives, the liberals implemented much of their program of privatization. But with the collapse of the Russian economy in the early 1990s and the rise of crime and corruption, liberalism became discredited. As a result, centrism ended up "by the late 1990s, the predominant representation of Russian identity." In the Putin years, the Russian Federation has come to understand itself "as a great power who can either join European social democratic civilization as a counterweight to U.S. liberal market hegemony, or bandwagon with that hegemony in order to pursue more narrow tactical considerations in defense of its own fissiparous periphery."[66]

The new Russian state lives in a different world from the Soviet state, a world that has been profoundly changed by the disappearance of the USSR. The likelihood of nuclear attack from the West, led by the United States, has been largely eliminated as a perceived threat, though there is much discontent in Russia over the George W. Bush administration's decision to abrogate the Antiballistic Missile Treaty and develop a national missile defense. The Soviet obligation to support national liberation movements and poor leftist developing states (including countries that had once been part of the Soviet Union, such as in Central Asia) evaporated with the demise of the USSR. And an entirely new challenge faced the Russian Federation: the competition for influence with the West (and Islamic powers) in the near abroad.

EMPIRE OR HEGEMONY? THE SOUTHERN TIER

Within the newly independent states lying to the south of Russia, what I call "the southern tier," the euphemisms "building a market economy" and "transition to democracy" hide more than they illuminate. The ending of the command economy almost everywhere resulted in a mammoth transfer of wealth from the state to a new "bourgeoisie" that enriched itself by dipping deeply into the coffers of the old system. In many cases "privatization" was code for looting of public and state resources, and the legitimacy of that transfer of wealth continues to be bitterly questioned throughout the former Soviet Union. One of the more unexpected developments in the post-Soviet period has been the power of the old Soviet system to reproduce itself in new ways, even after the Communist Party disbanded. What institutional continuity and actual authority remain in many republics are tied back to the Soviet system. The ability of the Soviet regime to suppress the emergence of alternative elites left the heirs of communism, stripped of their ideological baggage, the most effective political players in many of these republics.

Of the eight republics of the southern tier, five (Azerbaijan, Georgia, Kazakhstan, Turkmenistan, and Uzbekistan) were ruled through the 1990s by former communist first secretaries. In most of these countries, a democratic facade concealed the continuing power of the old apparatus. In at least two cases, Eduard Shevardnadze in Georgia and Nursultan Nazarbaev in Kazakhstan, the former party chiefs appeared to be presiding over quasi-democratic transitions, but the longer they remained in power, the more they were seen by their own populations and outside observers as hindrances to further democratization. In November 2003 the "street" spoke in Tbilisi, and Shevardnadze was overthrown in the Rose Revolution by Westernizing "democrats." Unreconstructed old communist rulers, now disguised as "leaders of the nation," still rule in Turkmenistan (Saparmurat Niyazov) and Uzbekistan (Islam Karimov). Heidar Aliev returned to power in Azerbaijan and maintained his position through the forceful containment of the opposition. Just before his death, he turned power over to his son, Ilham, in a kind of sultanist succession. In Tajikistan the Communist Party suffered a deep schism, but those currently in power, supported by Russia, are former communists (including the president, Imomali Rakhmonov). In Kyrgyzstan the former academic Askar Akayev skillfully maneuvered between democratic and former communist forces, allowing much local power to remain in the hands of clan leaders, but in March 2005 protestors swept him from office. Only in Armenia and Georgia have nationalist, and ostensibly democratic, oppositions come to power. In Armenia, however, President Robert Kocharian continues to rule by manipulating elections and suppressing demonstrations. Although there are differences of degree (in many ways, Russia is further along the democratic spectrum), the political order in the states of the southern tier looks a lot like that of Russia under Putin.

What resulted from the Soviet collapse was not the birth of fifteen fully formed nation-states, but the appearance of fledgling states that only in some cases coincide with relatively homogeneous, coherent, and nationally conscious nations within them. Where the nation and the state coincide most successfully, as in relatively homogeneous Armenia, internal ethnic conflicts are easily avoided. Where states are much more multinational or binational, as in Kazakhstan, serious issues of the inclusivity or exclusivity of what constitutes the nation arise. Several of the states—Azerbaijan, Georgia, and Tajikistan—fragmented, albeit for different reasons; however, problems of ethnicity, identity, and the appropriate political forms to sustain the new state in the future were at the base of the devastating and violent crises that fractured the new republics. These are legacies of empire that present both problems and opportunities for Russia.

Another legacy of the Soviet empire is the complex integration of this mixed multinational subcontinent, highly interdependent economically, with millions of people living outside what had become their "homelands." New minorities in republics, face to face with new dominant majorities, no longer have any appeal to an imperial center. Since the mid-1990s, a massive "unmixing of peoples" (the phrase is Rogers Brubaker's) has taken place, as hundreds of thousands of Russians, Armenians, Jews, and others have left one republic for their ostensible "homeland" or for a better life in Russia, Israel, or the West.[67] Still another, particularly pernicious inheritance from Soviet times is the ethnicization of politics that gave greater representation and enhanced rights to so-called titular nationalities than to others, whether or not they are majorities. In Soviet discourse the nation was real and primary, a fixed, primordially rooted, bounded group attached to a given territory. Nationality developed over time into a powerful source of advantages and disadvantages in the distribution of Soviet resources. So tightly linked were politics and nationality in the

Soviet system that post-Soviet players have found it difficult to imagine other ways of engaging in politics.

CONCLUSION

The ways in which policy makers and opinion shapers see the world have profound effects on the constitution of that world. In the post-Soviet space, metropolitan actors look upon the newly independent states differently from the way leaders of the new states look upon the former metropole. Distributions of power and resources also remain important to the formation of ways in which the real world is understood. Although the mere proximity of a mammoth state to much smaller ones does not necessarily lead to imperialism or even hegemony, because relations between states depend on the forms of national identity and discourse, the disparity in power and past imperial experience contributes to perceptions of threat.

Russia's problem is not one of a changing national identity, but one of a chronic failure to construct coherent national and state identities that are widely accepted by the population. Yet since the mid-1990s, there has been a growing consolidation of identification with an ideal of democracy (if not the actual practice) in Russia, the attractions of a modernity in large part defined by Europe, and a palpable need for a stronger state and more central authority (in response to internal threats such as the conflict in Chechnya and external threats from U.S. hegemony). The hold of the Soviet past on the Russian mentality has weakened over time, though the Russians' desire for greater influence, power, and security in the world has not diminished. There is a greater sense under Putin of shared interests with the West, as in the struggle against terrorism. The evolving and incoherent sense of national identity and interest complicates the ability of analysts to predict Russia's future intentions, and the uncertainty of Russia's intentions and behavior affects the calculations of its neighbors. Understandably, in an uncertain universe, leaders may rationally revert to the kind of paranoia and suspicion that realists predict. It makes more sense to think that everyone is out to get you when states have not yet solidified their idea of themselves and others. While Russia faces the problem of constructing a coherent national identity, other states must consider the consequences of whichever identity emerges.

No matter how weak it is at the moment, Russia will likely continue to identify itself to itself and others as a great power, and great powers seldom operate under the same rules and constraints as lesser powers. Although increasingly it is becoming a purely symbolic issue, as a great power Russia will probably continue to demand a role in protecting those it considers its co-nationals (the so-called *russkoyazychnye*) in the near abroad. Like the United States in the Western Hemisphere, Russia will seek to police its neighborhood and reserve the ability to guard frontiers that impinge on its security. For Russia, which now sees itself as a multinational nation-state that has eschewed empire at home and abroad, the near abroad will remain a sphere of interest. Even if momentarily Russia conceded the right of the United States to locate bases in Central Asia, it did so reluctantly and now wants to roll back U.S. influence in the southern tier. Russia has interests both in the near abroad and farther away that are distinct from, and at times opposed to, U.S. interests. Putin demonstrated this by his opposition to the United States' invasion of Iraq in 2003.

For the states of that region, the question is not whether there will be a strong Russian presence, but what kind of presence it will be. Russia is far more likely than the United States to remain a powerful presence in the region for simple geopolitical reasons. Although Russia is a much-reduced former superpower, even in its current weakness and domestic confusion, it remains far stronger militarily and economically than any of the other newly independent states. Besides the restraints and rewards offered by other powers, particularly the United States, the major obstacles to Russian dominance or direct imperial control of the southern tier are (1) the ability of the southern tier states to consolidate their identities as nations and establish legitimate and effective institutions of statehood, and (2) the internal generation of a Russian identity that includes genuinely democratic values, satisfaction with Russia's current boundaries, and respect for the sovereignty and territorial integrity of its neighbors.

An optimistic scenario for the future might envision strong republics in the south that would encourage more moderate Russian policies, and a democratic Russia limiting its major strategic interests in the region to maintaining stable, prosperous states on its southern border and a secure buffer against intrusions from China, Iran, or Turkey—not the full burden of colonizing a complexly mixed and resistant population. Yet because of its internal confusion and corruption, its occasional pretensions to empire, and the insecurity it engenders among its neighbors, Russia has been unable to acquire the kind of acquiescence from the other former Soviet states for exercising hegemony. Russia's identity crisis has left it without a clear justification for hegemony. It can no longer credibly claim to be filling a power vacuum, providing security, mediating conflict, aiding in economic development, or building democracy. Notwithstanding its pretensions to great-power status, a crisis-ridden chaotic Russia cannot exercise the special role it wants to play in the region.

Some prominent observers in the West fear the rise of a new Russian imperialism, point to Russia's self-image as a great power, and rehearse Russia's repeated interventions in the near abroad. In late 1994 and early 1995, Yeltsin and his foreign minister, Andrei Kozyrev, publicly declared their support for the reintegration of the countries of the former Soviet Union, first economically, but then militarily and perhaps even politically. This policy continued with Foreign Minister Yevgeny Primakov, who became prime minister in the summer of 1998. What might have been called the "Yeltsin doctrine" could be interpreted as recognition of the independence and sovereignty of the existing states (along with a paramount role for Russia in the southern tier), an explicit claim for dominance in the realm of security, and perhaps a special role in protecting Russians and other minorities. Although the Russian government stated repeatedly that it did not wish the dismemberment of the Transcaucasian republics, which could set "a most dangerous precedent" and lead to similar struggles at home, it was concerned about the spillover of unresolved ethnic conflicts into the country. Although Yeltsin did not have plans to reannex the states of Transcaucasia and Central Asia, he promoted a greater military and political presence, even hinting that the United Nations should give Russia exclusive rights as gendarme in the area. He also underscored the desire for Russian partnership in the exploitation and development of the natural resources of the region, the most important of which is the offshore oil in Azerbaijan. Moscow repeatedly claimed the right to protect rail lines in Transcaucasia, for the major link from Russia to Armenia passes through Abkhazia and Georgia, and the line to Baku passes through Chechnya.

Russia's reach into Georgia displays all the contradictions of its hegemonic policy in the near abroad. In many ways Georgia is a failed state, fragmented among its nationalities—Abkhaz, Ajars, Armenians, Azerbaijanis, Georgians, and Ossetians—with Russia playing the role of protector of minorities (largely with their consent). But Russia both suffers from Georgia's lack of central state authority (e.g., in the Pankisi Gorge, where Chechen fighters have found refuge) and perpetuates it (by its support of the minorities and its refusal until recently to give up its military bases in the country). Georgia is one of the few states where both Russian and U.S. soldiers serve, with both powers asserting their interests. The United States supports democratic development in Georgia, hopes to limit Russia's influence in the country, and is concerned about protecting the major oil and gas pipeline from Azerbaijan to Turkey (Baku-Cehan) that runs through Georgian territory. When the democratic opposition led by Mikhail Saakashvili launched its campaign against Shevardnadze in the fall of 2003, Russia's foreign minister, Igor Ivanov, flew to Tbilisi and negotiated with both sides. U.S. secretary of state Colin Powell was also involved by phone, and both ministers attended the inauguration of Saakashvili, elected early the next year. Neither the United States nor Russia wants a confrontation with the other in Georgia, yet their ambitions in that small land are pulling in different directions. Putin's Russia considers Georgia a test for its own responsible foreign policy; after all, it was Russia that mediated both the Ossetian and Abkhaz cease-fires with the Georgians. Moreover, Georgia borders on Russia and affects the security of the latter's southern border. Given both the emotional ties of Russians to the Great Caucasus (and to Georgia particularly) and what it conceives as vital strategic interests in the region, Russia imagines itself the fair-minded arbiter of internal Georgian affairs. Yet it is deeply distrusted by the Georgians, whose own national identity is intimately connected with the nationalist construction of Russia as its long-time colonial oppressor.

Russia wants to be the regional hegemon, not the imperial overlord, of the southern tier. But it exists in a world in which its major rival, the United States, not only is a regional hegemon but is as close to becoming a global hegemon as any power in several millennia. The United States faces no other regional hegemons in the world and wants to keep it that way. If Mearsheimer is right that a regional hegemon desires to be the only regional hegemon, Russia and the United States have fundamentally conflicting interests in the southern tier. Elsewhere in the world, Russia, like Europe, must find the means to contain the United States' global reach, though it currently lacks the material strength to achieve this objective. Russia has faced the hard fact that it is vulnerable to U.S. power, that the world it lives in is largely shaped by the United States, and that it no longer can contain its former adversary as the Soviet Union once did. As Mearsheimer puts it:

> Although that intense superpower rivalry ended along with the Cold War in 1990, Russia and the United States have not worked together to create the present order in Europe. The United States, for example, has rejected out of hand various Russian proposals to make the Organization for Security and Cooperation in Europe the central organizing pillar of European security (replacing the U.S.-dominated NATO). Furthermore, Russia was deeply opposed to NATO expansion, which it viewed as a

serious threat to Russian security. Recognizing Russia's weakness would preclude any retaliation, however, the United States ignored Russia's concerns and pushed NATO to accept the Czech Republic, Hungary, and Poland as new members.[68]

The West, with its own array of identities, holds out the prize of NATO membership to states with the right democratic and market credentials. NATO expansion to a select number of East European states, including the Baltic countries, sends a clear message to Russia that it is not fit for membership. As the border of the Western alliance moves eastward and Russia and the newly independent states are left unmanaged and undefined, Russia is left on its own to deal with the drug trade, Islamic fundamentalism, and terrorism.[69]

Russia's self-image as a great power is a highly imaginative one that does not correspond to its actual power. Again, as in the Gorbachev years, identity and imagination diverge from more realistic readings of Putin's Russia. Its leaders understand that it is no longer capable of reconstructing an empire in the near abroad, but they remain anxious to thwart outside contenders. Despite its internal divisions, since the early 1990s Russia has become a much more predictable and much more restrained foreign policy actor than many in the West had imagined it could be. To some degree, it may have learned from the conflict in Chechnya the heavy costs of empire. Although Russia is still caught in a quagmire in the Caucasus, there is reason to hope that its leaders are willing to show greater caution before choosing military options in the near future. Rather than a sign of a pattern of Russian expansionism, the Chechnya adventure is a bitter indication of the serious disease of state weakness and the narrowing of political decision making into the tight circle around Yeltsin and now Putin. The current president of Russia has made Chechnya a personal vendetta, and his policies have led to a bloody impasse that is having a profound effect on Russia's identity, international image, and relations with the Islamic world. The Chechen war is clearly an episode of imperialism, or what might more generously be called "empire repair," in what in many ways is becoming a multinational state.

Much like the United States was in the first half of the nineteenth century, Russia is today a regional power that seeks to consolidate state authority over its territory, define its borders, and police its neighborhood to prevent rivals from establishing influence in its sphere of interest. Since roughly the Primakov years of the late 1990s, Russia seems to have come to terms with the limits of its power. Putin has been eminently pragmatic, willing to deal sensitively with his U.S. counterpart, George W. Bush, while working assiduously to build a bloc with the European powers to constrain American unilateralism. Whether it is contingent or structural, the new forward policy of the Bush administration has presented Russia with a vital challenge. After the terrorist attacks against the United States on September 11, 2001, Putin quickly joined the so-called war on global terrorism, a move that both brought him closer to the United States, at a moment when Washington was determined to move militarily into Central Asia and the Middle East, and yielded international legitimation for Russia's own brutal suppression of the Chechens. Still, it is unclear whether Russian leaders have developed a coherent idea of what their state's interests ought to be. The lack of a clear, consistent, widely accepted national identity remains at the core of Russia's lack of clarity in foreign policy.

No longer imperial, the Russian Federation is a multinational state, but one with imperial pretensions in Chechnya and unrequited dreams of hegemony in the near abroad. The Russian state is a state in flux, its interests dependent on such contingent factors as the whims and preferences of a vigorous young president, the international economy, and the discontents and expectations of his still impoverished and disgruntled people. Russia's imperial past generates among its neighbors and foes suspicions of its present and future aims and ambitions, which, given the flux of Russia's own self-identity, remain extraordinarily difficult to predict. Even as Russia moves away from empire at home and abroad, the great state formed by autocrats from Ivan Groznyi to Joseph Stalin must cope with the legacies that weigh on the minds of the living.

NOTES

1. The actual quotation by Henry John Temple, 3d Viscount Palmerston (1784–1865), is "We have no eternal allies, and we have no perpetual enemies. Our interests are eternal and perpetual, and those interests it is our duty to follow." Remarks defending his foreign policy in the House of Commons, March 1, 1848, in *Hansard Parliamentary Debates*, 3d ser., vol. 97, 1848, p. 122.

2. Ernest B. Haas, "The Balance of Power as a Guide to Policy-Making," *Journal of Politics* (August 1953), pp. 370–398; reprinted in *Crisis and Continuity in World Politics: Readings in International Relations*, ed. George A. Lanyi and Wilson C. McWilliams (New York: Random House, 1966), pp. 324–325.

3. Ibid., p. 336.

4. John J. Mearsheimer, *The Tragedy of Great Power Politics* (New York: Norton, 2001), p. 2.

5. In a paragraph that could easily apply to Russia, Mearsheimer notes, "Every state might want to be king of the hill, but not every state has the wherewithal to compete for that lofty position, much less achieve it. Much depends on how military might is distributed among the great powers. A great power that has a marked power advantage over its rivals is likely to behave more aggressively, because it has the capability as well as the incentive to do so. . . . Before great powers take offensive actions, they think carefully about the balance of power and about how other states will react to their moves. They weigh the costs and risks of offense against the likely benefits. If the benefits do not outweigh the risks, they sit tight and wait for a more propitious moment." Ibid., p. 37.

6. For an appreciative statement of the constructivist approach, see Ted Hopf, "The Promise of Constructivism in International Relations Theory," *International Security* 23, no. 1 (Summer 1998): 171–200.

7. Ibid., p. 176. Similarly, Alexander Wendt points out, "Identities are the basis of interests. Actors do not have a 'portfolio' of interests that they carry around independent of social context; instead, they define their interests in the process of defining situations." Wendt, "Anarchy Is What States Make of It," *International Organization* 46, no. 2 (Spring 1992): 398.

8. Alexander Wendt, *Social Theory of International Politics* (Cambridge: Cambridge University Press, 1999), pp. 113–114.

9. Ibid., p. 114 (emphasis in original).

10. The first term is from an earlier version of Hopf's article "The Promise of Constructivism in International Relations Theory"; the second is from Ronald Grigor Suny, "Provisional Stabilities: The Politics of Identities in Post-Soviet Eurasia," *International Security* 24, no. 3 (Winter 1999/2000): 139–178.

11. Wendt, *Social Theory*, pp. 233, 235–237.

12. Ibid., p. 238.

13. Ibid., p. 241.

14. Ibid., p. 138.

15. The theory is indebted to my reading of Kenneth Waltz, Stephen Walt, and Ted Hopf and was most directly inspired by Paul Huth, *Standing Your Ground: Territorial Disputes and International Conflict* (Ann Arbor: University of Michigan Press, 1996), pp. 33–67. There is even a residue of Karl Marx in it.

16. Both Vladimir Lenin and Boris Yeltsin oversaw, and to a certain degree sanctioned, the loss of territory for both pragmatic and ideological reasons. In Lenin's case, the principle of national self-determination led him to recognize the right of Finland and Poland to independence, though in other cases his actions compromised that principle. To increase his power and eliminate his main rival, Mikhail Gorbachev, Yeltsin signed away the Soviet Union and permitted the fourteen non-Russian republics to form independent states. Yet both would have preferred to have kept intact the maximum possible territory under their rule.

17. I am indebted to Kenneth Schultz for the points made in this paragraph.

18. "Evil empire" is, of course, the famous phrase of U.S. president Ronald Reagan; "affirmative action empire" comes from Terry Martin; "empire of nations" is the title of a book by Francine Hirsch; and "imperialism as the highest stage of socialism" was employed by Yuri Slezkine. See Martin, *The Affirmative Action Empire: Nations and Nationalism in the Soviet Union, 1923–1939* (Ithaca: Cornell University Press, 2001); Hirsch, *An Empire of Nations: Ethnographic Knowledge and the Making of the Soviet Union* (Ithaca: Cornell University Press, 2005); Hirsch, "Toward an Empire of Nations: Bordermaking and the Formation of Soviet National Identities," and Slezkine, "Imperialism as the Highest Stage of Socialism," both in *Russian Review* 59, no. 2 (April 2000): 201–226 and 227–234, respectively.

19. Hirsch, "Toward an Empire of Nations," p. 204n15. Martin distinguishes his affirmative action empire as a "national entity" from ideal types such as nation-state, city-state, federation, confederation, and empire. Martin, *The Affirmative Action Empire*, pp. 18–20. Dominic Lieven reviews the various meanings of "empire" and adopts a broad definition that includes "a very great power that has left its mark on the international relations of an era," "a polity that rules over wide territories and many peoples," "not a democracy, . . . not a polity ruled with the explicit consent of its peoples," and often "linked to some great religion and high culture, thereby having a major impact on the history of world civilization." Lieven, *Empire: The Russian Empire and Its Rivals* (London: John Murray, 2000), p. xiv. Geoffrey Hosking contrasts empire, which he defines as a gigantic, ethnically diverse state with deep divisions between rulers and ruled, with nation-state, a "large, territorially extended and socially differentiated aggregate of people who share a sense of a common fate or of belonging together." Hosking, *Russia: People and Empire, 1552–1917* (London: HarperCollins, 1997), p. xx.

20. For the formulation of this definition, I am indebted to the work of John A. Armstrong and Michael W. Doyle. Armstrong, *Nations Before Nationalism* (Chapel Hill: University of North Carolina Press, 1982); and Doyle, *Empires* (Ithaca: Cornell University Press, 1986).

21. Doyle, *Empires*, p. 36.

22. As Alexander J. Motyl argues, the peripheries must be home to a distinct population—whether along class, ethnic, or religious lines—they ought to have a distinct territory, and they should have either a distinct polity or a distinct society. Motyl, "From Imperial Decay to Imperial Collapse: The Fall of the Soviet Empire in Comparative Perspective," in *Nationalism and Empire: The Habsburg Empire and the Soviet Union,* ed. Richard L. Rudolph and David F. Good (New York: St. Martin's Press, 1992), p. 18.

23. The distinction between "ethnic group" and "nationality/nation" need not be territory but rather the discourse in which they operate. The discourse about ethnicity is primarily about culture, cultural rights, and some limited political recognition. In contrast, the discourse of the nation is more often about popular sovereignty, state power, and control of a territorial homeland. But this is not

necessarily or exclusively so, for one can conceive of nonterritorial nationalisms, such as those of the Jews before Zionism, the Armenians in the nineteenth century, and the Gypsies to the present. For another view on the problems of definitions, see Lowell W. Barrington, " 'Nation' and 'Nationalism': The Misuse of Key Concepts in Political Science," *PS: Political Science & Politics* 30, no. 4 (December 1977): 712–716.

24. There are a few states in recent times that do not explicitly claim to be nation-states (e.g., the Soviet Union or states ruled as the patrimony of a hereditary ruler), but they are rare exceptions.

25. Rogers Brubaker, *Citizenship and Nationhood in France and Germany* (Cambridge: Harvard University Press, 1992), pp. 22, 27.

26. Benedict Anderson, *Imagined Communities: Reflections on the Origin and Spread of Nationalism* (London: Verso, 1991), p. 84.

27. Ibid., p. 85.

28. Ibid., p. 86.

29. Ibid.

30. Ibid., p. 87.

31. I thank Kenneth Church for raising this point following his careful and critical reading of an earlier paper from which this chapter is taken.

32. Joshua A. Sanborn, *Drafting the Russian Nation: Military Conscription, Total War, and Mass Politics, 1905–1925* (DeKalb: Northern Illinois University Press, 2003); Barry R. Posen, "Nationalism, the Mass Army, and Military Power," *International Security* 18, no. 2 (Fall 1993): 80–124; and Matthew Levinger, *Enlightened Nationalism: The Transformation of Prussian Political Culture, 1806–1848* (New York: Oxford University Press, 2000).

33. Sanborn, *Drafting the Russian Nation*, pp. 3–4.

34. Ibid., p. 71.

35. To explain the unique path of Russian social development—a peasant country that produced a radical working class that toppled the autocracy and brought a Marxist party to power—Tim McDaniel offers a model of what he calls "autocratic capitalism" as the source of the tsarist state's dismal fate. Once the autocracy attempted to promote economic and social modernization while maintaining the essential contours of the autocratic structure, both the state and its fostered capitalism were undermined. The autocratic polity hindered the development of private property and law, thus inhibiting entrepreneurial initiative and authority. At the same time, capitalism subverted autocracy by creating antagonistic classes and threatening patriarchal norms. The hybrid autocratic capitalism shaped a revolutionary labor movement by eliminating differentiation between economic and political issues; generating both traditional and modern opposition to capitalism; diminishing fragmentation and moderation within the working class; and facilitating a high degree of interdependence among mass workers, conscious workers, and radical intellectuals. McDaniel, *Autocracy, Capitalism, and Revolution in*

Russia (Berkeley: University of California Press, 1988). See also McDaniel, *Autocracy, Modernization, and Revolution in Russia and Iran* (Princeton: Princeton University Press, 1991).

36. Hubertus F. Jahn, *Patriotic Culture in Russia During World War I* (Ithaca: Cornell University Press, 1996), pp. 171–173.

37. Joshua A. Sanborn, "The Mobilization of 1914 and the Question of the Russian Nation: A Re-examination," and "More Than Imagined: A Few Notes on Modern Identities," both in *Slavic Review* 59, no. 2 (Summer 2000): 267–289 and 330–335, respectively. See also Scott Seregny, "Zemstvos, Peasants, and Citizenship: The Russian Adult Education Movement and World War I," *Slavic Review* 59, no. 2 (Summer 2000): 290–315.

38. S. A. Smith, "Citizenship and the Russian Nation During World War I: A Comment," *Slavic Review* 59, no. 2 (Summer 2000): 316–329.

39. Ibid., p. 329. For the nationalizing effects of the war on the empire, without an explicit argument that a Russian nation was being formed, see Eric Lohr, *Nationalizing the Russian Empire: The Campaign Against Enemy Aliens During World War I* (Cambridge: Harvard University Press, 2003).

40. Geoffrey Hosking, *Russia and the Russians: A History* (Cambridge: Harvard University Press, 2001), p. 505.

41. Moshe Lewin, *Lenin's Last Struggle*, trans. A. M. Sheridan Smith (New York: Random House, 1968), p. 54 (emphasis in original).

42. For contrasting views, see Richard Pipes, *The Formation of the Soviet Union: Communism and Nationalism, 1917–1923* (Cambridge: Harvard University Press, 1964); and Lewin, *Lenin's Last Struggle*.

43. Martin, *The Affirmative Action Empire*, pp. 3, 19.

44. Ibid., p. 20.

45. For discussion of economic and ethnic *raionirovanie*, see ibid., pp. 33–55. See also Hirsch, "Toward an Empire of Nations," pp. 205–213.

46. Stalin's lieutenant in Georgia, "Sergo" Orjonikidze, told his comrades that expertise was more important than nationality as a criterion for selecting economic officials: "It is necessary to work for the economic renaissance of our country, and for this it is not enough to be a Georgian, one must also know one's business." Quoted in Ronald Grigor Suny, *The Making of the Georgian Nation* (Bloomington: Indiana University Press, 1988), p. 230.

47. On the uses of history and heroes in building Stalin's vision of the USSR, see Ronald Grigor Suny and Terry Martin, eds., *A State of Nations: Empire and Nation-Making in the Age of Lenin and Stalin* (New York: Oxford University Press, 2001); David Brandenberger, *National Bolshevism: Stalinist Mass Culture and the Formation of Modern Russian National Identity, 1931–1956* (Cambridge: Harvard University Press, 2002); and Serhy Yekelchyk, *Stalin's Empire of Memory: Russian-Ukrainian Relations in the Soviet Historical Imagination* (Toronto: University of Toronto Press, 2004).

48. Yuri Slezkine, "The USSR as a Communal Apartment, or How a Socialist State Promoted Ethnic Particularism," *Slavic Review* 53, no. 2 (Summer 1994): 414–452; reprinted in *Becoming National: A Reader,* ed. Geoff Eley and Ronald Grigor Suny (New York: Oxford University Press, 1996), pp. 203–238.

49. Ted Hopf makes the point that, in foreign affairs, "understanding itself as nationally Russian, the Soviet Union presented itself as if it were Russian." Hopf, *Social Construction of International Politics: Identities and Foreign Policies, Moscow, 1955 and 1999* (Ithaca: Cornell University Press, 2002), pp. 90–91.

50. This is the argument of much of Moshe Lewin's work, stated convincingly in his *Soviet Century,* ed. Gregory Elliott (London: Verso, 2005).

51. For an elaboration of the argument in this paragraph, see Ronald Grigor Suny, *The Revenge of the Past: Nationalism, Revolution, and the Collapse of the Soviet Union* (Stanford: Stanford University Press, 1993).

52. Hopf, *Social Construction of International Politics,* p. 16; and Clifford Geertz, *The Interpretation of Culture: Selected Essays* (New York: Basic Books, 1973), p. 5.

53. Ted Hopf periodizes the last half century of Soviet (and Russian) identity into six segments: the Soviet Union as part of a great power condominium (1945–1947); the Soviet Union within capitalist encirclement (1947–1953); the Soviet Union as natural ally (1953–1956); the Soviet Union as the other superpower (1956–1985); the Soviet Union as normal great power in an international community (1985–1991); and Russia as European great power (1992–2000). Hopf, "Identities, Institutions, and Interests: Moscow's Foreign Policy from 1945–2000," in *Cambridge History of Russia,* vol. 3, *The Twentieth Century,* ed. Ronald Grigor Suny (Cambridge: Cambridge University Press, 2006).

54. Ibid.

55. Archival documents on the Soviet intervention into Afghanistan are available from the Cold War International History Project, Woodrow Wilson International Center for Scholars at http://www.wilsoncenter.org/index.cfm?topic_id=1409&fuseaction=topics.home.

56. Hopf claims that Gorbachev succeeded in changing identity politics in the Soviet Union in just six years, as evidenced by the failure of the coup, but that the new identity discourse remains weak. Hopf, "Identities, Institutions, and Interests."

57. Edward W. Walker, *Dissolution: Sovereignty and the Breakup of the Soviet Union* (Lanham, MD: Rowman and Littlefield, 2003).

58. Igor Chubais, "From the Russian Idea to the Idea of a New Russia: How We Must Overcome the Crisis of Ideas" (Cambridge, MA: Strengthening Democratic Institutions Project, John F. Kennedy School of Government, Harvard University, 1998), p. 1.

59. Hopf, *Social Construction of International Politics,* p. 160. Hopf writes, "In looking at the Soviet past, the new Russian identity rejected authoritarianism, arbitrary police powers, individual passivity before the state, ideological homogenization, atheism, and autarky." Ibid., p. 162.

60. *Sovok* (plural, *sovki*) literally means "dustpan," but in the late Soviet period, it referred negatively to something or someone "Soviet." It has come to be an ambivalent reference to a Soviet person.

61. Ronald Grigor Suny, "The State of Nations: The Ex-Soviet Union and Its Peoples," *Dissent*, Summer 1996, pp. 90–98.

62. Vera Tolz, "Conflicting 'Homeland Myths' and Nation-State Building in Postcommunist Russia," *Slavic Review* 57, no. 2 (Summer 1998): 268.

63. Ibid., p. 289.

64. Ibid., p. 293.

65. Ibid., p. 294.

66. Hopf, "Identities, Institutions, and Interests."

67. Rogers Brubaker, *Nationalism Reframed: Nationhood and the National Question in the New Europe* (Cambridge: Cambridge University Press, 1996).

68. Mearsheimer, *The Tragedy of Great Power Politics*, pp. 49–50.

69. I thank Ted Hopf for sharing this point.

CHAPTER 2

Russian Foreign Policy During Periods of Great State Transformation

Robert Legvold

IF HISTORY IS A RIVER, its currents often run treacherously. For nations caught in its flow, the rapids and waterfalls come as war, revolution, conquest, and sometimes violent liberation. Russia, however, alone among nations in four of the last five centuries and twice in the twentieth century has endured the turbulence differently. At these moments, its autocratic leadership out of fear or hope lays siege to the country's domestic order, upending institutions, social patterns, and even the hierarchy of society's core values. It happened in the sixteenth century under Ivan IV,[1] in the eighteenth century under Peter I, in the nineteenth century under Alexander II, in the twentieth century under Lenin and Stalin, and again at the century's close under Gorbachev and Yeltsin. These are times when the normal fare of politics—the struggle for power and over policy—fades, and the stakes become political life itself. What counts ceases to be the game's outcome, and instead becomes the game's rules—indeed, the choice of game in the first place. No longer is the issue, in Robert Dahl's venerable formulation, who gets what, when, and how, but the very structure of the political and economic system within which these questions are answered. They are revolutions, with revolutionary effects, but ones visited from above, not triggered by an explosion from below. Call them eras of "great state transformation."

Rupture and drama on this scale are bound to have a special effect on foreign policy, but precisely what this effect is, and how it is to be distinguished from the path of policy in less charged times, cannot be easily determined. The difficulty stems from the way events in the outside world also work their effect. Apportioning cause between impulses generated within and those coming from without is hard at any time for any country, but it becomes more so when the change under way within a country reverberates in the world outside. Often during these more extraordinary periods, foreign policy seems to be hyper-influenced by external challenges, challenges that at the same time are often accentuated by the transfiguration taking place inside the country. Russia's fears become self-fulfilling. Its anxieties produce defensive and often aggressive behavior.[2]

If such eras alter the normal course of events and have an impact beyond the normal tugging and hauling surrounding foreign policy, it then matters greatly when they end. Indeed, is that what the Putin interlude is all about? Has Russian foreign policy come to the end of a period of great state transformation? And is the significance of Putin's stewardship that he now presides over a more settled international engagement less subject to large-scale change at home?

What follows begins by describing periods of great state transformation and the qualities that make them different from less extravagant interludes in Russian history. Next comes an exploration of the three factors whose resonance intensifies the impact of these special periods on Russia's foreign policy: the role of war; the effect of Russian vulnerabilities, particularly when accompanied by extreme national weakness; and the uncertainties introduced by shifting trends in the world outside. Together the upheaval within the country and the complicating impulses from these three factors draw to the surface tensions over Russia's role and place in international politics that lie buried in more ordinary times, the subject of the third section. These tensions then surface in Russia's demeanor and real-world choices, in its ambivalent strategic location, and in its tortured relations with the West, all of which are the focus of the fourth and final section.

The Nature of Great State Transformation

Historically eras of great state transformation share four characteristics. First, they are moments when change from above, a common syndrome in Russian history, becomes particularly intense—when quantity changes into quality. Second, and partly as the embodiment of the first characteristic, they entail far-reaching change in not merely one, but multiple dimensions of the country's political, economic, and social life, usually as a consequence of which the country emerges from the period fundamentally altered, a different entity from what it was before, or at least seemingly so. Third, they recast the autocracy, sometimes making it more transcendent, at other times, the object of quasi-liberal reform, but never—at least until the Gorbachev and Yeltsin era—questioning the virtue and merit of autocracy itself. Fourth, in the trauma they impose, their immediate effect is almost always to weaken the country economically and sometimes in other spheres as well, such as the quality of the bureaucracy, the cohesion and effectiveness of the political elite, and the health and well-being of the broader population.

This is not to suggest that these massive assaults on the political status quo always reach fruition or are consistently and thoroughly pursued by their authors. On the contrary, from the first case (Ivan IV) to the last (Gorbachev and Yeltsin), reform qua imposed change is often started but not completed either because it runs afoul of prevailing realities or because it is misconceived and has to be abandoned or radically modified. Often the unintended consequences of reform are as powerful as the thrust of reform itself. But in either event, while the outcome hangs suspended, the struts and buttresses of the old system weaken and give way—although (and this is the perverse other side of the story) not entirely.

Take the case of Ivan IV (1533–1584): Whatever the historical disagreement over the nature of his innovations, more so over his purpose in introducing one or another, and still more over the effect of any one, few quarrel with the watershed that his rule represents. He transformed the Muscovite state that his father and grandfather had "gathered," to use the historical euphemism Russians prefer, into a consolidated entity. He gave it control of its eastern strategic parapet, the Volga River, and made it a player, albeit ultimately unsuccessful, in the scrum of European international relations, modernized militarily, and constructed around a fundamentally different relationship with the warrior caste that had been the regime's underpinning. What he began as a seventeen-year-old by liberating himself from the tutelage of the boyars, he finished three years before his death by taking the first steps toward tying the serfs to the land. First came the formation of an inner council of independent advisers and a *zemskii sobor*[3] of the gentry and merchants, followed by efforts to cleanse the Orthodox Church, to thoroughly revamp local administration, and to create a large, mobile, artillery-armed military force. His reform may have been in any one of its elements fitfully or partially pursued, but it left Muscovy a different state. It was, of course, the process by which he brought the boyar class to heel and rendered the nobility permanently locked into state service that shook the entire fabric of political society. Ivan upended and then forever changed the face of Russia, first by dictating the military duty and levy for all who held landed estates (1556)—thus underscoring that property, whatever may have been the rights once attached to the *votchina* estate, was held at the tsar's pleasure and only on condition of life service to the state—and then more severely during the seven years of the *oprichnina* (1564–1571) by seizing the estates of boyars and *udel* princes and exiling their owners to the newly conquered Kazan territories, eventually creating a literal private domain that totaled nearly half the claimed land in the realm.[4]

To say that Ivan changed the face of Russia does not mean that he changed the country's more basic sociopolitical physiology, which is simply to borrow Yuri Lotman's "insight that in Russia the most radical changes despite appearances, actually reinforce the traditions of the society they are meant to change."[5] Ivan may have taken to an extreme the unhindered and arbitrary power of the autocrat, but he acted within a tradition that "the Tsar's prime duty is to carry out God's will, as the mediator between God and his people, and make himself responsible for their salvation"—indeed, without constraints on his "right to punish the wicked in pursuance of their salvation," even by unrestrained cruelty.[6] Similarly, while he reinforced the notion that in his person the autocrat embodied the state (the antithesis of an institutionalized, law-defined state), he did not invent it. Nor were the shackles of lifetime state service that he imposed on the nobility of his devising. The award of land tied to military service, the *pomestie* system, was the innovation of his grandfather and father.

What Ivan did do was bring everything together in one giant crescendo, out of which emerged the omnipotent Russian state. Only under him was the "synthesis of the Moscow seigneurial system, of Mongol despotism, and of Byzantine Caesaropapism," to cite Tibor Szamuely, ultimately effected.[7] He consummated what the great nineteenth-century Russian historian Vasily Kliuchevsky called the "Russian Tradition," the merger of the autocrat as the state with the state as the possessor of all property, and with property as the currency by which all society was subordinated to military mobilization. In the process, he perfected the Muscovite state, the entity that "in the name of the common welfare, took into its full control all the energies and the resources of society, leaving no scope for the private interests of individuals or of classes."[8]

Historians from Paul Miliukov to Marshall Poe insist that the despotic Russian state emerged as the natural, indeed the only, form of government capable of mastering a vast, unwieldy territory in an exceedingly inhospitable environment, and squeezing from its scant resources the wherewithal to fend off formidable external enemies.[9] Poe calls the long ascendancy of this system the "Russian moment in world history," which began "when the Muscovite elite created the first sustainable society capable of resisting the challenge of Europe."[10] By the "challenge of Europe," he means literally conquest by Europe, something

Russia alone among non-European empires managed to elude over the next three centuries. In states to the west, "borders were relatively uncontrolled, the factors of production were relatively freely exchanged, and military reforms were undertaken in an organic fashion. Only in Muscovy were the borders closed, universal or near universal state ownership of land and labor imposed, and forced military reform undertaken." "Bits and pieces of this program," Poe says, existed elsewhere in the early modern world. "But Muscovy was unique in pursuing, and pursuing successfully, the entire suite of radical reforms."[11] The great state transformation occurring under Ivan IV can be thought of as bringing these three elements to fruition and, therefore, "the Russian moment" into full being.

Now, however, after a half millennium, has the Russian moment come to an end? Does the truly historic significance of Gorbachev and Yeltsin's revolution reside in its break with the "Russian Tradition"? Has the country at last been cut free from the legacy of autocracy, the patrimonial state, and the subordination of society to the ardors of military mobilization? If so, whatever else links this last great state transformation with those that came before, its implications are fundamentally different. Poe contends that "in 1991 the era of the Russian path to modernity ended, and a new epoch in world history began." Autocracy was replaced by an "evolving democracy." The "tightly controlled public sphere was opened." The command economy gave way to "a chaotic mix of banditry and capitalism." And the "once mighty armed forces were scaled back." The "Russian project" at the heart of the Russian moment was over.[12] Perhaps. But even if it was, its traces, as we shall see, constantly resurface in the life of Vladimir Putin's new Russia.

Finally, in Ivan IV's case, as in nearly all the great state transformations that followed, and in none more than the one in our own day, the culminating stages of his assault on society left the country weakened and broken. "War, casualties, plagues and famine, Crimean raids, taxation, the extension of the *pomestie* system which deprived the peasants of land, . . . the obligation to bring an armed and mounted *kholop* to battle as a military slave, and the depredations of the *oprichnina*," writes Isabel de Madariaga, "had depopulated the country, which became so impoverished that it could provide neither the manpower nor the money for the continuation of the war in Livonia, Ivan's long quest to displace Sweden, Denmark, and Poland in the Baltic." Near Pskov, "over 85 percent of the homesteads were deserted in 1585"; around Novgorod, 97 percent; in the area around the Oka River, nearly 95 percent. The fleeing peasantry left the lands of the service nobility uncultivated and bereft of human resources, in turn undermining the material basis of military mobilization, and, as Madariaga notes, leading "to the increasingly frequent suspension of the peasants' right of departure" and the first steps toward serfdom.[13]

Beyond the barriers that his excesses raised to the emergence of a modernizing, soundly institutionalized state open to the leavening of Renaissance ideas ("what he set in motion was not state-building, but the statization of personal dominance"[14]), Ivan's final harm was to the dynasty itself. By murdering his cousin Vladimir, Vladimir's heir, and his own eldest son, leaving his sickly and childless son, Fyodor, to succeed him, he reopened the way to the clan-based struggle for power that he, his father, and his grandfather had labored to end. In this and the environment of violence that he fostered in the last third of his rule, he prepared the ground for the near-fatal chaos that threatened Russia's very existence in the first decades of the seventeenth century during the Time of Troubles.

Peter the Great's reign (1696–1725), the second period of great state transformation, illustrates the phenomenon in its broadest and most comprehensive form. Not until Stalin would a Russian ruler attack so frontally, ambitiously, and brutally the existing political and social order. Beginning with the transformation of a semipermanent, semifeudal military into a permanent standing army of two hundred thousand men to which was added a navy of twenty-eight thousand and ending with the decision in 1721 to abolish the Orthodox patriarchate and replace it with a state-dominated Holy Synod, Peter lay siege to virtually every institution, from the administrative mechanisms of the state to the framework of social hierarchy, from public finance to education, science, and the arts.[15] More fundamental than the institutional upheaval, however, was the conceptual revolution behind it. Peter meant not merely to aggrandize Russian power, or to free his hand from the joint tenure of the church, or to drag his people into the world of Protestant Europe. Rather he sought to glorify, indeed make sacred the state itself, to alter the religious consciousness of his people, to transform the basis of Russian autocracy, and to insert Russia into the European international system as one of its architects, even with a *droit de regard* over the internal development of Sweden, a key actor within this system. In the words of Lindsey Hughes, he introduced into Russia "the very concept of an entity called the 'State' " and, indeed, the notion that this state and he as its sovereign servant were to benefit "the common good"; he brought to a society wedded to the medieval notion of time as "more or less static, and change as cyclical, geared to the seasons and the recurring events of the church calendar" a strong sense of time as linear and capable of yielding progress.[16] His church reform, claim others, was nothing less than a "Protestant Reformation."[17] For Vissarion Belinsky, he was "the most extraordinary phenomenon not only in our history, but in the history of mankind; he is a deity who has called us into being and who has breathed life into the body of ancient Russia, colossal but prostrate in deadly slumber."[18]

No matter that many of Peter's reforms faltered or were cut short, as had been Ivan IV's,[19] nor, even more fundamentally that, as Geoffrey Hosking and many others have contended, Peter could go as far as he did because "in many respects he was working *with* the grain of Muscovite society, perpetuating and even intensifying its archaic features"—"renewing the service state, not undermining it."[20] In the end, he is the divide between one period of Russian history and all that follows. With other countries one can speak of, say, pre- and post-revolutionary France or pre- and postwar Germany; with Russia the point of reference is pre- and post-Petrine. If Peter failed to rip Russia entirely from its ossified, premodern traditions, his sweeping and merciless onslaught on old customs, practices, and institutions gave birth to the torn Russia of the last three centuries, a country in but not of Europe or the West, divided over the merit of its past and the model for its future, bifurcated into two social worlds, and focused on economic over political modernization—thus, always a step behind.

Above all, Peter, like Ivan IV, carried Russia's unique form of autocracy to an even more imperious level. Ivan IV brought it to its first culmination by making the nation's patrimony his possession and subordinating all, including the most highborn, to it. Peter added the sacralization of the monarchy, in effect placing it, by means of ceremony and public representation, on the same level as the deity.[21] From then on, as one observer put it, Peter's innovation "provided a perfect illustration for one of the basic differences between Russian despotism and Western European 'absolute monarchy': The Russian ruler, with every justification, considered not only '*l'Etat, c'est moi,*' but '*l'Eglise, c'est moi,*' too."[22] True, under Ivan IV, religious sanction for the autocracy had already assumed a character fundamentally different from the "divine right" asserted by European kings. They located their power in God's will; he, in his likeness unto God.[23] Peter, however, literally subordinated the church to the state, deifying the state and turning the monarch from Christ's spirit on earth into Christ's equal.

Two centuries later Stalin carried the transfiguration to the ultimate extreme, not the least because no longer was there a God above or beside him. The hagiolatry that surrounded his cult of personality was, of course, severed from traditional religious belief, but the godlike—or at a minimum talismanic—figure that Stalin became fit within the tradition and certainly served to give autocracy a nonsecular source of legitimacy.[24] When schoolchildren sang, "He is the friend of the sun; he will disarm all his foes, your name is on our lips, your heart is in our hearts"; poets wrote, "O Great Stalin, O Leader of the Peoples / Thou who didst give birth to man / Thou who didst make fertile the earth"; and sculptors represented him as a father-deity figure, the worship was not a new and alien invention.[25]

Stalin would be the last Russian leader to bolster the autocracy by attaching transcendental significance to the ruler. His successors had neither the capacity nor the will to carry on and, indeed, faced with the harm of Stalin's cult, began the process of dismantling it. Nikita Khrushchev's de-Stalinization campaign, however, scarcely aimed to undo the autocracy; it was meant only to free it of its most brutal and pathological aspects. Mikhail Gorbachev went beyond. His perestroika sought, as the Russian word signifies, to reconstruct the system. Even he and his colleagues, however, did not at the outset wish to abandon all aspects of autocracy embodied in the one-party state—only to freshen and invigorate it with more room for initiative from below.

They lost control, however, and those parts of the autocracy that survived the collapse of the Soviet Union were, in their formal aspects, liquidated by Boris Yeltsin. The less formal aspects, however, proved more durable. In the concluding chapter of her book on the Yeltsin era, Lilia Shevtsova says of him and even more of the Russian environment, "In contrast to Western political tradition, in which power is based on rational ideas and institutions, the Byzantine tradition has always invested power with something sacred, irrational, and personal." His superpresidency, she writes, simply follows the "country's historic Byzantine model of governance, in which all power is concentrated in a leader—tsar, general secretary, president—who becomes the symbol of the nation and its arbiter as its main guarantor of stability."[26] In historical context, her point is, of course, figurative rather than literal, and, when one extends it to Putin's conception of the strong state, he scarcely has in mind "*l'Etat c'est moi*," but he does have a conception of authority and the state that honors this tradition far more than it does post-Enlightenment democratic theory. Thus, in his commitment to modernizing the Russian state by engaging and reinvesting his people, he faces a version—true, a heavily modified version—of a challenge tracing back to Peter. As Kliuchevsky said of him, "He wanted the slave [by which was meant literally the serving nobility as well as the rest of the population], while remaining a slave, to act consciously and freely."[27]

Finally, while Peter's period of revolutionary exertion is the only one that did not leave the country weaker economically than beforehand, the primitive industrialization that he sponsored set the country on a stultified and rigid path of economic development. In his time, the system of state-authored and state-protected foundries and factories served to stock the state's military needs, with enough iron left over to create an export base, but it was an inferior version of the European model it sought to imitate, inefficient and resistant to innovation. Its effects endured into the nineteenth century, where its legacy was to burden Russia's effort to join the Industrial Revolution. Moreover, while Peter's reforms added to the power of the state, they exacted an awful price from the Russian people, most vividly illustrated in the fact that the country's population was 25 percent smaller at his death than when he came to power. As a percentage this is a number greater than combined Soviet losses in World War II and the purges of the 1930s.

Even the era of Peter the Great, however, pales when compared with what Stalin wrought from 1928 to 1941. Never before or since has a Russian ruler so ravaged existing political, economic, and social structure. Not a single institution, from the family to the inner sanctum of political power—army, village, academy, police, and party, not to mention the press, diplomatic corps, and judiciary—escaped wholesale transmogrification. More than that, of course, the collectivization of agriculture, the forced-draft industrialization, and the purge of the party and military thoroughly rescripted the very underpinnings of society. In his case, while Stalin, too, scarcely succeeded in all respects and often in the respects with which his successes preserved historical continuities, he, more than any of his predecessors, followed through on what he started. As has been said, his was the real revolution (the "second" Russian revolution).

It was not the whole of the period of great state transformation, however, because the Leninist phase was also integral to it. The years after 1918 flow together with the Stalinist period because they cleared the way; they were the hammer that completed the destruction of the ancien régime. In this sense, the great state transformation in the first half of the twentieth century was a two-phased revolution, and, as such, it resembles the great state transformation at the end of the century—the dual revolution of Mikhail Gorbachev and Boris Yeltsin. Gorbachev, far less wittingly than Lenin, began the process of bringing the system down, not so much with consciously delivered blows as by cautiously pulling out bricks, but in the end with the same effect. Yeltsin picked up where Gorbachev left off, completing the destruction, but then like Lenin he also carved out the rough rudiments of a new economic and political order.

Lenin, however, in a far more self-conscious tribute to his predecessors, embraced the notion of change imposed from above, ruthlessly, unflinchingly. In

1918, in urging the Communist Party to copy from the "state capitalism of the Germans," he demanded that this be done "without sparing *dictatorial* methods," speeding the transfer "even more than Peter sped . . . the Westernization of barbaric Rus by not shrinking from barbarous means in the struggle against barbarity."[28] Yeltsin turned his back on the past, at least on the methods Lenin extolled. Still, he and the young economic reformers on whom he relied bore some resemblance to Lenin and his colleagues, albeit in far milder form, in their determination to smash the prior economic order—accepting that they, as Yegor Gaidar, his acting prime minister, put it, were kamikazes.[29] And the resemblance did not stop there. Despite their genuine desire to see Russia move toward a more democratic order, they were willing to rush through their economic reforms in relatively authoritarian fashion, circumventing a recalcitrant parliament and disdaining the need to build a popular political base for reform.

Thus, while historians write of Peter I's and Yeltsin's reforms, each has more in common with Lenin and Stalin's revolution, because in all three cases they were intended not to modify the ancien régime but to raze it. In this respect Ivan IV, Alexander II, and Gorbachev seem more alike in their aspiration to rid the system of its weaknesses and defects while breathing new life into it. Yeltsin, however, made no pretense of remaking the character of Russian society or the people in it. Peter, who did, at least regarding society's elite, nonetheless fell far short of Lenin and Stalin's totalitarian fantasy of molding a new human being, the "new Soviet man." Moreover, whereas Peter sought to emulate the West in overhauling the Russian system, and Yeltsin to accommodate the West, Lenin and Stalin meant to supplant it, a difference that had profound implications for Russia's relationship with the West. This imbued the Lenin-Stalin transformation with a messianism that none of the others had. The Bolshevik Revolution was not just for Russia, but for the remainder of mankind as well.

Stalin, however, took Lenin's conceptual framework into another realm by the content he gave to it. True, elements of his miscreate design were all present in the 1920s. The system of nomenklatura, bestowing on the state's command center control over the selection of *all* key personnel, not just in government but throughout society, from industry to the arts, originated in the appointment lists assigned to the party secretariat in 1922–1923. The displacement of religion with atheism and the physical destruction of the Orthodox Church traced back to the decrees of 1918 and the early 1920s' expropriation of the church's land and property. The collectivization of agriculture had its forerunner in the grain requisitions under war communism following the revolution. And the subordination to a monolithic state of all civic organizations, from writers associations to sports clubs, more than honored Lenin's dislike of any group or agency that wished to be independent of the party. But Stalin went far beyond. When added together, his initiatives produced a Leviathan that penetrated deeper into society, overturned institutions more thoroughly, and destroyed the dividing line between ruler and ruled more completely than any Russian state—or, for that matter, any state anywhere—ever had. Peter's Russia dictated to its elite and people; Stalin's atomized them. Ivan IV's Russia recast the relationship between property and state power; Stalin's crushed both and then reconstituted them in his own image. Ivan IV and Peter made society the state's servant; Stalin made it the state's fodder.

Although Stalin's revolution more imitated Peter's in the scale of the change it wrought, in many more respects it bore striking similarities to Ivan IV's, particularly in the person, methods, and pathologies of the *vozhd*.[30] In no respect was this truer than the role of terror. Lenin was not squeamish about commanding the indiscriminate murder of the revolution's supposed enemies, but Stalin turned terror into the system's armature. It became the principal mechanism by which he not only eliminated political opposition and brought to heel the party, military, diplomatic corps, and international communist movement, but also destroyed threats when still only imagined. It was meant to devastate its victims not only physically, but morally, guaranteeing that they would never reappear in any guise. When Ivan arrived in Novgorod on horseback with his son and band of executioners on July 25, 1570, and over the next four hours supervised the boiling, flaying, eviscerating, and beheading of 116 nobles, after ordering the townspeople to draw near as witnesses, he was pioneering a method Stalin would take to unimaginable lengths.[31]

Like that of Ivan IV, Stalin's savagery sprang from an immense paranoia. Each saw conspiracy and betrayal in the slightest criticism or unorthodoxy. Each was ready to condemn not merely an act, real or conjured, but an individual for who he or she was. Each lacked the most fleeting capacity for compassion, and did not hesitate to slaughter those who had been closest to them, along with family members—and, for that matter, their own family members as well. And each twisted and inflated monstrously the offenses they prosecuted. In Stalin's case dereliction or simple on-the-job failure became sabotage, questioning in any form was classed literally as treason, and, most preposterously, political opposition was reduced to "terrorism," with all of the attendant consequences.

Finally, the great state transformation authored by Lenin and Stalin, as those that preceded it and the one that would follow, exacted an enormous price from those sacrificed to it. By 1923–1924, six years into the revolution, total industrial production in the Soviet Union had reached barely half the 1913 level.[32] Those manning the factories were half the number before the war. Towns were without food and often abandoned by a now wandering population in search of employment. Infrastructure, including transport, had collapsed, and the countryside, raided and uncared for, was sullenly divorced from the wants and needs of the architects of the new order. In the next decade, the hothouse effect of the five-year plans did initially catapult the Soviet Union's industrial sector forward, more than doubling production by 1933 and creating whole new sectors of industry (automobiles, aircraft, machine building, tractors, etc.). Much as Peter with his forced industrialization, only on a massively larger scale, Stalin fattened the economic base for state power. Much like Peter, he also did it in a fashion that squeezed the life from his people. Five million died in the famines of 1932–1933 that swept Ukraine, Western Siberia, and the Volga region. More than three million died in the camps, although no one knows how many for sure, because, other than for executions within the formal Gulag system, Soviet authorities were sloppy in keeping track.[33] Nor can the emotional torment of those with loved ones caught in the "meat grinder" (as the Gulag was called) or the deprivations, hardships, and damaged health suffered by nearly all be tallied. Hosking's summary judgment: "The Communists had aimed to build an egalitarian system based on plenty; instead they created a hierarchical one based on scarcity."[34]

While the likeness between Stalin and Ivan IV stands out, the parallel for the great state transformation that began under Gorbachev is with Alexander II and the twenty-year period from 1861 to 1881. As did Gorbachev, Alexander rolled the dice by launching change in hopes of reinvigorating a calcified system. The 1861 emancipation edict, like perestroika in Gorbachev's day, was meant to remove the one burden seen as critical to the system's stagnation— serfdom in the first case, bureaucratic overcentralization in the second. But, to quote Dietrich Geyer, "The rights and duties of the various estates, the administrative, judicial and tax systems, the armed forces and the organization of the economy were all bound up with *krepostnichestvo*. The 'emancipation of the serfs' therefore undermined the entire traditional political and social system."[35] In much the same fashion, Gorbachev's effort to override bureaucratic resistance and inertia and reanimate an economy in decline ended by bringing down the entire Soviet political edifice, and then the country itself. Geyer says of Alexander's edict that between the Petrine reforms of the early eighteenth century and the "revolutionary convulsions of 1917," no other measure "so profoundly altered the social, economic and political foundations of Russia."[36] Of Gorbachev still more can be claimed: During no other era of radical change over the last four centuries of Russian history was the outcome more dramatic.

There are other similarities between Alexander's two decades and Gorbachev's half decade. Neither launched his reform with the intention of fundamentally altering the existing political system. The overriding objective of each was to modernize a faltering economic order, above all with the aim of preserving the country's power and standing in international affairs. Gorbachev's December 1984 warning that "only an intensive, highly developed economy . . . will permit [the Soviet Union] to enter the new century in a manner befitting a great and flourishing power" echoes the thoughts of Alexander's court, who worried that Russia's economic backwardness, exposed in the Crimean War of 1854–1856, unless corrected, would doom the country to a second-rate status among major powers.[37] Both leaders at the outset accepted modest political modifications as a prop for their larger economic goals; both also soon found themselves forced to take far more radical political steps to salvage their economic goals. In Alexander II's case, it turned out that emancipation required new forms of self-government in the countryside, reform of urban government, a reconstructed financial and tax system, the modernization of the court system, and the transformation of higher education. In Gorbachev's case, the attempt to push economic progress by exhortation and a shake-up of the bureaucracy failed, and by 1988 he moved to more decisive measures, including competitive elections, enhanced responsibility for enterprise directors, and decentralized decision making, albeit not at the very top.[38]

Both Alexander II and Gorbachev were, Dominic Lieven argues, "liberal modernizers." That is, their reforms allowed a "greater respect for the rule of law, much greater freedom of expression, and the liberation of the people's economic potential from the shackles of serfdom and the command economy."[39] But both also, in ways true to the Russian past, either sought to preserve the autocracy (Alexander) or could not entirely let go of it (Gorbachev). Alexander would not hear of ideas implying even modest movement toward constitutionalism because "it would limit his powers" and "provoke the disintegration of such a huge and diverse empire."[40] Gorbachev chose to replace the encumbered role of Communist Party general secretary with a presidency, but with the president selected by the Congress of People's Deputies, where the results could be more or less controlled, rather than through direct elections. As Michael McFaul suggests, he wanted this "to accord himself greater autonomous political power with which to pursue his ailing economic reform policies."[41] Perhaps even more symptomatically, in both cases, elections were for the lower reaches of government, not the top, and were meant to mobilize society behind government policy, not to control those designing the policy. Ultimately, in both cases, this clinging to comfortable forms of authority set the limits on how far reform could go, limits that eventually contributed to the reform's demise.

The two eras shared one other characteristic: In both cases, once the die was cast many within the ruling circle worried that what had been unleashed could not be controlled, and would lay ruin to Russia. Even friends of reform found themselves torn. As the liberal St. Petersburg professor A. V. Nikitenko agonized little more than a year after the Emancipation Edict, "The tyranny of freedom is no less dangerous than the tyranny of despotism."[42] Indeed, scarcely had the reform started when a deep sense of crisis swept through parts of the imperial court and ministerial circles. In much the same way, those who had initially signed on to economic reform, soon after the 1988 Nineteenth Party Conference, choked on the idea of speeding change by introducing electoral choice and allowing the formation of political groupings, thus imperiling the party's monopoly of power. Gorbachev's prime minister, Nikolai Ryzhkov, would grumble, "Many of the political leaders in the country, including myself, said that it was not necessary to rush things, that we should provide the opportunity to look at and work on these questions more deeply. But the haste continued."[43] Misgivings of this sort added to the drag of recalcitrant bureaucrats and open opponents, further burdening the prospects of reform.

Like the other periods of great state transformation, Alexander's and Gorbachev's experiments, too, levied a price on society. Both leaders inherited economies in crisis or decline, and then made matters worse. True, the massive railway construction program of the 1860s did stimulate a rapid rise in industrial production, but it did this only by increasing debts, taxes, and capital flight, plunging the state back into near financial crisis by the end of the decade, and leaving the peasantry re-enslaved to taxes and redemption payments. By the Soviet Union's last years, an economy that had been in slow descent for two decades was, as a result of half-implemented reforms, in free fall. By 1990 the growth of gross national product had long ceased to match the anemic rates during what had come to be called the "period of stagnation" under Leonid Brezhnev, and was falling by 2 percent per year; labor productivity by 3 percent; national income by 4 percent. State debt had soared by more than 25 percent; inflation had reached 11 percent. Crime was up; the supply of goods, including essential items such as bread, was down—indeed, so much so that bread lines formed, lines that were still longer for other basic goods, for example, toothpaste, matches, razor blades, teapots, and shoes. The poor in society, about 20 percent of the population, now consumed 30 percent less meat and dairy products than in 1970. And by 1988, meat was being rationed in twenty-six of the Russian Republic's fifty-five regions.[44]

When Yeltsin came to power and unleashed the second stage of this two-staged great state transformation, he demolished state, party, and economic structures in a way that Gorbachev simply could not. By abandoning administered prices on all but a few essentials and permitting a far greater range to private initiative, he filled empty store shelves with a cornucopia of goods, including fancy imported foods, electronics, and clothing. But, ravished by the so-called shock therapy of the young reformers, the country's economic life for most people grew harsher and more unpredictable. In Russia's first four years of independence, industrial production plunged 46 percent, a drop that followed a 5–8 percent decline in the Russian share of Soviet industrial production during the Soviet Union's last two years.[45] From 1993 to 1996, Russia's grain harvest shrank from 99.1 million tons to 69.3 million tons; tractor production, from 214,000 units in 1990 to 29,000 in 1994.[46] Capital investment in 1998 was 20 percent of what it had been in 1990. Gross domestic product (GDP) fell at rates from -2.5 percent in 1992 to -7 percent in 1996.

The effects radiated everywhere and to everyone. By 1996, 40 percent of the population was officially categorized as "impoverished" (earning less than fifty dollars a month); among those drawing a wage, 49 percent had not been paid in more than a month.[47] Corruption soared; public health plummeted. By 1994, 70–80 percent of Russian private businesses and banks paid protection money to racketeers equal to half of their profits.[48] Between 1991 and 1994, male life expectancy decreased from 63.5 years to 57.6 years; from 1990 to 1993, infant mortality rose from 17.4 per thousand to 19.3 per thousand.[49] Suicide rates soared from 26.5 per 100,000 in 1991 to 45 per 100,000 in 1995.[50]

GREAT STATE TRANSFORMATION AND FOREIGN POLICY

Change on this scale, as might be expected, left a distinctive mark on Russian foreign policy. It both deepened traditional patterns of Russian behavior and brought to the surface more fundamental responses less conspicuous during less wrenching times. It matters, of course, whether the revolution from above was driven by desperation or aspiration, whether Russia was recoiling from failure and decline, as in the case of Alexander and Gorbachev-Yeltsin, or girding itself for new conquests, as in the three other cases. Yet, even then, these periods all seem to have infused policy with three common qualities: a tendency to pursue defensive objectives by offensive and at times provocative means; a penchant for manipulating rather than cementing relationships, for maneuvering rather than committing; and a habit of jeopardizing prospective alliances by appearing to be an unreliable ally, even when the dynamic of international politics tolerated frequent shifting from one ally to another, as it did over much of the sixteenth through nineteenth centuries.

To understand the significance of these tendencies (and before turning to illustrations), one needs to start at a more essential level, where the unique effect of these special periods emerges. More than usual, Russia, while amid the upheaval, sinks back into a tortured quest to define its very identity, one manifestation of which is an ostentatious preoccupation with its great-power standing (or *derzhavnost*) and the other, a sharpened version of its permanently vexed relationship to the West. Then, to trace the issue one causal level deeper, much of this awkward soul-searching owes to a variety of factors that combine in often sharply different fashion, but always with a similar effect: war; Russia's vulnerabilities, sometimes augmented by excruciating internal weakness; and unnerving international trends.

War's Role

War has played an intimate role in shaping Russia's great state transformations in all but the last instance, a distinction of major consequence. Charles Tilly's celebrated insight is a useful place to begin. "War," he argued in describing the formation of European states from the tenth to the nineteenth century, "made the state, and the state made war."[51] It certainly can be argued that war made the Muscovite state. Such was the necessary consequence of the fact that in the two hundred years between 1480 and 1690, Russia was at war for eighty-five of them. During this time it fought six wars with Sweden and twelve with Lithuania-Poland. While Ivan III, Vasily III, and Ivan IV ruled, Russia was permanently embattled with the Turkic and Tatar tribes that regularly swept across its open steppe borders, capturing and sacking Russian cities, including Moscow (as late as 1571), plundering, and above all seizing Russians to be sold on the slave markets of the Near East. To meet this challenge, Russia "had to raise and maintain an armed force, much larger than . . . European armies in absolute figures and greater still in relation to her resources, not just for an isolated campaign, but for three hundred unbroken years."[52] Every year it mobilized 65,000 men in six regiments (compared with the 18,500 men the German emperor gathered in 1467 to fight the Turks or the 12,000 men that the king of France mustered for the battle of Crécy, the largest feudal army to that point). "This task," Szamuely writes, "demanded a total, unremitting and ruthless concentration of all national resources, both human and material, that for scope and intensity is probably unparalleled, over a comparable period of time, by any other nation."[53]

However, unless one argues that this state of permanent and, by the standards of its day, total war "caused" the vast internal transformation authored by Ivan IV—which poses the analytical problem, Why not under his father and grandfather?—the war-state sequence is reversed. Ivan, in fact, began his assault on Russia from within before he launched his assault on Kazan from without. Before sending his armies against the remaining segments of the Golden Horde as a twenty-one-year-old newly crowned tsar, he had already set about reforming the country's power base by replacing the old *kormlenie* system for raising revenue with another that transferred taxation and local administration to local village assemblies; he had already convened the church council of 1551, broaching change in church practice, standards, and title to land; and, most relevant, he had already begun to restructure the military and create his special force of one thousand elite musketeers. The decision to lay siege to the khanate of Kazan was a carefully premeditated move, prepared a year or two beforehand and aided by the construction of fortifications close to the target. The successful war that Ivan launched in 1552 against one of the most formidable successors to the Golden Horde, followed four years later by the capitulation of the khanate of Astrakhan at the southern end of the Volga, did more than give Russia control over the trade route to the south, more than open the way to the next phase of Russian expansion across the Urals into Siberia; it marked a critical advance toward the core objective of the Muscovite state—namely, to gain strategic control over the southern steppe gateway, underbelly, breadbasket, and strategic frontier. Ivan, of course, did not stop with his triumph in the east or follow the advice of his councilors, including Prince Andrei Kurbsky, to concentrate on defeating the other menace to the south, the khanate in Crimea. Instead, in 1558 he embarked on what would be a twenty-four-year war in the west against Sweden, Denmark, and by 1569 a reunited Poland and Lithuania, a war that ended badly, with Russia losing all that it had gained in its early stages.

How much Ivan's decision to force the issue with the Livonian knights—that is, to compel them to turn over trade through Riga and Reval to the Russians—was driven by a determination to open a Baltic pathway for the newly established trade with England; or how much it was the conceit of a leader determined to make his newly tumescent state an accepted part of the European system; or how much it was driven by an underlying desire to secure Russia's western front in the struggle against major European powers cannot be easily settled. What is indisputably salient, however, is that, as a result, during Ivan IV's reign, as during Peter's, Russia would be at war two-thirds of the time. In the thirty-seven years from his coronation in 1547 until his death in 1584, Russia waged war for twenty-eight of them. Thus, while war may or may not have been the immediate inspiration for the great state transformation that Ivan initiated, it was the crucible within which it was shaped.

Peter the Great does make Tilly's point. Whatever may have been Peter's restless disposition and inclination to shake up his slumbering empire, the initial impulse for reform came from military defeat. The failure of the 1695 campaign to drive the Turks from their coastal fort at Azov, a sally that Hughes portrays as "an attempt to recover Russian prestige [from his predecessors' calamitous Crimean campaigns of 1687 and 1689], gain a stronger bargaining position with his allies, and ward off Turkish attacks on Ukraine," produced a rush of activity to rectify military deficiencies. But it was the long Northern War with Charles XII of Sweden that drove the bulk of Peter's reengineering of Russia's institutions and ways. From the moment he moved his army to Narva in the Swedish province of Estonia in 1700 until the Treaty of Nystad in 1721, Russia's shifting wartime fortunes not only impelled Peter's changes, but also defined their content. Even the famous Embassy to Europe in 1697–1698, from which came so many of Peter's ideas, was war related. Its primary purpose was to explore the possibility of forming a European alliance against the Turks. In this it failed, but along the way, Peter began to entertain the prospect of challenging the Swedes. As George Vernadsky wrote, "So it turned out that Peter went to Europe with the idea of fighting the Turks and returned with the idea of fighting the Swedes."[54]

War, of course, provided the dramatic catalyst to the Great Reform of 1861—the emancipation of the serfs—in the era of Alexander II; not that sentiment against preserving the institution had not been building for some time, even in Nicholas I's circle. But the Crimean War, because it was seen to have been lost more from internal weakness than from the external strength of the adversary, united the political spectrum on the need to act at last. For the war had exposed as nothing else could how far behind Russia had fallen, not just in military technology, but also in industry, communications, transportation, organization, and a civic-based nationalism. "It called into question Russia's status as a great European power," writes Terence Emmons, "and brought to the fore as at no time, perhaps, since Peter came to the throne, the issue of overcoming Russia's backwardness."[55]

It need not be stressed how central war was to the Bolshevik Revolution. Never would Lenin and his allies have been able to gather the shards of power lying in the streets, as Adam Ulam once suggested, had the old regime not been broken by the disastrous effect of World War I.[56] Less noted but equally important, much in the format of the Bolsheviks' new political order extended the model that an embattled imperial Russia had put in place to prosecute the war.[57] If world war created the basis for revolution, the civil war from 1918 to 1922 heavily influenced the shape and character it then assumed. So, the Bolshevik Revolution both in its origins and in its early development was very much a war project.

War's role in the Stalinist phase of the Bolshevik great state transformation, however, is less clear-cut. Stalin used the 1927 war scare to aid in consolidating his power, but whether he actually feared becoming embroiled in war as a result of the recent political skirmishing with London, Paris, and Warsaw remains in dispute. He would say that summer, "It is hardly open to doubt that the chief contemporary question is that of the threat of a new imperialist war. It is not a matter of some indefinite and immaterial 'danger' of a new war. It is a matter of a real and material *threat* of a new war in general, and a war against the U.S.S.R. in particular." From there he insisted on the urgency of "strengthening the defensive capacity of our country, raising its national economy, improving industry," but whether this represented a genuine impulse or a convenient excuse for what he was about to unleash is hard to tell.[58] When he returned to the theme in his famous "the weak get beaten" speech to industrial managers in February 1931, he was launching in earnest his revolution and, thus, had still more reason to exploit the theme, but he also had before him compelling evidence that Europe and Asia were slipping toward war.[59] Throughout the 1930s, whatever are the unresolved arguments over the sincerity with which he pursued a collective security strategy to fend off the danger of war and however contradictory his authorship of the purges, particularly of the military, the shadow of war did shape, at least in part, his domestic course.[60] In a more essential respect, however, war reverberated through all of Soviet foreign policy, because Stalin, like Lenin, accepted as an article of faith that the very nature of capitalism produced it. Although the inevitability of the war they preached was between capitalist states, the fear was that the Soviet Union could not avoid being drawn in. With the rise of Hitler in Germany, Stalin and his circle persuaded themselves that this path was paved by French and British leaders too weak to defend their countries and too eager to see the predator turned to the east. This poisonous image ensured that Stalin's choice of allies had neither a moral nor a lasting basis.

In momentous contrast, not war but the absence of war forms the defining context of the great state transformation under Gorbachev and Yeltsin. It is too much to claim, as some have, that Gorbachev could embark on perestroika because the Soviet Union faced no clear and present danger in the outside world. In the first years (1985–1986), as he prepared his program, he and his entourage scarcely looked with equanimity on the defense policies of Ronald Reagan's administration, although the specter of nuclear confrontation featured and fed by his predecessors now faded. Gorbachev set off on his path, not because the other superpower made it safe to do so, but notwithstanding his misgivings over Reagan's aims. In general, however, war as Ivan IV, Peter I, Alexander II, Lenin, and Stalin had known it was no longer a force or constraint for Gorbachev. True, to proceed, he had to extract Russia from war as he all-too-painfully did know it: the imbroglio in Afghanistan and lesser entanglements in southern Africa. Still, as said, it was the receding prospect of core security threats generated by other great powers, especially the other superpower, once the West began to take Gorbachev's innovations seriously, that created an altogether different context from that of earlier periods.

It would be wrong, however, to assume that war has ceased to be a factor shaping Russian foreign policy this time around. Gorbachev sought to free Soviet foreign policy from the country's distended stress on war, its inflated notion of enemies, its hopelessly overdrawn notion of military tasks, and, above all, its paralyzing assumptions about the militarism inherent in capitalist societies. This transformation of the Soviet Union's national security agenda was at the heart of Gorbachev's foreign policy revolution, which in turn served as an essential prerequisite for his domestic reform.[61]

Initially Yeltsin continued and enlarged this metamorphosis by further downgrading the role of nuclear weapons, acknowledging the collapse of Russian military power (indeed, proposing major defense cuts), and declaring Russia to be without major military adversaries, including the United States and NATO. But the inertia of old and deeply entrenched attitudes within the military, the dissipation of excessively rosy expectations surrounding Russia's relations with the West, the rise of new security threats nearby for which Russia had no clear answer, and the delayed shock over the country's great-power demise exposed how durable or easily revived old attitudes could be. It turned out that Russia's military was unable to shed the image of NATO and the United States as the challenge, and continued to prepare to fight them. When other threats, such as Chechnya and instability in former Soviet republics, intruded, the military, rather than reorienting its priorities, simply layered the new tasks onto the old schema of fears.[62] The consequence was to impede military reform and leave Russia with a defense establishment both unsuited to its needs and unaffordable.

Under Putin, Russia appeared at last to accommodate a world whose principal challenges were economic, not traditional security concerns focused on opposing alliances and the military balance among major powers. Given the opportunity opened by the September 11, 2001, terrorist attacks on the United States, the Russian president cast aside his previous ambivalence, allied his country with the Americans, and made plain Russia's reordered preoccupations. Ahead of other tasks now came Russia's determination to integrate into the World Trade Organization, to sort out its economic relationship with the European Union, and to concentrate on rebuilding economic ties with the other post-Soviet states. Putin seemed to be saying that, with the exception of the struggle against terrorism, globalization, not war and its corollaries, henceforth would have priority. As if to prove his commitment, he raised scarcely a fuss when George W. Bush's administration announced its unilateral abrogation of the Antiballistic Missile Treaty in December 2001.[63] Five months later he signed off on a strategic arms treaty that did little more than codify the future attrition of Russian nuclear forces and next to nothing to constrain the U.S. side. And then at the end of May 2002 in Rome, Putin put prior frustrations and anger over NATO to the side and embraced a new joint NATO-Russia Council designed to give Moscow and Brussels a common agenda.

Appearances, however, concealed how hard it was for Russia to escape the accumulated weight of history and the biases that populated it. In the words of one observer, "traditionally, in Soviet and tsarist times, economic interests had ranked well down the list of foreign policy priorities, very much an ugly stepsister to the 'real' business of security and geopolitics."[64] Putin—or at least one part of him—wanted to change that. Many within the government, a growing number of foreign policy intellectuals, and his own instincts told him that this was more than ever an economic world, and, unless Russia reoriented its thinking, it would be left behind. His new mantra became "a fundamental feature of the contemporary world is the internationalization of the economy and society," and in the face of this reality, Russia "no longer had a choice of whether or not to integrate into the world economic space."[65]

For two reasons, however, Putin's admonition produced less change than many at first expected.[66] No matter how implacably the forces of economic globalization bore down on Russia, many among the political elite and nearly all of those tasked with security planning simply could not shake free of the notion that international politics remained a dangerous game, driven by forces able, even ready, to harm Russia, and at a minimum to roll back its international influence. Because they viewed the West, particularly the United States, as in the front rank of these forces, they instinctively regarded these countries as adversaries, not as partners (not even as self-interested partners trying to manage and reap the benefits from an ever more densely entwined global economy). They remained fixated on the idea that NATO, even if not poised to attack, had not changed its essence, and, therefore, both its expansion eastward and its role beyond Europe's borders represented a threat that somehow had to be countered. And the United States, even if an unavoidable presence in fighting terrorism and opening doors to the club of international economic players, was not to be trusted. Given the United States' arrogance of power and its desire to put Russia in a box, perhaps even under its thumb, and to commandeer its resources, Russia needed to stand up for itself, needed to find ways of checkmating U.S. ambitions.

The second reason Putin's new theme faltered had to do with Putin himself. He, it turned out, bowed to the imperatives of global economics but in traditional geopolitical terms. Russia's tribute to globalization was less in terms of enhancing national welfare than in terms of enhancing national power. Putin, like Gorbachev, remained preoccupied with restoring Russia's great-power status. He understood that this could be done only by reconstituting the country's economic base and forcing growth rates beyond 7 percent annually, which in turn could be done only if Russia merged more fully into the world economy. But this recognition paralleled rather than displaced his basically competitive view of the other major powers, especially the United States. As a consequence, crucial as his interest in WTO membership was or as sincere his desire to enhance Russia's energy partnerships with Europe and the United States, this still left room for geostrategic maneuvering. Indeed, he sought to draw Europe and the United States into Russia's energy orbit precisely because he saw gas and oil as his country's most potent foreign policy instrument—which in no small measure explained his moves to give the state greater control over these resources.

Moreover, Putin's lingering tendency to view the United States as a competitor rather than a partner showed in his testy reaction to U.S. activity in the post-Soviet space. Even his initial acceptance of U.S. military deployments in Central Asia as part of the war against Afghanistan's Taliban, perhaps the most striking evidence of the shift in Russian priorities, was less striking than it seemed. The United States might be an ally in the war against terrorism, but not one whose military power he wanted anywhere near his country. Hence, the adjective that he attached in his original telephone conversation with President Bush—yes to a "temporary" deployment—was formally spelled out in a July 2005 meeting of the Shanghai Cooperation Organization (SCO), when Russia, China, and the other members demanded that the United States set a timetable for closing down its bases in the region now that the Afghan war was drawing to a close.[67] His edginess erupted far more starkly during the 2004 Ukrainian presidential election. Only a deep suspicion of Washington and Brussels explains his crude, direct attempt to influence the electoral outcome and then his furious recrimination against the Americans and Europeans when his candidate lost to Viktor Yushchenko, whom he chose to see as the West's stalking horse.

Vulnerabilities

Russia's external vulnerabilities, permanent and passing, real and supposed, have also amplified the effects of great state transformation. They reverberate with special force when Russia is weak and feeling it, and never more than in our day. They begin with the hard reality of geography. Russia has neither mountains nor oceans behind which to fashion a national defense. From the moment in 1237 when Batu, the grandson of Genghis Khan, crossed the Volga and invaded the principality of Riazan, until June 22, 1941, when Hitler's armies surged across the Bug, the open steppe to the east and the soft marshes and fertile plains to the west served as an easy corridor for invasion. True, the same terrain allowed the Russians to push continually outward, first into Siberia, then to the Pacific, west to the Baltic, south to the Crimea, and ultimately through Central Asia to the Hindu Kush. But what started in the fifteenth and sixteenth centuries in the slave-seizing depredations of the Nogai Horde and the khans of Siberia and Astrakhan ends today with the Russian core again exposed to the threats that pass through weak, largely spectral strategic frontiers.

Ivan IV, even after conquering Kazan and subduing its sister khanate in Astrakhan, faced the constant ongoing assaults of the Crimean Tatars. Indeed, twice they reached and burned Moscow. The first time, in the summer of 1560, was said to have hastened the death of Ivan's young tsaritsa, Anastasia, an event many assume contributed to Ivan's inordinate cruelty in subsequent years.[68] Then in 1571 the Crimean khan, Devlet Girey, and his army again set Moscow ablaze, killing so many that it reportedly took more than a year to bury the dead.

Peter, it is said, came away from his famous Embassy to Europe in 1697 disarmed by Russia's economic and technological backwardness, even persuaded that "Russia faced the danger of falling into economic dependence on more advanced countries, turning into a colony or even being conquered by its neighbors."[69] Peter and Ivan IV both compounded Russian vulnerabilities by launching their northern wars—neither of which was, except by the loosest definition, defensive—and in the process adding territory whose borders were still harder to defend while promoting powerful anti-Russian coalitions that at times united Russia's European and Turkish adversaries. Alexander II, or sometimes freelancing military officers, pushed the imperial borders deep into Central Asia in the years after the Crimean War with much the same effect, in this case driven by a sense of weakness. They in part sought to offset their maimed position in Europe and the Near East by adding to Russia's imperial glory elsewhere. Stalin, too, shared this historical sense of vulnerability, and as early as 1925 stressed that the Soviet Union could be secure only if a belt, or cordon sanitaire, of socialist states existed on its western frontier. But, as in the past, when the Soviet Union drove its strategic frontier outward across Eastern Europe, it simply added another source of perceived vulnerability.

From Ivan IV to Stalin, Russian expansionism swept within the country's de jure and strategic frontiers an ever-expanding number of non-Russian peoples, most of whom remained on patrimonial lands, and in the process created a further internal source of vulnerability. This in turn tied the fate of the autocracy to the country's security. Autocrats from Ivan IV to Stalin believed unquestioningly that were the authoritarian state to falter, their polyglot empire would disintegrate (and in the end, of course, they were right). Even after the outer shells of the empire crumbled, however, an allied sense of vulnerability continues to haunt Russia's leaders. It echoes in the way Putin frames the stakes in Russia's war with Chechnya. He imagines a linked set of dominoes: If Chechnya is lost, the entire North Caucasus will be next, and then the Muslim territories in the middle of the country, severing Siberia and the Russian Far East from its European core.[70]

When a crushing sense of weakness compounds the ever-present sense of vulnerability, the effect is far more pronounced. The urgency and near desperation that agitated Alexander II and those around him flourished amid converging crises: a state facing massive deficits and, to quote Geyer, "on the brink of bankruptcy"; a spirit of revolt that quickly spread to Congress Poland and then the western provinces of Russia itself; and a shattering loss of the regime's authority among the privileged class.[71] Weakness is far more difficult to encapsulate in Stalin's case. That by the early 1930s the country was wracked with economic misery, including a famine that destroyed millions, and a society turned upside down by the frantic first stages of Stalin's fevered industrialization seems obvious. Stalin, however, did not judge weakness in these terms. Weakness he feared, but it was in the treachery he saw all around him—in colleagues plotting against him, in workers and managers "wrecking" the party's noble effort to speed the Soviet Union's modernization, in a military high command spoiling for revenge over past indignities at Bolshevik hands, and in entire nationality groups secretly disloyal and sure to betray the country at the first chance. His savage answer, including his murderous purge of the military, created a perception of Soviet weakness in the eyes of others, notably Nazi German leaders, and this subjective dimension of the threat Stalin does seem to have sensed.

In none of the five cases of great state transformation, however, was weakness as complete and searing as in Yeltsin and Putin's Russia. Even if the Soviet Union's superpower status turned out to be, in large degree, fraudulent, based only on nuclear weapons and a massive conventional military that almost certainly would not have performed as the West feared at the time, the plunge into the ranks of second-rate powers inflicted special pain. The collapse occurred in all domains (military, economic, and political, where alliances matter). It was both absolute (measured against what had been) and relative (measured against what others had).

After the free fall of the Soviet economy in Gorbachev's last three years and the massive shrinkage of the Russian economy in the first five years of the Yeltsin reforms, Russian GDP placed it not in the category of second-tier powers such as Germany, France, or Italy, but just ahead of Canada and Mexico. Russia's economy in 1996 was now considerably smaller than half that of India and scarcely one-seventh that of the United States.[72] Measured in terms of the United Nations Development Programme's Human Indicators Report (an index that incorporates poverty, literacy, mortality, and GDP), by 1995 Russia had fallen to sixtieth place, slightly above Malaysia and Mauritius.[73]

Economic collapse, of course, was both a source and a manifestation of the state's basic enervation and, in particular, of its incapacity to mobilize resources essential to the performance of basic governmental tasks, including the design of effective foreign policy. Under Yeltsin, the federal government initially collected less than 9 percent of a shrunken GDP in revenue, a ratio too small to sustain a national government whatever its condition.[74] Neither could the state ease the dislocations and pain caused the population by tumultuous economic change, nor could it protect society from the health, environmental, and personal security hazards of decaying infrastructure or even preserve intact human capital (e.g., the scientific community) and social resources (e.g., an education system) essential for renewal.

As a consequence, Russia's ability to shape even its most immediate external environment suffered continually from strained resources and a limited array of tools. Add to this the disintegration of the country's military power. Within a decade of the Soviet Union's demise, Russian spending on a bloated and misshaped military had fallen to less than 10 percent of that in the Soviet Union's last year and to about 2 percent of what the United States was spending.[75] By 1997 fewer than 10 percent of army divisions were 80 percent combat ready and the hardware available to them, other than fighter aircraft and helicopters, was less than half that in 1992, much of it in disrepair. Just how weak the Russian military had grown was on graphic display in its helpless effort to bring a single province to heel in the 1994–1996 Chechen war.

Finally, the demographic descent of the country, reflected in sharply declining male life expectancy, increasing infant mortality, and a population predicted to fall from 145 million to 102 million by 2050, created a unique sense of peril. Never had a postindustrial society experienced a retrograde slide of this kind, let alone magnitude, and Russia's national leadership treated it not merely as a social setback, but as a threat to national security. By 2003 Putin, in his "state of the nation" addresses to parliament, began openly discussing Russia's shrinking population and supplying numbers. He called it "one of the most serious threats" facing the country.[76]

Taken together, the ruination of Russian power in all its forms, save nuclear weapons, prompted outsiders to the cruelest of judgments. The bluntest among them put it directly: "There is," Lawrence Freedman wrote, "now no particular reason to classify Russia as a 'great power.'" He went on: It "cannot therefore expect the privileges, respect and extra sensitivity to its interests normally accorded a great power. Increasingly it lacks the clout to enforce its objections to developments it considers harmful or to take on the sort of responsibilities that can earn it international credit."[77] Russia's leaders and political elite hated the thought, but they knew it was true.

By 2006 the picture had begun to change. Weakness no longer remained the sole unrelenting backdrop of policy. High energy prices filled the Russian treasury, providing Russia with the world's third most sizable foreign reserves, freeing it from its debt burden to the West, and creating a sense of empowerment over those, including Europe, China, and Japan, who needed Russia's oil and gas. This, coupled with the impression that Putin had restored order after the chaos of the Yeltsin years, stirred a prickly new self-confidence. But Russia's rebuff of Western criticism over authoritarian trends within the country, its unapologetic use of sticks against balky neighbors, and the voice that it demanded on the crisis issues of the day co-existed with deep ongoing insecurities. Putin and those around him, at root, worried that Russia's position in the countries closest to its borders was under siege and vulnerable, that Russia's internal stability was not assured, and that other players beginning with the United States were on the prowl for ways to limit Russia's external influence or shape its domestic policies to their taste. Thus, with poignant effect, weakness limned the stirring of renewed Russian self-confidence.

Weighing the International Dimension

The shifting contours of the international setting constitute the third factor conditioning the foreign policy effects of great state transformation. When they are dramatic, as they have been for Yeltsin's and Putin's Russia, each of the other influences also etches its effects more sharply. Vulnerabilities cut more deeply or take on a strange, unfamiliar shape. Tensions with other states and the shadow of war loom larger or twist the pressures pushing in more positive directions. Above all, because they more often than not radiate multiple, frequently conflicting impulses, they deepen the uncertainties and stresses already inherent in the turmoil roiling the country from within.

Russia's world from the late Gorbachev years to the Putin era has been marked by three extraordinary circumstances. They start with the recrudescent force of geopolitics, because for the Russians the single most excruciating feature of international politics over the last two decades has been the shrunken reach of their country's writ and influence. From the lost war in Afghanistan and the lost empire in Eastern Europe to the collapse of the Soviet Union itself, the country has been in historic geopolitical retreat. Putin's Russia, shorn of the far-flung dominions that imperial Russia and the Soviet Union brought under its rule over a half millennium of war and conquest, has been reduced to the physical entity that it was in the sixteenth century.

This massive rollback has not simply left Russian pride lacerated, nor, still more significantly, has it simply demolished the strategic salients behind which Russia struggled to make itself secure. It has recast Russia's relationship to its external environment, altering fundamentally its standing and options vis-à-vis the major power centers in the world. For the first time in the modern era, China, Russia's giant neighbor to the east, is the ascendant force, and Russia in its shadow. As the discrepancy in standing and wherewithal grows, the possibility arises, to quote Dmitri Trenin, of "a situation unthinkable in the last 550 years," when Russia will again become "a vassal of an Asian empire."[78] To the west the Russians face a Europe physically more distant than at any time since before Peter the Great, separated by a wide swath of states straining to flee Russia by attaching themselves to a European economic and security enterprise from which the Russians are conspicuously excluded. With the United States, the deeper significance of Russia's fall from superpower status resides in the challenge that unipolarity poses when there is precious little that Russia can do about it.

Yet, simultaneously, another powerful, countervailing trend, one equally without match in the last four centuries, is also at work. For one of the few moments in the history of the modern state system, strategic rivalry among the greater powers is not the defining feature of international politics. None of them views another as the principal threat facing it; none of them strains to arm against another; and none of them labors to forge alliances against another. Never has this blessing existed in other periods of great state transformation, and it should offset much of the peril that the collapse of Russia's strategic position otherwise might entail. Alas, the blessing carries no guarantee that it will endure. Already traces of a return to the past lurk in the uneasy jostling between the United States and China and, with gathering speed, between China and Japan. In the post-Soviet space, Russia, too, has tended to see the U.S. and European role as a strategic challenge rather than an opportunity to work at prolonging this historic interlude of great-power civility.

The momentary absence of strategic rivalry among the great powers is a fact; Russia's geopolitical decay is a process. Globalization, too, is a process, and the third critical component of Russia's international environment. It also complicates the effect of the other two influences. As at the end of the nineteenth century, the vastly accelerated flow of goods, services, capital, ideas, and people through borders made porous by technological advances creates an imperative any country resists to its own distinct disadvantage. But globalization also has a dark underside. Not only does it pick winners and losers, with the strong growing stronger and the weak weaker, but it pumps growing quantities of a great many contaminants—drugs, arms, disease, trafficked humans, terrorism, crime, and the makings for weapons of mass destruction—across the same porous borders.

Russia dares not remain aside from the processes of globalization, for then it has no chance of surmounting the economic backsliding that cast it out of the category of great powers and brought it to this point of frustration and discontent over its geopolitical decline. Globalization, by the web of mutual dependence that it weaves, might even be thought of as buttressing this moment of quiescence in the rivalries among great powers. And it has the potential of shifting Russian preoccupations from counterproductive fields of competition to spheres where all sides stand to gain. But globalization, too, carries no guarantees. The last great phase of globalization a century ago did not prevent two deadly world wars and numerous lesser wars, the collapse of the international economic system in the 1930s, and a draining, tension-filled half century of Cold War. Despite the expectations of many of globalization's contemporary essayists, nothing says that the dynamic of international politics could not again become dangerously violent. Nothing says that globalization itself, given its negative features and uneven effects, may not become a source of trouble.

When the current great state transformation began in the 1980s, the first two of these factors had not yet materialized, and the third, globalization, remained a secondary consideration. Gorbachev's Soviet Union inhabited an international universe still defined by the rigidities of a now crumbling bipolar world. Although some have argued that the harshest features of the Cold War had eased enough to make the international setting an enabling condition for Gorbachev's perestroika, the truth is that had he not chosen to recast the Soviet Union's long-standing aims and apprehensions, there would have been precious little enabling about it.[79] The foreign policy revolution that Gorbachev carried out from 1986 to 1989 drained the superpower contest of its military intensity, neutralized the Sino-Soviet conflict, pushed regional crises into the background, and began to erase the divide that kept the two Germanies and the two Europes apart. Eventually the international environment did become permissive, but only after he made it so. In this case the causal arrow pointed from the subjective to the objective.

The dual revolution imposed by Lenin and Stalin occurred, in its first phase, in the ruins of an international system. World War I tore down the last remnants of the old order, dismantling empires, undermining a European-based balance of power, and creating a subset of critical pariah states. For a war- and revolution-weakened Russia, its unenviable lot in the victors' postwar order was as an object, not a subject, a wounded nation under an outlaw regime, to be disciplined by Europe's stronger states and assigned its place. By the time Stalin readied his assault on Soviet society, the international setting was slowly sliding from the shapeless tensions of the 1920s to the gathering threat from unchecked predator nations. In the next decade, while Stalin ravaged his country from the inside, the world around him settled into a deadly bipolarity—not the face-off between capitalism and communism of Lenin's imagining, but a fateful contest between democracy and fascism whose inexorable outcome was a war from which no machination could save the Soviet Union. It was, however, a war out of which the Soviet Union emerged as an architect and no longer merely an object of the new postwar order.

Alexander II's Russia operated in an international system at middle age, formed forty years earlier at the end of the Napoleonic wars and fated to survive another forty years before it would perish in the fury of World War I. True, the rise of Bismarck's unified Germany from 1864 to 1870 would, when combined with the decline of the Ottoman and Austro-Hungarian empires, lay the ground for a fateful contest among the great powers. But, while Alexander II ruled, Russia's external environment seemed in normal, albeit fluid, equilibrium. Britain stood as the principal bulwark against Russian ambitions—condemning its actions during the 1863 Polish insurrection, blocking its initiatives in the Balkans, enforcing the Paris Treaty that ended the Crimean War, threatening war over Russian expansion in Central Asia, and rolling back Russian gains in the 1877–1878 Russo-Turkish War. Prussia served as its principal ally, although scarcely unconditionally. France and Austria, at different times, collaborated with Russia, but always as a function of trends in relations with other key states. And each carried a taint in Russian eyes: France because it was too sympathetic to revolutionary currents, and Austria because it was a rival in the Balkans. So, for Russia there was play in the system, but not much scope for any given move.

There was, however, a new phenomenon that intruded on this setting, and, like globalization today, exerted new and conflicting pressures on Russian foreign policy. This was the rise of nationalism in the wake of the Industrial Revolution spreading across Europe. Its growth in Poland and Finland threatened Russian control in these regions and, when the Polish insurrection exploded in

1863, stimulated a conservative nationalist backlash in Russia that, too, had a negative side. Not only did it create unwanted pressure for more extreme measures than the regime cared to adopt, but it also had an increasingly anti-German cast that risked complicating the regime's strategic stake in cooperation with Prussia.

Peter the Great more altered Russia's international environment than the other way around, for it was in his time that Russia became part of the European system, and no longer merely Europe's hinterland. He not only drew Russia into Europe physically, enhanced Russia's commerce with it, and regularly made the rounds of its capitals. More significantly, he threw himself into Europe's dynastic politics, carefully calculating marriage strategies for his offspring as well as nieces and nephews, and still more vigorously into the alliance politics of the day. He, more than any of his predecessors, sought to forge coalitions as a counterfort of Russian foreign policy, and, to cite Evgeny Anisimov, struck "alliances with those states with which relations had been unthinkable in Orthodox pre-Petrine Russia."[80] But the alliances available to him were with secondary players. Hence, he went to war with mighty Sweden in 1700, with Denmark, Saxony, and eventually the Rech Pospolita at his side and Prussia off to the side, a venture made feasible by the fact that Sweden's traditional ally France was neck deep in the War of Spanish Succession. Once the major powers—Great Britain, France, and Austria—turned their full attention to checking Russian expansion in 1719–1720, they rather quickly isolated Russia by breaking up the "Northern Alliance." They could do so because alliances were unsteady props in the eighteenth-century European international system, and Russia's military appearance beyond Poland's western border, its role in destroying Swedish power, and its growing naval strength in the Baltic gave a country like George I's England every incentive to work to reconstitute the old balance of power as a check on the rise of Europe's new player.

Finally, if Peter gave shape to Russia's international environment by making it a part of the European system, the salient feature of Ivan IV's external world was a lack of shape. Although Russia grew much larger during his rule, extending beyond the Urals into Western Siberia, across the Volga basin, and south to the Caucasus Mountains, its new reach remained menaced by soft, ill-defined borders, which contributed much to Russia's ambiguous relationship with its larger surroundings. To the east Russia encountered an amorphous realm dominated by the rulers of nomadic Siberian tribes; to the south it faced the enervating threat of the marauding Crimean khanate, backed by the power of the formidable Ottoman Empire; and to the west, tempting as the opportunity to aggrandize Russia at the expense of a crisis-ridden Livonian Order of German knights was, Ivan IV's move to seize it brought the country into direct conflict with Poland, Lithuania, and Sweden, a conflict in which it could not prevail. Most significantly, however, it was under Ivan IV that Russia's international environment took on its most essential aspect, one that has been at the heart of Russia's agitated existence ever since. For it was in his time that Russian expansion brought the country alongside two of the three great civilizations Russia would come to border—the European, the Muslim, and the Asian—thus, creating the historically enduring pressures with which Russia struggles to our day.

From This Mix: The Search for Identity, Great Power Anxieties, and the Specter of the West

In the context of great state transformation, the effects of war, Russian vulnerability (particularly when heightened by national weakness), and the challenges posed by the outside world cut far deeper than at more ordinary moments. Not simply Russia's day-to-day actions and ideas are affected; its whole sense of being is at issue—not simply with whom to be or to what ends, but in the name of what and by what self-definition. Perhaps because the sense of loss and weakness has been particularly wrenching since the collapse of the Soviet Union, contemporary Russia has suffered this soul-searching with a special intensity.

Russia shorn of empire and doubted as a great power has been thrown back into swirling uncertainty over the most primal questions: Where in the universe of nations does Russia belong? Indeed, where among civilizations? Should it wish or even dare to imagine itself as part of the industrialized, democratic West? Or should it hold itself apart, insisting on what, in the eyes of Russians, makes it both incommensurable and superior to the West? The underlying divide, of course, has a long pedigree. Russian intellectuals, tracing back to the first part of the nineteenth century, split along fundamental lines. From those early days, the so-called Westernizers and their descendants have defended the notion that Russia's path to progress requires that Russia acknowledge its cultural affinity with Europe and dedicate itself to emulating Europe's values and institutions. The other camp, originally identified with a Slavophile philosophical and literary intelligentsia that flourished in the 1840s and early 1850s, sees Russia in a very different light. Russia, located at the confluence of three civilizations, European, Asian, and Muslim, and imprinted with elements of each but distinct from all, molded by a long history that has endowed it with qualities and institutions suited to the land and its people, constitutes a unique segment of humanity. The value that it attaches to community over the individual, to spirituality over materialism, to cooperation over competition, to tradition over "liberal modernism," and to Orthodox Christianity over Catholicism and Protestantism is to be celebrated and preserved against the encroachments of a less noble and spiritually impoverished West.

These dueling themes reacquired life amid the disarray of thought and emotion following the collapse of the Soviet Union. In the first years Yeltsin, his foreign minister, Andrei Kozyrev, and more casually the young reformers who filled his government embraced the liberal internationalism of Gorbachev at the height of his foreign policy revolution, and then went further. They imagined that Russia could and should seek a place among the countries of the West, or, as Yeltsin and Kozyrev put it, in their fanciful opening years, join in forming a strategic community "from Vancouver to Vladivostok." Even before their heedless optimism gave way and collapsed, other dissenting voices had emerged, put off by what seemed to them an unseemly and unnecessarily yielding approach to the Europeans and North Americans and convinced that Russia's first priority should be nearer to home. Russia, they believed, should focus on the pieces of what had been the Russian and Soviet empire and worry about reconstituting its voice among and within these new states on its borders. The simplified label attached to much of this was "Eurasianism," and there was a version of it that did hark back to the original school of thought in the 1920s, a quest that in its day also represented anguish over Russia's postimperial identity and that also traced its lineage back to the nineteenth-century Slavophiles.

However, the arguments of Alexander Dugin, Eduard Limonov, and, in a different vein, Elgiz Pozdnyakov captured only a portion of the spectrum of those struggling to sketch a Russian identity that was neither servile to the West nor shackled by the country's overpowering weakness. Pozdnyakov, a historian in the Slavophile tradition, saw Russia as not only a civilization apart and badly served by proponents of Russia's integration into either the East or the West, but a great power by definition, given its historic role of holding the balance between East and West, a balance as much cultural as strategic.[81] Dugin, the organizer of what he calls the International Eurasianist Movement, presents a far starker argument. His violently Manichean view of the world juxtaposes "our" (a universe of "tradition," "total superiority of the spiritual over the physical," the "assertion of [the] ethics of hero over [the] ethics of dealer," "material equality," "the principle of fairness over the principle of profit," etc.) with "not our" ("Western civilization starting with [the]

Enlightenment, humanism, Cartesianism and Kantianism, individualism, materialism, and domination of merchant society," "tranquility, cowardice, cautiousness, coolness, indifference, and [a] selfish fear of death," etc.). Between the two only one outcome is possible: The contest "will be decided by war, the 'father of things.'"[82]

Dugin explicitly takes as the roots of his movement the émigré Russian "Eurasianists" of the 1920s—Nikolai Trubetskoy, Petr Savitsky, George Vernadsky, Nikolai Alexeev, and others—who, in the wake of imperial Russia's destruction and the arrival of Russia's new Bolshevik masters, also struggled with the primordial. Like their Slavophile ancestors, they depicted Russia as a unique amalgam of Slavic and non-Slavic peoples, including Turks and Asians, occupying a unique space physically and culturally, and fated to fulfill a unique mission as a spiritual force transcending a morally desiccated Europe.[83] Although the movement would by the late 1920s splinter into factions—the members of one becoming apologists for Stalin's regime—their common ground remained a vivid Russian nationalism and an acceptance of despotism as Russia's natural lot.[84]

They in turn followed in the footsteps of the Pan-Slavists of Alexander II's day, whose nationalist loyalty to the Russian Empire also refashioned and incorporated the intellectual and cultural urgings of the Slavophiles. For them, too, Russia was marked to lead a grand Slavic civilization as a successor to the dominant but fading Romano-Germanic imperium of the day. Their prideful vision, however, masked a basic frustration over Russia's fall from grace. Thus, in a way, their project for protecting and uniting their Slav brothers to the West and their fellow Orthodox within the Ottoman Empire was deep down a means to "renew [Russia's] national identity and strengthen its standing in Europe."[85] At the same time, as Geyer argues of the general upsurge of Russian nationalism in the 1850s, "A deep craving for new ideals had been created by the hardships and the confusion of social roles which had accompanied the transformation of Russian society and which had been intensified by economic depression."[86]

Dugin and those like him, however, represent only an extreme point on the spectrum of Russian politicians and thinkers who, in their restless effort to invent a future for Russia, believe it must honor Russia's peculiar needs and characteristics—believe in a "third way" for Russia.[87] This leaves room for moderate Eurasianists, of which Putin may be one, at least when he rises on some mornings. On the eve of the Asia-Pacific Economic Cooperation summit in 2000, in an article carefully placed in multiple Russian newspapers, he announced that "Russia has always felt itself to be a Eurasian country. We have never forgotten that most of Russia's territory is in Asia."[88] Clearly, however,

Putin does not fit squarely in the Eurasian school, first, because on other occasions he has stressed Russia's European face and attachment—indeed, readiness to work for Russia's integration into Europe—and, second, because, faced with the challenges of globalization, he embraces them. Dugin and his sort reject globalism, or in their lexicon "mondialism," and insist that somehow Russia should stand against it.

Then there are those who some would call democratic Eurasianists.[89] As the label suggests, they reject Russia's autocratic traditions and want to see it become a liberal, open society. But they recognize that the loss of Eastern Europe and the Baltic states has moved Russia eastward and made Asia all the more central to Russian concerns. Because of this displacement, wrote one of them, "its stabilizing function is naturally converted from a predominantly European one into a properly Eurasian one."[90] Unlike their more radical counterparts, they are not anti-West. Most, in fact, favor close cooperation with Europe and the United States. Unlike Western-oriented liberals or *zapadniki*, however, they stress the post-Soviet space as the first priority of Russian foreign policy, not Europe or the United States.

On the other side of the divide are the *zapadniki,* whose preference for the West puts them very much in the tradition of the nineteenth-century Westernizers. The initial and most enthusiastic within this camp were the so-called Atlanticists, people such as Yeltsin's first foreign minister, Andrei Kozyrev, and many of the liberal economic reformers, who believed Russia could literally incorporate itself into the Euro-Atlantic community. The more democratic Russia became, the more acceptable to the West it would be; the more accepted it was, the more democratic it would become. By the mid-1990s, however, their voice had been largely lost, discredited by the failure of both Russia and the West to make Russia's Western option politically acceptable within Russia. Still, among politicians and foreign policy intellectuals, others after them continue to view the West as Russia's natural, indeed, necessary partner, even if membership in NATO and the European Union remains out of reach. They may disagree over whether Europe or the United States should be the axis of a pro-Western policy, but they share a conviction that Eurasianism, particularly in its harsher forms, is at best foolish nostalgia and at worst a dangerous misreading of where Russia's real interests lie.[91] They also divide over who is to blame for the obstructions keeping Russia from a closer relationship with the West, some insisting that overbearing, clumsy Western policies drive Russia away, others, that Russia's unsavory drift toward authoritarianism puts the Westerners off.[92]

This simple division does not, by any means, capture the full range of foreign policy views among Russians. Various commentators, when sketching the spectrum, usually propose five or six categories.[93] Their tally, however, blurs a distinction that I want to preserve in this chapter. There is a difference between the fault lines that set one Russian against another when the contrast is at the fundamental level of national identity versus the wider array of views on practical strategic choices. In this second, more prosaic realm the deeper distress over what Russia is to be can be sidestepped and replaced with the issue of how Russia is to proceed. Those whom Alexander Sergunin classifies as "realists," for example, spend less time agonizing over first principles and more focused on the hard security challenges facing Russia. They are less interested in sweeping philosophical debates than in determining the threats that Russia faces and then deciding on the best strategy for dealing with them.

They cannot escape, however, the fundamental ambivalence at the heart of Russia's struggle to define its place in the world, and at this level the universe is essentially two-dimensional: *with*, although not necessarily as part of, the West, or *without* and perhaps against the West. Although Russians can argue over alternative approaches to most foreign policy issues, from globalization to alliances, terrorism to trade regimes, and the role of nuclear arms to the role of international institutions without harking back to the rift over identity, in the end the underlying contrast sets boundaries. Dugin's anti-American focus and readiness to ally with any state willing to stand up to the United States, including in his reveries the "Romano-Germanic" powers of Europe, are the direct product of what he and the prior generation of Eurasianists took from the late-nineteenth-century geopolitical analyst Halford Mackinder. Russia, the great land power at the core of the Eurasian heartland, is fated to confront the great sea power, particularly when, as today, that power attempts to dictate the shape of the larger international order.

At the same time, however hard-nosed the "realists" wish to be, however pragmatic in their approach to strategic partners, few among them think alignment against Europe or the United States is either realistic or sensible, not the least because most of them see China as the longer-term threat rather than as a useful counterweight to U.S. preponderance. For their part the pro-Westerners—they would prefer to describe themselves as pro-Russians—can disagree over the best way to protect Russian interests in the post-Soviet space and even over the nature of the challenge posed by the United States, NATO, and the European Union within the region, but none of them advocates a response that would sacrifice a deeper and more productive relationship with the Western powers, including the United States. In contrast, those who tout the idea of allying with China, or with India and China, or with some angry subset of the third world, or who believe that the strategic threats facing Russia matter far more than the challenges of globalization in almost all instances, stress Russia's singularity and maintain that for it there is or must be a "third way."

In short, stances rooted in assumptions about national identity have an inner logic of their own. The nineteenth-century Pan-Slavists, in defining Russia as the unifier of Slavs and the protector of the Orthodox under Ottoman rule, were inevitably pushing Russia into war with the Porte and the Austro-Hungarian Empire. Lenin and Stalin, in casting the Soviet Union as history's instrument and the nemesis of the existing international order, guaranteed that a strategy of cooperation with the other major powers, as long as they remained capitalist, could only be circumscribed, temporary, and a means to an end, never an end in itself. Similarly, a sense of identity that views Russia as unique by nature, preoccupation, and mission creates very different imperatives from one that views Russia as a normal (would-be) great power, facing the same problems as others. And when definitions of national identity compete, the turbulence generated around Russian foreign policy is particularly great. With the arguable exception of Stalin's time, it is in the nature of great state transformations to generate this competition, leaving Russia twisting among multiple identities.

The core problem traces back to Peter the Great, whose revolution made Russia a European power, but without making it fully European. As Hosking suggests, until Peter, the unresolved cleavage in Russian identity—and never more than under Ivan IV—was a "threefold . . . split between the Third Rome, the steppe khanate, and the aspiring European power, between the pious, God-fearing Byzantine ruler, the horse-borne nomadic warlord, and the rational, ruthless Renaissance prince."[94] Peter pulled Russia from these misty currents and imposed a choice. Russia would be, to continue Hosking's thought, neither "the center for an East Christian ecumene" nor a "Russian nation-state for all East Slavs," but "a north Eurasian multiethnic empire and European great power."[95]

However, Peter's choice, conditioned as it was—that is, Russia *in* but not *of* Europe—and then thrust on a resentful society entrenched in its ways, created a natural and enduring tension between Russians frustrated by Russia's unconsummated nod toward Europe and those attached to Russia's past and determined to see the country prosper on its own terms. The effect, at moments when the ground falls out from under Russia, has been to stir an awkward sense of not belonging. It echoes in Dostoevsky's injured exhortation: "In Europe we were hangers-on and slaves, while in Asia we shall be the masters. In Europe we were Tatars, while in Asia we can be Europeans."[96] Orlando Figes is right to see this as "a perfect illustration of the Russians' tendency to define their relations with the East in reaction to their self-esteem and status in the West."[97] Dostoevsky wrote these words at a time when, under Alexander II, Russian self-confidence had vanished and popular resentment against Europe over the humiliation of the Crimean War pulsated. Similarly and unsurprisingly, a kindred doubt reappears in Putin's Russia. "Does Europe count Russia in or out?" Russian observers ask.[98] "Were we to choose the West, would they have us?" Or will they, as in Peter's day, continue to say that "the Russians should be feared more than the Turks. Unlike the latter, they do not remain in their gross ignorance and withdraw once they have completed their ravages, but, on the contrary, gain more and more science and experience in matters of war and state, surpassing many nations in calculation and dissimulation."[99]

The insecurity, however, parallels—indeed, may even stimulate—another emotion-laden reflex. From Ivan IV's to Putin's day, Russia has worn its great-power status on its sleeve, and, when it is called into question, its leaders and essayists sink into a narcissistic preoccupation with the country's decline. The Russians even have a name for it: *derzhavnost,* from the Russian word for "power." *Derzhavnost,* however, has a meaning all its own, one missing from the English language, simply because the phenomenon is missing. Only the Russians in moments of distress revert to an affectation of great-power standing— that is, to asserting their natural right to the role and influence of a great power whether they have the wherewithal or not.

The syndrome has been there from the beginning. One of the most striking aspects of Ivan IV's relationship with the outside world was his extreme sensitivity to his standing as a ruler among rulers and to the place his realm was accorded by Europe's monarchies. Anything less than full equality with the Holy Roman Empire he treated as intolerably demeaning. At every turn he insisted on the superiority of his crown (by inheritance) over those of Sigismund Augustus of Poland and John III of Sweden (by election). "You say Sweden is the patrimony of your father," he wrote to John, "and whose son was he, and was your grandfather on the throne?" For good measure he claimed, quite falsely, descent from Caesar Augustus "at the dawn of time as everyone knows."[100] With Poland, the Holy Roman Empire, and Sweden, a constant and large issue was their refusal to acknowledge his self-proclaimed title of tsar.

Both the feeling of exclusion and the indignant claim to a God-given place in the political firmament come through in notes that Peter the Great made near the end of his life for a sermon to be delivered at a commemoration of the Treaty of Nystad. "All other nations maintain the policy of keeping a balance of forces with their neighbor and were especially reluctant to admit us to the light of reason in all matters and especially military affairs, but they did not succeed in this. It is in truth a divine miracle," he then goes on, "that all human minds are nothing against the will of God and this must be emphasized."[101]

Derzhavnost in contemporary Russia thrives across a broad spectrum of groupings. Within the main Communist Party (for there are several), it serves as a curious rebonding with imperial Russia. The eternal values that its leader now insists Russia embodies—*derzhavnost, sobornost* (community), and *dukhovnost* (spirituality)—are a throwback to the sacred trinity celebrated by Nicholas I and his successors (Orthodoxy, autocracy, and *narodnost* [an untranslatable cross between nationality, national character, and the people]). The attachment of the Russian Orthodox Church, particularly its conservative spokesmen, such as Metropolitan Ioann of St. Petersburg and Ladozhkii, has more distant antecedents, tracing back to the priest, Iliaron, in the early eleventh century, who at the time of Kyivan Rus wrote of the "*derzhavnost* of the Great Prince and the Russian land."[102] Even Russia's first Western-oriented liberal foreign minister, Andrei Kozyrev, as he sensed support for his foreign policy disintegrating, came back to the theme. Rather plaintively in spring 1994, he wrote that "the only policy with any chance of success is one that recognizes the equal rights and mutual benefit of partnership for both Russia and the West, as well as the status and significance of Russia as a world power."[103] Or, take the representative comment by the omnipresent guru on the fringes of Putin's entourage, Gleb Pavlovsky, that "over the coming years, at least until the end of President Putin's tenure and probably until the end of the presidency of his immediate successors, the Russian foreign policy priority will be turning Russia into a world power of the twenty-first century." This, he confessed, "in spite of the fact that at present we have a weak regional power with a weak commodity-oriented economy."[104] Aleksei Pushkov makes the stakes starker still: "If Russia does not arise as a great power, economically and militarily, it may fall apart."[105] Compare that with Hu Jintao, the Chinese leader, speaking at the African-Asian summit a few months later: "China will always be a member of the developing world, and strengthening solidarity and cooperation with the other developing countries is the cornerstone of China's diplomacy."[106] The same words simply could not pass from Putin's lips, not because Russia is obviously not a "developing country," but because their self-effacing tone is alien.

With the exception of a tiny minority of Russian intellectuals who balk at the very idea, Putin, the communists, nationalists, the church, and even a good many liberals find common ground where injured pride, the ache to be a great power, and the sense that the path back requires a strong and directive state intersect. Putin has been clear on this score from the beginning. On the eve of Yeltsin's retirement, in a personal manifesto placed on the Internet, he argued that "traditionally, ideals of the strong state that cares for the people have dominated our society." Ideas of "social solidarity" have historically prevailed over "principles of individualism," and this, he said, must be kept in mind when formulating a "national strategy for the revival of Russia." At the base of such a strategy must be the concepts of "patriotism, *derzhavnost*, and *gosudarnichestvo*, as well as social solidarity."[107]

Putin was careful to distinguish patriotism from "national conceit and imperial ambitions," and to emphasize that *derzhavnost* should not be understood in terms of military might, but rather as the country's ability to be "a world leader in new technologies" and ensure the population's welfare, and "by the skill with which it defends its national interests in the international arena." But, while he has expended far less energy declaiming Russia's natural right to the status of a great power, he leaves no doubt that deep within burns a determination to restore his country to a special prominence, not merely as the equal of partially restored major powers such as Great Britain, France, or Japan, but to a role decisive in the post-Soviet space and weighty in other key areas of global politics. He feels the impulse intensely enough to subordinate nearly everything he does—whether mastering the Duma, bringing regional leaders to heel, waging war in Chechnya, wielding Russia's vast energy sources, limiting opposition, promoting foreign investment, or seeking admission to international economic institutions—to bringing this goal closer. *Derzhavnost* for Putin transcends economic revitalization as a means to a better life for the average Russian; it renders the self-realization of the individual secondary to the realization of the individual through a reenergized state capable of holding the country together, producing, as he says, "social solidarity," and reanimating collective national pride.

THE EFFECTS

Like large amplifying chambers, first the underlying force of war, weakness, and international complexity, and then more directly the intervening tumult over identity show up in the specifics of Russian foreign policy. When the country is weak and dazed by catastrophes inside or out, the instinct of leadership is, naturally and sensibly, to retrench; to avoid gambles leading to face-offs with states more powerful than it; and to eschew commitments or undertakings too great for its depleted resources. Take the case of Alexander II. Prostrate after the crushing defeat in the Crimean War and wracked by the stresses of the "Great Reform," Russia needed an extended respite from international conflict. Foreign policy became the servant of domestic imperatives. No longer could it, as was often the case before and after, indulge foreign ambitions divorced from requirements at home. Its task was to create conditions aiding the arduous effort of restoring Russia to health and refurbishing its power. This meant a policy whose fundamental thrust was defensive—what Geyer calls a "new 'realism' of international abstinence."[108]

Therein, however, was a cruel contradiction directly fired by the deeper, resonant effects of great state transformation. Alexander's Russia had every incentive—well-warranted concern over domestic political stability, the travail of troubled reform, and an only partially reconstructed military—to settle for a lower profile among the other great powers of the day. Yet, the passion to restore their country's great-power standing, the preoccupation with undoing the hamstring of the Paris Treaty, the irresistible temptation to score minor victories over the European powers most resented, combined with the reckless urgings of new nationalist voices and the adventures of free-booting governors and military officials, constantly led the Russians—and none more than Tsar Alexander—to acts seen by others as aggressive. Thus, eight years after the close of the Crimean War and three years after the Emancipation Edict, Russia began to extend its imperial reach over the former khanates of Central Asia, until in 1884 the final encroachment as far south as Merv nearly ended in war with Great Britain.

Military governors, acting on their own and contrary to instructions from St. Petersburg, took it upon themselves to bring the benefits of Russian rule to the locals. "General Chernyaev has taken Tashkent," Russia's minister of interior Peter Valuev wrote in his diary in 1865, "and nobody knows why."[109] Nonetheless, in the end, Russia's long-serving foreign minister and chancellor, Prince Alexander Gorchakov, the great advocate of the "new 'realism' of international abstinence," defended the aggrandizement. "The United States in America, France in Africa, Holland in her colonies, England in India," he argued in a formal defense, "were all forced to take the road of expansion dictated by necessity rather than by ambition, a road on which the chief difficulty is to know where to stop."[110] In truth, as Geyer suggests, Central Asia's significance "derived not from the intrinsic value of the conquered territories but from the role it played in European affairs."[111] For in Central Asia, a region England could "penetrate only with difficulty," Russia could in comparative safety "satisfy her own thirst for prestige and . . . prove, despite any lingering self-doubts, that the Tsar was still at the helm of a true world power."

In the Balkans, Russia bumbled into war with the Turks in spring 1877 even though the tsar, Gorchakov, and other key officials did not want one. As Dmitri Milyutin, the minister of war, confessed to his diary three months before the start of the war, "a war . . . would be a very serious misfortune for us. The terrible loss of inner strength would be magnified by external exertions, every useful kind of work would be paralyzed and the countless casualties of war could soon completely exhaust the country and even threaten Russia's greatness."[112] Indeed, as the Serbs sought to drag Russia into war in the years after 1875 and fashioned an alliance with Montenegro, more or less guaranteeing the Serbo-Turkish war that followed, the tsar and his men continually tried to warn the Serbs off, and when war began, they, with Austria, adopted a posture of nonintervention. Yet, two years later, they had maneuvered themselves into a belief that war was their only option.[113] So, they went to war, with Milyutin now saying to his diary, "Russia's honor forbids us to stand about any longer with lowered guns just for the sake of peace."[114] In the process, Russia overreached, won great gains and wrote them into the Treaty of San Stefano (March 1878), but provoked the British and Russia's sometimes supporter, Bismarck, to organize the Congress of Berlin, where four months later most of them were taken away—once more to great bitterness among the Russian elite.

Stalin's most recent biographer, Robert Service, maintains that for him "the primary aim of Soviet security policy was to stay clear of entanglement in conflicts between capitalist powers."[115] Adam Ulam concurs. He says of the early 1930s, "For the immediate and foreseeable future, the Soviet aims were not the punishment of aggressors or the preparation of a grand military alliance against them, but the noninvolvement of the Soviet Union in war."[116] Yet, for all the wariness of being sucked into war, there was nothing pacifist about Stalin's policy. On the contrary, he continued to believe that others' conflicts—particularly among the capitalist powers—would create opportunities for the Soviet Union, hence the militancy he whipped the Comintern to adopt in the wake of the 1930s' Great Depression. Readily as he sought in the 1920s to avoid provoking an anti-Soviet coalition between Japan and the West inspired by the prospect of a communist takeover in China, he at the same time maneuvered continually in search of wedges by which to undermine the British and Japanese position in China, even if it meant betraying the Chinese Communist Party. And much as he desperately needed to rally the British and the Americans to his side after Hitler attacked the Soviet Union in June 1941, he nonetheless, even at the moment of greatest peril, demanded U.S. and British recognition for the territorial grabs that he had worked out with Hitler. Nor, for that matter, as the danger of war mounted in the 1930s and he had good reason to try to erect floodgates against it, did this discourage him from contriving to seize territory in the Baltic area, Poland, and the Balkans.

In the case of Yeltsin's and then Putin's Russia, the same juxtaposition of a fundamentally defensive posture advanced in key instances by aggressive language and actions reappears. From the beginning it was evident that those at the helm of state, as opposed to some elsewhere in the political establishment, fully understood Russia's need to avoid confrontation with any of the several power centers (the United States, Europe, China, and Japan) that were now stronger than it economically or militarily or both. They presided over a foreign policy directed, often fitfully and clumsily, at making it safe to live with their weakness. They shied away from climbing too high up the ladder of escalation on political issues when they disagreed with one or more of these centers, whether over Bosnia, Kosovo, Kaliningrad, Iran, Iraq, NATO enlargement, national missile defense and the abrogation of the ABM treaty, or any of innumerable instances in the post-Soviet space. They withdrew from the Cam Ranh Bay air base and deepwater facility in Vietnam (in May 2002) and from the electronic surveillance station in Lourdes, Cuba (in 2001), Russia's largest foreign covert intelligence facility. The first had cast a shadow over relations with China and the United States; the second had been a serious source of contention with the United States, and withdrawing produced an angry public rebuke from Fidel Castro. And they did not seriously try to mobilize one great power against another (China or Europe against the United States or the United States against China), other than superficially over fleeting issues.

Yet Yeltsin, Putin, and others in their governments regularly chose harsh, even menacing language when they felt cornered, disregarded, or threatened. A startled Bill Clinton experienced it, when at the Budapest summit of the Conference on Security and Cooperation in December 1994, Yeltsin suddenly and without warning bitterly denounced talk of NATO enlargement as a reprise of Cold War divisions, a threat to European stability, even a threat to democracy in Russia. Until then Russian officials had seemed willing to talk quietly about their objections to NATO's move eastward, counting on Washington to heed their concerns, particularly in the lead-up to the 1996 Russian presidential election. The same reflexive anger spilled forth after the terrorist massacre at the Beslan school in September 2004, when Putin lashed out against those in the West who, in their eagerness to diminish a still powerful nuclear Russia, would not stop at encouraging those who want to "tear from us a juicy piece of pie."[117] Or, when Putin, having struggled to avoid hard choices before the U.S. invasion of Iraq in spring 2003, after the fact, for an inexplicable moment, outdid the Germans and French in mocking Washington for failing to find nuclear weapons in Iraq, and ridiculed the idea of "a new strategic alliance between the U.S., Europe, and Russia, saying that it would not work if the White House made all the decisions."[118] Here, too, the outburst came in public before a surprised and embarrassed guest, this time British Prime Minister Tony Blair. One saw it as well in the Yeltsin leadership's emotional response to NATO's attack on Serbia in the 1999 Kosovo war, topped off by a reckless gambit to rush Russian military into Priština at the war's conclusion in hopes of giving Russia a voice in the outcome, and only narrowly avoiding a direct clash with NATO forces.[119] And it erupted again in Putin's 2006 "state of the union" address to the Federation Council, when out of nowhere but with an unmistakable target in mind, he threw his knife at a "wolf" who knows "whom to eat," and "judging by everything" that "is not about to listen to anyone."[120]

For the most part, this was rhetorical flailing more than an active threat to those flailed against. True, there were exceptions when Moscow grew particularly frustrated: For example, in early 1994, when in response to what it saw as the West's one-sided anti-Serbian approach to the Sarajevo crisis, it unilaterally moved military forces into the area to block the West's threatened air strike on the Bosnian Serbs.[121] In one sphere, however, Russia consistently treated with testy mistrust the Americans and the Europeans and consistently stood ready to parry what it saw as the West's ill-intentioned designs in the post-Soviet space— Russia's former empire and now new neighborhood.

After an initial period of neglect, by 1993 Yeltsin's Russia had already begun reasserting a special right to keep order in the region, and for this it expected the United Nations' blessing. In February, Yeltsin told a Russian audience, "The moment has come when responsible international organizations, including the United Nations, should grant Russia special powers as a guarantor of peace and stability in the region of the former Soviet Union."[122] When the Western powers demurred, his up-to-this-point liberal foreign minister, Andrei Kozyrev, petulantly warned that, with or without international sanction, Russia intended to protect its national interests within what had once been its national patrimony.[123] By 1994 Yeltsin and those around him had grown much less receptive to outsiders, including international agencies such as the Organization for Security and Cooperation in Europe and the United Nations, playing a leading role in settling the simmering local conflicts that dotted the post-Soviet landscape.

With Kozyrev's ouster and Yevgeny Primakov's arrival as foreign minister in early 1996, Russia became still more serious about staunching the erosion of Russian influence in the new post-Soviet states and countering the faintest hint that outsiders, particularly the United States, were trying to muscle Russia aside. His energized diplomacy in the Caucasus, the increased pressure put on Ukraine, the effort to fashion some kind of architecture drawing key Central Asia states closer to Russia, and the push to advance a formal Belarus-Russian union all reflected a new determination to assert Russia's influence within the region; all fit with the harsh appraisal of the U.S. aims in the post-Soviet space issued by Russia's foreign intelligence agency when Primakov headed it; and all were more than vaguely consistent with Primakov's impatient insistence that multipolarity, not a U.S.-dominated unipolarity, should govern international politics.

Under Putin, Russia's edgy assertion of its stakes, even rights, in the post-Soviet space did not end, but it did undergo a noticeable shift in method. Gradually the underlying impulse driving policy grew clearer. No longer did half-baked notions of restoring Russian sway over parts or all of the former Soviet Union echo dimly at the back of Russian policy. Instead Putin's entourage seemed more taken with maximizing Russian influence than with resurrecting crude forms of control. To quote Dmitri Trenin, Russia became "post- rather than neo-imperialist."[124] Its instruments would be increasingly economic ties, direct foreign investment, and joint antiterrorist activity, not military bases or meddling in regional conflicts, although on the latter score Putin and his colleagues were not above using Russia's self-appointed role as broker in these disputes to pressure their new neighbors.

The adaptation did not come easily, however. Strobe Talbott, the deputy undersecretary of state in the Clinton administration, tells of an exchange he had in November 1999 with Boris Berezovsky, then still in the service of the new Putin government. When Talbott showed distinctly little enthusiasm for Berezovsky's proposal to allow Russia to " 'restore order to Chechnya and the surrounding region,' " evidently including Georgia, Berezovsky exploded. "You talk about the 'rights' of the Georgians! You have no rights of your own in those countries down there—no rights and no interests! They are *our* neighbors, not yours."[125] Talbott adds, "He said the word 'neighbors' as though it were a euphemism for satrapies."

Slowly, however, Russia under Putin was accepting the reality that, for good and ill, the new states on its border were here to stay. Maybe a country like Belarus would again submerge itself in Russia; maybe other countries, such as Kazakhstan and even Ukraine, would agree to new forms of economic integration; or maybe, more ominously, some would disintegrate in chaos. Still, in one form or another, all but Belarus were now beyond the reach of Russia's fading imperial dreams. Hence, Putin moved swiftly to complete the process of normalizing relations with countries that had been most leery of Russia in the prior decade, countries such as Azerbaijan and Uzbekistan (although notably not with Georgia). Yeltsin had begun this process with Ukraine in 1997, and Putin vigorously advanced it. He tolerated rather than fought the deployment of U.S., Canadian, Australian, and French forces in Central Asia as part of the war against Afghanistan's Taliban and so, too, the U.S. military "train and equip" program in Georgia, announced in April 2002. Eventually he even softened Russia's resistance to a greater role for international agencies in helping to deal with the "frozen conflicts" in the Caucasus and Moldova.

Yet, at a deep, visceral level, where the pain of loss and the turmoil of change ate away, Putin and those around him fought demons reflexively and aggressively. The Rose Revolution in Georgia in 2003 and the Orange Revolution in Ukraine in 2004 brought the frustration rushing to the surface, displaying it in its starkest form. But its starkest form—Putin's furious railing against Washington and Brussels for meddling in the Ukrainian election, stirring the public revolt, destabilizing the country, and "practicing double standards designed to isolate Russia"—obscured a deeper tension.[126] So did his own far more conspicuous personal intervention during the Ukrainian elections, because the real drama was in the corrosive impulse that triggered this reaction. At root the problem was not simply that Putin preferred one Ukrainian candidate over another or that he resented the West's role in the election. It was why he preferred one candidate over the other, and what this said about his view of the West's role in the post-Soviet space. More than ever he regarded it as mischievous, if not malevolent. The West's professed commitment to promoting democratic change was at best a careless challenge to stability in the region and at worst a conscious effort to weaken Russian influence, perhaps even to subvert Russia itself by organizing in it another "color" revolution.

It also turned out that Putin's acceptance of U.S. bases in Central Asia was less cool and collected than it first seemed. By summer 2005, following the falling out between Uzbekistan and the United States over the latter's sharp criticism of Tashkent's murderous actions in Andijon, the Russians seized the moment to rid the region of the Americans. At the July meeting of the Shanghai Cooperation Organization, Moscow and Beijing egged their partners to join in a declaration demanding that Washington set a timetable for getting out of Uzbekistan and Kyrgyzstan. And a few weeks later the Americans began evacuating the Khanabad base in Uzbekistan, although they would persuade the Kyrgyz to allow at least a temporary extension.

In another more subtle and baleful respect, the competitive urge born of insecurity plagued Russian policy with its new neighbors. Whether consciously contrived or the residue of an unconscious impulse, Russian policy had an internal, but dubious integrity. Putin's Russia had made itself the buttress of the domestic status quo throughout much of the former Soviet Union, alas, an often sterile, at times dangerous, and in too many places potentially ill-fated status quo. Whether in trying to perpetuate a Kuchma-like regime in Ukraine, in looking the other way as repression grew in Lukashenko's Belarus, in rallying to the Central Asian regimes as they cracked down on opposition, or in doing little to unfreeze the "frozen conflicts" in the Caucasus and Moldova, Russian leaders were tying the fate of their country to an unsteady and, in all likelihood, chaotic future. And here was the point: They were doing so in large part because they feared a loss of influence and the risk that others would steal a step on them in the region. Ultimately and sadly, the effects of great state transformation were to close the Russian mind to thinking of the Americans and Europeans as partners in promoting change in the post-Soviet space and equals in dealing with the sources of the region's instability.

The second major imprint of great state transformation on actual behavior could be seen in the inability of Russia to make clear strategic choices among potential major allies. Instead policy was marked by maneuvering rather than commitment, tactical accommodations rather than workable, long-term partnerships. Ultimately, of course, given Russia's contiguity to many different power centers, a balanced policy designed to build constructive relations in all directions, rather than one based on alignment with one power center (the United States, Europe, or China), made sense, particularly when the chances of integrating Russia into the formal institutions of the West or of drawing China (let alone China and India) into an exclusive alliance were near nil.

So, however, was integration *with* the West in lieu of integration *into* the West a plausible and historic strategic option. Russia could have chosen to ally itself with Europe and the United States, notwithstanding, indeed, perhaps more easily because of, the increasing range of policy views within the West. By joining the Europeans and the Americans in addressing the core long-term challenges to international peace and welfare, including the one sphere where Russia is crucial—*mutual* security and stability in and around the Eurasian landmass—Yeltsin and Putin could not only have served Russia's core strategic interests; they would also have addressed what since Peter's day has been the insoluble issue at the heart of Russian foreign policy—Russia's relationship with the West. And it need not have been a choice against China or India, countries of indisputably growing importance to Russia. On the contrary, a key objective of a Russia-West alliance would have been finding ways to integrate the rising power of China safely and constructively into an evolving international order.

Ironically Russia began independence by appealing for such an alliance. When Yeltsin visited George H. W. Bush at Camp David in February 1992, a month after the collapse of the Soviet Union, he wanted to know whether the United States still saw Russia as an adversary. "And Bush replied no. But Yeltsin pressed him, asking why the proposed joint statement did not say that the two countries were allies."[127] Bush's secretary of state, James Baker, noted that the statement did speak of "friendship and partnership." "But Yeltsin wanted more; he wanted the two leaders to say that the two countries were moving from being adversaries to allies." Bush's response: "We are using this transitional language because we don't want to act like all our problems are solved." Soon, however, the thought that Yeltsin or any other Russian leader would continue to insist on alliance became a distant and discredited fantasy. The pressures, passions, and problems of Russia's harsh transition had rendered it so.

A decade later, for a moment, the possibility—or perhaps only its shadow—reappeared. Following the September 11 terrorist attacks, when Putin threw Russia's full support behind the United States' new war against "global terrorism," he seemed to be making a larger strategic choice. He seemed to be embracing a broader and more basic alignment with the West, one featuring areas that Russia had in common with Europe and the United States, such as international economic cooperation, energy partnership, and the struggle against terrorism, while downplaying those that divided, such as NATO enlargement, the modernization and use of U.S. military power, and disputes over the proper handling of "rogue states" and regional conflicts. Again, the promise soon melted away. May 2002, the month of the Moscow U.S.-Russian summit and the Rome conclave that launched the new NATO-Russia Council, turned out to be the high point. Afterward the U.S.-Russian relationship lost momentum, marking time until knocked off course by the Iraq war. In truth the likelihood that Putin's dramatic choice would flourish was slim from the beginning, doomed by his failure to develop a strategy for giving it content and rallying a skeptical political elite behind it.

The failure of this option, however, did not validate the other. Rather, out of inertia and inefficacy, Moscow settled for a policy that simulated rather than constituted an attempt to balance among the major power centers. Russian leaders talked of a "multidirectional" foreign policy, and they looked for bits and pieces that would give a positive push to each relationship. But nothing suggested that Putin and his team were thinking hard about how over the long haul they would keep relations with China, Europe, and the United States in equilibrium and what this would require, beginning immediately. Had they been, they would have skirmished less with the European Union over secondary issues, paid more attention to a long-term strategy for coping with an ascendant China, and, above all, worried less about balancing against the United States in regions on their periphery. Thus did the chilling hand of great state transformation haunt Russian policy, inhibiting constancy, vision, and boldness.

By 2006, Russia seemed to be exiting the distress and confusion of the prior decade and a half. After five years of steadily reasserting the power of the state, throttling all opposition, and putting behind itself the mayhem and hardships of the Yeltsin era, and suddenly empowered by high oil prices and a commanding position as a supplier of energy, Putin's Russia appeared to have regained its self-confidence. No longer was Russia willing to be tutored by Western powers whose economic largesse it no longer needed, or to worry about the West's unhappiness over the course it chose at home and abroad. Russia, the voices of the cognoscenti said almost in unison, was again its own person. While it did not wish to face off against the Americans, or for that matter any of the other major powers, neither was it any longer ready to trim its foreign policy ambitions, particularly in those states that it saw as its natural sphere of influence. And no longer would it agonize over its prospects of being accepted by or into the West. If necessary it could and would stand by itself or fashion its own camp of like-minded states drawn from its post-Soviet neighborhood. Yet, this, too, seemed more an interlude than a denouement, as likely to be undone by a shift in Russian fortunes as any of the earlier phases. It, too, seemed a comforting but temporary resting point in lieu of a more fundamental strategic choice.

The half choices and narrow perspectives in the late-Yeltsin and Putin eras had their parallel more than a century before under Alexander II. Leadership then, too, found it difficult to settle on a clear strategic direction, and also let emotion buffet a relationship pivotal to the choices open to Russia—in this case with Austria. In the wake of the Crimean War, the Holy Alliance, the partnership among Russia, Prussia, and Austria that had been the backbone of Russian foreign policy for the first half of the nineteenth century, suddenly lost its luster, discredited by what to the Russians were Austria's predatory actions in the last phases of the war. For three years, from 1856 to 1859, therefore, Russia flirted with a Franco-Russian rapprochement, notwithstanding the distaste the tsar and his circle had for the France of 1789, and unaided by the awkward moments between Alexander and Napoleon III. Still, the inertia of St. Petersburg's conservative identification with Berlin and Vienna retained its influence, and in 1873 and 1881, the old tripartite alliance returned in the diluted form of the alliance of the "three emperors." During the peregrination, neither Gorchakov nor his sovereign ever managed to make a strategic choice. Their actions were what Baron Boris Nolde called "but a series of improvisations."[128]

During the Stalinist period, granted the underlying meaninglessness of strategic choice when the international order itself is rejected, at a working level the Soviet dictator refused to choose or was incapable of choosing between two courses—either solidarity with the Western democracies or collaboration with the fascist dictatorships. So, for the six years from 1933 to 1939 Stalin traveled two paths; only in August 1939 did he make his decision, and even then it was more tactical than strategic, driven more by momentary advantage than by a durable solution.

In the sixteenth century, Russia's international environment was too fluid to give much significance to the notion of strategic choice or to the distinction between commitment and maneuver. But even for Ivan IV, the centrality of the threat posed by the Turks to both Russia and Europe created more than a theoretical possibility of alliance. At times, either with the European powers or with the Vatican, Ivan discussed the idea, but never with an earnestness that allowed it to be consummated. So can it be argued that in the eighteenth century, Peter's fickle political alignments typified the international politics of the day. It is worth noting, however, that he began his reign by making Turkey his principal strategic focus, only to shift abruptly to targeting Sweden, and then after eighteen years of war against Sweden, in 1718, while the war continued, seriously entertained the notion of allying with Sweden, even if the compensations proposed to Charles XII betrayed the interests of Peter's anti-Swedish allies.

Russia's external actions under Peter, however, did illustrate a third characteristic common to these periods of upheaval, and a natural concomitant of a lack of long-term strategic clarity. In these times, Russia, while potentially an important ally for other major states, reduces or even loses that attraction by coming across as unreliable or, worse, as an adversary waiting to happen. Vasily Kliuchevsky writes, "Peter's interference in Germany [he is referring to his meddling in the state of Mecklenburg] completely changed the direction of his foreign policy. It turned friends into enemies but failed to turn enemies into friends."[129]

Alexander II and his deeply divided entourage, by their inconsistencies and conflicting initiatives, created among other European powers "a reputation of duplicity and half-heartedness," while regularly and increasingly leaving Bismarck's Prussia, Russia's key ally, nonplussed and wary.[130] The goodwill that Russia earned in Berlin by its firm support during the Franco-Prussian War was tested by the regime's hasty, peremptory decision to renounce unilaterally the Black Sea provisions of the 1856 Paris Treaty in October 1870, and then in 1875 further wounded by Gorchakov's incautious defense of France in what turned out to be a false alarm over a putative German plan to wage a new war on France. Three years later, Alexander II and his bumptious chancellor angered Bismarck by blaming him for the defeat they suffered at the Berlin Conference, despite the fact that, if anything, he had saved Russia from a more painful outcome. Although the two sides would put the pieces back together, and, after the assassination of Alexander II, in 1881 negotiate a secret alliance among Germany, Russia, and Austria, before that, in 1879, Bismarck had taken the precaution of arranging with Vienna a secret defensive alliance against Russia. In the meantime, in the course of the diplomacy at the close of the Russo-Turkish War, Russia had casually betrayed its commitments to its wartime ally, Romania. This is not to suggest that the behavior of other major European powers was altogether more stalwart or predictable, but the vanity, confusion, and narrow-mindedness of a leadership riven with internal jealousies and conflicts, dominated by an autocrat of many minds and weak will, prejudiced Russia's alignments more than need have been the case.

It is, of course, difficult to judge Stalin's Soviet Union by this standard, because the underlying ethos of Soviet foreign policy militated against anything other than tactical alliances of momentary convenience with the great powers. Yet, even when it came to alliances within the world of socialism, his ruthless expediency in dealing with communist parties taught Mao Zedong and Mao's Chinese comrades to mistrust their Soviet ally long before they captured power in 1949. As for his eventual British and American partners in the Grand Alliance, quite apart from Soviet behavior, the very essence of the system—its authoritarianism, alien values, oppressiveness, and worldview—made the country an unsavory, even unthinkable ally, and only the all-consuming threat posed by Hitler's Germany overrode that disqualification.

Sadly a weaker echo of the same perspective haunts contemporary Russian policy, and its weight has grown heavier rather than lighter in the passage of time from Yeltsin to Putin. Increasingly Western capitals view Russia through the lens of its internal development. From this angle Russia's trend toward illiberalism—the concentration of power in a single figure, the tightening grip of "bureaucratic authoritarianism," the stage management of civil society, and the substitution of "virtual" for competitive politics—stifles any thought of a deep and enduring partnership before it forms.[131] This scarcely means that Western governments disbelieve in the possibility of finding common ground with contemporary Russia on many issues or would discount the need to make the sphere of cooperation as large as possible. Nor does it rule out practical partnerships—even institutionalized ones—addressed to concrete problems. But it does mean that Washington, Brussels, Berlin, Paris, London, and Tokyo believe less than ever in Russia being accepted into—never mind, accepting—the kind of alliances they have had for most of the last half of the twentieth century and hope to continue. Scarcely a decade and a half ago, in the wake of the collapse of the Soviet Union, the idea did not seem at all far-fetched to Western leaders.

The idea did not fade overnight. The descent was by stages. By fall 1998 key figures in the Clinton administration had begun to question the steadfastness of Russia's commitment to liberal reform and worried about its spillover to Russian foreign policy. Secretary Madeleine Albright, speaking before the U.S.-Russian Business Council in Chicago, confessed that "a true and lasting transition to normalcy, democracy, and free markets in Russia is neither inevitable nor impossible. It is an open question, the subject of a continuing debate and struggle." Doubts over the course the new Primakov government would adopt at home suddenly swelled, accompanied by uncertainty over the prospects for U.S.-Russian relations. To this point Russia and the United States "had been able to advance our cooperation where our interests converge and to manage our differences honestly and constructively." "The question now is," she went on, "whether that cooperation can continue" when "there are many voices in Russia who want to shift the emphasis in Russia's interaction with America and our allies from one of partnership to one of assertiveness, opposition and defiance for its own sake."[132] Unease over the evolution of Russian foreign policy had begun to blend with concern over the direction of events inside Russia.

The misgivings grew in spring 1999, driven by the Yeltsin government's angry riposte to NATO's war against Slobodan Milošević's Serbia. When Wolfgang Ischinger, state secretary in the German Ministry of Foreign Affairs, spoke to a Berlin conference of the Institute of East-West Studies in April 1999, he started by upbraiding Moscow for having done too little to avert the current crisis in Kosovo, but his reservations ran much deeper. He referred to "the 'normative divide,' which has long distinguished Russia from the West." He wondered whether the West's standards of a "normal" Russia could "ever coincide" with Russia's own notion. He lamented Russia's leftover Cold War tendency to view the world through the "prism of Russian-American relations." Worse, he said, "countering American influence still holds a top place on the list of Russian foreign policy objectives."[133]

At this stage, the West's growing hesitancy stemmed mostly from what its leaders saw as Russia's uncertain foreign policy orientation. In this, parallels existed on the Chinese side. China's leaders, too, albeit for different reasons, began wondering about the constancy of Russian foreign policy and the utility of counting on it to defend positions that seemingly drew the two countries together. The first of these was Russia's initial opposition to NATO enlargement, a development the Chinese abhorred as much as Moscow did, not least because they tended to lump together NATO and the U.S.-Japan security relationship. So when in spring 1997 Russia caved and signed the Founding Act, accepting the first wave of new members, Beijing drew its own conclusions. Four years later when Putin meekly swallowed the Bush administration's unilateral abrogation of the ABM agreement, opening the way to the development of national missile defense, again the Chinese felt let down. Not only had the two countries over the last three years signed statement after statement condemning the idea, but a limited U.S. national missile defense system posed far more dangers for China than for Russia.

Russia's shrinking appeal as a plausible, long-term ally for Europe, the United States, and Japan, however, crossed a threshold only well into the Putin era. Gradually the doubts and misgivings that had earlier arisen over Russia's foreign policy priorities and preoccupations mutated into a deeper concern over the country's internal evolution. Bush and his European counterparts muffled their public criticism—far more than did other critics, who no longer hesitated to characterize Russia as an authoritarian state and a menace to its neighbors—but behind the facade the worry grew. Russia, they feared, was at best plagued with a confused and limited leadership unable to take decisive steps to push the country forward and sort out its basic foreign policy choices, and at worst headed in the wrong direction, making a lasting and durable working partnership ever more distant. Russia's leaders, for their part, accepted the West's rejection, and, while answering with a mix of steely patience and counterpunches, simply went their own way.

History is not a mechanism whose parts mesh to produce reliable effects or a process whose patterned moments yield large law-governed outcomes—not even moments as grandiose as those discussed in this chapter. Nothing says that the consequences for Russian foreign policy of the turbulence and drama in Ivan IV's day should be the same under Alexander II, let alone under Yeltsin or Putin. Too much in the revolutions they wrought, not to mention the larger world in which they lived, is different to pretend that these vastly separated historical eras dictated common foreign policies. But each generates considerable turmoil at the roots of Russian foreign policy, which reverberates in Russia's aspirations, attitudes, and actions in the outside world. When a society is turned upside down by the wholesale recasting of its institutions and the ruling caste by brutal assault or disorienting change, unsurprisingly the underpinnings of foreign policy come loose. Russia's rulers and elite alike return to the most primal questions: Where in the international constellation does Russia fit? How should it position itself vis-à-vis other major players both near and far? And to what forces in the international environment should it respond and by what priority?

When preceded or accompanied by war, as all the great state transformations were except the last, war adds its own complicating influence. Ironically, the fact that war neither caused nor followed Gorbachev and Yeltsin's revolution has not freed Russia from its influence. Because the Soviet Union was not vanquished in war or those who managed its military establishment discredited, as was true, for example, of Germany and Japan after World War II, the country has found it difficult to separate itself from traditional ways of defining national security or even who poses a threat. Many of its politicians and commentators sense the counterimperatives of a changed world, including those created by the accelerating effects of globalization, but they cannot quite give themselves over to featuring them. For adjusting requires not simply shifting the lens through which the world outside is judged, but also setting an internal course that abandons the comforting familiarity of the strong state. Similarly, fully rethinking the meaning of security in the twenty-first century or capitalizing on the historic absence of strategic rivalry among the great powers entails far greater reliance on a strategy of reassurance than on one of deterrence, let alone of coercion. Disconcerted by the swirl of events and unnerved by the weak hand Russia holds, its leadership and much of the political elite simply cannot turn their minds in this direction. Trusting the creative energy of unhindered souls, political parties, and groupings seems too risky in a society unfamiliar with civic freedom, cleaved into sharply contrasting socioeconomic and ethnic categories, and whose institutions totter between the old that are in ruins and the new that are unformed. Dealing with Russia's new neighbors by seeking to reassure them through word and deed, rather than coerce them, conflicts with deeply embedded imperial habits and the difficulty of accepting the give-and-take of international politics in territories that once formed the homeland. Russia in the near term may wield its foreign policy resources, including its growing power as an energy supplier, with greater self-assurance, and it may succeed in recouping its influence in several of the post-Soviet states, but the process of transforming its neighborhood into a community of trusting, constructively enmeshed states will be delayed.

Thus, as in the past, great change within Russia clouds and twists the meanings attached to events and trends in international politics. Simultaneously unfamiliar, sometimes intimidating new trends in international politics reverberate through Russia's charged domestic political milieu, deepening the divisions over Russia's place in the world and leaving those who guide its foreign policy less sure-handed, less consistent in their judgments, and less given to a long-term vision. Although always with important differences, as a result Russia ultimately emerges during these interludes less well anchored in the international order of the day, less predictable as an international actor, and less willing or capable of making fundamental strategic choices.

Which leaves the ultimate question posed at the outset: Has a historic chapter closed, has the most recent period of great state transformation ended, and does Putin preside over a foreign policy no longer sent spinning by primal forces? Is the foreign policy confidence that he and his colleagues began to show by 2006 proof that the new era has dawned? The short answer is almost surely no. The rapid, powerful, convulsive turns of the kaleidoscope that marked the intense phases of great state transformation from 1985 to 1998 seem to have passed. But the basic question of where Russia is headed remains unanswered. Indeed, if anything, the answer has become less clear. If, in the last years under Yeltsin, Russia's transition to democracy seemed an increasingly complicated affair, buffeted by setbacks and retreats, seven years into the new century no longer is it obvious that this is even the path Russia is on. Instead, say many, Russia resembles less an "unconsolidated democracy" than an "unconsolidated autocracy," slowly sliding toward a cumbersome, self-preoccupied form of bureaucratic authoritarianism with power again concentrated in the hands of a single figure. Few who share this view, however, see this as a sustainable situation. Either the regime will, under the pressure of inevitable policy failure, lurch toward a purer form of authoritarianism, or it will, checked by social forces even now gathering in the interior of society, desist and slowly move in the other direction.[134]

Dmitri Trenin occupies one of the more arresting middle positions, arguing that Putin's regime is less authoritarian ("which evokes the image of a traditional trains-running-on-time dictatorship") than "openly tsarist." Russia's defining characteristic inheres in "the presidency, or rather the president, a modern tsar," the country's "only functioning institution." Putin's Duma, like Nicholas II's, is "docile and acquiescent, while many of his governors are also like Nicholas' governor-generals." Russia's capitalists are "dependent on the authorities and [play] no independent role in politics." Indeed, he says, "politics in Russia today is court-driven and essentially Byzantine."[135]

From this, however, he takes hope. Comparing modern Russia to the Russia of 1913 "does not mean that there is no difference," but "it does mean that Russia is back on its historical path of development—roughly at the point where things started to go wrong—and has a chance of doing better this time." And, because so much of what is happening in Russia today has escaped the regime's capacity to control, freedom has arrived, even while democracy remains a distant prospect: freedom "to worship, make money, and move around."[136] The freedom to make and spend money has spread sufficiently to create a thickening strata of consumers—something Soviet Russia did not have—even if they are not yet citizens. As the numbers of those making and spending money inexorably grow, so in all likelihood will the demand for good, or at least more effective, governance. The demand for democracy will come only later. But come it should.

Two things are to be said about this portrait, assuming it is correct. First, it underscores how much of Russia's past survives into the present, and, therefore, for all the indisputable differences between then and now, how much the insights drawn from history add to a narrowly contemporary analysis. But, second, so does it warn one how many miles Russia has yet to travel before its political identity takes on a more definitive shape. The stages through which Russia must still pass are likely to be dramatic, some perhaps radically so, agitated by powerful crosscurrents, leaving the attributes of great state transformation intact, including the unresolved, wrenching question of national identity. Russia will overcome the effects of this passage only when it again feels itself a subject, not merely an object, of international politics; when it again has pacified the demons that inhabit its insecurities; and when it again has the self-confidence to make clear, farsighted strategic choices, not merely the momentary assurance to assert itself. And that will not happen until Russia has restored a sustainable vitality to its society and economy, made peace with the loss of empire, begun to trust its ability to hold the country together, and come to terms with what the trauma of great state transformation has wrought.

NOTES

1. Years ago Sir Bernard Pares argued that the better translation of Ivan's epithet was Ivan the Dread, not Ivan the Terrible, bringing it closer to one Russian meaning for the adjective *groznyi* as "inspiring awe or fear." Because Ivan the Dread is foreign to most readers, I use Ivan IV in this chapter.

2. With apologies to those, especially among my historian colleagues, who bridle against reifying "Russia," or, for that matter, "history" and "foreign policy," Russia in my use normally refers to national leadership. When the reference is to a somewhat broader cohort, including relevant parts of the political elite, I think it is clear from the context.

3. *Zemskii sobor* is the name these so-called assemblies of the lands were given much later by historians, not a label used at the time, nor should they be understood as a permanent, let alone representative, institution.

4. For the details on the transformation of the *pomestnaya* system, see V. O. Kliuchevsky, *Sochineniya: Kurs russkoi istorii*, vol. 2, part 2 (Moscow: Gosudarstvennoe isdatelstvo politicheskoi literatury, 1957), pp. 220–225.

5. Geoffrey Hosking, *Russia and the Russians* (Cambridge: Harvard University Press, 2001), p. 213, referring to Iu. M. Lotman and B. A. Uspenskii, "The Role of Dual Models in the Dynamics of Russian Culture (up to the End of the Eighteenth Century)," in *The Semiotics of Russian Culture*, ed. Ann Shukman, Michigan Slavic Contributions, no. 11 (Ann Arbor: Department of Slavic Studies, University of Michigan, 1984), p. 5.

6. Isabel de Madariaga, *Ivan the Terrible* (New Haven: Yale University Press, 2005), p. 368.

7. Tibor Szamuely, *The Russian Tradition* (New York: McGraw-Hill, 1974), p. 30.

8. V. O. Kliuchevsky, *Sochineniya: Kurs russkoi istorii*, vol. 6 (Moscow: Gosudarstvennoe izdatelstvo politicheskoi literatury, 1956–1959), p. 462.

9. In Miliukov's formulation, "Compelling national need resulted in the creation of an omnipotent State on the most meager material foundation; this very meagerness constrained it to exert all the energies of its population—and in order to have full control over these energies it had to become omnipotent." P. Miliukov, *Ocherki po istorii russkoi kultury*, 3d ed., vol. 3 (St. Petersburg, 1909), pp. 22–23, cited in Szamuely, *The Russian Tradition*, p. 28.

10. Marshall Poe, *The Russian Moment in World History* (Princeton: Princeton University Press, 2003), p. 58.

11. Ibid., p. 57.

12. Ibid., p. 86.

13. Madariaga, *Ivan the Terrible*, pp. 370–371.

14. Hosking, *Russia and the Russians*, p. 127.

15. For a brief summary, see Michael T. Florinsky, *Russia: A History and Interpretation*, vol. 1 (New York: Macmillan, 1963), pp. 355–427.

16. Lindsey Hughes, *Russia in the Age of Peter the Great* (New Haven: Yale University Press, 1998), pp. 378, 385–387.

17. Hosking, *Russia and the Russians*, p. 200, referring to the work of G. V. Florovskii, *Puti russkogo bogoslovii* (Paris: YMCA, 1937), p. 84; and A. V. Kartash, *Ocherki po istorii russkoi tserkvi*, vol. 2 (Moscow: Terra, 1992), pp. 323–330.

18. Quoted in Florinsky, *Russia*, vol. 1, p. 428.

19. For a concise summary, see Lindsey Hughes, *Peter the Great: A Biography* (New Haven: Yale University Press, 2002), pp. 210–214.

20. Hosking, *Russia and the Russians*, p. 195.

21. See Richard S. Wortman, *Scenarios of Power: Myth and Ceremony in Russian Monarchy*, vol. 1 (Princeton: Princeton University Press, 1995), pp. 61–78.

22. Szamuely, *The Russian Tradition*, p. 105. This is not to overlook Hosking's point that one of Peter's most significant innovations was for the first time to set the state apart from the person of the sovereign, a "first hesitant step away from the patrimonial state toward a functional or bureaucratic one." Hosking, *Russia and the Russians*, pp. 201–202.

23. On this extraordinary conflation, see Madariaga, *Ivan the Terrible*, pp. 378–381, who in turn relies on Priscilla Hunt, "Ivan IV's Personal Mythology of Kingship," *Slavic Review* 52, no. 4 (Winter 1993): 769–809.

24. "Talismanic" is the characterization of Robert C. Tucker in *Stalin in Power: The Revolution from Above, 1928–1941* (New York: Norton, 1990), p. 331.

25. The illustrations are numberless. These come from Howard Swearer, "Bolshevism and the Individual Leader," *Problems of Communism* 12, no. 2 (March–April 1963): 87. For the rich context of this hero worship, see Jeffrey Brooks, *Soviet Public Culture from Revolution to Cold War* (Princeton: Princeton University Press, 1999), especially pp. 198–209 and 233–238.

26. Lilia Shevtsova, *Yeltsin's Russia: Myths and Reality* (Washington, DC: Carnegie Endowment for International Peace, 1999), p. 281.

27. Kliuchevsky, *Sochineniya: Kurs russkoi istorii*, vol. 4, p. 233.

28. V. I. Lenin, "O 'levom' rebyachestve i o melkoburzhuaznosti" (May 1918), in *Polnoe sobranie sochenienii*, 5th ed., vol. 36 (Moscow: Izdatelstvo politicheskoi literatury, 1969), p. 301 (emphasis in original).

29. Indeed, one particularly critical study compared their approach quite literally to the Bolsheviks. See Peter Reddaway and Dmitri Glinski, *The Tragedy of Russia's*

Reforms: Market Bolshevism Against Democracy (Washington, DC: United States Institute of Peace Press, 2001).

30. This is scarcely an original comparison. Many others have commented on the similarities, including one of the most distinguished students of Ivan IV. See Edward Keenan, "Muscovite Folkways," *Russian Review* 45 (1986): 115–181.

31. Ivan's use of terror, of course, was applied many more times than this, although usually in smaller clusters. Indeed, on this occasion, in the days that followed "some fifty to seventy prisoners brought from Novgorod were dealt with, together with some eighty of their wives and children." Madariaga, *Ivan the Terrible*, p. 259. Nor was the vengeance exacted against Tver and Novgorod in late 1569 and early 1570 out of character. The *oprichniki* butchered nine thousand in Tver alone, cutting off limbs and shoving bodies beneath the ice of the Volga.

32. S. N. Prokopovich, *Narodnoe khozyaistvo SSSR*, vol. 1 (Moscow: Chekhov Publishing House, 1952), pp. 174–175.

33. Anne Applebaum, *Gulag: A History* (New York: Doubleday, 2003).

34. Hosking, *Russia and the Russians*, p. 458.

35. Dietrich Geyer, *Russian Imperialism: The Interaction of Domestic and Foreign Policy, 1860–1914* (New Haven, CT: Yale University Press, 1987), p. 18. *Krepostnichestvo* is Russian for "serfdom."

36. Ibid., p. 17.

37. Gorbachev's comment is in a speech unpublished at the time and delivered three months before he came to power. See M. S. Gorbachev, "Report to the All-Union Scientific-Practical Conference," December 10, 1984, in *Izbrannye rechi i stati*, vol. 2 (Moscow: Izdatelstvo politicheskoi literatury, 1987), p. 86.

38. See Michael McFaul, *Russia's Unfinished Revolution: Political Change from Gorbachev to Putin* (Ithaca: Cornell University Press, 2001), pp. 43–60; Archie Brown, *The Gorbachev Factor* (Oxford: Oxford University Press, 1996), pp. 155–211; and Seweryn Bialer, "The Changing Soviet Political System: The Nineteenth Party Conference and After," in *Politics, Society, and Nationality inside Gorbachev's Russia*, ed. Seweryn Bialer (Boulder, CO: Westview, 1989), pp. 196–241.

39. Dominic Lieven, *Empire: The Russian Empire and Its Rivals* (London: John Murray, 2000), p. 300. Lieven adds the qualification, "by Russian standards."

40. Hosking, *Russia and the Russians*, p. 292, quoting *Dnevnik P. A. Valueva, ministra vnutrennikh del*, vol. 1 (Moscow: Izdatelstvo Akademii Nauk SSSR, 1961), p. 181. Or, to be still clearer, in response to an 1865 appeal from a Moscow assembly of gentry urging the convocation of a general assembly, he wrote, "The right of initiative . . . belongs exclusively to ME, and is indissolubly bound to the autocratic power entrusted to ME by GOD. . . . No one is called to take upon himself before ME petitions about the general welfare and needs of the state. Such departures from the order established by existing legislation can only hinder me in the execution of MY aims." Quoted in Terence Emmons, *The Russian Landed Gentry and the Peasant Emancipation of 1861* (London: Cambridge University Press, 1968), p. 411.

41. McFaul, *Russia's Unfinished Revolution*, p. 53.

42. A. V. Nikitenko, *Zapiski i dnevnik, 1804–1877*, vol. 2, p. 87, as quoted in Geyer, *Russian Imperialism*, p. 24.

43. Personal interview of Ryzhkov with Michael McFaul, quoted in McFaul, *Russia's Unfinished Revolution*, p. 59.

44. All of this data is from Stephen White, *Gorbachev and After* (Cambridge: Cambridge University Press, 1991), pp. 123–128.

45. David Kotz, *Revolution from Above: The Demise of the Soviet System* (London: Routledge, 1997), p. 174. This drop was one and a half times as large as the collapse in the United States during the Great Depression (1929–1933).

46. Reddaway and Glinski, *The Tragedy of Russia's Reforms*, pp. 250–251.

47. Shevtsova, *Yeltsin's Russia*, p. 206.

48. Thane Gustafson, *Capitalism Russian-Style* (Cambridge: Cambridge University Press, 1999), p. 199.

49. Ibid., p. 183.

50. Ibid., p. 184.

51. Charles Tilly, *Coercion, Capital, and European States: 990–1992* (Cambridge, MA: Blackwell, 1992); and Charles Tilly, ed., *Formation of National States in Western European States* (Princeton: Princeton University Press, 1975).

52. Szamuely, *The Russian Tradition*, p. 26.

53. Ibid., p. 25.

54. George Vernadsky, *History of Russia* (New Haven: Yale University Press, 1969), p. 153. The path to war was considerably more involved than this suggests, including the role of the Danes in drawing Peter in this direction. For greater detail, see Paul Bushkovitch, *Peter the Great: The Struggle for Power, 1671–1725* (New York: Cambridge University Press, 2001), pp. 213–226.

55. Terence Emmons, " 'Revolution from Above' in Russia: Reflections on Natan Eidel'man's Last Book and Related Matter," in *Reform in Modern Russian History: Progress or Cycle?* ed. Theodore Taranovski (Cambridge: Cambridge University Press, 1995), p. 47.

56. Ulam writes, "The Bolsheviks did not seize power in this year of revolutions. They picked it up. First autocracy, then democracy capitulated to the forces of anarchy. Any group of determined men could have done what the Bolsheviks did in Petrograd." Adam B. Ulam, *The Bolsheviks* (New York: Collier Books, 1965), p. 314.

57. Peter Holquist, *Making War, Forging Revolution: Russia's Continuum of Crisis, 1914–1921* (Cambridge: Harvard University Press, 2002).

58. Quoted in Jane Degras, ed., *Soviet Documents on Foreign Policy*, vol. 2 (New York: Oxford University Press, 1951), pp. 233–237.

59. J. V. Stalin, *Problems of Leninism* (Moscow: Foreign Languages Publishing House, 1953), pp. 454–458. In Stalin's words, "those who fall behind get beaten. But we do not want to be beaten. No, we refuse to be beaten! One feature of the history of old Russia was the continual beatings she suffered because of her backwardness. She was

beaten by the Mongol khans. She was beaten by the Turkish beys. She was beaten by the Swedish feudal lords. She was beaten by the Polish and Lithuanian gentry. She was beaten by the British and French capitalists. She was beaten by the Japanese barons. All beat her because of her backwardness, military backwardness, cultural backwardness, political backwardness, industrial backwardness, agricultural backwardness. They beat her because to do so was profitable and could be done with impunity. Do you remember the words of the pre-revolutionary poet: 'You are poor and abundant, mighty and impotent, Mother Russia.' Those gentlemen were quite familiar with the verses of the old poet. They beat her, saying: 'You are abundant; so one can enrich oneself at your expense.' They beat her, saying: 'You are poor and impotent' so you can be beaten and plundered with impunity. Such is the law of the exploiters—to beat the backward and the weak. It is the jungle law of capitalism. You are backward, you are weak—therefore you are wrong; hence, you can be beaten and enslaved. You are mighty—therefore you are right; hence, we must be wary of you."

60. On the debate, see Max Beloff, *Foreign Policy of Soviet Russia, 1929–1941*, vol. 1 (New York: Oxford University Press, 1947–1949); Louis Fischer, *The Soviets in World Affairs* (Princeton: Princeton University Press, 1951); Jonathan Haslam, *The Soviet Union and the Struggle for Collective Security, 1933–39* (Cambridge: St. Martin's Press, 1984); and Jiří Hochman, *The Soviet Union and the Failure of Collective Security, 1934–1938* (Ithaca: Cornell University Press, 1984).

61. On this score, see Coit D. Blacker, *Hostage to Revolution: Gorbachev and Soviet Security Policy, 1985–1991* (New York: Council on Foreign Relations, 1993).

62. Pavel K. Baev, "The Trajectory of the Russian Military: Downsizing, Degeneration, and Defeat," in *The Russian Military: Power and Policy*, ed. Steven E. Miller and Dmitri Trenin (Cambridge, MA: MIT Press, 2005), pp. 51–55. See also Alexander M. Golts and Tonya L. Putnam, "State Militarism and Its Legacies: Why Military Reform Has Failed in Russia," *International Security* 29, no. 2 (Fall 2004): 128–129.

63. For the behind-the-scenes effort of the administration to make this bitter pill go down more easily, see Peter Baker and Susan Glasser, *Kremlin Rising: Vladimir Putin's Russia and the End of Revolution* (New York: Scribner, 2005), pp. 134–135.

64. Bobo Lo, *Vladimir Putin and the Evolution of Russian Foreign Policy* (Oxford: Blackwell, 2003), p. 51.

65. This is from his April 2002 "state of the union" address to the Federal Assembly, Russia TV, BBC Monitoring, April 18, 2002.

66. Here I include myself. See, for example, Robert Legvold, "All the Way: Crafting a U.S.-Russian Alliance," *National Interest*, no. 70 (Winter–Spring 2002): 21–31.

67. The account of the telephone conversation appears in Bob Woodward, *Bush at War* (New York: Simon and Schuster, 2002), pp. 117–120. For a report on the Astana SCO meeting, see C. J. Chivers, "Central Asians Call on the U.S. to Set a Timetable for Closing Bases," *New York Times*, July 6, 2005.

68. Madariaga suggests the first and joins others on the second point. Madariaga, *Ivan the Terrible*, p. 142.

69. Hughes, *Russia in the Age of Peter the Great*, p. 23.

70. See Jonathan Steele, "Candid Putin Offers Praise and Blame," *Guardian*, September 8, 2004; and, more extensively, Matthew Evangelista, *The Chechen Wars: Will Russia Go the Way of the Soviet Union?* (Washington, DC: Brookings Institution Press, 2003).

71. Geyer, *Russian Imperialism*, pp. 22–23, 25, 33.

72. Index Mundi, "Country Comparison: GDP," http://www.indexmundi.com/g/r.aspx?c=rs&v=65.

73. United Nations Development Programme, "Human Development Index Trends," *Human Development Report, 2003*, http://hdr.undp.org/reports/global/2003/?CFID=2724905&CFTOKEN=39201310.

74. In the United States, where the share of GDP spent on national government is among the lowest, it is still nearly 20 percent.

75. Rajan Menon, "Russia," in *Strategic Asia 2001–02: Power and Purpose*, ed. Richard J. Ellings and Aaron L. Friedberg (Seattle, WA: National Bureau of Asian Research, 2001), p. 181.

76. This characterization was in his 2003 "Annual Address to the Federal Assembly of the Russian Federation," May 16, 2003. For both the 2003 and 2004 addresses, see the Web site, "President of Russia," http://www.kremlin.ru/sdocs/appears.shtml?type=63372.

77. Laurence Freedman, "Traditional Security," in *Russia and the West: The Twenty-First Century Security Environment*, ed. Alexei Arbatov, Karl Kaiser, and Robert Legvold (Armonk, NY: Sharpe, 1999), p. 26.

78. Dmitri Trenin, "Russia's Foreign and Security Policy under Putin," Carnegie Moscow Center Publications, June 24, 2005, http://www.carnegie.ru/en/print/72804-print.htm.

79. Daniel Deudney and G. John Ikenberry, "The International Sources of Soviet Change," *International Security* 16, no. 3 (Winter 1991/1992): 74–118.

80. E. V. Anisimov, "The Imperial Heritage of Peter the Great in the Foreign Policy of His Early Successors," in *Imperial Russian Foreign Policy*, ed. Hugh Ragsdale (Cambridge: Cambridge University Press, 1993), p. 23.

81. E. A. Pozdnyakov, "Russia Is a Great Power," *International Affairs* 39, no. 1 (January 1993): 3–13. His ideas are elaborated in several collections of essays, including *Balans sil v mirovoi politike: teoriya u praktika* (Moscow: IMEiMO RAN, 1993).

82. This comes from an "editorial" in his own journal *Elementi* (no. 7 [n.d.], http://www.feastofhateandfear.com/archives/dugin_01.html), but he has used this characterization many times in many places. Dugin not only is widely discussed in some Russian circles, but earlier served as an adviser to Gennady Seleznev, when he was speaker of the Duma.

83. Of the many accounts examining the phenomenon, several are particularly useful: Nicholas Riasanovsky, "The Emergence of Eurasianism," *California Slavic*

Studies 4 (1967): 39–72; and Ilya Vinkovetsky, "Classical Eurasianism and Its Legacy," *Canadian-American Slavic Studies* 34, no. 2 (Summer 2000): 125–140.

84. Because there were, as Trubetskoy once commented, as many Eurasianisms as Eurasianists, this overstates the case. Trubetskoy himself decried a conventional Russian nationalism ("separatism," he would call it), and half predicted, half exhorted a new statehood among the peoples of Eurasia, of which the Russians would merely be one. On this point, see Mark Bassin, "Classical Eurasianism and the Geopolitics of Russian Identity" (unpublished paper, 2001). For detail of the splits, particularly between Petr Savitsky and the left Eurasianist Petr Suvchinsky, see Dmitri V. Shlapentokh, "Eurasianism: Past and Present," *Communist and Post-Communist Studies* 30, no. 2 (1997): 129–151. Eventually the movement would produce a splinter profascist branch, which tellingly entertained the notion that Stalin would yet turn into the fascist superhero-leader, doing for Russia what Hitler was doing for Germany.

85. Hosking, *Russia and the Russians*, p. 313.

86. Geyer, *Russian Imperialism*, p. 61.

87. Russia's new Eurasianists were of many stripes, with various observers creating multiple classifications. One even divided the "hard-line Eurasianists," such as Dugin and the editor of *Den*, Alexander Prokhanov, into subgroups of "modernizers" and "expansionists." Andrei Tsygankov, "Hard-Line Eurasianists and Russia's Contending Geopolitical Perspectives," *East European Quarterly* 32, no. 3 (Fall 1998): 315–334.

88. V. V. Putin, "Rossiya: novye vostochnye perspektivy," *Nezavisimaya gazeta*, November 14, 2000.

89. Alexander A. Sergunin, "Discussions of International Relations in Post-Communism Russia," *Communist and Post-Communist Studies* 37 (2004): 19–35.

90. Alexei Bogaturov, "The Eurasian Support of World Stability," *International Affairs*, February 1993, p. 41, quoted in David Kerr, "The New Eurasianism: The Rise of Geopolitics in Russian Foreign Policy," *Europe-Asia Studies* 47, no. 6 (1995): 981.

91. One of the most thorough and sophisticated critiques is Dmitri V. Trenin, *The End of Eurasia: Russia on the Border Between Geopolitics and Globalization* (Washington, DC: Carnegie Endowment for International Peace, 2002). Many others, for all their differences on specific issues, fit into this category, including Sergei Rogov, director of the Institute USA and Canada; Nikolai Smelov, director of the Institute for the Study of Europe; Sergei Karaganov, director of the Council on Foreign and Defense Policy; Alexei Arbatov, former Duma deputy and scholar; Vladimir Baranovsky, deputy director of the Institute of World Economy and International Relations; Andrei Piontkovsky, director of the Center for Strategic Research; Lilya Shevtsova, senior fellow at the Carnegie Moscow Center; Andrei Melville, deputy rector of the Moscow State Institute of International Relations; and a number of leading politicians such as Anatoly Chubais, Irina Khakemada, Andrei Kokoshin, Boris Nemtsov, Vladimir Ryzhkov, and Grigory Yavlinski.

92. For the first view, see Konstantin Kosachev, "Rossiya mezhdu Evropeiskim vyborom i Aziatskim rostom," *Mezhdunarodnye otnosheniya*, no. 12 (December

2005): 54–67; for the second view, Alexei Arbatov, "Rossiya: osobyi imperskii put?" *Rossiya v globalnoi politike*, no. 6 (November–December 2005): 20–57.

93. For example, Margot Light, "Foreign Policy Thinking," in *Internal Factors in Russian Foreign Policy*, Neil Malcolm, Alex Pravda, Roy Allison, and Margo Light (London: Oxford University Press, 1996), pp. 33–100; Leon Aron, "The Foreign Policy Doctrine of Postcommunist Russia and Its Domestic Context," in *The New Russian Foreign Policy*, ed. Michael Mandelbaum (New York: Council on Foreign Relations, 1999), pp. 23–53; Alexei G. Arbatov, "Russia's Foreign Policy Alternatives," *International Security* 18, no. 2 (Fall 1993): 5–43; Alexei Tsygankov, "From Liberal Internationalism to Revolutionary Expansionism: The Foreign Policy Discourse of Contemporary Russia," *Mershon Center International Studies Review* 41 (November 1997): 247–268; and Bobo Lo, *Russian Foreign Policy in the Post-Soviet Era: Reality, Illusion, and Mythmaking* (New York: Macmillan, 2003), pp. 40–65.

94. Hosking, *Russia and the Russians*, pp. 125–126.

95. Ibid., p. 149.

96. Fedor Dostoevsky, *Diary of a Writer*, vol. 2 (New York: C. Scribner's Sons, 1949), p. 1068.

97. Orlando Figes, *Natasha's Dance: A Cultural History of Russia* (New York: Metropolitan Books, 2002), p. 415.

98. Vladimir G. Baranovsky and Alexei G. Arbatov, "The Changing Security Perspective in Europe," in Arbatov, Kaiser, and Legvold, *Russia and the West*, p. 47. See also Vladimir Baranovsky, "Russia: A Part of Europe or Apart from Europe?" *International Affairs* (London) 76, no. 5 (July 2000): 447–451.

99. British official under George I, quoted in Hughes, *Russia in the Age of Peter the Great*, p. 56.

100. Quoted in Madariaga, *Ivan the Terrible*, p. 295.

101. Quoted in Lindsey Hughes, *Peter the Great: A Biography* (New Haven: Yale University Press, 2002), p. 195. This brooding sentiment did not come to him only late in life. In 1703 in *The Discourse on the Just Reasons of the War Between Sweden and Russia*, he wrote, "The past times are not like the present, for then the Swedes thought of us differently and considered us blind. . . . And not only the Swedes, but also other and remote peoples, always felt jealousy and hatred toward the Russian people, and have attempted to keep the latter . . . in ignorance, especially in the military and naval arts. . . . [Now] those, who, it seems were the fear of all Europe, were defeated by us. And I can say that no one is so feared as we are. For which one should thank God." Quoted in Astrid S. Tuminez, *Russian Nationalism Since 1856: Ideology and the Making of Foreign Policy* (Lanham, MD: Rowman and Littlefield, 2000), p. 32.

102. A. N. Lazereva, *Intelligentsya i religiya: k istoricheskomu osmyslenniyu problemmatiki "Vekh"* (Moscow: IFRAN, 1996), http://philosophy.ru/iphras/library/lazareva/intelg2.html#.

103. Andrei Kozyrev, "The Lagging Partnership," *Foreign Affairs* 73, no. 3 (May–June 1994): 61.

104. "Press Conference with Effective Policy Fund President Gleb Pavlovsky," RIA Novosti, February 3, 2005, Federal News Service, http://fednews.ru.

105. Quoted in Arkday Ostrovsky, "From Freedom a Pliant Return to Propaganda," *Financial Times*, June 27, 2006, p. 17.

106. Quoted in Donald Greenless, "Japanese Premier Reiterates Apology to China for World War II," *International Herald Tribune,* April 22, 2005.

107. Quoted in Marina Volkova and Nikolai Ulyanov, "Po mneniyu premier-ministra, Rossiya nuzhdaetsya v silnoi gosudarstvennoi vlaste i dolzhna imet ee," *Novaya gazeta*, December 30, 1999. The word for "state" is *gosudarstvo,* or "statehood" *gosudarstvenmost. Gosudarnichestvo* is a somewhat awkward word, rarely used, but evidently with a connotation that rather glorifies the state.

108. Geyer, *Russian Imperialism,* p. 31.

109. From *Dnevnik Valueva,* vol. 2, pp. 60f., quoted in Geyer, *Russian Imperialism,* p. 89.

110. Quoted in Michael T. Florinsky, *Russia: A History and Interpretation,* vol. 2 (New York: Macmillan, 1963), p. 982.

111. Geyer, *Russian Imperialism,* p. 94.

112. *Dnevnik Milyutina,* vol. 1 (Moscow, 1947–1950), p. 47, quoted in Geyer, *Russian Imperialism,* p. 76.

113. The details are recounted in many places, but one particularly useful account is David MacKenzie, "Russia's Balkan Policies Under Alexander II, 1855–1881," in Ragsdale, *Imperial Russian Foreign Policy,* pp. 229–246.

114. Quoted in Geyer, *Russian Imperialism,* p. 77.

115. Robert Service, *Stalin: A Biography* (Cambridge: Harvard University Press, 2005), p. 381.

116. Adam B. Ulam, *Expansion and Coexistence: The History of Soviet Foreign Policy, 1917–67* (New York: Praeger, 1968), p. 217.

117. Quoted in "Obrashchenie prezidenta Rossii Vladimira Putina k grazhdanam strany," *Izvestiya,* September 6, 2004, p. 1.

118. Rosemary Bennett and Robin Shepherd, "Putin Challenges Allies to Find Nuclear Weapons," *Times* (London), April 30, 2003.

119. The story is told most completely in John Norris, *Collision Course: NATO, Russia, and Kosovo* (Westport, CT: Praeger, 2005), pp. 237–287.

120. "Poslaniya Federalnomy sobraniyu," May 10, 2006, from the Web site of the "President of Russia," http://president.kremlin.ru/appears/2006/05/10/1357_type63372type63374type82634_105546.shtml. It is worth noting that the line stirred applause.

121. Reneo Lukic and Allen Lynch, *Europe from the Balkans to the Urals: The Disintegration of Yugoslavia and the Soviet Union* (Oxford: Oxford University Press, 1996), pp. 327–349.

122. He was speaking to the Congress of the Civic Union. "Russia" TV, February 28, 1993, recorded by the BBC Summary of World Broadcasts, SU/1626B, March 2, 1993.

123. As he said to a meeting of Russian ambassadors to the Commonwealth of Independent States and Baltic countries on January 18, 1994, "We should not withdraw from those regions which have been the sphere of Russian interests for centuries and we should not fear these words about [our] military presence." At the time, the reference was to Russian bases in the Baltic states. In *Diplomaticheskii kyrer,* no. 2 (1994).

124. Dmitri Trenin, "Reading Russia Right," *Policy Brief* (Carnegie Endowment for International Peace), no. 42 (September 2005): 6.

125. Strobe Talbott, *The Russia Hand* (New York: Random House, 2002), p. 365 (emphasis in original).

126. Putin attacked from many directions—not just over Washington's alleged interference in the Ukrainian election but also over the disgrace of forcing elections in a war-ravaged Iraq, the United States' own marred presidential election, and more. In Turkey in early December, he fumed, "I do not want to see a situation where, as happened in Germany, we divided Europe into 'Westies' and 'Easties,' into first- and second-class citizens, where those in the first category could live under democratic, stable laws and those in the second category, the people, figuratively speaking, with 'dark skin,' were expected to obey a kind but strict uncle telling them under what conditions they will live. And if, God forbid, one of the ungrateful natives disobeys, he will be punished with the help of a club of missiles and bombs as was the case in Belgrade." Vladimir Putin, press conference with Russian journalists in Ankara, Turkey, December 6, 2004, http://www.kremlin.ru/appears/2004/12/06/1409_type63380_80827.shtml. He also returned to Primakov's dyspeptic view of unipolarity. To an Indian audience three days earlier he said, "Attempts to restructure the God-given diversity of modern civilization along the army barracks principles of a unipolar world seem extremely dangerous. . . . Even when dictatorship [in international affairs] is beautifully gift-wrapped in pseudo-democratic phraseology it has never been capable of resolving such systemic problems. On the contrary, it can only make them worse." Quoted in Yulia Petrovskaya, "Moskva i Vashington polemiziruyut zaochno," *Nezavisimaya gazeta,* December 6, 2004.

127. James M. Goldgeier and Michael McFaul, *Power and Purpose: U.S. Policy Toward Russia After the Cold War* (Washington, DC: Brookings Institution Press, 2003), p. 54.

128. Quoted in Florinsky, *Russia,* p. 952. Indeed, it may be thought that Russia's most fundamental strategic myopia during this period was a shortsighted willingness to alienate Great Britain, when greater foresight would have recommended working with London and Paris to block Bismarck's plans for a united Germany, a development sure to shake the prevailing international order.

129. Vasili Kliuchevsky, *Peter the Great* (New York: Vintage Books, 1961), p. 70.

130. Florinsky, *Russia,* vol. 2, p. 1008.

131. Andrew Wilson explores in depth the rise of "virtual politics" in Russia and Ukraine in *Virtual Politics: Faking Democracy in the Post-Soviet World* (New Haven: Yale University Press, 2005).

132. Secretary of State Madeleine K. Albright, "Address to the U.S.-Russian Business Council" (speech, Chicago, Illinois, October 2, 1998).

133. The speech can be found at the Web site of the "Foreign Office of the Federal Republic of Germany, http://www.auswaertiges-amt.de/diplo/en/Startseite.html.

134. Lilia Shevtsova, *Putin's Russia* (Washington, DC: Carnegie Endowment for International Peace, 2005), pp. 322–351, 396–407; Michael McFaul and Nikolai Petrov, "Russian Democracy in Eclipse: What the Elections Tell Us," *Journal of Democracy* 15, no. 3 (July 2004): 20–31; and Michael McFaul, Nikolai Petrov, and Andrei Ryabov, *Between Dictatorship and Democracy* (Washington, DC: Carnegie Endowment for International Peace, 2004), pp. 292–298.

135. Trenin, "Reading Russia Right," p. 2.

136. Ibid.

CHAPTER 3

Domestic Conjunctures, the Russian State, and the World Outside, 1700–2006

David McDonald

VLADIMIR PUTIN'S PRESIDENCY HAS brought a long-missing stability to Russian political life, but not much comfort to many Western observers and their democratic friends in Russia itself, both of whom shared great expectations for Russian democracy immediately after the collapse of the Soviet Union in 1991.[1] Yet, the foreign and domestic policies of this nascent order defy easy categorization. They certainly do not fit neatly within the old Cold War framework that had in mind only Soviet post-totalitarianism or Western-style "rule of law" constitutional democracy.

Domestically, the Russian economy and political system have stabilized following a fifteen-year crisis in which the very existence of a Russian state and the form it might take preoccupied elites and citizens alike.[2] The Putin administration has brought order to the chaos of the Yeltsin years. It has solidified the institutional structures by which Yeltsin and his team attempted to govern Russia and surmount the social, economic, and political unraveling that overtook the Soviet Union under Mikhail Gorbachev in the 1980s. Led by a popular president who has won two electoral mandates, however tainted, an increasingly domineering state power has begun to take hold of the various facets of domestic economic and political life that displayed a refreshing, or alarming, lack of control during the 1990s, depending on one's point of view. Through a series of aggressive démarches, Putin has subordinated to the state's writ the oligarchs created by the suspect privatizations of the Yeltsin era, and placed much of their assets under state control. He has attacked entrenched post-Soviet elites in the provinces by converting governorships from electoral offices into positions filled by Moscow's appointees. Through fair means and foul, he has assured himself a legislative partner in the form of a pliant Duma, while imposing new restrictions on the mass media.

Yet, this reassertion of state authority still falls short of the standards set under Soviet rule. Crackdowns on the media do not match the full-scale censorship of the ancien régime. The Soviet press would never have published the critiques of Putin's policies that appeared in print and online during the Ukrainian Orange Revolution of late 2004 or after the catastrophe in the northern Caucasus city of Beslan, where the seizure of a school by Chechen militants in September resulted in the mass slaughter of both the hostage takers and their hostages—schoolchildren and staff.[3] Putin has asserted the state's respect for the market economy, private property, and civil rights,[4] however unconvincing he may sound after the arrest, trial, and imprisonment of Mikhail Khodorkovsky, an energy magnate who supported the president's opponents. And, despite efforts at recentralization, local and regional governments still operate with more autonomy than did their tsarist or Soviet predecessors.

This newfound vitality in the exercise of state power has also led to an increasing assertiveness in Russia's international conduct, disappointing expectations rooted in Cold War perspectives. Since 1999, Russia has moved away from the Sturm und Drang of Boris Yeltsin's presidency.[5] President Putin and his advisers appear reconciled to the postwar status quo in post-Soviet Europe that so rapidly rose from the USSR's wreckage in the early 1990's. While he has deplored the dismantling of the Soviet empire as a "geopolitical disaster,"[6] Putin, like Yeltsin before him, has accepted the enlargement of NATO and the European Union (EU), both marking the definitive demise of what many knew as the "Brezhnev Doctrine," when, for more than a half century, Soviet leaders three times used Warsaw Pact forces and the Red Army to enforce the maintenance of state-socialist regimes in Eastern Europe.

Putin's foreign policy has also manifested a definitive "turn to the West,"[7] including membership in the Group of Eight and the consultative NATO-Russia Council established at the Rome summit in 2002.[8] Since the terrorist attacks against the United States on September 11, 2001, U.S.-Russian relations have entered a period of unprecedented, if often fractious, mutual cooperation. President Putin was among the first world leaders to offer his condolences and support to President George W. Bush on the day of the tragedy. Moreover, the Russian government shared intelligence information with its U.S. counterparts and acquiesced in the establishment of American bases on former Soviet territories in Central Asia as part of the U.S.-led operations against the Afghan Taliban government, an agreement that would have been inconceivable a scant fifteen years previously. Perhaps nothing so reflects the transformation in

U.S.-Russian relations as the warm personal relations between Putin and Bush, who famously "looked [Putin] in the eye . . . and got a sense of his soul."[9]

On the other hand, the Putin government's foreign policy has often acted at apparent cross-purposes with the Western alliance or the United States. Russia has continued its own "war on terror" in Chechnya despite Western criticism, which also greeted the Putin government's support for favored candidates in the Ukrainian and Belarusian presidential elections of 2004 and 2006, respectively. Similarly, Russia has pursued an independent course in its contributions to Iran's nuclear energy program, arms and energy sales to China, and pursuit of special relations with North Korea and other "rogue" states. Most notably, despite his strong expressions of solidarity in the "war on terrorism," President Putin joined President Jacques Chirac of France and Chancellor Gerhard Schröder of Germany in opposing the U.S.-led invasion of Iraq in 2003.

In this chapter, I argue that the increasing assertiveness and independence of Russia's foreign policy has resulted from the consolidation of state power within Putin's Russia. Stated briefly, Putin and his allies have reestablished the state *per se* as a relatively autonomous and self-contained agent, standing "above" and "managing" life in the domestic sphere, while harnessing the latter's material and human resources to augment the state's ability to assert its interests as a player in international affairs. In doing so, they have re-created, albeit with new elements, a relationship between domestic politics and foreign policy that has predominated in Russia since at least the early nineteenth century. The language and imagery that Putin has employed in describing the role of the Russian state, as well as his use of state power, honor the logic of an impressively durable worldview among Russian statesmen and political thinkers concerning the attributes and raison d'être of the state at home and abroad—that is, a specific understanding of Russian statehood (*gosudarstvennost*).

The reappearance of this dirigiste and mobilizational Russian state as a freestanding agent in both the foreign and domestic spheres was historically determined by the continued hold of the absolutist worldview on successive generations of Russian statesmen. The assertive state that Putin inherited from Yeltsin in 1999 did not result, as some have contended, simply from a series of politically necessary or expedient decisions during the institutional turmoil of the 1990s.[10] Doubtless, specific junctures and conflicts during the 1990s played a role in the elaboration of the new political order—for example, the conflict between the Duma and the presidency in 1993 or the presidential elections that gave Yeltsin his second term in 1996. Yet, Russians themselves, not least Putin and other national leaders,[11] have looked back past 1917 in search of a usable history by which to build a brave new Russia.

Observers, however, frequently misattribute continuity in Russian conduct to such metahistorical forces as the Third Rome trope, geopolitical necessity, innate expansionism, predisposition to authoritarian rule, or the "Russian idea."[12] These explanations often treat such considerations as innately Russian, without demonstrating how they have worked their causal effect over the long haul of history. As a corrective, it is better to think in terms of "persistent factors"—to use Alfred Rieber's term—as long as they are understood to be operational only within the mediating and interpretive framework provided by the perspective and logic of Russian statehood as interpreted and practiced by leaders steeped in its traditions.

From this point of view, the protracted crisis that began with perestroika (i.e., the economic and governmental reform policies of the late 1980s) and its ongoing resolution during the early twenty-first century raise a series of important questions about the connections between Russia's international conduct and its domestic order. On the face of it, the intertwined political, social, and economic crises of the late twentieth century bore some connection to a sea change in Russian activity abroad. During the 1990s, the relationship between Russia's domestic order and its international conduct stood at the very center of the larger debates over Russia's identity as a state.[13] Many in the West and in Russia thought that the new federation would enter into an ever-closer relationship with its partners in Europe's "common home," making for peace abroad and strengthening the development of market capitalism and democracy within Russia itself. Others, particularly in the communist "red" and right-wing "brown" ranks of Russian politics, lamented the sudden disappearance of the country's superpower status and called for the restoration of its traditional might (*derzhavnost*) through the creation of a nationalist, authoritarian state.[14]

This newfound awareness of the ties binding domestic and foreign policies has also penetrated the ruling circles of the Russian Federation, in ways that depart markedly from older and largely abstract Soviet formulae about class relations or socialist construction. The foreign policy concept that Putin promulgated in June 2000 stated the need "to create favorable external conditions for the steady development of Russia, for improving its economy, enhancing the population's standard of living, successfully carrying out democratic transformations, strengthening the basis of the constitutional system and observing individual rights and freedoms."[15] More concretely, since shortly after

Gorbachev's appointment in 1985 as general secretary of the Communist Party, the link between the two realms has found various expressions: the more thorough integration of the Ministry of Foreign Affairs into general organs of government—as opposed to the practices of the last forty-odd years of Soviet rule and much of the imperial period—and the public discussion of foreign policy in the new legislative organs and the emergent public spheres.

Thus, to explain the links binding foreign and domestic policies in the post-Soviet Russian Federation, I explore the role played by what I term the "statehood discourse" as a conceptual means of explaining the relationship of the state to both spheres. This discourse first took hold in Russian political thought and practice under Peter the Great—inaugurating a tradition that W. Bruce Lincoln labeled "bureaucratic absolutism."[16] A rival to other modes of economic and political thought—including the strain of liberal thought associated with the Scottish Enlightenment—this perspective involves a specific understanding of the state, not simply as the font of power and authority, but also as an agent juxtaposed between the two distinct realms of its domestic domain and an international realm of competing fellow-states. In its domestic policies, this state mobilized resources, administered, dispensed justice, and unified manifold social, confessional, ethnic, and other particularistic groups under its universalizing aegis. Abroad, this state behaved most of the time with apparently little regard for its domestic capacities—reflected in a marked segregation of foreign policy making from institutions and individuals presiding over domestic affairs. With Russia's entry into the European state system under Peter and his successors, however, it also sought "greatness" or "glory" as an indispensable condition of statehood.[17] Thus, for example, from the materialist or cost-benefit perspective that governs Western ways of understanding this problem, Russian states have often indulged the luxury of grounding their conduct in one or another ideology at the expense of physical or social costs—whether Nicholas I's legitimism at home and abroad or the undeniable detriment to the Soviet economy inflicted by the allocation of resources during the Cold War. Interestingly, both periods represented as well the high-water mark of Russian prestige and might in international political life.

Despite repeated challenges to this understanding of Russian statehood, it has proven more adaptable and flexible than its critics might have expected. Since the seventeenth century, Russian history has been punctuated by moments of dramatic change following military and political setbacks, most often at the hands of Western competitors—European states and, more recently, the U.S.-led Western alliance anchored in NATO. Peter the Great's reign serves as the best-known example of such moments of crisis and renewal, which also include the aftermath of Russia's Crimean defeat, as well as the Great War, which brought down the Romanovs amid conditions in which the Bolsheviks could imagine and construct Soviet socialism. At these moments of literal crisis, Russian leaders have returned repeatedly to the strategic logic of the statehood discourse as they consolidated and turned their incontestable and centralized power to domestic transformation—institutional, economic, and social—at least partially in support of restoring Russia as a leading participant in the international order.

In a process hypothesized by Alexander Gerschenkron, Russian rulers have used state power as a "substitute" for more spontaneous or historical processes in order to replicate those factors to which they attributed their competitors' success—for instance the administrative structures of Charles XII or the industrial economies of nineteenth-century Europe.[18] Gerschenkron's metaphor captures the logic of substitution but leaves unaddressed the actual conceptualization of the state and its uses that has made substituting it an attractive strategy for generations of Russian rulers and governors. To explain both, one must take into account the actors' understanding of the state as a historical or political agent or, more specifically, the languages that have explained and legitimated state power to its users.

In this context, the late twentieth century stands out as a specific moment in the relationship between the domestic and foreign spheres—in some ways resembling other times of domestic transformation, but also distinctive for at least two reasons. First, this period was defined by a thoroughgoing systemic crisis, during which the very bases of Russian *gosudarstvennost* came under active, often violent, debate, before the reemergence by the late 1990s of an apparently viable regime based on the 1993 constitution.[19] Second, the acuteness of this crisis led Soviet and Russian leaders to subordinate Russian foreign policy goals, or even the conduct of an active policy, to the urgent necessity of domestic reform and reconstruction, in contrast to most other periods of reform. Significantly, to judge from their actions and the outcomes they achieved, Russian leaders saw the reestablishment of an authoritative state as a necessary condition for the domestic reforms required to return Russia to the ranks of leading world powers. In addition, their understanding of the relationship between domestic and foreign policies underwent an important change, as they sought to accommodate the *gosudarstvennost* worldview to a new appreciation for the power to be gained from an engaged and patriotic population, alongside a market economy.

To better understand these changes, it is worth comparing the crisis of the late twentieth century with the years following Russia's defeat in the Russo-Japanese War and the revolution of 1905, the other moment in Russian history when leaders responded to a similar challenge through a similar set of responses. This period was dominated by the figure of Pyotr Stolypin, who served from 1906 until his assassination in 1911 as minister of internal affairs and premier. In both positions, Stolypin sought to extirpate the forces of revolution that had almost overthrown the autocracy in 1905. Yet he also sought to revive the Russian Empire through domestic reconstruction—including a sweeping land reform and the forging of a partnership with the men of property and the rural gentry from the right and center of the State Duma. If, in the short term, he insisted that Russia avoid any and all "foreign complications" of the sort that had sparked revolution in the first place, he nonetheless envisioned the emergence from these reforms of a "Great Russia," able to "speak with its former voice" in international relations. If he failed to achieve these goals, for a variety of reasons, he nonetheless articulated a clear understanding of the relationship he saw between a vital state, Russia's domestic order, and its international position.

A comparison of these two periods demonstrates Russian statesmen's continuing preference for this venerable notion of statehood, which they chose instead of the numerous alternatives on offer from within the state itself as well as civil society. By emphasizing continuities, I do not suggest that Russian states have not changed—each regime differed significantly in its respective uses of technologies of rule, the application of violence, as well as claims to legitimate areas of intervention. Thus, despite the real differences separating, say, Stalin's USSR from Alexander I's Russia, the persistence of the ways in which successive Russian rulers have thought about state power and its uses at home and abroad is striking.[20]

Finally, my emphasis on the survival and self-reinvention of Russian statehood should not be misconstrued as an apology for it—the experience of Western Europe and North America offers more than ample vindication for the liberal rule-of-law state. Nor do I subscribe to a historical fatalism dooming Russians to a foreordained existence under a regime that flouts Western standards of legality and good government. Economic and social transformations could yet create the conditions for a normal state order on Western terms. Yet, the statehood discourse has proven much more adaptable and viable than critics since Adam Smith or Karl Marx have expected. Inspired by Bismarck's Germany, Sergey Witte inaugurated a period of unprecedented economic growth during the 1890s, convinced that an industrial economy could serve as the buttress for a flourishing autocracy. Putin and his colleagues appear to share this perspective, in defiance of arguments linking markets, an emergent bourgeoisie, and liberal democracy.

In view of these considerations, I argue that observers have to take historical continuity and alternative traditions as seriously as do the agents themselves. Only in this way can one come to a well-grounded assessment of the policies and interests that Russian leaders pursue. Putin and his colleagues appear to have concluded that Russia has arrived at that moment in its recovery when, assured of the restoration of order and the promise of economic growth, it can reclaim its place as a "leading world power."[21]

THE RUSSIAN STATE AS AGENT AT HOME AND ABROAD

The interpretive claims laid out above require several qualifications or amplification. First, rather than focus on foreign policy details, this discussion addresses the relative willingness of Russian governments to pursue their objectives in the international sphere. The Gorbachev and Yeltsin years saw Russian diplomacy accept, with good or ill grace, revisions to the international status quo that Soviet leaders had defended forcefully under the Brezhnev Doctrine. One need merely compare the reunification of Germany in 1990 or the eastward expansion of NATO with the consequences of the Prague Spring or the Hungarian rising of 1956 to appreciate the difference. At the same time, the term "domestic policy" broadly connotes what might be understood as not only internal politics, but also questions related to the social and economic orders under which the population lives.

Second, an emphasis on the importance of historically constructed discourses—that is, sets of ideas and arguments grounded in their own apparent inner logic—might seem an unconventional means by which to explain the relationship of the foreign and domestic spheres in Russian policy making. Usually, historians connect these two realms of activity through structural explanations. Thus, the Rankean logic of the Russian "state school" long dominated the writing of Russian history, with its emphasis on the *Primat der Aussepolitik* for a state confronted with unceasing threats along a series of highly permeable boundaries.[22] Marxist and post-Marxist historians of the late empire in particular incorporated domestic issues in their analyses of Russian foreign policy in one of two ways. Some explained the course of Russian diplomacy as a result, in part, of decision makers' efforts to balance or satisfy competing economic or ideological interests among elite groups—hard- or soft-liners, constitutionalists, and adherents of the "monarchical principle." Others saw in Russia's eastward expansion and involvement in the Balkans during the last years of the empire an attempt by the leadership to divert growing ferment in a rapidly changing society by appealing to international triumphs as a way to generate support for the existing state order, an argument that could conceivably apply as well to the post-Stalin Soviet Union.[23]

Other scholars see the "domestic" sphere as comprising the views, relationships, and activities of groups within the governing structures, as well as expert opinion in the academy or educated society. Such scholarship seeks determinants for foreign policy making or given policy directions—vis-à-vis Europe and the United States or defense policy—in a consensus springing from domestic political alliances,[24] in the political attitudes and orientations of experts in and out of government,[25] or, in some cases, in public opinion.[26]

Certainly, ideas and learning matter greatly in political environments shaped by a high degree of centralized power, but where factions and policy advocates compete within and among the institutions of centralized power. These conflicting groups gain entrée to policy making, and advantage over their rivals, when leadership changes or the previously dominant view is discredited, with accompanying changes in policy.[27] Thus, for more than twenty years, the Brezhnev-era Politburo largely ignored academic and Communist Party reports documenting the economic costs of the arms race—declining productivity and mounting social problems—while continuing to pursue strategic and political parity with the United States.[28] Yet, on their arrival in power barely five years after Brezhnev's death, Gorbachev and his supporters interpreted this same evidence as signaling the urgent necessity to embark on what became perestroika, to the extent of abandoning by 1989 virtually every foreign policy position of the Soviet state since World War II.[29] In the nineteenth century, convinced of autocracy's superiority or necessity, Nicholas I based his domestic and foreign policies on the defense of order: serfdom, "official nationality," the Holy Alliance with Prussia and Austria founded on the "monarchical principle" in post-Napoleonic Europe. Within two years of his death and Russia's defeat in the Crimea, however, "enlightened" officials who had come of age during his reign persuaded his son, Alexander II, that thoroughgoing reform of Russia's social, administrative, and legal structures was necessary to its continued existence as a great power.[30]

The emphasis these studies place on the role of varying layers of context—experience, institutional politics, and socialization—as mediators for decisions by specific groups or individuals answers many questions about how domestic and international arenas interact in Russian history. But, in addressing short-term or institutional-political circumstances leading to given outcomes, these analyses often ignore the larger conceptual framework through which participants in these decisions understood the nature and purposes of the state to whose service they devoted their careers. Yet, for most of Russian and Soviet history, these figures, their rivals, and their conflicting ideas operated inside the structures of the state or the Communist Party and agreed on the prerogatives and imperatives attaching to their authority.

Third, such a narrowly circumscribed view of the domestic element in the creation of foreign policy omits two related areas of consideration. The first is how the very idea of the "domestic" writ large (i.e., rulers' and policy makers' understanding and valuation of the country's domestic circumstances—political, social, and economic) shaped the state's conduct in the international arena (i.e., how a Nicholas or a Brezhnev might have seen their states as strong, when their successors saw besetting weakness). The second area of consideration involves the rather surprising fact that, for much of the last three centuries, Russian leaders and institutions have treated domestic and foreign policy as separate, united only at the apex of the political system—in the person of the ruler or leadership. Indeed, to judge from the historical record, Russian and Soviet governments during periods of institutional and social stability have tended to conduct policy with little regard for the material capacity of their society or economy to sustain such a course of action.

During the last century of Romanov rule, from 1801 to 1917, with the notable exception of the Stolypin era, Russian rulers consulted directly and exclusively with their foreign ministers, themselves drawn from the ranks of a ministry noted for its insularity, even in the Balkanized world of Russian bureaucratic politics.[31] One need only recall such figures as Karl Nesselrode or Prince A. M. Gorchakov to appreciate the gulf separating the foreign policy establishment and the rest of the imperial government.[32] This isolation of diplomats from their country's real circumstances provoked criticism of the imperial foreign service and its Russian policy as socially isolated and divorced from the empire's national interests and domestic life—much as elsewhere in Europe in the early twentieth century.[33] It even survived the revolution of 1905, and the autocracy's concession of an elective legislature and limited freedoms in the October Manifesto, when the empire's Fundamental Laws—revised in April 1906 to reflect these and other constitutional changes—stipulated that foreign policy, along with military and court affairs, remain the sovereign emperor's exclusive prerogative, immune from Duma interpellations.[34] A similar separation between the two realms of policy prevailed during much of the post–World War II period, when foreign policy became the bailiwick of a select group within the Politburo, who discussed these issues isolated from their comrades, as Gorbachev observed with dismay on joining that body.[35]

This combination of circumstances under both the imperial and Soviet orders (i.e., retention of virtually exclusive prerogative in all realms of policy, alongside the tendency to treat domestic and external affairs separately) draws attention to the position of the state in Russian tradition as a relatively autonomous actor interposed between these two spheres—a position in sharp contrast with modern Western states. For long stretches of time—during the era of Nicholas I or from the mid-1860s until 1905 and certainly for much of the Cold War—historians were satisfied to explain Russian diplomacy with little reference to domestic circumstances, beyond the influence of certain ideologies or individuals. At home, equally, the state has figured as the great demiurge in Russian history, whether as a force for upheaval and transformation under such figures as Peter I or Joseph Stalin, or as the defender of order and imposer of unity and direction over its ethnically, geographically, and socially heterogeneous territories—a role associated with much of the nineteenth century and the post-Stalin years.

This understanding of the Russian or Soviet state as a Janus-faced and powerful agent vis-à-vis its population and in the world outside explains the importance of ideas and perceptions as the basis of foreign policy. In this context, the important connections between domestic affairs and foreign policy are those that are "imagined"—to use Benedict Anderson's image—by those in power at a given time. When events have brought the relationship between the realms of foreign and domestic policy under scrutiny, however, Russian leaders have acted within the framework of a surprisingly stable and long-standing worldview regarding the state and its purposes when seeking to regulate, balance, or reform this relationship. The most obvious examples of such activity are associated with periods of reform or revolution from above: the reign of Peter the Great; the Great Reforms under Alexander II; the crisis and revolution from 1900 to 1917; the period that saw the construction of the Bolshevik-Stalinist order; and, finally, the last two decades of the twentieth century. Each instance involved setbacks or challenges to Russia's position as a dominant international player. Each in turn elicited a related set of responses from the leadership: a recognition that Russia had fallen behind or could not compete against its Western rivals; and a corollary recognition that this circumstance demanded a reordering of domestic life to reestablish Russia as a viable competitor for influence or interest in international affairs, but also the assumption that the state would direct this reordering.[36]

Not accidentally, this syndrome and this fixation on competitiveness with the West began, as so much else in Russian history, with Peter the Great and his twenty-year conflict with Charles XII in the eastern Baltic. This period also saw the first articulation of a new, secular, and instrumental definition of the state as an agent in domestic and foreign affairs. This definition's explanation of the state's role and raison d'être have since displayed a remarkable persistence through the imperial, Soviet, and post-Soviet regimes.[37]

THE LANGUAGES AND PRACTICES OF RUSSIAN STATEHOOD

An appreciation that the state is a conceptual construct—a form that has harbored differing ideologies—is more than a frivolous or postmodern claim. It helps to resolve the perplexity and disappointment that pervade so much comment on Putin's Russia. Part of the problem lies in the historic or philosophical perspective of many observers.[38] Critics of this new order have tended to believe that in bursting asunder the integument of Soviet rule, Russian leaders and citizens had or should have embarked on a historical developmental path characteristic of what intellectual historians know as the *doux commerce* or its successor, the political economy discourse.

Best exemplified by Adam Smith's brief discussion of the bourgeoisie's triumph in book 3 of the *Wealth of Nations*, this discourse argues that markets, the rule of law, and prosperity develop hand in hand in a law-governed process, spreading both rationality and an understanding among participants in the marketplace that they share a mutual dependence and a reliance on a law-regulated environment for the production and distribution of goods. It has also incorporated from theories of natural law the principles of popular sovereignty, inalienable rights, and strict limits on the state's ability to intervene in the individual's life, as the historical by-products of economic growth and the rise of the middle classes.[39] According to this view, the state marks out and enforces the playing field and rules to ensure fair and transparent exchanges, leaving questions related to property and privacy to agreements among individual actors. Doubtless this vision of historical development, when used as the benchmark to measure Russia, has inspired more than a century of Western critiques of Russian and Soviet rule.

Still, this intellectual tradition constituted only one approach to explaining the creation of society, sovereignty, and political authority, one that has prevailed in a relatively small group of contemporary states, however obvious its benefits to them. Commentators often forget that Smith and his colleagues were engaged in polemics with other theories—Physiocratism, mercantilism, and varieties of thought associated with absolutism.[40]

Absolutist tradition stressed the centrality of state power as the guarantor of order and security for its citizens, necessary for the creation of the benefits of civilized life. As stated in Hobbes's *Leviathan,* state power stood as a reified agent or "artificial animal" above and outside the members of the society that created it.[41] Through laws and the application of incontestable coercive power, this body protected subjects from one another's depredation while defending them collectively from other states. As adapted by the monarchies of Central Europe to the rigors of unremitting conflict during the seventeenth century, absolutist ideology also acquired an economic perspective. Leaders in the various German states and Sweden developed an administrative philosophy dedicated to organizing the population to maximize the kingdom's revenues—and thus military capacity—while also rationalizing administrative structures to extract and mobilize to directed ends the human and material resources provided by the estates of the realm.[42] Strikingly, the state's ambit of mobilization and transformation extended to regulating conduct and dress among its subjects.

Emulating these states, including Sweden, his adversary in the Great Northern War, Peter sought to transform Russia into the model absolutist state, a task simplified by the absence in Russia of social estates endowed with entrenched rights or ideologies of resistance.[43] Despite the turmoil his efforts created during and after his reign, Peter became for such Enlightenment admirers as Voltaire and Catherine II the apotheosis of absolutism as a civilizing force, able to wrest Russia from its former barbarism, a project that Catherine embraced as her own.[44] She and her French admirer, too, regarded the state as the maker of *historical* transformation, taking a now-backward Russia into a future embodied by its European counterparts, while applying European standards of efficiency and rationality in statecraft.[45] Peter thrust this role onto his government and society not only through institutional reform, but also with laws on dress, education, and mixed-gender social gatherings—not

to mention through the construction of St. Petersburg, his new capital mod-
eled on Amsterdam. The same perspective motivated the Great Reforms and
Sergei Witte's industrialization, which used the state's power and position to
replicate the transformations and new modes of power wrought in Europe by
the Industrial Revolution; indeed, for Witte, this process was of such significance that only the state could direct and coordinate it.[46] Soviet leaders likewise acknowledged this sense of historicity when pledging to "catch up to and
surpass" (*dognat i peregnat*) the capitalist states of the West.[47]

The absolutist discourse envisions a different world than that of *doux commerce*. Explicitly rejecting the contract myth—in which subjects voluntarily
surrendered some of their power to sovereigns in exchange for security or the
protection of certain rights[48]—the Russian absolutist tradition derived the ruler's or state's sovereignty from various sources, including God and the laws of
history. If political economy theories emphasized society as a venue in which
market exchanges among individuals produced expanding rationality, prosperity, and civility, absolutist theory—while often recognizing the benefits of
commerce—stressed the centrality of the state as an overarching unitary force,
mobilizing and ordering society at home, while protecting and advancing its interests abroad. Within the realm, the state preserved order and security by mediating and directing the activities of a population composed of particular
social, confessional, or ethnic groupings. Only state power could unify these
distinct groups and coordinate their efforts to improve and enrich the empire.
To this end, the state passed "positive" laws mandating conduct or obligations,
as opposed to the regulatory laws conceived in *doux commerce* discussions.[49]

In this worldview, only the state could articulate and define the universal-
ized goals toward which to coordinate and mobilize subjects' efforts. Such a
view guided the crafters of the Great Reforms under Alexander II in the 1860s[50]
and, in a different mode, the Communist Party, as the vanguard of Soviet society.[51] This rhetoric has survived in post-Soviet Russia. On his elevation to the
presidency in 1999, Putin declared:

> Here the state, its institutions and structures always played an exception-
> ally important role in the life of the country and the people. For a Russian,
> a strong state is not an anomaly, not something with which to struggle,
> but, to the contrary, the source and guarantor of order, the initiator and
> main driving force of any changes. Modern Russian society does not iden-
> tify a strong and effective state with a totalitarian one. We have learned to
> value the benefits of democracy, a law-based state, personal and political

freedom. At the same time, people are alarmed by the obvious weakening of state power. Society desires a restoration of the guiding and regulating role of the state to the necessary degree, proceeding from the traditions and present state of the country.[52]

Common to both the reformist/mobilizational and the order-oriented motifs in this worldview was the state's role as a discrete and self-contained agent in both domestic and international spheres, an image Peter invoked when distinguishing between the state and his person as its "first servant." Peter acted *upon* his society as a virtual Leviathan or deus ex machina, a stance most trenchantly symbolized in his "shearing" of the boyars' beards and the subjugation of the Orthodox Church to the government through the creation of the Holy Synod.[53] In these instances, as well as through successive attempts at transformation across three centuries, the state has stood as the active subject shaping, cajoling, taxing, and organizing—generally standing above its social and economic object, the inhabitants of its domain.[54]

This self-imposed separation was also reflected in social practice and identity. As the bureaucracy expanded in the nineteenth century, officialdom came to constitute a separate social milieu, bound by education, uniforms, and the badges of rank and intermarriage.[55] The Soviet party-state and its leaders set themselves at numerous removes from the population, a divide already implicit in Lenin's vision of the party in *What Is to Be Done?* which distinguished the class-conscious vanguard, able to read and even manipulate history's laws, from a proletariat mired in "spontaneity," doomed to eternal subjection without the vanguard's intervention on its behalf.[56]

This notional distance became institutionalized in the form of the governing Communist Party. More concretely, the regime imposed it through the violence that characterized the relationship of the state with much of the population, most notably the peasantry, nationalist dissenters, and intellectuals. And, in a society wracked by chronic goods shortages, party leaders enjoyed access to scarce goods, living space, superior health care, travel abroad and, especially as the "class of '38" became ensconced in power during the 1950s and 1960s, educational and career privileges for their children.[57] These attitudes became politically entrenched as well. Recalling the 1980s, Yegor Ligachev wrote that he had worried that perestroika would face "difficulties of an objective 'external' nature," referring to the conditions in the country resulting from "stagnation." He had not anticipated the acerbity of what he called "internal" (i.e., intraparty) intrigues that the reformers encountered.[58]

More recently, Vladimir Putin decried the state's self-enclosure when criticizing bureaucratic corruption and self-serving behavior—an interesting echo of early-twentieth-century critiques—in his "state of the union" address to the Federal Assembly in May 2005.[59]

Nineteenth- and twentieth-century critics of state power themselves underscored this separation between state and population. Such literary works as the *Bronze Horseman* and Gogol's stories emphasized the cloistered social contours of officials' lives. Political thinkers such as Peter Chaadaev, the "Westernizers," and the Slavophiles added a moral and historical element to this critique, as they emphasized the state's divorce from its subject society, a distance defined by coercion and by its active preemption of the development of self-consciousness or unity in the population.[60] These terms of analysis framed radical and liberal criticism of the autocracy throughout the rest of the nineteenth century, before finding concrete expression in the revolution of 1905. That upheaval and the quasi-constitutional order it engendered were grounded in a notional opposition of "state and society."[61] During the Soviet years, a similar critique appeared, albeit in Marxist terms. Echoing a formulation first advanced by Leon Trotsky, Milovan Djilas wrote of *The New Class* in the post-Stalin USSR,[62] while popular parlance referred to the Communist Party leadership collectively as the "bosses" (*nachalstvo*). Those inside the charmed circle shared this perspective.

THE DILEMMAS OF CHANGE, THE "RULES OF THE GAME," AND MAKING RUSSIA GREAT

These self-isolating states claimed a monopoly of political deliberation—indeed, of virtually all independent volition in areas identified as involving the state's interest. Still, this monopoly brought its own dilemmas. Most pressingly, administrators and rulers in the autocratic and Soviet eras sought to reconcile the linked but often contradictory missions of maintaining order alongside historic transformation. Nicholas I genuinely deplored the abuses of serfdom but feared that reform would unleash a peasant uprising.[63] The "enlightened bureaucrats" who brokered the Great Reforms of the 1860s and 1870s reclaimed the state's role as a transformer; they also quickly limited the participation of representatives of nonofficial society in the framing of their reforms.[64] Witte's industrialization took place alongside policies designed to immobilize the peasantry in the commune (*obshchina*).[65] The Communist Party confronted a similar dilemma with the wave of reforms associated with Nikita Khrushchev, ranging from the temporary loosening of censorship associated with the "thaw" of the late 1950s and early 1960s to the solicitation of popular input in social policy, the reconstruction of the Party, and proposals for economic reorganization that many saw as desperately needed.[66]

Perceived threats to order came from various quarters. Imperial and Soviet regimes actively repressed claims to national or religious self-determination that threatened to shatter imperial integrity. Intellectual elites, whose knowledge was vital to the formation of policy and the creation of military technology, stirred deep ambivalence among both imperial and Soviet leaderships.[67] More often, though, both orders concentrated on the threat to stability posed by the Russian people (*narod*), seen as primitive and given to a dangerous spontaneity, a view rooted in the historicity of the statehood discourse. The masses represented a distinctly backward element in need of tutelage and guidance into the future: this view underlay, in turn, apologies for serfdom,[68] the "tutelary" regime in the countryside after serfdom's abolition,[69] and, arguably, collectivization. The history of each period offered examples of the peasantry's explosive force: the Pugachev rising of the 1770s, the widespread and violent peasant unrest of 1905–1906, and the rural wars that raged intermittently during the revolutions and the civil war from 1917 to the early 1920s, culminating with the assault on the countryside during the 1930s.

The spontaneity of unregulated market relations also inspired suspicion among imperial and Soviet administrators alike. Nineteenth-century conservatives feared both the spatial movement that accompanied the market's circulation of goods and people as well as the market's effects as a social solvent, encouraging people to think beyond their station in a society founded on ascriptive-legal estates.[70] Even during the years of the Stolypin reform, and in the effort to provision the empire's troops and population during the Great War, officials rejected market mechanisms, preferring instead to use bureaucratic means to control the distribution of land and produce.[71] The Soviet order's opposition to the marketplace sprang directly from ideology, as well as political apprehensions about threats from foreign enemies and the domestic saboteurs in the black market.[72]

These attitudes toward the ordering of Russian society also point to a fundamental dilemma that has confronted Russian leaders since the middle of the nineteenth century: how to enhance the creation and mobilization of resources while retaining the requisite degree of control over social changes and the political pressures they engender. This question forms the pivot in relations between the foreign and domestic realms of Russian state activity. If leaders have demonstrated a marked diffidence toward the market, the same holds a fortiori for the exploitation of nationalism in support of the regime's international goals. Both forces have proven critical to the international success of Russia's international rivals—most notably the United States during the second half of the twentieth century—but both also rest on the same concession of initiative to "society" broadly conceived that has dogged attempts to introduce free markets to Russia.

In its aspiration to political self-determination for a community defined by particularistic attributes, nationalism challenges the broader universalizing contentions underpinning Russian leaders' authority. Claims to popular sovereignty and separatism present an obvious threat to a supranational, multiethnic imperial state—as was the challenge posed by tsarist Poland or among many of the nationalities of the Soviet period. But social peace could be jeopardized as well by ethnic Russian nationalism, or at least the variant that exalted the Russian people and their state, while regarding both the West and domestic religious or ethnic minorities with suspicion or hatred.[73]

In recognition of nationalism's compelling attraction, Russian officials have tried to appropriate its arguments, either in defense of the existing order or in an attempt to cultivate loyalty. Count S. S. Uvarov's famous formulation of "orthodoxy, autocracy, and nationality" in the 1830s represents the classic instance of the former.[74] The cult of Stalin as well as attempts to nest local national identities in an ultimate Soviet patriotism were designed to cultivate loyalty to Stalin and his regime.[75]

Yet, Russian and Soviet governments have resorted to nationalist appeals relatively rarely. Both regimes recruited their officials from the empire's non-Russian nationalities, while grounding the "center's" authority in an alliance with local non-Russian elites. Baltic Germans played a prominent role in the imperial state, as did Ukrainian Cossacks, converted Tatars, and Caucasian nobles, as attested by such names as Benkendorf, Kochubei, Shirinsky-Shikhmatov, and Loris-Melikov. The Soviet regime showed a similar inclusiveness, incorporating Jews, Georgians, Armenians, Azeris, and even Karelian Finns alongside ethnic Russians. Post-Soviet efforts to devise a vocabulary suitable for the new polity—including the revival of the supra-ethnic term *Rossyanin* as a designation for the Russian Federation's citizens—demonstrate the difficulties of establishing a national identity in such a heterogeneous state. Historically, Russian governments resorted to "national" mobilizational rhetoric at times of acute foreign threat to the state edifice: the Napoleonic wars and the two world wars.

Indicatively, during World War I, such appeals unleashed the sort of spontaneous and virtually irresistible violence—in pogroms directed against Jews, Germans, and refugees—that fueled larger concerns about disorder.[76]

Still, whatever the ambiguities or contradictions in the rhetoric of Russian absolutism and statehood, Russians from virtually all sections of society and on either side of the state-society divide agree that Russia is "fated to be a Great Power."[77] Stolypin promised to build a Great Russia, much as President Putin has called for Russia's reestablishment as a leading international power, a call echoed in successive foreign policy concepts as well.[78]

The breadth of popular and elite consensus on Russia's "greatness" as a sine qua non of its identity as a state appears clearly in the crises that have arisen from international failure. Invocations of Tsushima and Mukden after the Russo-Japanese War, and recriminations over the loss of empire since the USSR's demise, attest to the broad resonance of Russian claims to a grand destiny. Challenges to Russia's great-power status have frequently provided the opening allowing those in the state and their allies among intellectual elites to argue for the necessity of domestic restructuring.[79] Analysts of the imperial Great Reforms and the Gorbachev period have long appreciated this fact.[80] Responding to criticism of his policies from noble landowners, Witte argued that only a policy of state-directed industrialization could save Russia from becoming a second-class power.[81] Most significantly, even during moments of systemic crisis—when the existence of the state itself has come into question, as after 1905 or during the 1990s—Russian leaders have defended domestic reform and external restraint as temporary but necessary conditions for the restoration of Russia's greatness. As is often noted, Stolypin argued that Russia required twenty years of peace for internal reconstruction; elsewhere, he spoke of building a Great Russia. A similar sense of temporary retreat dominated Russian statements during the 1990s about the relationship between domestic reform and foreign policy. However individual actors may differ over the necessary means to reestablish Russia's greatness—whether through marketization, liberalization, or the reimposition of state discipline—they all agree on the ultimate goal.

These parallels in structure and practices suggest strong continuities in the way Russians have thought about the state and its role, despite the real differences distinguishing the three regimes. The image of the state as an agent of historic transformation from above has long formed a central theme in Russian historical literature. State school historians, most notably S. M. Solovev and his disciples, established this perspective in the classrooms of universities throughout the nineteenth-century empire. Of course, this view of the state also anchored the historical philosophy of G. W. F. Hegel, who exerted an indelible influence on Russian historical thought in the mid-nineteenth century, as well as on the first generation of the Russian intelligentsia.[82] Many late imperial radicals and revolutionaries—including Lenin—took a view of state power and its role as transformer that prompted their critics to call them "Jacobins."[83] Lenin's *State and Revolution* epitomized this perspective, arguing that the dictatorship of the proletariat, led by the vanguard party, could use state power to create socialism and then communism by expropriating and eliminating the old possessing classes.[84]

Continuities connecting imperial-era and Soviet understandings of statehood also flowed along more practical paths. Many Bolshevik practices during the civil war—including expropriation of factories, food-supply policies, and surveillance of potentially hostile elements in the population—merely continued policies devised by the imperial and provisional governments as they prosecuted the Great War.[85] The numerous "bourgeois specialists" who aided the Bolsheviks in the civil war and the construction of the new Soviet state order represented yet another source of continuity. More symbolically, Stalin's embrace of such figures as Peter the Great and Ivan the Terrible as his precursors underscored the dictator's views about continuities between his vision of the state and theirs.[86] More recently, Putin himself has cited Stolypin as a figure he admires.[87]

These continuities have also defined the "rules of the game" among generations of Russian and Soviet leaders, who have learned them through the various patterns of socialization that brought them along the corridors of power to the heart of the imperial or Soviet political orders. Taken together, these strands of historical and conceptual continuity have combined in Russian political culture to form a surprisingly strong consensus about state power, the discreteness of the state as director, and its role vis-à-vis Russian society and in the world at large, even despite competing notions of the ends to which state power should be put and the permissible means for achieving them. It is a consensus that survived across both the imperial and Soviet periods.

Thus, to assess how domestic developments have traditionally affected Russia's international conduct, and to estimate how this interaction might continue to frame Russian foreign policy in the future, it is necessary to understand this relationship in two related contexts. First, one must examine the way in which these two spheres of state activity, traditionally treated separately by Russian statesmen, were brought together by the actions of particular national leaders.

Second, these perceptions and the conclusions or responses they elicited were themselves framed within a worldview that understood the state, in ideal terms, as a freestanding and independent actor, in terms inherited from the rhetorical traditions of absolutist statehood.

FOREIGN POLICY AND THE DOMESTIC ORDER

For extended periods, the history of Russian foreign policy demonstrates the relative absence of domestic factors as either a restraint or an impetus on Russia's conduct. Compared with its European and U.S. rivals, Russia has played a prominent role in the European and global state systems despite an often conscious adherence by its statesmen and rulers to the maintenance of a domestic regime regarded as barbarous and underproductive in much of the West by the nineteenth century, and even by its monarchical Prussian/German and Austrian allies by the 1840s, if not earlier—a view that assumed new variations in relation to the Soviet Union.[88] A by-product of the absolutist worldview, this regime rested on serfdom and its legacies for a huge rural population regarded with fear and suspicion by noble officials and Communist Party functionaries. It was the paradox of highly centralized rule hobbled by ineffectual local governance,[89] with strict controls over public expression and the extra-governmental dissemination of technical knowledge, and consequently contentious relationships with technical elites.

Until the Crimean defeat, Russian leaders abjured for ideological reasons the processes associated with modernization in nineteenth-century Europe—most notably, the development of national, industrial economies and the spread of increasingly participatory forms of government. Afterward and until the 1890s, a lack of available capital combined with fear of conceding too many prerogatives to local society retarded the course of modernization, grudgingly accepted in state circles following Russia's Crimean setbacks and signaled by the adoption of the Great Reforms. These measures abolished serfdom, while maintaining communal land tenure, and created the local, elective zemstvos—bodies of local self-government whose powers and composition were increasingly restricted by the state, as well as reforming the legal order.[90] Russia's belated industrialization stands out even more starkly when one recalls Prussia's, and later Germany's, own experience, inspired by the writings of Friedrich List beginning in the 1830s and ultimately finding expression in Bismarck's famous appeal to "blood and iron" as the means for imperial unification. Russian leaders accepted national electoral politics only under the duress of revolutionary pressure in 1905—and even under the Duma monarchy and its relatively free press, public opinion played a much less decisive role than in Germany, let alone in other the Western powers.[91] Similarly, the Soviet state after World War II managed to maintain notional parity with the United States in Europe and around the world despite the growing evidence that the Soviet economy, technological development, and the well-being of the population itself were falling farther behind similar measures in the United States, Europe, and Japan.

The seeming paradox of Russian might combined with relative backwardness becomes less puzzling when one considers its geographical position on the eastern end of the European state system in addition to its sheer magnitude: these attributes, as much as "General Winter," afforded a protection not enjoyed by many other continental states, as attested by the failures of Charles XII, Napoleon, and Hitler. Likewise, the prospect of encirclement—*pace* Stalin—did not present the sort of threat to Russian strategists that preoccupied, for example, German military planners after 1871. For much of the nineteenth century, Russia's western border was secured through its good relations with the neighboring monarchies; the Ottomans had declined as a threat by the late eighteenth century, while Asia played most often a secondary role in Russian calculations.[92] The Soviet state under Lenin and Stalin could build "socialism in one country" protected by the fragmented and weak states of the Eastern European cordon sanitaire created at the Paris Peace Conference.

These periods of Russian and Soviet predominance produced similar, and interesting, conceptual relationships between the domestic and foreign policies of each state order. International success or prominence served to legitimate each regime to domestic and foreign critics, in a sort of totalizing discourse, linking international stature with a vindication of each order's approach to domestic governance. Through such doctrines as "official nationality" and the "monarchical principle," Nicholas and his advisers openly championed Russia's difference from the liberal powers of Western Europe.[93] Similarly, members of the Brezhnev Politburo repeatedly rejected recommendations for reform from Soviet economists and other experts, grounding their resistance partly in the triumph the system had realized in the victory over fascism and the USSR's resulting superpower status.[94] Like Nicholas, the leadership emphasized the Soviet Union's difference from, and superiority to, decadent Europe and America.[95] Conversely, they interpreted as virtually congruent—and connected—challenges to their authority in either the foreign or domestic spheres. From the 1820s into the 1850s, both Alexander I and Nicholas I—like their ally Metternich—perceived intimate links between upholding the constitutions established by the Congress of Vienna and the protection of order at home against the spirit of revolution. A similar sort of linkage appears to have operated during and after the Warsaw Pact invasion of Czechoslovakia in 1968—an event followed by mounting harassment of dissidents within the Soviet Union.

For much of this period, considerations of the domestic realm, whether as a material restraint on foreign political options or as an impetus to a more energetic or expansionist policy, rarely figured in discussions among Russian governments. Pan-Slavism, nationalism, and even orientalism in the late nineteenth century played only a limited role in impelling what foreign observers regarded as Russian expansionism; acknowledging such demands of public opinion would constitute a concession to that same opinion, which Russian leaders often vigorously resisted.[96] Soviet leaders pursued the expansion of their sphere for reasons of ideology or simpler considerations of "face" or status, as when Khrushchev argued for the retention of Soviet troops in Budapest at the end of October 1956, lest the Western "imperialists . . . perceive it as weakness on our part and go on the offensive."[97] In these instances, leaders measured their ability to act according to relatively crude indicators: the ability to levy sufficient troops to maintain the army and expertise from a regimented population organized, at least in state laws, according to the duties they were to discharge for the government.[98] Following the precepts of statehood rhetoric, leaders seldom engaged in cost-benefit analysis when requesting more soldiers, taxes, or armaments technology.[99] Even when ministers or experts warned them of the economic or social problems they were creating, they used their power to divert the resources necessary to achieve their ends.[100] Gorbachev saw such disregard as the besetting vice of the Soviet system; as a provincial official, he witnessed the real costs of such decisions.[101]

At certain times, however, events conspired to dissolve the barrier between these two spheres of policy and to bring Russian leaders face-to-face with very real domestic limits on their capacity to act abroad. Most often, this occurred at times of military defeat, which laid bare the insufficiencies of the existing order. Peter I's reforms originated as a desperate reaction to Russian military defeats by Sweden. Alexander II's decision to abolish serfdom, while modernizing Russia's administration and its economy, originated at least in part from the shock of the Crimean defeat. With important qualifications, the history of the Soviet state during its laborious construction between the civil war and the outbreak of World War II also constitutes such an episode, albeit an extreme one. For reasons of ideology and political exigency, Soviet foreign policy reflected the simultaneous processes of state building and social transformation that characterized not only this era, but also the period of political and social fracture from the end of World War I through the Depression in Europe.[102] Given its relative isolation in European politics, and in relation to a population that Communist Party leaders often regarded as shot through with hostile elements—especially the peasantry—the new Soviet state conducted two foreign policies during these years: one toward a population it sought to conquer, to take an uncharitable view, and one toward a hostile or suspicious Europe.

In most of these cases, reforms involved domestic society only as a passive participant or object. Reform originated with officials whose ideas or recommendations had gone rejected or unheeded by those exercising authority during the prereform situation, but who subsequently gained influence through changed circumstances associated with political defeats or challenges that demonstrated the flaws in their bureaucratic opponents' defense of the established order: Nikolai Miliutin and Mikhail Gorbachev and their respective allies in the imperial and Soviet systems represent such figures. These reformers believed as strongly as their ministerial or party rivals and opponents in the instrumentality and centrality of the state as the director of reform—and as the only forum for judging what measures the situation required. Through their policies, the reformers also sought to enhance the state's ability to fulfill its role within the empire and abroad. Russian and Soviet leaders have initiated reform from above, both to catch up to the West and to strengthen the power and efficacy of the state itself, in terms and measures that combine the demands of Russian statehood and Western measures of successful performance, a notion related to Gerschenkron's image of "substitution." In this context, standing above and outside the society, reformers (and revolutionaries) used state power as a notional surrogate for processes that occurred "spontaneously" in Western Europe; Russian leaders used laws or mustered and applied economic resources to replicate what they understood as developmental strategies that had brought strategic advantages to their Western rivals. The Great Reforms took place under the aegis of the state, managed by reforming officials who rejected the arbitrariness, irrationality, and corruption they associated with the government under Nicholas I; they believed they could reform Russian laws, social relations, the army, and the economy on models adapted from contemporary Prussia and elsewhere to render more efficient the production and extraction of resources required by the state.[103] The Soviet state of the 1920s and 1930s represented a Promethean effort at substitution, using the

Communist Party and the Red Army to build a new state, which in turn became the means to catch up to and surpass by rapidly engineering the transition from capitalism into socialism.

In most cases, these efforts did not exert serious or lasting impact on the foreign policy pursued by individual leaders or on Russia's status as a great power. Peter the Great continued to fight, and eventually defeat, Sweden at the very height of his reforming activity, despite significant unrest. Following the Crimean War, Alexander II's government sought to break out of its isolation through cooperation with Napoleon III in Eastern European questions. This rapprochement lasted only until the Polish rising of 1863—a rebellion that enjoyed the Second Empire's moral support. In addition, Russia became active once again in European and Asian diplomacy, abetting German unification, conquering Turkestan, and waging war against the Ottoman Empire in 1877 (i.e., barely three years after the initiation of a comprehensive military reform).[104] During the 1930s, amid the turmoil of the "revolution from above" and facing the rise of Nazi Germany, Stalin and his advisers fortified the USSR against external threat by mobilizing all the levers at their disposal: in addition to the Comintern, these included appeals to collective security, and more conventional international agreements, such as those loosely binding Czechoslovakia, France, and the Soviet Union in the mid-1930s.[105] Certainly, during both periods of relative weakness, Russian and Soviet leaders benefited from broader dynamism or ferment in the European order—in part created by Russia's partial eclipse as a participant—but it also bears noting that these did not necessitate the stark subordination of short- and middle-term foreign policy goals to demands from the domestic sphere.

DOMESTIC COLLAPSE AND FOREIGN RETREAT: THE CRISES OF THE LATE IMPERIAL AND LATE SOVIET STATES

At the beginning and the close of the twentieth century, however, domestic crises challenged the state's hegemony so seriously that the very issue of Russian statehood came into question, with direct and dramatic consequences for foreign policy. Despite their considerable differences, the crises that faced officials under Nicholas II—particularly Stolypin—and the leaderships of the Soviet Union and the Russian Federation that succeeded it in 1991 bear important and illustrative resemblances, most significantly the fact that both periods saw active and conscious efforts on the part of leaders to subordinate Russia's foreign policy to the demands of domestic reconstruction.

Each regime simultaneously faced redoubtable external *and* domestic challenges. In the early twentieth century, these came with a military defeat in the Far East that catalyzed a revolution lasting from 1905 through 1907. In the Soviet Union, the political and social forces unleashed by Gorbachev's prosecution of perestroika, "democratization," and "new thinking" culminated in the collapse of the old party-state and de facto defeat in the Cold War. There ensued a decade of institutional fracture and social and economic dislocation for several generations of post-Soviet citizens, leading to frequently bitter political conflict over the nature of the Russia that would succeed the defunct USSR.

In both periods, turmoil wracked every facet of political and social life, including foreign policy, during which several processes unfolded simultaneously. In foreign policy, each regime embarked on evident retreat. The Gorbachev administration pulled Soviet troops out of Afghanistan, abandoned its East European satellites, accepted German unification, and acceded to the dissolution of the USSR. Boris Yeltsin and his successive assistants labored to construct a new Russian Federation in the face of daunting economic and political challenges at home, themselves exacerbated by a volatile international environment—including the first Gulf War, the dissolution of Yugoslavia, and the expansion of European security and political institutions into the Soviet Union's former sphere. The debacles of 1905 and their aftermath obliged Stolypin and his colleagues to reconcile with their traditional British adversary and to accept, albeit temporarily and reluctantly, a passive role in an increasingly unstable Balkan arena.

In domestic politics, imperial, Soviet, and the new Russian leaders conducted what amounted to two sets of negotiations. The first entailed the restoration of the state's authority as the director of social and economic reform in a political arena that included representative bodies with legislative functions and a much more uncontrolled public sphere than had existed previously.[106] This task also entailed acceptance of the necessity for a fully developed market economy. Second, Stolypin and Russia's leaders in the late twentieth century recognized that they had to forge a loose contract of sorts with the population, guaranteeing the conditions in which Russians could pursue prosperity. Both calculations were intended to engender social support for the recast political order, but within limits set by the state itself. This new relationship found expression in a dialogue between government and an elective legislature and in efforts to mobilize a civic patriotism, grounded in appeals to Russian tradition and uniqueness.

Finally, the severity of each crisis forced Stolypin and Russian leaders in the late twentieth century to alter radically the relationship between foreign and domestic policies through two related measures. These leaders insisted on dissolving the institutional and conceptual barriers that had traditionally separated foreign and domestic policy making, going so far as to sacrifice Russia's great-power status, if need be, to domestic renovation. To assure compliance with these priorities, each asserted his direct control over the framing of Russian foreign policy, marking a strong departure from conventional practice. These measures arose from the conviction shared among the leaders of both regimes that the severity of the domestic situation jeopardized the state's very existence; the necessity of reconstituting the domestic order and a viable state in each case convinced Stolypin, Gorbachev, and his successors that they had to avoid at virtually all costs international complications that could divert economic and political resources from the project of domestic reconstruction. Finally, Stolypin and the leaders of the Russian Federation regarded this subordination as a temporary expedient, necessary to restoring a greatness that they all understood as an indispensable adjunct to Russian statehood.

Stolypin's insistence on the subordination of foreign policy to domestic considerations arose directly from the revolutionary threat that still confronted the imperial state when he became minister of internal affairs in the spring of 1906; he assumed the leadership of the Council of Ministers that summer.[107] By the fall of 1905, rising social protest, exacerbated by defeat in the Far East against Japan, had unleashed an all-Russian revolution. To save his throne, in October 1905 Nicholas promulgated a manifesto that granted drastic concessions: an elective legislature, civil liberties, religious tolerance, and relaxed controls over public expression. Two days later, he decreed the formation of a "united" Council of Ministers.[108] Led by a chairman charged with "unifying" ministerial activity, this last body would coordinate and oversee decision making among the various ministries. Before 1905 Russian ministries had functioned independently, united only in their accountability to the emperor, resulting in contradictory initiatives that had given rise, in the view of many officials, to the twinned catastrophes of war in the Far East and revolution at home.[109]

The result of these reforms would look familiar to students of Russian politics and society since the late 1990s. Once accustomed to dealing with the population through orders, discipline, and mobilization, the imperial state now confronted an elective legislature with limited powers of the purse.[110] Although still serving at the emperor's pleasure, ministers appeared before the Duma and answered interpellations on points of policy. For their part, Duma deputies and their various parties represented an impressively broad array of political positions, including the revolutionism of Marxist and populist parties on the far left, the moderate-to-republican constitutionalism of such groups as the Octobrists and Kadets, and the virulently chauvinistic and monarchist sentiments echoing from the benches on the right. Shifting configurations also marked Russian foreign policy following the loss to Japan.[111] Russia's French ally had by late 1904 entered the Entente Cordiale with Great Britain, while Germany and Austria-Hungary had both extended support to Russia during the recent war. German ports in the Baltic and Southwest Africa supplied Russia's Baltic Fleet, which met its end at Tsushima in May 1905; Austria-Hungary had agreed to respect the status quo in the Balkans, despite Russia's engagement in Asia.

The problem of Russia's international orientation—whether toward France and the new entente or toward the Central European monarchies—aroused widespread discussion in the government and the press, much like that heard in Moscow ninety years later.[112] All sides sought a policy that would strengthen the developmental path they desired in domestic life. Liberals and moderates supported closer relations with France and Great Britain, while conservatives wanted to buttress the "monarchical principle," which the revolution and its aftermath had brought into question, by restoring good relations with the German and Habsburg empires. Within government, ideological differences over these issues coexisted with more pragmatic views. In early 1906, Foreign Minister Count V. N. Lamzdorf suggested that Russia seek closer ties with Germany and Austria-Hungary as fellow exponents of monarchical rule.[113] His replacement, A. P. Izvolskii, a self-described liberal, like many in his ministry,[114] favored closer relations with Great Britain.

Stolypin took a more pragmatic and uncompromising view. Echoing a widely shared belief among educated Russians in state and society, Stolypin blamed the revolution of 1905 on the disastrous war with Japan.[115] This perspective sprang directly from his professional experience. A noble landowner from the western provinces, Stolypin had received legal training before entering imperial service, where he made his career as a local administrator in the Ministry of Internal Affairs.[116] He came to the attention of his superiors, and eventually Nicholas II, for his performance as governor of Saratov Province (*guberniya*), an area of intense agrarian and constitutionalist unrest before and during 1905.

In his attitude to reform and state policy, Stolypin drew on his experience as the state's "man" in the provinces. His service as governor of Saratov Province, where he worked with the leaders of the local zemstvos to contain peasant unrest, had convinced him not only of the necessity for social order, but also of the state's need to cultivate those patriotic and loyal elements that would support order and measured reform. Despite his reputation as a high-handed reactionary, Stolypin sought a Duma he could work with, even as he employed draconian methods against any threats of recurrent unrest. When he dissolved the second Duma on June 3, 1907, he also revised electoral laws to ensure strong representation from the property-holding classes in cities and, particularly, in the countryside. His land reform, based on earlier projects in his ministry, aimed at the creation of a freehold peasantry as a bulwark of government support in rural Russia.

Stolypin's view of Russia's interests abroad necessarily reflected his preoccupation with domestic concerns. He repeatedly insisted that Russia had to avoid all foreign complications. In August 1907 he stated categorically, "Our internal situation does not allow us to conduct an aggressive foreign policy. The absence of fear from the viewpoint of international relations is extremely important for us, since it will give us the opportunity to dedicate with full tranquility our strength to the ordering of matters [*ustroenie*] within the country."[117] In early 1908, at a meeting to discuss responses to the extension of Austrian railways across the Balkans, Stolypin argued forcefully against an assertive response: Any "mobilization" would only "lend strength to the revolution from which we are just beginning to emerge." After the restoration of domestic order, Russia might once again speak in "its former voice," but anything other than a "purely defensive" policy would represent the "delirium of an abnormal Government" and would endanger the dynasty. As he told Foreign Minister Izvolsky, "There is now in his hands a lever without a fulcrum, but Russia must have a respite after which it will become strong, and again occupy its appropriate rank as a Great Power."[118]

Guided by this perspective, Stolypin advocated a foreign policy that eliminated any complications. In 1907, ending a rivalry of nearly a century's standing, Russia concluded an entente with Great Britain on outstanding questions in Central Asia. Yet, to balance this rapprochement, he also advocated good relations with Germany.[119] In the meantime, the alliance with France assured the capital necessary for economic development and military renewal.

Stolypin, however, had to wage an active campaign to gain a decisive role in foreign policy making, a struggle that culminated during the Bosnian crisis of 1908–1909, which broke out when Austria-Hungary annexed two Balkan provinces nominally under Ottoman rule. The annexation had resulted in part from an agreement between the Austrian foreign minister, Count A. Aehrenthal, and

Izvolsky, without Stolypin's knowledge, but with Nicholas's permission.[120] News of the annexation created an outcry among Stolypin's allies in the Duma and the makers of public opinion. Appalled by the foreign minister's actions in "a matter of such immense national historical significance, which affected the interest of the Empire's internal political conditions,"[121] Stolypin threatened to resign unless foreign policy was discussed in the Council of Ministers.[122] Nicholas acceded to these demands. By the spring of 1909, the Russian government officially recognized the Austrian act. For the duration of his premiership, until his assassination in 1911, Stolypin and the council oversaw foreign policy discussion.[123] Additionally, to succeed the disgraced Izvolsky, he secured the appointment of S. D. Sazonov in 1910. Despite his lower position and inexperience in the foreign ministry, Sazonov also possessed the distinct advantage of being Stolypin's brother-in-law.

Several aspects of Stolypin's policies offer insight into how systemic crisis, domestic policy, and Russia's international conduct have interacted since the 1980s. When he took office, Stolypin saw himself placed in charge of a volatile domestic order threatened by a recurrence of revolution unless and until reconstruction had taken root. He responded to these apprehensions with a series of measures which, taken together, amounted to a long-term strategy for Russia's domestic regeneration. While encouraging the continuation of the industrialization bequeathed by Witte, he also moved to solve the chronic problems associated with the "agrarian question" in the countryside—land shortage and underproduction. His land reform of 1906, which wagered on the "sober and the strong" by encouraging prosperous peasants to leave the commune for individual farms, sought to create a loyal class of small landholders. Likewise, a Duma dominated by mature political forces—rooted in urban and rural propertied elements—would provide the necessary order and social support for his program.

At the same time, Stolypin regarded the state and the restoration of its authority as an indispensable guarantee of order and as the proper director of this project, the creation of what he termed "Great Russia."[124] His measures in defense of order and reform reflected his understanding—shared by reformers in previous generations—that only the state could direct and implement the great reforms whose need had found such dramatic expression in the recent revolution.[125]

Above all, this period stands out as an instance in which the reconstitution of state authority at a time of social and political crisis brought a marked retrenchment in Russia's foreign policy and its active subordination to domestic demands. As such, Stolypin's domestication of foreign policy, so to speak, represented a marked departure from conventional practice, including the making of foreign policy during the Great Reforms. To be sure, Stolypin and his successor V. N. Kokovstov faced resistance to their views: Izvolsky's conduct in 1908 represented an egregious instance, as did the "Charykov demarche" to open the straits during the Italo-Turkish War of 1911. At the same time, S. D. Sazonov subscribed to these procedures and the outlook informing them, most notably in the fall of 1912, when he expressed unfeigned outrage at the initiation of war against Turkey by Serbia and Montenegro, under an alliance that the Russian government had brokered.[126]

As one turns to the end of the twentieth century, it also bears remembering that Stolypin's reform strategy sought the creation of a more vital Russia, sustained by the prosperity and patriotism of a new nation,[127] under the aegis of a state that upheld the domestic order on which that prosperity depended. This Great Russia would serve in turn as the basis on which Russia could once again "speak in its former voice" abroad.

Critical differences distinguish the Stolypin years from the late twentieth century, but they do not outweigh the salient similarities, particularly the discursive logic of statehood that appears to have guided Gorbachev, Yeltsin, and Putin in their dealings with Russia's domestic and foreign political spheres. Stolypin's authority rested on the pleasure of his master, Nicholas II.[128] The notorious vagaries of that ruler created the possibility for defiance to Stolypin's preferences—as Izvolsky had shown in 1908; ultimately, Nicholas acceded to the idea of unified decision making, even during the July Crisis of 1914, during which deliberations over the Austrian ultimatum to Serbia occurred within the Council of Ministers. Gorbachev, Yeltsin, and Putin, too, have had to deal with a diffusion of power and authority that rival for their unpredictability the arbitrary inclinations of an autocrat. Gorbachev's years as general secretary and president witnessed a chronic battle with conservatives in the Central Committee and the Politburo, climaxing in the failed putsch of August 1991. He also faced redoubtable social forces, whether in the mining towns of Siberia and the Donbass, in the streets of Tbilisi and Vilnius, in the Congresses of People's Deputies, or, most important, in the form of Boris Yeltsin's election to the presidency of the Russian Republic in the summer of 1991.

For their part, Yeltsin and Putin have contended with numerous challenges, themselves a consequence of the party-state's disintegration in December 1991: an often fractious electorate, a revived Communist Party and

Vladimir Zhirinovsky's Liberal Democrats; the rise of local political elites that defy central authority, particularly in those provinces dominated by non-Russian populations; and the appearance in Russian politics of wealth as a potential political force.

In these respects the Stolypin years and the late twentieth century resemble each other in that the leaders under discussion asserted the necessity of maintaining the authority of the state as a directing center at times when the very bases of Russia's statehood drove all political discussion and activity. After 1905, in the Duma, in the press, and even within the government itself, the foundations of Russia's existence as a political order came under repeated and far-ranging scrutiny. Revolutionaries propagandized their vision of a socialist or communalized state. Liberals regarded the post-1905 accommodation as a step on the path to a constitutional rule-of-law state. Conservatives and Nicholas himself considered the post-1905 regime a temporary concession, at best, or a betrayal, at worst, to be reversed at the soonest possible moment.[129] From the mid-1980s, debates over the foundations of Russian statehood divided governors and governed in Russia, even leading to violence, as in August 1991 and October 1993.

The severity of these existential crises, in each case, convinced leaders of the necessity to pursue two separate but related goals: to reestablish state authority and, in so doing, assert its traditional role as director of Russia's domestic social, political, and economic restoration. To this view, only state power, representing a universalist perspective above the particularistic aspirations of constituent social, economic, or regional actors, can direct this process, a view that Stolypin would have endorsed and that Putin has expressed frequently.

These crises also created situations in which, willy-nilly, Russian governments had to avoid undue complications abroad while the state and its agents pursued domestic restoration that would eventually permit Russia to "speak in its former voice," despite the differences in sequence by which this occurred. To be sure, unlike Stolypin, Gorbachev did not inherit an explicitly revolutionary situation. However, to judge from his own testimony, even before becoming general secretary, he saw the Soviet Union entangled by a challenge of such dimensions that domestic reform would demand a radical alteration of the USSR's foreign policy. Like Stolypin, Gorbachev's perspective on the USSR's condition stemmed from his professional experience as a provincial Communist Party official; indeed, much of his early support came from such fellow provincial secretaries as Yegor Ligachev, Boris Yeltsin, and Nikolai Ryzhkov. All of these men were significantly younger than the Brezhnev cohort and had received much more thorough educations, winning their intellectual and political spurs during the reformist Khrushchev era. This generation assessed the Soviet Union's domestic well-being in much different terms than had the Brezhnev leadership.[130]

By his own account, Gorbachev had reached a clear understanding of the Soviet Union's problems by the early 1980s, after conducting with Ryzhkov and several scholars a study on the Soviet economy, at Yuri Andropov's request.[131] This study only confirmed the view among Gorbachev and his colleagues that economic rationality, systematic planning, and the population's economic welfare had been sacrificed to the sustenance of the military-industrial complex. Upon becoming general secretary, Gorbachev embarked on a program of systemic reform that he and his supporters in the Politburo and Central Committee regarded as urgently necessary. Convinced that he could not pursue the restructuring he envisioned while expending the resources to maintain the USSR's superpower status,[132] Gorbachev made the same choice Stolypin had earlier and subordinated foreign policy to the needs of perestroika. His "new thinking" sought to decrease the burdens of empire and the arms race, so that the state could focus on providing the necessary resources for domestic renewal.

As important, Gorbachev also gained control over Soviet foreign policy, effectively integrating it with the needs of domestic policy. Even before becoming general secretary, he had deplored Andrei Gromyko's long-time monopoly over foreign policy—and the exclusion of much of the Politburo from discussion of these issues.[133] To remedy this shortcoming, Gorbachev replaced Gromyko with another provincial secretary, the Georgian Eduard Shevardnadze. With Gorbachev's support, Shevardnadze quickly reorganized his new ministry and actively recruited contributions to policy discussions from academics and members of Communist Party think tanks, whom the previous leadership had largely ignored.[134]

There followed a breathtaking diminution of the Soviet Union's role in Eastern Europe and the world at large: In addition to reaching understandings with the Ronald Reagan and George H. W. Bush administrations on a range of long-standing sticking points, Gorbachev presided over the withdrawal of Soviet forces from Afghanistan and then from the "fraternal" socialist republics in the Warsaw Pact, triggering a series of revolutions, velvet to violent, throughout much of the former Eastern bloc. By the fall of 1990, Germany's reunification signaled the end of the onetime Pax Sovietica in Cold War Europe.

If these retreats had begun as tactical calculations in support of domestic reform, they assumed new momentum once political conflict overtook the

Communist Party and then the country. Hard-liners within the party began to mobilize against what they considered Gorbachev's assault on a system whose values had been vindicated by socialist construction, the victory over fascism, and the USSR's status as a superpower.[135] These clashes soon spilled over into the tribunes of party conferences and Congresses of Peoples' Deputies.[136] Finally, amid demonstrations, social and political unrest, economic destabilization, and increasing self-assertion against the center by union republics (including Russia), supporters of the old notions of statehood tried to end the ferment with the attempted putsch of August 1991.[137] Their failure doomed Gorbachev's and, ultimately, the party's version of statehood.

THE NEW ACCOMMODATION: THE RUSSIAN STATE, ITS DOMESTIC SPHERE, AND FOREIGN POLICY SINCE 1996

Despite the turmoil, great expectations, and dashed hopes associated with the Yeltsin years, in retrospect they marked a period of transition between the late Soviet era and the relative stability of the Putin presidency. The virtual collapse of state power and the dramatic decline of Russia's international standing that characterized Yeltsin's first term as president gave way, after the presidential elections of 1996, to the coalescence of the presidential state that Putin inherited and Russia's reemergence as an important international power. Certainly, the new republic's foreign policy seemed to reflect the volatility of Russian domestic life. Both Yeltsin and Putin saw adjustments to the void left by the disappearance of a Soviet state that, whatever its undeniable vices, had provided a sort of stability to its subjects and the international order. Throughout much of the 1990s, politics in Russia revolved about the very bases of the new formation's statehood and, indeed, the nature and purposes of state power. The instability and social costs inflicted by market reform fragmented politics and society over the question of "whither Russia."[138] This volatility, which exploded in the violent conflict between the Yeltsin government and the Duma in 1993, was exacerbated by the mercurial personality of Yeltsin himself. Pervasive corruption, political infighting, and the rise of strong and autonomist governments in many of the federation's provinces all attested to the near collapse of the state as an administrative force.

Abroad, the turmoil of the 1990s accelerated Russia's decline as an arbiter of international affairs, even in Europe, in a rapidly changing environment whose dynamism itself sprang from the fact of the Soviet collapse. In need of Western capital to finance marketization, possessed of a dilapidated and demoralized military, and preoccupied with the task of state building amid domestic ferment, the new Russian state lacked the physical ability to act, even as it gained recognition as the successor to the USSR in international organizations and retained the trappings of nuclear power status inherited from the Soviet state. Still, the swiftly changing environment, particularly in Europe, challenged any claims to Russian greatness. Russian leaders endured criticism from their opponents for going cap in hand to the Western powers and banks for money. The same critics also deplored the Yeltsin administration's seeming acquiescence to a series of faits accomplis by the United States and its allies in areas where the Soviet Union had once played a determinative role: the post–Persian Gulf War Middle East; an Eastern Europe rapidly reorienting to NATO and the European Union; and the post-Yugoslav Balkans, where NATO and President Bill Clinton's administration acted with little regard for Russian concerns.[139]

The weight of domestic concerns burdened Russian foreign policy in two related fashions. Most obviously, the social and political turmoil of these years signaled the patent incapacity of the post-Soviet state to mobilize any meaningful response to the rapid crystallization of a "new world order." Much as during the years following defeat and revolution in 1905, the new Russian state simply could not respond to these alterations in the prior status quo. Also, as after 1905, the Yeltsin government had to define its domestic and foreign policies with an eye on a newly empowered civil society. In the strident debates over statehood, disagreements over Russia's international role and destiny took on an unusual asperity, largely for the sheer fact that they occurred in the public sphere, and electoral outcomes depended on them directly or indirectly.[140]

As in the "orientation" debates after 1905, the proponents of various positions drew strict links between Russia's role in the world and the future structure of the domestic realm, guided by their own theories of the laws of historical development and by their hopes for the shape the new Russia might take. The liberals who dominated the first Yeltsin government, including Foreign Minister Andrei Kozyrev, advocated close ties with the United States and European states to gain the financial aid that would promote a market economy and its inevitable concomitant, a law-governed constitutional democracy. On the other end of the spectrum, nationalists and Communists invoked peculiarly Russian heritages to urge the restoration of squandered glory through the resurrection of a powerful state at home and abroad.[141]

At the time, these debates appeared to gain some purchase on Russian foreign policy. This occurred through two conduits. First, in an environment of rough-and-ready electoral politics—punctuated by three legislative and two presidential elections—Yeltsin showed himself responsive to calls for an end to Russian acquiescence to Western (i.e., U.S.) encroachment in traditional areas of the state's interest. Certainly, such criticism seems to have played a part in his replacement of Kozyrev with Yevgeny Primakov in January 1996, during preparations for the impending presidential election.[142] The lack of appreciable Western economic aid also played a part. Earlier, the surprising success of Zhirinovsky in Duma elections sprang at least in part from his unabashed appeals to the restoration of Russian *derzhavnost*.

The appointment of Primakov, a onetime intelligence agent with expertise in the Middle East, indicated a shift toward a more centrist or pragmatic foreign policy, less automatically oriented toward good relations with the Western powers in favor of "multipolarity."[143] The Yeltsin government protested strongly Western initiatives in the Balkan wars of the 1990s, eventually gaining a role in the international peacekeeping forces. Likewise, it objected to the pace and process of NATO enlargement. Interestingly, these démarches, which led to little assertive action and, at best, to face-saving compromises, constituted only a faint echo of the actions one might have expected from the Soviet state of the Brezhnev years. Rather, as one scholar plausibly argues, Russian foreign policy seemed to emphasize the "primacy of participation over results."[144] Even so, these actions, in the context of the continuing turmoil in Russian economic and political life, provoked in a Western audience (itself seeking the seeds of Russia's future statehood) misgivings as to whether the process of democratization might not heighten the belligerence of such states, rather than encourage the pacific policies that traditionally prevail among liberal democratic states.[145]

The sheer disunity of Yeltsin's government provided the second conduit for the influence of domestic voices on foreign policy. In these circumstances, and given the weakness and volatility of the administration, a nearly unprecedented variety of views and prescriptions—tied to the visions of Russia's future development advanced by liberals, nationalists, and pragmatists alike—gained purchase in foreign policy deliberations. This occurrence, exacerbated by continuing domestic disarray, provides yet another explanation for the paralysis or reactive quality of Russian foreign policy during the first half of the 1990s. Although he traveled extensively—with often embarrassing consequences—and took a visible role as Russia's face abroad, Yeltsin showed little interest in the substance of foreign policy. His 1994 memoir, for instance, contains little mention of foreign policy beyond statements of his confidence in Kozyrev and his personal reflections on the various foreign leaders whose acquaintance he cultivated.[146] Yeltsin sought to impose some coordination of effort on Russian diplomacy through a presidential council devoted to foreign policy issues and by elaborating a foreign policy concept as a guiding document for policy makers.[147] If unity in decision making only began to develop after 1996, the 1992 concept did indicate an appreciation of the changed relationship between foreign and domestic spheres, when it identified the creation of a "dynamic" economy and the maintenance of the Russian Federation's territorial integrity as key tasks for the government's foreign policy.

Yeltsin's reelection as president in 1996 signaled a turning point in post-Soviet history and began the consolidation of a new Russian state. In retrospect, this election marked the final acceptance by Russian voters and politicians of a market economy—this, despite the real abuses that accompanied privatization and the economic crash of the late 1990s. In addition, by facing down repeated threats to his authority and developing at least routine relations with the legislature, Yeltsin helped to establish a widely accepted political playing field. To be sure, this new order foreclosed in many ways the democratic developmental option that many expected as a matter of course after August 1991. But, through presidential and Duma elections from 1996 through 2004, the "super-presidential" constitution withstood repeated challenges: for better or worse, by the turn of the millennium, a viable state had reemerged in Russia.[148] This state still faced many challenges, identified in numberless presidential speeches—among them, bureaucratic inertia, corruption, insubordination in the regions, and economic weakness. Nonetheless, the cohort that came to power with Putin inherited a network of institutions and a constitutional order that had successfully weathered nearly ten years of controversy and contestation.

Putin's accession to the presidency saw the Russian administration move aggressively to bring to heel the various constituencies that arose during the turmoil of the 1990s: the general electorate; educated society; and such new actors as the oligarchs, the regions, and the many ethnic and confessional minorities within the federation. From the very inception of his presidency, Putin has called for a strong state to manage Russia's continuing progress toward prosperity and civilization—echoing generations of Russian reformers. Thus, in an address to the Russian people published on December 30, 1999, the day before he succeeded Yeltsin, Putin laid out his vision of a Russian way to modernity, grounded in the country's historical traditions. This path included "a strong and effective state" alongside "personal and political freedom," a regime rooted in Russia's traditions and its present needs.[149] Rejecting factional "political squabbling," Putin referred to the desire of the "bulk of Russians" for stability, peace, and Russian greatness, aspirations grounded in their embrace of "supra-national universal values that are above social, group, or ethnic interests."[150]

CONCLUSION

When viewed through the prism of *doux commerce*, Putin's presidency has tried to accommodate contradictory imperatives.[151] Despite his emphasis on building a strong civil society, a market economy, and democratic values, his acts suggest the restoration of an authoritarian state.[152] His government has gained control over much of the electronic media, once the property of such entrepreneurs as Boris Berezovsky and Vladimir Gusinsky. While honoring the principle of popular elections, his government has also used the state's power and influence to gain desired results. The arrest of Mikhail Khodorkovsky at the end of 2003 and the subsequent turmoil in Russia's resource industries sent powerful signals to those in the private sector that they will come to grief if they seek to use their wealth for political ends properly reserved to the state's purview. And, through the centralization associated with the policy of the "power vertical," the Putin administration has resurrected the state as the decisive player in Russian politics, against local cliques as well as the Duma and opinion makers.

Yet, when seen in the context of the statehood or post-absolutist discourse, the tensions between the assertion of high-handed state prerogative and gestures toward democratic values or civil society become, at the very least, more comprehensible. Like Stolypin, Putin made a strong state and order the watchwords of his administration,[153] voicing priorities shared even by liberals seeking a truly democratic rule-of-law political order.[154] Putin's perspective distinguishes between the form of the state as a certain type of actor in domestic and international politics, on one hand, and the ideological content with which this form is invested—for example, totalitarianism—on the other. Putin's electoral successes suggest that the Russian population largely endorses his view of the state's role, his confrontation with the oligarchs, and his public resolve in the war against terrorism. After fifteen years of political tumult, economic chaos, palpable decline, and uncertain prospects, the promises of order and national renewal cannot help but gain support.

Regarded in historical context, Putin's state has honored the strategies of national statehood traditions. He has made the state a dominant player in Russian domestic life, managing from "above" relationships with particular constituencies, encouraging—by its lights—processes for the generation of wealth, welfare, prosperity, and the inculcation of civic values, all matters of state interest to this view.[155] In this regard, Putin can be seen as continuing and completing in different historical circumstances the program that inspired Stolypin before he fell victim to Nicholas II's resentment and an assassin's bullet in 1911: the use of state power to impose order on a fractured society; the creation of a partnership—albeit hierarchical—with a loyal, patriotic citizenry; and the encouragement of a vibrant economy as the necessary conditions for Russia to "speak in its former voice" in international affairs.[156]

What are the implications of this new domestic conjuncture for the course of Russian foreign policy in the next decade? In some ways, Putin has proven "fate's darling," to cite a description of Stolypin.[157] The consolidation of the post–Cold War European order under expanded NATO and EU structures had largely taken hold before his presidency, a consequence of Soviet collapse. He also took over a Russia that had recovered from the economic travails of the late 1990s, while enjoying the fiscal and political benefits of rising oil prices after 2001.

Similarly, Putin's rise to the presidency coincided with changes in international affairs that afforded Russian diplomacy the opportunity to stake out the independent course he has advocated in his declarations on foreign policy. Although the United States continued to dominate the international order as the sole surviving superpower, alternative poles of economic and political power began to emerge in China and Europe, as became clear in the challenges posed by North Korea's development of nuclear weapons and, more concretely, in controversies between the United States and "old Europe" over trade and subsidies, but most acutely in the lead-up to the U.S.-led invasion of Saddam Hussein's Iraq in 2003.

Most important, according to Putin, domestic stability and economic well-being have entered a new phase, exiting the preceding periods of chaos and uncertainty. This new phase will allow Russia to be independent in world affairs, while enabling the leadership to develop policies looking ahead for a decade or more.[158] Commenting on the country's stabilization in 2003, he stated, "I think that our ultimate goal should be to return Russia to its place among the prosperous, developed, strong, and respected nations," thus linking the two projects of domestic renewal and regaining great-power status abroad. In support of the latter goal, Putin advocated that the government help to strengthen international economic and political organizations, continue as a partner in the struggle with terrorism, deepen ties with Europe, and revitalize Russia's ailing armed forces.[159]

In comparison with the Yeltsin years, Russian foreign policy reflects the stabilization and economic growth that marked the transition to the Putin administration. As the embodiment of a new Russia, Putin has earned respect through participation in such bodies as the Group of Eight; in 2002 he fostered a new framework for relations with NATO, ending for the time being the tensions remaining from reactions to the Western alliance's campaign against Serbia in 1999; he continues to seek Russian membership in the World Trade Organization; and he states repeatedly Russia's civilizational and economic belonging in Europe.[160]

As a diplomatic persona, Putin exudes an authority that commands a respect not enjoyed by his predecessor since 1991, to judge from George W. Bush's insight into his soul or the impressive international turnout at the tercentenary celebrations for his birthplace, St. Petersburg, in 2003. On an institutional level, the high turnover in executive and ministerial offices that typified the Yeltsin administration has given way to more stability, with regard to both personnel and institutional structures. Once a blend of Yeltsinites and Putinites (themselves divided by economic liberals and *siloviki* [strongmen]), the higher decision-making bodies, such as the Security Council, are composed of Putin appointees.[161]

At the same time, the confidence inspired by renewed domestic stability and the reestablishment of state authority has also found reflection in a more independent or assertive defense of Russian interests. The government's pursuit of the second Chechen war over criticism from the West offers one instance. Other examples include ongoing resource and military technology sales to China; relations with Iran, Cuba, and North Korea; and, in a more unfortunate line, the misbegotten saber rattling that marked the Russian government's initial reaction to the Orange Revolution in Ukraine in late 2004. Still, Moscow's belated or grudging acquiescence to President Viktor Yushchenko's victory, abetted by support from Washington and Europe, attests to the relative priority the Putin administration places on partnership and cooperation with the Western allies. The same applies to his agreement to the stationing of U.S. forces in Central Asia.

In historical context, much of the current situation suggests the possibility for future Russian states to follow the pattern that marked previous eras of domestic reconstruction in pursuit of greatness. In the cliché long associated with "realism," these projects have sought through domestic reconstruction to restore the state's ability to behave like the realists' "billiard ball" in international affairs, as it had in the times before reform became urgently necessary (e.g., during the Nicholas I era or the Brezhnev years). Certainly, the processes of recentralization, concentration, and increasing assertiveness against the oligarchs and the media would argue for the prospects of a reassertion of this tradition of Russian *gosudarstvennost,* to be accompanied by the assertion of *derzhavnost* abroad.

Yet, to judge from Putin's statements and from the ways in which his administration has engaged with the new world order, the present moment is also pregnant with potential for a departure from older Russian tradition. The ongoing program to enhance Russia's economic competitiveness—in resources, but also in civilian and military technologies—suggests that future Russian governments will pursue a policy characterized by much greater complexity and fluidity than found in the Hobbesian and geopolitical worldview of their Soviet and imperial predecessors. At the same time, the conceptualization of Russia's relations with the global economy contained in policy documents suggests a much more dynamic interaction between the domestic sphere, the state, and the international order than that of the Soviet or imperial eras. Thus, the Russian government seeks closer ties with the West—Europe and the United States—to encourage further development of Russian domestic prosperity, as well as the federation's ability to compete with its partners in export markets.[162] These economic relationships offer two benefits. First, increasing domestic wealth and its spin-offs for the development of intellectual capital in Russia can provide new resources and power for the state as an international player. Second, at the same time, the global economy offers a new sphere of operations for Russian foreign policy, in which it can reinforce—through the leverage afforded by its assets in natural resources, armaments, and, eventually, technology—the multilateralist thrust that now informs Russia's conventional diplomacy.

The years since the collapse of the Soviet Union have witnessed a drastic recasting not only of that state's domestic arrangements and international standing, but also of the interrelationship between the two. The acknowledgment by Russian leaders that the state's power as an international actor derives from a domestic sphere conceived in terms of economic development and "managed" popular support represents an almost unprecedented acknowledgment of the interrelation between both spheres as a basis for the conduct of the state's foreign policy. Having reestablished order and stable relationships with the legislative branch and civil society, the new Russian state has also restored its position as an agent able to mobilize the necessary resources—and public support—for the pursuit of the greatness that has long stood at the center of the Russian statehood discourse.

Whatever the shifting complexions that have characterized successive regimes in post-Soviet Russia, each has publicly asserted Russia's great-power status as a primary attribute of the federation's statehood and its foreign policy. These statements reflect the traditions of statehood rhetoric and form an important source of legitimation for any Russian government. Russian protection of the state's territorial integrity in Chechnya and Kaliningrad, despite the high human and diplomatic costs, has illustrated the state's willingness to undertake sacrifices in defense of fundamental strategic and security claims.

The question that remains is, will this new statehood persist beyond the Putin presidency, given the volatility of the new world order and the resource economy, Russia's own partial progress toward a market economy, persisting challenges in the creation of a professional administration, and the uncertainty that stalks the constitution and general question of the rule of law? Conceivably, under certain adverse circumstances, Russians could elect a president who espouses the achievement of Russian greatness through reversion to command-administrative means along the Soviet model and an aggressive assertion of Russian power abroad. Such an outcome seems unlikely. Russian voters have repeatedly rejected that option. Moreover, given the new emphasis on economic development that has driven Russian domestic and foreign policies since the early 1990s and the reestablishment of the state as director and agent of reconstruction, it appears more likely that the managerial model embodied by Putin—sober, professional, and "serious," to use the Russian locution—will prevail. Should this be the case, historians, political scientists, and national leaders in the West will face a state and society that combine both continuity and change: Continuity will appear in the persistence of a powerful, managerial state, acting with relative autonomy at home and abroad; yet, this state will frame policies in both spheres in the context of a much more nuanced understanding of power as the product of a healthy economy and a supportive electorate.

Whether guided by the *doux commerce* perspective or the Marxist inversion of the same historical narrative, observers of contemporary Russia confront paradoxes undreamt of in their philosophies, most notably an assertive or "managerial" state using the operations of a market economy as a source of its power. Witte's vision of industrialization under an absolutist state order and the career of Wilhelmine Germany both suggest at least the possibility of reconciling economic modernization with a strong and directing state authority. Modern China and, in a softer fashion, Singapore offer similar examples in the contemporary world.

As Russian leaders have stated repeatedly, they seek a stable, prosperous society at home and an independent Russia abroad, able to pursue its economic and political interests as a leading power in a multilateral international environment. At the very least, the new emphasis on the domestic benefits of economic development and the recognition of the interdependence arising from the global economy promise a softer competitor than the old Soviet state; but the pursuit of these benefits and the restoration of a great Russia promise that Russia will be a competitor nevertheless. The greatest challenge facing Western analysts and policy makers in dealing with this new Russia is to view this country on its own terms and those of a surviving absolutist tradition, rather than through the norms dictated by the *doux commerce* tradition.

NOTES

1. For the most thorough and critical view of the Putin presidency, see Lilia Shevtsova, *Putin's Russia,* trans. Antonina W. Bouis, 2d ed. (Washington, DC: Carnegie Endowment for International Peace, 2005). Wherever possible, citations refer to English-language materials for the convenience of nonspecialists. For a contrary, but persuasive, view, see Richard Sakwa, *Putin: Russia's Choice* (New York: Routledge, 2004).

2. See Putin's remarks on this process and Russia's new stability in his message (*poslanie*) to the Russian Federal Assembly, May 26, 2004, *President of Russia,* http://www.president.kremlin.ru/sdocs/appears.shtml?value_from=/includes/appears/2004/05/26&value_to=/includes/appears/2004/05/27.

3. See *Nezavisimaya gazeta, Kommersant,* or the Web site of "Polit.ru," http://www.polit.ru for documents dated November and December 2004. Notably, however, the publication of a photograph depicting victims of the Beslan raid led to the dismissal, under government pressure, of *Izvestiya's* editor.

4. See, for example, his "introductory remarks" to the Fourteenth Congress of Russian Industrialists and Entrepreneurs, November 16, 2004, on the presidential Web site, President of Russia, http://www.kremlin.ru/eng/speeches/2004/11/16/2045_type82912type82913_79525.shtml.

5. One need only recall the president's own metabolic misadventures in Germany and Ireland in 1994. In the former, he conducted a brass band at an official luncheon;

in the latter, he proved unable to leave his airplane for a scheduled meeting with the Irish premier. Similarly, in late 1992 then Foreign Minister Andrei Kozyrev delivered a strongly anti-NATO speech at a meeting of the Council of Security and Cooperation in Europe, which he subsequently explained was a joke meant to demonstrate how much Russian policy had changed since the mid-1980s. In March 1999 a later foreign minister, Yevgeny Primakov, ordered the airplane flying him to Washington for talks to perform a dramatic U-turn as a protest against the initiation of NATO's aerial campaign against Serbia. Bobo Lo, *Russian Foreign Policy in the Post-Soviet Era: Reality, Illusion, and Mythmaking* (New York: Palgrave, 2002); Andrei Kozyrev, *Preobrazhenie* (Moscow: Mezhdunarodnye otnoshennia, 1994), p. 506; and Craig R. Whitney, "Cold War Words Jolt the West," *New York Times*, December 15, 1992. On Primakov, see John Broder, "A Phone Call from Gore and a U-turn to Moscow," *New York Times*, March 24, 1999.

6. President Vladimir Putin, "Annual Address to the Federal Assembly," April 25, 2005, President of Russia Web site, http://www.president.kremlin.ru/sdocs/appears. shtml?value_from=/includes/appears/2005/04/25&value_to=/includes/appears/2005/04/27.

7. Dmitrii Polikanov and Graham Timmins, "Russian Foreign Policy Under Putin," in *Russian Politics Under Putin*, ed. Cameron Ross (New York: Manchester University Press, 2004), pp. 223–235.

8. For the official presentation of this agreement, see *NATO*, http://www.nato.int/docu/comm/2002/0205-rome/rome-eng.pdf.

9. Frank Bruni, "Leaders' Words at First Meeting Are Striking for Warm Tone," *New York Times*, June 17, 2001.

10. Michael McFaul, "Lessons from Russia's Protracted Transition from Communist Rule," *Political Science Quarterly* 114, no. 1 (Spring 1999): 111.

11. The appeal to "Russian traditions" forms a motif in Putin's speeches, particularly to the legislative bodies. In the first section of his memoir, Andrei Kozyrev cites in turn the classic Russian historians Vasily Kliuchevsky and Pavel Miliukov, in addition to the Russian émigré religious thinkers Pavel Florensky and Nikolai Berdyaev.

12. For the classic example from the height of the Cold War, see Ivo Lederer, ed., *Russian Foreign Policy: Essays in Historical Perspective* (New Haven: Yale University Press, 1962). See also Theodore von Laue, *Why Lenin? Why Stalin? Why Gorbachev? The Rise and Fall of the Soviet System* (New York: HarperCollins, 1993); Marshall Poe, *The Russian Moment in World History* (Princeton: Princeton University Press, 2003); and, in an idealist vein, Nikolai Berdyaev, *The Russian Idea* (New York: Macmillan, 1947).

13. Neil Malcolm, Alex Pravda, Roy Allison, and Margot Light, eds., *Internal Factors in Russian Foreign Policy* (Oxford: Oxford University Press, 1996); Michael McFaul, *Russia's Unfinished Revolution: Political Change from Gorbachev to Putin* (Ithaca: Cornell University Press, 2001); Kozyrev, *Preobrazhenie*; Lo, *Russian Foreign Policy*, chap. 3; and Alla Kassyanova, "Russia Still Open to the West? The Evolution of the

State Identity in Foreign Policy and Security Discourse," *Europe-Asia Studies* 53, no. 6 (September 2001): 821–839.

14. Malcolm, Pravda, Allison, and Light, *Internal Factors,* chap. 2. A good selection also appears in T. A. Shakleina, *Vneshnyaya politika i bezopasnost sovremennoi Rossii, 1991–2002,* vol. 1 (Moscow: ROSSPEN, 2002).

15. "The Foreign Policy Concept of the Russian Federation, Approved by the President of the Russian Federation, V. Putin, June 28, 2000," *Federation of American Scientists,* http://www.fas.org/nuke/guide/russia/doctrine/econcept.htm. The Russian original is in *Vneshnyaya politika i bezopasnost sovremennoi Rossii, 1991–2002 v 4-kh tomakh,* vol. 4 (Moscow: ROSSPEN, 2002), pp. 109–121.

16. Marc Raeff, *Michael Speransky: Statesman of Imperial Russia, 1772–1838* (The Hague: Martinus Nijhoff, 1969). Raeff's student W. Bruce Lincoln made this concept the centerpiece of his many works on the nineteenth- and early-twentieth-century autocracy.

17. For a clear statement of this view, see, for example, the "Instruction" (*Nakaz*) addressed by Catherine for the future members of her commission to revise the empire's law code, particularly chapter 2, in Paul Dukes, ed., *Russia Under Catherine the Great,* vol. 2 (Newtonville, MA: Oriental Research Partners, 1978), p. 44.

18. For a concise statement of a theory he iterated several times, see Alexander Gerschenkron, "Russia: Agrarian Policies and Modernization: 1861–1917," in *Continuity in History and Other Essays* (Cambridge: Harvard University Press, 1968), pp. 142–143. Although economists have refuted many of his other theories, "substitution" seems an image well suited to Russia and itself an intellectual outgrowth of the state school.

19. McFaul, *Russia's Unfinished Revolution.*

20. Given its focus on the connections between foreign and domestic policies, this discussion also downplays both the social grounding of Russian states and the undeniable disparity between claims to agency and a real world in which the efficacy of state power was attenuated by distance, inefficiency, corruption, or lack of resources.

21. See Putin's address to the Federal Assembly of the Federation, May 26, 2003, President of Russia Web site, http://www.president.kremlin.ru/eng/sdocs/speeches.shtml?type=70029.

22. N. M. Karamzin, *Istoriya gosudarstva rossiiskogo,* published serially beginning in 1818. S. M. Solovev, *Istoriya Rossii s drevneishikh vremen,* 2d ed., 29 vols. (St. Petersburg: Obshchestvennaya polza, n.d.), available in English as Hugh Graham, trans. and ed., *History of Russia* (Gulf Breeze, FL: Academic International Press, 1976). For a synopsis of his arguments, see N. M. Karamzin, "Memoir on Old and New Russia," trans. with an analysis by Richard Pipes (Cambridge: Harvard University Press, 1959).

23. For the best example of this approach, see Dietrich Geyer, *Russian Imperialism: The Interaction of Foreign and Domestic Policy, 1860–1914,* trans. Bruce Little

(Leamington Spa, NY: Berg, 1987), first published in German in 1977. In Russian, see I. V. Bestuzhev, *Borba po voprosam vneshnei politiki v Rossii, 1906–1914gg* (Moscow: Nauka, 1961); and V. A. Emets, ed., *Istoriya vneshnei politiki Rossii. Konets XIX-nachalo XX veka* (Moscow: Mezhdunarodnye otnosheniia, 1997). The American historian Adam Ulam espoused a non-Marxist version of this interpretation, arguing that an assertive foreign policy helped legitimate the Soviet regime to its domestic population. See, for example, Ulam, *Expansion and Coexistence: Soviet Foreign Policy, 1917–1973* (New York: Praeger, 1974).

24. See, for example, Jack Snyder, *Myths of Empire: Domestic Politics and International Ambition* (Ithaca: Cornell University Press, 1991).

25. Sarah Mendelson gives a strong demonstration of this theory in "Internal Battles and External Wars: Politics, Learning, and the Soviet Withdrawal from Afghanistan," *World Politics* 45, no. 3 (April 1993): 327–360. See also Matthew Evangelista, "The Paradox of State Strength: Transnational Relations, Domestic Structures, and Security Policy in Russia and the Soviet Union," *International Organization* 49, no. 1 (Winter 1995): 1–38. In a related vein, see Jeffrey Checkel, "Ideas, Institutions, and the Gorbachev Foreign Policy Revolution," *World Politics* 45, no. 2 (January 1993): 271–300. For an allied approach, see Ted Hopf, "The Promise of Constructivism in International Relations Theory," *International Security* 23, no. 1 (Summer 1998): 171–200.

26. For the Yeltsin years, Bobo Lo takes public opinion seriously as a determinant of foreign policy. See Lo, *Russian Foreign Policy*, pp. 27–29. He also cites *Pravda*'s work in this connection.

27. Mendelson's discussion of the Soviet withdrawal from Afghanistan offers an excellent example of the ways in which leadership change in the mid-1980s led to the adoption by the Gorbachev leadership of recommendations long proposed by Soviet experts who had gone unheard by the Brezhnev–Konstantin Chernenko regime. Jeremi Suri makes related arguments from the viewpoint of a historian of international relations in his survey article "Explaining the End of the Cold War: A New Historical Consensus?" *Journal of Cold War Studies* 4, no. 4 (Fall 2002): 60–92. Similar, equally dramatic shifts occurred during the tsarist era—also characterized by centralization, powerful personalities, and ideologically heterogeneous official and semiofficial elites who gained or lost authority and support for their proposals with shifting imperial favor or "confidence." N. G. O. Pereira, "Alexander II and the Decision to Emancipate," *Canadian Slavonic Papers* 12, no. 1 (1980): 99–115; W. Bruce Lincoln, *The Great Reforms: Autocracy, Bureaucracy, and the Politics of Change in Imperial Russia* (DeKalb: Northern Illinois University Press, 1990); and Ben Eklof, John Bushnell, and Larissa Zakharov, eds., *Russia's Great Reforms, 1855–1881* (Bloomington: Indiana University Press, 1994).

28. Michael Ellman and Vladimir Kontorovich, "The Collapse of the Soviet System and the Memoir Literature," *Europe-Asia Studies* 49, no. 2 (March 1997): 260–261. The future reformers claim to have appreciated these problems acutely: M. S. Gorbachev, *Memoirs* (New York: Doubleday, 1995), pp. 93, 114, 117; and Yegor Ligachev,

Inside Gorbachev's Kremlin: The Memoirs of Yegor Ligachev, trans. Catherine A. Fitzpatrick, Michele A. Berdy, and Dobrochna Dyrcz-Freeman, with an introduction by Stephen F. Cohen (New York: Pantheon, 1993), pp. 14–17.

29. M. S. Gorbachev, *Zhizn i reformy*, 2 vols. (Moscow: Novosti, 1995), p. 269; and Mendelson, "Internal Battles and External Wars," p. 352.

30. W. Bruce Lincoln, *Nikolai Miliutin: An Enlightened Russian Bureaucrat* (Newtonville, MA: Oriental Research Partners, 1977).

31. Michael Hughes, *Diplomacy Before the Russian Revolution: Russia, Britain, and the Old Diplomacy, 1894–1917* (Basingstoke: St. Martin's Press, 2000), pp. 124–139; and Dominic Lieven, *Russia and the Origins of the First World War* (New York: St. Martin's Press, 1983), pp. 84–101.

32. See the memoirs of S. D. Sazonov, A. P. Izvolsky, and N. V. Charykov, among others, for descriptions of career paths that unfolded entirely within the Ministry of Foreign Affairs—in contrast to the professional experiences described by V. N. Kokovtsov or S. Iu. Witte, who served in a variety of institutions. Sazonov, *Fateful Years, 1909–1916: The Reminiscences of Serge Sazonov* (London: Cape, 1928); Izvolsky, *The Memoirs of Alexander Iswolsky, Formerly Russian Minister of Foreign Affairs and Ambassador to France*, trans. and ed. Charles Louis Seeger (London: Hutchinson, 1920); Charykov, *Glimpses of High Politics: Through War and Peace, 1855–1929* (London: Allen and Unwin, 1931); Kokovtsov, *Out of My Past: The Memoirs of Count Kokovtsov*, trans. Laura Matveev, ed. H. H. Fisher (Stanford: Stanford University Press, 1935); and Witte, *The Memoirs of Count Witte*, trans. and ed. Sidney Harcave (Armonk, NY: Sharpe, 1990). A similar specialization seems to have operated in the Soviet period. See Anatoly Dobrynin, *In Confidence: Moscow's Ambassador to America's Six Cold War Presidents (1962–1986)* (New York: Random House, 1995), particularly his discussion of his own career and that of long-time Soviet foreign minister Andrei Gromyko. Under Nicholas II especially, the ruler consulted special conferences (*osobye soveshchaniya*), bringing together representatives of several interested ministries to discuss foreign policy questions, among others. But these meetings were, by their very definition, "special" and did not change the prevailing institutional division of labor.

33. Hughes, *Diplomacy Before the Russian Revolution*, pp. 3–19.

34. For an English translation of the revised Fundamental Laws, see Marc Szeftel, *The Russian Constitution of April 23, 1906: Political Institutions of the Duma Monarchy* (Brussels: Librairie Encyclopédique, 1976), pp. 84–109. For articles on "excluded" ministries, see ibid., pp. 85–86.

35. Gorbachev, *Memoirs*, p. 160; Gorbachev, *Zhizn i reformy*, vol. 1, p. 266; and Mendelson, "Internal Battles and External Wars," p. 357.

36. In a plausible discussion, Gerschenkron sees this pattern extending back to Muscovite times.

37. O. Kharkhordin has written a helpful *Begriffsgeschichte* of the "state" as a concept in Russia. See Kharkhordin, "What Is the State? The Russian Concept of *Gosudarstvo* in European Context," *History and Theory* 40, no. 2 (May 2001): 206–240.

38. Alla Kassianova addresses a similar problem in examining discussions of identity, in Kassianova, "Russia: Still Open to the West? Evolution of the State Identity in the Foreign Policy and Security Discourse," *Europe-Asia Studies* 53, no. 6 (2001): 821–839.

39. This intellectual tradition is closely associated with the Scottish Enlightenment of the eighteenth century. For an introduction to these debates and the relationship between trade, cultivation, and virtue, see Istvan Hont and Michael Ignatieff, eds., *Wealth and Virtue: The Shaping of Political Economy in the Scottish Enlightenment* (New York: Cambridge University Press, 1983); Laurence Dickey, "Doux-commerce and Humanitarian Values: Free Trade, Sociability, and Universal Benevolence in Eighteenth-Century Thinking," *Grotiana* 22–23 (2001–2002): 271–318; and the more popularly pitched discussion by Arthur Herman, *How the Scots Invented the Modern World* (New York: Three Rivers Press, 2001).

40. See Laurence Dickey's appendices cum commentaries in his edited abridgement of *Wealth of Nations* (Indianapolis: Hackett, 1993), pp. 213–259.

41. Thomas Hobbes, "The Introduction," *Leviathan*, ed. C. B. MacPherson (Markham, Ontario: Penguin, 1983), p. 81. Marc Raeff offers an excellent discussion and analysis of the intellectual genealogy of absolutism and *Polizeiwissenschaft*, the term used to refer to the science of administration. Raeff, *The Well-Ordered Police State: Social and Institutional Change Through Law in the Germanies and Russia, 1600–1800* (New Haven: Yale University Press, 1983), part 1. For brevity's sake, "absolutism" occurs as shorthand to describe the variant referred to generally as "bureaucratic absolutism" to underscore the partnership that evolved between royal/autocratic rulers and their cadre of professional administrators. As Donald Ostrowski rightly notes, Raeff was also one of the first to emphasize this variant as a hallmark of absolutism in Russia in his political biography of Mikhail Speransky. See Ostrowski, "The Façade of Legitimacy: Exchange of Power and Authority in Early Modern Russia," *Comparative Studies in Society and History* 44, no. 3 (July 2002): 560n105.

42. Ibid.

43. Indeed, as Raeff notes in the third part of *Well-Ordered Police State*, a distinguishing—and ironic—attribute of absolutism's history in Russia consisted in the necessity for Catherine II to use law to create and give institutional form to social estates in Russia.

44. Voltaire, *Histoire de Russie sous Pierre le Grand* (1761); see also Catherine II's *Nakaz*, chap. 1, art. 7, in Dukes, *Russia Under Catherine the Great*, vol. 2. Catherine II provided the frankest and clearest statement of these purposes in the preface and first six chapters of her *Nakaz* (instruction) to the representative commission she convened to revise the law code in 1767. The *Nakaz* has been published in various editions and translations since the empress first published it.

45. Cynthia H. Whittaker, "The Reforming Tsar: The Redefinition of Autocratic Duty in Eighteenth-Century Russia," *Slavic Review* 51, no. 1 (Spring 1992): 77–98.

46. Theodore von Laue, *Sergei Witte and the Industrialization of Russia* (New York: Columbia University Press, 1963).

47. For a fuller discussion in a theoretical vein, see Alexander Gerschenkron, *Economic Backwardness in Historical Perspective* (Cambridge: Harvard University Press, 1962), chaps. 2, 6.

48. Cf. discussion of Romanov installation in N. M. Karamzin, *Memoir on Ancient and Modern Russia*, trans. and ed. Richard Pipes (New York: Atheneum, 1966).

49. Catherine II's *Nakaz* discusses at great length the relationships between and the duties of Russia's constituent social group, most specifically in chapters 15 and 16 (see Dukes, *Russia Under Catherine the Great*, vol. 2). See also Raeff's discussion of Catherine's "Statute on Good Conduct" (*Ustav blagochiniya*) from 1782, which sought to regulate dress, hygiene, and social mores. Raeff, *Well-Ordered Police State*, p. 243. On Russian legal traditions, see N. M. Korkunov, *General Theory of Law*, trans. W. G. Hastings (Boston: Boston Book, 1909); and Richard Wortman, *The Development of a Russian Legal Consciousness* (Chicago: University of Chicago Press, 1976).

50. Lincoln, *The Great Reforms;* and F. W. Wcislo, *Reforming Rural Russia: State, Local Society, and National Politics, 1855–1914* (Princeton: Princeton University Press, 1990).

51. Thus, the minutes of the Central Committee meeting that appointed Gorbachev as general secretary in 1985 declared that "the party is that force that can unify society, and propel it [*podniat*] to the enormous changes that are simply necessary." Cited in Gorbachev, *Zhizn i reformy*, vol. 1, p. 271.

52. V. V. Putin, "Rossya na rubezhe tysiacheletii," in *Vneshnyaya politika i bezopasnost*, vol. 1, pp. 25–26. Richard Sakwa translated the speech and included it as an appendix in *Putin*, pp. 251–262. Translations in this text are mine.

53. Lindsey Hughes, *Russya in the Age of Peter the Great* (New Haven: Yale University Press, 1998); Paul Bushkovitch, *Peter the Great: The Struggle for Power, 1671–1725* (New York: Cambridge University Press, 2001); and James Cracraft, *The Church Reform of Peter the Great* (London: Macmillan, 1971).

54. The state's autonomy from and even juxtaposition against the population found reflection in the first generations of Russian historiography (e.g., Karamzin's popular *History of the Russian State*), but, more important, in the establishment of the "state school" in the 1840s. The latter proceeded from the premise that the vast expanses of Russia's geography, its vulnerability to invasion, and the area's sparse and scattered population all required the state to act as organizer, mobilizer, defender, and surrogate of a national development that had occurred more "naturally" elsewhere. One could well argue that this interpretation of Russian history anticipated in important ways Gerschenkron's theory of substitution. Cf. Gerschenkron, *Economic Backwardness in Historical Perspective*, chap. 1. Interestingly, in chapter 2 of *Nakaz*, Catherine argued that Russia's sheer physical extent required an "absolute" sovereign to maintain its integrity. In the *Social Contract*, Jean-Jacques Rousseau made a similar argument. Both echo a commonplace in European political thought.

55. P. A. Zaionchkovskii, *Pravitelstvennyi apparat samoderzhavnoi Rossii v XIXv* (Moscow: Mysl, 1978); Walter M. Pintner, "The Evolution of Civil Officialdom, 1755–1855," in *Russian Officialdom: The Bureaucratization of Russian Society from the Seventeenth to the Twentieth Century,* by Walter M. Pintner and Donald K. Rowney (Chapel Hill: University of North Carolina Press, 1980), pp. 190–226.

56. V. I. Lenin, *What Is to Be Done?* rev. ed., trans. J. Fineberg and G. Hanna (London: Penguin, 1988), especially pp. 89–92, chap. 2.

57. For an exhaustive examination, see Elena Osokina, *Our Daily Bread: Socialist Distribution and the Art of Survival in Stalinist Russia, 1927–1941,* trans. K. Transchel and G. Bucher (Armonk, NY: Sharpe, 2001).

58. Ligachev, *Inside Gorbachev's Kremlin,* pp. 79–80. In the Russian-language edition, Ligachev uses the terms *vneshnii* and *vnutrennii* to distinguish the two spheres—in Russian, these terms are used to connote, respectively, foreign and domestic politics. Ligachev, *Zagadka Gorbacheva* (Novosibirsk: Interbuk, 1992).

59. Vladimir Putin, "Annual Address to the Federal Assembly," April 25, 2005, President of Russia Web site, passage beginning "First, about the state" in the English-language text, http://www.president.kremlin.ru/eng/sdocs/speeches.shtml?type=70029.

60. P. Ia. Chaadaev's first "Philosophical Letter" stated this relationship most bluntly. For a translation, see James M. Edie, James P. Scanlan, and Mary-Barbara Zeldin, eds., with the collaboration of George L. Kline, *Russian Philosophy,* vol. 1 (Knoxville: University of Tennessee Press, 1984), pp. 106–125. The most dense and evocative articulation of this view occurs in Alexander Herzen's memoir, *Byloe i Dumy,* discussing the origins of the Russian intelligentsia among the "boys" of the 1830s. For a good translation, see "Young Moscow," in *Readings in Russian Civilization,* vol. 2, ed. Thomas Riha (Chicago: University of Chicago Press, 1969), pp. 321–331.

61. P. N. Miliukov, *Russia and Its Crisis* (Chicago: University of Chicago Press, 1905). V. A. Maklakov expresses the division explicitly in his memoir entitled *Vlast i obshchestvennost* (Paris: n.p., 1936). Until 1911, Octobrists and "moderate Rights" constituted a partial exception.

62. L. D. Trotsky, *The Revolution Betrayed: What Is the Soviet Union and Where Is It Going?* (Garden City, NY: Doubleday, Doran, 1937); and Milovan Djilas, *The New Class: An Analysis of the Soviet System* (New York: Praeger, 1957).

63. W. Bruce Lincoln, *Nicholas I: Emperor and Autocrat of All the Russias* (Bloomington: Indiana University Press, 1978), pp. 187–188. This tension forms the central theme of A. E. Presnyakov, *Emperor Nicholas I of Russia: The Apogee of Autocracy, 1825–1855,* trans. and ed. Judith Zacek (Gulf Breeze, FL: Academic International Press, 1974).

64. This forms a central argument of Daniel Field, *The End of Serfdom: Nobility and Bureaucracy in Russia, 1855–1861* (Cambridge: Harvard University Press, 1976).

65. Wcislo, *Reforming Rural Russia,* chaps. 2, 3.

66. Interestingly, such a reading of events can be found in Gorbachev, *Memoirs*, pp. 80, 138. Ligachev's memories coincide in their critique but differ in their depiction of the timing. *Inside Gorbachev's Kremlin*, p. 14.

67. This conflict forms an entire genre in a tragically rich memoir literature, from Alexander Herzen's *My Past and Thoughts* through those of the surviving "dissidents" of the Soviet era. Herzen, *My Past and Thoughts: The Memoirs of Alexander Herzen*, trans. Constance Garnett, 6 vols. (London: Chatto and Windus, 1924–1927). Douglas Weiner, Loren Graham, and other historians of Soviet science have written extensively on this theme.

68. N. M. Karamzin articulated the most prevalent argument during the prereform era in *Memoir on Ancient and Modern Russia*, pp. 162–167.

69. Wcislo, *Reforming Rural Russia*, chap. 3. Yanni Kotsonis documents a similar view among liberal and reforming nonstate elites in *Making Peasants Backward: Agricultural Cooperatives and the Agrarian Question in Russia, 1861–1914* (New York: St. Martin's Press, 1999).

70. Gerschenkron cites Nicholas I's finance minister, E. Kankrin, who regarded railroads as the "malady of our age" for their encouragement of mobility and egalitarianism. Gerschenkron, "Russia: Agrarian Policies and Industrialization, 1861–1917," *Continuity in History and Other Essays* (Cambridge: Harvard University Press, 1968), p. 145; and K. P. Pobedonostsev, *Reflections of a Russian Statesman* (Ann Arbor: University of Michigan Press, 1965), pp. 75–84.

71. Peter Holquist, *Making War, Forging Revolution: Russia's Continuum of Crisis, 1914–1921* (Cambridge: Harvard University Press, 2002).

72. Osokina, *Our Daily Bread*.

73. For one approach to the genealogy of such a nationalism, see Liah Greenfeld, *Nationalism: Five Roads to Modernity* (Cambridge: Harvard University Press, 1992). On the problems presented by Russian nationalism, as well as its uses by Russian and Soviet leaders, see Theodore R. Weeks, *Nation and State in Late Imperial Russia: Nationalism and Russification on the Western Frontier, 1863–1914* (DeKalb: Northern Illinois University Press, 1996); and John B. Dunlop, *The New Russian Nationalism* (New York: Praeger, 1985). For an overview of the growing literature on the topic, see David Rowley, "Russian Nationalism and the Cold War," *American Historical Review* 99, no. 1 (February 1994): 155–171; and Yitzhak Brudny, *Reinventing Russia: Russian Nationalism and the Soviet State, 1953–1991* (Cambridge: Harvard University Press, 1998).

74. See Uvarov's justification of the doctrine as a defense against "destructive ideas" in Nicholas Riasanovsky, *Nicholas I and Official Nationality in Russia, 1825–1855* (Berkeley: University of California Press, 1967), pp. 74–75. See also C. H. Whitaker, "The Ideology of Sergei Uvarov: An Interpretive Essay," *Russian Review* 37, no. 2 (April 1978): 158–176.

75. Francine Hirsch, *Empire of Nations: Ethnographic Knowledge and the Making of the Soviet Union* (Ithaca: Cornell University Press, 2005). This is not to deny the parallel growth of a Russian-centered nationalism whose cultivation Stalin

approved. D. L. Brandenberger and A. M. Dubrovsky, " 'The People Need a Tsar': The Emergence of National Bolshevism as Stalinist Ideology, 1931–1941," *Europe-Asia Studies* 50, no. 5 (1998): 873–892.

76. Eric Lohr, *Nationalizing the Russian Empire: The Campaign Against Enemy Aliens During World War I* (Cambridge: Harvard University Press, 2003).

77. Kozyrev, *Preobrazhenie,* p. 79.

78. This theme recurs throughout Putin's statements to the Federal Assembly and elsewhere, accessible via the presidential Web site, President of Russia, http://www.president.kremlin.ru. Russian texts of the foreign policy concept are published in *Vneshnyaya politika i bezopasnost sovremennoi Rossii v 4-x tomakh,* vol. 4 (Moscow: ROSSPEN, 2002), sec. 2.

79. For a more detailed and thoroughgoing discussion of this problem, see Robert Legvold's chapter in this volume, chap. 2, "Russian Foreign Policy During Periods of Great State Transformation."

80. This appreciation is implicit in Mendelson's study, as in studies of foreign policy debates during the 1990s. It forms the central theme in all modern explanations for the advent of the Great Reforms. Both literatures also underscore the often overlooked point that such reorientation in response to challenge or crisis reflects the existence of diverse clusters of opinion and orientation within state institutions—a diversity that attests in its own way to the contending strains accommodated in the absolutist tradition. Mendelson, "Internal Battles and External Wars."

81. T. H. von Laue, "A Secret Memorandum of Sergei Witte on the Industrialization of Russia," *Journal of Modern History* 26, no. 1 (March 1954): 60–74.

82. Martin Malia, *Alexander Herzen and the Birth of Russian Socialism, 1812–1855* (Cambridge: Harvard University Press, 1961); and D. I. Chizhevskii, *Gegel v Rossii* (Paris: Dom knigi, 1939).

83. Lenin's critics astutely noted his affiliation with a line of Russian radical thought often referred to as Jacobinism, advocating the takeover of state power as the necessary means of effecting social transformation, rejecting the gradualist approach of the social revolutionaries. Leopold Haimson, *The Russian Marxists and the Origins of Bolshevism* (Cambridge: Harvard University Press, 1955), pp. 36–37, 194–195; and Robert Service, *Lenin: A Biography* (Cambridge: Harvard University Press, 2000), pp. 296–297. It is also worth noting parenthetically that the rhetoric of the intelligentsia—and later of the Communist Party in the Soviet Union—emphasized its transcendence above particular divisions along traditional class, estate, or other ascriptive lines. See Ivanov-Razumnik, *Chto takoe intelligentsiya?* (Berlin: Skify, 1920).

84. Vladimir Lenin, *State and Revolution* (New York: International Publishers, 1932, 1943), especially pp. 51–54, 71–78. Lenin's pamphlet constituted in another context yet one more contribution to a wide-ranging debate over the question of Russia's statehood that had begun in the late 1890s. See, for example, P. B. Struve, *Patriotica: politika, kultura, religiya, sotsializm. Sbornik statei za pyat let 1905–1910* (St. Petersburg:

Izd. D. E. Zhukovskago, 1911); K. Arsenev, N. Gredeskul, and M. Kovalevskii, eds., *Intelligentsiya v Rossii* (St. Petersburg: Zemlia, 1910), especially the chapter by P. Miliukov, "Intelligentsiya i istoricheskaya traditsiya," pp. 89–191; P. D. Dolgorukii and I. I. Petrunkevich, eds., *Politicheskii stroi sovremennykh gosudarstv* [The political structure of contemporary states], 2 vols. (St. Petersburg: Slovo, 1905); and Andrzej Walicki, *Legal Philosophies of Russian Liberalism* (New York: Oxford University Press, 1986).

85. See, for example, Holquist, *Making War, Forging Revolution;* and Peter Holquist, "To Count, to Extract, to Exterminate: Population Statistics and Population Politics in Late Imperial and Soviet Russia," in *A State of Nations: Empire and Nation-Making in the Age of Lenin and Stalin,* ed. Terry Martin and Ronald Grigor Suny (New York: Oxford University Press, 2001), pp. 111–144.

86. Even in the late Soviet period, one finds evidence of the affinities between the two orders in the minds of contemporaries. In a private conversation, the onetime democrat Sergei Stankevich recalled an episode that took place when he worked with the "interregional group" that had formed during the Second Congress of People's Deputies, in 1989. Anatoly Lukyanov, substitute chair for the congress and future putchist, invited Stankevich to a meeting about the upcoming session. Stankevich noticed that his host had on his desk the published proceedings of the late imperial State Duma, presumably for guidance in dealing with this equally novel political conjuncture. Stankevich, conversation with the author, Moscow, August 1989.

87. Vladimir Putin, interview in *Der Bild,* September 18, 2001. Other observers have also noted the similarities. Dmitri Trenin, interview in *Business Week,* May 31, 2004, http://www.businessweek.com/magazine/content/04_22/b3885096_mz054.htm; and Mauro Martini, "Il cavaliere di bronzo," *Testimonianze,* http://www.testimonianze.org/cavaliere_di_bronzo.htm.

88. Rieber, "Persistent Factors in Russian Foreign Policy"; for an excellent general discussion of such perceptions, see Martin Malia, *Russia Under Western Eyes* (Cambridge: Harvard University Press, 1999).

89. The imperial historian S. Frederick Starr writes of "undergovernment" in Russia's provinces as a basis for the zemstvo reform of 1864: *Decentralization and Self-Government in Russia, 1830–1870* (Princeton: Princeton University Press, 1972). *Pace* those who regarded the Soviet Union as a successful totalitarian state, continual complaints in Soviet times about "localism" and "family building" in Soviet provinces and republics, as well as the persistent difficulties in finding reliable national cadres, all exacerbated chronic underperformance in the agricultural sector and suggest that Soviet governments never reached a satisfactory resolution to this challenge either. Of course, these apprehensions and the concessions they forced vis-à-vis social constituencies also helped contribute to leaders' concerns over order.

90. Steven Hoch, "The Banking Crisis, Peasant Reform, and Economic Crisis in Russia, 1857–1861," *American Historical Review* 96, no. 3 (June 1991): 795–820. For a useful and comprehensive discussion of the Great Reforms, see Eklof, Bushnell, and Zakharov, *Russia's Great Reforms.*

91. Caspar Ferenczi, *Aussenpolitik und Oeffentlichkeit in Russland, 1906–1912* (Husum: Matthiesen, 1982) and, I. V. Bestuzhev, *Borba v Rossii po voprosam vneshnei politiki, 1906–1910* (Moscow: Izdatelstvo Akademii Nauk, 1961). Interestingly, the collapse of tsarism amid the Great War resulted not a little from the reluctance to concede prerogative to the leading strata in civil and commercial society. Equally interesting, the Bolshevik regime that eventually succeeded the Romanovs invested the older idea of the state with the practices learned during "total war" and the Russian Civil War to address the challenges of backwardness once for all. For this argument, see Holquist, *Making War, Forging Revolution.*

92. This is the central argument in Poe, *The Russian Moment in World History.* For a less controversial and more substantive discussion, see Rieber, "Persistent Factors in Russian Foreign Policy," especially pp. 344–356, which underscore Russia's "cultural marginality" as a consequence of its spatial marginality.

93. "Why change the political system that made [Russia] a first-class power? . . . To undermine its foundations, everything that constitutes its strength and essence, is ill-advised and dangerous." Cited from the manuscript memoirs of Gen. A. E. Tsimmerman, in Lincoln, *The Great Reforms,* p. 29. This represents an interesting and significant recasting of the quasi-mystical impulse that had driven Alexander I across Europe in pursuit of his arch-foe during the campaigns of 1812–1814. See also the suggestive citation to this effect in Daniel Field, *The End of Serfdom: Nobility and Bureaucracy in Russia, 1855–1861* (Cambridge: Harvard University Press, 1976), p. 49.

94. On rejection of recommendations, see Gorbachev, *Memoirs,* pp. 114–118, 127–138.

95. During the Cold War, these claims came to define a mutually engaged competition with the United States, most notably in the realms of popular culture, high culture, and athletics. It says something about the ideologically charged atmosphere of the Cold War that victory in a chess match or a hockey game, or the defection of ballet dancers, was routinely read as a definitive statement about one or another "system."

96. See, for example, Pobedonostsev, *Reflections,* pp. 62–74. Similarly, see P. A. Zaionchkovsky's account of Pobedonostsev's harsh response to Ignatiev's proposal for a *zemskii sobor* in the early 1880s, in Pobedonostsev, *The Russian Autocracy in Crisis,* trans. Gary Hamburg (Gulf Breeze, FL: Academic International Press, 1979), pp. 287–303. Of course, such ideas *could* become instrumental when the ruler accepted them, as Nicholas II did in the case of Russia's destiny in the Far East; see David Schimmelpenninck van der Oye, *Toward the Rising Sun: Russian Ideologies of Empire and the Path to War with Japan* (DeKalb: Northern Illinois University Press, 2001).

97. Transcript of "working notes" of Communist Party of the Soviet Union CC Presidium, meeting, October 31, 1956, published by the Cold War History Project, http://www.wilsoncenter.org/index.cfm?topic_id=1409&fuseaction=va2.document&identifier=6915E4D2-C619-6304-6860C0E2046814AC&sort=Collection&item=195

6%20Hungarian%20Revolution. See also William Taubman, *Khrushchev: The Man and His Era* (New York: Norton, 2003), pp. 296–297.

98. Raeff, *Well-Ordered Police State,* part 3.

99. In a stark illustration of this point, Anatoly Dobrynin recalls Gromyko telling him that, after returning from Potsdam, where he had learned of the existence of a U.S. atomic bomb, Stalin ordered a hastening of Soviet efforts to build one. Upon hearing that the project faced shortages of electricity "in our war-devastated country," Stalin simply decided to divert electricity from "several large, populated areas" and to devote tank divisions to help clear Siberian forests for the project. Dobrynin, *In Confidence,* p. 23.

100. Such apprehensions arose even under Nicholas I. Future reformer Count P. D. Kiselev complained in 1828 that, without "funds and industry," Russia resembled a "colossus with feet of clay." Lincoln, *Nicholas I.* See also Ellman and Kontorovich, "The Collapse of the Soviet System," pp. 260–261.

101. Gorbachev, *Memoirs,* p. 127.

102. Jonathan Haslam, *Soviet Foreign Policy, 1930–1933: The Impact of the Depression* (New York: St. Martin's Press, 1983); Jonathan Haslam, *The Soviet Union and the Struggle for Collective Security in Europe, 1933–1939* (New York: St. Martin's Press, 1984).

103. Wortman, *The Development of a Russian Legal Consciousness.*

104. Barbara Jelavich, *St. Petersburg and Moscow: Tsarist and Soviet Foreign Policy, 1814–1974* (Bloomington: Indiana University Press, 1974).

105. Haslam, *The Soviet Union and the Struggle.* Some may argue that the Soviet Union had lost its great power position until 1939 through exclusion by the Versailles powers and by virtue of its internal weakness—a factor that French and British policy makers found persuasive in 1938–1939. On the other hand, interwar Europe was characterized by a general diffusion or dissipation of power until the emergence of Nazi Germany—given U.S. isolationism and the impact of the Depression on Western economies, in addition to the chronic war weariness among the Western allies that helped to support the policy of appeasement.

106. Abraham Ascher, *P. A. Stolypin.* Putin expressed this view when remarking that people regard the state "as a source and guarantor of order and the initiator and main driving force of any change." V. V. Putin, "Rossya na rubezhe tysyacheletii," in *Vneshnyaya politika i bezopasnost,* vol. 1, pp. 25–26.

107. Ibid., pp. 115–116.

108. McDonald, *United Government and Foreign Policy in Russia, 1900–1914,* chap. 5.

109. Nicholas II, memorandum of August 6, 1905, discussed in ibid., pp. 83–85.

110. The best history of the Duma is still Geoffrey Hosking, *The Russian Constitutional Experiment: Government and Duma, 1907–1914* (London: Cambridge University Press, 1973).

111. Barbara Jelavich, *St. Petersburg and Moscow: Tsarist and Soviet Foreign Policy, 1814–1974* (Bloomington: Indiana University Press, 1974), pp. 249–279; George

F. Kennan, *The Fateful Alliance: France, Russia, and the Coming of the First World War* (New York: Pantheon, 1984); and Lieven, *Russia and the Origins of the First World War.*

112. Lieven, *Russia and the Origins of the First World War,* pp. 119–140; and Hans Heilbronner, "An Anti-Witte Diplomatic Conspiracy, 1905–1906: The Schwanebach Memorandum," *Jahrbuecher fuer Geschichte Osteuropas,* vol. 14 (1966), pp. 347–361. The best study in Russian is still Bestuzhev, *Borba po voprosam vneshnei politiki v Rossii, 1906–1914gg.*

113. McDonald, *United Government and Foreign Policy in Russia, 1900–1914,* p. 105.

114. A. P. Izvolskii, *Recollections of a Russian Foreign Minister* (Garden City, NY: Doubleday, Page, 1921), p. 20; and Charykov, *Glimpses of High Politics,* pp. 268–269.

115. McDonald, *United Government and Foreign Policy in Russia, 1900–1914,* chap. 5. During the Bosnian crisis in 1908–1909, one conservative diarist wrote, "God grant that there be now war, for there would be another revolution." A. V. Bogdanovich, *Tri poslednikh samoderzhtsa* (M-L, 1924), p. 460, entry for March 13/26, 1909.

116. Ascher, *P. A. Stolypin.*

117. Cited in McDonald, "Izvolskii and Russian Foreign Policy," in *New Perspectives in Modern Russian History,* ed. R. B. McKean (London: Macmillan, 1992), p. 184.

118. Cited in ibid., p. 188.

119. Emets, in *Istoriya vneshnei politiki Rossii,* argues that this constituted a policy of *lavirovanie* (alternating directions) to prevent the emergence of a hostile coalition while Russia required peace for domestic purposes. Allen C. Lynch makes a related argument about the conduct of Russian foreign policy under Yeltsin in "The Realism of Russia's Foreign Policy," *Europe-Asia Studies* 53, no. 1 (2001): 7–31.

120. Izvolsky had agreed not to oppose the annexation, in exchange for Aehrenthal's support for a revision of the convention regulating the egress of Russian ships from the Black Sea. Aehrenthal's announcement caught Izvolsky by surprise and deprived him of any chance to prepare his colleagues or to conduct discussion on the strait with other governments. For a detailed account of the Bosnian crisis, see Bernadotte Schmitt, *The Annexation of Bosnia, 1908–1909* (Cambridge: Cambridge University Press, 1937).

121. Cited in McDonald, "Izvolskii and Russian Foreign Policy," p. 192.

122. Ibid.

123. McDonald, *United Government and Foreign Policy in Russia, 1900–1914,* chaps. 7, 8. During the fall of 1911, then premier V. N. Kokovtsov gained Nicholas's formal approval for this arrangement. Ibid., pp. 171–175.

124. Government declaration to the third Duma; available in English translation in Riha, *Readings in Russian Civilization,* vol. 2. Stolypin used this famous phrase to close an address on the land question to the second State Duma. This address delivered May 10, 1906, defended the government's land reform against calls for expropri-

ation or nationalization. In his concluding remarks, Stolypin stated: "The opponents of statehood [*gosudarstvennost*] would like to choose the path of radicalism, the path of liberation from Russia's historical path, liberation from cultural traditions. They need great shocks [*potryaseniya*], we need a great Russia!" *Gosudarstvennaya Duma, vtoroi sozyv: Stenograficheskie otchety 1907 god, sessya vtoraya, Tom II* (St. Petersburg: Gosudarstvennaia tipografiia, 1907), pp. 436–445. Thomas Riha published an edited translation of this speech in *Readings in Russian Civilization, Volume II: Imperial Russia, 1700–1917* (Chicago: University of Chicago Press, 1969), pp. 457–464.

125. This view also drew a line between those in state power and the forces of "society" represented in the State Duma and public opinion. To be sure, when Stolypin first assumed the premiership in the summer of 1906, he and Izvolsky conducted talks with moderate public figures to construct a cabinet of "social confidence." But these discussions foundered on both the latter's insistence on receiving portfolios to one of the important ministries—for example, Internal Affairs—as well as Stolypin's unwillingness to cede such areas of policy and authority to nongovernmental actors. Izvolsky, *Recollections of a Russian Foreign Minister,* pp. 183–186, 189–191. Later, in the "western zemstvo" controversy, Stolypin pushed through an important legislative bill with emergency legislation, rather than try to work with his Duma supporters. Hosking, *The Russian Constitutional Experiment,* pp. 134–139.

126. On Charykov, see McDonald, *United Government and Foreign Policy in Russia, 1900–1914,* p. 172; on Sazonov and the Balkan allies, see McDonald, *United Government and Foreign Policy in Russia, 1900–1914,* pp. 180–181.

127. Wcislo, *Reforming Rural Russia;* and Ascher, *P. A. Stolypin,* p. 256.

128. David McDonald, "United Government and the Crisis of Autocracy, 1905–1914," in *Reform in Modern Russian History: Progress or Cycle?* ed. Theodore Taranovski (New York: Cambridge University Press, 1995), pp. 204–205.

129. Walicki, *Legal Philosophies of Russian Liberalism;* Struve, *Patriotica;* and Dominic Lieven, *Nicholas II: Emperor of all the Russias* (London: John Murray, 1993).

130. Gorbachev, *Memoirs,* 138; and Ligachev, *Inside Gorbachev's Kremlin,* pp. 14–17.

131. Gorbachev, *Memoirs,* pp. 215–216.

132. Ibid., p. 401.

133. Ibid., p. 160.

134. Mendelson, "Internal Battles and External Wars."

135. This struggle broke into the public sphere in Nina Andreeva's notorious broadside, published in *Sovetskaya Rossiya* in April 1988.

136. McFaul, *Russia's Unfinished Revolution.*

137. In addition to McFaul, *Russia's Unfinished Revolution,* on the national element in the Soviet collapse, see Mark Beissinger, *Nationalist Mobilization and the Collapse of the Soviet State* (New York: Cambridge University Press, 2002); Alfred Senn, *Gorbachev's Failure in Lithuania* (New York: St. Martin's Press, 1995); and Anatol Lieven's studies.

138. See McFaul, *Russia's Unfinished Revolution.* Boris Yeltsin gives his own account in Yeltsin, *The Struggle for Russia,* trans. Catherine Fitzpatrick (New York: Random House, 1994), chap. 6.

139. Lo, *Russian Foreign Policy in the Post-Soviet Era;* these concerns form a major theme in Kozyrev, *Preobrazhenie.*

140. Kozyrev, *Preobrazhenie,* part 1; Malcolm, Pravda, Allison, and Light, *Internal Factors in Russian Foreign Policy,* chap. 2; and Lo, *Russian Foreign Policy in the Post-Soviet Era.*

141. Ibid. For a selection of essays by officials and scholars that give a good cross-section of views in this connection, see *Vneshnyaya politika i bezopasnost,* vol. 1, sec. 2.

142. Lynch takes a different view, arguing that Russian policy had already shifted before Primakov's advent. Despite other differences, most observers agree that Yeltsin replaced Kozyrev with Primakov with an eye toward domestic audiences. See, for example, Michael McFaul, "A Precarious Peace: Domestic Politics in the Making of Russian Foreign Policy," *International Security* 22, no. 3 (Winter 1997/98): 5–35.

143. "Kontseptsiya natsionalnoi bezopasnosti Rossiiskoi Federatsii" (1997), *Vneshnayaya politika i bezopasnost,* vol. 4, p. 51; and Lo, *Russian Foreign Policy in the Post-Soviet Era.*

144. Lo, *Russian Foreign Policy in the Post-Soviet Era.*

145. Edward Mansfield and Jack Snyder, "Democratization and the Danger of War," *International Security* 20, no. 1 (Summer 1995): 5–38.

146. Yeltsin, *The Struggle for Russia,* chap. 5.

147. Text of concept in *Vneshniaia politika i bezopasnost,* vol. 4, pp. 19–51.

148. See McFaul's ruminations in the conclusion to *Russia's Unfinished Revolution.*

149. Putin, "Rossiya na rubezhe," pp. 24–26. Richard Sakwa refers to this important document as Putin's "manifesto," formulated when he already knew of his impending replacement of Yeltsin. Sakwa, *Putin,* pp. 43–47.

150. Putin, "Rossiya na rubezhe," p. 25.

151. Brian Taylor, "Putin's State-Building Project: Issues for the Second Term," PONARS Policy Memo 323, November 2003, *Center for Strategic and International Studies,* http://www.csis.org/media/csis/pubs/pm_0323.pdf.

152. Shevtsova, *Putin's Russia,* passim. This concern has emerged as a particular theme in the Western press as well. The *Economist's* leader on Putin in the December 9, 2004, issue provides a good example.

153. Ibid. See also the official transcript of a radio "dialogue with the population" on the presidential Web page, President of Russia, http://president.kremlin.ru/eng/speeches/2003/12/18/1200_57480.shtml, in the passage beginning "We are all expecting something from the state, but what do we need the state for?"

154. Andrei Kozyrev attested to the hold of the statehood worldview when, in 1994, he recognized that historical circumstances, geopolitical realities, and the

challenges of introducing unpopular measures required a strong state that would provide democratic leadership against those forces seeking the restoration of an authoritarian and "imperial" Russia. Kozyrev, *Preobrazhenie,* pp. 26–32. Interestingly, much Western advice and policy toward post-Soviet Russia rested on a similar paradoxical premise: A powerful state apparatus that had levied tyranny and irrationalism on its population for centuries was now supposed to use that same power in the service of rational goals, for the good of a people who would in turn understand such concepts as rights, franchise, freedom, and law.

155. These themes dominated his "state of the union" addresses to the Federal Assembly in 2004 and 2005. For English-language translations, see the presidential Web page, President of Russia, http://www.kremlin.ru/eng/sdocs/speeches.shtml?type=70029.

156. Putin, "Rossiya na rubezhe." In addition to his declarations to legislative bodies, see also his address to Russian ambassadors and diplomatic representatives in July 2004, Embassy of the Russian Federation, http://www.russianembassy.org/Putin/address_at_Mid_july_2004.htm.

157. S. E. Kryzhanovskii, cited in McDonald, *United Government and Foreign Policy in Russia, 1900–1914,* p. 102.

158. Putin, "Declaration to the Federal Assembly," May 26, 2004, presidential Web page, President of Russia, http://www.kremlin.ru/eng/sdocs/speeches.shtml?type=70029.

159. See Putin, presidential Web page, President of Russia, http://www.kremlin.ru/eng/sdocs/speeches.shtml?type=70029.

160. Studies of Putin-era foreign policy include Sakwa, *Putin,* chap. 9; and Bobo Lo, *Vladimir Putin and the Evolution of Russian Foreign Policy* (Oxford: Blackwell, 2003).

161. On relations between the two factions, see Shevtsova, *Putin's Russia.*

162. Putin, "Address to the Federal Assembly," May 16, 2003, President of Russia Web site, http://www.kremlin.ru/eng/sdocs/speeches.shtml?type=70029.

Acknowledgment: I would like to acknowledge those colleagues who commented and critiqued successive iterations of this essay. My fellow contributors to this volume offered valuable advice on framing the initial draft. Peter Holquist, Francine Hirsch, Jeremi Suri, and Bill Reese helped greatly during later stages. Throughout, Bob Legvold combined great patience with acute perception in guiding this piece to press. I owe him a special debt of gratitude.

CHAPTER 4

How Persistent Are Persistent Factors?

Alfred J. Rieber

R ECENT COMMENTATORS HAVE REVIVED the idea that expansionism and exceptionalism are the driving forces of Russian foreign policy. As evidence they cite the use of oil and gas exports as a political weapon, the support of separatist or pro-Russian movements in neighboring states, and the modernization of an aging nuclear arsenal. They link these symptoms of an aggressive foreign policy to signs of a retreat from market capitalism and democracy in domestic affairs. Familiar questions have been raised regarding whether Russia is "a normal country" worthy of full membership in the newest exclusive club of the international community, the Group of Eight. Does Russia's status as a "civilized" nation require reexamination? Or are recent events a response by the new leadership to problems that periodically reoccur in the making of Russian foreign policy?

Fifteen years ago I sought to define and apply the concept of persistent factors in order to dispel three myths about the forces shaping the foreign policy of imperial Russia. The geopolitical myth attributed unlimited Russian expansion to the absence of physical barriers in the great Eurasian plain and the search for warm-water ports; the leadership myth perceived Russian expansion as an extension of the autocratic power of the ruler; and the ideological myth found the key to Russian expansion in a messianic urge originally rooted in Russian Orthodox culture and subsequently transformed by Marxism-Leninism. Although the myths are no longer widely held, they have left a legacy of suspicion and a fear of "the Russian menace." This chapter accepts the premise of continuity in Russian foreign policy but rejects single-factor, determinist theories. It offers instead an analysis that combines four long-range persistent factors and two middle-range conjunctural factors in order to accommodate both continuity and change in Soviet and post-Soviet foreign policy.

PERSISTENT FACTORS REDEFINED

Russia is no exception to the rule that the makers of foreign policy define state interests within a context of geographical and cultural factors,[1] but these factors are not fixed and immutable. They are not permanent. The physical environment shapes and modifies social organization, cultures, and the projection of power without determining them, just as purposeful human action shapes and modifies the environment by overcoming the limitations they place on action.[2] Spatial concepts are revised to create new symbolic geographies such as "Europe," "Eurasia," and the distinction between "West" and "East" that have so deeply influenced perceptions about Russia's place in the world.[3] Like space, culture is contested, but it is not imaginary. Changes in the geo-cultural configuration of a state proceed slowly over time, if at all, and then only under great external pressure or internal upheaval.

Persistent factors are not artificial constructs; nor did they suddenly materialize at some magic moment in Russian history. They are the result of an evolutionary process, features of historical life that have their origins in the period of state formation in the fifteenth and sixteenth centuries. The four persistent factors that shape the following analysis of foreign policy are relative economic backwardness, porous frontiers, a multinational society, and cultural alienation.[4]

First, definitions of economic backwardness depend on the object of comparison, the standards of measurement, and the mutual perceptions of domestic and foreign observers. In the case of Russia the object was always "the West," which meant the more highly commercialized and industrialized countries of Western Europe and later the United States. The standards of measurement were often subjective in the early centuries of Russian history before accurate statistics were available; later they were based on quantitative data, although in the case of the Soviet Union these have proven to be highly unreliable.[5] Mutual perceptions were reflected in the accounts of foreign travelers, diplomats, and journalists writing as external observers and Russian statesmen and intellectuals writing from the inside. From the period of the gathering of the lands and the concentration of power under the grand prince of Muscovy in the fifteenth century, economic life was severely restricted by climatic and geographic factors, short growing seasons, poor soil, extreme temperatures, a landlocked location, and the lack of easily accessible stone for building. Muscovy controlled the headwaters of great rivers—the Western Dvina, Dniepr, and Volga, but not their outlets in the Baltic, Black, and Caspian seas. So the production of agricultural surpluses and international trade were inadequate to provide the foundations for a great power or even to mount a strong defense against external enemies. These conditions changed only slowly over time.

The acquisition of good arable land (the famous black earth, or *chernozem*), access to natural resources such as furs, gold, salt, and later coal and iron ore, and outlets to the inland seas were secured only in the course of several centuries of expansion and colonization: from Siberia and left-bank Ukraine in the seventeenth century to the conquest of the Baltic and Black seas littoral in the eighteenth century. But their exploitation was hampered by the means by which they were acquired. Only Siberia was an easy conquest. To the west and south, long and costly wars from the early sixteenth to the late eighteenth century were required to establish Russia as an imperial power of European rank. To extract the surpluses from its initially meager resource base, the state imposed heavy obligations on all strata of the population, organized as corporate estates (*soslovie*). Through state subsidies and outright ownership of factories it controlled the production of weapons and equipment for the army. From the time of Peter the Great military expenditures swallowed most of the budget. Resorting to these extreme administrative and fiscal measures, the Russian Empire succeeded in adapting to the gunpowder revolution of the sixteenth century and the military revolution of the seventeenth century. But it fell behind during the third, industrial revolution in technology and weaponry in the second half of the nineteenth century.

Despite renewed efforts to reform all the major institutions of Russian society to create a modern fiscal system and an army of citizens rather than serfs, imperial Russia in its late stages lost three out of four wars, something that had not happened since the seventeenth century. The drive to catch up with the West had become more urgent.

Russia's industrialization, however, was slowed by the absence of capital, the social conservatism of its merchantry, and the economic attachment of the peasant to the commune after the abolition of serfdom. Economic backwardness never translated into dependency on the West as it did with other Eurasian empires. But foreign loans, technology transfer, and patterns of trade did expose Russia to pressures from abroad that sparked nativist reaction and influenced the formation of alliances. During the First World War Russia's need for loans obliged the government to make concessions to foreigners that encroached upon its sovereignty. Thus, economic backwardness was the first legacy of the persistent factors inherited by the Bolsheviks.

Second, porous or vulnerable frontiers have existed since the formation of the Muscovite state in the late fifteenth century. For four centuries the frontiers were ill defined, unstable, underpopulated, and contested by rival multicultural states all along the state's extended periphery. From the sixteenth to the nineteenth century Russia and its imperial rivals—Sweden, the Polish-Lithuanian Commonwealth, the Ottoman, Safavid (Iranian), and Qing empires—engaged in a prolonged struggle over the borderlands. During the same period the steppe nomads resisted incorporation into the competing empires and remained a serious threat to stability along Russia's southern frontier into the eighteenth century.

By the end of the eighteenth century Russia had established its ascendancy over its long-standing continental competitors and subdued the steppe nomads. This was due in major part to the superiority of Russian arms achieved by introducing Western military techniques and imposing harsh measures to mobilize men and resources. But these efforts seriously distorted economic growth. Colonization also played a part in consolidating the borderlands despite the government's ambivalence in promoting it. The authorities perceived the advantages of populating the expanding margins of empire, yet they sought to prevent the illegal flight of peasants from the center and the formation of autonomous frontier communities such as the Cossack brotherhoods. Neither conquest nor colonization, however, guaranteed security on the frontiers. Having gained ascendancy over its imperial continental rivals, Russia faced a new set of external challenges in the nineteenth and early twentieth centuries.

As early as the late eighteenth century the British began to perceive Russian overland expansion in Southeastern Europe and Central Asia as a potential threat to its possessions in India and its imperial sea lanes. The Anglo-Russian rivalry in Central Asia, popularized by Kipling as "the Great Game," was only one sector in the long arc of an extended if a low-level competition that stretched along Russia's porous frontiers from the Balkans in the Ottoman Empire through the North Caucasus, Iran, Afghanistan, Tibet, and Xinjiang. The "first Cold War" between Britain and Russia erupted into an armed conflict only once, during the Crimean War. But several other collisions were narrowly averted. Even after the Anglo-Russian Treaty of 1907 partitioned Iran into spheres of influence, their rivalry continued unabated.

A second and more direct threat to Russian control over its borderlands came from two latecomers to imperialism, Germany and Japan. In both countries patriotic societies, military planners, and business interests saw opportunities to expand their influence and power along Russia's vulnerable frontiers.

After having defeated Russia in the 1904–1905 war, the Japanese Kwantung Army regarded Korea and Manchuria as stepping-stones to annexing the Russian maritime provinces, an aim they pursued vigorously during the period of civil war and intervention (1918–1922). Similarly, the German army during the First World War envisaged integrating parts of Russia's western borderlands into a greater Mitteleuropa, while granting the rest specious independence under German domination. Russia's defeat in the First World War and the intervention stripped Russia of its imperial borderlands and reduced the core to the frontiers of 1618. This was the second legacy of the persistent factors inherited by the Bolsheviks.

Third, with the conquest of the Muslim Khanates of Kazan and Astrakhan in the sixteenth century, Russia became a multicultural state. As a result of further expansion, migration, and colonization, the Russian periphery acquired the characteristics of a "shatter zone," inhabited by a complex mix of ethnic groups, religions, and cultures. Imperial officials were neither systematic nor successful in their attempts to assimilate the borderlands by imposing either Orthodoxy or linguistic Russification on the non-Russian peoples. In some cases, such as that of Poland, they confronted the resistance of a people with a strong Catholic identity and a proud statist tradition of their own. In other cases, such as that of Finland and the Baltic provinces, a long association with Sweden and Protestantism had sunk deep roots that were difficult to extirpate. The Muslim peoples of the Volga, Siberia, the Caucasus and Central Asia and the large Jewish population brought into the empire through the partitions of Poland adhered stubbornly to the customs and beliefs of their corporate religious life. The nomadic populations resisted efforts to turn them into agriculturalists.

The borderlands were highly unstable regions, and the history of this multicultural empire is replete with rebellions. The most serious of these were those of the Cossacks throughout the seventeenth century; the Bashkirs, three times in the eighteenth century; and the Poles twice in the nineteenth century. It was difficult for the central government to control the movement of peoples on the periphery. Nomadic tribes crossing frontiers, runaway serfs, and religious dissenters fleeing persecution continually added to a large floating population on the frontiers outside government control. In the eyes of the ruling elite the loyalty of peoples in the "shatter zone" was always in question.

By the turn of the twentieth century, nationalist sentiment began to coalesce in the borderlands, spreading from small circles of intelligentsia to larger groups in the population and increasing concerns for stability among the leadership. In 1905 nationalism erupted with explosive force along the western and southwestern periphery as a consequence of Russia's defeat in the war with Japan. Consequently, following the outbreak of the First World War, the Russian government and army command regarded certain ethnic groups such as the Jews and Germans as security risks and ordered their massive deportation from the western frontier provinces. The process of national awareness intensified during the civil war and intervention, when many nationalities sought to separate from the empire under foreign protection. It represented the third legacy with which the Bolsheviks had to deal.

Fourth, cultural alienation refers to an amalgam of geographical, political, and historical factors that have contributed to perceptions of Russia by natives and foreigners alike as a state and society engaged with but distinctive from Europe. Two centuries of Mongol rule, acceptance of Christianity from Byzantium rather than Rome, and sheer physical distance from the centers of European civilization have often been given as the reasons that Russia did not participate in the Renaissance, Reformation, and early stages of the rise of capitalism. These perceptions had practical consequences for Russia's belated entry and incomplete integration into the international system.

From the time of Ivan IV "the Terrible" until Peter the Great, Russia's rulers were unsuccessful in their efforts to gain European recognition as a full-fledged member of the Christian commonwealth. Ivan's conquest of the Muslim khanates of Kazan and Astrakhan turned the state into a multicultural empire. But the pope denied its imperial claims because the conquered lands were not recognized as belonging to the European state system. Its subsequent conquest of Siberia, inhabited mainly by nomadic peoples organized along tribal lines, reinforced the image of Russia in Europe as an Asian empire. Throughout the sixteenth and seventeenth centuries, Russia was omitted from official registers of Christian states and celebrated peace plans for Europe like those of William Penn. It was ignored in the Treaty of Westphalia in 1648, which laid the foundations of the European balance of power. Peter the Great and Catherine the Great expended great efforts to demonstrate that Russia was part of Europe in both a political and cultural sense. But neither they nor their successors were able to convince large segments of European opinion. Western observers such as the Marquis de Custine in the nineteenth century continued to explain Russia to Europe in much the same terms as foreign diplomats, soldiers of fortune, and merchants had done in previous centuries. The land was mysterious, exotic, "oriental," even a "rude and barbarous kingdom." Moreover, the work of the Marquis de Custine was hailed in the mid-twentieth century by such diplomats as George Kennan as a reliable guide to the contemporary Soviet Union.

Europeans often regarded Russian diplomatic practices as irregular or deceitful. In part this was the result of misunderstandings arising from Russia's need to conduct relations with societies possessing very different political cultures, ranging from nomadic empires and tribal confederations to imperial China and the European state system. In part, too, European chanceries misinterpreted the activities of Russian proconsuls, loose cannons in the distant reaches of empire, who ignored instructions from St. Petersburg in order to take advantage of local conditions or to advance their own careers. Many of these impressions had weakened but still lingered on the eve of World War I. It was the fourth legacy inherited by the Bolsheviks.

Although this chapter takes up each persistent factor separately, they have been closely related throughout Russian history. No single periodization can be applied to all of the factors, and the development of each may vary asynchronously with the others. Attempts to resolve problems arising from one such factor may set back efforts to solve problems related to others. For example, the defense of long-permeable borders might be strengthened by deportation of reputedly unreliable frontier people and their replacement by settlers from the interior—at least Stalin thought so. But his policy imposed heavy costs in terms of discrediting Soviet nationality policy and disrupting economic development on the periphery without resolving the problem of frontier security.

Conjunctural Factors for Change

An interpretation of foreign policy that privileges continuity but rejects determinism needs to provide an explanation of the conditions under which change takes place. This chapter attributes change to two conjunctural factors, one external and one domestic: the international system and leadership. Persistent factors have a long time horizon; they make up the geographical and cultural dimensions of Russian foreign policy. Conjunctural factors have a shorter time span; they are the source of immediate and specific problems imposed from the outside and of the policies formulated and implemented by the domestic policy makers to solve those problems. The international system underwent more radical changes during the twentieth century than in any previous comparable period of time. During the transformation of the system and Russia's position within it, dramatic changes also took place in the quality and style of domestic leadership as well as the composition of the ruling elites.

During the twentieth century, the relative distribution of power among the major players, including Russia, shifted not only within Europe but also between Europe and extra-European powers. Three times, in 1917–1920, 1941–1943, and 1989–1991, the very existence of the Russian state stood in the balance. In the first half of the twentieth century the most significant change for Russia and the Soviet Union was the rise and expansion of the two flank powers, Germany and Japan. Late in shaping their national identities and in industrializing, they repeatedly challenged Russian and Soviet hegemony in the borderlands of Eastern Europe and Northwest Asia. A second no less decisive challenge was the sudden emergence of the United States as a world power in 1945 and its rapid assumption of the role played so long by the British Empire in challenging Russian influence along a wide arc from Turkey to Korea. Following the defeat of the flank powers and the decline of the traditional European powers, including France, this change introduced a bipolar world, a unique phenomenon in international politics.

The third transformation occurred when the Chinese Communists completed the reunification of China in 1949. By the 1960s they revived old border disputes between the two states and emerged as an unexpected rival of the Soviet Union within the international communist movement. The fourth transformation in the international system was the process of decolonization and the creation of scores of new sovereign states. Lacking well-developed administrative and economic infrastructures, often poverty-stricken, and governed by radical politicians or military dictators, they formed a new contested ground for the two dominant global powers. Added to this, the creation of nuclear weapons and intercontinental delivery systems completely altered the strategic balance and constituted a fifth important shift in the international setting. Henceforth all frontiers were porous. By introducing the ultimate weapon, one that imposed the risk of mutual annihilation, the two powers locked themselves into a deeply dialectical relationship, marked by a profound and enduring rivalry but at the same time requiring significant cooperation in order to avoid Armageddon.

And the changes continued after the collapse of the Soviet Union. The emergence of the European Union as an economic superpower harnessed to a NATO alliance and steadily marching eastward confronted the new Russia with a prospect that has in the past represented the ultimate security nightmare—a frontier with a unified European "empire." Finally, American triumphalism expanded the influence of the United States into regions of long-standing Russian interest all along its shrunken frontiers. Throughout these shifts, Soviet and post-Soviet policy makers were forced to deal with circumstances that were beyond their immediate control and, in the process, to adjust their strategic posture.[6] The question is, How deep were the adjustments and how lasting are they?

As for leadership, there were major changes in the basis of legitimacy and the social composition of the ruling elite following the two radical transformations of 1917 and 1991. After 1917 the tsarist ruling elite and the entire class from which it had been recruited were eliminated from political life. In the Stalinist purges the elite of the revolution was destroyed. Perestroika introduced a new generation of Soviet leaders prepared for extensive change. Since then there has been more continuity in the elites but sharply different leadership styles.

In this chapter leadership style signifies the mode of rhetorical expression, presentation of self, ideological pronouncements, and setting of strategic priorities. Styles were distinctive and in the case of Stalin monstrously so. But it should be kept in mind that up to the present all Soviet and post-Soviet leaders since Lenin's death have emerged from the same political milieu. Moreover, changes in style have often been more striking in appearance than in reality due to the tendency of successive leaders to discredit or denounce their predecessors, always excepting Lenin. The role of leadership has revolved around two basic issues: innovation versus continuity in tactics and strategy and passive versus active response to the challenge of the persistent factors.

Major policy innovations have been associated with the dominant personalities who succeeded Lenin. Yet in all cases the epigone laid claim to his legacy. Central as this was to legitimizing succession in the case of Stalin, Khrushchev, Brezhnev, and Gorbachev, it was not without foundation in fact. Justification can be and was found in Lenin's thoughts and action for the concepts of socialism in one country and peaceful coexistence, the Brezhnev Doctrine, and perestroika. To be sure, the original versions of these ideas were modified to fit changes in the international environment, but they also should be viewed as a response to problems arising from the persistent factors. So should the policy departures of their post-Soviet successors, Yeltsin and Putin.

SETTING THE SOVIET STAGE

It is both an irony of Russian history and testimony to Lenin's political genius that the conjuncture of the Bolshevik seizure of power and the collapse of the international system in 1917–1918 offered the best opportunity to resolve the major questions in Russian foreign policy arising from the persistent factors. The Bolsheviks' initial approach to foreign policy was to reject any links to the past and to deny that they were heirs to previous policies and traditions. Yet, their revolutionary stance and repudiation of historical continuity represented an attempt, however unintended, to transform the problems created by the persistent factors into advantageous conditions for the achievement of their original aims. First, they would seek to create a federation of soviet republics that, in Lenin's version, would be based on equal, voluntary, and open membership. Even Stalin supported the creation of multinational institutions at the republic and local levels. In both cases, the aim was to transform the nationalities problem that had persistently weakened the tsarist empire into a powerful force for unifying the state and attracting other countries to join it.

Second, the Bolsheviks would throw open the frontiers to two-way traffic, accepting revolutionary refugees from outside and dispatching revolutionary proconsuls in all directions, thus terminating the long-standing efforts of the tsarist government to seal Russia's porous frontiers that persistently sapped the internal resources of the state and exposed it to penetration by alien influences. Third, they would impose drastic, indeed unprecedented, controls over the economy that would enable them to mobilize, manage, and direct human and material resources to compensate for the economic backwardness that persistently hampered the vigorous and independent conduct of foreign policy. Fourth, by redefining Russia as the weakest link in the imperialist chain, they would claim to have initiated socialist revolutions in the advanced, industrialized countries of the West and at the same time to have inspired progressive anticolonial revolutions in the East, thus resolving both the internal conflicts over identity and external perceptions of strangeness that persistently contributed to Russia's cultural alienation. In sum, the original vision of Bolshevism projected on an international system shattered by four years of war and revolution would transcend the persistent problems by abolishing national frontiers and nation-states, opening the way for economic modernization through domestic planning and massive assistance from the proletariat of the advanced industrial countries undergoing their own revolutions inspired by Bolshevism, placing Russia at the center rather than at the margins of global societies and social change. But the apparent breakthrough failed to take place. The Bolsheviks lacked the necessary strength, and the European powers, having recovered their equilibrium, excluded them from the new international system. The transforming moment was over.

The Bolsheviks were forced to retreat from their utopian goals by foreign intervention, the outbreak of civil war, and the failure of revolution to secure a foothold beyond the borders of the former Russian Empire.[7] They then faced the daunting prospect of constructing a state order and a foreign policy from an isolated, ruined country encircled by hostile forces ranged along disputed borders. More than one astute observer compared the situation with Russia's Time of Troubles in the early seventeenth century, when internal rebellions, external intervention (by Poles, Swedes, and Tatars) and "false pretenders" came close to destroying the state altogether.

By 1917 the war had seriously eroded the achievements of tsarist reformers such as Count S. Iu. Witte and P. I. Stolypin who had sought in the two preceding decades to reduce economic backwardness. The Bolsheviks inherited a wartime economy that had achieved remarkable results in a few sectors of industry but failed to solve the problem of food procurement and distribution. By the time of the February Revolution, administrative chaos more than shortfalls in productivity brought the regime to the brink of collapse.[8] Russia's international debt had sharply increased, and further economic assistance from its Western allies came only at the high price of sacrificing some of its national sovereignty. The economic foundations of a great power had been destroyed. Strained by more than three years of war, industry collapsed, the working class melted away, and Russia suffered a demographic disaster. Losses among the general population to war, disease, and famine may have reached a total of eight million.[9] The country was plunged into a state of primitive autarky. Deindustrialization and a collapse of the transportation system broke apart the urban-rural nexus. In the eyes of European statesmen, the Bolshevik government was virtually an international outlaw. The state-building potential of the alternative White governments was even less promising. They controlled the economically underdeveloped and multicultural borderlands contested by separatist movements, which strongly opposed the restoration of a Great Russian centralized state. The persistent factors cramped the Bolsheviks but crippled the Whites.

The need to survive forced the Bolsheviks to adopt a series of improvisations in domestic policy called war communism. These measures resembled some of Peter the Great's most stringent programs and foreshadowed those of Stalin. The Bolsheviks intensified and broadened the policies adopted by both the tsarist and provisional governments to extract resources by coercive means but gave preference to the industrial over the agricultural sector.[10] Economic backwardness in the Soviet Union, however, posed more serious problems for the Bolsheviks than it did for the statesmen of imperial Russia.

First, unlike the tsarist elites, the Soviet leadership unanimously, openly, and repeatedly declared its intention to catch up with the West and, for that purpose, supported a proindustrial developmental Weltanschauung. Second, the pattern of substitutions, in Alexander Gerschenkron's formulation, shifted: Among late industrializers in nineteenth-century Europe the state had taken over the guiding role played by industrial entrepreneurs in early capitalism; in the Soviet Union in the 1930s an administrative command economy was imposed by the Communist Party with initially very high levels of coercion.[11] Third, in the Soviet experience, the difference in both the supply and quality of domestically produced military and civilian goods increased to the point where the former achieved near parity with the West beginning with World War II, while the latter steadily fell behind in almost every category. In Vasili Kliuchevskii's famous aphorism, "The state grew fat and the people lean." The Soviet leadership's determination to conduct the foreign policy of a great power and to serve as the model for building socialism was constructed on an inadequate economic base at the expense of impoverishing the population.

Moreover, in the separate peace negotiations between the fledgling Soviet republic and the Central Powers, ideology ran up against reality. The treaty of Brest-Litovsk, signed with Germany in March 1918, was the first major decision taken by the Bolshevik leaders when elements of the persistent factors threatened to overwhelm them.[12] During and immediately after, Lenin drafted the main outlines of Soviet foreign policy with two guiding principles, both of which reflected the impact that the persistent factors had on him: first, to split the capitalist powers and the socialist parties of Europe.[13] The immediate Bolshevik aim at Brest-Litovsk was to negotiate a separate peace with the Central Powers to secure the frontiers on the western and southern frontiers from further penetration even at the cost of surrendering the entire glacis of the non-Russian borderlands. Once this had been done, the Bolsheviks could build a new Red Army to defeat the Whites and separatist movements in the borderlands.

Second, by signing the treaty, Lenin sought to underscore Soviet Russia's commitment to the doctrine of self-determination. The object here was twofold: first, to win the support or at least the neutrality of peoples of the imperial borderlands by reassuring them that the Bolsheviks did not intend to reimpose the repressive tsarist policies toward the nationalities, what Lenin called "Great Russian chauvinism"; and second, to reserve the right for the center to decide which movements for self-determination were in the interests of the new Soviet state. Although the treaties signed at Brest-Litovsk were abrogated by the defeat of Germany in the West, they left an enduring legacy. They laid the basis for the post–World War I independence of Finland, the Baltic republics, Ukraine, and the Caucasian republics. Although an independent Ukraine did not survive the civil war, after 1991 Ukrainian nationalists celebrated its brief existence as the symbolic foundation of the new state.

By creating a new, Third International in 1919, the Bolsheviks forced a split in the European socialist parties with two important implications for their foreign policy. First, they aimed to disrupt a common front of the European Left dominated by "revisionists," who regarded the Bolshevik revolution as a Russian distortion of Marxism and an alien intrusion into civilized Europe. Second, they created a unique instrument of foreign policy by subordinating the activities of foreign communist parties to the political control and interests of the Soviet state as the self-proclaimed base of world revolution.[14] However, attempts by the Soviet leaders to manipulate the activities of the foreign parties whether through the Comintern (1919–1943), the Cominform (1948–1955), or some form of communist commonwealth were never entirely successful. Once in power, communists in Eastern Europe and China began to perceive the cultural distance that separated them from the Soviet Union. After 1917, the persistent problem of cultural alienation resurfaced in a new and unexpected form.

Soviet leaders perceived opportunities as well as dangers stemming from porous frontiers. If their frontiers were vulnerable to outside penetration because of the presence of a nationalist bourgeoisie in the borderlands and a petty bourgeois peasantry throughout the country, then frontiers of the capitalist West could also be penetrated by mobilizing its working class. On balance, however, the Bolsheviks' fears of foreign penetration took precedence over their hopes for revolution. Until and unless potential domestic enemies were eliminated, there was always the danger that they represented a reservoir of support for foreign intervention. This fear, fed by the memories of the civil war and intervention but exaggerated to pathological proportions under Stalin, helps to explain the war against the kulaks in the 1930s, the deportations before and during World War II, and the distrust of Russian Jews after the creation of the state of Israel. As had been the case under tsarist rule, porous frontiers running along the perimeter of multinational borderlands created problems that blurred the distinction between foreign and domestic policies.

The Soviet state had survived the civil war and intervention in a weakened condition and faced a barrage of problems in its relations with the external world. The most pressing concerns were related to problems arising from the persistent factors. The first was to attract trade and investment without running the risk of capitalist restoration or "the enslavement of the Russian working people by foreign capital." This could be done by appealing to the commercial interests of the Entente powers, an idea that the foreign commissar, Georgii Chicherin, dubbed "one of the most outstanding in Lenin's foreign policy."[15] The second was to stabilize the frontiers by reaching agreements with neighboring states. The third was to gain diplomatic recognition from the major powers and secure its status in the international community without, however, abandoning its long-term commitment to revolution. The fourth was to integrate the populations of the borderlands so as to disarm the local nationalists in both a political and cultural sense and to serve as a magnet for peoples across the frontier who belonged to the same ethnic group.

Economic Backwardness: The Road to Autarchy and Back

> My future is blank, but I feel
> A longing to see beggared Russia
> Become a Russia of steel
> —Sergei Esenin, 1925

In the 1920s, foreign economic relations of the Soviet Union were shaped by a complex interplay among three factors: the international monetary system, domestic production for export, and the incompatibility of the capitalist and socialist systems. Attempts to attract foreign concessions and foreign loans, controversial as they were among the Soviet leaders, went nowhere. Although a decree on foreign concessions had been adopted in 1920, it never fulfilled its potential. This was due in large part to the difficulty of maintaining a stable currency based on gold, a problem that had existed throughout Russian history except for the two decades before the revolution.[16] Another obstacle was the refusal of the Soviet government to repay debts incurred by the tsarist government and to compensate foreign owners for property confiscated during the revolution.

High hopes for foreign trade did not materialize despite Soviet willingness to sign agreements, such as the Anglo-Soviet trade treaty of 1921, which did not grant diplomatic recognition. Throughout the 1920s Soviet exports continued to depend on agricultural products and raw materials that were vulnerable to slumps in commodity prices, unfavorable harvests, and, more ominously from the government's perspective, difficulties in collecting grain from the peasantry. In the mid-1920s the value of foreign trade was equal to one half the 1913 level.[17] If the export trade was quantitatively insignificant in the overall Soviet economy, it was necessary, nonetheless, in order to purchase vital machinery and equipment from abroad. But the party and state leaders were increasingly attracted to the ideas of self-sufficiency and industrialization. Commercial relations continued to be troubled by recurrent political differences with foreign powers, especially Great Britain and the United States, because of mutual suspicions and distrust. The Western powers were convinced that the main object of Soviet representatives abroad was to subvert the capitalist system. The Soviet leaders feared that foreign economic contacts, especially when linked to domestic bourgeois specialists, carried the germ of capitalist infection.[18]

The Soviet leadership expressed grave concern over the impact of economic backwardness on weapons technology and the preparedness of the armed forces. Like the epigone of Peter the Great, Lenin's successors were obliged to lift the crushing burden of military expenditures at the expense of weakening the army. Massive demobilization after the civil war cut the size of the Red Army from its peak of four and a half million to 560,000 in 1923. This figure amounted to one-third of the prewar standing army of Nicholas II. The Soviet military chiefs acknowledged that although their artillery was by this time a match for Poland's, it lagged far behind that of the "bourgeois states." The Soviet government was willing to take great risks to close the gap. It turned for assistance to the other loser at Versailles, Weimar Germany.

For a decade after the end of the civil war and intervention, the Reichswehr provided the Red Army with advanced military hardware and professional training. In exchange the Soviet Union helped the Germans to avoid the restrictive clauses of the Versailles Treaty by manufacturing and testing new weapons on Soviet territory. It is difficult to determine who gained the most from these dangerous deals. Russia had traditionally borrowed much of its military technology from the West, but never before had it gambled for such high stakes with a potential antagonist. The final reckoning came in World War II when the Soviet Union paid a fearful price for its assistance in building a modern German army. With the rise of Hitler to power in Germany, the Soviet leadership was determined to overcome its dependence on foreign weapons technology by constructing its own military-industrial complex.

In the great industrialization debates of the 1920s, different proposals advanced by Soviet leaders shared the imperative of overcoming economic backwardness. All had ramifications for Soviet foreign policy. In developing his ideas of economic autarky Stalin insisted that the country had to rely on its own resources, but he did not spell out how this was to be done. Evgeny Preobrazhenskii, a left-wing economist, was less inhibited, or less politically astute, in advocating a policy of squeezing surplus grain out of the peasantry at a time when the party was still hesitant to accept such a radical course. Nikolay Bukharin perceived the need for technological innovation and rationalization linked to international contacts. Leon Trotsky also favored the importation of high technology from Western Europe and the United States and even supported a policy of concessions to foreign capital to help develop the Soviet Union's natural resources.[19] The growing sense of urgency over the need to industrialize was driven in part by foreign events, the break in diplomatic relations with Great Britain, and the war scare of 1926–1927.[20] But no single policy commanded unequivocal support.

At the Fifteenth Party Congress in 1926 a compromise was hammered out that endorsed a faster pace based on advanced technology, importation of sophisticated machinery, and expansion of foreign trade. But compromise was possible only so long as two conditions continued to prevail: first, that the economic infrastructure largely inherited from the past was capable of sustaining further growth without large-scale capital inputs and, second, that the Soviet Union would continue the process of integration into the international community. Neither condition held firm. By the late 1920s the legacy of economic backwardness began to produce bottlenecks that jeopardized further development, increasing the perception of the country's cultural alienation rather than diminishing it, as had been the case a few years earlier.

On the eve of the First Five-Year Plan, industrial capacity and technical infrastructure did not differ much from the situation in 1913. According to R. W. Davies, the Soviet leadership faced a stark choice: either squeeze the peasant or "open the geographical and ideological frontiers to foreign specialists, foreign investment, technology transfer and trade."[21] Both courses carried high risks for the stability of the Soviet system.

In the Second Five-Year Plan, the linkage between industrialization and defense grew stronger. Once the industrial infrastructure had been created, the military sector steadily increased its share of investment, highly trained technical cadres, and transfer of foreign technology—a trend that continued throughout the Soviet period.[22] As a result, relative economic backwardness, always an uneven phenomenon, grew in the area of consumer goods and housing while it had virtually disappeared in the production of military hardware. The outbreak of war merely intensified this trend. The expansion of arms production to full capacity was nearly completed by the end of 1942, demonstrating how extensive the prewar planning had been. A combination of supercentralization, heroic improvisation, and mobilization of the scientific as well as technical intelligentsia enabled the Soviet economy to recover in part from the initial catastrophic losses of men, material, and productive capacity. Nevertheless, even in certain sectors of military hardware the Soviet Union still lagged behind Germany, Britain, and the United States and depended upon foreign technology to close the gap. For example, the Lend-Lease Act, passed by the U.S. Congress in 1941, provided the trucks, jeeps, and radio equipment that made possible a rapid advance of the Red Army after the great defensive victories at Stalingrad and Kursk won by arms and armaments produced in the Soviet Union.[23]

The Pyrrhic victory over Nazi Germany and the short campaign against Japan vaulted the Soviet Union into the ranks of the superpowers, but they also intensified the problem of relative backwardness. Stalin estimated that the enormous war losses in productive potential were equivalent to two five-year plans. The demographic disaster caused by the deaths of twenty-eight million Soviet citizens and an estimated shortfall in births of eleven million was too shattering to be revealed for more than forty years. The psychological devastation was incalculable. The Soviet Union's attempt to recover drew upon three sources: the mobilization of domestic resources, including millions of demobilized soldiers; the stripping of industrial plants located in the occupied territories in the Soviet zone of East Germany, Manchuria, and Romania; and the acquisition of foreign economic assistance, mainly in the form of credits.

Despite the terrible destructiveness of the war, the Soviet Union no longer felt the same pressure to obtain foreign aid that had complicated its foreign policy in the prewar period. Still, its economic recovery could have been speeded up through the purchase of advanced technology from abroad with the assistance of low-cost foreign loans. The problem was the persistent one of a political trade-off. Moscow interpreted the abrupt U.S. cancellation of Lend-Lease as an unfriendly act. It appeared to presage the use of economic weapons to extract political concessions. The impression was reinforced by the failed negotiations with the United States over a postwar loan, and confirmed in Stalin's eyes by the U.S. conditions for participation in the Marshall Plan.[24] In the event, the United States' dollar diplomacy, designed to take advantage of Soviet economic backwardness, proved as unsuccessful as its atomic diplomacy. Both tactics contributed to a policy of autarchy in reconstructing the Soviet economy, intensifying its campaign to catch up with and surpass the United States, and developing its own atomic and nuclear weaponry.

In the post-Stalinist era, the Soviet leadership periodically undertook reforms to repair the obvious shortcomings of the state economy. These included Khrushchev's orgy of administrative reorganization, Brezhnev's timid tinkering, and Gorbachev's more radical reorganization of the foundation blocks of Soviet institutions.[25] All labored under widespread economic and cultural restraints. Under Khrushchev, the drive to overcome economic backwardness coincided with a more adventurous foreign policy. His aim was to achieve superpower equality with the United States as the prerequisite to resolving all outstanding differences. What amounted to *Primat Aussenpolitik* in budget allocations created serious infrastructural problems, primarily in agriculture, and resulted in a persistent lag in the standard of living of the average Soviet citizen compared with those in the industrialized West. By the mid-1970s the growth rate of the Soviet economy turned down sharply and "the process of catching up came to an abrupt end."[26]

The slowdown coincided with structural changes in the global economy that once again forced the Soviet leadership to confront the problem of relative backwardness in their relations with countries in the developing world. By the mid-1970s, Soviet industrial goods and technology no longer satisfied the needs of developing countries. In light of its growing technological lag, the Soviet Union had to embark on a program of modernization with the West and reassess the mechanical application of the Soviet model in overcoming backwardness in the postcolonial world. This process opened a gap between the kinds of technology the Soviet Union could provide and what the radical movements in Asia and Africa needed.[27]

At the same time, the Soviet Union sought to compensate for its declining economic influence through a massive increase in arms exports, the one area where the persistent asymmetry of Soviet economic development continued to make it competitive on a world scale.[28] But this in turn created tensions with the West, especially the United States, its putative partner in arms control and détente. The Soviet foreign policy elite began to express doubts about the correlation-of-forces theory not only with respect to the efficacy of national liberation movements, but also from the perspective of foreign military assistance.[29] The conjuncture of concerns over these two aspects of the persistent factors foreshadowed Gorbachev's "new thinking," stressing less the "correlation of forces" and focusing more on common ethical norms and economic interdependence in an integrated world.[30]

Persistent attempts by Soviet leaders to overcome the debilitating effects of economic backwardness on foreign policy repeatedly ran into the same problem: how to preserve the Soviet system yet overcome long-standing structural weaknesses. All of the economic reforms rested on a number of cultural assumptions. First, according to the "campaign mentality" generated by the civil war, codified by Stalin, and followed by his successors (including Gorbachev), fundamental problems could be resolved by concentrating resources and propaganda on a single sector to achieve a breakthrough. In every case, this meant creating new or reorganizing existing bureaucracies with all the concomitant waste and confusion. In agriculture, the abolition of private landowning through Stalin's collectivization (admittedly more of a political than an economic measure) and Khrushchev's virgin soil program were the most egregious examples. But even under the conservative Brezhnev, the massive injection of capital into the countryside without establishing priorities or coordinating among different sectors backfired. Second, the state discouraged or penalized initiative and innovation at the local level. The expulsion of the "kulaks" was only the most spectacular of such measures. Khrushchev curtailed the collective farmers' right to use their private plots for growing produce. Under Brezhnev, enterprising collective farm managers were punished rather than rewarded.[31] With no opportunities for fresh talents to make improvements and in the absence of the amenities of modern life, the most enterprising peasants began to leave the land. The massive outflow of labor that began in the early 1970s continues today, leaving the countryside even more backward and impoverished.

To address this shortfall, the Soviet Union had to import grain, making it vulnerable to economic pressure from abroad. Starting in the early 1970s the United States attempted to link trade and Soviet political behavior—with mixed results. There were indications that what some Western observers called the "tactic of positive linkage" moderated Soviet policy toward Jewish emigration and more generally in the Middle East. But by the 1980s, it also created a backlash among the Soviet leadership. In dealing with national security along Soviet frontiers, as in Afghanistan and Poland, the Soviet leaders reacted to Western economic pressure by rejecting positive linkage. Since the 1930s the Soviet leaders had feared that relying on foreign trade to overcome domestic shortcomings could lead to further compromises and concessions in the area of security.[32] The same concerns surfaced in connection with technology transfer as a means of overcoming economic backwardness. The governing elites split over the desirability of continuing to rely on foreign trade and technology transfer to solve domestic problems.[33] In this respect the dilemma and ensuing internal debates parallel the controversy over the Witte system in late imperial Russia.

Although foreign critics had long maintained that the Soviet system had failed to overcome its relative economic backwardness, it was left to the Soviet economists during the era of glasnost to reveal the severity of the lag and the desperate need for reform.[34] Early in this period, Gorbachev made clear that his main aim was "the removal of everything that hampered development." He emphasized "the necessity for far-reaching change and reorganization (*preobrazovanie*), to create a high-quality society" in every sense of the word. Above all, this meant a scientific-technological renewal of production and "attain[ment] of a high world level of productive labor."[35] By 1988 Gorbachev had come to realize that the achievement of this goal would be out of reach as long as military expenditures remained the top priority (amounting by his estimate to two and a half times that of the United States), thus continuing to hamper research and development and distorting the economic development of the civilian sector. This meant "an ideologically conscious retreat from orthodox class theory and methodology in analyzing international relations and so in formulating our foreign policy."[36]

In the post-Soviet period the Russian leadership continued to search for a policy that would promote the integration of the Russian economy into the global economy but protect the commanding heights of the economy against foreign control. Under Yeltsin, market reformers were disappointed by the lack of real economic assistance from the West. The statists viewed radical reform as a loss of control over the levers of power.[37] The tug of war between the two generated a series of hesitant, confused, and inconsistent economic policies. The result was a deepening domestic crisis that widened the gap between the Russian and Western economies.[38] Throughout the decade of the 1990s Russia's gross domestic product (GDP) fell in real terms almost every year, ending up at 57 percent of what it had been in 1990. The decline was sharper in the twenty-one republics than in the predominantly Russian center. Within the republics the non-Russian population suffered from higher levels of poverty and unemployment than the Russians. All this contributed to a rise in ethnic tensions.[39]

President Vladimir Putin's formula for catching up with the West is to impose state control over the ownership and management of mineral resources as a means to enter the global market economy. This is to be accomplished by creating "vertically integrated financial-industrial corporations capable of competing with Western multi-nationals." Cracking down on errant oligarchs, building pipelines to enhance Russia's geopolitical interests, striking deals with European firms that give Russia 51 percent control, and raising gas and oil prices in neighboring states (Belarus, Ukraine, Georgia, and Moldova) to world market levels are so many aspects of his foreign economic policy.[40] The strong state sector of the economy and controlled market mechanisms in domestic and foreign trade appears to be a variation on policies first introduced by tsarist finance ministers such as Mikhail Reitern and Sergei Witte, and subsequently proposed by Bolsheviks such as Trotsky, Bukharin, Krassin, and others in the 1920s but never fully implemented.[41] The use of mineral resources as a basis for the restitution of Russia as a great power requires a delicate calibration to succeed. Its overly zealous implementation runs the risk of tilting heavily toward the statist side, scaring off Western investors and alienating Western governments.[42] A crucial obstacle to Russia's membership in the World Trade Organization was long Putin's concern that the establishment of directly owned local branches of foreign banks would not allow Russia to control flows of capital in and out of the country.[43] This is another example of the recurrent contradiction between overcoming economic backwardness and defending porous frontiers.

Although the Russian economy is recovering from the wild 1990s, culminating in the crisis of 1998 when the Russian government defaulted on its foreign debt, it ranks only sixty-third in the world on the scale of "competitive ability outlook." Still reeling from the distorting effects of deindustrialization, Russia remains overly dependent on the export of raw materials, primarily oil and gas. The change in Russia's political system has aggravated the lag between research and development in the technology sector, while a brain drain has further reduced the pool of talent necessary for innovation. In 2003 only 3 to 5 percent of Russian products were competitive in the markets of industrial nations, and only 25 percent of Russian technological products met world standards.[44] These sober conclusions underline Russia's dilemma in having to choose yet again between full integration into the international economic system and movement toward greater autarky. Under Putin's administration, there have been moves in both directions. But in both cases, the tendency of the economic oligarchs to accumulate, rather than reinvest, their profits has strengthened the state's role in the economy. It is still a matter of debate whether Russia's decision to eliminate gas subsidies to members of the Commonwealth of Independent States and ban Georgian wines is part of an effort to exert political pressure or an economic necessity.[45]

POROUS FRONTIERS: SEALING, EXPANDING AND CONTRACTING

A great new age is born
Have faith in it! Receive it from our hands!
Both ours and yours, it will efface all boundaries
—Ilya Ehrenburg, 1920

The problems that permeable frontiers posed for Soviet foreign policy were partly inherited from the prerevolutionary period and partly the making of the new regime. The most serious of these, common to both eras, were encirclement, penetration, and flight. One of the first tasks facing the Soviet Commissariat of Foreign Affairs was to seal the borders of the new state against a possible renewal of intervention from bases in neighboring countries. Foreign troops had penetrated the space of the old empire from multiple points along its periphery from Finland to the maritime provinces. For the Bolsheviks the pressing need was to establish diplomatic relations with the smaller states that might serve as staging grounds for future interventions. Between 1920 and 1921 the Soviet government signed treaties with Estonia, Latvia, Finland, Turkey, Afghanistan, Iran, Mongolia, and, following a brief war, Poland. Yet almost at once the hope faded that these measures would blunt the efforts of émigré groups and the more powerful states of the Entente from using these countries as springboards for future intervention. In December 1921 Poland, quietly encouraged by France, took the lead in forging a mutual assistance pact with Finland, Estonia, and Latvia. To Stalin this was an additional sign that neither commercial nor diplomatic agreements with foreign states were reliable guarantees of state security. Rather, in his words, they opened Soviet borders to "spies of the world bourgeoisie," who were also busy in Turkey, Persia, Afghanistan, and the Far East building "an economic (and not only economic) fence" around the Soviet Union.[46]

Meanwhile, the Bolsheviks were constructing their own metaphorical fence along the inner perimeter of the country. Its purpose was to stem the outflow of people and the importation of ideas. There had been precedents throughout Russian history. Before Peter I, travel abroad was made very difficult. Following a relatively open period in the eighteenth century, Russian rulers reacted strongly to revolutionary events abroad in 1789 and 1848. Paul forbade students from attending foreign universities and Nicholas I imposed strict regulations on young people studying abroad.[47] Russian university curricula were purged of courses dealing with European constitutionalism. The importation of books from the West was subjected to severe censorship. Yet at the same time Russian engineers were sent to the United States to study railroad construction and French engineers were recruited to teach in St. Petersburg and supervise public works projects, including the construction of railroads. From Peter the Great to Gorbachev there were persistent attempts to promote economic development and technology transfer without opening the frontiers to subversive political ideas or direct foreign influence. To acknowledge economic backwardness and simultaneously to claim some kind of spiritual or ideological superiority repro- duced the dilemma faced by tsarist bureaucrats in the nineteenth century.

In the early years of the revolution the Bolshevik frontier policy was in- spired briefly by the idea of proletarian internationalism. The borders were thrown open to supporters of the revolution, and revolutionary proconsuls fanned out from Germany to China. In-migration brought hundreds of intel- lectual sympathizers and thousands of foreigners seeking jobs.[48] War-torn Russia's need for skilled workers and agriculturalists complemented Bolshevik ideology. In the 1920s the government also attempted to woo back rank-and- file participants in the civil war who had fled for their safety by offering them amnesty. The objective was to weaken anti-Soviet organizations abroad. But in seeking to make open frontiers work to their advantage, the Bolsheviks were unable to reconcile proletarian internationalism with the need for state secu- rity. Contradictions multiplied over practical issues, such as settling the emi- grants, incorporating them into the economy, and granting them citizenship. Soviet attitudes toward migrants eventually shifted as the prospects for the spread of revolution diminished and Stalin's ideological linkage between capi- talist encirclement and socialism in one country reinforced the importance of secure borders.

As early as May 1918, concern over the implications of Russia's open fron- tiers had prompted Lenin to approve the formation of a special border guard, which in 1920 was reorganized into the internal security forces. One of its ini- tial tasks, to prevent illegal emigration, was marked by failure. One and a half million people passed into exile, draining the country of much irreplaceable talent.[49] Over the following two decades the border guard, recruited selectively and paid well, developed into an elite unit. The annexations of 1939–1940 cre- ated a new western frontier, with territories that included Western Galicia, which had never been part of the Russian Empire, and territories such as Kare- lia, the Baltic states, and Bessarabia, where substantial parts of the population were of dubious loyalty. In 1939 the growing tension along the western frontier caused by German pressure on Poland and Romania prompted the Soviet government to undertake a major reorganization of the border guards, to increase their number to 158,000, and to renew emphasis on the importance of ideology in their training.[50]

In the 1920s Stalin introduced three ideological proposals aimed at strengthening frontier defenses that marked a further shift away from international revolution to territorial expansion as the basic goal of Soviet foreign policy. First, he asserted that contrary to the internationalist viewpoint Soviet Russia would be "transformed in the course of building socialism into a base for the further unfolding of the world revolution, into a lever for the further disintegration of imperialism."[51] Second, in giving overwhelming priority to strengthening the Soviet state as a prerequisite for spreading world revolution, Stalin took the final, decisive step in imposing upon foreign communist parties a primary obligation to defend the Soviet state, even if this meant sacrificing their own revolutionary prospects in the short term. Third, Stalin declared that though the Soviet Union could build socialism it could not guarantee immunity against the dangers of "intervention and consequently against a restoration of the bourgeois order without the victory of the revolution in at least a number of countries."[52] He did not specify which countries or how the revolution would be carried out, implicitly leaving the choice of ends and means in his hands. By giving the Soviet state preeminence in creating the external conditions for building socialism, he set the stage for a new relationship with the external world. He opened the way for the possibility of signing of nonaggression pacts and even treaties of alliance between the Soviet Union and imperialist powers.

To secure the frontiers during the turmoil of the five-year plans, Stalin continued to pursue the traditional policy of keeping Russia's potential enemies divided at a time of domestic crisis. The foreign policy of the state represented one arm and the Comintern the other arm of that policy. When the threat from German fascism and Japanese militarism appeared greatest, the Soviet government supported collective security, entered the League of Nations (that "den of imperialists") in 1934, signed treaties of alliance with Czechoslovakia and France in 1935, and negotiated seriously with France and Britain into the summer of 1939 for a pact of mutual assistance. But the exclusion of the Soviet Union from the four-power negotiations that led to the Munch Pact in 1938 raised the ancient specter of Russia's isolation. Stalin turned toward the alternative option of reaching agreements with Germany and Japan in order to avoid the nightmare of fighting a war on two fronts separated by thousands of miles without substantial aid from the West.

Toward the same end the Soviet Union orchestrated Comintern activities in Spain and China to keep Germany and Japan engaged in conflicts far removed from Soviet frontiers. In addition, Soviet diplomats sought to gain international support from the Western democracies. But the deeper the Comintern and the Soviet Union became involved in supplying military aid and volunteers to Spain and China, the more the Western democracies feared that encouraging antifascist activities would fulfill Stalin's prediction of "the victory of the revolution in at least a number of other countries."[53]

Stalin's decision to sign a pact with Hitler may have shocked the communist faithful outside the Soviet Union, not to mention noncommunists, but it was not fundamentally different from Russia's traditional approach to challenges on its western frontiers. Many called the Nazi-Soviet pact "the fourth partition of Poland," echoing the three-stage partition of Poland in the eighteenth century. It was that, but something more as well. It delineated spheres of influence all along the western perimeter of the Soviet Union, and it represented an approximate restoration of the old tsarist frontier. Would an agreement with France and Britain have provided the same guarantees? Quite possibly, although the outcome might have been more similar to what happened after World War II. In the negotiations with the French and British in the summer of 1939 Stalin had sought access rights for the Red Army in Poland and Romania.[54] He also insisted that any treaty guarantee the Soviet Union against "indirect aggression" launched from the Baltic states. One could easily imagine, in the event of a coalition war to check Nazi aggression, that these arrangements would have led to Soviet-inspired political changes in the countries "hosting" the Red Army as they did after 1945.

Moreover, the results in either case represented another in a series of Russian war aims (or frontier rectification, to use Stalin's preferred phrase) stretching back to the secret treaty of Rome in 1915, the Vienna settlement following the Napoleonic Wars, Elizaveta Petrovna's plans to crush Prussia during the Seven Years War against Frederick the Great, and Peter the Great's attempt to break down the "barrier states" in the early eighteenth century—to go back no further in time. In other words, the Soviet leaders shared with their predecessors (and with their successors) the belief that the porous western frontiers presented the most serious threat to the security of the state. Yet there seemed to be no permanent solution to this persistent problem, the reasons for which are discussed in the next section on the multinational character of the Soviet state.

Until very late in the Second World War, Stalin aimed at a restoration of the territories seized under the Nazi-Soviet pact with some strategic modifications.

These included obtaining bases in Finland, annexing the northern half of East Prussia and Sub-Carpatho Ukraine, securing economic and military concessions in Manchuria, and occupying North Korea. There is no evidence that he foresaw any immediate radical socioeconomic transformation of the "liberated" countries of Eastern Europe.[55] In the postwar years no master plan emerged. Rather a combination of internal struggles for power, Western political intervention, and Soviet manipulation of armistice agreements created opportunities for local communists to turn their countries into "popular democracies" as adumbrated by Stalin in the 1930s.[56] At the same time Stalin sought to create spheres of influence along the southern frontier of the Soviet Union. His prime aims were to prevent British and American penetration of frontier areas in Iran and China, weaken Chinese control over Xinjiang and Manchuria, and obtain Nationalist China's recognition of independence for Outer Mongolia.[57] But he did not foresee a communist revolution in China and was surprised at its success. The postwar formation of a territorial belt of "friendly countries" on the Soviet periphery did not solve the problem of its permeable frontiers. On the contrary it worsened the problem by increasing the porousness of the empire's outer limits.[58]

During the Cold War, new challenges to the security of Soviet frontiers emerged in a number of areas: economic, military, ideological, and technological. They originated both outside and within the Soviet bloc. In the negotiations preceding the adoption of the Marshall Plan, Stalin displayed his renewed concern over the vulnerability of the Soviet Union to capitalist penetration. In Paris in July 1947 a high-powered Soviet delegation led by Molotov attended the economic discussions among the European powers. But it soon became clear that economic cooperation would mean economic coordination. Soviet planning would have to be subordinated to a European plan. Stalin quickly concluded that this was "a scheme to organize a Western bloc against the USSR." He gave orders to the governments of Eastern Europe not to participate.[59]

The U.S. policy of containment posed even greater problems. In 1949 the Western European states under U.S. leadership signed an unprecedented peacetime military alliance. Although defensive in character, NATO was routinely denounced by the Soviet Union as aggressive and anti-Soviet in its aims. The United States extended its ring of alliances to include a treaty with Japan, the Baghdad Pact, and the Southeast Asia Treaty Organization (SEATO) in Southeast Asia. The latter two were short-lived but no less threatening in Soviet eyes. The permanent presence of American air bases and ground forces stationed around the outer perimeter of the Soviet Union gave a wholly new meaning to capitalist encirclement. The problem for the Soviet leadership then became how to break the ring or vault over it.

Only after West Germany joined NATO did the Soviet Union react in kind by organizing the Warsaw Pact in 1955. Although article 8 required members to respect the independence and sovereignty of other members and practice nonintervention in their internal affairs, there was an ambiguity about the precise limitations this placed on joint action by members of the pact in order to maintain its unity. The Soviet leadership repeatedly attempted to resolve the ambiguity by linking intervention to an appeal from a group of local communists. In this way the operation would have the appearance of supporting the "legitimate" representatives of the socialist state against its internal enemies. As Stalin had learned in the break with Tito, it was not enough to have a communist party in power to guarantee Soviet predominance. What was needed was "a Russian party," as it had been known at times during the tsarist period, for example, in the case of relations with Poland and the Kazakh nomads in the eighteenth century or with Iran in the nineteenth century. Lacking any internal support in Yugoslavia, Stalin could "snap his little finger" all he wanted, but when no Yugoslavs responded, he chose not to intervene.[60] In the post-Stalinist period the Soviet leadership generally opted to intervene, despite initial hesitations and even disagreements, rather than accept the defection of a communist regime on its borders. In the case of Poland in 1956 and again in 1980 they took a chance in allowing the local party leadership to restore order rather than risk triggering a national uprising by sending in Soviet troops.

The Soviet decision to intervene in Afghanistan in 1979 differed only in details from the general pattern. During the civil war and intervention and into the 1930s Afghanistan had been a sanctuary for Turkmen resistance fighters (called Basmachi or bandits by the Bolsheviks) opposing the Soviet reconquest of Central Asia. A low-keyed British-Soviet competition for influence gave way in the 1950s to a more intense competition between the United States and the USSR. Soviet involvement suddenly increased following the establishment of a pro-Soviet government in April 1978 and the outbreak of a rebellion against it at a time when the Iranian revolution threatened great instability in the region. Although Afghanistan was not part of the Soviet alliance system, its strategic location, the danger that the Afghan communists would be overthrown by Muslim radicals to the benefit of the Americans, and memories of the transborder Basmachi revolt combined to draw a reluctant Soviet leadership into an armed intervention.[61] The occupation of Afghanistan was never completed, and a new frontier with Pakistan opened. It was another case of attempting to close a porous Soviet frontier by territorial expansion that ended by creating another frontier even more difficult to seal.

Earlier, by moving the western border of its political dominion to the Stettin-Trieste line, the Soviet Union established a frontier that in the long run proved fatefully permeable. The United States was able to exploit social and economic problems in the East European communist bloc to create difficulties for the Soviet leadership. In the early years of the Cold War, both U.S. threats to destabilize Eastern Europe and the East German refugee crisis spread apprehension in Moscow. The Kersten Amendment to the Mutual Security Act, passed in the summer of 1951, authorized $100 million for inciting insurgency in Eastern Europe, prompting a strong Soviet protest against subversion as a violation of the Roosevelt-Litvinov agreements that preceded U.S. recognition of the Soviet Union in 1933.[62]

Responding to economic crisis and the lure of the West, a mass exodus of Germans—one hundred thousand in March 1952 alone—threatened the stability of the Communist regime. A more porous frontier could not be imagined, and Stalin recognized that the danger was not confined to East Germany. Writing to the East German communists in April 1952, he noted that the division of Germany had created "a dangerous frontier" between the two blocs. "One must strengthen the protection of this frontier," the Soviet leader concluded.[63] Attempts to stem the tide were only temporarily effective. From January 1951 through April 1953, 447,000 people fled to West Germany.[64] Following the 1956 Hungarian revolution, 175,000 refugees crossed into Austria and another 20,000 fled to Yugoslavia, most of them young and well educated.[65] In 1961 another large wave of East Germans prompted the Communist leader Walter Ulbricht to write Moscow: "If the present situation of open borders remains, collapse is inevitable."[66] The construction of the Berlin Wall in 1961 was an admission that only a physical barrier could seal the most permeable land frontier of the expanded Soviet system.

The final, fatal breach in the extended frontiers of the Soviet bloc was made by the decision of the Hungarian government in September 1989 to open their borders with Austria to the citizens of the GDR. Within a few weeks tens of thousands of Germans crossed into the Federal Republic by this route, putting pressure on the Czech government to follow suit.[67] The GDR could no longer resist the demands of its own population to travel freely, and gave up its efforts to defend the Berlin Wall. Earlier the same year Soviet forces completed their withdrawal from Afghanistan after ten years of costly and futile efforts to close the porous frontier with Central Asia. It was all part of the great retreat.

Gorbachev's decision to renounce force in maintaining the outer perimeter of Soviet power abandoned a basic principle of Soviet foreign policy since 1945. Pulling back the Soviet political frontier to the 1945 territorial boundary was not, however, the end of the great retreat. In the end Gorbachev also chose not to use force to prevent the inner borderlands from breaking loose—first the Baltic states and then the rest of the western Caucasian and Transcaucasian republics. The western frontiers now bore a striking resemblance to those dictated at Brest-Litovsk. Gorbachev did not plan on this outcome, but at each moment of choice he opted for the solution that would end cultural alienation, enhance Soviet integration into the world community, reduce the economic burden of the arms race, and open the way for economic development and technological transfer by achieving partnership with the advanced Western states. Transcending the persistent factors is what the "new thinking" was all about.

The ideological penetration of Soviet frontiers came from within the socialist camp as well as from the capitalist world. Stalin himself was partially responsible for the problems. By preaching socialism in one country Stalin had been the first prophet of national communism. By dissolving the Comintern in 1943 he had opened "separate roads to socialism."[68] Tito was the first to take one, but not by departing from Stalinism, which he continued to follow for several years after the Yugoslav-Soviet break in 1948. Rather his break with the Soviet Union was the result of his ambition to become the Stalin of the Balkans.

Mao Zedong was already moving along his own path before the Chinese Communists took power in 1949, and he and his successors continued to do so after Stalin's death.[69] Others followed. From the death of Stalin to the collapse of communism, every socialist state in Eastern Europe plus China engaged in a major conflict with the Soviet Union that ended in violent repression, an armed clash, or an outright break with the international communist movement.

Porous frontiers joined cultural alienation as the two sources of the Sino-Soviet conflict. Both had deep historical roots. The origins of their border disputes go back to the Muscovite-Ming period and evolved into a full-blown competition during the great expansion of the Qing dynasty into Central Eurasia during the eighteenth century.[70] Throughout the second half of the nineteenth century, as Qing power declined, Russian penetration into the northern tier of China—Xinjiang, Mongolia, and Manchuria—set precedents that would haunt the relationship between the Soviet and Chinese Communist regimes. Mao resented Stalin's policies of independence for Outer Mongolia, Soviet bases in Manchuria, and economic penetration of Xinjiang. Although Khrushchev pulled back from Xinjiang and Manchuria, the Chinese began in 1959 to reopen the entire border question by denouncing Russia's unequal treaties with China, imposed centuries earlier.[71]

Border incidents multiplied and tension mounted, reaching a peak in 1969 with large border clashes. By the early 1970s there were more Soviet divisions along the Chinese frontier than in Central Europe, and the Chinese deployed the bulk of their small nuclear strike force in the northeast, aimed at Soviet targets.[72] The dissolution of the USSR weakened Russia's bargaining position and increased the pressure to reach economic agreements with China. In another trade-off between the demands of persistent factors, the Russians signed a border agreement in 1991 that was disadvantageous for them but cleared the way for the sale of arms to China. Russia accounted for 91 percent of China's arms imports in the period from 1993 to 2002.[73] However serious, the border dispute was also symptomatic of a deeper cultural divide between the two erstwhile allies, a point discussed in the section on cultural alienation.[74]

In Eastern Europe the Soviet attempt to seal the USSR's porous frontiers by constructing a protective glacis of "fraternal countries" crumbled under the dual impact of Marxist revisionism and nationalism. In all the major crises that rocked the bloc, ideological deviation from the Soviet model was backed by the joint action of intellectuals and workers, who in theory constituted the social base for building socialism. This was true in the Berlin insurrection of 1953, the Hungarian Revolution of 1956, the Prague Spring of 1968, and the Solidarity movement in Poland in the early 1980s.

A second common aspect linking these events was the "spillover effect." The problems facing Soviet leaders attempting to deal with insurrections within the bloc were similar in two respects to those faced by their imperial predecessors within the empire. First, there was the danger that uprisings in the borderlands could lead to foreign intervention. Second, there was the concern that an uprising in any one of the borderlands could touch off similar outbreaks in others. There is good evidence that these considerations played a crucial role in the decision of the Soviet leaders to intervene in Hungary in 1956. Similarly, the Soviet intervention in Czechoslovakia in 1968 was related in part to fears that the Ukrainian population of eastern Slovakia could serve as a conduit for the ideas of the Prague Spring into the Soviet Ukraine.[75] In the wake of the Soviet intervention in Czechoslovakia, Leonid Brezhnev made explicit an unspoken assumption underlying Soviet foreign policy in the bloc:

> When internal and external forces hostile to socialism seek to reverse the development of any socialist country whatsoever in the direction of the restoration of the capitalist order, when a threat to the cause of socialism arises in that country, a threat to the security of the socialist commonwealth as a whole—this not only becomes a problem of the country concerned, but also a common problem and concern of all socialist countries.[76]

It is illuminating to compare this statement with the justification offered by Nicholas I in 1849 for his decision to order Russian forces to suppress the Hungarian revolution against Habsburg rule.

> As in the past I foresee only envy, malice and ingratitude [on the part of the Habsburg Monarchy] and probably would not intervene if the shirt was not so close to my body, that is if I did not see in [Polish General Jozef] Bem and other scoundrels in Hungary not only enemies of Austria, but enemies of universal tranquility and order . . . that would destroy our tranquility.[77]

One of the landmarks of Gorbachev's foreign policy was to repudiate the so-called Brezhnev Doctrine by invoking the new ideal of a "common European home," a bid to end the cultural alienation of the USSR.[78] But there was a trade-off. After 1989 local communist leaders could no longer count on Soviet support against popular uprisings. This was a decisive step toward the disintegration of the protective band of territories along the western Soviet frontier.

The changes in leadership after Stalin's death and the momentum of decolonization in the third world created new possibilities for the Soviet Union to attack the problem of encirclement by vaulting over the alliance system that the United States had erected around the bloc. Khrushchev claimed and many Western observers agreed that his policy of supporting national liberation movements was a return to Leninist principles and a rejection of Stalin and Zhdanov's "two-camp doctrine." It proved to be something more and something less. It was a fusion of both with an admixture of Khrushchev's own views. Khrushchev launched his new policy at the Twentieth Party Congress in 1956, stressing the need to establish friendly ties with "peace-loving states," while at the same time promoting peaceful coexistence with the imperialists. What had changed since Lenin's day, he argued, was that war was no longer inevitable due to changes in the international system.[79] For the next ten years Soviet diplomatic and military support went exclusively to established sovereign states, not revolutionary movements. In other words, the leapfrog strategy aimed at supporting, not overthrowing, existing governments. The object was to relieve pressure on the periphery of Soviet continental power by creating a new line of frontier states beyond the American perimeter of containment. The most dramatic bid to exercise this pressure directly on the United States led to the Cuban missile crisis in October 1962.[80] The shift in Soviet policy to outright support of revolutionary movements occurred in the 1970s only after the Soviet Union had achieved de facto nuclear parity with the United States.[81]

By projecting its ideological frontiers into the third world the Soviet Union created new problems in defining and defending them. It became clear by the late 1960s that the number and variety of national liberation movements required a revision of outworn theoretical conceptions and a more flexible set of policy options. The result was a low-key debate among bureaucratic intelligentsia and different levels of support for the movements by the Soviet leadership that did not quite mesh into a consistent and comprehensive approach.[82] The specialists had become increasingly sophisticated, the third world had become increasingly complex, and the defense of the land frontiers and those overseas had become increasingly entangled and contradictory. Throughout the Brezhnev years, Soviet foreign policy increased its political and military involvement in the developing countries, providing greater support for anticolonial movements than for separatist movements. In most cases, the Soviet Union engaged in active competition with China for influence over both national liberation movements and foreign communist parties. But Moscow's concerns that local conflicts might antagonize the United States, undermine détente, and possibly escalate into a wider war appeared to exercise a restraining influence on its policy.[83] By the mid-1980s it was increasingly clear that the growing Soviet involvement in national liberation movements had imposed a heavy burden on the Soviet economy without having achieved its aim of putting pressure on the United States to reach agreements on other outstanding issues that were more vital to Soviet security, such as arms limitations.

The problems of porous frontiers acquired a wholly new dimension with the development of nuclear weapons, technologies of penetration and surveillance, such as shortwave radios, supersonic aircraft, and satellites. In the postwar years the traditional means of guarding the frontiers by securing strong points on the periphery or influence beyond it were less effective. U.S. long-range bombers carrying atomic or hydrogen bombs were capable of penetrating Soviet air space and inflicting terrible damage. The development of more powerful bombs and more sophisticated delivery systems operating at even greater range compounded the problem. Soviet foreign policy developed a two-pronged strategy. On the one hand Moscow attempted to overtake the U.S. lead in nuclear weapons and develop delivery systems capable of reaching the United States. On the other hand it sought to negotiate a settlement of all outstanding questions on the basis of military equality. At the same time, the Soviet leadership remained alert to any danger that new technologies could penetrate its frontiers.

Throughout the 1950s and 1960s the Soviet Union reacted violently to repeated penetration of its air space by U.S. aircraft engaged in electronic surveillance. According to semiofficial sources, twenty-five such aircraft were attacked and destroyed during this period. But it was not until 1982 that a comprehensive Law of the USSR State Borders set new restrictions on the violation of Soviet air space that arguably went beyond the commonly accepted practices of international law. Two incidents, the shooting down of the U-2 in 1961 and that of the KAL 007 in 1983, seriously disrupted Soviet-American relations at potentially crucial turning points in the ragged course of détente.[84]

Western shortwave radio broadcasts in Russian from powerful long-range transmitters began first in 1946 with the British Broadcasting Corporation (BBC) and the following year with Voice of America (VOA). Radio Free Europe followed in 1950 and Radio Liberation (eventually Radio Liberty) and Deutsche Welle three years later.[85] As early as 1948 the Soviet Union began to close the ether frontier by jamming VOA and then the BBC. It employed this technique more or less consistently with mixed results over the next forty years. In a sign of the seriousness with which the Soviet Union regarded the penetration of its airwaves, the government devoted more resources to jamming than to broadcasting its own domestic and foreign programs. By 1968 there were more than twenty million shortwave receivers in the hands of the Soviet public. The government belatedly sought to forbid the sale of sets that could get the high-frequency bands, but individuals with the know-how were able to adapt their receivers.[86] In 1988 Gorbachev permanently ended jamming.[87] His decision may have diminished the image of the Soviet Union as culturally marginal. But the failure to reform the character of Soviet broadcasting left it to Western radio to inform the Soviet public of the dissident national movements, particularly in the Baltic states. Here the confluence of problems stemming from three persistent factors—porous frontiers, a multinational state, and cultural alienation—contributed to bringing down the entire Soviet structure.[88]

Multinational Society: Revenge of the Borderlands

> We were in Georgia. You can get to this land
> If Hell is multiplied by paradise.
> —Boris Pasternak, 1931

The peculiarities of a multinational society common to the Russian Empire, the Soviet Union, and the Russian Federation posed problems for foreign policy makers that were closely related to porous frontiers. If the outer perimeter of the state was exposed to the penetration of foreign ideas and foreign armies, the inner perimeter remained, as it had been under the empire, the most vulnerable to subversion and invasion. But in the decade between 1914 and 1924 three important changes had taken place between the periphery and the center that affected the conduct of Soviet foreign policy. First, during the civil war and intervention the nationalities had experienced periods of autonomy, independence, or foreign protection. The collective memory of these episodes was never completely repressed. Separatist aspirations rose to the surface in 1941 and again in 1991. Second, the relative weight of the Great Russians in the Soviet population represented only slightly more than half of the total population, although that percentage had increased as a result of the loss of non-Russian territories such as Finland, Poland, and two Armenian provinces.[89] Third, the Bolsheviks endorsed a three-part nationalities policy that in the long run stimulated national sentiments rather than bringing them under control. They condemned Great Russian chauvinism, recognized the right to national self-determination, and undertook to build a state along federal lines. This signaled a sharp departure from the most recent policies of the tsarist government. That the Communist Party leadership steadily moved over the following decades toward a greater degree of concentration of power at the expense of the nationalities cannot detract from the residual, psychological effect of the original theories and structures. It should not be forgotten that the Soviet nationalities policy, no matter how vacuous or repressive it may have been, delimited the boundaries of the future members of the Commonwealth of Independent States, established cultural institutions such as local branches of the Academy of Sciences, trained cadres of local leaders, and promoted cultural symbols that played a vital role in the formation of nation-states after 1991.

As a man of the borderlands, Stalin forged a nationalities policy linked to his concepts of state building and his conduct of foreign policy. Its contours were shaped by his early life as a Russified Georgian revolutionary in a frontier region and his experience in the civil war as commissar of nationalities and an active participant in the reintegration of Ukraine and Transcaucasia into the new multinational Soviet state. During and after his rise to power he showed tactical flexibility in adjusting his policies to fit his domestic agenda and responding to changes taking place in the international environment.[90]

For Stalin the civil war and intervention threw into bold relief two aspects of security—the constitutional structure of the state and its territorial boundaries. The key to both in Stalin's mind was the geographic location and social composition of the nationalities. Throughout the 1920s he repeatedly warned that the socioeconomic backwardness of the periphery created a "zone of foreign intervention and occupation" where indigenous bourgeois nationalists and foreign capitalist powers had cooperated during the civil war to detach the periphery from the Russian center and stifle the fledgling Soviet republic.[91]

Consequently, in the constitutional debates of the early 1920s, Stalin opposed Lenin's "liberalism," as he called it, and won the argument in favor of a more centralized federal system. Stalin's insistence that all the constituent union republics share an international border has generally been interpreted as an empty gesture designed to conform with a spurious right to self-determination. More likely, however, it reminded communists that any sign of excessive nationalism would be treated as a breach of external security, the equivalent of treason, and an offense punishable by death. For this reason, the chief Soviet prosecutor in the show trials of the 1930s, Andrei Vyshinsky, justified the arrest and execution of so-called national communists within the USSR on the basis of their intercourse with foreign powers.[92] In the 1940s the same accusations were leveled against communists such as Josip Tito, Władysław Gomułka, Lázsló Rajk, and Rudolph Slansky for the East European parties.

Stalin's creation and incorporation of four new union republics (Estonia, Latvia, Lithuania, and Moldavia) in the wake of the Nazi-Soviet partition of Eastern Europe in 1939 all but completed Stalin's state-building project. The criteria for inclusion were in part strategic and in part political. The three Baltic republics would guard the approaches to Leningrad and provide additional naval bases; the acquisition of Moldavia (Bessarabia) would make the Soviet

Union a riparian power on the Danube. In political terms these territories had once been part of the Russian Empire, and, as such, Stalin considered them part of the country's historical patrimony, a point of pride with him. They were also home to many who had been educated in prerevolutionary Russian schools, mirroring his own experience in his native Georgia.[93]

In the 1930s and 1940s, years of relative military weakness versus the Soviet Union's western neighbors, Stalin dealt with the problem of ambiguous loyalty among the nationalities living in the borderlands by granting them cultural autonomy and establishing local soviets based on the principle of ethnicity. The process became known as "*korenizatsiya*," although Stalin preferred the term "*nationalizatsiya*."[94] This administrative innovation may have been inspired by both domestic and foreign concerns. But internal and external security has been closely intertwined throughout Russian history. Stalin's perception of the borderlands as the most vulnerable point of interaction between internal enemies and international capitalism injected new vigor into the idea.

That *korenizatsiya* had a direct relation to Soviet foreign policy emerged most clearly with respect to the so-called Piedmont principle. The concept, mentioned in contemporary Soviet documents, refers to the role played in the nineteenth century by the Kingdom of Piedmont-Savoy as the focus for attracting the loyalty of all patriots living under foreign domination. Throughout most of the 1920s the Soviet government aimed to strengthen the impression among Belarusians and Ukrainians outside the USSR and various national groups in Bessarabia that their co-nationals across the Soviet frontier enjoyed a high degree of political and cultural autonomy. In 1934 the Soviet government launched a campaign to reverse the prerevolutionary image of Galicia as a Piedmont for Ukraine and transform Soviet Ukraine into a Piedmont for Ukrainians living in Poland. In addition, to attract the allegiance of nationalities beyond its frontiers, Stalin ordered the transfer of large territories of the Russian Soviet Federated Socialist Republic to enlarge the Belarus republic and to create the Moldavian Autonomous Soviet Socialist Republic. Stalin defended both political and cultural *korenizatsiya* until it became clear that the policy was intensifying, rather than reducing, ethnic conflict within the country.[95]

The breakdown of political *korenizatsiya* coincided with the 1926–1927 war scare with Great Britain, a complex episode when strands of the intraparty struggle became intertwined with Soviet foreign policy. A series of international incidents during these years, including Soviet aid to British workers in the general strike of 1926, British raids on Soviet trade offices leading to a break in diplomatic relations, the collapse of the communist-nationalist united front in China, and the assassination of the Soviet ambassador in Warsaw, raised fears among the Soviet leadership that war was imminent. It is now clear that these fears not only were groundless but were manipulated by Stalin in his campaign to destroy the Right Opposition.[96] Stalin was convinced, nonetheless, that frontier people could not be counted on in the event of war with Poland or Romania. At the beginning of the war scare in 1927, OGPU (secret police) reports described the Polish border villages as "defeatist," waiting impatiently for liberation that would achieve "the great power ideas of Poland."[97] To forestall Polish intervention during agricultural collectivization in the Soviet Union, the Politburo pursued alternate policies; on one hand it ordered repression and deportation of Polish peasants; on the other, it created in 1932 a Polish national region in the Belarus republic to fight Polish "chauvinism." The pendulum swung rapidly back again with the repression of Polish cultural organizations in Ukraine and Belarus and in 1934 with the abolition of the Polish Communist Party.

For the same reasons, a similar uncertainty characterized the policy of the center toward Ukraine. But in this case, the local Ukrainian communists believed it their duty to challenge Polish imperialism, while the center envisaged joint Soviet-Polish repression of the Ukrainian Liberation Movement as the basis for a nonaggression pact.[98] This well-documented episode is just one illustration of the convoluted and contradictory nature of Soviet policies, as the leadership struggled to overcome economic backwardness through collectivization, secure the loyalties of the nationalities, and defend the state's porous frontiers. At the same time they exploited the nationalities question to penetrate the porous frontiers of neighboring countries.

The multinational character of the Soviet state created fresh problems for the Soviet leaders following Adolf Hitler's rise to power. Stalin was slow to recognize the implications of Nazi racial policies for his nationality policy, but he soon realized that the political aspects of *korenizatsiya* and the doctrine of national self-determination endorsed by the Comintern were vulnerable to Nazi manipulation.[99] German minorities (Volksdeutsch) throughout Eastern Europe, including the Soviet Union, were high-profile targets for Nazi propaganda. At home Stalin adjusted his nationality policy to fit the changed international situation by emphasizing the role of the Great Russians in holding together the multinational Soviet state and adopting two guiding "law-governed" principles first articulated by Lenin. Stalin argued that the dialectical process of drawing together (*sblyzhenie*) and fusing (*sliyanie*) the nationalities had to be held in creative tension, implicitly to be sure by his own guiding hand. This meant promoting greater integration and unity of the nationalities, particularly in the face of external threats, without imposing linguistic Russification, which he knew from his own experience in the Caucasus could only drive them apart. Against this backdrop, Stalin introduced the concept of the "great friendship" of nations with Great Russia as big brother.[100] At the same time, he continued to permit the celebration of cultural traditions as long as they did not cross the line into bourgeois nationalism, a line that only he could draw.[101]

Stalin's policy of cleansing the frontier regions of non-Russian ethnic groups appeared to have a double aim: as a precautionary security measure and as punishment for resistance to collectivization that had been strongest in Ukraine and the North Caucasus. In the first years of collectivization, even before the full implications of the Nazi threat were clear to him, his definition of unreliable elements conflated class and ethnic identities, that is, "kulaks" and "nationalists," as the source of opposition.[102] As a result, the rate of de-kulakization was greater among ethnic minorities such as Greeks, Bulgarians, and Germans living in the Black Sea frontier districts.[103] Once the class danger had receded, on the eve of war, he focused his suspicions exclusively on ethnic groups. The ethnic turn intensified as the perceived threat from Nazi Germany increased and Poland adopted an ambivalent attitude toward its two powerful neighbors. As a consequence of the Sovnarkom decree in April 1936 on the need to "display revolutionary vigilance," fifteen thousand Polish and German households were accused of being politically "unreliable" and uprooted from their homes in the western oblasts of Ukraine. Ethnic Poles were also excluded from living in an eight-hundred-kilometer frontier zone. A year later the government expanded special closed zones to include regions adjacent to Iran, Afghanistan, and Turkey. Following a separate order on "resettlement of undesirable elements with the aim of strengthening state frontiers," new frontier districts were created in Armenia and Azerbaijan. Next, it was the Koreans. By the late 1920s eight thousand to ten thousand Koreans a year were migrating across the Soviet frontier with Manchuria. As the international situation in the Far East heated up in the late 1930s, Stalin, viewing the Koreans as potential Japanese agents, ordered the deportation of more than 173,000 from the territory of the Buryat-Mongol Autonomous Republic, Khabarovsk, and the Primurskii krai. At about the same time, the frontier zone of Azerbaijan was cleared of Iranian families.[104]

Reproducing patterns established during tsarist times, the expansion and contraction of the Soviet Union's borders led to large-scale forced population movements. The pace of deportations and migration of frontier peoples accelerated in 1939–1940 following the Winter War with Finland, and the annexation of west Belarus, west Ukraine, and Bessarabia. After the Finnish defeat, virtually the entire population of the Karelian territory, destined to be annexed by the USSR, about 420,000 people, left for Finland. Roughly two-thirds had returned with the Finnish armies in 1941–1944 and left again following the armistice. In two separate waves, approximately 243,000 Poles were deported from the western regions.[105]

Following the outbreak of war with Germany, the tempo of deportations became frenzied in a massive campaign to deport all Germans from European Russia. By the end of 1941 more than 438,000 people from the German Volga Republic were sent east. Even ethnic Germans in the Red Army, numbering over 33,000, were demobilized and reassigned to labor battalions. There was no letup at the end of the war. In 1945, 1946, and 1949 the Ministry of Interior ordered Germans in the frontier regions of the Baltic republics, Belarus, Ukraine, and Moldova resettled in Siberia.[106]

The German invasion of the Soviet Union in 1941 intensified these practices, having exposed the weakness of Stalin's 1939–1940 policy of annexing territories of the former Russian Empire. Instead of consolidating the frontier along ethnic lines, the annexations introduced a number of Trojan horses into the Soviet citadel and touched off civil wars all along the western periphery in a replay of the civil war and intervention. Stalin responded by launching a massive deportation campaign of non-Russians from the Soviet periphery and by intervening in the domestic politics of East European countries, where civil wars, actual or threatening, greeted the advance of the Soviet army.[107]

Stalin, prompted by his chief of secret police, Lavrenti Beria, interpreted any sign of anti-Soviet activity among the nationalities in the face of the German advance as a sign of wholesale defection. Beginning in 1943 the counteroffensive of the Red Army signaled a policy of massive deportation of peoples in the borderlands, including: the Crimean Tatars, Chechen-Ingush, Kalmyks, Balkartsy-Kabardintsy, and many other smaller nationalities.[108] In the orgy of frontier cleansing, merely belonging to a small national minority was grounds for deportation. So, for example, the Greek and Bulgarian populations of the northern shores of the Black Sea and Transcaucasia were deported to Central Asia. Full juridical rehabilitation and permission to return did not occur until forty years later. Gradually the right to return was extended to the Balkartsy-Karachaevtsy, the Kalmyks, and the Chechen-Ingush; in the 1960s and 1970s the right of return was granted to the Crimean Tatars and Meskhetian Turks.[109] But the government's attempt to repair damage to the multinational image of the

Soviet Union backfired in the postcommunist period. Rehabilitated and returned to their homeland, the Chechens rose in rebellion, reviving a tradition of resistance to Russian rule that stretches back to the mid-nineteenth century and reopening the persistent problem of the porous Caucasian frontier.

Stalin applied the same punitive policy in the wake of the Red Army's advance into Central Europe. His efforts to redraw the ethnic map of Central and Eastern Europe, aimed at eliminating potential "nests of subversion," initiated the organization of a mass deportation of Volksdeutsch from countries bordering on the Soviet Union—Poland, Czechoslovakia, Hungary, and Romania. He encouraged the Czech and Yugoslav governments to expel or resettle the Hungarians in Slovakia and the Voevodina. He promoted the resettlement of Poles from their prewar marchlands in the East (*kresy*) to the former German provinces of Pomerania, Silesia, and the southern half of East Prussia.[110] The result was the reconfiguration of postwar states in the region along more ethnically homogeneous lines than at any time since the Middle Ages.

The threat of a Trojan horse within the body politic of the multinational Soviet Union was not eliminated by territorial expansion after World War II. On the contrary, the Soviet leaders faced a new situation with the emergence of a politics of internal resistance and ethnic emigration. The existence of Baltic governments in exile, the underground resistance in Lithuania and West Ukraine lasting into the early 1950s, and the enthusiastic reception by Soviet Jews of the first diplomatic representatives of the newly created state of Israel persistently raised the question in the minds of Soviet leaders of dual or divided loyalties among their citizens.

The role of the Jews in Russian foreign policy had a history going back to the Congress of Berlin in 1878. Foreign Minister A. M. Gorchakov attempted to persuade the West European delegates not to extend legal guarantees to the Jews in Serbia or Romania because, like the Jews in Russia, they were different from the Jews in Western Europe and "the equalization of their rights would have harmful consequences for these countries."[111] The same issue surfaced in the 1950s. When the initial Soviet support for Israel as part of its anti-imperialist strategy shifted to a pro-Arab foreign policy, Soviet Jews with Zionist sympathies, and many without, found themselves consigned to an oppositionist camp. The closer Israel drew to the United States, the more Soviet Jews fell under suspicion as agents of imperialism. When Soviet Jews expressed sympathy with Israel during the Six Weeks War, a new wave of anti-Semitism erupted in the Soviet Union. This led to a sharp increase in Jewish applications to emigrate, which in turn triggered a Soviet reaction.

The Soviet leader Leonid Brezhnev was now caught in a bind. To allow Jews to emigrate freely would lead to the loss of a highly educated group in the population, particularly those with advanced degrees in the exact sciences, a brain drain that would seriously affect the Soviet effort to overcome economic backwardness. Emigration to Israel, the preferred goal of the Soviet Jews, would arouse the ire of the Arab states being actively courted by the Soviet Union. But to oppose emigration would antagonize the United States and jeopardize détente, which Brezhnev needed to solve other problems related to the persistent factors: reducing the cost of the arms race, obtaining Western technology necessary to overcome economic backwardness, gaining a free hand to deal with the Chinese threat on his Asian frontier, and securing Western recognition of the frontiers established after World War II.[112] The Soviet compromise—to allow Jews to leave but impose an education tax on them—fell short. The Jackson-Vannik Amendment to the Soviet American Trade Treaty of 1973 linked the most favored nation clause to unrestricted Jewish immigration. The Soviet Union denounced the treaty. The amendment complicated Soviet-American relations for decades and has yet to be repealed.[113]

In the last years of the Soviet Union the eruption of the multinational question not only took the leadership by surprise but also reopened the question of the government's stability and legitimacy. Despite a flurry of straws in the wind, the Soviet leadership, including Gorbachev, continued to believe they had essentially solved the national question. Repeating Brezhnev's "dialectical" formula on the eve of being blown away by the force he thought benign, Gorbachev stated, "The development of our multinational state is naturally accompanied by a growth in national consciousness. This is a positive phenomenon."[114]

The nationalist protest movements in the late 1980s would not have acquired the force and momentum they did without the endorsement by the Communist Party's central apparat of glasnost and *zakonnost,* the principles of openness and legality. Glasnost and *zakonnost* were attempts "to end the state of stagnation" by freeing the society from the ideological fetters that defined Soviet cultural alienation, and in Gorbachev' words "to remove everything that was holding back development," that is, to overcome economic backwardness.[115] Under new conditions of openness, isolated incidents of national protest began to coalesce into "a cycle of mobilization and . . . a tide of nationalism."[116] The first autonomous political organizations to emerge in the late 1980s were the popular fronts. Emulating the model of the Baltic peoples, they were emblematic of a multicultural society where the only viable reference group outside the discredited Communist Party was ethnoterritorial.

There was no alternative transnational source of legitimacy and allegiance. The fate of the USSR was sealed.[117]

CULTURAL ALIENATION

It was a German town that we awoke in
Endless the long, long roads that stretch behind me
And only alien cities lie ahead.
                    —Mikhail Matusovskii, 1945

The initial Bolshevik commitment to spread world revolution opened a cultural distance between the Soviet Union and the rest of the world that waxed and waned but did not disappear until the demise of communism. Afterward a strong residue remained while deeper and older currents rose to the surface. Measuring the cultural alienation of the Soviet Union encounters difficulties of interpretation on three levels: the discourse of international politics, diplomatic practice, and the philosophical underpinnings of science, scholarship, and the fine arts. For example, what was the meaning and relationship between "peaceful coexistence" and the "correlation of forces?" Were changes in Soviet foreign policy tactical or strategic? Were Soviet norms and models for creativity different from those of the international community? These questions became more complex as the interaction developed between the Soviet Union and the international community and as different styles of leadership emerged to cope with new situations.

Confusion and suspicion within the international community over the norms and aims of Soviet foreign policy stemmed from the earliest ideological pronouncements of the leadership and the creation in 1919 of a communist international that quickly showed itself to be an instrument of that policy. The discourse of Soviet foreign policy created the impression that the leadership played by two sets of rules or spoke to two different audiences. The tropes of competition and conflict run through the public statements of communist leaders from Lenin to Gorbachev, as if they were the permanent conditions of international relations. Of the many examples that could be cited, Khrushchev's famous statement about the demise of capitalism is the most striking. Were his much-quoted words on the demise of capitalism to be translated "We shall bury you"? Or did they mean, "we shall be present at your funeral," as he subsequently insisted? And what was the real difference between the two versions?[118] The discursive dichotomy in Soviet foreign policy did not cease with the advent of perestroika. As part of his "new political thinking" Gorbachev declared that "alienation is evil." Yet he insisted that "*perestroika* requires Party leaders who are very close to Lenin's ideal of a revolutionary Bolshevik."[119] How were Western students of Marxism-Leninism or Gorbachev's Soviet audience, for that matter, supposed to resolve the contradiction?

The rhetoric of alienation in Soviet foreign policy was institutionalized by the creation in 1919 of the Third International, the Comintern, signaling a radical departure from international norms. The impression that the Soviet Union was an alien actor on the international scene was reinforced when in 1919 the Second Congress set rigid criteria for membership in the form of the twenty-one demands that imposed upon the members an organizational model based on Bolshevik experience. The effect on the external perception of the Soviet role in world politics was twofold. On the one hand it reinforced the impression among European statesmen and diplomats that the Bolshevik dictatorship had passed beyond the limits of civilized nations. On the other hand it permanently split the Left into revolutionary and reformist camps.[120] These events had a profound influence on most of the major foreign policy issues between the two world wars.

The victorious allies were determined to treat the Bolsheviks as an international pariah. They refused to invite Soviet Russia to participate in the Peace Conference of 1919, the first time that Russia had been excluded from an international congress since the seventeenth century. They imposed a blockade and launched an intervention, however uncoordinated and ineffective, to overthrow the new regime. It took fifteen years for all the major powers to extend diplomatic recognition to the Soviet Union, the last being the United States, in 1933. The Soviet Union was admitted to the League of Nations only in 1934 and then for the brief span of six years before it was expelled, the only country to suffer that indignity. The Soviet attack on Finland was the cause, legitimate enough under the Covenant of the League. But the same sanction was not imposed on Japan in 1931 for its occupation of Manchuria or on Italy in 1936 for its attack on Ethiopia. Clearly Soviet policy was being judged on different grounds.

The deep and bitter split between communists and Social Democrats facilitated Hitler's rise to power and hampered the formation in Europe of a strong popular front to oppose fascism. Suspicions of Soviet motives during the Spanish Civil War helped discourage Britain and France from assisting the republican forces. The same attitudes led to the exclusion of the Soviet Union from the discussions over the fate of Czechoslovakia leading to the Munich Conference and to the breakdown of talks in Moscow in 1939 between the Anglo-French mission and the Soviet leaders.

In most of these cases external interpretations of Soviet foreign policy collected around two extremes. It was regarded either as purely opportunistic, that is, lacking any principles, or as purely ideological, that is, based solely on principles, although of the wrong kind. The fact that it consistently pursued a goal of revising the Versailles system, which revived old security problems on the western frontier linked to both its multinational society and its porous frontiers, was largely ignored. Yet, it should have been clear from the Soviet inclination to align with the Germans in the 1920s, then the French in the mid-1930s, Germany again in 1939, and *par la force des choses* against Germany after 1941. In all cases the object was to prevent a European "crusade" against communism (a function of cultural alienation) by dividing the capitalists or to restore lost imperial territories and reestablish a more defensible ethnic and strategic frontier. Was this so very different from the policies of the nineteenth century, particularly after the Crimean War?[121]

Maxim Litvinov, Soviet foreign commissar from 1929 to 1939, may well have been sincerely committed to a policy of collective security, but his strategic aims were similar, if more subtle, than those of his predecessor, Georgii Chicherin, or his successor, V. M. Molotov, a point not lost on Stalin. Litvinov calculated that if war came, the Soviet Union must have strong allies and the fighting should be done outside Soviet space. Although his policy failed in the end, he had succeeded for a while in narrowing the cultural gap that separated Soviet diplomatic practice from that of the capitalist powers. His long residence in Britain, his English wife, and his cadre of cosmopolitan diplomats all contributed to the reputation he enjoyed at the League of Nations and with foreign diplomats. However, at home his main rivals in the Soviet leadership, Molotov and Andrei Zhdanov, adopted a more isolationist position. Their views on strengthening security by acquiring a territorial buffer to cover the porous frontier to the west carried the day, when the British and French backed away from collective security as defined by Litvinov.

Once the war had broken out, Stalin sought to pursue both collective security and territorial guarantees simultaneously. In talks with Eden and Churchill in 1942 and 1944, at Yalta in 1945, and in the armistice negotiations with Finland and Romania, he proposed only slight revisions in the territorial agreements he had signed with Hitler. He flirted with the idea that he might exploit a different kind of split in the capitalist world by mediating between the United States and Great Britain. However, he also committed himself to a new international system based on a rough division of the world into spheres of influence and participation in Roosevelt's plan for the United Nations. Stalin's policy may be seen as an attempt to realize his vision of replacing capitalist encirclement with a belt of "friendly countries" and to maintain the wartime alliance with the United States and Great Britain. It was a difficult balancing act, and Stalin lacked Litvinov's subtlety to make it work. Litvinov attributed the breakdown to Stalin's inability to understand the West.[122]

The replacement of Litvinov by Molotov and later Vyshinsky as foreign minister inaugurated major changes in Soviet diplomatic practice that reinforced Western perceptions of Russia's cultural alienation. The "Litvinovtsy," most of whom were purged in the late 1930s, were professionals—cultivated men and women with a good knowledge of foreign languages and cultures. Their successors displayed none of these characteristics. Molotov later admitted that without experienced diplomats who understood foreign languages, the Soviet leaders feared "being swindled." As a result, he went on, Soviet "diplomacy in the thirties, forties and fifties was highly centralized . . . the ambassadors were only executors of specific orders."[123]

Nikita Khrushchev's free-wheeling leadership style gave a fillip to well-established Western perceptions of Soviet foreign policy as culturally alien. His bullying of President Kennedy at Vienna, his antics at the UN, and other incidents culminating in the Cuban missile crisis convinced many Western observers and his Soviet associates as well that he was prone to impulsive and at times irrational behavior that had a damaging effect on the Soviet image abroad. It was only after the late 1960s, when Andrei Gromyko and other diplomats who had entered service as novices in the 1940s began to take hold, that foreigners expressed a more balanced appreciation of Soviet diplomatic practice.

Khrushchev's style should not obscure his contributions to a reduction of problems stemming from cultural alienation. His revival of the doctrine of peaceful coexistence, albeit under the threat of a nuclear holocaust, as the basis for negotiations over outstanding problems reduced the unremittingly hostile environment in which diplomats had been forced to operate during Stalin's last years. Similarly, the opening of cultural and scientific exchanges between the Soviet Union and the West and the developing countries contributed to the erosion of cultural marginality. But by this time the belief in incompatible ideological differences had become so deeply rooted in the cultural life of both the West and the Soviet Union that only a major change such as the crisis that inspired Gorbachev's "new thinking" could shake the established stereotype of Soviet cultural alienation.[124]

As the cultural distance between the liberal, capitalist West and the USSR diminished, it increased within the international communist movement. Lenin's definition of Russia as "the weakest link in the imperialist chain" recognized its intermediate position between the industrial West and the colonial East. The success of its revolution enabled its leaders to claim special knowledge in promoting revolution in societies that were in socioeconomic terms the most advanced and the most backward. As the home of the first successful socialist revolution, the Soviet Union exercised throughout most of its history a powerful attraction for many throughout the world who were disillusioned with capitalism, fearful of the rise of fascism, and hostile to colonial rule; it served as an inspiration, a model for development, a military power, and a source of material support for a wide spectrum of the Left. A broad spectrum of sympathizers identified with Soviet policies that promoted socially progressive causes, fought the good fight in Spain, liberated Eastern Europe from Hitler, and supported anticolonial revolutionary movements. In their eyes the Soviet Union had moved from the cultural margins of the dominant international power structure to an imaginary center of a new world civilization.

In the long run, however, Soviet determination to maintain its centrality within the communist movement had the unintended and paradoxical consequence of spreading disunity.[125] Four major components tipped the balance toward the alienation of the Soviet Union within the international communist movement. The first was the insistence of Soviet leaders on the primacy of Soviet interests in their strategy of world revolution. This was implicit in the twenty-one demands of the Second Comintern Congress in 1920 and made explicit in Stalin's doctrine of socialism in one country. The Soviet-first view survived throughout the existence of that organization and its truncated successor (the Cominform) and withstood abortive attempts by, for example, the Conference of Sixty-One Communist Parties to establish a communist commonwealth, socialist interstate agreements such as the Warsaw Pact, and the Council for Mutual Economic Assistance (COMECON).

The second component was the unique character of the Russian Revolution. Soviet leaders and political analysts made it clear to other communist, anticolonial, and social revolutionary movements that only the Soviet Union, because of its revolutionary experience, was capable of making the direct leap from a capitalist to a socialist society. Lenin had suggested the possibility of a transitional democratic dictatorship of the proletariat and peasantry as early as 1905 but then abandoned the idea. Stalin and his successors revived, revised, and applied the concept of a transitional stage to socialism first to Spain during the civil war and then after World War II to Eastern Europe, and finally in the 1960s as "revolutionary democracies" in the third world.[126] When the Communist Party (CPSU) was building socialism in the Soviet Union, other parties were struggling to launch a revolution; when the CPSU was building communism in the Soviet Union, other parties were building socialism, always one step behind and lacking the leading role of the most advanced state within the movement.

A third component was the purges of foreign communist parties at the instigation of the Soviet Union. The most serious so-called blood purges took place under Stalin in the late 1930s and late 1940s. In the first instance, whole parties were either wiped out (e.g., the Polish Communist Party) or virtually crippled by the arrests and executions (e.g., the German and Yugoslav parties) and had to be rebuilt from the bottom up. In the late 1940s, the emphasis shifted toward show trials of leading communists in the people's democracies of Eastern Europe, many of whom were later executed. Although the executions ceased with Stalin's death, expulsions from foreign parties did not. They remained part of the Soviet interventionist arsenal.

The fourth component was direct intervention by Soviet armed forces in states either under the control of a communist party or, as in the case of Afghanistan, a revolutionary regime. These interventions were in a way an extension in the post-Stalinist period of the purges in that they aimed to remove from power communists or social revolutionaries who were regarded as dissident or, in Soviet parlance, "counterrevolutionaries" (i.e., anti-Soviet). The list is well known: East Germany in 1953, Hungary in 1956, Czechoslovakia in 1968, Afghanistan in 1979, and Poland in 1980.[127] A declaration spelling out the right to intervene to maintain a socialist state was articulated only under Brezhnev, but it had existed implicitly since the creation of the first non-Russian socialist state. In fact, the precedents were set in the post-1917 civil war when the Red Army overthrew socialist governments in Ukraine and Transcaucasia.

An inherent tension existed in the Soviet cultural monopoly of revolution. On the one hand, Soviet leaders emphasized the unique (and superior) character of their state's revolutionary tradition, implying that other socialist revolutions could not duplicate it. On the other hand, they disputed or rejected efforts by other revolutionary movements to define their own ideological course. Following Stalin, Soviet leaders (including Gorbachev) reserved the right to revise Marxism-Leninism within the Soviet context, as they assumed that the Soviet Union had the right to define it in the international movement. But communists in other countries expressing different cultural traditions took issue with this view. Philosophical revisionism within the bloc began within the communist parties themselves.[128] Popular disturbances in East Germany in 1953, Hungary and Poland in 1956, and Poland in 1980 were initiated by workers. Soviet intervention or threats of intervention revealed the fears among the leadership that reopening "separate roads to socialism," closed since 1948, might spill over into the non-Russian borderlands that could also claim cultural distinctiveness.[129]

The last Soviet attempt to create a communist commonwealth, which occurred during a meeting of the eighty-one communist parties in Moscow in 1960, produced more than an open Sino-Soviet split. What emerged was a wide range of political attitudes.[130] The most revisionist of these crystallized in the late 1970s when the Spanish and Italian parties launched what the Spanish communist leader Santiago Carillo first called "Euro-communism." Under that rubric, they rejected several of the fundamental tenets of Marxism-Leninism such as the one-party system and the centrally planned economy. Although the Soviet leaders found such actions distressing, they lacked the will and authority to extirpate the heresy, adopting what Robert Legvold called an "agnostic" position, critical but not inquisitorial.[131]

Some similarities but also important differences characterized relations with Chinese and other Asian communist parties, reflecting another dimension of the Soviet Union's cultural alienation. Recognizing the vast cultural differences that separated China, Europe, and Russia, Mao Zedong and Ho Chi Minh staked out their own revolutionary positions. By the mid-1930s Mao had already laid claim to a place in the communist pantheon of original thinkers by stressing China's "unique and original development in the course of human history."[132] The Soviet Union (and the Comintern) did not challenge Mao openly, but they did attempt to moderate his revolutionary activity to accommodate the changing international situation beginning in 1934 and continuing to 1949, first by adhering to unity of action with the Kuomintang against Japan; then by avoiding a direct clash with the United States; and finally by bringing China's northern borderlands (Manchuria, Outer Mongolia, and Xinjiang) into the Soviet sphere of influence. The communists' victory in China's civil war in 1949 reinforced Mao's belief in the correctness of his course. Although he was willing to defer to Stalin even on matters that ran against China's interests, he was not so accommodating with the old dictator's successors. Changes in leadership and the pressure within the international system weakened the centripetal forces and accelerated the centrifugal forces that characterized the cultural alienation of Soviet foreign policy.

Paradoxically, the cultural distance between the Communist Party in the Soviet Union and those in Asia widened at a time when their interests appeared to draw them closer. No doubt this explains why most Western specialists initially doubted the seriousness of the Sino-Soviet split. Even now, when archival materials reveal the fierce debates between representatives of the Chinese and Soviet communist parties from 1957 to 1963, their disputes about real policy issues, such as the possibility of surviving a nuclear war or the need for détente with the United States, do not appear to provide sufficient reasons for the depth of the conflict. Or to put it another way, the cultural dimensions of the conflict, rooted in differences over conflicting claims of equality and supremacy within the communist movement, help to explain why specific issues were so difficult to resolve.

A long-standing cultural bias existed among Soviet leaders going back to Lenin, who adopted it from Marx's theory of the Asiatic mode of production. Stalin for one had always perceived Asia through a different lens. When the Chinese Communists approached him about joining the Cominform, he replied that the fundamental differences between Europe and Asia made it infeasible. He emphasized that the popular democracies of Eastern Europe and the "democratic dictatorship of the workers and peasants in China" were separated by "not so small differences" from one another and implicitly from the Soviet Union.[133]

Despite efforts to consolidate the partnership with China, Stalin's successors were continually confronted with Beijing's demand for equality within the Sino-Soviet relationship. This showed up most clearly in the long, acerbic discussions in the late 1950s and early 1960s between representatives of the Soviet and Chinese communist parties. There were real policy differences over détente, nuclear disarmament, disputed borders, and migration. But standing in the shadows of all these differences were the fundamental issues of equality and the meaning of history. Mao made this unmistakably clear in his 1957 speech to the Chinese Communist Party Politburo when he stated that Soviet "ways of thinking, behavior and historical traditions differ from ours."[134] As Chen Jian has pointed out, Khrushchev and Mao talked about equality on the assumption that each occupied the position of cultural superiority. The failure of a discussion led by Mikhail Suslov and Deng Xiaoping over specific issues resulted in mutual denunciations of a principled kind and dealt a mortal blow to the international communist movement.[135] Unable to convert détente into a "steady state" or to consolidate the international communist movement, the Soviet Union, like its tsarist predecessor, remained suspended between several cultural worlds and at home in none of them.

Another aspect of Soviet cultural alienation emerged most clearly during an intense debate from 1958 to 1964 over cultural contacts with the outside world as part of a general discussion on the relationship between the party and the creative intelligentsia. Two Ideological Commissions of the Central Committee invited representatives of the intelligentsia to present their views at closed meetings and, from them, produced a series of instructions to the party apparat. One of the goals of the commissions was to issue detailed instructions on limiting foreign cultural contacts as part of the party's general mission to reassert control over the arts.[136] What was unusual about the discussions was the employment by each side—the creative intelligentsia and the party's ideological watchdogs—of a distinctive discourse replete with contrasting tropes. A semiotic analysis of the exchange reveals the extent to which both sides occupied a culturally alien position vis-à-vis Western norms.[137] Although the representatives of the intelligentsia argued for the right to express themselves freely, to be sure without using such explicit language, they were often sharply critical of Western "abuse" of that same freedom.[138]

The discussions and resolutions of the Central Committee split Russian political culture into three unequal parts: the official, the dissenters, and the dissidents.[139] The latter group refused to abide by the tacit agreement following the debates of 1963–1964, namely, no persecution if no open confrontation. The trials, imprisonment, or expulsion of Josif Brodsky, Andrei Siniavsky, and Yury Daniel were followed in the 1970s by the departure of other major cultural figures who refused to accept the tacit agreement. The arrival of each celebrated émigré in the West strengthened the external perception that an unbridgeable gap separated Soviet culture from that of "the civilized world." By failing to enlist the intelligentsia as a partner in reform, the Communist Party drove many dissenters into open dissidence. In the case of Solzhenitsyn, the publication of *Gulag Archipelago* devastated the Soviet Union's image abroad, particularly among French intellectuals on the Left, who concluded that the Soviet system was rotten to the core.[140]

That the Soviet leaders never fully appreciated the damage inflicted by their cultural policies on the prestige and perception of their country abroad emerges clearly from their willingness to sign the Helsinki Agreements in 1975. The Soviet decision was intended to deal with one aspect of the permeable frontiers by obtaining de facto recognition of the postwar borders of Europe. In exchange, the Soviet Union agreed to observe a series of human rights provisions, which, in light of its repressive cultural policies, was tantamount to opening itself to foreign intervention in its domestic affairs.

PERSISTENT FACTORS AND CONTEMPORARY VARIATIONS IN POST-SOVIET RUSSIA

The realignment of global power relationships and the transformation of the Russian state and society after 1991 raise questions about the extent to which the persistent factors continue to influence the formation of Russian foreign policy. The main problem is to identify which elements of continuity survived the radical transformation of Russia's institutional and social structures as well as changes in the leadership and the international environment since the collapse of the Soviet Union. With Russians now comprising 90 percent of the population of the Russian Federation, what remains of the former Soviet Union's multinational society? With Great Russia having adopted a free market economy and abandoned notions of autarchy, is not economic backwardness a thing of the past? With the end of the one-party system and reigning Marxist-Leninist ideology, as well as the introduction of elections and open access to world communications, have not the problems of cultural alienation and porous frontiers substantially diminished in their impact on the conduct of foreign policy?

The four persistent factors have left their mark on Russia's foreign relations as legacies of empire not only in specific cases but also in their interaction, which if anything has become more focused. The loss of the non-Russian periphery with the collapse of the Soviet Union created one new problem and revived another related to both the tsarist and Soviet constructions of a multinational state with porous frontiers. For the first time in modern history, a large Russian population lives across the frontiers in neighboring countries. Although often referred to as the "Russian diaspora," the term is somewhat misleading. Its members were caught up in a process of internal resettlement that was sometimes voluntary but at other times forced—a phenomenon that extended back to the early years of the Muscovite state in the sixteenth century. They did not emigrate and were cut off from their homeland when the

Soviet Union fell apart. But the new Russian Federation did not abandon them, and therein lay the problem. The Russian government has lobbied hard to obtain special status for ethnic Russians living in the successor states even to the point of granting them dual citizenship. Moscow has used the presence of substantial Russian populations in Kazakhstan, Moldova, and Ukraine to press for closer integration of the CIS.

By far the most serious legacy of the multinational state has been the rebellion in Chechnya and its connection to Islamic fundamentalism, especially in the six Muslim successor states of Azerbaijan, Kazakhstan, Kyrgyzstan, Tajikistan, Turkmenistan, and Uzbekistan. The Chechens were conquered by Russian forces in the mid-nineteenth century, but only after a long and bloody war. They were never assimilated into the tsarist or Soviet state. They fiercely resisted collectivization until the eve of World War II. Armed bands reappeared during the German invasion. The Soviet government deported the entire population in January and February 1944. Rehabilitated by Khrushchev, the Chechens gradually returned to their homeland embittered and impoverished. Following the collapse of the Soviet Union they declared their independence, which Moscow refused to recognize. Since 1992 the post-Soviet governments have been unable to repress the rebellion or satisfy Chechen demands.

The wider significance of the Chechen War for Russian foreign policy is related to Moscow's efforts to stabilize the weak, post-Soviet Muslim states and to find a modus vivendi with Muslims outside former Soviet territory.[141] Over the last three decades, Soviet and Russian troops have fought Islamic forces in Afghanistan (1979–1989), Tajikistan (1992–1993), Chechnya (1994–1996 and again since 1999), and Dagestan (1999). When the Chechens invaded the Russian republic of Dagestan in 1999, the Taliban in Afghanistan raided Tajikistan. Russian efforts to mediate in conflicts involving Muslims both inside and outside the CIS include the resolution of the civil war in Tajikistan in 1997 with the good offices of Moscow and Tehran. At the time, Russia's ambassador in Tajikistan warned, "If religious radicals strengthen their positions in Central Asia, a 'holy war' might create a Muslim state on the Russian territory as well."[142] Russia's relations with Iran and Arab states in the Near East are conditioned in part by its vulnerability on the Chechnya conflict. Russian policy toward the entire Muslim world must be carefully calibrated to oppose Islamic extremism both within and across Russia's frontiers and, at the same time, to cultivate good relations with stable governments of large Muslim populations such as Iran. Superficially, it would appear that this balancing act would bring Russia in line with U.S. policy. But the differences in perception and interests over the key issue of who within the region constitutes the greater danger and how it should be managed have divided Russia and the United States as much as they have united them.

The breakup of the Soviet Union has made it more difficult for Russia to police its frontiers than at any other time since the eighteenth century. One reason is that the new external boundaries were not originally designed to be international. They were drawn in the 1920s or, in many cases, even earlier under tsarist rule to serve internal administrative functions. Another reason is that the decline of central authority in the 1990s allowed the growth of regional identities, particularly on the periphery. Certain border regions have shown signs of exploiting their geographically marginal position and reinventing their historical identity to gain an advantage in bargaining with the center.[143] As a result, Russia's frontiers have become once again ill defined and contested. They have become the sites of massive, illegal border crossings of people, drugs, arms, and terrorists—a situation that has prompted Russia to reach reciprocal arrangements with its neighbors over frontier security. It is no wonder that President Vladimir Putin has repeatedly stated, first in 2001 and again in September 2004, that Russia's relations with the countries of the CIS are the highest priority.[144] Nor is it surprising that he is determined to reduce regional autonomy and reimpose centralized authority.

A third reason closely related to the other two is the emergence of a new constellation of powers on the Russian periphery composed of the European Union, China, and the United States, each of which constitutes both a potential challenge to Russian security and an opportunity for "partnership." The enlargement of the European Union to include Ukraine, the military and economic presence of the United States in the Middle East and Central Asia, and the population pressure on Siberia from China's northern provinces have been cause for concern in Moscow. The Russian response has been pragmatic but not without problems. As in the past, the defense of Russia's frontiers forces its interaction with three different cultural and political systems—the European, Middle Eastern, and East Asian. In addition there is the need to deal with the United States, which, for different reasons, is also involved in all three areas. Difficulties arise for Moscow in seeking to maintain equilibrium among the competing demands of this complex international environment. Reactions abroad, particularly in the West, to tactical shifts in Russian foreign policy are often expressed in terms of cultural alienation. Even the most optimistic Russian observers have concluded that "in the foreseeable future Russia may be *with* the West but not *of* it."[145]

Interpretations differ over the motivation for Putin's policies in dealing with the western borderlands. What cannot be denied is how closely they resemble historical Russian responses to frontier problems in the region. Putin has supported a pro-Russian regime in Belarus that is odious to the West but in Russian eyes may be preferable to a liberal government that leans the other way, in the direction of Poland and NATO. His policy toward Ukraine appears to be similarly motivated by concerns over external penetration. For example, Moscow denounced foreign nongovernmental organizations (NGOs) for having supported the Orange Revolution and criticized representatives of Poland and Lithuania for playing a mediating role in the Ukrainian political crisis. The renewed interest of Poland in Belarus and Ukraine can only remind the Russians of their long competition with the Poles over influence in the borderlands, assumed to have ended in 1945. Similar problems have complicated relations with Estonia and Latvia, countries with large Russian populations. Russia long refused to negotiate a final boundary with them in a vain attempt to prevent or slow their joining NATO and the European Union.

The U.S. penetration of Russia's strategic space along its southern flank has opened a new, potentially vulnerable frontier with territories that were once Soviet republics or clients. U.S.-Russian rivalry in the region has both military and economic ramifications. The armed interventions of the United States in Afghanistan and Iraq, the establishment of U.S. bases in Kyrgyzstan and Uzbekistan, and the introduction of training groups in Georgia have gone far beyond any challenge to Russian interests in the region mounted by Great Britain during the Great Game. Throughout the 1990s Russian and U.S. companies engaged in fierce bidding for contracts to build oil pipelines from Central Asia and Caucasian fields to the West. Although the battle of the pipelines has ended, the competition for oil resources continues. The Soviet response has been to form with China and the four Central Asian states the Shanghai Cooperation Organization (SCO). It has maintained a low profile and its representatives deny they have any ambitions to emulate NATO. They have stated clearly that the organization is opposed to the U.S. policy of creating a military cordon around Russia and China and in 2005 called for a timetable for the withdrawal of U.S. bases from Central Asia. But there are rifts in the group. The ongoing struggle for spheres of influence between Russia and the United States changes the political alignment of the Central Asia states from one year to the next. In 2004 one analysis showed Russia predominant in Armenia, Kazakhstan, and Tajikistan, and the United States in Azerbaijan and Uzbekistan, with Georgia and Kyrgyzstan open to influence from both.[146] Two years later the configuration held true in scarcely any of its parts.

The growth of the power of the state in regulating domestic and foreign economic relations has given rise to perceptions that Russia is once again displaying the features of a culturally alien society. In the immediate post-Soviet period, the country's leaders eagerly claimed that they had accepted a new system of values based on individual liberties and the free market. In a whirlwind propaganda campaign, Foreign Minister Andrei Kozyrev explicitly linked his pleas for Russia's new cultural centrality and specific foreign policy aims. He argued that a new Marshall Plan for Russia would facilitate its entry into "the family of civilized states." It would further clear the way for the Conference of Security and Cooperation in Europe (later the Organization for Security and Cooperation in Europe, or OSCE), with Russian participation, to address the security problems produced by border conflicts around the new state. At the same time, he maintained that Russia ought to be recognized as a great power and an equal partner with the West on the basis of its human and intellectual resources, vast natural resources, and geographical location and size. The goal of nuclear disarmament meant the establishment of a "special kind of relationship" with the United States.[147] By the mid-1990s, however, a reaction had set in, partly in response to the disillusionment over the lack of substantial Western economic aid and partly because of the deteriorating conditions of the Russian economy during the process of privatization, a process it appeared to many in Russia that had been engineered and mismanaged by Western economists. The reaction was associated with an ideological shift dubbed the "new Eurasianism."

New Eurasianism simply meant avoidance of excessive dependence on the West and a retreat from an untrammeled free market at home and abroad. It appeared that the Russian economy was moving toward an intermediate position between Western and Asian models of economic development: on the one hand, an emphasis on the role of the free market, mass consumption, and state social services; on the other, a focus on rates of growth, government support and protection of enterprises, and encouragement of accumulation. In the mid-1990s the terms "individualist values" versus "collectivist values" were widely invoked in the Russian media. In foreign economic policy, the new Eurasianism took the form of substituting energy for declining military power as a means of reasserting Russia's traditional influence over the successor states of the CIS.[148] Since 2003 Putin's attack on the wealth and influence of the oligarchs, like his attempts to reduce the authority of the regional barons and to control the media, has been part of a campaign to enhance the power of the state and to control and manage the economy.

Putin's actions have often been interpreted in the West as a retreat from democratic practices and respect for human rights. Russia's attempts to intervene diplomatically, economically, and, on occasion, militarily in the "near abroad," a term employed by the Russian leadership to define the territory of the former Soviet Union but rejected by those to whom it is applied, have complicated relations with the European Union, which perceives such activities as lacking in sophistication and not being "civilized."[149] For the first time since the fall of communism, Russia has slipped into the category of "not free" in the international rankings established by Freedom House.[150] But overall, the consensus has been that in all areas of foreign policy a new pragmatism prevails and that "Eurasianism is over."[151] Although this may be true at the highest levels of policy making, it is not easy to alter cultural perceptions that have become embedded in educational institutions and the popular mentality.[152] There is ample evidence in the Russian media and on the floor of the State Duma that Eurasianist, as much as Western, sympathies continue to attract vocal advocates as well as others who, for pragmatic reasons, champion both.

The major foreign policy problems facing the Russian leadership in the post-Soviet period continue to arise from the four persistent factors analyzed in this chapter, although their specific features and patterns of interaction have undergone changes. The loss of the majority of the federation's non-Russian population has not ended the security problems of a multinational society with porous frontiers, but instead has merely transposed them. The Islamic factor and the so-called diaspora, both legacies of empire, have created threats to Russia's security along its southern frontier as well as opportunities to intervene in the affairs of its immediate neighbors. Efforts to repress the Chechen revolt and strengthen ties with the CIS invariably raise the specter of Russian imperialism in the international community, mainly in the United States and Europe, and jeopardize Russia's efforts to be accepted as a normal, "civilized" member of that community. Similarly, attempts to overcome Russia's relative economic backwardness, exacerbated by a crash program of "Westernization" in the early 1990s, have led to a greater concentration of power in the hands of the president and predictable criticism from abroad. If post-Soviet Russia fails to meet its international obligations under the terms of membership in the OSCE and the Council of Europe, then what differentiates its behavior from past actions such as Soviet violations of the Helsinki Agreements or the Yalta Declaration on Liberated Territories? Or so the question may be posed. Thus, Russia's endeavors to solve problems arising from one of the persistent factors have created or intensified problems related to one or several of the others. Can the present leadership break the cycle?

Following in the footsteps to Gorbachev and Yeltsin, President Putin has launched a series of initiatives aimed at resolving the conundrum. But changing circumstances in the international system and in the nature of leadership itself further complicate his problems. First, the United States has taken advantage of its new position as the sole superpower to press vigorously for a global transformation of political systems in its own image. It has also taken a lead in defining the rules of the war against terrorism. Through international agencies such as the World Bank and International Monetary Fund, as well as its own powerful export instruments, the United States is having an unprecedented impact on the global economic environment in which Russians must operate. Its cultural exports, particularly in the field of pop culture, now flow unimpeded into Russian space. This new form of "capitalist encirclement," whether perceived by Russians as benign or aggressive, exercises a powerful influence on Russian policy makers and the public.

Second, Russia must deal with the growing power of China and its renewed interest in Central Asia as an energy source, a trading partner, and a potentially dangerous locus of support for Muslim separatism in Xinjiang Province. As the Russian population of eastern Siberia declines and the Russian diaspora shrinks in Central Asia, Chinese migration into the border provinces increases. As yet, there are no signs that China intends to expand territorially. But to replace Russian influence in Central Asia or Siberia, that may not be necessary.

The third major factor of change in the complex equation of Russian foreign policy is domestic and structural. Since the fall of communism, the leadership has had to operate in a public sphere that, in the West, may appear to be cramped or even shrinking. But interest groups and political parties still contend with one another as policy shifts and ministerial appointments continue to demonstrate. Current evaluations in the West of President Putin's policies range from pragmatic (positive) to chaotic (negative). These policies might better be perceived as attempts by a new kind of leadership to devise solutions within a changing international environment to problems arising from the interaction of persistent factors that have restrained and shaped Russian foreign policy for centuries.

NOTES

1. George Kennan restated this truism in his testimony before the U.S. Senate Foreign Relations Committee, *New York Times*, April 5, 1989. "Hearing of the Senate Foreign Relations Committee Chaired by Senator Clairborne Pell (D-RI): Testimony of Professor George Kennan," *New York Times*, April 4, 1989.

2. Lucien Febvre with the assistance of Lionel Bataillon, *La terre et l'évolution humaine* (Paris: Michel, 1970), chap. 1; Andre-Louis Sanguin, *Vidal de la Blache, 1845–1918: Une génie de la géographie* (Paris: Belin, 1993), p. 127; Paul Vidal de la Blache, *Tableau de la géographie de la France* (Paris: Tallandier, 1979), pp. 1–7.

3. Denys Hay, *Europe: The Emergence of an Idea,* 2d ed. (Edinburgh: Edinburgh University Press, 1968), pp. 57–60. See also Geoffrey Barraclough, *The Medieval Empire: Idea and Reality* (London: Historical Association, 1950); and Denis de Rougemont, *The Idea of Europe* (New York: Macmillan, 1966); Nicholas V. Riasanovsky, "The Emergence of Eurasianism," *California Slavic Studies,* no. 4 (1967); Ilya Vinkovetsky, "Classical Eurasianism and Its Legacy," *Canadian American Studies 34,* no. 2 (Summer 2000): 25–140.

4. The following is based on Alfred J. Rieber, "Persistent Factors in Russian Foreign Policy: An Interpretive Essay," in *Imperial Russian Foreign Policy,* ed. Hugh Ragsdale (Cambridge: Woodrow Wilson Center and Cambridge University Press, 1993), pp. 315–359. I have slightly altered some of the terminology. "Multicultural" has given way to "multinational" in order to reflect the evolution of ethnic into national identities in the twentieth century, and "cultural alienation" replaces "cultural marginality," which was criticized for implying inferiority; this had not been my intention.

5. For a devastating critique of the failure of American academic and government officials to uncover the massive distortions of Soviet statistics, see John Howard Wilhelm, "The Failure of the American Sovietological Economics Profession," *Europe-Asia Studies 55,* no. 1 (2003): 59–74.

6. Marshall D. Shulman, *Stalin's Foreign Policy Reappraised* (Cambridge: Harvard University Press, 1963) is a good case study of how these changes had already influenced Stalin's latter-day policies.

7. Soldiers' soviets were briefly established in a few cities in Germany, the crumbling Habsburg monarchy, and even Bulgaria, but aside from the short-lived Hungarian Soviet Republic, these were ephemeral events, although they sparked considerable enthusiasm among the Bolsheviks at the time.

8. Peter Gatrell, "The First World War and War Communism, 1914–1920," in *The Economic Transformation of the Soviet Union, 1913–1945,* ed. R. W. Davies, Mark Harrison, and S. G. Wheatcroft (Cambridge: Cambridge University Press, 1994), especially pp. 220, 222, 224, 228–229. The amount of railroad track laid down from 1914 to early 1917 (eleven thousand kilometers) actually exceeded the Soviet performance during the Second World War (nine thousand kilometers). During both world wars,

rising productivity in defense industries and transportation was accompanied by a sharp decline in civilian industrial production.

9. Moshe Lewin, *Russia/USSR/Russia: The Drive and Drift of a Super State* (New York: New Press, 1995), pp. 48–50, summarizes the Soviet literature demonstrating that key sectors of industrial production fell to pre-1861 levels.

10. Peter Holquist, *Making War: Forging Revolution in Russia's Continuum of Crisis, 1914–1921* (Cambridge: Harvard University Press, 2002).

11. Alexander Gerschenkron, *Economic Backwardness in Historical Perspective* (Cambridge: Harvard University Press, 1962), chap. 6. Later Gerschenkron characterized the Soviet economy as a throwback to the mercantilist state of Peter the Great with its subjugation of the peasantry and "self perpetuating force of an inherently unstable dictatorship." Alexander Gerschenkron, *Europe in the Russian Mirror: Four Lectures in Economic History* (Cambridge: Cambridge University Press, 1970), p. 121. In like spirit Moshe Lewin used the term "superstructure suspended in air." Moshe Lewin, *The Making of the Soviet System: Essays in the Social History of Interwar Russia* (New York: Pantheon, 1985), pp. 260–261.

12. There were actually two treaties signed at Brest; the first recognized a breakaway, anti-Bolshevik Ukrainian government.

13. V. I. Lenin, *Sochineniya*, 2d ed., 35 vols. (Moscow: Gosizdat, 1930–1935), vol. 25, pp. 498, 501; vol. 26, pp. 14, 15; vol. 30, p. 384; E. H. Carr, *The Bolshevik Revolution, 1917–1923*, vol. 3 (New York: Macmillan, 1953), chap. 25, "Revolution over Europe."

14. The foreign policy volumes of E. H. Carr, *A History of Soviet Russia*, remain indispensable for the early years. See *The Bolshevik Revolution, 1917–1923*, vol. 1 (London: Macmillan, 1950), part 3; vol. 3, *The Interregnum 1923–24* (London: Macmillan, 1953), part 2; *Socialism in One Country, 1924–1926*, vol. 3 (London: Macmillan, 1964), parts 1 and 2; *Foundations of a Planned Economy, 1926–1929*, vol. 3 (London, Macmillan, 1971), part 3. For more recent interpretations, see Teddy Uldricks, *Diplomacy and Ideology: The Origins of Soviet Foreign Relations, 1917–1930* (London: Sage, 1979); Branko Lazitch and M. Drashkovitch, *Lenin and the Comintern*, 2 vols. (Stanford: Stanford University Press, 1972); Richard Debo, *Revolution and Survival: The Foreign Policy of Soviet Russia, 1917–1918* (Toronto: University of Toronto Press, 1979); Richard Debo, *Survival and Consolidation: The Foreign Policy of Soviet Russia, 1918–1921* (Montreal: McGill-Queen's University Press, 1992).

15. Louis Fischer, *The Soviets in World Affairs: A History of the Relations Between the Soviet Union and the Rest of the World, 1917–1929* (Princeton: Princeton University Press, 1951), vol. 1, p. 463.

16. Carr, *The Bolshevik Revolution*, vol. 3, p. 283; E. H. Carr, *Socialism in One Country* (New York: Macmillan, 1958), vol. 1, pp. 454–455.

17. Carr, *Socialism in One Country*, vol. 1, pp. 273–279, 293–297, 443–445.

18. Robert Lewis, "Foreign Economic Relations," in *The Economic Transformation of the Soviet Union, 1913–1945*, ed. R. W. Davies, Mark Harrison, and S. G. Wheatcroft (Cambridge: Cambridge University Press, 1994), pp. 198–215. In staging trials of

bourgeois specialists, Stalin sought to link their alleged sabotage to foreign engineers and the threat of foreign intervention. Kendall E. Bailes, *Technology and Society Under Lenin and Stalin: Origins of the Soviet Scientific Intelligentsia, 1917–1941* (Princeton: Princeton University Press, 1978).

19. The key instrument for obtaining foreign technology was the state monopoly on foreign trade. As L. B. Krasin repeatedly stated, its object was not "narrowly commercial" but "productive-economic." V. A. Shishkin, *Polosa priznanii i vneshne-ekonomicheskaya politika SSSR (1924–1928 gg.)* (Leningrad: Nauka, 1983), pp. 81, 94.

20. It turned out that the war scare was manipulated by Stalin to discredit the Right Opposition, another instance of blurring the differences between domestic and foreign policy.

21. R. W. Davies, *The Soviet Economy in Turmoil, 1929–1930* (London: Macmillan, 1989), pp. xiv–xviii, 34–35, quotation at p. xiv.

22. The share of defense in the total budget expenditure rose in the following pattern: 1933: 3.4%; 1934: 9.1%; 1935: 11.1%; 1936: 16.1%; 1937: 16.5%; 1938: 18.7%; 1939: 25.6%; 1940: 32.6%. Alec Nove, *An Economic History of the USSR, 1917–1991* (London: Penguin, 1992), p. 230. After a postwar decline, the defense share began to creep back up from 18.7% in 1950 to 21.2% in 1952 and 23.9% in 1953. Ibid., p. 328. From 1950 to 1955 the Soviet Union devoted a higher percentage of its GNP to defense than the United States did. R. W. Davies, *Soviet Economic Development from Lenin to Khrushchev* (Cambridge: Cambridge University Press), p. 71.

23. James Barber and Mark Harrison, *The Soviet Home Front, 1941–1945: A Social and Economic History of the USSR in the Second World War* (London: Longman, 1991), pp. 189–190.

24. As late as September 1945 Stalin frankly outlined Soviet economic needs to a visiting group of American senators. He dismissed his earlier views on self-sufficiency and stated that "the greater the economic development of a country, the greater its foreign trade potential." He estimated a need for six billion dollars to pay for five million tons of rail, 10,000 locomotives, 150,000 railroad cars and 40,000–50,000 machine tools. U.S. Department of State, *Foreign Relations of the U.S.: The Soviet Union, 1945*, vol. 5 (Washington, DC: U.S. Government Printing Office, 1955), pp. 882–883. For different interpretations of American motives, see John Lewis Gaddis, *The United States and the Origins of the Cold War, 1941–1947* (New York: Columbia University Press, 1972), pp. 178–182, 194–197, 215–220; and Gabriel Kolko, *The Politics of War: The World and United States Foreign Policy, 1943–1945* (New York: Random House, 1968), pp. 335–338.

25. George W. Breslauer has characterized the three ruling strategies of Khrushchev, Brezhnev, and Gorbachev as "reforming," "adapting," and "transforming." Breslauer, *Khrushchev and Brezhnev as Leaders: Building Authority in Soviet Politics* (London: Allen & Unwin, 1982); and Breslauer, *Gorbachev and Yeltsin as Leaders* (Cambridge: Cambridge University Press, 2002). For the application of Khrushchev's and Brezhnev's approach to foreign policy, see James Richter, *Khrushchev's Double*

Bind (Baltimore: Johns Hopkins University Press, 1994); and Richard D. Anderson, *Public Politics in an Authoritarian State: Making Foreign Policy During the Brezhnev Era* (Ithaca: Cornell University Press, 1993). With their combined emphasis on personal styles of leadership and the Soviet political system, these are good examples of injecting social science methods into the historical school of great men. Although Richter asserts that both Khrushchev and Brezhnev endorsed a similar policy of "offensive détente," he does not show how persistent factors might have helped shape those choices. Richter, *Khrushchev's Double Bind*, chaps. 7, 8.

26. Mark Harrison, "Economic Growth and Slowdown," in *Brezhnev Reconsidered*, ed. Edwin Bacon and Mark Sandle (Basingstoke: Macmillan, 2002), p. 45.

27. Elizabeth Kridl Valkenier, *The Soviet Union and the Third World: An Economic Bind* (New York: Columbia University Press, 1983).

28. R. Craig Nation and Mark V. Kauppi, eds., *The Soviet Impact on Africa* (Lexington, MA: Heath, 1984), especially pp. 233–235.

29. Rajan Menon, *Soviet Power and the Third World* (New Haven: Yale University Press, 1986).

30. Mikhail Gorbachev, *Perestroika: New Thinking for Our Country and the World* (New York: Harper & Row, 1987), pp. 141, 146.

31. Alec Nove, *An Economic History of the USSR, 1917–1991* (London: Penguin Books, 1992), pp. 378–379.

32. Bruce Parrott, ed., *Trade, Technology and Soviet-American Relations* (Bloomington: Indiana University Press, 1985).

33. Bruce Parrott, "Soviet Foreign Policy, Internal Politics, and Trade with the West," in Parrott, *Trade, Technology, and Soviet-American Relations*, pp. 41–57.

34. For a selection of excerpts by Soviet critics, see Alec Nove, *Glasnost in Action: Cultural Renaissance in Russia* (Boston: Unwin, Hyman, 1989), chap. 8. Significantly, Nove identifies the reformers with a "cultural revolution," thus linking attempts to overcome economic backwardness with the elimination of the mental gap that lay at the heart of cultural alienation.

35. He further recognized that this reform would entail other deep changes in the bureaucratic structure and social conventions. Mikhail Gorbachev, *Zhizn i reformy*, vol. 1 (Moscow: Novosti, 1995), pp. 280–281. Acknowledgment of economic backwardness was widespread among his close advisers. See, for example, Anatoly S. Chernyaev, *My Six Years with Gorbachev*, trans. Robert English and Elizabeth Tucker (University Park: Pennsylvania State University Press, 2000), p. 24. Chernyaev writes, "Science and technology are reaching new frontiers worldwide while we lag ten to thirty years behind." Ibid.

36. Chernyaev, *My Six Years with Gorbachev*, pp. 192–201, quotation at pp. 200–201. For an analysis of the "intractable military-industrial sector," see William E. Odom, *The Collapse of the Soviet Military* (New Haven: Yale University Press, 1998), chap. 11.

37. Archie Brown, *The Gorbachev Factor* (Oxford: Oxford University Press, 1996), chap. 5.

38. There is wide disagreement among scholars over the seriousness of the problems facing the late Soviet and early post-Soviet economy as well as the reasons for the collapse of the command economy. For recent revised views on both topics see Andrei Shleifer and Daniel Treisman, "A Normal Country," *Foreign Affairs* 83, no. 2 (March–April, 2004): 20–38; Gerard Roland, "The Russian Economy in 2005," http//www.econ.berkeley.edu~groland/pubs/The Russian Economy in the Year 2005.pdf; and Mark Harrison, "Are Command Economies Unstable? Why Did the Soviet Economy Collapse?" *Warwick Economic Research Papers*, no. 604 (May 3, 2001). There is no denying, however, that the late Soviet and early post-Soviet economy lagged far behind the most advanced industrialized countries, now multiplying in Asia as well as Europe, against which Russian leaders have always measured their achievements.

39. Donna Bahry, "Ethnicity and Equality in Post-Communist Economic Transition: Evidence from Russia's Republics," *Europe-Asia Studies* 54, no. 5 (2002): 673–699.

40. Harley Balzer, "The Putin Thesis and Russian Energy Policy," *Post-Soviet Affairs* 21, no. 3 (2005): 210–225, quotation on p. 217.

41. Alfred J. Rieber, "Zheleznye dorogi i ekonomicheskoe razvitie: istoki sistemy Reiterna," *Stranitsy rossiiskoi istorii. Problemy, sobytie, lyudi. Sbornik statei v chest' Borisa Vasilevicha Ananicha* (St. Petersburg: Dmitrii Bulanin, 2003), pp. 150–178.

42. When Andrei Ilarionov resigned as Putin's top economic adviser he noted unhappily that "the state has evolved in quite different directions" from pursuing a liberal economic policy. Quoted in Peter Gumbel, "Putin's Power Surge," *Time Europe* May 9, 2006; for potential problems for Western investors see Timothy Frye, "Credible Commitment and Property Rights: Evidence from Russia," *American Political Science Review* 98, no. 3 (August 2004): 453–466.

43. For a comparative treatment unfavorable to Russia's international financial position see Michael S. Bernstam and Alvin Rabushka, "China versus Russia: International Bankers Run a Natural Experiment," *The Russian Economy* (Stanford: Hoover Institution, April 13, 2006), http://www.russianeconomy.org/comments/041306.html.

44. Vladimir Yevtushenko, "Russian Petrodollars Will Have to Move Back," *Russia in Global Affairs*, March 24, 2003, http://eng.global.affairs.ru/numbers/2/467. html. In 2004 the per capita GDP of the Russian Federation was 24 percent of that of the United States (as compared with 43 percent in 1975), leading Putin's economic adviser, Andrei Illarionov, to conclude: "By modern standards of well-being, Russia remains a fundamentally impoverished country." Quoted in "A Long-Term Project for Russia," *Russian Global Affairs*, no. 3 (July–September 2005), http://eng.globalaffairs. ru/numbers/12/939.html. Opposing Illarionov's proposals for Russia to follow the U.S.–Hong Kong model of development, the spokesman for a return to autarky as the means for Russia to catch up with the West without losing its sovereignty is Mikhail Yaryev, "Fortress Russia," *Russian Global Affairs*, no. 3 (July–September 2005), http://eng.globalaffairs.ru/numbers/12/939.html.

45. David G. Victor and Nadejda M. Victor, "Axis of Oil?" *Foreign Affairs* (March/April, 2003), pp. 47–61; and Nadejda M. Victor, "Russia's Gas Crunch," *New York Times,* April 6, 2006, where she argues that the price increases reflect "problems connected by [Gazprom's] inefficient management and a looming decline in gas production."

46. Stalin, *Sochineniya,* vol. 5, pp. 117–120.

47. Nicholas I was convinced that young people traveling abroad "sometimes returned to Russia with the most incorrect (*lozhnyi*) notions about it, not understanding its real needs, laws, customs, norms and frequently language." The law of 1851 set strict limits on the time that anyone could remain abroad and attached severe penalties. During the period of the Great Reforms most of these restrictions were lifted. A. E. Ianovskii, "Pasporty zagranichnye," *Entsklopedicheskii slovar,* ed. F. A. Brogauz and I. A. Efron (St. Petersburg: Efron, 1897), pp. 925–926.

48. Yuri Felshtinsky, "The Legal Foundations of the Immigration and Emigration Policy of the USSR, 1917–1927," *Soviet Studies* 34, no. 3 (July 1982): 327–348. Children of these immigrants could still be encountered in Moscow in the 1950s.

49. Marc Raeff, *Russia Abroad: A Cultural History of the Russian Emigration, 1919–1939* (New York: Oxford University Press, 1990). The full story remains to be told. For a valuable bibliography, see *Bibliothèque russe de l'institut d'études slaves— L'émigration russe: Revues et recueils, 1920–1980, index général des articles* (Paris: Institut d'Études Slaves, 1988).

50. I. I. Petrov, "Zabota partii ob ukreplenii pogranichnykh voisk (1939–1940)," *Voprosy istoriya KPSS,* no. 1 (1985): 94–99.

51. Stalin, *Sochineniya,* vol. 6, p. 396.

52. Stalin, *Sochineniya,* vol. 8, p. 265.

53. Stanley G. Payne, *The Spanish Civil War, the Soviet Union and Communism* (New Haven: Yale University Press, 2004), argues strongly the position that this was precisely Stalin's goal in Spain.

54. If successful, this policy would have confronted Hitler with the potential of a three-front war. The question of how seriously Stalin was committed to fulfilling the terms of this alliance has recently been reviewed and revised to suggest that it was Romanian opposition to transit rights of the Red Army, not Soviet reluctance to oppose Hitler, that blocked the conclusion of a grand alliance to stop German aggression. Hugh Ragsdale, *The Soviets, the Munich Crisis, and the Coming of World War II* (Cambridge: Cambridge University Press, 2004).

55. According to Litvinov, "our commission, with the approval of the government was to prepare its work without considering (*ignoriruya*) the possibility of serious social upheavals (*perevorotov*) in Europe and taking as its point of departure the existing structure." *Arkhiv vneshnei politiki. Ministerstvo inostrannykh del,* fond 0512, opis 2, dela 4, protocol 5, list 31. See also Aleksei M. Filatov, "Problems of Post-War Construction in Soviet Foreign Policy Conceptions During World War II," in *The Soviet Union and Europe in the Cold War, 1943–53,* ed. Francesca Gori and Silvio Pons (New York: St. Martin's

Press, 1996), pp. 3–23; and A. A. Danilov and A. V. Pyzhikov, *Rozhdenie sverkhderzhavy SSSR v pervye poslevoennye gody* (Moscow: Rosspen, 2001), pp. 15–17.

56. For specific case studies of where these combinations succeeded and where they failed for the communists, see Alfred J. Rieber, "Zhdanov in Finland" (Carl Beck Papers, no. 1107, University of Pittsburgh, 1995), and Rieber, "The Crack in the Plaster: Crisis in Rumania and the Origins of the Cold War," *Journal of Modern History* 76, no. 1 (March 2004): 62–106. For evidence that communist parties in Western Europe were pursuing similar goals under much less favorable conditions, see Rieber, *Stalin and the French Communist Party, 1941–1947* (New York: Columbia University Press, 1962).

57. On Iran, see David Nissman, *The Soviet Union and Iranian Azerbaizhan: The Use of Nationalism for Political Penetration* (Boulder, CO: Westview, 1987); Stephen L. McFarland, "A Peripheral View of the Origins of the Cold War: The Crisis in Iran, 1941–1947," *Diplomatic History*, no. 4 (Fall 1980): 333–351, and Rouhallah K. Famazani, *Iran's Foreign Policy, 1941–1973* (Charlottesville: University of North Carolina Press, 1975). Russian military intervention and Bolshevik penetration of Azerbaijan had long and complex histories. See "Iranian Relations with Russia and the Soviet Union," in *Cambridge History of Iran*, vol. 7, eds. Peter Avery, G. R. G. Hambly, and C. Melville; Firuz Kazemzadeh, *Russia and Britain in Persia, 1864–1914: A Study in Imperialism* (New Haven: Yale University Press, 1968); and Chosroe Chaqueri, *The Soviet Socialist Republic of Iran, 1920–1921: Birth of the Trauma* (Pittsburgh: University of Pittsburgh Press, 1995); for Xinjiang, see Alan S. Whiting and Sheng Shih-ts'ai, *Sinkiang: Pawn of Pivot?* (East Lansing: Michigan State University Press, 1958), which makes the comparison with Azerbaijan; for Outer Mongolia, see Robert A. Rupen, *Mongols of the Twentieth Century*, part 1 (Bloomington: Indiana University Press, 1964); for China, see Odd Arne Westad, *Cold War and Revolution: Soviet-American Rivalry and the Origins of the Chinese Civil War* (New York: Columbia University Press, 1993).

58. Maxim Litvinov made the argument to an American reporter that Soviet foreign policy was still guided by the antiquated belief that security was synonymous with expansion and control of territory. Vojtech Mastny, "The Cassandra in the Foreign Commissariat: Maxim Litvinov and the Cold War," *Foreign Affairs* 54 (January 1976): 373.

59. This included Czechoslovakia, which was not yet under full communist control. G. P. Murashko, T. V. Volokitina, T. M. Islamov, A. F. Nosova and L. A. Rogavaia, eds. *Vostochnaya Evropa v dokumentakh rosiiskikh arkhivov, 1944–1953 gg.* 2 vols. (Novosibirsk: Sibirskii khronograf, 1997–1998), vol. 1, p. 675.

60. I. S. Girenko, *Stalin-Tito* (Moscow: Izd. Politicheskoi literatury, 1992); Ivo Banac, *With Stalin Against Tito: Cominform Splits in Yugoslav Communism* (Ithaca: Cornell University Press, 1988), 110–116, 123–124.

61. Odd Arne Westad, "Concerning the Situation in 'A': New Russian Evidence on the Soviet Intervention in Afghanistan," *Bulletin* (*Cold War International History Project* [*CWIHP*]), nos. 8/9, pp. 128–130, 137–144.

62. *Documents on International Affairs* (London: Royal Institute of International Affairs, 1951), pp. 317–318. Although the actual effect was minimal, the U.S. administration's rhetoric of liberation stressed the need, in John Foster Dulles's words, "to break up [the Soviet Union] from within." Robert Divine, *Foreign Policy and U.S. Presidential Elections, 1940–1960*, vol. 2 (New York: New Viewpoints, 1974), p. 51.

63. Quoted in Norman Naimark, "The Soviet Occupation: Moscow's Man in (East) Berlin," *Bulletin (CWIHP)*, no. 4 (Fall 1994): 48.

64. USSR Council of Ministers Order, "On Measures to Improve the Health of the Political Situation in the GDR, 2 June 1953," *Bulletin (CWIHP)*, no. 10 (March 1998): 79.

65. Ferenc A. Vali, *Rift and Revolution in Hungary: Nationalism Versus Communism* (Cambridge: Harvard University Press, 1961), pp. 438–439.

66. Quoted in Hope Harrison, "Ulbricht and the Concrete Rose: New Archival Evidence on the Dynamic of Soviet–East German Relations and the Berlin Crisis, 1958–1961" (Cold War International Working Papers, no. 5, Woodrow Wilson International Center for Scholars, Washington, DC, 1993), p. 39.

67. Stephen Szabo, *The Diplomacy of German Unification* (New York: St. Martin's Press, 1992); and Hans-Herman Hertle, "The Fall of the Wall: The Unintended Self-Dissolution of East Germany's Ruling Regime," *Bulletin (CWIHP)*, nos. 12/13 (Fall and Winter 2001): 133, 154–158.

68. Stalin repeatedly reminded the communist parties of Eastern Europe after the war that they did not need to establish a dictatorship of the proletariat because the Soviet Union would prevent the outbreak of civil war and foreign intervention in their countries. See, for example, his comments to the Polish communists in May 1946. Murashenko, *Vostochnaya Evropa*, vol. 1, pp. 456–458; and discussion in Alfred J. Rieber, "Stalin as Foreign Policy Maker," in *Stalin: A New History*, ed. Sarah Davies and James Harris (Cambridge: Cambridge University Press, 2004), p. 154.

69. For the early history of the growing alienation, see Sergei N. Goncharov, John W. Lewis, and Xue Litai, *Uncertain Partners: Stalin, Mao, and the Korean War* (Stanford: Stanford University Press, 1993), especially pp. 26–28, 121–122.

70. Peter C. Perdue, *China Marches West: The Qing Conquest of Central Eurasia* (Cambridge: Harvard University Press, 2005), pp. 51–94, 133–173, 511–531.

71. Thomas W. Robinson, "The Sino-Soviet Border Dispute: Background, Development, and the March 1969 Clashes," *American Political Science Review* 66, no. 4 (December 1972): 1175–1202.

72. Robin Edmonds, *Soviet Foreign Policy: The Brezhnev Years* (Oxford: Oxford University Press, 1983), pp. 104–105, 112.

73. Jeanne L. Wilson, *Strategic Partners: Russian-Chinese Relations in the Post-Soviet Era* (Armonk, NY: Sharpe, 2004), p. 116.

74. China had its own history of porous frontiers that was older and more turbulent than that of Russia. The persistence of this factor shows up in the multiple frontier wars fought by the Chinese Communists after 1950 on their frontiers with Korea,

India, and Vietnam as well as their occupation of Tibet, repression of Muslim dissension in Xinjiang, and little cold war with Taiwan.

75. Simultaneous with the disturbances in Hungary in June 1956 the Poznan riots in Poland moved Khrushchev to declare that the violence had been provoked by the imperialists with the aim of "fomenting disunity" within the bloc and "destroying [the socialist countries] one by one." Cited in Mark Kramer, "New Evidence on Soviet Decision Making and the 1956 Polish and Hungarian Crises," *Bulletin (CWIHP)*, nos. 8/9 (Winter 1996–97): 361.

76. *Pravda*, November 13, 1968. Brezhnev later denied that this constituted a new doctrine of "limited sovereignty." *Pravda*, September 23, 1971.

77. E. A. Chirkova, "Revoliutsiia 1848–1849 godov i politika Rossii," in O. V. Orlik, V. N. Vinogradov, A. G. Ignat'ev and V. N. Ponomarov, *Istoriia vneshnei politiki Rossii. Pervaia polovina XIX veka (Ot voin Rossii protiv Napoleona do Parizhskogo mira 1856 g.)* (Moscow, Mezhdunarodnye otnosheniia, 1995), p. 357.

78. R. Craig Nation, *Black Earth, Red Star: A History of Soviet Security Policy, 1917–1991* (Ithaca: Cornell University Press, 1992), p. 308; Michael Beschloss and Strobe Talbott, *At the Highest Level: The Inside Story of the End of the Cold War* (Boston: Little, Brown, 1994), p. 134.

79. As "peace-loving states" Khrushchev singled out India, Burma, Afghanistan, Egypt, and Syria. But he made no mention of revolutionary national liberation movements, referring only to a disintegrating colonial system. *Pravda*, February 15, 1956. It was more difficult for Molotov to change course. He conceded that capitalist encirclement no longer existed, yet he denounced "the ring of bases situated around the Soviet Union" and the U.S. talk of finding "a principal use for atomic weapons in Europe." *Pravda*, February 20, 1956.

80. This move was preceded less than a year earlier, in August 1961, by the construction of the Berlin Wall, which plugged the last serious loophole in the porous frontiers of the continental Soviet bloc.

81. Bruce D. Porter, *The USSR in Third World Conflicts: Soviet Arms and Diplomacy in Local Wars* (Cambridge: Cambridge University Press, 1984), pp. 26–27, 58–59, and Edmonds, *Soviet Foreign Policy*, pp. 117–126, agree on the great significance of 1973 for the joint recognition of equality as the basis for détente, but are more reluctant to make a direct connection with the development of a more radical Soviet policy toward national liberation movements.

82. The main innovative character of the debate introduced two revisions of Stalinism by placing greater emphasis both on subjective factors in defining nation and on intrinsic factors (as opposed to the inspiration of the October Revolution) in sparking national liberation movements. Galia Golan, *The Soviet Union and the National Liberation Movements in the Third World* (Boston: Unwin Hyman, 1988), pp. 16–22, 37–38.

83. Ibid., pp. 162–166, 262–265, 323.

84. Alexander Dallin, *Black Box: KAL 007 and the Superpowers* (Berkeley: University of California Press, 1985), pp. 67–68, 119–120. Dallin characterizes the long his-

tory of Russian and Soviet sensitivities to border violations as constituting "an almost visceral response" that remained even after Stalin's death "tenaciously persistent in at least some parts of the population and the elite in particular." Ibid., pp. 70–72. For the U-2 incident, see David Wise and Thomas B. Ross, *The U-2 Affair* (New York: Random House, 1962).

85. There were wide swings in the tone of the U.S. broadcasts. For a highly critical view of the quality of programming and especially the political role of émigrés in Radio Liberty, see Ludmilla Alexeyeva, *U.S. Broadcasting to the Soviet Union* (New York: Helsinki Watch Committee, 1986). Alexeyeva had been an active dissident until her emigration from the Soviet Union in the 1970s.

86. Martin Nelson, *War of the Black Heavens: The Battles of Western Broadcasting in the Cold War* (Syracuse, NY: Syracuse University Press, 1997), pp. 91–93.

87. The decision to come clean came only after Gorbachev won a heated debate within the Politburo. Gorbachev, *Zhizn i reformy*, vol. 1, pp. 302–303. Gorbachev's decision to stop the jamming was unilateral, although it was preceded by negotiations between his close adviser Alexander Yakovlev and Charles Z. Wick, head of the United States Information Agency. Arch Puddington, *Broadcasting Freedom: The Cold War Triumph of Radio Free Europe and Radio Liberty* (Lexington: University Press of Kentucky, 2000), pp. 222–223.

88. Puddington, *Broadcasting Freedom*, pp. 297–299; and Mark R. Beissinger, *Nationalist Mobilization and the Collapse of the Soviet Union* (Cambridge: Cambridge University Press, 2002), p. 63.

89. Given the enormous problems of establishing ethnic identity in Russia, the Soviet Union, and the Russian Federation, population statistics on the nationalities can only be approximate. See the discussion in Sven Gunnar Simonsen, "Inheriting the Soviet Policy Toolbox: Russia's Dilemma over Ascriptive Nationality," *Europe-Asia Studies* 51, no. 6 (September 1999): 1069–1087; and Eric D. Weiz, "Racial Policies Without the Concept of Race: Reevaluation of Soviet Ethnic and National Purges," *Slavic Review* 61, no. 1 (Spring 2002): 1–43.

90. Alfred J. Rieber, "Stalin: Man of the Borderlands," *American Historical Review* 106, no. 5 (December 2001): 1651–1691.

91. Stalin, *Sochineniya*, vol. 4, pp. 74–75, 162, 236–237, 372. See also Rieber, "Stalin," pp. 1683–1684.

92. To be sure, such accusations were also leveled at major figures in the great purge trials, but this does not invalidate the claim that they were originally designed to transform a right, that is, to self-determination of the proletariat as a class, into an obligation, that is, to repress national aspirations associated with the class enemy, the bourgeoisie.

93. In response to a question from an Azeri member of the Mussavet Party, who asked Stalin why he believed that socialism did not suit Iran while he supported the establishment of a Soviet republic in the far more backward Turkestan, the Soviet leader stated, "Nonetheless, in Turkestan there is an intelligentsia who completed Russian schools." Quoted in M. E. Rasuladze, "Vospominaniya o I.V. Staline,"

Vostochnyi ekspress, no. 1 (November 1993): 49. Rasuladze perceptively replied, "However, you agree this is not a Marxist reason."

94. Terry Martin, *The Affirmative Action Empire: Nations and Nationalism in the Soviet Union, 1923–1939* (Ithaca: Cornell University Press, 2001), pp. 12–13 and passim. For the abandonment of political *korenizatsiya* in the 1930s, see Gerhard Simon, *Nationalism and Policy Toward the Nationalities in the Soviet Union: From Totalitarian Dictatorship to Post-Stalinist Society* (Boulder, CO: Westview, 1991).

95. Martin, *The Affirmative Action Empire*, pp. 9, 31, 41. In 1929 Stalin rebuffed proposals to transfer additional districts of the Russian Soviet Federated Socialist Republic to Ukraine: "We change our borders too often. We must be especially careful since such changes provoke enormous resistance from some Russians." Quoted in ibid., p. 70.

96. L. N. Nezhinskii, "Byla li voennaya ugroza SSSR v kontse 20-x -nachale 30-x godov?" *Istoriya SSSR*, no. 6 (June 1990): 14–30.

97. O. N. Ken and A. I. Rupasov, *Politbiuro TsK VKP (b)i otnosheniya SSSR s zapadnymi sosednimi gosudarstvami (konets 20–30-kh gg.). Problemy. Dokumenty. Opyt kommenariya*, part 1: 1928–1934 (St. Petersburg: Evropeiskii Dom, 2000), pp. 484–485. A special commission of the Politburo for studying the security of the frontier zone had been established as early as 1925. Ibid., p. 486.

98. The defensive position of the Narkomindel was that Soviet diplomacy should seek to prevent the Poles "from exploiting West Ukraine and West Belarus as 'Piedmont' in the struggle against the Ukrainian and Belorussian Soviet Republics." Stalin made the connection more explicit when he warned the Poles, "We will judge your relations with the Germans and us by your 'work' in the Soviet Ukraine." Quoted in ibid., pp. 491, 497, citing material from archives.

99. Abroad he imposed a new Comintern line at the Eighth Congress, reversing the policy of national self-determination aimed at the dismemberment of countries such as Czechoslovakia and Yugoslavia into their component national parts, denouncing it as another form of nationalist deviation that could only pave the way for the expansion of Germany into Eastern Europe.

100. For the major shift in historiography and the teaching of history along these lines, see Lowell Tillet, *The Great Friendship: Soviet Historians on the Non-Russian Nationalities* (Chapel Hill: University of North Carolina Press, 1969).

101. Yuri Slezkine, "The USSR as a Communal Apartment, or How a Socialist State Promoted Ethnic Particularism," *Slavic Review* 53, no. 2 (Summer 1994): 414–452; Roman Szporluk, "History and Ethnocentrism," in *Ethnic Russia in the USSR*, ed. Edward Allworth (New York: Pergamon, 1980), pp. 41–54; and Terry Martin, "The Origins of Ethnic Cleansing," *Journal of Modern History* 70, no. 4 (December 1998): 813–861.

102. Andrea Graziosi, *The Great Soviet Peasant War: Bolsheviks and Peasants, 1917–1933* (Cambridge: Harvard University tPress, 1996), pp. 20, 27, 54, 63, 67.

103. Hiroaki Kuromiya, *Freedom and Terror in the Donbas: A Ukrainian-Russian Borderland, 1870s–1990s* (Cambridge: Harvard University Press, 1998), pp. 231–235.

104. N. F. Bugai, *L. Beria—I. Stalinu: Soglasno Vashemu ukazaniyu* (Moscow: AIRO XX, 1995), pp. 8–25; and Pavel Polian, *Ne po svoei vole: Istoriya i geografiya prinuditelnykh migratsii v SSSR* (Moscow: OGI-Memorial, 2001), pp. 84–94. Officials of the Ministry of Interior later described the resettlement "not as a measure of repression but as a precautionary measure with respect to cleansing (*ochishchenie*) the frontier region with Japan." Bugai, *L. Beria*, p. 22.

105. S. T. Verigin and L. V. Suni, "Pereselenie ingermandtsev v Kareliiu v kontse 1940-kh godov," in E. I. Klementev and V. N. Birin (eds.), *Karely, Finny: Problemy etnicheskoi istorii* (Moscow, Institut etnologii i antropologii RAN, 1992), pp. 200–215; V. S. Parsadanova, "Deportatsiya naseleniya iz Zapadnoi Ukrainy i Zapadnoi Belorussii v 1939–1941 gg.," *Novaya i noveishiya istoriya*, no. 2 (February 1989): 26–44; and N. S. Lebedeva, "The Deportation of the Polish Population to the USSR, 1939–41," *Journal of Communist Studies and Transition* 16, nos. 1/2 (March–June 2000): 28–45.

106. Bugai, *L. Beria*, pp. 27–47; and Polian, *Ne po svoei vole*, pp. 215–216. For a thorough exploration of the parallels with the tsarist expulsion of hundreds of thousands of Jews and Germans from the western frontier zone from 1914 to 1916, see Peter Gatrell, *A Whole Empire Walking: Refugees in Russia During World War I* (Bloomington: Indiana University Press, 1999).

107. Alfred J. Rieber, "Civil Wars in the Soviet Union," *Kritika* 4, no. 1 (Winter 2003): 129–162; and Amir Weiner, *Making Sense of War: The Second World War and the Fate of the Bolshevik Revolution* (Princeton: Princeton University Press, 2001).

108. Bugai, *L. Beria*, pp. 61–68, 96–101, 119–131, 143–154, 163–169. The prospect of war with Turkey in 1943 automatically touched off fears about the Muslim population along the border between Georgia and Turkey, a highly mixed frontier zone. In one district, for example, the census of 1926 counted 24,353 Georgians, 29,170 Turks, 15,565 Armenians, 3,094 Kurds, and only 167 Russians, with a scattering of Greeks, Tatars, and Jews. Ibid., p. 164. For a selection of documents indicating the sensitivity of the People's Commissariat of Internal Affairs (NKVD) to border incidents along the Turkish and Iranian frontiers in the first year of war, see E. D. Solovev and A. I. Chugunov, eds., *Pogranichnye voiska v gody Velikoi otechestvennoi voiny. Sbornik dokumentov i materialov* (Moscow: Nauka, 1976), pp. 601–609.

109. Bugai, *L. Beria*, pp. 198–199; and Polian, *Ne po svoei vole*, pp. 157–180. But the longer the process of rehabilitation, the slower the rate of return. According to the census of 1989, only 10 percent of the Meskhetian Turks had returned to the Azerbaijan Republic. Except for a small number in the Russian Republic, the remainder still reside in Kazakhstan, Kyrgyzstan, and Uzbekistan. Ibid., p. 178.

110. See Alfred J. Rieber, ed., *Forced Migration in Central and Eastern Europe, 1939–1950* (London: Frank Cass, 2000); and Norman Naimark, *Fires of Hatred: Ethnic Cleansing in Twentieth-Century Europe* (Cambridge: Harvard University Press, 2001).

111. Cited in John Klier, *Imperial Russia's Jewish Question, 1855–1881* (Cambridge: Cambridge University Press, 1995), p. 395. Klier concludes that "Externally [the Jews] were linked to the foreign foes of Russian national interests." Ibid.

112. Alvin Z. Rubinstein, *Soviet Foreign Policy Since World War II: Imperial and Global,* 3d ed. (Glenview, IL: Scott, Foresman, 1989), pp. 341–342.

113. Minton Goldman, "United States Policy and Soviet Jewish Emigration from Nixon to Bush," in *Jews and Jewish Life in Russia and the Soviet Union,* ed. Yaacov Ro'I (Ilford, Essex: Frank Cass, 1995), pp. 338–358; Marshall Goldman, "Soviet-American Trade and Soviet Jewish Emigration: Should a Policy Change Be Made by the American Jewish Community?" in *Soviet Jewry in the 1980s: The Politics of Anti-Semitism and Emigration and the Dynamics of Resettlement,* ed. Robert O. Freedman (Durham: Duke University Press, 1989).

114. *Pravda,* January 8, 1988, as cited in Zvi Gitelman, "Ethnopolitics and the Future of the Former Soviet Union," in *The Politics of Nationality and the Erosion of the USSR,* ed. Zvi Gitelman (New York: St. Martin's Press, 1992), p. 5.

115. Gorbachev, *Zhizn i reformy,* vol. 1, p. 280. Gorbachev's simultaneous calls for speeding up (*uskorenie*) scientific and technological innovation and introducing economic reform that would contain some elements of the market economy make this connection abundantly clear. See ibid., pp. 203, 294. See also Archie Brown, *The Gorbachev Factor* (Oxford: Oxford University Press, 1996), pp. 122–123.

116. Beissinger, *Nationalist Mobilization and the Collapse of the Soviet Union,* especially pp. 27–32, 48, 68, 74, quotation at p. 29. As key moments in the process, he cites the protest of the Crimean Tatars as having given it structure; the Armenian movement to politicize the Karabakh issue as having constituted the first major wave; and the Baltic peoples as having undertaken a secessionist mobilization for the first time. Ibid., pp. 60–62, 64, 160–162. For similarities and differences in the case of the Central Asian republics, see Yaacov Roi, "Nationalism in Central Asia in the Context of Glasnost and Perestroika," in Gitelman, *The Politics of Nationality,* pp. 50–76.

117. Gorbachev's failure to understand the profound emotional and political importance of nationalism can be exaggerated. He was not as ignorant of the problem as many observers have maintained. Cf. Chernyaev, *My Six Years with Gorbachev,* pp. 181–185, 226–227, 382–383.

118. Rubinstein, *Soviet Foreign Policy Since World War II,* pp. 343–344.

119. Mikhail Gorbachev, *Perestroika: New Thinking for Our Country and the World* (New York: Harper and Row, 1987), pp. 54, 222. At the same time Gorbachev denounced the use of selective "quotations" to prove that Lenin intended to impose world revolution. Ibid., p. 150.

120. For the repeated failure of "organic unity" of the Left, see Paolo Spriano, *Stalin and the European Communists* (London: Verso, 1985).

121. Immediately after the Crimean defeat, Russia attempted to align with its former enemy France. When the Polish issue disrupted that policy, it turned to Prussia-Germany, and by the 1890s it had returned to a French alliance.

122. Vojtech Mastny, "The Cassandra in the Foreign Commissariat: Maxim Litvinov and the Cold War," *Foreign Affairs* 54 (January 1976), pp. 366–376.

123. F. Chuev, *Sto sorok besed s Molotovym. Iz dnevnika F. Chueva* (Moscow: Terra, 1991), pp. 98–99. Even a cursory comparison of Soviet diplomatic dispatches written in the 1930s with those composed in the 1940s and 1950s confirms Molotov's verdict. The differences begin to show up most clearly in Ministerstvo Inostrannykh del Rossiiskoi Federatsii, *Dokumenty vneshnoi politiki, 1942–22 iyunya 1941* (Moscow: Mezhdunarodnye otnosheniya, 1998). They became more pronounced through the war years. See Murashenko, *Vostochnaya Evropa*. Western diplomats registered similar if harsher views on the indifference or ignorance of Soviet diplomats toward established standards of international conduct. George F. Kennan, *Memoirs, 1925–1950* (Boston: Little, Brown, 1967); Gen. John Deane, *The Strange Alliance* (New York: Murray, 1946); Raymond Dennett and Joseph E. Johnson, eds., *Negotiating with the Russians* (Boston: World Peace Foundation, 1951); and W. Averill Harriman, *Special Envoy to Churchill and Stalin, 1941–1946* (New York: Random House, 1975).

124. This is not the place for a full-scale review of the extensive changes that took place in the intellectual and cultural life of Western Europe and the United States as a response to the nature of the Soviet system and Soviet foreign policy. The centerpieces were the theory of totalitarianism and the grand narrative of Western civilization. For the best introduction to the former, see Abbott Gleason, *Totalitarianism: The Inner History of the Cold War* (New York: Oxford University Press, 1995). There is no good analysis of the latter phenomenon, but see Gilbert Allardyce, "The Rise and Fall of the Western Civilization Course," *American Historical Review* 87, no. 3 (June 1982): 695–725.

125. At the end of his life Lenin acknowledged that it was an error to have imposed on foreign communist parties an organizational resolution "permeated through and through with the Russian spirit. . . . It is completely incomprehensible to foreigners and they will not be satisfied to hang it in the corner like an icon and pray to it." Lenin, *Sochineniya*, vol. 27 (Moscow: Partizdat, 1937), pp. 354–355. But his warning was ignored.

126. H. Gordon Skilling, "People's Democracy in Soviet Theory," *Soviet Studies* 3, no. 1 (July 1951): 16–33; and Karen Brutents, *National Liberation Movements Today*, vol. 2 (Moscow: Progress, 1977), pp. 9–55. The concept of "revolutionary democracy" was a Khrushchev innovation.

127. In each of these cases strong elements within the local communist parties resisted or denounced the Soviet model as incompatible with their own cultural traditions.

128. The literature on this subject is extensive. I have drawn insights in particular from Leszek Kolakowski, *Main Currents of Marxism*, vol. 3, *The Breakdown* (Oxford:

Oxford University Press, 1978); and James H. Satterwhite, *Varieties of Marxist Humanism: Philosophical Revisionism in Postwar Eastern Europe* (Pittsburgh: University of Pittsburgh Press, 1992).

129. Kramer, "New Evidence on Soviet Decision Making." For concerns about the effect of the Prague Spring on internal stability in Ukraine, see Grey Hodnett and Peter Potichnyj, "The Ukraine and the Czechoslovak Crisis"; Kramer, "Ukraine and the Soviet-Czechoslovak Crisis of 1968," pp. 234–247; and Mark Kramer, "Soviet Moldavia and the 1968 Czechoslovak Crisis: A Report on the Political 'Spill-Over,' " *Bulletin (CWIHP)*, no. 11 (Winter 1998): 263.

130. Alexander Dallin, "Long Division and Fine Fractions," *Problems of Communism* 11, no. 2 (March–April 1962): 7–16.

131. Robert Legvold, "The Soviet Union and West European Communism," in *Eurocommunism and Détente*, ed. Rudolph L. Tokes (New York: New York University Press, 1978), pp. 314–384. See also Jiri Valenta, "Eurocommunism and the USSR," in *Eurocommunism Between East and West*, ed. Vernon V. Aspaturian, Jiri Valenta, and David P. Burke (Bloomington: Indiana University Press, 1980), pp. 103–123.

132. Schwartz also made clear that the Chinese Communist Party was neither a vanguard of the proletariat nor a peasant party, but "an elite of professional revolutionaries which has risen to power by basing itself on the dynamic of peasant discontent." Benjamin Schwartz, *Chinese Communism and the Rise of Mao*, 2d ed. (Cambridge: Harvard University Press, 1958), pp. 199, 201. Although Ho never made such extravagant claims, he, too, was critical of Eurocentrism and quietly shaped an eclectic revolutionary movement that blended Marxism-Leninism with Confucianist and patriotic, rather than class, elements. Huynh Kim Khanh, *Vietnamese Communism, 1925–1945* (Ithaca: Cornell University Press, 1982), pp. 62, 74–85, 141.

133. I. V. Kovalev, "Dialog Stalina c Mao tze-tung," *Problemy dalnogo vostoka*, no. 2 (February 1992): 79–80. After meeting Mao, Molotov told Stalin that he was not really a Marxist but some kind of Chinese Pugachev. Chuev, *Sto sorok besed s Molotovym*, p. 114. For details on Stalin's diplomatic dance with Mao, see Sergei N. Goncharov, John W. Lewis, and Xue Litai, *Uncertain Partners: Stalin, Mao, and the Korean War* (Stanford: Stanford University Press, 1993), especially chap. 4 and appendix, docs. 6, 7, 8.

134. Quoted in Odd Arne Westad, ed., *Brothers in Arms: The Rise and Fall of the Sino-Soviet Alliance, 1945–1963* (Stanford: Stanford University Press, 1998), p. 345. Mao's explanation that they could win over the Soviet leaders by persuasion was, in his view, simply an acknowledgment of Chinese superiority.

135. Chen Jian, "Deng Xiaoping, Mao's 'Continuous Revolution,' and the Path Toward the Sino-Soviet Split: A Rejoinder," *Bulletin (CWIHP)*, no. 10 (March 1998): 162–164, docs. 165–182. In February 1965 Mao told Soviet premier A. N. Kosygin that the struggle with the Soviet "revisionists" would last nine thousand years. Ibid., p. 164.

136. For example, Central Committee resolutions of July 28, 1958, and June 4, 1959, ordered severe cutbacks in subscriptions by official state organs to foreign periodicals aside from technical and scientific material, in addition to careful screening and reduction of translations and publication of foreign literature. V. Iu. Afiani, chief ed., *Ideologicheskie komissii TsK KPSS 1958–1964: Dokumenty* (Moscow: Rosspen, 1998), pp. 64–72, 172–175. Similar instructions dealt with foreign films. Ibid., pp. 186–189.

137. Karl Aimermakher, "Partiinoe upravlenie kulturoi i formy ee samoorganizatsii (1953–1964/67)," in Afiani, *Ideologicheskie komissii TsK KPSS 1958–1964*, pp. 19–22.

138. See, for example, the testimony of Dmitri Shostakovich, in Afiani, *Ideologicheskie komissii TsK KPSS 1958–1964*, pp. 499–503.

139. The failure of the ideological commissions to arrive at any theoretical guidelines for artistic expression left room for enlarging the parameters of socialist realism. In painting, a wide array of styles emerged under the umbrella of socialist realism. See Susan Reid, "The 'Art of Memory': Retrospectivism in the Soviet Painting of the Brezhnev Era," in *Art of the Soviets: Painting, Sculpture, and Architecture in a One-Party State, 1917–1992,* ed. Matthew Cullerne Brown and Brandon Taylor (Manchester, NY: Manchester University Press, 1993), pp. 161–187. In the 1970s it was possible to hear the most advanced avant-garde music, at least for small ensembles, in private recitals at the Union of Soviet Composers. Poets and writers encountered more restrictions, but even here, limits were tested.

140. Sabrine Dullin, "Les interprétations françaises du système soviétique," in *Le siècle des communismes,* ed. Michel Dreyfus (Paris: Les Editions de l'Atelier, 2000), pp. 50–51, nn. 22, 24.

141. See the analysis in Dmitri Trenin and Aleksei V. Malashenko with Anatol Lieven, *Russia's Restless Frontier: The Chechnya Factor in Post-Soviet Russia* (Washington, DC: Carnegie Endowment for International Peace, 2004).

142. Ibid., p. 166.

143. Andrey Makarychev, "Pskov at the Crossroads of Russia's Trans-border Relations with Estonia and Latvia: Between Provinciality and Marginality," *Europe-Asia Studies* 57, no. 3 (May 2005): 481–500; and Vladimir Kagansky, "Tsetr-Provintsiya-Granitsa. Osnovnye zony kul'turnogo landshafta. 1997," http//www.inme.ru/previous/Kagansky/Kagansky.htm.

144. *Pravda,* September 7, 2004.

145. Dmitri Trenin, "Integrating Russia into the European Security System," *U.S.-Russia Relations: Opportunities for Cooperation. Thirtieth Conference, August 10–16, 2003* (Washington, DC: The Aspen Institute, 2003), p. 26.

146. Paul Kubicek, "Russian Energy Policy in the Caspian Basin," *World Affairs* 166, no. 4 (Spring 2004): 207–217. For the battle over the pipelines, see Robert Ebel and Rajan Menon, *Energy and Conflict in Central Asia and the Caucasus* (Lanham, MD: Rowman and Littlefield, 2000).

147. Quoted in Leszek Buszynski, *Russian Foreign Policy After the Cold War* (Westport, CT: Praeger, 1996), pp. 4–5.

148. David Kerr, "The New Eurasianism: The Rise of Geopolitics in Russia's Foreign Policy," *Europe-Asia Studies* 47, no. 6 (1995): 977–988; and Peter Rutland, "Paradigms for Russian Policy in the Caspian Region," in Ebel and Menon, *Energy and Conflict in Central Asia and the Caucasus*, pp. 171–173.

149. For an excellent analytical summary of the growing tension between Russia and the European Union, see Olga Vlasova, "Pochemu nas razlyubila Evropa," *Ekspert* 7, no. 410, February 23, 2004. Following the enlargement of the European Union the Russians complained that the new East European members were bringing "phantoms of the past" into the organization. *Financial Times*, May 22, 2006.

150. Jennifer Moll and Richard Gowan, *Losing Ground? Russia's European Commitment to Human Rights* (London: Foreign Policy Center, 2005).

151. Dmitri V. Trenin, *The End of Eurasia: Russia on the Border Between Geopolitics and Globalization* (Washington, DC: Carnegie Endowment for International Peace, 2002).

152. Jutta Scherrer analyzes the role of *kulturologiya*, a required subject in Russian universities though not official policy, which interprets Russia as a unique civilization that differs from Europe in many of its values. Scherrer, *Russland auf der Suche nach einer zivilisatorischen identität* (Göttingen: Wallstein, 2003).

CHAPTER 5

Russian Concepts of National Security

Lawrence T. Caldwell

W HY SHOULD A VOLUME that attempts to place contemporary Russian foreign policy in its historical context devote a chapter to Russian concepts of national security? And how does it propose to differentiate national security from more traditional explorations of foreign policy? The answer to the first question is straightforward: Nowhere is the discrepancy between Russia's historical context and the factors that shape most countries' foreign policies more evident than in the means available to secure its ambitions. Today's Russia continues to experience the wrenching process of imperial collapse. The tragedy of the Beslan schoolchildren held hostage by Chechen militants in the fall of 2004 was, in part, a product of Moscow's inability to find peace with its loss of empire and its confusion about how to combine the demands of building a new Russian nation and accepting the contraction of Russian and Soviet ambitions abroad. This problem was painfully obvious in mid-2006, when Kremlin efforts to pressure Ukraine over natural gas, as well as to interfere in both Georgian and Moldovan politics during the first months of the year, strained relations with Europe and the United States. In early May Vice President Dick Cheney gave a speech at the Vilnius meeting with heads of state from the "new Europe" that attacked Kremlin policies at home and in the region. His speech precipitated a vituperative exchange between Russia and the United States before President Vladimir Putin stepped in to calm the tone of relations prior to the July St. Petersburg Summit of the Group of Eight. This rhetorical strain in Moscow-Washington relations developed over a region Moscow had long considered to be within its "sphere of influence."

President Boris Yeltsin's futile efforts to block the eastward expansion of NATO, Russia's clumsy attempts to interfere in the Serbian crises of the 1990s, and President Vladimir Putin's complete inability to affect U.S. policy in Iraq all underlined the greatly diminished role of Russia in world affairs. And, as this chapter argues, in an effort to compensate for its new impotency, Moscow has attempted in the first years of the twenty-first century to showcase new nuclear technologies and has altered its declaratory nuclear doctrine to suggest a diminished inhibition about using nuclear weapons. Both the Chechen tragedy and the "nuclearization" of Russian military policy reveal the Kremlin leadership's struggle to combine military means and perceived requirements of foreign policy. The art of constructing national security policy is the art of matching external ambitions to domestic resources.

The answer to the second question, then, derives from the first. The study of national security adds to the study of foreign policy an explicit analysis of means—military forces, doctrines that define their use in wartime, the economic power of the state on which military capabilities depend, and the critical and difficult relationship between the front and the rear. This distinction draws attention to how qualities of the nation-state affect military power. In Russia's case, almost all historians agree that foreign policy has strained inadequate domestic institutions. Russian military power has often been formidable in the field, at least in the initial phases of conflict, but foundered on the shoals of perilous statehood.

This chapter explores the interplay of state structures, foreign policy, and military power. It does so by explicitly analyzing the Russian state's military power and the doctrine that sets the stage for the use of that power. It tests its ideas by paying particular attention to those periods that Robert Legvold calls, in his contribution to this volume (chapter 2), the "great transformations" of Russian society. While the discussion makes reference in a less structured way to a number of these turning points in Russian history, it also addresses this interplay in three such cases.

There are multiple stereotypes of Russian national security interests. Like most stereotypes, many of these have some basis in truth, but they provide little help in understanding Russia's policies in particular contexts. For example, one persistent generalization posits a "drive for warm water ports."[1] This idea has been used to explain such diverse Russian behavior as Peter I's establishment of St. Petersburg after defeating the Swedes in 1703; imperial Russia's push to build forts and railroads southward into Central Asia in the nineteenth century, not only to contest British policy in South Asia but also to probe for a geostrategic position on the Indian Ocean; tsarist support for the exploration of Siberia, including the building of forts along the California and even the Hawaiian coasts; various efforts to create or maintain a military foothold in

the Caucasus, including the Black Sea littoral; and the decision by Leonid Brezhnev to invade Afghanistan in 1979. This explanation has covered such diverse policies under such widely varying political and economic circumstances
that it loses almost all of its explanatory power.

Another such generalization asserts that the vulnerability of Russian frontiers induced a seven-hundred-year drive for secure borders.[2] This outward
push from a relatively small, inconspicuous border town in the early fourteenth century, by which time political and ecclesiastical power increasingly
had gravitated to Moscow, has explained an almost unbroken string of military successes and defeats—Dmitri Donskoy's victory over Mamai's Tatar
troops at Kulikovo in 1380; Ivan IV's conquest of Kazan with the help of Cossacks in 1552; Alexei's Treaty of Pereiaslavl, establishing Russian claims to
Ukrainian and even Polish territory; Peter I's struggles with Charles XII of
Sweden and his subsequent war with Turkey; Catherine II's push southward to
the Black Sea and her partition of Poland; and even Stalin's absorption of the
Baltic and East European states after 1940. This view posits an outward geopolitical thrust from Moscow, ever expanding Russian territory in a seemingly
endless thirst for secure borders. In the Cold War, this explanation of Soviet
military behavior had considerable currency. Some observers even drew the
parallel between Russia's impossible search for geopolitical security in the inevitably fluid movement of ethnicities and states that have characterized the
Eurasian landmass since the first Indo-European peoples pushed across the
steppes twenty millennia ago with the Roman Empire's similar inability to establish stable and secure borders on some of this same territory. Other participants in the Cold War debates tried to explain away phenomena such as the
brutal domination of Eastern Europe as a partially logical consequence of the
sacrifices made by the Soviets in World War II and Stalin's wartime demands
for friendly governments along his borders. Although Russian, like Roman, expansion is undeniable, the idea that insecure geopolitical space imparts an inevitable predisposition to imperial conquest of other peoples or justifies brutal
domination of neighboring states misses the richness of choices made by Russian governments and by those of surrounding peoples over this long period.

A more difficult but also slippery and unsatisfying generalization suggests
that Russian behavior can be seen as a response to a kind of national psychological sense of inferiority. It posits that much of Russian behavior grows out
of its economic backwardness and sense that it lagged behind other powers
both technologically and in level of economic development.[3] This idea, too,
has some beguiling plausibility but is ultimately not very useful. This view of

Russian national security observes imitative behavior from Ivan IV's military reforms establishing the fateful *streltsy* (troops skilled in the use of musketry) to Peter I's obsession with the creation of a modern navy and Stalin's resolve to acquire nuclear weapons by mobilizing every means possible, especially covert ones. But this view, too, distorts a record that has multiple successful innovations at home and military innovation that was often ahead of that in other states, not imitative. During the 1930s a group of capable military officers around Chief of the General Staff M. N. Tukhashevsky developed tactical doctrine that was extremely innovative, and the Commissariat of Armaments developed a 76-millimeter gun that became the ZIS-3. When this gun was mounted on the T-34 tank, the Russians had a weapon that surpassed those of the Americans, British, French, and Germans.[4] Khrushchev's encouragement of missile technology, then his efforts to force political gains from the narrow window of apparent Soviet advantage between 1957 and 1960, demonstrated both technological sophistication and an appreciation that it might be exploited for political purposes. These examples are not alone, but they represent interesting counterexamples of Russian innovation and technological advance. Moreover, the Politburo's drive for successive generations of a wide range of military technologies in the 1960s and 1970s cannot satisfactorily be made to fit the generalization of technological backwardness. Nonetheless, an orthodoxy has gained surprisingly wide currency that President Ronald Reagan so raised this traditional specter of technological inferiority with his Star Wars missile defense challenge that he forced radical change onto the Soviet agenda.[5] Such assertions overestimate U.S. influence on Russian behavior in several ways, but they are also based on assumptions about the technological and military balances that were not obvious in 1983, or 1986, among specialists either in Washington or in Moscow.

Although Russia and the Soviet Union were economically and technologically underdeveloped from the sixteenth through the twentieth century, the picture of economic backwardness and a sense of technological inferiority oversimplify both reality and Russian perceptions of it. Even though Ivan IV's and Peter I's reforms may have grown out of a sense of Russian backwardness, they were also perceived as at least partially successful. It would be a terrible oversimplification to say that a sense of international inferiority characterized the national security policy of either tsar. Ivan's success against Kazan and Peter's victories against Sweden were at least partly the fruits of military reform, and Russia emerged from each with a sense of national confidence that was reflected, among other ways, in the glorious architectural monuments these rulers raised to their power—St. Basil's Cathedral on Red Square in the former case and the unsurpassed city of St. Petersburg in the latter. Even the undoubted concessions made by Mikhail Gorbachev in arms control negotiations with the United States and NATO in the late 1980s can be interpreted as the product of confidence. These concessions can be interpreted as reflecting Soviet military achievements more easily than they can be seen as driven by fear that U.S. superiority would make it impossible for Moscow to compete in new military technologies.

Nor has Russian behavior been only competitive and autarkic. From World War I to the early 1950s, Russian and Soviet governments alike had no difficulty in accepting technological assistance that came with an intrusive presence of their allies that at less urgent times would have been unthinkable. In World War I, Russia's allies maintained military and other nondiplomatic missions in St. Petersburg that interacted extensively with Russia's political, military, and economic elite.[6] In World War II, while the naval convoys that brought U.S. and British aid to Russia constituted a serious disagreement among Stalin, Winston Churchill, and Franklin Roosevelt, memories of American "Fords" and "Spam" persist into the twenty-first century among Russians who have had little additional contact with U.S. culture.

These and other generalizations concerning Russian national security behavior fail to explain in ways that go beyond the simple limitations of historical stereotypes. This chapter suggests that a few general patterns can be observed, although they are not always present and almost never are they present in exactly the same mix from one period to another.

First, Russia has demonstrated a keen sense of strategic distance. It almost invariably has looked at the world as a series of concentric circles spreading outward from its own borders and established priorities based on its appreciation of geographical proximity.

Second, Russian diplomacy has been creative and fluid at almost all times and under every kind of political leadership. It has applied principles of national interests, alliance building, and power balancing, on the whole, as successfully as any other world power. Russian strategists have also demonstrated a sharp eye for identifying the main threat to national security. The interplay between priorities based on geographical proximity and policy designed to balance principal adversaries has often produced the richest challenges for policy makers, irrespective of the kind of regime that rules the country.

Third, for at least eight hundred years, Russia has mixed these considerations of realism with a strong dose of ideology. Even though ideology has shifted across time—from a strongly religious Third Rome, to a far more secular kind of nationalism in the eighteenth and nineteenth centuries, to Marxism-Leninism in the twentieth century—it has always been in the mix. In part, the challenge of understanding contemporary Russian foreign policy—that exercised by presidents Yeltsin and Putin—has been a product of a struggle among competing ideologies to take the place of the socialist one that dominated three-quarters of a century following the revolution of 1917.

Fourth, as a focus on ideology suggests, foreign and security policies have often been driven by, and constrained by, domestic political and economic conditions. Ivan IV modernized his state before undertaking his crusade against the Tartars. Peter I experienced defeat in his first skirmishes with Charles XII, then understood better than he had previously the need to reform his state and used that necessity as a club to introduce what were at the time perceived as draconian changes. The first great debate in Bolshevik Russia was over whether survival at home depended on revolution abroad and whether the dictates of promoting world revolution should take precedence over consolidation of political power at home. Stalin used the backdrop of the rise of fascism as a justification for introducing a paranoid, totalitarian political experiment during the 1930s. And Khrushchev attempted to use his successes in foreign and security policy as a lever against a recalcitrant political opposition in the Communist Party elite. Thus, a symbiotic relationship has long existed and has been seen to exist between the state of domestic politics and foreign policy. An ability to elevate Russian survival to a kind of supreme moral value has often pushed Russian behavior to extremes—what other observers have frequently perceived as unusual brutality or obsession with secrecy and covert measures. This same identification of Russian security with absolute and total social value has also often produced particularly brutal regimes for the Russians themselves and what some observers have long found to be a kind of national propensity to equate suffering with good. This Russian perspective on national security has combined with such diverse ideologies as the Third Rome of Orthodox tsars, the eighteenth and early nineteenth centuries' struggle to preserve stability and order in what became Europe's Congress system, and the communist commitment to world revolution.

Fifth, while a sense of peril in foreign policy has often been the driver of domestic politics, Russia has shown a powerful resistance to reform. The society has, for centuries, demonstrated a kind of native conservatism. The rulers who attempted great change (Peter I, Alexander II, Lenin, Khrushchev, and Gorbachev) all experienced a society that has pushed back and resisted, sometimes powerfully and bloodily. That conservative nature of society has often meant that rulers inclined to make reforms have looked for, and found, external threats that justified a sufficient concentration of power to achieve their purposes.

Sixth, Russian and Soviet generals have developed a distinctive style of combat in wartime: They have substituted quantity for quality. Russia has consistently emphasized the "teeth" of its armies and navies, giving less successful attention to their "tail," to logistics, or to what modern armies call "lift" and "mobility." In other words, there has been a persistent bias against investment in favor of procurement. Russia has mortgaged future technology to the needs of current military consumption. It has also shown a consistent interest in surprise, in striking its adversaries first and in achieving overwhelming superiority in manpower and firepower. Russia's history at the Narva in the late seventeenth century, with Napoléon in the nineteenth century, and with Adolf Hitler in the twentieth century would suggest both a reason for this preoccupation and a reminder that Russian practice has not always been successful. Even if a surprise first strike—"preemption," in the language of the early twenty-first century—is not the operational intention, Russian military doctrine has shown consistent interest in the first phases of combat and the need to concentrate forces rather than disperse them. Again, this can be seen as a product, for example, of Russia's need to spread forces along its frontiers, and the degree to which its biggest military disasters (in 1812 and 1941) have been caused in part by dispersal and intermittency rather than concentration in time and space. These long-standing preferences pose the greatest challenges of military power in the twenty-first century, and if Putin is to be successful in reforming the Russian military forces, he will have to overcome these traditions.

This chapter takes these six propositions and examines them with respect to three disparate periods in Russian security policy. First, it analyzes the period from the establishment of the Franco-Russian alliance in 1892 through the first, tentative steps of the new Bolshevik leadership onto the world stage. Second, it considers the circumstances between Khrushchev's Twentieth Party Congress in 1956 and the collapse of the first efforts at peaceful coexistence with the United States in 1961. Finally, it tests these propositions against the policies of the postcommunist governments of presidents Yeltsin and Putin, focusing especially on the latter's efforts to redefine Russian security policy after his election in 2000. All three of these cases meet the criteria of great transformations established in the Legvold chapter of this volume (chapter 2), albeit imperfectly. Each is characterized by significant changes in Russian domestic politics as well as by powerful challenges to adapt to changes in the international system. And while the current chapter includes illustrations from others of those transformations identified by Legvold, it concentrates its analysis on these three periods: 1892 to 1917, 1953 to 1964, and 1991 to the present.

WORLD WAR I AND THE FIRST STEPS OF BOLSHEVIK FOREIGN POLICY

The mix of geopolitical realism, diplomatic flexibility, nationalist ideology, and the need for domestic reform in Russia in the years leading up to World War I is among the most commented upon in history. There is little that is fresh to be added, but partly because it is such a familiar case, it serves as a useful starting point for examining Russian national security traditions. The relatively short time span between the Franco-Russian entente of 1892 and Lenin's first steps onto the international stage (1917–1918) provides a sufficiently compressed case study to illustrate this chapter's basic argument. Indeed, the case study may be too ambitious, attempting as it does to encompass the periods both before and immediately after the Bolshevik seizure of power. But because it is so obviously a period when the great forces of change were compressed into a short time frame, it also exposes all the factors that this study argues form the essence of Russian national security style.

Foreign Policy and the Domestic Context

The loss of Russia's traditional sense of strategic distance cost the reign of Tsar Nicholas I dearly. To be fair, he was not the first ruler to lose his way in these matters. Although the sixteenth, seventeenth, and eighteenth centuries can be said to focus most Russian exertions in national security on a ban of geographically distant territories, the ambitions inherited from Catherine II, and even Peter I, drew Russia inexorably farther away from her immediate frontiers. Peter fought battles along his western, northwestern, and southern frontiers. Like his father and his grandfather, he made Poland a central focus of foreign and military policy. From the Time of Troubles (the late sixteenth and early seventeenth centuries), Polish interference in Russian affairs had grated on Kremlin leaders. Peter's decisive victory over Sweden's Charles XII (partly on Polish territory) and his symbolic movement of the capital of his empire to the Gulf of Finland demonstrated that he had inherited this unerring sense that Russia must first secure its peace by dominating its borders on the west. While his wars against Turkey were partially derivative of his war with Sweden (Charles XII had taken refuge with the Porte after Peter's armies defeated him at Poltava), Peter was far less successful against his southern adversary and showed the good sense to make concessions where his armies could not assert his will. His successors, notably Empress Elizabeth, became embroiled in European affairs, occasionally to the neglect of matters closer to home. Catherine II, while involving herself in intellectual and diplomatic matters far from home, focused the bulk of her foreign and military policy on those same border issues: Poland, which she partitioned three times, and the southern steppes and Caucasus, where she continued Petrine policy against the Turks.

Napoléon was the first to draw Russian armies far from home, and eventually Alexander I's forces found themselves encamped on the Champs-Élysées. In fairness, the French Revolution and Napoléon upset the security traditions of all European powers. And, as the nineteenth century proceeded, it proved that not the least of his effects on Russia was to fan Russian nationalism along with the nationalisms of all Europe. The "nationalist century" largely reflected Napoléon's demonstration of what a mobilized nation could accomplish, and the mobilization of French economic and military capabilities had affected all of Europe, Russia included. But Napoléon fanned Russian nationalism earlier than his invasion of 1812. Following his famous meetings with Alexander I at Tilset in May 1807 and at Erfurt in September 1808, a nationalist backlash rose against what was perceived as the tsar's pro-French policy. This Francophobic nationalism grew until it created a need for war among a segment of the Russian nobility. Thus, Napoléon both demonstrated the military usefulness of a mobilized state and launched the Slavophile movement among the Russian intelligentsia that influenced so much of the remainder of the nineteenth century. By the end of that century, another powerful force—imperialism—had begun to sweep Europe, and although it came late to Russia, it nevertheless had a profound effect. In the years prior to World War I, Nicholas was partly the victim of these two powerful forces—nationalism and imperialism—that had inundated the entire world.

Germany's emperor, William II, had fed his cousin's dreams of empire and his anxieties about Russia's late arrival in the global struggle for imperial sway. He encouraged Nicholas II to push Russian claims in the Far East, and while the causes were complex, the country found itself embroiled in imperial competition with the Japanese in the Far East during the last decade of the nineteenth century. Nicholas's finance minister, Count Sergey Witte, had pushed for the development of Siberia and for greater trade with China. The Trans-Siberian and the Chinese Eastern railways were the products of this policy. Before this competition with Japan broke into a hot war in February 1904, there were strong voices in the Ministry of War, notably War Minister A. N. Kuropatkin, who argued against this Far Eastern policy because it diverted attention from the main danger: the European powers of the Triple Alliance.[7]

Following the decisive defeat of Russian forces by the Japanese, when the Baltic Fleet was destroyed in the Strait of Tsushima in May 1905, cooler heads in the tsar's government prevailed. Led by Foreign Minister A. P. Izvolsky, Russia repaired relations with Great Britain and Japan, signing agreements with the latter in July and the former in August 1907.[8] The great rapprochements of that year constituted a positive rejection of the imperialist ambitions that had embroiled St. Petersburg in a disastrous Far Eastern war. They returned Russia's attention to its main adversaries and to its geographically closest dangers.

The story, then, of Russian policy in Asia in the ten to twenty years prior to World War I was, in part, a struggle over the country's sense of strategic distance. It also demonstrates Russia's sometimes artful, sometimes dangerously clumsy foreign policy. Izvolsky's reversal after the Russo-Japanese War and the signing of the treaties with Japan in 1907, 1910, and 1912 effectively neutralized the Far Eastern theater for Russia until Japanese intervention against the Bolsheviks in 1918 to secure allied interests along the Trans-Siberian Railway. To be sure, the Far East had not been the only imperialist diversion that had drawn Russian attention from the main focus of its geopolitical interests at the end of the nineteenth century. Russia had also experienced repeated temptations in Central Asia, the Mediterranean, and the Bosporus since the reign of Catherine II. This interest was partially derivative of ongoing competition with Turkey and Austria-Hungary for influence in the Balkans, but it also brought Russian imperial ambitions into direct conflict with Great Britain. It was again a sign of Izvolsky's good judgment that he settled these conflicts in the 1907 Anglo-Russian convention.

Russia's diplomacy in Central Europe had been no less creative and flexible. Here it grew out of the Treaty of Paris of 1856, which had been highly unfavorable to Russia after its defeat by the French and British in the Crimean War. Thereafter, for nearly a quarter of a century, Russia's European policy was affected more by the actions of Germany's chancellor, Otto von Bismarck, than by any other variable. His diplomatic footwork, of course, is legendary. Just one widely observed variant included his negotiation of an anti-Russian

Austro-German alliance in 1879, which he followed with a proposal for the return to the Three Emperor League, which reassured St. Petersburg and led to a
Russo-Austro-German treaty in 1881. The treaty that established this alliance
was renewed in 1884 and, after some tensions that led Bismarck to explain the
text of the 1879 treaty, again in 1887. This delicate minuet—an anti-Russian alliance with Austria simultaneously with a series of three treaties between Germany and Russia—proved too delicate for German diplomacy after Bismarck
was ousted in March 1890. It was one of those great realignments of European
states—the French fleet visited Kronstadt; the tsar and Russian public gave it a
rousing welcome; and on August 27, 1892, Paris and St. Petersburg exchanged
notes that formalized the Franco-Russian alliance, which was formally ratified
in August 1894.[9]

As is outlined above, Russia's ambitions in the Far East and its competition
with England in Central Asia delayed a final solidification of the entente that
was to fight the Triple Alliance in World War I. Once Japan had defeated Russia
and more sensible heads prevailed in St. Petersburg, it was possible in 1907 to
construct the alliance among France, Great Britain, and Russia. The point here
is that Russian diplomacy proved able both to grasp the fundamental conflict
of interest with Germany and Austria and to overcome powerful, albeit less
central, conflicts of interests (particularly with London) to forge the alliance
on which it would fight World War I. Russia proved flexible at the end of Bismarck's diplomatic system in 1890 and again after its failed attempt at empire
in the Far East by making accommodations with the Japanese and British in
1907.

Nowhere in all of Russian history is the linkage between inadequate domestic structures and security policy more clear than in this story prior to World
War I. The tsar's government proved incapable of adjusting the geopolitical focus of Russian foreign policy until after a humiliating defeat at the hands of
Tokyo and the intervention by U.S. president Theodore Roosevelt, who personally helped to negotiate the 1905 Portsmouth treaty, which resolved Russo-
Japanese hostilities. One of the many indictments against Tsar Nicholas II's
system of governing was that no one other than the tsar himself was responsible for coordinating the complex policies of empire, economic imperialism, diplomacy, and domestic rule. He failed, and failed obviously, in 1905. The
autocracy faced a serious challenge in widespread domestic violence during the
revolution of 1905. It was resolved in part because the political opposition,
while extensive and determined, was inchoate. S. J. Witte returned from his
successful negotiation of the Portsmouth treaty in September of that year to be

given the title of "count" and to write an "October Manifesto," which the tsar reluctantly accepted. This document pointed toward a constitutional monarchy and included a legislature: the Duma. The failure of these institutions over the next eleven years spelled the doom of the autocracy. The story is complex and oft told, but, in the end, the revolution of 1917 cast final judgment on the failure of tsarist political institutions to adapt to the multiple crises of political and economic modernization, world war, and a steady drumbeat of new classes demanding political participation, including a radical revolutionary elite led by Lenin.[10]

Russian politics in the fifteen years prior to 1917 were intensely ideological. The tsar was nothing if not committed to his own view of autarchy, a view that was in itself ideological and ill suited to necessary adaptation. This ideology, in turn, contributed to the rise of Bolshevik ideology. The tsar's ideas discouraged the emergence of alternative, moderate leadership to Lenin and his small group of revolutionaries. His nationalist ideology, with its fatal attraction to the ideas of empire, especially in the Far East between 1896 and 1904, contributed to the rise of political alternatives, discouraged large segments of his loyal elites, and fanned radical fires. Lenin, when he came to power in October 1917, found that the dictates of his ideology colored everything, at least initially. Upon seizing power, he issued two decrees, one on peace and the other on land. He had come to power in part because, when he arrived back in St. Petersburg in April of that year, he had taken strong positions against Russia's continued participation in World War I and against cooperation with the provisional government that had come to power when Nicholas II abdicated in March. He had been an antiwar candidate for six months. These decrees were his first attempts to turn his pre-revolution positions into state policies.

No one in the diplomatic community in St. Petersburg doubted the Bolshevik commitment to peace, but turning a revolutionary slogan into a state policy proved very difficult. Marxist-Leninist ideology dictated that the war was an imperialist one, hence one against the class interests of the proletariat, in whose name the Bolsheviks had seized power. That the Bolshevik leadership took their ideology seriously in this matter of critical foreign and security policy quickly became painfully evident. Leon Trotsky, called upon to establish the Commissariat of Foreign Affairs, believed that the revolution could not succeed in Russia unless it was quickly subsumed into the world revolution that Marxism predicted. Even during the months of December, January, and February, as the new leadership hammered out ad hoc policies on almost every imaginable issue, they hotly debated whether to sign a separate and annexationist peace with Germany, whose military forces took advantage of the dis-integration of the Russian army to advance virtually at will. Lenin prevailed over Trotsky and Nikolay Bukharin—both of whom wanted to refuse a peace agreement with Germany—because he correctly saw that if the Bolshevik rev-olution were to have any chance of success in Russia, it had to have breathing space—that is, peace with Germany. What is particularly revealing about this debate over the Brest-Litovsk treaty was that Lenin, Trotsky, and Bukharin all agreed that they would fail in Russia unless the predicted world revolution were to materialize. Their difference, and the slim thread of Lenin's success, was over the timing of the larger, global proletarian uprising. Lenin saw more clearly than his policy opponents that the timing of the world revolution could not be predicted; hence Russia had to buy time to address political survival at home.[11]

This was not the end of Lenin's pragmatic adjustment of ideological pre-cepts. The period from the seizure of power in 1917 into 1920 was defined by an intense ideological struggle against those who wished for a return to the autoc-racy (often called the Whites), but also against the Constitutional Democrats, who had dominated the provisional government from March to October 1917. And, as was characteristic of Lenin, the greatest ideological vituperation and political repression were reserved for those political forces that had been clos-est to the Bolsheviks before the October coup—for example, the Menshevik faction of Lenin's own Social Democratic Party and the Social Revolutionaries, another left-wing organization with its roots in that same socialist tradition that influenced Lenin himself.[12] By the time of the Tenth Party Congress, in the spring of 1921, Lenin's patience with ideological factions within his own Bolshevik Party had worn thin. The preceding summer he had begun system-atically to trim his expectation of a world revolution at the Second Comintern Congress by requiring that the communist parties of other countries support the Russian revolution, an implicit acknowledgment that the proletarian revo-lution's future was tied to communist survival in Russia. At the Tenth Party Congress, he adjusted his ideology to embrace the New Economic Policy, an explicit return to some forms of capitalism and markets. As he made this tack to the right, he also tightened control over the more orthodox factions in his own party—what had come to be called the Democratic Centralists and the Workers Opposition. In response to these ideological opponents and a more popular uprising against the Bolsheviks by the Kronstadt workers and sailors during the Party Congress itself, Lenin introduced the first measures of politi-cal control that were to be taken to extremes by Stalin a decade later—a purge of recalcitrant party members and the use of prison camps to incarcerate his opponents. Lenin moved Russian foreign policy away from its more extreme ideological formulations; sought legitimacy in world affairs that would subsequently be rewarded by a treaty with Germany at Rapallo in 1922; and at the same time imposed a tight, even draconian dictatorship over political opposition of all kinds. As they sought to tighten controls at home and move toward international legitimacy, Lenin and his Politburo colleagues used a variety of external threats from the imperialists and capitalists to justify their policies. Hence, domestic repression, in part, was done in the name of national security.

Throughout this turbulent and fateful period, the traditionally conservative Russian society pushed back. The tsar distrusted the new, urban, and bourgeois elites who became politically organized early in the century. His repeated scaling back of political rights that appeared initially to be granted by the October Manifesto in 1905, by regressive disenfranchisement of the electoral base for the Duma, revealed his (mistaken) belief that autocracy better served the great, uneducated, and backward masses of Russia than did the new political forces that came forward in the last decade of the nineteenth and the first decade of the twentieth centuries. Lenin, too, revealed his distrust of popular will in his seminal political writing of the time, *What Is to Be Done?* In it he joined his Marxist beliefs with the radical Russian populist (*narodnik*) traditions of the 1860s and 1870s. While the story is a complex one, even the title of this important publication in 1902 tied Lenin's ideas to those of Nikolay Chernyshevsky forty years earlier. What Lenin took from these *narodnik* thinkers was his great skepticism about the revolutionary potential of the Russian masses and his commitment to an elite of professional revolutionaries. Lenin and Nicholas II shared the view that the great bulk of Russians were conservative, a force against political and economic change.[13]

Military Power, Doctrine, and War

The fate of Russia's army played a very large role in this overall political story. On the one hand, it seems a tale of utter and complete failure. The Japanese had defeated the Russian army decisively in 1904–1905. The army performed unevenly, but mostly inadequately as part of the entente between 1914 and 1917; disintegrated throughout the summer and early fall of 1917; and gradually melted away into a civilian population embroiled in the October Revolution. Lenin's great service was that he recognized early and acted decisively on his perception that the army could not be kept in the field against the Germans. He sued for peace at any price at Brest-Litovsk in early 1918. Russia was finished in World War I. That was reality. The German and Austrian armies had scored unprecedented victories in face of the Russian collapse. As Chief of the German General Staff Erich Ludendorff prepared for what was to be the last great offensive of the war on the western front, one that attempted to drive the British from the Somme beginning on March 21, the aircraft of the Central Powers bombed Venice, London, and Paris. The Germans occupied Odessa on the Black Sea and later Nikolayev, virtually capturing the Russian Black Sea Fleet. One historian has summarized the perspective from Berlin as the Russians abandoned the field: "For the first time in history, one power's control of Europe stretched from the North Sea to the Black Sea, something even Napoleon had not achieved."[14]

On the other hand, Russian military power was undercut by weakness in civil political structures. There simply is no more persuasive case of foreign and security policies being driven by domestic politics. The chaos at home left the Bolsheviks with no real choices but to sue the Germans for whatever peace they could get. As for the military itself, despite not performing brilliantly on the field of battle during the first three years of World War I, it was still a serious armed force, one whose capabilities repeatedly influenced the military decisions of the Supreme Allied Council on the western front. John Mearsheimer has measured the power of European states on the eve of World War I in his study *The Tragedy of Great Power Politics*.[15] Table 5.1, based on Mearsheimer's work, measures power using several variables. These data describe a macroview of Europe immediately before World War I, and they give some sense of why Russia was considered a "great power." Before the collapse of the tsarist autocracy, Russia both expected and was expected to play a major role in any European war.

Russian military planning was always ambivalent. Russia saw itself both as a great power and as an extremely vulnerable one, although some planners saw its very vulnerability and backwardness as strategic advantages. During the 1880s Russia's generals certainly understood the complicated and tenuous character of Bismarck's diplomacy. They assumed that they would have to fight both Austria and Germany in any European war. Some powerful figures guided this policy: Foreign Minister N. K. Giers; Chief of the General Staff Gen. N. N. Obruchev; and Minister of War P. S. Vannovsky. The strategy of the 1880s changed at various times, but overall it assumed that Russia would go on the offensive against Austria in Galicia, while conducting defensive operations against Germany in Poland and East Prussia.[16] These plans were not too far

Table 5.1 Measures of Russia's Great Power Status

	1900	1913
GNP		
Russia [billions of $]	32.0	52.4
Britain	36.3	44.1
France	23.5	27.4
Germany	35.8	49.8
Total industrial production		
[UK in 1900 = 100]		
Russia	47.5	76.6
Britain	100	127.2
France	36.8	57.3
Germany	71.2	137.7
Relative Share of European Wealth		
Russia	10%	11%
Britain	37%	28%
France	11%	12%
Germany	34%	40%
Standing Armies/War Potential		
Russia	1.1 m/4.6 m	1.3 m/1.8 m
Britain	231 k/677 k	247 k/110 k
France	598 k/2.5 m	736 k/1.07 m
Germany	600 k/3.0 k	880 k/1.7 k

SOURCE: John Mearsheimer, *The Tragedy of Great Power Politics*, W.W. Norton, New York, 2001. A composite of tables 3.1, 3.2, 3.3 and 6.1. War potential represents the total number of men who would be in the army immediately after mobilization.

from what the Russian army actually tried during the early stages of World War I. They reflected an appreciation for the interplay among warning provided by intelligence, forward versus rear defenses, readiness, and mobilization. A vigorous debate had taken place among the General Staff and in the government of Alexander III during the development of these plans, and agreement on these matters had been hard earned.

The exchange of draft notes between the French and the Russians in 1891–1892 revolved around the question of Russian mobilization. The French wanted a Russian commitment to mobilize when intelligence told the two allies that Germany had mobilized; St. Petersburg, however, realized that such an arrangement would both tie its hands and commit it to early combat against Berlin. Foreign Minister Giers, in particular, saw that such a commitment carried the danger of the kind of escalation that actually occurred in August 1914. The French still pushed for a military convention, and the Russian Foreign Ministry resisted. Obruchev wrote a memorandum in May 1892 that carried many of the traditional assumptions of Russian military doctrine.[17] He argued that the earlier Russia mobilized, the greater its chance of success in the first battles of the war, on which the entire outcome might well depend. German mobilization was tantamount to a declaration of war, and agreeing to the French demand for a military convention that pledged countermobilization simply recognized this reality. While the French wanted a Russian commitment to military action against Germany, Obruchev urged flexibility. It might, he argued, be more effective to strike Austria-Hungary with a devastating first blow, knock it out of the war, then turn to face Germany. Here he emphasized both the importance of the earliest stages of any European war and the advantages of striking first, propositions that continued in Russian military planning well into the nuclear age. He said, much as V. D. Sokolovsky would say seventy years later, "Success on the battlefield now depends . . . on the most rapid possible deployment of the greatest possible mass of troops and on beating the enemy to the punch. Whoever first concentrates his forces and strikes against a still unprepared enemy has assured himself of the highest probability of having the first victory, which facilitates the successful conduct of the entire campaign."[18] Russia was technologically ill prepared for modern war. It had underfunded its military. A first strike that would end the war quickly, going on the offensive, taking preemptive action, all held out the hope—or illusion—that Russia's weaknesses would be less exposed. It had better ready forces than reliable reserves. It did not have the means of prolonged mobilization or the transportation assets to bring fresh troops quickly into the battlefield.[19]

Elements of this planning influenced Russian defense thinking down to World War I. As might be expected, after the disastrous defeat at the hands of Japan in 1905, some elements in the Ministry of Defense and General Staff argued for a reorientation of defense eastward. They expressed a genuine worry about the possibility of renewed hostilities with Japan. There were two important issues: One was redeployment of forces away from the western frontier, and the other was a debate over the role of Russia's system of fortresses in the western regions. A vigorous debate took place in 1909–1910 on both issues, resulting in the development of a report in December 1909 by War Minister V. A. Sukhomlinov, "Mobilization Schedule 19."[20] The plan altered the doctrine of the early 1890s, anticipated a redeployment of Russian forces backward from the western regions, and carried mobilization plans that contradicted the Russo-French military conventions of 1893. "Schedule 19" carried the potential for a real reversal of Russian strategy, but it was altered again in May 1912 after much debate by the General Staff's Main Directorate in ways that carried it back to the assumptions of the 1880s and 1890s. Variant A of these 1912 plans supposed that Germany would strike to the west against France, and Russia could assume the offensive against Austria in much the same way that Obruchev had planned twenty to thirty years earlier.[21]

Analysis of National Security Style

In some ways, the period prior to World War I is a litmus test for whether a style of Russian national security exists. Of course 1917 constitutes a great divide, so qualities of style found on both sides of 1917—in the late tsarist period or the earliest Soviet one—suggest a pattern for Russian conceptions of security. There are similarities in some variables, but in others the postrevolutionary context simply diverges too dramatically from the period prior to 1917 to justify generalization.

In terms of *strategic distance,* Russia's imperial ambition drew it into a nearly disastrous adventure in Asia, resulting in a loss of the country's normally strong sense of strategic distance. This was not an inadvertent consequence. A debate had raged in the General Staff and the tsar's court for twenty years over the primacy of the European theater, and Germany had made a deliberate effort to deflect Russian diplomacy and military forces eastward. The Bolsheviks, on the other hand, had learned the lesson of the Kerensky government in early 1917. In contrast, Lenin and his new leadership did not continue to wage a war beyond Russia's means. Hence, they pared down even Russia's European ambitions to gain what they called a "breathing space" for survival at home. They signed the humiliating Brest-Litovsk treaty with Germany in early 1918, buying time to organize the new revolutionary society. In crisis, time to sort out domestic institutions trumped all foreign and military policy.

With respect to *diplomatic flexibility,* the governments of both Nicholas II and Lenin proved adept at diplomatic and military retreat in the exigency of extreme necessity. Russia made peace with Japan and reorganized its alliances after 1905. In 1918 it withdrew from World War I, and in 1922 signed the Treaty of Rapallo with a capitalist German state, an act contrary to Bolshevik ideological principles. In both cases, Russia sought allies where it could find them, even at the cost of swallowing national pride or proletarian ideology to create the best available balance of power.

Although the content varied, *ideology* was a salient issue both before 1917 and afterward. Nationalist ideology got Russia into its Far Eastern troubles before 1905, and it was against more orthodox Marxist-Leninist ideology that

Lenin fashioned the pragmatic compromises of Brest-Litovsk and the Tenth Party Congress in 1921. While ideology mattered, it did not prevent either the tsarist or Bolshevik governments from adopting pragmatic diplomatic adjustments and realist policies.

As for *domestic constraints,* in no periods of Russian history did they drive foreign and security policy more than in 1902–1905 and 1917–1921. The perception of inadequate political institutions was one cause of the Japanese debacle. The defeat in the Russo-Japanese War provoked what at first appeared to be radical reform of those institutions in October 1905. Inadequate domestic institutions greatly impeded Russian military performance in World War I, demoralized the tsar's court, and contributed to the collapse of the autocracy. Lenin's need to consolidate and rebuild at home drove all his foreign and security policy decisions from October 1917 until his incapacitation in 1922.

On the issue of *conservatism,* the innately conservative nature of Russian society, and the political leadership's perception of it, affected everything done by both St. Petersburg and those trying to overthrow the autocracy. It also provided the excuse for Nicholas II's retreat from his reforms in 1905 and for Lenin's introduction of increasingly authoritarian politics within his party and between it and society.

Finally, concerning *military style,* although the exigency of survival prevented the immediate postrevolutionary army from having the luxury of defining its military doctrine, those instincts so evident in the planning of the 1890s and in the years just before 1914 would reemerge in the 1930s under Stalin. Russia's military doctrine before World War I demonstrated a clear preference for the offensive, even surprise. Almost all observers saw how underinvested the army was in the means of mobility, and for that matter in the means of static defense. Logistics were a persistent shortcoming from 1914 to 1918. The inadequacy of Russia's efforts to supply its forces, especially its reserves after the initial battles in the summer and fall of 1914, contributed to the disillusionment that eventually spread through the streets of the cities in 1917 and brought down the tsar's government.

THE TWENTIETH PARTY CONGRESS AND THE SOKOLOVSKY DOCTRINE

A look backward to the twentieth century reveals that few moments in Russian history stand out as important as does the Twentieth Party Congress of the

Soviet Union in 1956. One might argue that the events of 1917 themselves, or the great victories of the Red Army from late 1942 through the summer of 1943, or Lenin's attempt to redefine national policy under extreme duress in March 1921, or Mikhail Gorbachev's reforms in the 1980s were periods of similarly momentous consequence for the fate of twentieth-century Russia, but surely the months immediately following the Congress of 1956 rank among these few supremely important periods of time. Nikita Khrushchev, having consolidated his own power only during the previous year, laid out a policy course of enormous consequence and great promise. He corrected Stalin's (and Lenin's) doctrine on war, which had heretofore held that war was both inevitable and an engine of progressive historical development. In doing so, he acknowledged what only a few of his most forward-thinking military specialists had been arguing in the years right after Stalin's death: that nuclear weapons constituted a technological change of political consequence. That recognition required an adjustment in Soviet foreign relations with other nuclear powers—and Khrushchev selected and began to elaborate a Leninist idea of "peaceful coexistence." He also broke from the orthodoxy of Stalin's attempt to control the international socialist camp from Moscow by applying a "Russian model" for revolution. This, in turn, positioned Soviet foreign policy to catch the wave of national liberation, which was at that moment the most significant feature in global affairs. And he put these significant alterations of foreign policy in the context of a radical, albeit partial and ambiguous, adjustment in domestic policy by exposing the depths to which Stalin's abuse of power had gone. The fact that Khrushchev used these maneuvers against his opponents and to further his own political ambitions in no way diminishes their significance for society or for international politics. These ideas dominated his era at home and abroad in a way that the ideas of few other Russian leaders have.

Such a radical alteration of the national political course had powerful consequences. In the months following the Twentieth Party Congress, old-guard elements in the Communist Party that opposed, or whose interests were threatened by, Khrushchev's policy changes came together in an attempt to overthrow him; he survived an attempted coup by this "antiparty group" by the slimmest of margins.[22] Many scholars have focused on Khrushchev's own contradictions. He seemed to call for, or at least to accept, diversity in the world socialist movement, but he crushed the attempt by Hungarian reformers to cut out a distinctly national variant of socialism only eight months later. He seemed to break out of the bipolar model of international politics and to appreciate the richness of the movement to break from nineteenth-century colonialism and to forge new ties of national liberation. But his policies in Africa, Latin America, and Asia were often clumsy, devoid of a sense of texture among the diverse movements and personalities that rode this wave not so much as a global revolution but as a response to local conditions.[23] And, while his policy toward the West was arguably more creative than Stalin's, he was forging new relationships based on an imperfect understanding of societies that he still perceived through a lens of Marxist-Leninist class dogma. Perhaps most significantly, his disclosure of Stalinist abuses and his incomplete attempts to steer Russia onto a new course sent shock waves throughout the ruling elite. In the immediate aftermath of these events, Khrushchev's efforts to adjust Moscow's priorities appeared to have failed, but those waves continued outward and culminated thirty years later in Yuri Andropov's and then Mikhail Gorbachev's parallel efforts to correct the direction of Russia's socialist revolution.[24]

Nonetheless, in February 1956 Khrushchev launched one of the richest and most significant periods in Soviet history. Much attention has been given to the limitations of his experiment in domestic affairs.[25] He appeared to call for a new course for the economy but failed to institute appropriate reforms of economic policy. He nurtured the thaw in the arts but proved to have no liberal preferences himself and alienated the intelligentsia by persistent evidence of his peasant roots—by his provincial patterns of speech and manners. Clear as these and other limitations were, no objective observer can fail to note the quick pace he set for national change. He beat back the coup by aggressive and creative means. In doing so he forged an alliance with the Soviet military, then moved to curb its power. He used the partly fortuitous timing of Russia's great scientific success in rocketry, symbolized by the launching of the world's first satellite, *Sputnik,* in 1957, in an attempt to vault his country into global leadership. He traveled to Europe and the United States and spoke at the United Nations. He returned to the enduring institution of summitry with other world leaders, a pattern reluctantly created by Stalin during the exigencies of war but subsequently abandoned.

The Twentieth Party Congress: Foreign Policy and Domestic Context

Khrushchev's Central Committee Report to the Twentieth Party Congress on February 14, 1956, in retrospect, probably represents the most confident assessment of world and national trends in the seventy-seven-year history of the Bolshevik experiment. Although Khrushchev continued to beat the drum of optimism over the next six years, his ebullient words were issued in greatly different circumstances. Soviet power was greater when Leonid Brezhnev faced the Twenty-Fourth (1971) and Twenty-Fifth (1976) Party Congresses, but by then optimism had waned—on developments both globally and nationally. Khrushchev set the tone by stating that "the chief feature of our epoch is the emergence of socialism from the confines of one country and its transformation into a world system."[26] Then, in a trick worthy of the accounting offices of the cleverest corporation facing its board of directors, the statisticians of the Central Committee produced a table showing industrial growth rates in the USSR and the leading capitalist states, using 1929 as a base. Soviet rates were shown at 429 percent in 1937 and recorded a steady increase until 1955, when they reached 2,049 percent of what they had been twenty-six years earlier. In contrast, U.S. rates had been at 103 percent in 1937, and had climbed back to only 234 percent in 1955. Despite the statistical sleight of hand by using 1929 as a base, Soviet industrial growth was undeniable and impressive. These achievements served as a powerful bragging right for the Communist Party and its leadership.

Khrushchev could not expect his audience to accept these data uncritically, and he observed that capitalist output had grown by 93 percent from 1929 to 1955. However, he offered four explanations for capitalism's resiliency, the most important of which was the militarization of the economy. In retrospect, the standard Marxist language of his explanation seems odd to read in the twenty-first century. For example, one of his four explanations for capitalism's continued success was that capitalist states continued to increase their output by "sharply intensifying the exploitation of the working class and reducing the living standard of the working people." Nonetheless, even without this standard ideological rationalization for capitalism's resiliency, the Communist Party elite could take pride in the industrial achievements of the 1930s and 1940s, a nationalist pride that continued to shape politics fifty years later.

Domestic achievements were only the baseline of Khrushchev's optimism at the Twentieth Party Congress. Here he first articulated the concept that would come to dominate much of Soviet foreign policy over succeeding decades—the zone of peace. He noted the policy of the Truman and Eisenhower administrations to forge a ring of alliances around the Soviet Union (he specifically cites NATO, the Southeast Asian Treaty Organization, the Baghdad Pact, and the West European Union) and attacked the arms buildup that accompanied these alliances. He characterized Western policy as one based on "positions of strength" and "aggressive blocs." Against these dangers, he proposed the establishment of a "vast peace zone" that would include "both socialist and nonsocialist peace-loving states in Europe and Asia." This zone, he argued, would embrace "tremendous expanses of the globe, inhabited by nearly 1.5 billion people." This optimistic assessment, of course, was more than propaganda. It represented Moscow's real view of world affairs and was rooted in objective changes then sweeping the post–World War II international system. Anticolonialism, even in the hands of an ardent nationalist who persecuted his own communists such as Gamal Abdel Nasser in Egypt, was strongly anti-Western, as Nasser would soon prove by nationalizing the Suez Canal in 1956 and inviting a French and British attack that complicated world reactions to Soviet intervention in Hungary. It was not only from Moscow's perspective that the tide of history seemed to be running against Western interests in 1956.[27]

To provide an ideological blanket that recognized this diversity of positive developments in world affairs, Khrushchev made one of his most creative adjustments to Stalinist orthodoxy. That his formulation was potentially controversial was suggested by his attachment of it to Lenin's own: "All nations will arrive at socialism—this is inevitable—but not all will do so in exactly the same way." He called Lenin's precept "brilliant" and observed that "alongside the Soviet form of reorganizing society on a socialist foundation, we have the form of people's democracy." He explicitly mentioned Albanian, Bulgarian, Chinese, Czech, Polish, and Yugoslav forms of "socialist construction." Although the omission of East Germany and Hungary from his list is interesting, his conclusion seemed inclusive: "It is quite probable that the forms of transition to socialism will become more and more varied." He then proceeded to a remarkably frank discussion of the role of violence in a transition to socialism, acknowledging that many roads to socialism included peaceful ones, even transitions in which the proletariat "has an opportunity to win a firm majority in parliament." Some revolutions would continue to require violence, even civil war; others could be peaceful. But the critical variable was "the more favorable conditions for the triumph of socialism in other countries having arisen because socialism triumphed in the Soviet Union and is winning in the people's democracies."

Khrushchev saw a world where socialism was growing and imperialism was in retreat. His ideological adjustment placed Soviet foreign policy in a position to support a broad range of "favorable developments," from purely nationalist, anticolonial movements to a broad variety of socialist experiments in China, Cuba, Egypt, Ghana, India, Indonesia, and Yugoslavia, as well as in members of the Warsaw Pact that were more tightly tied to Moscow's policies.

This growing power of socialism and the "zone of peace" had possibilities for inhibiting the most dangerous qualities of capitalism. Again Khrushchev returned to a Leninist thesis: "As long as imperialism exists, the economic base giving rise to wars will also remain. . . . But war is not a fatalistic inevitability." This was a delicate point for Khrushchev. Members of his foreign policy elite continued to believe that Leninism's observations regarding war still prevailed: that in the case of war, the cause of the working class would be advanced, as indeed it appeared to have done after both world wars. A small group of thinkers in the Soviet General Staff, however, had been working since Stalin's death on a different appreciation of the new "military-technical revolution," meaning in the first instance the appearance of nuclear weapons.[28] There had been a lively, if limited and classified, debate regarding the interplay between this new technology and class warfare. Now Khrushchev cautiously and partially tied his position to that identified with those who had argued that the new technology changed the role of war in the advancement of class struggle. His arch rival, Georgy Malenkov, had taken that position a year earlier, and the Politburo's rejection of it had contributed to Khrushchev's political victory over him. At the Twentieth Party Congress he used a neat but not unusual communist rhetorical trick. He stated that "in recent times prominent bourgeois figures more and more often admit frankly that 'there can be no victor in an atomic war.'" He then proceeded to tie bourgeois inhibitions concerning the use of nuclear weapons to the general trend of growing socialist strength and the defeats experienced by the "imperialist colonial system." It is possible that Khrushchev, or his speech writers in the Central Committee, still felt some ambivalence on this crucial matter of the role of war in the modern era. But he laid out the basis of what was the most "progressive" formulation on the subject: that nuclear weapons created conditions in which no one would win a modern war. This, combined with his formulation that wars were no longer inevitable, laid the basis of his new policy of peaceful coexistence.

Here Khrushchev explicitly called for the "establishment of firm, friendly relations between the two largest powers of the world—the USSR and the United States." He used a formula that had been advanced in a 1955 meeting of third world countries in Bandung, Indonesia; the principles of peaceful coexistence would be "mutual respect for territorial integrity and sovereignty; nonaggression; noninterference in each other's internal affairs; equality and mutual benefit; peaceful coexistence; and economic cooperation." This program not only justified the first steps toward détente in the next few years but linked Soviet policy to a growing nonaligned and third world movement.

In short, Khrushchev's foreign policy at the Twentieth Party Congress was as revolutionary as was his attack on Stalin's cult of personality. The implications of both were potentially profound.

Military Doctrine and Civil-Military Struggles

It should be emphasized that thinking about the implications of the nuclear/missile age had not progressed very far by the mid-1950s. In the West, Bernard Brodie had published his pathbreaking study, *The Absolute Weapon: Atomic Power and World Order,* in 1946, but these ideas were developed more fully only in his 1959 *Strategy in the Missile Age,* which attempted to assess a world in which two powers had deliverable nuclear weapons.[29] Henry Kissinger's *Nuclear Weapons and Foreign Policy* was first published in 1957. Thomas Schelling published *The Strategy of Conflict* in 1960.[30] In other words, thinking about the implications of mating nuclear warheads to missiles did not develop in the United States until the late 1950s and early 1960s. It developed among a group of "defense intellectuals" who worked outside government for the most part, although a distinction between "inside" and "outside" had by then begun to blur significantly with the central role played by nongovernmental think tanks such as the Rand Corporation.

This tradition of nonmilitary defense thinking did not develop in the Soviet Union until a decade later, when Georgy Arbatov established the Institute for the USA and Canada in Moscow. The first, and most important, Soviet thinking about the implications of the nuclear missile age was done entirely by professional military officers. Much of this thinking remained highly classified at the time, but the Soviets published two editions in 1962 and 1964 of a work entitled *Military Strategy,* of which Marshal V. D. Sokolovsky was the lead author. Although the two editions differ in important ways, they agree on many key concepts, and those constitute a valuable window into Soviet military thinking at the time.[31] Their publication signaled consensus among Soviet military and political authorities that nuclear weapons had become the decisive means of combat. The books had an explicit role to play in the larger political dialogue between Moscow and Washington, and they were publicly acknowledged as having, in part, the role of warning the West of Soviet capabilities, hence reinforcing their deterrent effect.[32] On the whole, therefore, both books tended to discount U.S. thinking at the time, which increasingly emphasized the possibility of counterforce targeting or limited nuclear options. This posture in the Sokolovsky volumes probably suggested a sense that Soviet technology for limited targeting lagged behind that of the United States.

These subtleties, however, which may have been part of the volumes' intended purpose, did not obscure its more central message: In wartime the Soviets would need to destroy both military and civilian-economic targets. If war broke out in, say, the European theater, Soviet forces would use extensive nuclear strikes before sending in conventional forces. In subsequent U.S. debates over Soviet doctrine, a number of observers argued that the description of nuclear strategy in Sokolovsky resembled the use made of massive artillery on the eastern front in World War II. It was also asserted in the West, as Soviet strategic forces grew and were modernized during the 1960s and 1970s, that Moscow believed that a surprise first strike would achieve potentially significant wartime advantages. But Sokolovsky and most Soviet discussion in the early 1960s tended to minimize the possibility of surprise or the danger that a first strike would "destroy all counterstrike means."[33] This implied the possibility of a relatively stable second-strike deterrent, although confidence that Soviet forces were sufficient to that end probably was uncertain until a decade later, when Moscow engaged in negotiations leading to the first series of Strategic Arms Limitation Talks from 1969 to 1972.[34]

The strategic realities strained this doctrine, and the tensions generated spilled over into the political arena. One fairly reliable set of estimates for Soviet strategic capabilities in the period shows this comparison early in the U.S.-Soviet strategic contest (see Table 5.2). Some Central Intelligence Agency estimates at the time have been made public, and although they differ in detail and include a worst-case analysis that projected much more rapid Soviet deployments than in fact happened, the National Intelligence Estimates of first-generation Soviet intercontinental ballistic missiles (ICBMs) and of hardened launchers for these SS-6 and SS-7 missiles did not differ significantly from these International Institute of Strategic Studies' data.[35] While these intelligence estimates are fascinating for a variety of reasons having to do with U.S. politics and policy, including the impact of the alleged missile gap on the U.S. presidential election of 1960, they also provide a rough estimate of how Khrushchev looked at the strategic balance and the calculations he made as he attempted to gain political leverage out of perceptions of Soviet power. Of course, Khrushchev and the Politburo knew the true number of Soviet missiles and bombers. His public exaggeration of Soviet power demonstrated a kind of risk taking that came to characterize his entire national security policy.

Table 5.2 Estimates of Soviet and U.S. Strategic Power

	1959	1960	1961	1962	1963	1964
Soviet						
ICBMs	some	35	50	75	100	200
SLBMs	none	none	none	none	100	120
US						
ICBMs	none	18	63	294	424	834
SLBMs	none	32	96	144	224	416

SOURCE: Institute for Strategic Studies, *The Military Balance, 1969–70,* London, 1969.

Soviet strategic doctrine in the early 1960s emphasized the deterrent effects of nuclear/missile weapons. If war were to break out, however, this doctrine demonstrated skepticism that targeting could be constrained or that fighting could be limited. On the contrary, it seemed to imply that an advantage would go to the side that launched a first strike. It also indicated that, if war were to occur, Soviet forces would use massive nuclear strikes against a wide variety of targets from military ones to economic infrastructure that would, inevitably, put large populations of civilians at risk. This Sokolovsky doctrine had at least two purposes. First, by emphasizing the early phase of a general war as being decisive, the General Staff strengthened its argument for military spending and deployments of weapons. Second, this was in many ways the most threatening posture that the Soviets could take, and in that sense official doctrine seemed to complement the political leadership's efforts to seek leverage from world perceptions of Soviet power. If the early phase of a general war would require decisive nuclear blows, the Russians seemed to edge toward a doctrine of strategic surprise. Since the world perceived Russian nuclear capabilities as greater than they were in fact, coupling those exaggerated capabilities to a doctrine that seemed to threaten a surprise first attack created conditions of extreme instability. This perception was part of the fear generated by the Cuban missile crisis in 1962. The degree to which the Sokolovsky volumes stressed the early stages of a war and the need to take offensive action that would end a general war quickly repeated some of the ideas developed by the Russian General Staff in the 1880s and 1890s. The new doctrine was alleged to show an interest in a surprise attack that seemed to some observers close to advocating preemption of the kind that General Obruchev had envisioned against Austria in World War I.

These military realities emerged in a political context. Khrushchev had elaborated at the Twentieth Party Congress a view of the world in which the forces of socialism were engaged in a global struggle with the forces of capitalism and imperialism. Moreover, he interpreted the economic successes of capitalism as dependent on the role of its military-industrial complex. Consequently, while the possibility of peaceful coexistence existed, the chance of war was significant. And he regarded the growing power of the Soviet Union and its socialist allies as the principal deterrent to military adventures by the imperialists.

Such a view of the world required a demonstration of Soviet military power, and the successful launching of an ICBM with a small satellite payload in October 1957 provided just the dramatic and public demonstration that Khrushchev sought. Once demonstrated, he knew that the window of perceived Soviet advantage might be narrow. Certainly, he could count on strong U.S. efforts to deny it. Hence, his problem was how to convert this apparent Soviet superiority into a political lever. In this, Khrushchev was exceedingly aggressive. He threatened to use Soviet nuclear rocket technology or he exploited world perceptions of those capabilities in a series of crises from Taiwan in 1958 to Berlin in 1961. This political manipulation of Soviet military forces brought him into conflict with elements of the professional military. He had used the armed forces to overcome his opponents in defeating the antiparty group in 1957, and his relationship with the military was tenuous without this policy of attempting to exploit perceptions of Soviet power.[36]

There was a second element of Khrushchev's military policy that caused strain in party-military relations. The Sokolovsky volumes had made the argument that nuclear weapons had assumed the central role in military affairs. Marshal R. Ya. Malinovsky revealed in 1961 that a separate branch of the armed forces had been created—the strategic rocket forces (SRF).[37] From 1960 onward their importance among the various branches of Soviet military forces became controversial. Khrushchev consistently argued that the SRF held primacy among the branches, and in January 1960 he called for a significant reduction of ground forces.[38] This almost certainly was part of a political strategy to find economies in the overall defense budget, or, at a minimum, to shift resources within that budget. Inevitably these proposals created a backlash, forcing Khrushchev to back down in the late spring of 1960, following a notorious episode in which the Soviets shot down an American U-2 spy plane.[39] The revelation that the United States had been violating Soviet airspace was itself an embarrassment for Khrushchev. He had to cancel his planned summit with the outgoing American president, Dwight Eisenhower. But public disclosure of the U-2 overflight program implied that the Americans had a good idea that the Soviets had decided not to deploy as many *Sputnik*-generation ICBMs as had been feared. In the 1960 U.S. presidential election, the Democratic candidate, John Kennedy, made telling effect of the charge that a missile gap had developed between the USSR and the United States, but a few months after he had moved into the White House and announced his programs for upgrading U.S. strategic nuclear forces, his administration quietly but publicly revealed that the Soviets had fewer ICBMs than had been feared.[40]

The fact of the U-2 program and the public disclosure that U.S. intelligence had reduced their estimates of Soviet capabilities created a huge political problem for the Kremlin. Undoubtedly the emplacement of medium-range and intermediate-range ballistic missiles on Cuban soil in the summer and fall of 1962 was partly a response to Khrushchev's political problem with his own military.[41] This gamble that he could alter the strategic balance cheaply and clandestinely no doubt contributed to his removal from power two years later. It was a creative, even brilliant political-military move, but it failed and Khrushchev never recovered, although he typically moved quickly and aggressively to retake the initiative by signing the first real arms control treaty, the Nuclear Test Ban, in 1963.

Analysis of National Security Style

Regarding *strategic distance*, in some ways the period from 1956 to 1961 represents a case of overreach in national security policy. This was not, of course, the only time that security policy has been extended beyond Russia's immediate border regions. Alexander I's chosen role in the Holy Alliance, then in the Congress system of the early nineteenth century, also demonstrated a focus beyond the immediate geographical concentric ring, but he scaled back his Polish ambitions when his allies in Vienna objected. Catherine the Great, too, had flirted with a more distant policy but quickly retreated when the "Greek project" aroused opposition. In this she had envisioned an elaborate reorganization of the Balkans and the eastern Mediterranean. Her son had conceived a "mad" project to invade India, and that may have contributed to his assassination. In other words, Russian adventurism beyond the landmass contiguous to the space Moscow has controlled was not without precedent, but in every case Russian rulers chose diplomatic retreat when faced with any determined opposition by a foreign power. Nonetheless, Khrushchev's policy pushed beyond Soviet borders in a way that has been rare in Russian experience. While his focus on the socialist camp in the Twentieth Party Congress follows traditional geopolitical priorities, his concern for socialist revolutions around the globe and his challenges to the West suggest ambitions that exceeded Moscow's capabilities. He, too, retreated in the face of determined opposition—tactically, as in the case of Cuba when faced by a determined foreign power; tactically also when faced by strong domestic opposition, as was the case in early 1960 when his security establishment objected to his plans for reducing ground forces. While his view of world trends and Russia's place in them constitutes one of the most optimistic moments in Russian history, as that optimism waned in the two decades after his removal, that retreat gradually became strategic.

Both the theoretical basis in Khrushchev's report to the 1956 Congress and his behavior reveal an appreciation that U.S. power represented the greatest threat to Soviet interests. His development of nuclear and ballistic missile capabilities and the twists and turns of his efforts to exploit their deterrent effect and to gain political leverage from them suggest his uncompromising vision that the United States was his principal foreign policy challenge.

In terms of *diplomatic flexibility,* Soviet diplomacy in this period was exceptionally varied and creative. Khrushchev took the dictates of peaceful coexistence seriously. He was the first Soviet leader to travel to the United States, and he probably staked his own political fortunes on a special relationship with President Eisenhower. After the unanticipated crisis over the U-2 incident in May 1960, however, he made a nearly 180-degree turn, breaking up the Paris summit, saying that he could not do business with the U.S. president, and assuming leadership over a much more confrontational policy. Even as relations descended into outright hostility when he met the new U.S. president in Vienna in 1961, in the construction of the Berlin Wall that fall, and in the emplacement of missiles in Cuba in 1962, Khrushchev kept the door of U.S.-Soviet peaceful coexistence open just a crack. After his failure in Cuba, he reversed himself still again and signed the Nuclear Test-Ban Treaty with Britain and the United States in the summer of 1963.

Khrushchev's double reversal on Berlin alone suggested his tactical flexibility. First he attempted to exploit the high-flying perception of Soviet power in the late fall of 1958 by issuing an ultimatum that demanded a treaty to end the Western presence in West Berlin. He then postponed the six-month deadline that he had given and agreed to a foreign ministers' conference in Geneva the following May, and although little substantive progress was made at Camp David in September of that year, the tone clearly had changed. This moderation of the Berlin crisis was again reversed at the Vienna summit in 1961 when Khrushchev reiterated a deadline for a peace treaty with East Germany by the end of the year. In this harsher climate, he built the Berlin Wall as a tactical response to a hemorrhaging border. What some of his colleagues in the Politburo saw as unstable behavior was, in fact, a resourceful adaptation to challenging circumstances. Soviet diplomacy under Khrushchev was as tactically flexible and creative as it was at any time in Russian history.

As for *ideology and domestic constraints,* although it is not difficult to find a traditional strand of "messianic" thinking in the words of the Twentieth, Twenty-First, and Twenty-Second Party Congresses during this period, Khrushchev's actions in the arena of national security policy demonstrated unusual pragmatism. There was some loosening of political controls at home, although many of the signals that some observers in the West thought they perceived in Communist Party actions turned out to be less a turn toward liberalism than had been hoped. For example, the publication of Alexander Solzhenitsyn's *One Day in the Life of Ivan Denisovich* in the fall of 1961 turned out to be more about Khrushchev's own struggles with conservatives in the party than about any relaxation of censorship. In fact, the best evidence for considering Khrushchev a "radical" in post-Stalin Soviet politics was the domestic opposition that he provoked. In 1957 the so-called antiparty group represented a kind of "Stalinist" resistance by the party apparatchiki to his program. The military opposition to his plans for increasing the role of strategic rocket forces and decreasing traditional ground forces represented a parallel conservative backlash in the Soviet context. Even the failure of his economic reorganizations—his initially successful opening of "virgin lands" to agriculture in the early 1950s, his division of the party into agricultural and industrial sections in the early 1960s—demonstrated the "push back" by an inherently conservative society.

Russian *military style* was a central feature of controversy during this period. Even the Sokolovsky volumes seemed partially wedded to traditional Russian efforts to substitute quantity for quality (i.e., to overwhelm opponents with massive force). In fact, it can be argued that Khrushchev's effort to upgrade the role of the SRF over the ground forces was an attempt to change this traditional Russian approach to national security. Khrushchev substituted quality for quantity in 1960 by reducing Soviet ground forces, and having been forced to retreat in the face of opposition from more traditional military and economic interests, he attempted to recoup his losses quickly and cheaply by his Cuban missile gamble. This chapter argues in a later section that Vladimir Putin may be engaged in a similar gamble, which began in 2000, and it remains to be seen whether Russian traditions will again force Moscow to choose quantitative over qualitative military power.

PUTIN'S SECURITY POLICY

Shortly after he was elected president in March 2000, Vladimir Putin signed a general statement of Russian foreign policy strategy called the "Foreign Policy Concept." This document explicitly denounced an earlier one that had been issued by President Boris Yeltsin's Foreign Ministry in 1993.[42] Some observers actually interpreted its appearance to the new administration's desire to "correct" the foreign policies of the 1993 foreign minister, Andrei Kozyrev.[43] Despite internal controversy regarding the content of Russian foreign policy during the 1990s, the two documents have much in common, and they reveal the contours of Russian foreign policy after the collapse of communism. The new Russia faced some hard realities about its capabilities and attempted to maintain its security with greatly reduced means and influence.

In addition to the June 2000 Foreign Policy Concept, President Putin had approved another document even before he was officially elected president. As acting president in January of that year, he had issued Presidential Decree no. 24, which authorized a new national security concept for the Russian Federation. This document, too, was paired with another promulgated by the Yeltsin administration in 1997, and a comparison of these two documents provides insights into the Kremlin's thinking about its national security policy at the turn of the new millennium and at the beginning of President Putin's administration.[44]

In parallel with these large statements of national security policy, the administrations of presidents Yeltsin and Putin also made public documents on military doctrine. The Russian Security Council approved one of these, "The Basic Provisions of Military Doctrine of the Russian Federation," on November 2, 1993. This document was updated by a "Draft Russian Military Doctrine" in October 1999.[45] The "new national military doctrine" was reported to have been approved by the Security Council in February 2000.[46] It was this document, or rather the pieces of it, that were commented on in the public media and led to controversy outside Russia about whether Russia had, in fact, lowered its nuclear threshold.

It is possible that still a further emendation of Russian military doctrine took place in October 2003. There was a brief flurry of controversy in international media about what came to be dubbed the "Ivanov doctrine," so named after Defense Minister Sergei Ivanov. Some stories referred to a "new military doctrine," and most were based on public statements made by the defense minister in which he argued that "we cannot absolutely rule out even the pre-emptive use of force if such a measure is dictated by the interests of Russia or by commitments to our allies."[47] These statements carried extra weight because they were made at a meeting at the Ministry of Defense attended by President Putin on October 2. Despite numerous references to documents handed out at that meeting, however, they have not been accompanied by publication of a new doctrine on the scale of those released in November 1993 and October 1999. The publicity surrounding this meeting and its emphasis on Russia's SS-19 ICBM, which carries multiple independently targetable re-entry vehicles, suggest that it had to do with the U.S.-Russian strategic balance. The timing of the public meeting just after President Putin returned from meetings at Camp David with President George W. Bush also suggests that the Ivanov doctrine was a piece in the complicated bilateral bargaining over the U.S. plans for developing a national missile defense (NMD). This chapter does not, therefore, treat it as a new military doctrine on par with those of 1993 and 1999.

Instead, it weaves an interpretation of contemporary Russian national security policy from the following documents: (1) "Basic Provisions of the Military Doctrine of the Russian Federation," November 1993; (2) "Russian Federation National Security Blueprint," December 1997; (3) "Draft Russian Military Doctrine," October 1999; (4) "National Security Concept of the Russian Federation," January 2000; (5) "Foreign Policy Concept of the Russian Federation," June 2000; and (6) "New Military Doctrine," October 2003.

A number of cautions must attend any effort to reconstruct a national policy from published, or in this case partially published, documents. First, in matters of national security reliable information is always difficult to obtain. Although the Cold War briefly provided the incentive for the United States to make public a great deal of information concerning Russian military affairs, the traditions of secrecy in that society are deeply rooted. Transparency is inadequate even for members of the Russian political elite to understand these issues or for parliament to exercise oversight of the military budget, and the problems faced by external observers in obtaining this kind of information have increased since the end of the Cold War.

Second, there is a particular history in the West in using open sources to discern Russian military policy. During the Cold War, many political battles were fought over the utility of what Western skeptics called "declaratory doctrine." They cautioned that there existed a huge gap between what Moscow claimed its policy to be (e.g., its declaration that it would not be the first to use nuclear weapons) and what its military forces actually prepared to do in wartime. Nonetheless, most analysts agreed that even under conditions when there was deliberate obfuscation for political purposes, published doctrine and open sources were useful in assessing Soviet policy.

Third, now more than then, these public documents are the product of political compromise among various players—the professional military, the security forces, the Ministry of Defense, the Foreign Ministry, the president's own staff, and key members of the legislative branch of government, to name only a few. The behavior of the Russian leadership in any given crisis would depend more on the alignment of these same forces at the time than on what documents they agree to in peacetime.

Fourth, the language itself is inevitably ambiguous. For example, on the crucial question of the role the Kremlin leadership assigns to using nuclear weapons, interpretation is difficult and inevitably tentative.

Finally, statements of national security policy, even if they represent a consensus of the best thinking among key players, still must be made operational. This requires that the vast bureaucracies whose work is affected by the content of the documents must give them effect. And the process of translating words into deeds inevitably offers many opportunities to interpret general statements of doctrine.

A sense of just how far declarations of national security policy are from actual practice can be gained by thinking of a well-known U.S. example. The Bush administration released its version of a national security strategy in September 2002. Although the document stirred a huge controversy by explicitly promising what it called "preemption" and rejecting the concept of deterrence as its authors conceived that concept to lie at the heart of U.S. national security policy during the Cold War, the skeleton of those words had no real flesh on them. They were given meaning by momentous decisions taken by the president in January–March 2003 to launch a war in Iraq that it defined as preemptive. The written policy did not equate with U.S. actions, but it also was not by any means irrelevant to them. The policy reflected the thinking of key players in Washington, and that thinking had momentous consequences. The same can be argued for the Russian documents listed here. They are a window into the thinking of key players in Moscow. They do not equate in any simplistic way to prescriptions for actual policy behavior, but they are not irrelevant either.

Much of the language of these documents follows the general concepts that any state would be expected to follow—for example, "ensuring the security of our country," "protecting the rights and interests of Russian citizens," "creating favorable external conditions for Russia's ongoing" economic development, and "influencing world processes with the aim of forming a stable, just, and democratic world order." These phrases are unremarkable, but there are a number of particular references to real problems confronted by the Russian state. The most important of these are references to the new states that had developed in former Soviet space, possibilities for a new European policy, tensions in U.S.-Russian relations, Russia's relationship to multilateral institutions, and how Russian military power might be conceived to serve these broader geopolitical goals.

Thus, in terms of the *domestic context of foreign policy,* no feature of the collapse of the Soviet empire so galled a broad spectrum of elite opinion in Russia as the loss of leverage among those new states that had evolved out of former Soviet republics. From 1991 forward, the Yeltsin administration and then the Putin administration sought to staunch the flow of Moscow's ebbing influence in the Baltic, Caucasus, Central Asia, Ukraine, and Belarus. This priority has been revealed in a variety of ways. During its losing battle to stop NATO expansion, the Kremlin initially attempted to prevent former Warsaw Pact states from joining; then, in the late 1990s, when it was evident that it did not have the resources to prevent the Czech Republic, Hungary, and Poland from becoming members of NATO, the Yeltsin government attempted a variety of threats and inducements to dissuade NATO from starting the process of offering admission to the Baltic three.[48] Moscow expended a great deal of emotional energy and diplomatic effort into preventing, then proscribing NATO's move eastward. This policy, too, failed, and in the spring of 2004, a second wave of new states joined that alliance, including three former Soviet republics: Estonia, Latvia, and Lithuania. In 2006 the Kremlin's awkward manipulation of the gas supply to Ukraine, its clumsy attempts to pressure Georgia and Moldova by boycotting their wine, and its seemingly irrational support for the Belorusian regime of Alexander Lukashenko represented, in part, a continuation of this impulse to see the states shaped out of the former Soviet space as part of a de facto Russian sphere of influence. These policies caused a sharp conflict with Europe and the United States that to some degree was the by-product of Moscow's efforts to manage relations with the nearest belt of states along its borders.

In parallel, going back to Gorbachev's policy in 1989–1991, successive Russian governments have attempted to develop the Commonwealth of Independent

States (CIS) as an alternative structure for retaining a primary relationship between Moscow and these former Soviet republics. The 2000 Foreign Policy Concept identifies this set of relationships as a top priority. It pledges to pursue multilateral and bilateral cooperation with these states. As examples of the former, it cites the Customs Union (Belarus, Kazakhstan, Kyrgyzstan, Russia, and Tajikistan) and the Collective Security Treaty (these same countries plus Armenia). These states are seen as a kind of inner ring of positive relationships among states formerly part of the Soviet Union, but the document explicitly ties them to a process of integration occurring at various rates and on various levels. Both institutions are therefore seen as elastic, and bilateral efforts will be made to draw more of the former republics into them.

The Baltic states represent a special concern for Moscow, and the 2000 Foreign Policy Concept approaches the problem very carefully. By the time Putin assumed the presidency, these states were clearly headed toward NATO membership. After Russia was forced to accept the first wave of accession to NATO by its former Warsaw Pact allies, President Yeltsin drew a line in the sand that prohibited a second or third wave that would include former Soviet republics. The 1997 blueprint maintained that "[the] creation by major powers (and their coalitions) of powerful groupings of armed forces in regions adjacent to Russia's territory remains a threat to Russia's national security in the defense sphere." It went on to warn that "NATO's expansion to the East and its transformation into a dominant military-political force in Europe" would be "extremely dangerous," and it singled out NATO's rapid-deployment forces and their nuclear weapons as the reasons that expansion posed such dangers. The 2000 concept documents both back down from these positions. While the 2000 Foreign Policy Concept states that "Russia retains its negative attitude toward the expansion of NATO," it also suggests that the "outlook for development of the Russian Federation's relations with Lithuania, Latvia, and Estonia is good" and calls their treatment of the Russian-speaking population within their borders the litmus test of good relations. The 2000 National Security Concept refers to the "eastward enlargement of NATO" as one of the "main threats" to Russian national security in the "international sphere," but it does not specify what countermeasures it considers appropriate. Thus, these documents from 2000 anticipated what by that year was probably already seen as unstoppable. On March 29, 2004, seven states became NATO's newest members: the Baltic three, Bulgaria, Romania, Slovakia, and Slovenia. In the Baltic case, Russian policy proved flexible. The documents reflect these tactical adjustments of Russian policy.

The 2000 National Security Concept documents pointedly do not single out the Caucasus or Central Asian states in the way they do the Baltic states. The 2000 Foreign Policy Concept does make reference to the interests of littoral states in the Caspian region in developing "shared rational use of natural resources," and it does so in the context of a proposed free-trade zone; otherwise, it is largely silent about this region. The 2000 national security document discusses the Caucasus and Central Asian regions only with regard to the CIS, especially the danger that "conflicts close to the state borders of the Russian Federation" and the borders of CIS might escalate. The relative paucity of specific reference to the region along Russia's southern border in these documents undoubtedly reflects the delicacy of the 1999–2000 Putin policy toward Chechnya. By late 2005, after the Beslan tragedy of 2004 and the Nalchik raid of 2005, the second Chechen war clearly threatened to spread to a North Caucasus civil war. It is this kind of "regional conflict" that the 1999 Draft Military Doctrine anticipates might escalate.

What can be said, therefore, about this inner ring of foreign policy relationships? First, in only a decade Russia has moved a long way from its early presumption of its paramount interests in these regions. Its acceptance of normal state-to-state relations with those political entities that have emerged from its former Soviet territory has been remarkable, one that few observers in the early 1990s predicted would happen so quickly or peacefully. The 2000 documents exclude language contained in the 1993 Foreign Policy Concept, which asserts Russia's role as "guarantor of stability" in the "system of positive relations among the states that used to make up the Soviet Union." This transition from "guarantor" to a state among states, one that seeks to develop multilateral institutions of cooperation, both reflects the realities that Moscow has encountered and may reveal a profound change in mental outlook. This conclusion is not yet certain, however, as President Putin's clumsy attempts to interfere in the Ukraine elections of 2004 and 2006 and his pressure on Georgia in 2006 demonstrated. Russia has habits of domination that do not atrophy easily, and Western diplomacy clearly has an obligation to encourage the less interventionist inclinations among Kremlin leaders.

Second, Russia has developed a kind of maturity, a longer time frame for asserting its influence in this region. The Kremlin view seems to assert that time will permit "natural" processes to evolve. Russia will continue to be the largest state in the region, and its gravity will inevitably affect the orbits of all these new states in the first ring of concentric circles about it. The documents of 2000 suggest that Moscow realized that it need not threaten the way it did in the more uncertain times of the early to mid-1990s, nor does it need to assert its special rights and obligations. These will emerge naturally without special effort to secure them, and modesty concerning them will lessen unease among Russia's immediate neighbors. The documents of 2000 seem to suggest a gradual process—first promoting integration with Belarus while maintaining closer cooperation within all CIS states during the crisis in the Caucasus. Then, in the future, Moscow can tend to its relationships with states along the CIS border, the second ring outward from Moscow. In the meantime, economic and defense cooperation with this outer ring of states will suffice. Putin's misstep on Ukrainian politics in late 2004, however, suggests the inevitable tension between the maturity of allowing Russia's gravitational pull to secure its interests over time and old habits of domination. The latter will inevitably resurface from time to time, and a firm diplomatic response from Europe, especially, and the United States will be needed to ensure that the balance of forces in the Moscow leadership continues to view its interests to be served by the gradualist approach that the Security and Foreign Policy Concepts of 2000 articulate.

As the Foreign Policy Concept of 2000 looks westward, toward the developed states of Europe and North America, it carefully adopts the language of realism. It forthrightly observes that "the chief priority of Russia's foreign policy in the area of international economic relations is to foster the development of its national economy." This objective grows out of the frank realization that negative tendencies in the international system, including some in the Euro-Atlantic region, "are compounded by the limited nature of the resources available for the support of the Russian Federation's foreign policy." The National Security Concept of 2000 begins with contrasting "two mutually excluding trends" that dominate post–Cold War international relations. One is perceived as positive, and the second, a negative trend from Moscow's perspective, is "the attempt to create a structure of international relations based on the domination of developed Western Countries, led by the USA."

The foreign policy document cites European integration as one of these dangerous tendencies that limited resources force Moscow to accept. It criticizes this process as being "often selective and limited in scope," which apparently means that it excludes Russia. The document notes a series of integrative developments in Europe that pose dangers for Russia. It would oppose "any narrowing of the functions of the Organization for Security and Cooperation in Europe (OSCE), in particular attempts to refocus its activities on the post-Soviet space and the Balkans." Thus, it explicitly sees OSCE peacemaking activities in the Caucasus and the Balkans as running counter to Russian interests. Similarly, it observes the growing tendency of the European Union to formulate a common foreign and security policy, especially its initial efforts at creating a common defense entity. These developments represent objective realities, and the document pledges to work to secure appropriate consideration of Russian interests.

The larger issue from Moscow's perspective is posed by developments in NATO. The Foreign Policy Concept recognizes the "importance of cooperating with it in the interests of security and stability on the continent" but lays out very specific conditions. NATO, it argues, must adhere to the May 1997 Founding Act on Russia-NATO relations, especially its provisions against the deployment of conventional forces and nuclear weapons on the territories of new members. Russia has very consistently argued that such forward deployments could have as their objective only hostility toward its interests.[49] The overall tone of the document's discussion of NATO is quite negative. It observes conflict between the alliance and Russian security interests "in terms of a whole variety of parameters." It criticizes, in particular, NATO's eastward expansion and what that alliance calls "out of area" military operations, which had been the focus of NATO's new Strategic Concept adopted at its Washington summit in April 1999.[50] Moscow's 2000 National Security Concept was even more pointed and succinct: It identifies NATO's eastward enlargement as one of the main threats to Russia's security and lists it above all among negative developments in military-political alliances.

Even this defensive and negative tone in the 2000 documents reflects changes in Russian thinking over that advanced in 1993. The earlier version still referred to Russia's special relationship with Eastern Europe as being within its "historical sphere of interests." And one supposes that a new policy concept, if it were written in 2003 or 2006, would demonstrate a more positive frame of mind with respect to Europe generally. President Putin skillfully joined Russian interests to those of France and Germany in resisting U.S. leadership in the Iraq war. In fact the 2000 document itself seems to lag behind the actual practice of the Kremlin leadership in Europe, where Putin waged aggressive diplomacy throughout 2000 and 2001 and scored some successes in aligning Russian policy with the foreign policy preferences of Germany and France. These efforts bore fruit in joint opposition among the three European powers to the war in Iraq and in their mutual suggestion that the United Nations Security Council play a central role in that country after the U.S. military "victory."

The 2000 Foreign Policy Concept has a decidedly negative tone with respect to relations with the United States. Perhaps this should not be surprising given the context in 1999–2000—conflict over the U.S.-led NATO campaign in Kosovo, the decision by Bill Clinton's administration to press for NATO expansion, and strain over U.S. policy in the Middle East. Nonetheless, the document observes "an increasing tendency toward the creation of a unipolar world under the economic and military domination of the United States." It elsewhere refers to "serious and, in some instances, fundamental disagreements" with the United States. This negative tone was balanced by the realism observed earlier, and by a pledge to "maintain the infrastructure of Russian-American cooperation that has been nearly ten years in the making." Yet this shared objective will not be easy to achieve, as escalating tensions in the spring of 2006 made clear. Vice President Dick Cheney's Vilnius speech to leaders from former Soviet states provoked harsh responses from President Putin and other Russian leaders and turned up the volume of what had been the background music of complaints and countercomplaints between Moscow and Europe as well as with Washington during late 2005 and early 2006. It will take hard work and persistence to cultivate the goodwill and calls for cooperation contained in earlier national security documents. But these possibilities exist, as was demonstrated within a month after the rhetoric of early May. The Bush administration reversed its approach to the Iran problem and the two former superpowers found a way to cooperate within a multinational approach to that country's nuclear ambitions.

The content of that cooperation is laced through the 2000 foreign policy document. The Conventional Forces in Europe Treaty is identified as a Russian interest. It mentions Moscow's continued willingness to "make further reductions in its nuclear arsenal on the basis of bilateral agreements with the United States." But it also calls the 1972 Antiballistic Missile (ABM) treaty "a cornerstone of strategic stability" and threatens to "respond with appropriate measures to maintain its own national security" if Washington goes forward with an NMD system. Of course, George W. Bush's administration would, within a year, both renounce the ABM treaty and move aggressively to deploy NMD. Additionally, the hints in 2003 of a new Ivanov doctrine were clearly tied to the Kremlin's failure in heading off U.S. NMD deployment.

Nonetheless, nowhere are the limits of Russia's power more evident than in its relationship with the United States. The Bush administration has made a great deal of its management of the Russian relationship, something that Secretary of State Condoleezza Rice, a former director of the National Security Council, takes a special interest in and has devoted personal attention to nurturing. Despite flurries of top-level consultations between the White House and the

Kremlin, relations have deteriorated since 2000. Disagreement over the Iraq war and Iran's nuclear policy were only the most visible policy disagreements as the United States moved into its 2006 election cycle; the process itself has deteriorated appreciably, as a reading of the 2000 Foreign Policy Concept makes clear. Washington has ignored Moscow's interests in each of the issues that document singles out as especially important—the ABM treaty, NMD, and even cooperation over the reduction of nuclear arms, which the Bush administration has moved far down on its policy agenda. Arguably the direction of the U.S. revolution in military affairs has so reduced its dependence on and interest in nuclear weapons that the administration has simply abandoned the urgency with which eight previous administrations had approached this central element of cooperation between the two powers between the early 1960s and the 1990s.

It cannot have been lost on important segments of the Russian political elite that the content of the relationship has shifted away from their country's interests to the Bush administration's agenda. On every element singled out by the 2000 Foreign Policy Concept, President Bush's policies have moved away from the agenda set forth by President Putin's team when they first came to power. The element of the 2000 Foreign Policy Concept that most aggressively positions Russian foreign policy in contrast to its historical pattern is the use made of multilateral institutions, although Mikhail Gorbachev, too, had experimented with a policy that made greater use of the multilateral instrument. The document poses these institutions, especially the UN Security Council, as a constructive alternative to a unipolar world in which U.S. power creates hegemony. And in that sense, it can be said that the document itself sets Russian policy on an opposite course to the policy preferences of the U.S. president and especially the neoconservatives who have played such a prominent role in his national security policy. In fact, the 2000 National Security Concept explicitly poses its analysis of international affairs in this manner. It sees two trends—a positive one toward "strengthening of economic and political positions of a considerable number of states and their integration associations, and in the improvement . . . of multilateral . . . international processes"—and a negative one toward "unilateral solutions of the key problems of global politics, above all with the use of military force." Moscow clearly supports the multilateral process and warns about the unilateral one.

These documents from 2000 state this difference both clearly and repeatedly. Right after asserting Russia's commitment to its own security, the Foreign Policy Concept ascribes to the aim of "forming a stable, just, and democratic world order that is based on the generally accepted norms of international law, including first and foremost, the goals and principles of the UN Charter." It contrasts the vision of a "unipolar world under the economic and military domination of the United States" with Russia's intention to "promote the formation of a multipolar system of international relations." When the document turns to Russian priorities, it lists first the "creation of a new world order" and identifies the United Nations and its "principle center." Although it calls for rational reforms and "enhancing the effectiveness" of the Security Council, it makes a thinly veiled challenge to what the Kremlin knows to be strong reservations about the efficacy of the council to meet the challenges of the contemporary security environment: "The Russian Federation will firmly oppose any attempts to downgrade the role of the UN and its Security Council."

While this emphasis on the UN is a striking component of the document, it mentions favorably a variety of multilateral institutions. It singles out international economic institutions—the Group of Eight, the International Monetary Fund, the World Bank. It calls the Nonproliferation Treaty "an important factor in Asian-Pacific stability." It calls for "stepping up Russia's participation in the major international organizations of the Asian-Pacific region." And, as indicated earlier, it devotes careful attention to European multilateral institutions such as NATO and the European Union.

Finally, the 2000 Foreign Policy Concept observes that a "distinctive quality" of Russian foreign policy is its "balance" between Europe and Asia. This derives "from Russia's geopolitical position as the largest Eurasian power, a position which necessitates an optimal combination of its efforts on all fronts." This position "imposes a responsibility on Russia for maintaining world security on both global and regional levels." While this identification of Russia's "special position" is a great deal less messianic than Ivan IV's declaration in his correspondence with Ivan Kurbsky that Moscow had become the "Third Rome," or the early Bolsheviks' claims to lead the "world proletarian revolution," or even the pretensions of the Twentieth to the Twenty-Third Party Congresses that the tide of history was moving inexorably in the direction of the world socialist movement, it does continue this tradition of exceptionalism in Russian consciousness. Interestingly, Russia's special mission is now identified with its geopolitical position, straddling Asia and Europe.

The document singles out relations with China and India, with whom Russia has long had a "traditional partnership." It calls for the "steady development" of good neighborly relations with Japan and notes with "greatest concern" the Korean problem, in the solution of which it lays claim to "full and equal participation."

The Kremlin has made considerable progress in developing its special relationship with Beijing, even if relations with Tokyo have, once again, stalled on the difficult issue of the Kuril Islands. In September 2004 Russia's prime minister, Mikhail Fradkov, and China's premier, Wen Jiabao, signed a series of important economic agreements at the Bishkek meeting of the Shanghai Cooperation Organization. Then President Putin went to Beijing in October for bilateral talks with the Chinese leadership. He and President Hu Jintao signed thirteen agreements, including an important one that delineated the border in the Amur region and completed the work of a "framework treaty" signed in 2001. From Moscow's perspective, Putin achieved valuable Chinese support for Russia's entry into the World Trade Organization. That significant cooperation is underlined in a declaration signed between the two presidents in Moscow on July 1, 2005, which, arguably, brought Moscow's and Beijing's foreign policies into closer condominium than at any time in recent history and was interpreted by some observers in Russia as sending a clear warning to Washington that a Sino-Russian alliance would create a formidable barrier to U.S. foreign policy unilateralism.

While some observers played down the anti-American implications of the Moscow declaration and the Bush administration naturally attempted to diminish its significance, the steady improvement in Russia's relations with China and its careful diplomatic coordination with China in the six-nation framework over the North Korean problem do suggest another line of diplomatic activism that promises to increase both countries' flexibility and leverage in international affairs. It suggests that President Putin has begun to make adjustments such as those called for in chapter 6 in this volume, by Gilbert Rozman—for example, pursuit of a "balanced and balancing" strategy and of a more normal approach to the "political and cultural ethos of Northeast Asia."

At a time when Washington has been preoccupied with the war in Iraq and the domestic fallout from it, Russian diplomacy has shown resilience and creativity in extending Moscow's influence. The China policy in the second Putin administration has shown an appreciation for the intricacies of balance-of-power diplomacy. Even in the 1990s, some foreign policy specialists in Russia, most notably former prime minister Yevgeny Primakov, had tried to compensate for reduced leverage in U.S.-Russian relations by creating an alternative opening for influence—in his case, in the Middle East. While independent Russian policies toward Iraq and Iran are reminders of that ambition, Putin seems to have landed on a potentially far more promising line of global balancing. In this case, Russia is at least showing an interest in achieving influence by diplomatic means that its power position seems unable to earn.

This is a sophisticated and highly differentiated foreign policy. In its response to Moscow's diminished influence in Washington, it attempts to use multilateral institutions and to practice balance-of-power tactics on several fronts, China and Europe foremost among them. Along its borders it has alternated between a mature, diplomatic policy that counts on the sheer weight of Russia to secure its interests and a more impatient policy that interferes directly in the economies and political life of its neighbors. In Russia's dealings with this inner belt of states formed from the former Soviet Union and in its policies toward Europe and the United States, old habits of conflict coexist with impulses of cooperation. This ambiguity is the starting point for Russia's relations with Washington and Europe. Nurturing the latter and resisting the former will, for some time, be the challenge facing U.S. and European policy toward Russia.

Toward a Leaner, Meaner Military Force

Even as acting president in early 2000, Putin was identified with national security reform. In late 1999 he presided over a full-scale debate concerning military doctrine. A draft document had circulated in the Ministry of Defense that was designed to supplant one issued by President Yeltsin in 1993.[51] The new version had been approved by the Russian Security Council on October 6, 1999, and was signed into law on January 6, 2000.[52] This document received considerable attention at the time, largely because it seemed to lower the nuclear threshold by expanding the circumstances in which Russia might initiate nuclear strikes. This development was not surprising, given the widespread perception in Moscow that its military power lagged significantly behind that of the United States. Moreover, lowering the nuclear threshold had been suggested as a possible response to U.S. NMD policy as it evolved at the end of the Clinton administration, a trend that was then certain to continue, however the U.S. presidential election of 2000 turned out.

After this new security policy was adopted in the Kremlin, debate on all of its principal issues continued. One such debate was over ending the draft and moving to an all-volunteer force, an idea that had military logic if Russia were to move toward a more professionally trained force but was abandoned because of the prohibitive costs. Putin himself ended this debate in his address to the Federal Assembly on May 16, 2003.[53]

The issue of military reform was placed at the center of the national agenda in that same address. In it Putin thrust military modernization to the forefront of the government's tasks, calling it one of three top priorities of national policy for the coming decade. He said that in 2008 the term of the draft will be reduced to one year, and he reaffirmed the goal of moving toward a professional military force. His establishment of priority for military modernization grew naturally, if uncomfortably, out of the demonstration of U.S. capabilities in the quick victory over Saddam Hussein's forces in Iraq during the weeks prior to this address. Criticism among some political observers had grown over the failure of Russian military officials to appreciate how quickly the U.S. armed forces would win the military battle for Baghdad.[54] That failure, in turn, suggested a broader and more important lack of understanding of the role of modern military technology. Public indications of dissatisfaction with Russia's military almost certainly suggested private reservations as well. What had already become clear by U.S. employment of technology in the war in Afghanistan against the Taliban in the fall of 2001 is made evident to all attentive publics and to defense ministries everywhere. Putin seemed to be saying that Russia's role in the future of international affairs requires military modernization.

A sense of how these military matters stood from the Kremlin's perspective seems clear in view of some rather simple military facts, outlined in Table 5.3. The data in this table provide a general overview of the military reality with which the Kremlin dealt in the first decade and a half after the beginning of communism's unraveling. In all dimensions, Moscow's military power was greatly diminished, suggesting several conclusions.

First, although one perception of this reality is that Russia's declining power would inevitably mean a reduced voice in international affairs, this conclusion has perhaps been drawn in too facile a manner by too many outside observers. Russian military power, and not only nuclear power, remains considerable. The number of tactical fighters, ground attack aircraft, and main battle tanks are only crude indicators of residual Russian military capabilities. But they also suggest a material basis for state power that is far from insignificant even without Moscow's real efforts to modernize its forces.

Second, the 2000 Military Doctrine is suffused with the concept of "sufficiency." It alleges that the Russian state is "maintaining a sufficient level" of military power to avert a "threat of direct military aggression" against it. The 1993 Military Doctrine was unequivocal: "It is stressed that the immediate threat of direct aggression being launched against the Russian Federation has

Table 5.3 Some Measures of Russian Military Power After the Collapse of Communism

	1989 [Soviet]	1995	2000	2003
Total Military Manpower	4.26 M	1.52 M	1.01 M	.96 M
Total Tactical Aircraft [fighters and ground attack]	4595	2150	1455	1514
Total ICBM	1,451	928	766	735
Total Main Battle Tanks	53,350	19,000	21,820	21,870
Total Surface Fleet Combat	264	150	35	32

Data taken from IISS, *The Military Balance* for years 1989/90; 1995/96; 2000/01; and 2003/04. These are very crude indicators. They do not account for operational arms control treaties, nor for qualitative technical capabilities. A more nuanced analysis of the 1989 data is available in *Soviet Military Power: Prospects for Change, 1989*, Washington, 1989.

considerably declined in contemporary conditions." That document was, in retrospect, amazingly optimistic, given the political chaos into which the country was soon to plunge. On the whole, it indicated that it regarded "no state as an enemy" and was explicitly restrained concerning the conditions under which Russia might employ military force.

Third, some outside observers have concluded that Russia is no longer a significant military power. While the illustrative data cited in Table 5.3 suggest caution in drawing such an assessment, the kinds of mobility and integration of intelligence, command and control, special operations, and coordination of air, ground, and naval assets demonstrated by the U.S. military in Afghanistan and Iraq underline severe limitations in Russian capabilities. Confronted with the demonstration of capabilities that Russia lacks, some of these observers have concluded that Moscow has little recourse but to lower the nuclear threshold and to attempt to achieve leverage from its strategic arsenal. There was a flurry of such commentary with the publication of the 2000 National Security Concept and again in the fall of 2003 in response to Defense Secretary Ivanov's comments on preemption.[55] Indeed, there does seem to have been a verbal shift toward greater emphasis on a nuclear deterrent in published Russian military doctrine. The 1993 Basic Provisions of Military Doctrine anticipated a modest role for Russia's nuclear forces, which it placed in the context of arms reductions "to a minimum level." The 2000 document tied the absence of a "threat of direct military aggression" to Moscow's "active foreign policy course" and its nuclear deterrence. The distinction is subtle but significant. By the start of Putin's presidency, enough negative trends had emerged in Russia's security environment that the Kremlin adopted something similar to a classical concept of deterrence. Indeed, the 2000 Military Doctrine found many scenarios that could lead to nuclear conflict. It argued that a "conventional world war" would have a "high probability of escalating into a nuclear war with inevitable mass victims and destruction." It indicates that in such a war "the sides will set radical military-political goals." This sounds considerably like the military doctrine of forty years earlier. The 2000 doctrine also anticipates that a "conventional regional war, if nuclear states or their allies participate in it, will be characterized by a constant threat of use of nuclear weapons." Altogether, then, the mood of the 2000 document was considerably more pessimistic about the chances of nuclear war than the 1993 document. In this context, the Ivanov doctrine of 2003 continues this trend. It attempted to extend Russia's nuclear umbrella to non-nuclear scenarios by inducing ambiguity about the possibility of preemption. While all three documents, and surely operational planning, explicitly anticipated the use of nuclear force if the national security of Russia were at risk, at least it seems evident that between 1993 and 2003 the public doctrine moved increasingly toward hedging conditions under which nuclear strikes might be used. By 2006, however, partly reflecting a significant improvement in Russia's financial picture as a result of rising energy prices, the Kremlin leadership seemed to appreciate that it might use non-nuclear military power as a lever in world affairs. President Putin used his annual message to Parliament on May 10, 2006, to outline plans for modernizing Russian strategic nuclear forces, but he also emphasized plans for modernizing and professionalizing the army. He explicitly linked these ambitious plans not only to potential combat scenarios but also to "resisting any attempt to exert foreign policy pressure on Russia."[56] This is a sophisticated politico-military policy. Moscow has created the impression that it would lower the threshold at which it would use nuclear weapons at a time when its military power is weak, but it has also embarked on significant and long-term force modernization.

To the degree that the 2000 National Security Concept reveals widespread consensus among the Kremlin's strategic thinkers—that is, the document's linkage of the "active foreign policy course" to a reduction in the danger of military aggression—it also illuminates Putin's foreign policy toward the U.S. and European problems. Both his aggressive efforts to foster closer ties with France and Germany and his nurturing of the Russo-Chinese relationship undoubtedly find their roots in this broader appreciation of Moscow's tools for achieving national security. Russian military options have narrowed, requiring a more creative foreign policy. Putin has a sophisticated appreciation of the interplay of military and political factors in world affairs. His use of foreign policy to strengthen a weak military hand has complemented a policy that uses an ambiguous nuclear policy to improve deterrence, while Russia pursues a long-term program of vigorous force modernization.

Analysis of National Security Style

Thus, President Putin turns out to be among the most interesting of Russian leaders in his national security policy. In some of this chapter's six variables he continues historic practice—his sense of strategic distance and his diplomatic creativity, for example. But in others—for example, his secular aloofness from ideology and the direction of his military policy—he seems to break from the patterns observed in the pre–World War I and post–World War II periods.

On the first quality, coping with *strategic distance*, Russian foreign policy after the fall of communism has returned to traditions that preceded the bipolar pretensions of the Cold War. Nowhere is this more evident than in Moscow's preoccupation with those states in closest geographical proximity. In fact, the Chechen wars, the Abkazian diversion, the Tajik intervention, and the attachment to close relations with Belarus despite the often odd behavior of its president, Alexander Lukashenko, all suggest that both Yeltsin's and Putin's Kremlin leaderships have focused on problems in states of closest geographical proximity. Indeed the policy seems to have some of the characteristics of one planned from a map with concentric circles of intensity, diminishing as they move outward from Moscow. The greatest effort, expense, and heartache have been made in Chechnya, but it is difficult to shake the impression that NATO's intervention in Kosovo and Russia's repeated efforts to protect Serbia from the dictates of a military solution also carried a somewhat irrational preoccupation with tsarist and Stalinist claims of a sphere of influence along Russia's western borders. Even Russian resistance to NATO expansion seemed imbued with this concept of geographical proximity: German unification and the inclusion of the new state in NATO seemed to be accepted with surprisingly less difficulty than the invitations for membership to the Czech Republic, Hungary, and Poland in 1997. And these, too, seemed to cause less heartburn than the possibility that the Baltic states would join in the second wave following NATO's Prague summit in 2002. After the collapse of communism, Moscow appeared to be thinking of Russia's interests as concentric circles spreading outward from the capital.

As for *creative diplomacy*, all the documents from 1993 to 2000 that form the basis of this analysis leave no doubt that the United States continues to be the central problem for Russian security policy. While relations between Moscow and Washington have waxed and waned since the danger of a communist return faded in the fall of 1993, they have frequently been highly strained and have turned decidedly more sour since the election of George W. Bush. Bush, like his predecessor, has frequently ignored fundamental Russian interests, has acted unilaterally and against Russian advice in world crises, and has made repeated references to the growing disparity between Russian and U.S. power. While Putin has candidly addressed this disparity, he has also made some progress toward fashioning an alternative to bipolarity—by cultivating an axis with Germany and various combinations of other European states as opportunities permit. His visits to Germany and Italy in 2000 signaled and probed for receptiveness to this strategy. His ad hoc siding with Chancellor Gerhard Schröder and President Jacques Chirac over the war in Iraq moved the strategy forward.

Putin's diplomacy in Europe, then, shows both a creative response to a growing American problem and an emerging strategic choice for the long term. Russia's resistance to the United States' vision for Iraq, its independent stance on Iraq's external debt, and its persistence in supporting Iran's nuclear program suggest a continued effort to gain traction in the international system. Moscow's careful cultivation of China and its tacit alliance with that country in the Beijing negotiations over North Korea in the fall of 2003 demonstrate that Putin has a global interest in forging pragmatic alliances to work on discrete international problems. His summits with President Hu Jintao in Beijing in 2004 and Moscow in 2005 have nudged policy beyond a tacit alliance, at least holding open an Asian foreign policy orientation to supplement his European policy. This diplomacy has been imaginative and relatively successful within the limits of Russian power. Nowhere are both sides of this strategy more evident than in the way the foreign policy and national security documents tie Russian interests to multilateral institutions, first of all the UN Security Council. On the one hand, Moscow has increasingly been alarmed by what it regards as U.S. unilateralism and has attempted to become a leading voice for multilateralism as an alternative. On the other hand, President Putin has attempted to forge a complex web of bilateral and multilateral relationships that seek also to reduce the role of international organizations in which the Russian voice is perceived as marginal—for example, NATO, the European Union, and possibly even the Group of Eight. This sophisticated strategy reminds one of Lenin's "dual policy." In the first five years after the 1917 revolution, Moscow attempted to conduct normal diplomacy with the major powers while promoting revolution within them by various instruments, including the Comintern. Now Putin seems to welcome opportunities to demonstrate Russian cooperativeness with other major powers at the same time that Russia attacks the very institutions in which that cooperation is framed. For example, Russia has used the NATO-Russian Council to obtain a place at the table in NATO's decision making while pursuing a consistent policy of attacking NATO's aggressive expansion eastward. Similarly, Putin enjoys Russian inclusion at major economic summits, such as Sea Island in the spring of 2004 and St. Petersburg in July 2006, while occasionally using those occasions as opportunities to fan the backfires of French, German, or other countries' resistance to U.S. policies.

With respect to *military style*, Putin has attempted to reinforce this emerging geopolitical strategy by making solid efforts to modernize Russia's military forces in a way that more closely mirrors the American appreciation for the revolution in military affairs.[57] The entire thrust of his new emphasis on a highly trained professional military equipped with modern weapons and technology runs counter to traditional Russian approaches. Although it is still early and there are signs of traditional resistance to adopting new ways, and although the behavior of the Russian military forces in Chechnya demonstrated persistent habits from past traditions, it is not easy to see how Russia can avoid modernization. It will be a long time before it can compete again with the United States in that complex of technologies on which modern warfare seems to depend, and there is evidence that Russia has thought out its short- and intermediate-term strategies for dealing with what will be a persistent inferiority. What this chapter has called the "nuclearization" of Russian military doctrine between 1993 and 2003 represents that temporary fix to multiple demonstrations of reduced Russian power. But in President Putin's second term in office, there is evidence that he is serious about correcting traditional Russian dependence on quantity to compensate for quality in military affairs. Whether Russian armed forces can learn the mix of intelligence, command and control, and precision-guided weapons that constitute the contemporary revolution in military affairs remains to be seen, but Putin's intention is to drive reforms in that direction. There is great skepticism among external experts that he can make real progress in this direction, and there are substantial constraints in economic resources and political will to increase radically the share of gross national product that supports defense.

When it comes to *ideology and realism,* Putin's policies do seem to run counter to several national security traditions. Both his pragmatic foreign policy and his realistic appreciation of the limitations on Russian military power have demonstrated the ability to adapt. While other members of the political and military elite may carry the messianic strain in Russian security policy, Putin himself has not yet shown that he has imbued his policy with moral passion. Of course, national survival is not at stake, as the documents analyzed in this chapter suggest, and a wide spectrum of the Russian elite seems to appreciate the need for a prolonged "breathing space," like the one Lenin chose in 1918 and 1921, in which attention to domestic economic and political affairs will take priority over military matters. Indeed, in this sense there are parallels between the current period and Lenin's policies at the Tenth Party Congress in 1921. Yuri Andropov, during his short time in power more than two decades ago, showed a keen interest in Lenin's adaptation during the early 1920s, and perhaps Putin has some of that same sense of Russian requirements. But there is a widespread sense of Russian vulnerability and wide-ranging disaffection from what is often termed "U.S. unilateralism" and "arrogance." External vulnerability has often been accompanied by an instinct toward internal repression. The Kremlin's turn toward tougher domestic controls since 2003 worries important domestic and international constituencies precisely because of the traditional correspondence between a perceived weakness in national security and tightening political reins.

While this discussion has emphasized the *domestic constraints* on Russian power since the collapse of communism in 1991, it requires an important qualification. President Putin has made considerable progress in turning the economy around. Rates of economic growth have been impressive, despite obvious disruptions at the intersection of the economy and the political system such as the arrest and trial of Mikhail Khodorkovsky, the chief executive officer of the giant oil company Yukos, who in 2005 was tried for and found guilty of tax violations. Much of this economic success has come because of the increased value of Russia's large energy production as world prices have increased. This is not new in Russian national security. Even during the Napoleonic and world wars, Russia's sense that its natural resources gave it significant geopolitical advantages affected elite perceptions of Russia's international role. During Khrushchev's and Brezhnev's thrust onto the global stage in the 1950s and 1960s, oil permitted Moscow to establish patron-client relations with ideologically compatible regimes such as that of Fidel Castro in Cuba. Now, in the first decade of the twenty-first century, global petroleum markets are very much front and center. Russia's oil production once again thrusts it onto the international stage, and rapid increases in international oil prices since Putin was re-elected to a second term undoubtedly both strengthen Russia's global position and extend Kremlin political and economic options. For example, access to Russian oil markets has become a major incentive for China and Japan to improve ties. Nonetheless, it cannot be said in retrospect that previous Kremlin leaders used their oil reserves wisely, nor did they achieve long-term benefits in international affairs by their energy advantages. It remains to be seen whether the current Moscow leadership will do better with the windfall profits from world energy markets during the new millennium's crisis in the Islamic world.

In one final way, Putin's mix of this chapter's six variables differs from those of his predecessors—that of *reform and reaction.* He has not experienced the traditional "push back" from a conservative society. On the contrary, his approval ratings have remained high relative to those of his democratic counterparts elsewhere. That could mean, of course, that in this sense he is simply in the "conservative, nationalist tradition" of other leaders—say, Nicholas I, or Alexander III, or Stalin. And in some senses he has seemed to capture the wave of reaction against the market and democratic transformations of the 1990s—he has attacked the financial oligarchs and adopted a foreign policy in particular that explicitly rejects the most imitative pro-Western policies of Yeltsin's early years. But it is too simple to say that he has joined the nationalist opposition. He has not proven to be ideologically nationalistic, at least not xenophobic, and he has proven to be a policy innovator. His national security policy is a complex mix. He is clearly not a "democrat" in the usual Western usage of that term, but he is also not quite in the tradition of dictators or autocrats. He has bullied and manipulated the Duma, but he also appears to expect his succession to be by electoral process, no matter how "managed." He has sought leverage in the international system by improving bilateral ties in Asia and Europe. Those policies have been partially anti-American, but he has also worked with President Bush on a variety of issues.

What can be said of Putin is this: He has practiced a foreign policy that reflects traditional preoccupations with the states along Russia's borders, but he has also been creative and flexible in dealing with the great transformations of NATO and the European Union. He has been mostly skillful in dealing with what many observers consider "American unilateralism." He has moved slowly and purposefully in all things but has committed himself to a mix of doctrinal change and technological innovation in military affairs. In these matters he seems to be prepared to break with Russia's traditions of giving quantity priority over quality.

CONCLUSION

This chapter examines several distinctive elements in the Russian style of national security. In making this analysis, it interweaves more general comments about Russian history into a fabric of three case studies: the years just before and after the Bolshevik seizure of power; the years following Khrushchev's bold policy initiatives at the Twentieth Party Congress in 1956; and the years in which President Vladimir Putin, like his predecessor, Boris Yeltsin, has wrestled with reconstructing national security after the fall of communism. The chapter, then, explicitly analyzes roughly 125 years of security policy, and it does so through periods of tsarist autocracy, Soviet communism, and post-collapse reconstruction. The range of political and economic circumstances certainly provides a sufficient test for generalizations about a Russian style. Similarly, the first and last of these cases meet Robert Legvold's criteria for great transformations. The Khrushchev period does not meet that standard, although this chapter argues that in some ways it envisioned changes as radical as those attempted since 1991—for example, the proposed reductions in ground forces and elevation in the role of the strategic rocket forces in early 1960 were not attempted again until after the collapse of communism. That Khrushchev sought so radically to transform Russian foreign and security policies, and failed, makes that case especially useful for testing the six propositions that form the analytical heart of this chapter. What conclusions, then, have been reached?

First, the cases examined here exhibit that quality of Russian national security policy established for hundreds of years—a preoccupation with immediately contingent geographical space. Two exceptions were explored—the Far Eastern policy at the turn of the twentieth century and Khrushchev's assertion of Soviet interests in the global "zone of peace" in the middle of it, which carried him far from Soviet boundaries into Asia, Africa, and Latin America. In both cases, Russian resources were not up to the task. Tsar Nicholas II reluctantly adjusted his Asian ambitions, or rather the Japanese navy did it for him in the Strait of Tsushima, and then reoriented both his diplomacy and his military policy. Khrushchev did not survive to see his global ambitions completely scaled back, but was clearly in military and political retreat after the U-2 crisis of 1960. In their readiness to sacrifice more distant ambitions to more proximate requirements, they followed a long tradition.

Second, although the conditions differed widely, Russia made the necessary diplomatic adjustments preparing to face Germany before World War I. Khrushchev designed his so-called peaceful coexistence policy in an attempt to define the rules for Soviet engagement with the United States, demonstrating both ideological and diplomatic light-footedness. And like his predecessor, Boris Yeltsin, Putin has returned to traditional balance-of-power diplomacy after decades in which the Soviet Union sought to create the basis of a global superpower, but has attempted to craft a policy toward the United States that maintains Russian independence for diplomatic maneuver while avoiding power confrontations. Putin, in particular, has explored a wide variety of foreign policy adjustments to reduce the primacy of U.S.-Russian relations. His efforts to nurture bilateral relations with Germany and France in Europe in his first two years as president and his efforts to cultivate a strategic alternative in Russo-Chinese relations both testify to his sense that creative foreign policy can compensate for diminished Russian military power—at least in the short run.

Third, in each period explored in this chapter, Russia has struggled to balance the often conflicting demands of realism and ideology. While the mix has varied since the 1880s, Nicholas I, Lenin, Khrushchev, and Putin have all chosen pragmatic compromise over ideological advance.

Fourth, foreign and security policies have often reflected domestic constraints and have been designed to accomplish domestic objectives. The tsar's security policies triggered collapse at home—twice, in 1905 and 1917. Lenin traded land and national humiliation at Brest-Litovsk to keep his thin grip on power at home. Khrushchev linked his great foreign policy vision and his creative use of missile diplomacy to his domestic struggle against the remnants of Stalinism. He ultimately lost, but he saw the symbiotic relationship between domestic change and foreign policy dynamism as surely as did Peter I. The "nuclearization" of Russian military doctrine under Putin has come as both the political and economic pictures have stabilized following the 1998 financial collapse. As this chapter argues, however, it is a rational response to the realities of power. And thus, once again, security policy reflects domestic constraints.

Fifth, Russian society pushes back against reform. At all times in Russian history, part of its elite and its *narod* have demonstrated strong, conservative preferences. Leaders who have tried reform have used foreign and security policy as a lever on internal politics, and the fate of change has often been determined by the conservative center of gravity in society. The Duma in 1905–1907, Lenin in 1918–1921, Khrushchev in 1956–1961, and democrats in 1992–1998 all were forced to retreat before the resistance of entrenched interests opposing change. Even Putin's retreat from democracy and capitalism reflects society's push back against postcommunist reforms. Domestic retrenchment has provided the latitude for diplomatic and military innovation, and the Kremlin's national security policy has legitimized, in part, his paring down of civic space.

Sixth, Russian military doctrine has consistently substituted quantity for quality and emphasized the early phases of combat to hide perceived weaknesses in organization and technology. The debates in the Russian General Staff of the 1880s and again after 1909 reflected a perceived need in the event of a European war to mobilize quickly, take the offensive, and prevail in the decisive early stages of combat. That tradition also drove military doctrine under nuclear conditions when the Sokolovsky volumes were published in the early 1960s, and fueled the arms race with the United States during the 1970s and 1980s. These doctrinal preferences emphasize forces in being, combat "teeth" rather than logistical "tail," a weakness in Russian military power that goes back to Ivan IV and Peter I. Putin's re-emphasis on nuclear weapons in the National Security Concept of 2000 and the Draft Military Doctrine of that same year reveals an appreciation that the modern revolution in military affairs has severely disadvantaged Moscow's power. And, if the so-called new military doctrine of 2003 does emphasize preemption, that development reflects a response to preemption in the Bush doctrine of 2002, a traditional Russian emphasis on the early stages of combat, and a traditional preoccupation with striking first. President Putin's detailed discussion of his military policy in addressing Parliament in May 2006 also demonstrated the Kremlin's determination to build modern military forces. He carefully trimmed expectations that Russia could match American power, but he explicitly scaled Russia's military ambitions to the more manageable dimensions of Britain and France, two major and nuclear world powers.

Is there a distinctive Russian national security style? Yes, in some ways. This chapter argues that these six characteristics are found across quite different political and economic circumstances in Russian experience. The chapter attempts to question some more traditional generalizations on the topic and to advance an alternative way of thinking about Russian security policy. Are there exceptions? Certainly. For example, the author is well aware that he has avoided the 1930s, the rise of Nazi Germany and Stalin's response to it. Some readers might accuse the author of faintheartedness for avoiding this difficult "exception" to the generalization about Russian concerns for the early stages of combat, the risk of surprise, and the necessity to strike first. The same could be said about 1807–1812. But these two obvious exceptions are only partial, and they provide a big part of the incentive for the thesis on military style advanced here. The exceptions do not refute the argument; rather, they are a part of the historical experience that drives the distinctive style of Russian national security.

Notes

1. The early Cold War provided the context for a rich literature examining the sources of Russian foreign policy. See, for example, the chapters by Michael Karpovich, "Russian Imperialism or Communist Aggression," Arnold Toynbee, "Russia and the West," and Edward Crankshaw, "Russian Imperial Design," all in *Readings in Russian Foreign Policy*, ed. Robert Goldwin (New York: Oxford University Press, 1959), pp. 657–666, 680–688, and 705–719, respectively. See also Ivo Lederer, *Russian Foreign Policy: Essays in Historical Perspective* (New Haven: Yale University Press, 1962).

2. Although their emphases and policy prescriptions sometimes differed widely, two scholars—George F. Kennan and Richard Pipes—have been widely associated with the perception of Russian expansionism. See, for example, the Kennan "Long Telegram" of 1946 or his *Foreign Affairs* article written under the pseudonym "X" in 1947. For an especially interesting insight into Ambassador Kennan's thinking at this crucial stage in the origins of the Cold War, see Kennan, *Measures Short of War: The George F. Kennan Lectures at the National War College, 1946–47* (Washington, DC: Superintendent of Documents, 1991). Representative of extensive writing by Pipes a generation later, although the volume had an implicit policy objective, is Pipes, ed., *Soviet Strategy in Europe* (London: Macdonald and Jane's, 1976), pp. 3–44.

3. Four important historians who have written general histories of Russia have been especially attentive to the relationship between domestic reform and foreign policy, on the one hand, and economic backwardness and military expansion, on the other. V. O. Kliuchevsky, *A History of Russia*, trans. C. J. Hogarth, 5 vols. (New York: Russell and Russell, 1960), especially his treatment of Ivan IV in vol. 2, chaps. 4, 5; George Vernadsky, *A History of Russia*, 4 vols. (New Haven: Yale University Press, 1972), especially vol. 4; and Michael Florinsky, *Russia: A History and Interpretation*, 2 vols. (New York: Macmillan, 1954), especially chaps. 8 and 13, on Ivan IV's and Peter I's military and foreign policy. Nicholas V. Riasanovsky has written a popular one-volume history, *A History of Russia*, 6th ed. (Oxford: Oxford University Press, 1999); see especially his summary analysis of Peter I's reforms.

4. The story of technological innovation prior to World War II is found in an easily accessible translation by Col. Gen. B. L. Vannikov, "In the People's Commissariat of Armaments," in *Stalin and His Generals: Soviet Military Memoirs of World War II*, ed. Seweryn Bialer (New York: Western Publishing, 1969), pp. 152ff. For an excellent analysis of the 1930s and 1950s, see David Holloway, *The Soviet Union and the Arms Race* (New Haven: Yale University Press, 1983).

5. To get beyond partisan hagiography and find a balanced discussion of the origins of the Star Wars idea and an effort to understand its impact on U.S.-Soviet relations, see Frances Fitzgerald, *Way Out There in the Blue* (New York: Simon and Schuster, 2000).

6. The degree of Western involvement in Russia during World War I is little appreciated in general histories. Two of the leading scholars of the period have a general appreciation: George F. Kennan, *The Decision to Intervene* (New York: Atheneum, 1967); and Richard H. Ullman, *Intervention and War* (Princeton: Princeton University Press, 1961). Both these works, however, focus on the intervention by the Allies against the Bolsheviks, not the cooperation prior to the Bolshevik seizure of power. The current author has an article in manuscript, "Major General F. C. Poole and the Intervention in Northern Russia," that discusses the British presence in St. Petersburg in 1917–1918. A good primary source is General Poole's "General Report for 1917 of British Military Equipment Section in Russia," CAB 27/189/13. This reference is to the Cabinet Papers found in that file at the British National Archives.

7. This interpretation depends heavily on William C. Fuller Jr., *Strategy and Power in Russia, 1600–1914* (New York: Free Press, 1992), pp. 376–377. Many scholars find the minister of war less committed to opposing the Japanese adventure. The problem seems to be that he was clearly in favor of an expansionist foreign policy in the Far East, while taking a Eurocentric view of Russia's military interests. Nonetheless, he commanded Russian forces against Japan. For an alternative interpretation to Fuller's, see Florinsky, *Russia: A History and Interpretation*, vol. 2, pp. 1272ff.

8. Fuller, *Strategy and Power in Russia, 1600–1914*, pp. 412–418.

9. This story, too, has been told by numerous scholars, but by none better than William Langer, *The Franco-Russian Alliance, 1890–1894* (Cambridge: Harvard University Press, 1929), reprinted by Octagon Books, New York, 1967. Two books by George Kennan explore this story with scholarly care: *The Decline of Bismarck's European Order: Franco-Russian Relations, 1875–1890* (Princeton: Princeton University Press, 1979); and *The Fateful Alliance: France, Russia, and the Coming of the First World War* (New York: Pantheon, 1984).

10. It is time here to acknowledge an important source for this study, although occasionally more significant as a foil. Few modern studies of Russian history have provoked more thoughtful analysis than that of Geoffrey Hosking, *Russia and the Russians* (Cambridge: Harvard University Press, 2001). His account of these years and his explanation for the failure of Russian institutions is brilliant and challenging.

See also Orlando Figes, *A People's Tragedy* (New York: Viking, 1997), especially chap. 1; and Adam Ulam's excellent discussion of prerevolutionary intellectual politics in *The Bolsheviks* (Cambridge: Harvard University Press, 1998).

11. No one has told this story better than Edward H. Carr, *The Bolshevik Revolution, 1917–1923*, vol. 3 (New York: Macmillan, 1961). See also Adam Ulam, *Expansion and Coexistence: Soviet Foreign Policy, 1917–73*, 2d ed. (New York: Praeger, 1976).

12. Richard Pipes details and analyzes Lenin's struggles with various opposition groups as well as anyone in *The Russian Revolution* (New York: Knopf, 1990). His *Formation of the Soviet Union* (New York: Atheneum, 1968) is still a classic for its analysis of the Bolsheviks' policy toward other nationalities. Another excellent source for the entire Soviet period of Russian history is Robert Service, *A History of Twentieth Century Russia* (Cambridge: Harvard University Press, 1999), especially his chapters on the civil wars and the New Economic Policy for the struggles of 1920–1921.

13. Ulam, *The Bolsheviks;* and Hosking, *Russia and the Russians.*

14. Martin Gilbert, *The First World War* (New York: Holt, 1994), p. 403. Gilbert's discussion of the military events of the Great War is as good as any, and places Russian behavior in the broader picture of global developments.

15. John J. Mearsheimer, *The Tragedy of Great Power Politics* (New York: Norton, 2001).

16. Kennan, *The Fateful Alliance*, pp. 157–192. Fuller's discussion of these important decisions in *Strategy and Power in Russia, 1600–1914* does not differ in important substance from Kennan's, *Strategy and Power,* pp. 328–393.

17. Kennan translates this memorandum from Vannovsky to Giers, May 7–19, 1892, in *The Fateful Alliance*, pp. 264–268.

18. Ibid., p. 264.

19. By far the most careful discussion of these developments known to the author is that of Bruce W. Menning, in *Reforming the Tsar's Army: Military Innovation in Imperial Russia from Peter the Great to the Revolution,* ed. David Schimmelpenninck van der Oye and Bruce W. Menning (Cambridge: Cambridge University Press; Washington, DC: Woodrow Wilson Center, 2004), pp. 215–231.

20. Bruce W. Menning, *Bayonets Before Bullets: The Imperial Russian Army, 1861–1914* (Bloomington: Indiana University Press, 1992), pp. 238–271. Menning's discussion of Russian adjustments to "Schedule 19" was pathbreaking in its detail and attention to Russian archival resources, but it is consistent with the devotion to the offensive that Kennan and Fuller found in their study of the 1880s and 1890s.

21. Fuller, *Strategy and Power in Russia, 1600–1914,* pp. 426ff.

22. The basic elements of this story were long ago pieced together by a pioneering group of "Kremlinologists." See Carl A. Linden, *Khrushchev and the Soviet Leadership, 1957–1964* (Baltimore: Johns Hopkins University Press, 1990); Robert Conquest, *Power and Policy in the USSR* (London: St. Martin's Press, 1961); and Wolfgang Leonhard, *The Kremlin Since Stalin* (New York: Greenwood Press, 1975).

23. For a good general discussion by a scholar who always demonstrated sensitivity to Soviet policy in what was then called "the third world," see Alvin Z. Rubinstein, *Soviet Policy Since World War II*, 2d ed. (Boston: Little, Brown, 1985). For samples of studies of Khrushchev's policies toward specific regions, see Robert Legvold, *Soviet Policy in West Africa* (Cambridge: Harvard University Press, 1970); and Raymond W. Duncan, *Soviet Policy in Developing Countries*, 2d ed. (Melbourne, FL: Krieger, 1981).

24. Mikhail Gorbachev, *Memoirs* (New York: Doubleday, 1996). See also a thoughtful interpretation by Jack Matlock, *Reagan and Gorbachev: How the Cold War Ended* (New York: Random House, 2004). One of the most insightful explorations of the Gorbachev period is David Remnick, *Lenin's Tomb* (New York: Vintage, 1994).

25. See, for example, Service, *A History of Twentieth Century Russia*. For a discussion of Khrushchev, see William Taubman's prize-winning biography, *Khrushchev: The Man and His Era* (New York: Norton, 2003). Taubman's discussion of the Twentieth Party Congress, despite its fresh details concerning the composition of the Central Committee Report, does not provide much analysis of its consequences for foreign policy. See also Jerry F. Hough, *How the Soviet Union Is Governed* (Cambridge: Harvard University Press, 1979). This editing of the classic *How Russia Is Ruled* by Merle Fainsod created controversy, as any revision of a classic will, but Hough's analysis of Khrushchev's politics within the Kremlin has stood the test of time.

26. N. S. Khrushchev, "Report of the Central Committee," appeared in *Pravda* on February 15, 1956; many of the documents associated with these party congresses have been translated in a series published by the Current Digest of the Soviet Press, in this case, Leo Gruliow, ed., *Current Soviet Policies*, vol. 2, *The Documentary Record of the Twentieth Communist Party Congress*, Sponsored by the Joint Committee on Slavic Studies (New York: Praeger, 1957). N. S. Khrushchev's "On Control Figures for Development of the USSR National Economy," at the Extraordinary Twenty-First Congress of the Communist Party of the Soviet Union, appeared in *Pravda* on January 28, 1959; and his "Report of the Central Committee," to the Twenty-Second Congress of the Communist Party of the Soviet Union, appeared in *Pravda* on October 17, 1961. Leo Gruliow, ed., *Current Soviet Policies*, vol. 3, *The Documentary Record of the Extraordinary Twenty-First Communist Party Congress* (New York: Columbia University Press, 1960); and Leo Gruliow, ed., *Current Soviet Policies*, vol. 4, *The Documentary Record of the Twenty-Second Congress of the Communist Party of the Soviet Union* (New York: Columbia University Press, 1962).

27. Rt. Hon. Sir Anthony Eden, *Full Circle* (London: Cassell, 1960); and Dwight Eisenhower, *The White House Years: Mandate for Change* (New York: Doubleday, 1963).

28. Raymond L. Garthoff, *Soviet Strategy in the Nuclear Age* (New York: Praeger, 1962), pp. 61–96; and H. S. Dinerstein, *War and the Soviet Union* (New York: Praeger, 1962), pp. 1–64.

29. Bernard Brodie, *The Absolute Weapon: Atomic Power and World Order* (Manchester, NH: Ayer, 1946); and Bernard Brodie, *Strategy in the Missile Age* (Princeton: Princeton University Press, 1959). For an excellent general discussion of the early thinking about the political implications of atomic weapons, see Lawrence Freedman, *The Evolution of Nuclear Strategy* (New York: St. Martin's Press, 1981).

30. Henry Kissinger, *Nuclear Weapons and Foreign Policy* (New York: Harper, 1957); and Thomas C. Schelling, *The Strategy of Conflict* (New York: Oxford University Press, 1960). Another excellent discussion, especially of U.S. thinking in the late 1950s and early 1960s, is Jerome H. Kahan, *Security in the Nuclear Age* (Washington, DC: Brookings Institution Press, 1975); and Janne E. Nolan, *Guardians of the Arsenal: The Politics of Nuclear Strategy* (New York: HarperCollins, 1991).

31. V. D. Sokolovsky, *Voyennaya Strategiya* (Moscow: Voyenizdat, 1960, 1962). Raymond L. Garthoff published an English translation of the second volume, *Military Strategy: Soviet Doctrine and Concepts* (New York: Praeger, 1963). A third edition was published in 1968, and Harriet F. Scott published a substantial translation and analysis as V. D. Sokolovsky, *Soviet Military Strategy* (New York: Crane, Russak, 1975).

32. Thomas W. Wolfe, *Soviet Strategy at the Crossroads* (Cambridge: Harvard University Press, 1964). See also H. S. Dinerstein, *War and the Soviet Union* (New York: Praeger, 1962). This point was made explicitly in the preface to the second edition. Soviet interest in using declaratory policy to increase deterrence was suggested in Marshal R. Ya. Malinovskii, "The CPSU Program and Questions of Strengthening the Armed Forces of the USSR," *Kommunist*, no. 7 (May 1962), pp. 3–25.

33. L. Glagolev and V. Larionov, "Soviet Defence Might and Peaceful Coexistence," *International Affairs*, no. 11 (November 1963), pp. 27–33.

34. Raymond L. Garthoff, *Détente and Confrontation: American-Soviet Relations from Nixon to Reagan* (Washington, DC: Brookings Institution Press, 1985), pp. 53–69, 127–188. See also Lawrence T. Caldwell, *Soviet Perceptions of Détente*, Adelphi Paper (London: Institute for Strategic Studies, 1972).

35. See especially NIE-11–5-58 and NIE 11–8-62 in Donald P. Steury, ed., *Intentions and Capabilities: Estimates on Soviet Strategic Forces, 1950–1983* (Washington, DC: History Staff Center for Study of Intelligence, Central Intelligence Agency, 1996), pp. 65–89, 181–190.

36. Michel Tatu, *Power in the Kremlin* (New York: Viking, 1969). Tatu was the correspondent of *Le Monde* in Moscow during the late 1950s and early 1960s. His discussion of Khrushchev's use of military power has stood the test of time remarkably well. Another good source is J. M. Mackintosh, *Strategy and Tactics of Soviet Foreign Policy* (New York: Oxford University Press, 1963). Malcolm Mackintosh was an adviser to the British Cabinet during these years, and he has an excellent sense both of detail and of Western perceptions of Khrushchev's challenges.

37. Marshal Malinovsky, report to the Twenty-Second Party Congress, *Pravda*, October 25, 1961.

38. See Tatu, *Power in the Kremlin;* and Thomas W. Wolfe, *Soviet Strategy at the Crossroads* (Cambridge: Harvard University Press, 1964), especially pp. 153–188.

39. An excellent source for the entire period, but especially the complicated civil-military relations of 1960, is Arnold L. Horelick and Myron Rush, *Strategic Power and Soviet Foreign Policy* (Chicago: University of Chicago Press and Rand Corporation, 1966), pp. 71–82. See also Tatu, *Power in the Kremlin.*

40. Horelick and Rush, *Strategic Power and Soviet Foreign Policy,* pp. 83–104.

41. This interpretation, too, has stood the test of time, despite any number of interpretations that focus less on Soviet motives. See ibid., pp. 105–158. On this key question, Tatu agrees. See also Elie Able's excellent demonstration of journalistic reporting very near the events themselves in Able, *The Cuban Missile Crisis* (New York: Lippincott, 1966). A large number of pertinent documents have now been published on the U.S. side. See, for example, Laurence Chang and Peter Kornbluh, *The Cuban Missile Crisis, 1962* (New York: New Press, 1992).

42. Foreign Minister Igor Ivanov presented the new document at a press conference in the Foreign Ministry on July 10, 2000, "The Foreign Policy Concept of the Russian Federation," *Nezavisimaya gazeta,* July 11, 2000. For the first extensive public discussion of the 1993 document that the author has found, see Vladislav Chernov, deputy director, Russian Security Council Strategic Security Administration, "Russia's National Interests and Threats to Its Security," *Nezavisimaya gazeta,* April 29, 1993, pp. 1, 3.

43. For an article particularly critical of former foreign minister Andrei Kozyrev's role in shaping the 1993 document, see Sergei Guly, "Déjà vu," *Novie Izvestiya,* July 11, 2000. This criticism of Kozyrev was widespread. See, for example, Aleksei Pushkov, "The Evolution of Our Foreign Policy Concept from Early Yeltsin to Early Putin," Nezavisimaya gazeta, July 18, 2000, p. 3.

44. For the two documents, see *Rossiiskaya gazeta,* December 26, 1997, and January 18, 2000. For English translations of both, see Federation of American Scientists Web site, http://www.fas.org/nuke/guide/russian/doctrine.

45. The 1993 document was widely reported. "The Basic Provisions of the Military Doctrine of the Russian Federation" was adopted by a presidential edict, no. 1833, on the same day that it was approved by the Russian Security Council. The only place that this author has found a full copy of this document is on the Federation of American Scientists Web site, http://fas.org/nuke/guide/russia/doctrine/russia-mil-doc.html. The 1999 "Draft Russian Military Doctrine" was published in *Krasnaya zvezda,* October 9, 1999, and translated by BBC Worldwide Monitoring on October 11, 1999. It, too, can be found at the Federation of American Scientists Web site, http://fas.org/nuke/guide/russia/doctrine.

46. Two such articles are found in a Reuters dispatch by David Storey on January 19, 2000, and by Interfax analysts Aleksei Aleksandrov and Igor Denisov on January 14, 2000. See Johnson's Russia List, no. 4051, January 20, 2000, Center for Defense Information, http://www.cdi.org/russia/johnson/4051.html.

47. See, for example, Mikhail Vorobyov, "Sergei Ivanov Threatens Preemptive Strikes Against Potential Aggressors," *Vremya novostei*, October 3, 2003, p. 1. For an extensive discussion of Russian commentary in ITAR-TASS News Agency, see *Rossiyskaya gazeta, Krasnaya zvezda*, and *Parlamentskaya gazeta*, among others; and FBIS Media Analysis, October 20, 2003, http://www.dialogweb.com/cgi/document?docKey=3-985-17900015&docFormat=full&fo. There was also an interesting press conference by several influential Russian analysts on October 6, 2003, including Sergei Karaganov, Andrei Kokoshin, Mikolay Mikhailov, and Vitaly Shlykov. See Federal News Service, http://www.fednews.ru/.

48. Moscow initially opposed NATO's offer of a "Partnership for Peace" in 1993–1994. The government delayed signing that agreement so that then foreign minister Andrei Kosyrev could obtain leverage over NATO expansion. He failed. Once NATO seemed likely to expand, after mid-1994 and throughout 1995, the Yeltsin administration engaged in harsh rhetoric in an effort to block the process. Having failed again, between December 1996 and May 1997, it sought to impose conditions for accepting the NATO-Russia Council. In this, too, it failed. Finally, it retreated to opposing the admission of the Baltic states. See Yeltsin's comments on the eve of the Paris summit in 1997, as reported by Carol J. Williams, "Yeltsin Walks Softly on Eve of Pact with NATO," *Los Angeles Times*, May 27, 1997, p. 10; Yeltsin and Foreign Minister Yevgeny Primakov were both quoted in the Russian press prior to signing the Founding Act in Paris as saying that if NATO were to admit former Soviet states, the entire relationship would be "undermined." Quoted in *RFE/RL Newsline* 1, no. 38, part 1, May 26, 1997.

49. For a sampling of tough Russian statements, see Craig R. Whitney, "Russia Tells NATO It Accepts Offer on a Formal Link," *New York Times*, December 12, 1996, p. A1, and reports on an interview with Foreign Minister Primakov in *Rossiiskaya gazeta*, December 17, 1996. William Drozdiak reported even harsher statements by Defense Minister Igor Rodionov in "Russian Defense Chief Blasts NATO's Plans," *The Washington Post*, December 19, 1996, p. A29. That the issue was still highly charged was revealed by the different positions taken by presidents Clinton and Yeltsin on the eve of the Paris summit. See Paul Goble, End Note, *RFE/RL Newsline* 1, no. 31, part 1, May 15, 1997; and Georgy Bovt, "U pozhiznennykh garantii zhizn mozhet okazatsya korotkoi," *Segodnya*, May 16, 1997, p. 3.

50. The document, "The Alliance's Strategic Concept," was adopted by NATO's heads of state at the Washington summit, April 23 and 24, 1999, NATO, http://www.nato.int/docu/pr/1999/p99-065e.htm.

51. A good discussion of the process within the Ministry of Defense that led to the new doctrine is found in an article by Andrei Korbut, "In Places, Draft Military Doctrine Would Supplant the Constitution," *Nezavisimaya gazeta*, October 13, 1999, p. 3. The best Western source on a wide range of these reform issues is found in Steven E. Miller and Dmitri Trenin, eds., *The Russian Military: Power and Policy* (Cambridge: MIT Press, 2004).

52. See Ivan Safranchuk, *Moskovskiye novosti*, no. 2, January 18–24, 2000, p. 5. Safranchuk refers in this article to a "previous version of principles, signed in 1997." The author cannot find a published version of those principles, although 1997 was a year of enormous conflict over military issues. President Yeltsin did sign a document on the "Basic Principles of . . . Military Development," in July 1998, although the author did not find a public version of that document either. See Ilya Bulavinov, "Russian Arms No Longer World's Strongest," *Kommersant-Daily*, August 4, 1998, p. 12. Bulavinov also comments specifically on the earlier version, which he says was approved by the Russian Security Council in May 1997 and consisted of thirty-eight pages. See his article in "National Security Goes Defensive," *Kommersant*, October 6, 1999, p. 2. The chapters in the Miller and Trenin book by Pavel K. Baev and Alexei G. Arbatov provide interesting context and a slightly different argument on the role and fate of military reform, especially its economic constraints. Arbatov's perspective is important because he had served as deputy chairman of the defense committee in the Duma. A.G. Arbatov, "Military Reform: From Crisis to Stagnation," in Miller and Trenin, *The Russian Military*, pp. 95–119. P. K. Baev, "The Trajectory of the Russian Military: Downsizing, Degeneration, and Defeat," ibid., pp. 43–72.

53. This was a major address, full of content on the same themes as the 2000 documents. RTR Russia TV, BBC Monitoring, May 16, 2003, Center for Defense Information, http://www.cdi.org/russia/johnson/7186-1.cfm. See also reports by Yekaterina Grigoryeva, "Vladimir Putin Talks About How to Make Russia Strong Again," *Izvestiya*, May 17, 2003 pp. 1, 3; and Dmitry Kamyshev and Ivan Safronov, "What Vladimir Putin Told Russians About the Future," *Kommersant*, May 19, 2003, p. 3.

54. See, for example, Andrei Lebedev, "If You Want Peace, Prepare for the Right Kind of War," *Izvestiya*, May 7, 2003, p. 3; and Aleksandr Babakin, "Tells Where the Russian Army Is Headed," *Rossiiskaya gazeta*, May 14, 2003, pp. 1, 5.

55. See, for example, Martin Nesirky's Reuters dispatch, "New Security Concept Sees Greater Threat to Moscow," Johnson's List, no. 4036, January 14, 2000, Center for Defense Information, http://www.cdi.org/russia/johnson/4036.html; and Anna Dolgov's AP piece, "Russia OKs Draft Military Doctrine," February 4, 2000, Center for Defense Information, http://www.cdi.org/russia/johnson/4091.html. Nikolai Sokov at the Center for Nonproliferation Studies in the Monterey Institute for International Studies has done some excellent analysis of this literature. See his January 2000 assessment in Nuclear Threat Initiative, http://www.nti.org/db/nisprofs/over/concept.htm.

56. *Rossiiskaya gazeta*, May 11, 2006, pp. 1–3. A substantial translation is found in BBC Monitoring, from RTR Russia TV, Moscow, in Russian 0800 gmt, May 10, 2006. See also an AP dispatch by Vladimir Isachenkov. The latter two are found in Johnson's List, #109, May 10, 2006 at www.cdi.org/russia/johnson.

57. This emphasis has long been a central theme of Russian military literature. For a recent popular discussion, see a report of comments by First Deputy Secretary of

the Russian Security Council Vladislav Sherstyuk in ITAR-TASS, in English, February 25, 2003, in English February 25, 2003. FBIS-SOV-2003-0225. For a perspective on the role of nuclear weapons from an informed American scholar who participated in the strategic arms control negotiations during the Clinton administration, see Rose Gottemoeller, "Nuclear Weapons in Current Russian Policy," in Miller and Trenin, *The Russian Military*, pp. 183–216. Her chapter is especially good in discussing the debate between Minister of Defense Igor Sergeev and Chief of the General Staff Anatoly Kvashnin in 1999 and 2000, just as Putin was taking hold of the reins of power.

CHAPTER 6

Russia in Northeast Asia: In Search of a Strategy

Gilbert Rozman

R USSIANS FACE THREE FUNDAMENTAL challenges in developing a
strategy toward Northeast Asia, an area that includes China, Japan,
South and North Korea, and, despite its distant location, the United States.
First, they must determine an effective balance among their strategic, economic, and civilizational objectives, the last of which refers to their adjustment to Asian traditions and social networks. Second, they have to decide
how much attention to give to each of the five states active in the region.
Third, they must find a new balance among nationalism, localism, and globalization in order to shape emergent regionalism, taking care to prevent
nationalism from overwhelming the others. An effective strategy would simultaneously address all three challenges.

Prior strategies left Russia overextended in its political and military ambitions, underfunded and unrealistic about its economic standing, and un-
comprehending about mutual enmity. A new path is needed in the early
twenty-first century, as Northeast Asia is coalescing as a center of global economic dynamism with a mixture of rapid economic integration and anxious
balance-of-power maneuvering. Strategically, this region is moving toward a
new multilateral framework that in important respects will set a pattern for
relations among many of the global powers, as seen in the struggle over the
six-party talks in Beijing about North Korea's nuclear weapons. In these circumstances, Russians are facing an urgent need to set priorities, to balance
anew strategic, economic, and civilizational goals, and to adjust domestic
policies that impact each.

Past strategies no longer offer a clear guide to a rapidly changing region.
Militarization of the Russian Far East and costly incentives to lure migrants
from European Russia to populate and develop the area are two examples of

measures that are no longer feasible and have been discredited. After stumbling through the 1990s with little benefit from its existing ties to Northeast Asia, Russia has begun to formulate a regional strategy based foremost on China, raising the role of political as well as economic ties to that country. For the moment, ties to Japan remain in a holding pattern, while Russian leaders await an opportunity for a political breakthrough following discussions over how to establish an energy partnership. Further, Moscow is attempting to use personal leadership ties with Pyongyang as well as Seoul's eagerness for its help to become an indispensable force in forging stability on the Korean peninsula. In addition, by gradually integrating North Korea into the regional economy, Russia seeks to build energy and transportation bridges that would resuscitate its own Far Eastern regions. In 2003–2006 a peripheral role in the nuclear crisis that produced a standoff between the United States and North Korea as well as divisions within the Kremlin over where to lay an oil pipeline underscored the absence of a regional strategy. As others in Northeast Asia put regionalism on hold, Russia also postponed some critical choices. Yet, rising reliance on China and a forward-looking vision for a peace regime and regional cooperation over the Korean peninsula are starting to reveal the contours of a new Russian strategy.

As a continental power with maritime aspirations, Russia has sought at times to be the primary geopolitical force in Northeast Asia and at other times of relative weakness to prevent any other power from achieving dominance. Other goals pale in comparison, but economic realities matter too. Russia aims both to cover the extraordinarily high costs of provisioning a sparse population scattered across a spacious and inhospitable territory and to enlist neighboring states, whether Japan, China, or Korea, in jointly developing its Asiatic resources, especially, in recent years, oil and gas. To date, Russia's efforts to move away from the Soviet Union's command economy have not been very successful in the Far East. The legacy of Stalin's deportation of Chinese and Koreans combined with recent Russian duplicity in cross-border dealings— many investors in joint ventures lost their assets—continue to plague ties with neighboring peoples. Russians' pride as Europeans often confronts the suspicions of Asian neighbors with scant understanding on either side to bridge the two perspectives.

For more than three hundred years, Russians have considered themselves vulnerable in isolated outposts distant from their main population and production centers but not very far from the borders of densely populated and culturally distinct Northeast Asian states. About 150 years ago, the situation acquired new urgency for two reasons: (1) the other great powers, including Great Britain, France, and the United States, pressed to advance their presence in the region by forcing open what had been largely closed countries; and (2) Russia's continued expansion led to a need to formalize boundaries with China, Japan, and Korea. For Russians, the challenges became defined largely in geopolitical terms: to secure exposed borders, to project national power in compensation for weakness elsewhere, and to establish spheres of influence in an era of imperialist rivalry. The legacy of this thinking endures despite the enormous changes across the territory of Northeast Asia.

From St. Petersburg or Moscow, East Asia looms in the distance as a solid mass in China and two jutting peaks in Japan and the Korean peninsula. Russian elites can either concentrate on smoothing the path to China as the dominant regional partner politically and economically or seek to balance it by broadening linkages to China's neighbors. Thus far, they have made China their primary focus, rarely exploring possibilities for regional balance. Other options had opened with the building of the Trans-Siberian Railroad after 1891 and the lead-up to the 1904–1905 Russo-Japanese War, but in the forty years of Japanese expansionism that followed, including the colonization of Korea, Russians soon realized that they had little choice but to concentrate on reinforcing ties to China.

Indeed, from 1945 to 1960 the Soviet Union's ambitions peaked, as it sought to remake the region by providing assistance to the Chinese communists, led by Mao Zedong; by supporting North Korea and China in the Korean War in an effort to oust the United States from continental Asia;[1] and by offering massive economic assistance, and briefly the promise of transferring nuclear weapons, to a resurgent China.[2] Yet, despite the Sino-Soviet dispute from 1960 into the 1980s, when each side claimed to be the only true socialist country and harshly criticized the other, Moscow did not alter its geopolitical priorities. Without making overtures to Japan and South Korea, it remained obsessed with pressuring China, erecting border fortifications, and approving military offensives along China's borders. The Soviet Union sought superior military power against any combination of the United States, Japan, South Korea, and China, while keeping alive the North Korean threat that pinned tens of thousands of American soldiers to the south side of the thirty-eighth parallel. This strategy favored closed borders and military pressure, not trade and trust, which could come only through sustained negotiations and compromise.

Beginning in the mid-1980s with Mikhail Gorbachev's "new thinking"—a different outlook on international relations that highlighted rapprochement with the United States—Russian analysts criticized the existing strategy toward Northeast Asia as outdated, costly, and failing to take advantage of the region's economic dynamism.[3] Having abandoned sponsorship of third world revolutions, accepted the integration of Europe, and even countenanced independent states among remnants of the former Soviet Union, Russia has found it difficult to devise a new strategy in Northeast Asia. Despite ample opportunities, it has been slow to make far-reaching adjustments, such as welcoming foreign investment in many sectors of the economy and normalizing ties with Japan. After favoring a path focused on "multilateral security" that had little appeal to other states, such as the United States and Japan, which were already secure in their own bilateral alliance, Russian leaders joined China in calls for "multipolarity" that again seemed to challenge the United States' role in Asia. Eventually, Russians must find a new concept to highlight integration more than division in the region.[4] A surge in oil prices by 2006, however, had restored Russia's swagger. Its leaders seemed persuaded that they now held the cards to resist outside pressure, and they appeared ready to revert to what many regard as Russia's instinctive pursuit of expanded power and influence.

Five factors help to explain Russia's lack of success in breaking away from its traditional geopolitical orientation vis-à-vis Northeast Asia. First, instead of feeling pressure on all sides to change course, Russia has been encouraged by China's geopolitical reasoning to view the region as a stage for great-power maneuvering. Nowhere else in the world has there been such a clear and consistent call by a major power for Moscow to resume its divisive policies. This shows up frequently in great-power summitry featuring declarations in favor of building a multipolar world order, backed by international relations experts on both sides who stress the need to work together to balance American power. In addition, China's appeal to buy arms and gain access to military technology resonates across Russia's half-closed military-industrial complex.[5] While China's own example might encourage Russia to open its doors to foreign investment and bide its time as it rebuilds its economy and technological know-how, China cynically plays on Russian apprehensions of weakness to use Russia in a strategy for accelerating the recovery of Taiwan.

At times, Moscow appeared to distance itself from Beijing. In the summer of 1999, for instance, Boris Yeltsin calculated that it would be better to work out an arrangement with the United States to end the Kosovo War that gave at least some scope for Russia to exert its influence. In the fall of 2001 Vladimir Putin supported George W. Bush's first moves in the war on terror that helped to eliminate a regime in Afghanistan dedicated to spreading Islamic fundamentalism and terrorism into Central Asia. Yet, especially after the U.S. invasion of Iraq in 2003 raised anew the specter of unilateralism, Russia's geopolitical orientation has swerved back toward China.

Second, North Korean saber rattling to coerce foreign economic aid has handed Russia an opportunity to benefit from strategic tensions. As the United States in 1993–1994 pressed Pyongyang to abandon its nuclear weapons programs, threatening economic sanctions or even preemptive attack, Russians felt helpless. After Russia was excluded from the arrangements that resolved this first North Korean nuclear crisis, including the establishment of KEDO (Korean Energy Development Organization) for the construction of light-water reactors in exchange for North Korea's suspension of plutonium production, nationalists bitterly denounced this sign of Russia's impotence. By the later 1990s, however, Russian officials were actively pursuing North Korea.[6] Building on this momentum, from 2000 to 2002 Putin completed the process of restoring relations and met three times with Kim Jong Il. In this way, Putin established himself as the foreign leader with the closest personal ties to North Korea's reclusive leader. When after discovering a secret North Korean uranium enrichment program the United States precipitated a second nuclear crisis in October 2002, Russian officials believed that they were positioned to play an intermediary role. After nearly a decade, they were optimistic that Moscow had regained its voice in Northeast Asian geopolitics. Russian analysts also were quick to accentuate the regional economic consequences, including energy and transportation projects, which would come from maneuvering over the Korean peninsula no less than the great-power balance. While such gains have yet to materialize, there remains hope in Russia that the regional endgame of the nuclear crisis will give it a good chance to play its "North Korean card."

A third reason for Russia's short-term orientation focusing on geopolitics more than economic integration is the paralyzing repetition in discussions with Japan over the four disputed islands. While Russians argue that the southernmost part of the Kuril Islands became its territory in accord with the Yalta agreement, which Roosevelt approved, Japanese counter that the Soviet Union seized the islands in 1945 in contravention of the principle that there would be no war gains of land indisputably belonging to a defeated power. When diplomatic relations were finally reestablished in 1956, no peace treaty was signed due to this dispute, which continued to bedevil bilateral relations throughout the Cold War. Despite upbeat negotiations in 1997–1998 and again in 2000–2001, an acceptable solution continues to elude Moscow and Tokyo.[7] Although few observers expressed optimism in January 2003 when Prime Minister Koizumi Junichiro and President Putin pledged a fresh start, at least both sides agreed on their common interests: finding a diplomatic solution to the North Korean crisis, working with China toward regional stability, and building oil and perhaps gas pipelines across the Russian Far East to supply Japan. Some suggested that the two sides had an even deeper interest in limiting any future Chinese move to become the regional hegemon, and even in gaining some joint leverage that could limit U.S. unilateralism in the region. Still, Koizumi's renewed emphasis on the recovery of all four islands in the second half of 2004 along with his penchant for nationalist symbols clouded prospects for regional cooperation. Putin responded to Koizumi's provocative September 2004 boat trip near the islands with rhetoric of his own, backtracking from the compromise posture he took in 2000–2001. And in November 2005 he went to Tokyo with one hundred businessmen in tow, but with no intention to discuss the territorial issue, which led to no communiqué at the end of the summit.

Fourth, the political leadership in the Russian Far East has sought to play on the local population's fears of foreign domination, emphasizing in particular the so-called China threat.[8] Newly conscious of their great distance from Moscow as a result of costlier transport and energy supplies, local populations nervously measure their declining fortunes against the relative prosperity and dynamism of the rest of the region, excluding North Korea. Criminalized elites try to divert their attention from vast illegal gains acquired by a few from the export of crabs, other marine products, lumber, and precious metals that are not put to use as investments or social welfare benefits. After a decade in power, these elites show little sign of adjusting policies in order to offer a true economic payoff for local citizens. The situation may be changing now that Putin appoints the governors. The governors have lost any say in international affairs, unlike, for example, Evgenii Nazdratenko of Primorskii krai, who until the final stage of border demarcation with China in 1997 had delayed and even promised to block the process, or Igor Farkhutdinov of Sakhalinskaya oblast, who as late as 2001 was striving to prevent even a compromise that would have transferred two islands to Japan.[9] Putin has demonstrated how the new appointment power adds to his clout, for instance by obliging Khabarovskii krai governor Viktor Ishaev to countenance the loss of some territory in the final demarcation of Russia's border with China. Perhaps Russian entry into the World Trade Organization, the terms of which were already approved by China and Japan in 2005, will smooth cross-border ties and alleviate some of the anxiety aroused by protectionist political and economic elites.

Fifth, the long-standing Eurocentric thinking of Russian elites does much to explain their lack of interest in economic integration with Asia.[10] Most also appear to be stuck in a mold of focusing on U.S. power and perceiving Northeast Asia largely as a venue for blocking it. To many Russians, the rise of China serves Russia's global objectives, even as regional implications seemed secondary. Under Putin, however, after September 11, 2001, there appeared to be a shift toward acceptance of U.S. power as inevitable, which opened the way for Russian leadership to look anew at Northeast Asia. This led some to focus on balancing China's power and others to concentrate on Russia's economic priorities. Yet, from 2003 Putin has led the way in cooperating with China to challenge U.S. power, seizing the initiative, while leaving little room for doubters to exert any influence. His appeals to nationalism may raise doubts about Russia's place in Europe, but they also make it hard for Russia to accept a secondary role in another region that appears much more foreign.

Still groping for a regional strategy, Russians must begin to reassess their national priorities. These include securing the Russian Far East in the face of huge economic and demographic challenges; increasing Russia's regional and global influence; calibrating Russia's relations with other regional actors; and, above all, assessing the role of the U.S. presence in the region and the relative balance in Sino-Japanese relations. Russia's ability to achieve success depends on its leadership's calculations about the relative weight of global and regional forces in Asia and the balance of central and local forces within Russia. And, in fact, in contrast to Moscow's short-term outlook in the late 1990s, the contours of a long-run, balanced approach are beginning to emerge—even if the leadership's immediate focus remains on China. Especially in 2005, when Russian leaders agreed to start spending part of the vast stabilization fund that was accumulated through high oil prices, prospects were brightening for large infrastructure projects in the Russian Far East as the basis for opening the area to closer regional ties.

In developing a new regional strategy, the Kremlin cannot ignore Russia's diminished military influence and negligible economic presence. It must build on recent analyses that accurately assess the influence of globalization.[11] Through the supply of energy, Russia can influence both regional security and the regional economy. By becoming a reliable large-scale supplier of oil and gas, it could emerge as a provider of energy security in a region where this has become a vital interest. By seeking a regional balance of power, Russia could maximize its fragile position by preventing any one country from dominating. Most difficult, it must accept the region's Confucian civilizational heritage and adjust to the fact that growing regional integration and heterogeneous communities will leave Russians an even tinier minority than they are now.

Coping with weakness amid regional dynamism and division poses a tough challenge. Yet, the failure of the United States to coordinate closely with regional actors in dealing with North Korea and Taiwan and its reluctance to accept advancing trends toward regionalism, as seen in last-minute skepticism toward the December 2005 East Asian summit, leave room for Moscow to maneuver as it strives for a stable place in the region. In addition, Japan's recent alienation from China and South Korea, without seeking to enhance ties with Russia, encourages the Russian leadership to settle for a continental strategy that may offer short-term satisfaction but not serve as a lasting regional approach.

Each of the three main sections of this chapter starts with the broad sweep of history and finishes with a close look at recent developments and what they portend for Russia's place in Northeast Asia. The first section depicts Russia's difficulties in balancing multiple objectives on its eastern borders. It argues that so far it has failed to find balance, remaining quite removed from the exceptional economic dynamism linking the Chinese, Japanese, and South Korean economies, and unwilling or unable to establish a favorable regulatory environment for cross-border ties, including the normal movement of traders and tourists. On many occasions in the nineteenth and twentieth centuries Russia had a chance to strike a new balance among its objectives, but it was too confident of its own superiority and placed too little value on the benefits of regional integration. It still needs to reduce the emphasis on geopolitics. Given the fluidity of the current situation, however, Russia still has a chance to act.

The next section explores Russia's struggle to find an enduring partnership in the region. Ties to China have historically been the starting point for assessing other states, and Russia's recent shift toward closer ties again is influencing the weight it assigns to the other four states in the region. Yet, other factors matter, too, in a fast-changing environment. Concern over China's long-term rise could still nudge the Kremlin to boost ties to Japan as well as to accept a greater role for the United States in Northeast Asia. To judge the prospects for change, Russian views of Sino-Japanese relations and of the Korean peninsula as part of the regional context are then examined. As one of the participants in the six-party talks over the North Korean nuclear crisis, Russia is eyeing its options if implementation of an agreement leads toward a regional program for reconstruction as well as a lasting security framework. A lasting approach to balancing five states in pursuit of peace and development awaits critical decisions.

The final section discusses the forces that have heightened Russian nationalism and the prospects for finding some balance in localism and globalization. Fear of a Russian Far East overridden with Asian migrants competes with the awareness of a need for foreign labor in order to realize the development projects under discussion. Migration is but one theme in the search for cultural understanding, a search impeded by a growing sense among Russians that they are outsiders, outnumbered and even marginalized by the regional dynamism around them. The strong sway of nationalism in past regional policies had led to serious misjudgments, such as the disastrous war with Japan in 1904–1905, the increased isolation of Russia in Asia in 1960–1985, and the unnecessary delay in regional integration in 1990–2000. In 2006 hesitant globalization and abortive localism as well as little trust in regionalism still offer no match for resurgent nationalism.

The challenges seen from European Russia have in most respects not changed fundamentally from those of a century and a half ago, when Russians intensified their advance into Northeast Asia. Indeed, to an unexpected degree, conditions have reverted to what they were then. With its weakness in Europe exposed, Russia seeks compensation in Asia. Its focus is again on China, yet, as before, its leadership is uncertain about how and in what measure cooperation with this large neighbor should be pursued. A rivalry with Japan seems to be rising, but it could turn into a partnership. The Korean peninsula again tempts Russia to prove its value as a friend in the hope of major rewards. In contrast with the past, however, instead of outside powers competing for advantage in a region of weak and declining states, today Russia may be the most exposed state before the rapid ascendancy of China and the states of Northeast Asia as a whole. While for long periods it appeared to be the main beneficiary of the region's weakness, past approaches had built-in limitations. The region's rise now offers many new opportunities, but it also carries the risk that Russia may become the principal loser of political influence, economic clout, and even territory.

BALANCING OBJECTIVES IN NORTHEAST ASIA

From the earliest years of its presence in Northeast Asia in the seventeenth century, Russia has sought economic ties with the established states, beginning with purchases of supplies to sustain its new distant settlements. By the time of its expansion in the 1860s to the coastal area just north of China and Korea and the founding of the port city of Vladivostok, many observers assumed that after suffering military reversals in the West, such as in the 1854–1856 Crimean War, Russia was seeking, above all, geopolitical glory. In the late nineteenth century, among the Russian intelligentsia, there was much talk of the civilizational challenge in Northeast Asia, encouraging Russia either to become the vanguard of a Western civilizing mission or to champion the cause of Asiatic resistance to it.[12] These economic, strategic, and civilizational themes persist today. Unsettled in security and edging its way toward economic regionalism, Northeast Asia still poses fundamental civilizational questions for a transitional Russia searching for its national identity and global role. Respect for East Asian culture means appealing to the educated elite with an appreciation for their traditions, while encouraging heterogeneous work and residential communities. The three choices are interdependent. Opting for narrow nationalism interferes with open borders necessary both for economic integration and for building civilizational bridges.

Geopolitically, Northeast Asia has undergone significant transformation from a region whose foreign affairs were guided by the Sino-centric tribute system, in which China commanded respect and occupied the central place; to one marked by great-power rivalries begun as imperialism and evolving into the Cold War; and, more recently, to one that has witnessed the rise of China and U.S.-led efforts to limit that rise. In the first case, Russia became a bridge outside of the tribute system but was able to maintain an ecclesiastical mission in Beijing as a window to Europe, while biding its time until its access to the West's advancing power would enable it to press for new boundaries and influence. In the second case, Russian and Soviet efforts to expand military influence peaked in 1905, 1945, and 1985 without much consideration of other objectives, especially economic ones. Even in the third period, that of China's rapid rise, Russian leaders have been slow to accept the logic of economic regionalism; they have stopped at ritualistic claims of seeking close relations, while stirring up anxiety over the danger of lowering "civilizational" barriers by accepting "Chinatowns" or including outposts on the borders of dynamic Northeast Asian cities in heterogeneous regional communities. Maldistribution of cities, or the "Siberian curse," has led to large-scale out-migration and dying cities.[13] At the same time, however, the prospects in some areas—mostly along Russia's southern borders—appear brighter for regional integration. As northernmost cities shed excess residents, while some nodes in the southeast are reborn, a streamlined system of cities could emerge if Russia were to focus on facilitating investment, good governance, and regional trust.

The origins of Russia's unbalanced approach to Northeast Asia are found in the eastward advancement of Russians in search of bountiful resources as well as glory, with fur traders leading the way. Miners followed, seeking rare and precious metals, including gold and diamonds. The region's untrammeled expanses and bountiful seas opened vistas for lumber, marine products, and specialty items such as ginseng, which were in high demand among Chinese. Protecting these resources from poachers demanded tight border controls along long frontiers. Thus, it was probably inevitable that vast areas rich in resources but burdened by climates able to support only sparse populations would have to be guarded as fortresses.[14] If Russia had not limited access to the region, Japan's century-long quest for resources to spur modernization, followed by South Korean and Chinese economic growth spurts, would have produced much more extensive resource exploitation. China's population has tripled since the end of the nineteenth century and its subsequent mass migration to the northeast would likewise have spilled farther northward, transforming the landscape much more than Russians have.

At the start of the twentieth century Russians began to panic at the prospect of the "yellow peril," allowing racism to poison their relations with Chinese small businessmen and construction workers who had been invited into the Russian Far East as builders of a foundation for its future, but whose presence left a residue of fear lasting to the present.[15]

Under Stalinism in the 1930s the Soviet Union expelled all the Chinese and Korean minorities, forcing the former to return to China and transporting the latter to Central Asia. This left the Far East to be developed by those from labor camps and recently released convicts. After capturing more than 600,000 Japanese soldiers in August 1945, after entering the Pacific War in its final days, the Soviet Union kept many of them for years as forced labor in the region. When Nikita Khrushchev released most of the inmates, and in 1956 finally sent the last of the Japanese home after reestablishing diplomatic relations with Japan, another approach was needed. Yet, Russia's leadership remained focused on closed borders and security concerns. Even when post–World War II prosperity boosted Japan's demand for coal, lumber, and other resources, Moscow put economic cooperation a distant second to military fortification, investing in the ill-fated Baikal-Amur Railroad, which even today carries little traffic despite the enormous outlays of funds, while keeping the port of Vladivostok a closed city. The geopolitical narrow-mindedness of the Soviet leadership continued through the Brezhnev era, when the Kremlin's fortress mentality reached its apogee. Meanwhile, Japan, then South Korea, and eventually China were opening their economies to the world.[16]

In 1987 the rhetoric from Moscow promised a new era of economic integration, bolstered by a program for massive investment in the Russian Far East. Gorbachev's new thinking on foreign policy and perestroika reforms were gathering force, and a bold program appeared to be in keeping with the spirit of the time. Russian reformers seized on the spirit of glasnost to repudiate the past, including the charge that economic regionalism, for its proponents, was only a smokescreen for political dominance and exploitation. They also condemned negative views of China, Japan, and South Korea that demonized them without crediting their reforms and development or their potential as economic partners. And they criticized the rejection of local initiative in Russia that had been designed primarily to serve the interests of a centralized military sector.

Gorbachev's new thinking, however, was long on criticism but short on action, or even attention to the pitfalls ahead. Ultimately, the program for the Russian Far East failed: The Russian government did not appropriate the necessary funds; no new personnel were hired to manage it; and no laws and regulations conducive to foreign investment were passed. Despite the desire to harvest the fruits of economic integration, few in the Kremlin were ready to abandon deeply embedded ways of doing business.[17] The military delayed opening Vladivostok until 1992. Local officials and criminal groups siphoned sudden profits from the border crossings in the Russian Far East that had opened by 1991. In Moscow leaders were too busy struggling for power to plan a coherent Asian strategy.

By 1990–1991 the Soviet Union's economic situation, including in the Russian Far East and Siberia, had deteriorated to such a degree that the government was obliged to shift from top-down planning for opening borders through large-scale investment and rush through measures to bring desperately needed consumer goods from abroad, selling surplus industrial goods and, in the process, creating a sense of "border fever."[18] The result was a windfall for industrial managers and the officials who facilitated their deals, as domestic prices remained fixed at low levels, while foreign buyers reckoned in terms of world market prices. Collusion brought rich rewards to a few, but no prospect of development. In turn, Russian consumers had little to spend and virtually no choice in what they bought, leaving them vulnerable to unscrupulous Chinese shuttle traders, who went back and forth across the border carrying only a few suitcases of goods and lacked established business ties. Although the crisis of consumer shortages passed, Russian distrust lingered.

As early as the summer of 1992 the new Russian state began to backtrack from its one-sided orientation to the West, but it only compounded early neglect of the forces resistant to regional integration by now offering them direct support. In September 1992 President Yeltsin abruptly shifted direction, canceling a visit to Japan at the last moment and turning toward China instead. His visit to Seoul in October was seen by many observers as playing the "Korea card" against Japan, but Yeltsin failed to resolve differences over the remainder of the $3 billion in loans promised by South Korea on which Russia was already refusing to pay interest. Having assured regional administrations that they could take all the power they wanted, watching uneasily as newly elected regional legislatures flirted with establishment of a "Far Eastern republic," Yeltsin did little to reestablish a clear division of authority. Instead, he cut deals with the old nomenklatura that put in place powerful, corrupt governors and presidents of republics who bled their populations, while failing to promote an environment conducive to investment and cross-border trust. "Border fever" with China yielded to hysterical accusations against Chinese traders and illegal migrants, often with the implication that a national conspiracy was operating to undercut Russia's hold on its territory. At the same time, business and governmental interests colluded to strip Japanese and South Korean investors of assets, such as through joint ventures whose legal status suddenly became dubious. By 1994 trade along the border was declining, joint ventures were closing, and plans for major projects such as the Tumen River area development and the Nakhodka industrial park had been exposed as unwelcome to vested interests that wielded a veto.[19]

In the mid-1990s Russia made one more attempt to achieve economic integration in what Russians called the "Asia-Pacific region," but which Chinese, Japanese, and Koreans saw much more narrowly as the Northeast Asian region or in terms of subregional economic zones. The Russian notion framed the territory on a grand geopolitical scale, where Moscow's interests could more easily be expressed. Russian leaders successively embraced the offers of each of these nations: the 1996 Chinese proposal to quadruple trade to $20 billion by the year 2000 based on partnerships between established Chinese and Russian enterprises as well as local governments; the 1997 Hashimoto-Yeltsin plan emphasizing Japanese investment in major projects as well as training for small businessmen; and the South Korean commitment made prior to the Asian financial crisis of late 1997 to build a business center in Vladivostok and an industrial park in Nakhodka as well as to play a leading role in large energy projects, such as the East Siberian gas fields north of Irkutsk. Russia's oligarchs and criminal syndicates, however, showed little interest in pursuing any of these offers, once they had succeeded in luring unsuspecting investors or state planners into funding the projects. Since investments were not backed by unequivocal property rights, these Russians found ways to strip the assets of investors foolhardy enough to rely on the protection of Russian officials and courts. While governors in the Russian Far East held conferences and issued high-sounding appeals to woo investors,[20] most of the action continued to come in the form of massive untaxed exports of Russian resources and shuttle traders improvising small marketing deals. If cross-border ties appeared stabilized at last, the reality remained one of pervasive criminal connections, high levels of distrust, and an uncertain future—all of which left both the local population and Russia's neighbors demoralized.

Political instability on the Russian side delayed economic integration, while a flood of investment from Japan and South Korea into China rapidly raised the potential for economic regionalism from which Russia would be excluded. In addition, Tokyo, Seoul, and Beijing began negotiations to establish free trade areas. Russians, meanwhile, paid little heed to this new dynamism as they sought to address geopolitical uncertainties. Yet, Russian reasoning had become increasingly contradictory. As talk of Chinese expansionism accompanied warnings of massive illegal migration, Russia's strategic partnership with China had become the principal political framework for its ties in the region. While grandiose designs for pipelines and an "iron silk road" terminating in Pusan demonstrated Russia's shared outlook with South Korea, Moscow's support for North Korea may have delayed that country's willingness to reform and reduce tensions in the region. Growing Russian interest in laying an oil or gas pipeline to serve the Japanese market does not seem to be accompanied by more serious exploration of a compromise on the Kuril Islands in a dispute that still blocks the signing of a peace treaty between the two states.

In 2006 Moscow positioned itself for an outcome of the Korean nuclear crisis that would convert geopolitical trouble into economic cooperation.[21] At the same time that the Seoul-Pyongyang axis was to become the node for new economic growth (a reconnected railroad, the Gaesong industrial park, highways beginning with the route to the Kumgang Mountain tourist and conference center), the Vladivostok-Pyongyang axis was expected to extend development into the Russian Far East. Despite Beijing's rejection of Pyongyang's attempt to establish an economic zone at Sinuiju on China's coastal border, Moscow still seeks agreement to develop a transportation corridor along North Korea's other coastal border. Its goal is the long-distance movement of oil, gas, and containers that are transferred from ships to railroad cars, rather than cross-border trade and investment. This requires a commitment to multilateral economic ties and political stability if Russia is to realize its objectives. Since August 2003, when North Korea asked Russia to deliver the message that it would join the six-party talks in Beijing, Russia has retained a tenuous place in the tense search for a solution to nuclear weapons development on the peninsula, supporting in principle the U.S. stance that North Korea must abandon these weapons, and at the same time siding with Pyongyang in insisting that the United States make many concessions.

If Russia continues to see an opportunity in geopolitical tensions in Northeast Asia, such as the nuclear standoff between the United States and North Korea, this does not mean it has something to gain from exacerbating those tensions. Indeed, while Moscow takes advantage of troubled situations, it does not see benefit in aggravating them. Should the North Korean regime collapse, leaving Seoul with the monumental task of paying for the costs of absorbing millions of people and their devastated land under one state, Russia could easily be overlooked by the concentration on intra-Korean affairs. If Sino-Japanese and Sino-U.S. relations proceed more smoothly, the need for Russian arms would be reduced. Yet, if these ties deteriorate sharply, there may be little prospect for Russia's regional economy, as an underpopulated and economically troubled Russian Far East could be easily ignored by a prosperous regional community focused on economic integration, or could be left to stagnate if tensions rile the region. A gradually improving regional environment in which geopolitical concerns recede into the background may be best for Russia. Putin could elevate his special friendship with Kim Jong Il to a position of economic benefit in the drawn-out soft landing that Pyongyang demands as the price to end its weapons of mass destruction threat. He could calibrate arms sales to Beijing and abrasive Russo-Chinese great-power rhetoric in proportion to U.S. and Japanese recognition of Russian interests. Even as its own Pacific fleet rusts near Vladivostok and its Far Eastern Command in Khabarovsk seems preoccupied more with suicides and revenge murders by harassed conscripted soldiers than with military readiness, Russia retains a say in Northeast Asian security. It needs to convert that foothold into economic standing and growing trust in a fast-changing region.

After making geopolitics the cornerstone of its approach to Northeast Asia for three hundred years and failing to change even after Gorbachev announced a new approach with promise for economic integration in his Vladivostok speech of 1986, Russia must realign its regional strategy. Over the next several decades the Russians may anticipate supplying two million barrels of oil a year to a thirsty region (through pipelines to Daqing in China and to the Pacific, including the Korean peninsula, as well as from tankers operating from Sakhalin's offshore oil fields); becoming the principal source of gas for a region only now beginning the shift to this cleaner fuel; building electrical transmission lines; and forming heterogeneous communities on or near national borders for processing natural resources and for specialty high-technology industries, such as those that support the development of outer space. The economic gains associated with such projects should take priority in Russia's regional strategy. Geopolitical objectives can be narrowed to securing borders by rooting out corruption among the border guards and striving for a stable balance of power.

Under Putin this search for a new direction intensified, as the gaze of all nations was fixed on the U.S.-North Korean showdown over nuclear weapons development. On September 26–27, 2003, at Camp David, presidents Putin and Bush discussed both security and energy issues, including participation in the next round of the six-party talks—once Russia awakened to the seriousness of the crisis. Yet, by the time Bush traveled to Moscow for the sixtieth anniversary of the Allied victory in Europe, U.S.-Russian energy cooperation was in doubt, since energy prices had risen sharply and Russia had more options, and both North Korea and Iran were divisive issues on a growing agenda of clashing interests. Moscow naturally turned to Beijing. In the fall of 2004 the two had settled their last territorial dispute and clearly were striving to project an image of solidarity vis-à-vis the United States.

Still, no matter how benign Chinese intentions may be, Moscow is likely increasingly to view China as the major potential national threat to security along its borders. A rising power with a huge population troubled by problems of poverty and unemployment, China would be a concern even if it had not earlier and often voiced territorial grievances. Regardless of the Russian media's exaggerations over the negative consequences of illegal Chinese migration for the ethnic population balance in Russia's Far East and the threat to sovereignty, the reality remains that only a managed flow of foreign workers and businesspeople will assuage Russian apprehensions. To prevent fears of geopolitical danger, Russia must draw on a mixture of peoples, including North Koreans and Vietnamese, as balance to the Chinese. To meet a need for talented and entrepreneurial young people, it must strive harder to establish mixed communities of middle-class Asians. An outpost of European civilization that tries to shield itself from Asian culture will have difficulty finding common ground with its neighbors. Only by becoming knowledgeable about the area around them and learning to live amid their neighbors will Russians be able to shed their fortress mentality in the Far East. So far, they have made even less progress than earlier in addressing this civilizational challenge. Claims by Russian officials of working closely together with their neighbors are belied by recurrent tensions in ongoing interactions.

In the 1860s, 1900s, 1920s, and 1950s, Russia faced opportunities to rebalance its objectives in Northeast Asia. On each occasion it sought to expand its power and stood a good chance of doing so; however, it consistently overrated its superiority and underappreciated ways to draw on the assets of a region that was little understood. Now Russia must start from a position of inferiority that is only likely to worsen due to the gap in economic dynamism and its demographic decline. Given current divisions between China and Japan and in the Korean peninsula as well as the uncertain U.S. role, it may miscalculate that, unlike in its dealings with the European Union, it need not take integrative forces seriously. Instead, it should recognize that its hand is even weaker in these circumstances. It cannot allow local autonomous actors, such as the governors who earlier stirred up fears of neighboring nations or criminal organizations, to block breakthroughs on demarcation and economic integration. If in 1991–1993 this message did not stick, in 2001–04 it became clearer, albeit still resisted. With Putin firmly in control over the governors in 2005, the issue was less one of contradictions interfering with central policies than one of the preoccupation with geopolitics at the center without a regional economic strategy or policies conducive to regional trust.

Whatever Putin's intentions, the policies of Bush, Kim Jong Il, and Koizumi made reaching a compromise in choices for the region difficult. For example, if Bush had been quick in 2003 to offer North Korea an unambiguous security guarantee and if Kim had been serious about agreeing to abandon all nuclear weapons programs, then Putin might have gained an important say over the shape of economic reintegration and a long-term security framework. Likewise, if Koizumi had prioritized relations with Russia and had resumed negotiations over the disputed islands where they had ended in 2001, then Putin could have explored a major upgrading of Russo-Japanese relations to enhance the geopolitical balance and open the door to more globalized economic dealings. It was not Russia alone that failed to find balance in the region. Yet, second only to North Korea, Russia stood out for its absence from the regional economic dynamism and for its fear of normal cross-border networking.

When Vice President Dick Cheney traveled to Lithuania and then to Kazakhstan on May 4–5, 2006, he warned Putin against growing authoritarianism and new tendencies to use energy as a source of pressure or even blackmail.[22] Against advice from some officials in the U.S. government who continued to hope for Moscow's support on critical problems, such as the nuclear weapons programs of Iran and North Korea, Cheney's words revived images of the Cold War. Attention quickly turned to the impact on Sino-Russian relations. If Russia became more isolated in the West, did it have a viable option in Northeast Asia for an alliance-like partnership with China? Although the Bush administration's efforts to avoid inflaming the question of Taiwan independence made it unlikely that China would revive a Cold War environment, its quest for advanced arms and expanded oil supplies from Russia meant that it would do little to discourage Moscow's emphasis on geopolitics.

DECIDING HOW MUCH WEIGHT TO GIVE TO THE FIVE STATES ACTIVE IN THE REGION

Although Russia has forged brief alliances among its neighbors in Northeast Asia, it has no enduring partner to the east. It has been too much of an outsider whose motives are suspect and whose cooperation seems at best expedient. From the seventeenth to the mid-nineteenth century, as Russia was establishing its presence near their borders through expeditions and then settlements, China, Korea, and Japan were anxious to keep all Europeans away and allowed little access to their countries. An arrangement for a Russian ecclesiastical mission in Beijing and trade through one border crossing from early in the eighteenth century were the sole exceptions to the self-seclusion practiced in the region. In the last decades of the nineteenth century, Russia achieved important inroads with China, then Japan, and finally Korea. During this period the best chance arose for partnership. Yet, a preoccupation with empire and later with revolution compounded Russia's troubles in creating an appealing image as a model, until violent opposition against imperialism or domestic misrule rose to the fore in Asia, giving Russia an opportunity. Only after communist parties gained power with Soviet assistance, first in North Korea and then in China, did the tide turn in Moscow's favor. Despite much hyperbole about the meaning of fraternal bonds, in Russia's case they proved to be ephemeral.

Lacking an occupation army, Russians found that, after the first phase of assisting a state in establishing socialism, they were put at arm's length as their closest associates were purged by the communist leadership in China and North Korea. Future ties depended on narrow great-power interests, and by the 1960s Moscow was relying heavily on these as its position deteriorated in the region.

For a half century after its defeat in the Crimean War, Russia engaged in imperialist intrigues along its borders in Asia. While an exclusive bridgehead in Korea or a close partnership for dividing the spoils with Japan were possibilities, China was the main target. Russia seized the opportunity of China's dual defeats at the hands of Great Britain and France to pose as its sole European friend, parlaying its status as the one country with longstanding representation in Beijing into a deal on the northeastern boundaries before other powers could interfere. While convincing itself that its behavior was just and would solidify long-term friendly relations with China, Russia proceeded to take advantage of ill-prepared and even corrupt Chinese negotiators as well as China's civil strife to gain control of the maritime zone. This important acquisition became the site of the port city of Vladivostok, giving Russia warm-water access to the Pacific Ocean and vital strategic benefits.

The decaying Qing empire continued to provide tempting targets. Having extended its rule into Central Asia only in the eighteenth century, China was ill equipped in the 1880s to prevent Russian meddling. As the Russian Empire consolidated its hold over Central Asia, it took advantage of separatist movements inside China's Xinjiang Province, where it also established a presence. As chaos gripped China at the time of the revolution that ended two millennia of imperial rule in 1911, other opportunities arose. Mongolia's liberation from Chinese rule offered Russia a chance to gain ascendancy, which was finalized by the imposition of a loyal communist puppet state in the 1920s. Other intrigues across the entire northern flank of China from Port Arthur on the Yellow Sea to Central Asia's Ili valley continued.[23] It would not be until Mao Zedong had unified China and negotiated with a new leader, Nikita Khrushchev, eager to build better relations with the Soviet Union's most important communist partner, that such meddling across the border would cease. That, however, would not prevent Mao, once he had decided for other reasons to break with the Soviet Union and split the international communist movement, from charging that tsarist imperialism had stolen vast Chinese lands. Even after the Chinese reduced their demands to demarcating islands in shared rivers rather than changing borders, following violent clashes in March 1969, heated rhetoric over this issue continued until 1983. Russia's delusion that territorial extension at China's expense was no different from its past settlement of Siberia and most of what became the Russian Far East made it hard to grasp the fallout, however belated, in a resurgent China.

The legacy of tsarist policies toward Northeast Asia endures. Even after the demarcation agreement of the eastern border in 1989, its fulfillment in 1997, and a demarcation of the most sensitive three islands in 2004, the fact that leaders in Moscow and Beijing agree that the border problem has been completely resolved does not stop many Russians, particularly residents of the Far East, from suspecting that some day Chinese feelings of injustice will come back to haunt them. They know that the Chinese do not share their perceptions of the fairness of the historical division of territory under what the Chinese call the "unequal treaties," as is evident from historical maps still found inside China. Thus, they suspect that once the balance of power, with the full force of demographic weight, has swung heavily in China's favor, the border issue may be revisited. Such fears were prominently on display in the 1990s and continue to fuel paranoia about any Chinese actions impinging on realities along the border.

Russian debates about how to conduct relations with China were intense in the second half of the nineteenth century, and so, too, in the early twentieth century, when both countries were convulsed by political turmoil and revolutionary movements. Russians recognized the vulnerability of their expansion far from the European core of the state. There was even some realization that China would revive, raising new challenges. Yet, a mind-set focused on immediate advantages prevailed over forward-looking preparation for a different balance of power. The musings of many intellectuals about the future of bilateral relations and the calculations of leading officials regularly displayed overconfidence and civilizational arrogance. More often than not China loomed as a symbol, judged more by stereotypes than by actual circumstances or China's prospective evolution.[24]

For a time Russian attention turned to Korea, which, like China, seemed ripe for outside influence or even domination and was the source of many migrants traveling into the newly opened maritime zone. As in the case of Japan, Russians plying the Pacific in search of logistical support for new encampments had long had their eyes on Korea. When other states, especially Japan, showed an interest in opening Korea, so did Russia. No intense debate erupted until Japan won the Sino-Japanese War (1894–1895) and showed its intent to take charge of Korean affairs. When Western powers resisted Japan's moves, the door was open for Russia to expand into Korea. After King Kojong fled to the Russian embassy legation in Seoul, where he remained for more than a year (1896–1897), this influence reached its peak. Subsequently the Russians agreed with Japan to a division of spheres of influence, but the arrangement did not last. Disillusioning Koreans about Russian support for their country's full independence and also disappointing some officials in Russia who demanded more vigorous pursuit of political and commercial interests, the outcome led to intrigues in Korea and provocative moves toward Japan. For example, Russia built a fortified region on both sides of the Russia-Korea border. Count Witte and others known as the pro-Manchuria group were mainly concerned with protecting the transportation and industrial projects inside China and did not mean to challenge Japan's interests, but their compatriots' Korean adventurism undermined their caution, leading to the Russo-Japanese War.[25] After Japan's victory in 1905, it was futile to try to stop its full annexation of Korea, and new deals were made, leading to a rapid improvement in relations. Yet, the temptations created by a state on Russia's border without the authority to defend itself or assert its own nationalism would draw Moscow back into Korean affairs, once Japan again became vulnerable.

Russians have long failed to recognize their negative role in both Korea and China. They often rationalize their involvement by stressing their support for Korean independence and insist that they have simply reacted when obliged to respond to Japanese expansionism. Notwithstanding Lenin's anti-imperialist pose, the Bolsheviks only briefly and incompletely renounced the evils of tsarist imperialism before resuming Russia's expansionary ways, camouflaging Soviet ambitions under the slogan of spreading communism through revolutions. Taking advantage of the U.S. success in the war against Japan, in the waning days of fighting Stalin sent the Red Army into China and down the Korean peninsula.[26] First China and then North Korea became allies in which Russia sought to meddle as communist "big brother." With Japan, resentment over roughly six hundred thousand men being kept for long periods as prisoners of war and other misdeeds left a bitter postwar legacy.

From the mid-1960s to the mid-1980s North Korea was the Soviet Union's sole partner in Northeast Asia. Preoccupied with military security, the USSR continued adding to its forces to keep the pressure on the United States, Japan, and China. Moreover, North Korea served Moscow's interests by putting pressure on the United States and Japan, while menacing South Korea above all. Responding angrily to the 1978 Sino-Japanese treaty of peace and friendship that condemned the threat of (Soviet) hegemony, Moscow continued to build up its military forces in the region and pointedly transferred military aircraft to the islands disputed by Japan.

In fact, Moscow had become increasingly isolated from the economic dynamism spreading throughout much of the region. After Japan and South Korea reestablished diplomatic ties in 1965, triangular economic ties reaching to the United States produced a bonanza in trade and economic growth. When China started its economic reforms in 1978, the boom spread to its coastal areas. Unlike the period culminating with the "oil shock" of 1973, when the withholding of supplies in the Middle East brought a spike in oil prices, rapid industrial growth did not stimulate interest in the resources of Asiatic Russia. The countries of the region found ample supplies of natural resources elsewhere and largely ignored their bellicose neighbor. Moscow's strategy left its eastern areas barricaded, with little chance of emerging from stagnation in the midst of increasingly prosperous neighbors. In 1979 China sent troops against Vietnam in protest of its invasion of Cambodia, as tensions with the Soviet Union also mounted. In 1981 Japan's Diet proclaimed a day of remembrance for the occupied "Northern Territories," escalating public hostility toward the Soviets. This raised the territorial dispute as a national priority. In 1983 the Soviets shot down a South Korean civilian airliner that had strayed off course. By comparison to its growing economic ties and political contacts with the capitals of Western Europe, Moscow remained an outcast in Eurasia's other showcase of capital and technology.

From 1982 to 1988, Moscow acted tentatively to redress this imbalance in its foreign policy. It began normalization talks with China in Leonid Brezhnev's final year. Indisputably, China was the centerpiece of its regional strategy, which was aimed more at changing the balance of power than at economic reform and regional integration. Yet, because of the Soviet Union's delay in addressing China's "three obstacles"—removing troops from Afghanistan, reducing troop concentrations on China's northern border including Mongolia, and pressuring Vietnam to withdraw its troops from Cambodia—the normalization of Sino-Soviet relations occurred only in 1989. Communist Party officials hostile to China and eager to boost North Korea's threat capacity versus the United States and Japan continued to create new obstacles until 1986, when Gorbachev changed the direction of Soviet diplomacy. In the meantime, Soviet hesitation to consider Japan's territorial demands and to challenge North Korea's insistence that no ties be developed with South Korea added another decade of Soviet policy paralysis in Northeast Asia. Soviet unilateralism dug itself an ever-bigger hole.

In the second half of 1992, Boris Yeltsin made the strategic decision to seek better relations with China. This set the tone for Moscow's relations with Northeast Asia over the next decade. Yeltsin hoped that the results would magnify Russia's global standing as it sought more leverage against the United States, while delivering an unmistakable message to Japan that Russia would not yield due to its economic troubles, reducing expectations that intensified pressure would lead to concessions on the territorial issue. At the same time, Moscow's improved relations with Beijing bolstered border security, making it easier for Russia to convert its arms plants to civilian use. The benefits, however, paled before the lost opportunities.[27]

Projected gains from Yeltsin's China partnership may have been exaggerated. If in 1991–1993 calls for separatism by local administrations in the Russian Far East reached their peak, stronger ties with China did not quell them. Forces behind them were mostly hostile toward China and were not reassured by Moscow and Beijing drawing closer. Nor did the partnership produce significant economic gains. While in 1991–1993 bilateral trade rose quickly as Chinese companies led the way in establishing joint ventures in the Russian Far East, the level of trade between Russia and China fell precipitously in 1994 as a result of a backlash against shoddy Chinese goods. Their bilateral trade failed to recover until the end of the decade. Moreover, the new investments were puny and soon they, too, were in retreat. Left largely on their own in a declining region of Russia to face a rising Chinese power, the residents of the Russian Far East suffered the psychological costs of Yeltsin's strategy.[28]

At the end of the Yeltsin era, Russia had little to show for its efforts to partner with China. Large economic projects did not advance, except for the offshore oil and gas projects near Sakhalin, in which China was uninvolved. Russia gained little leverage over China for shaping developments in Northeast Asia. As Chinese relations with the United States stalled, Russia's arms sales to China and bravado in summit meetings simply increased American suspicions of something like the communist-era pact. Japan, South Korea, and the United States, which in the 1990s had shown interest in building new ties with Asiatic Russia, were all reluctant to proceed.[29]

Russian interest rests to a considerable degree on protecting and developing a narrow swath of land from Blagoveshchensk to Vladivostok. Approximately half of the seven million residents of the Russian Far East inhabit this belt, and most of the urban residents and political and economic elite are concentrated there. The military commands of both the Pacific fleet and the Far Eastern district are located there as well. Each local administration has its own outlook on

China, complicating policies on security, trade, and border control.[30] Increasingly, Russian leaders are preoccupied with the proximity of Russia's regional security assets and human resources to China. Putin has taken a greater interest in this problem than Yeltsin did and appears to be convinced of the need to overcome the damage of depopulation and deindustrialization by developing a regional strategy. His approach to China and the United States, brought to the fore by the events of September 2001, created the strategic underpinning for a regional balance of power, one in which Russia would seek to elevate ties to Japan and both Koreas. Yet, by the end of 2005, after the United States had invaded Iraq without UN authorization and Russo-American relations had suffered from clashing interests in such countries as Ukraine and Georgia, Putin again began relying on China in a close regional partnership.

The key to the revival of the corridor north from Vladivostok to Khabarovsk and then west to Blagoveshchensk is investment in pipelines and railroads. For investment funds to reduce Russia's exclusive dependence on China, they must come largely from other sources and cover the additional costs of circumventing the hump of Heilongjiang Province. The country most eager to see the project completed appears to be North Korea, although it scarcely has the money to make it happen. Its leaders are fearful not only of the prospect of short-term U.S. military pressure but also of long-term Chinese economic pressure. In addition, they are anxious to resist being absorbed by the South Korean economy. This leads to plans for reviving their economy through transportation and energy linkages to the Russian Far East. The Seoul-Pyongyang-Vladivostok corridor serves their interests as well as Russia's. South Korea may be more enthusiastic about direct, short linkages across the thirty-eighth parallel, which separates it from North Korea, but Seoul's leaders have expressed support for the megaprojects from Russia across North Korea. Without directly raising alarm in China that this could serve South Korea's long-term goal of not becoming too enmeshed in the Chinese economic sphere, Seoul can justify these projects as a mechanism to connect the two Koreas as well as to enhance energy security.[31] Yet, Putin's post-2000 success in rallying both Koreas to this vision of regionalism has meant little without resolution of the North Korean nuclear crisis. And it has little prospect without the involvement of Japan, which is not inclined to make massive outlays unless they can give it an edge in the strategic competition with China or come on the heels of a breakthrough in relations with North Korea.

Japan has multiple reasons for looking favorably on a Russian Far East–Korean peninsula corridor. It would shape the transition of North Korea through economic integration, relieving Japan of its most immediate security fears. Moreover, it would turn the Koreas away from unchecked integration with China, offering the prospect of balanced regionalism. It would tend to mitigate Tokyo's and Beijing's jockeying for leadership in the halting advance toward regional economic integration. Finally, Japan's worries that the Russian Far East would become China's sphere of influence and that Sino-Russian relations could solidify would be alleviated. Indeed, Japan could, with one stroke, contain China through forging closer ties with Russia, while establishing itself in North Korea, benefiting South Korea in the process.

Since Japan recognizes that it cannot avoid paying roughly $10 billion to North Korea in the course of normalizing relations, as the equivalent of the financing it provided to South Korea in lieu of reparations for decades of occupation, the costs of loans and investments in the pipelines, railroads, and other infrastructure along this proposed corridor may not appear exorbitant. As it bid against China for a pipeline route from Taishet, Eastern Siberia, Japan had to decide, at a cost of billions of dollars in infrastructure investments in Russia, whether it really wanted to make such a commitment. Zigzags in Russia's plans for the pipeline, as it considered the Japanese option and the Chinese counter-offer, made a decision difficult.[32] Yet, Japan, too, was torn; linkage to territorial demands kept reappearing on the agenda without any diplomacy for finding a compromise solution. The absence of a reliable feasibility study demonstrating the volume of oil available made it hard for Japan to proceed. In December 2004 Putin decided to take a two-stage approach: First Russia would build the oil pipeline to a point near the Chinese border, from which China promised to extend the line to its refineries at Daqing in Heilongjiang Province, and only then, provided enough oil remained, would Russia build the line to the Pacific. This plan favors China, but it leaves some hope for Japan. In 2006, after Putin intervened to force a detour away from Lake Baikal, pipeline construction began, but there was still no clarity on how to reach the desired destination.

Russia's strategy remains to sell this arrangement to Japan without having to pay a price by returning the islands under dispute. In 2003, analysts in Moscow had argued that Japan was so concerned about the rise of China and instability in Korea that it was likely to make this deal. Yet, few in Japan would accept the logic that their country was more desperate than Russia or more in need of a breakthrough for economic and geopolitical reasons. A compromise agreement featuring the return of the two islands as promised in 1956 and some mutually acceptable arrangement for the other two more important islands would be a more secure foundation for a bilateral partnership.[33] After all, only this would ensure the signing of a peace treaty that has been in abeyance since 1945. Yet, Prime Minister Koizumi decided when he took office in the spring of 2001 not to pursue such a compromise. When he met Putin in November 2005 he spoke of improving bilateral relations even without a peace treaty. This was the time when Japan signaled its support for Russia's entry into the World Trade Organization, a tangible sign of progress in addition to the rapid increase in trade between the two countries, which was likely to reach $10 billion for the year. Yet, this meeting could not dispel the image that bilateral relations were still troubled. Even as both sides show growing appreciation for the logic of a closer relationship strengthened through energy pipelines, neither has articulated a strategic vision that incorporates any meaningful path to a compromise.

In the second half of 2005 Putin's meetings with Asian leaders did not suggest any change in direction. The most positive outcome occurred in meetings with Chinese leaders, especially through the Shanghai Cooperation Organization. The fact that he and Hu Jintao embraced Islam Karimov after his massacre of Uzbek crowds in May 2005 and warmly backed Karimov's decision to oust the United States from the Khanabad air base seemed an echo of Cold War maneuvering. Putin's visit with Koizumi reversed a downturn in relations, but it did not suggest that an upturn would soon follow. At the Asia-Pacific Economic Cooperation summit in Busan, Korea, Putin joined Roh Moo-hyun, Bush, Hu, and Koizumi in reaffirming the goals of the six-party talks, the brief fifth round of which had just deepened concerns that no solution was in sight. Then Putin's meeting with Asia-Pacific Economic Cooperation leaders in Kuala Lumpur on the eve of the East Asian summit, to which he had not been invited, indicated that regionalism is proceeding without Russia. Security is still Russia's priority, and it may better reflect genuine strategic thinking than the views of narrow interest groups that held sway before.

In the first half of 2006 the Shanghai Cooperation Organization acquired a more ominous appearance with the presence of Iran's president at the summit in Shanghai, seeking full membership for his country at the same time as he was thwarting the global community with his nuclear program. Yet, talk of some sort of expansive, alliance system was far-fetched. India and Pakistan also had observer status, but their differences as well as Sino-Russian divisions over them kept them outside. Indeed, a split remained between Russia's geopolitical interest in dominating Central Asia and China's economic interest in integrating with it, as well as rival notions of how to develop its energy resources.

More than before, Sino-Russian ties were becoming enveloped in Pan-Asian geopolitics.

RUSSIAN VIEWS OF SINO-JAPANESE RELATIONS

To calibrate a strategy for Northeast Asia, Russia must consider the combination of two great powers vying for leadership. In the eighteenth century, Russians were unique in having a mission in Beijing that provided news about China as they sought ways to expand trade through the caravan crossing at Kiakhta and extend their influence beyond the border set in the Treaty of Nerchinsk (1689).[34] As the century drew to a close, Russians also grew bolder in seeking to pry open Japan for maritime settlements along the Okhotsk Sea and to develop a small naval presence.[35] China and Japan appeared as reclusive states with little direct contact to the outside world. Russians recognized that they were the pursuers, anxious to draw these Asian countries into international exchange, even as they were hopeful that proximity would justify a special relationship. Identifying their country as European, Russians aimed to lead the way in incorporating the countries of East Asia into association with the European-led order. In contrast to other European states, which were focused on maritime trade, the Russians viewed the region as a source of support for their country's territorial expansion. They were more interested in using these borderlands to allow frontier outposts to prosper and to reinforce the security of Russia's increasingly stretched frontiers.

By the mid-nineteenth century, Russia's objectives had changed as a result of its deteriorating position in Europe, when other countries, already far advanced in the Industrial Revolution, had become increasingly formidable military rivals in a new age of imperialism. Russian views of China and Japan grew more negative, contrasting their closed and stagnant states with the dynamism of a more attractive Europe.[36] Ambivalent about their nation's own identity suspended between Europe and Asia, Russians distanced themselves from China and later from Japan. The so-called Westernizers embraced the civilizing mission of Europe; some even viewed China as a future threat. In contrast, the "Slavophiles" suggested not only that would Russia find its own path of development and rival the West, but also that China offered lessons about a different historical trajectory that might lead to a special relationship between the two countries.

China and Japan remained largely passive objects, dealt with separately until the 1850s, when Russia followed England, France, and the United States in opening borders and forcing modern diplomacy and economic relations on these countries. By 1860 Russia had scored its biggest coup, wresting the maritime zone, later called Primorskii krai and centered around the city of Vladivostok, from China's Manchu lords. The treaty allowed it to present its success as an act in defense of China in the struggle against the maritime European powers.[37] Russia now bordered Korea, possessed a window on the Sea of Japan, and had an incentive to seek a direct land route connecting Siberia to the Pacific coast through Chinese territory.

In the final decades of the nineteenth century, a triangular pattern of relations in Northeast Asia emerged. Russia grew more aggressive in its approach to China, while Japan became a rival in Manchuria. As Chinese nationalism gathered strength, Russians were torn among three courses of action. First, they could drop the image of a special relationship with China and place their country at the center of the civilizing mission needed to transform that country. Compared to rival Japan, Russians thought they had an advantage in assisting China's global emergence. Second, they could claim to be close to China and could work with that country to oppose the Europeans and the Japanese, from which the real dangers of imperialism came. This justified a patronizing attitude by Russia as the sponsor of China and an image of China beholden to Russia. Third, they could indulge their fear of China's rise, adopting an assertive position sooner rather than later. The growing presence of Chinese in the new cities of the Russian Far East fueled apprehension about a "yellow peril," which could lead to a demographic and even a military threat to this exposed territory. The second course of action eventually predominated, but the third continued to resurface. Both left a negative legacy among Chinese, evident as late as the 1960s and 1970s when Mao Zedong's China launched its most vicious attacks on the legacy of tsarist expansionism.[38]

In 1895 Moscow led a group of countries in pressuring Japan to abandon territorial claims on the Liaodong Peninsula after Japan defeated China. It cultivated an image as China's defender. Farther north, in Manchuria, Russian construction of the Chinese Eastern Railway as the link between Siberia and Vladivostok on land voluntarily leased by China enabled Russians to argue that their troops could now come to China's assistance. Yet, the political elite in Russia discussed an alternative view, making use of the faster transport to join with Japan in dividing Manchuria into spheres of influence. Neither view prevailed. Tsar Nicholas II sided with those who would go to war with Japan over the spoils of Korea and parts of China. The competition between the two expansionist powers culminated in the Russo-Japanese War of 1904–1905.[39] When Russia was defeated, it had to set its sights lower, cooperating with Japan for a share of control in Manchuria and making deals with weak Chinese governments. By the 1917 October Revolution, Russia had secured Mongolia's independence from China, had built the large city of Harbin striding the transportation arteries of Heilongjiang Province in northern Manchuria, and was firmly implanted in Xinjiang Province, adjacent to its own Central Asian territory. This temporary equilibrium would be disrupted by the rise of communism in Russia and of militarism in Japan, each targeting China in its sights.

Under communist control the Soviet Union substituted an ideological agenda for Russia's earlier expansionist inclinations. As Tokyo demanded ever more concessions from China, Moscow intensified its sponsorship of revolutionary activity not only to oppose imperialism and class exploitation but also to make China the front line in its tightly controlled international movement. After misjudging support for urban class struggle, Moscow used opposition to Japanese aggression against China to win favors from the Nationalist government as well as to sponsor the communist opposition. Of course, Moscow's great power and wartime strategic needs also influenced its decision making. Whether it solidified ties with the Nationalists or encouraged the Chinese Communist Party to launch more guerrilla attacks, it continued to have in mind the rivalry with Japan through 1945 and, in the first postwar years, when China was split by civil war, the new Cold War rivalry with the United States. Particularly, at the end of World War II, Moscow's objective was to outflank the United States and gain control over Northeast Asia.

The Sino-Soviet alliance and split occurred when Japan was essentially out of the picture in the 1950s to 1970s. For several decades the strategic triangle with the United States took center stage, while as a defeated power, Japan was left in the shadows. Only during the 1970s did Moscow begin to take note of newly normalized ties between Beijing and Tokyo, although it doubted the significance of the two acting together in the face of Moscow's enormous military might or the superpower rivalry with the United States. The first test of Moscow's interest came in 1973 at a summit following a rush of diplomatic activity in 1972, when Tokyo as well as Washington had taken advantage of the rift between Moscow and Beijing to renew ties to Beijing. Having been outflanked, Moscow could have been expected to respond with an overture to Tokyo. The timing seemed promising. The two sides had been making progress on projects to export natural resources from Siberia and the Russian Far East to Japan in return for large Japanese investments in infrastructure. Confident that they could sustain high rates of growth labeled the "economic miracle," Japanese officials sought greater energy security and diversification of supplies from a nearby source. Prior to the summit between Leonid Brezhnev and Tanaka Kakuei there was much talk that this first visit by a Japanese prime minister to Russia would be remembered as a historic visit similar to the 1972 summits opening China to the United States and Japan. Yet, Brezhnev brushed aside Japan's attempt to reopen territorial talks, and in a confusing conversation may have said yes to the prime minister's key question—or merely coughed. Moscow decided not to pursue a balance-of-power policy with Japan assigned an important role. Instead it chose to rely on growing military muscle by which, if necessary, it could overwhelm both of its Northeast Asian neighbors.[40]

The Soviet Union's miscalculation in 1973 can be traced to an erroneous analysis of the Japanese situation as well as of its own prospects. Censored writing on Japanese politics and economics left leaders with an inadequate understanding of the stability of the ruling Liberal Democratic Party and the dynamism of what was already the second largest capitalist economy.[41] Flawed extrapolation of growth rates in the Soviet command economy left the faulty impression that militarization of the Russian Far East could be sustained without integrating the area with the Japanese economy and also that a (misperceived) rapidly rising GDP would continue to swing the global balance in Moscow's favor. Given harsh images of China's lingering Cultural Revolution and Japan's exploitative foreign investments, Moscow failed to appreciate that Sino-Japanese economic ties would soon be advancing rapidly as part of a booming region.

In 1977–1978 Moscow miscalculated again. This time, however, it took a proactive approach as Japan and China prepared a peace treaty indirectly critical of Soviet hegemony. It resorted to threats and bluster, and when the treaty was signed Brezhnev chose to intensify the Soviet Union's military buildup near the border of each country. The stationing of a squadron of planes on the disputed islands just north of Hokkaido became one more thorn in Japan's side, leading to a deterioration of bilateral relations that was not reversed until Gorbachev came to power. Rather than compromise, the Soviets hurled charges of rising militarism at Japan.[42] Insisting that China had not changed the radicalism and xenophobia characteristic of the Cultural Revolution, despite Mao Zedong's death and the rise of Deng Xiaoping, Moscow isolated itself and delayed normalization with China. Instead of responding cautiously to flux in

China and recognizing Japan's growing leadership role in Asia, the Kremlin went on the offensive from Cambodia to Afghanistan. Its threatening behavior helped to drive China into the arms of the United States and Japan, despite inherent tensions left from Japan's invasion in the 1930s and 1940s.[43]

In 1982 Moscow at last turned to Beijing with the goal of normalizing relations. Its overture was not matched, however, by a pullback from the offensive operations and buildup in Afghanistan, Cambodia, and Mongolia that Deng labeled the "three obstacles." Despite obvious Chinese interest in balancing ties to the United States and making common cause on behalf of reform socialism, the aged Soviet leadership did not alter its priorities. And it showed little interest in Japan, dismissing it as committed to the U.S. alliance and driven by imperialist intentions of its own. Stagnating economically, Russia felt increasingly isolated internationally, unable to launch meaningful political or economic reforms until Gorbachev's advent in 1985. Moreover, it stifled debate about Japan and China that might have prepared the way for new approaches to Northeast Asia.[44]

Traditional notions of security imposed by the party's ideological guardians were slow to change. Only when Mikhail Gorbachev boldly introduced new ways of thinking, and Boris Yeltsin came to power rejecting communism and the Soviet mind-set against integration into Europe and Northeast Asia, did the Russian approach to the region begin to change. At this point, however, the Russian people became disconcerted by the rapid loss not only of Soviet superpower status but also of great-power leverage. Suggestions that economic security had assumed priority faltered in the face of uncertainty over compromises proposed in hopes of integrating Russia into the region. Nontraditional security challenges such as illegal migration, environmental damage, and crossborder criminality failed to elicit a strategic long-term response from Moscow.[45] Ambivalence toward China and the United States reached a crossroads as Putin entered office intent on ending the vacillations of the Yeltsin period.

Since the second half of the 1990s, Russian dreams of large-scale industrial sales to the growing Chinese market have failed to materialize. Apart from arms, Russia has little to offer that is commercially competitive. Instead of taking orders for civilian aircraft, it found China prohibiting charter flights of the Il-76 during the second half of 2000 due to noise pollution.[46] A few years earlier, Moscow had been disappointed when no Russian firms were chosen to build the huge turbines for power generation in China's Three Gorges dam project. Beijing would not pay the price of subsidizing Russia's aging industries. Russia was left with no alternative but to rely on exports of natural resources and eventually to find a way to attract investments in processing plants. China had started its manufacturing buildup with the creation of special economic zones. The Russian Far East drew attention as the area most suited to this model, but the necessary laws were never enacted; infrastructure was not built; and steps to weaken state authority led to corruption and tax evasion, not to investment. The Russian Ministry of Finance doubted whether new ideas for special zones in 2003 would lead to different results; yet, some continued to think that the Far East and other areas would benefit from simplified customs procedures, order in registrations and inspections, and accelerated decisions on investment projects.[47]

In 2006 there were at last some signs that change was coming. The Kremlin tightened controls over border crossings, which had long been regarded as criminalized and cumbersome. Moscow business interests gained greater control over the ports of the Far East. They provided access to new capital and more efficient management, even while squeezing out legitimate foreign investors. A gas pipeline from Sakhalin to Khabarovsk was under construction, with plans to extend it to Vladivostok in a few years. At last, those in the Kremlin who had resisted large-scale support for the Russian Far East as too far removed from a market economy had been persuaded that market forces were gaining control and that Russia's vast oil revenues would be well employed here as one of the country's priority development areas. They envisioned massive infrastructure spending on ports, roads, pipelines, and power grids. Also, they planned to attract foreign investment as well as money from Moscow for processing industries that would make use of the new energy supplies. Fish and lumber processing would lead the way, reviving local economies, which would no longer be limited to the export of natural resources.

Plans for revitalization of the Russian Far East accompanied bilateral agreements to boost trade and investment. Trade with China had climbed above $20 billion in 2004 and was projected to rise rapidly, as the Chinese promised investment in industrial parks along the border and inside Russia. Trade with Japan, after Putin's meeting with Koizumi at the end of 2005, was also projected to increase substantially. South Korean trade rose to $6 billion. On a much smaller scale, growth in trade with North Korea from $100 million to $160 million in 2005 completed the picture of an all-around improvement in Russia's economic ties in Northeast Asia. Yet, many of the projects required for large-scale growth, such as an electrical grid and a gas pipeline down the Korean peninsula, depend on a regional program for integration of North Korea and can only come after the nuclear crisis is resolved. Other plans would rely on massive Japanese investment, which remains uncertain at best. If China alone may be ready to provide many of Russia's needs, due to the high complementarity of the two economies, it is not clear that the Russians dare risk this degree of dependence on a rising and long-feared power.

The January 2003 summit between Prime Minister Koizumi and President Putin left the impression among some Chinese that Japanese-Russian relations were improving, even as Sino-Russian relations were falling short of their potential. If Japanese leaders continued to mention the territorial question, the fact that energy cooperation was at the top of the agenda led Russian analysts to assume that Japan actually was leaning toward a more flexible position. Attention focused on discussions of large-scale economic projects that had the potential to break the logjam in relations.

Many saw geopolitics behind the talks. They depicted Koizumi as competing for Russian oil as a means to prevent China from obtaining it, forcing China to become increasingly dependent on vulnerable sea-lanes. The larger concern is that Russia and Japan might find common cause in containing China. Having sought since 1994 to build a closer partnership with Russia and since 1999 to convince Japan through "smile diplomacy" and "new thinking" that regional ties can grow much closer, some Chinese wondered whether instead what they were getting was two declining powers joining to check the rise of the emerging regional power. They could not miss the eagerness with which Koizumi appealed to Russians to give new life to bilateral relations during his 2003 visit,[48] but they also found solace in his decision in 2004 to give priority again to the territorial issue. As over the past twenty years, Japanese intransigence again ensured an edge for China, and China played its hand skillfully. Only if Japan were to change course (and the United States, to shift to a more multilateral foreign policy approach) might Russian strategy confirm China's worst fears; more likely Russia will continue maneuvering, hoping to maximize the advantage of a third party to the regional triangle wooed by the other two. Great-power balancing is alive and well in Northeast Asia.

RUSSIAN VIEWS OF THE KOREAN PENINSULA IN A REGIONAL CONTEXT

All four of Russia's Northeast Asian neighbors beckoned to it after the Soviet Union's collapse. China proposed a closer embrace, offering open borders and economic integration but with the danger of making Russia deeply dependent on its large neighbor. Japan insisted on too steep a price, fixating on the disputed islands. In contrast, South Korea made clear that, if Russia could help it develop contacts with North Korea, it would be a steadfast suitor, and Pyongyang, once it was reassured that Moscow regretted the abrupt separation in 1990, when the alliance was severed by Moscow's normalization with Seoul, was prepared to give it first priority as a go-between. Putin's early initiative to Pyongyang helped smooth the way to the Korean summit of June 2000. His meeting with Kim Jong Il in Vladivostok in August 2002 led directly to the trip by Koizumi to North Korea a few weeks later. In January 2003 Putin sent a foreign ministry official to Pyongyang in an unsuccessful attempt to initiate talks with the United States over the nuclear crisis, after the Bush administration had accused Pyongyang of cheating on the 1994 Agreed Framework by secretly enriching uranium.

Russian diplomacy had become an essential factor in dealings with the reclusive Kim Jong Il. Its goals were not only to play a decisive role in guiding North Korea to a soft landing but also to reshape the strategic, economic, and civilizational environment of Northeast Asia. It sought somehow to stem the march of Asian migrants and ways of doing business into its exposed frontier. Sandwiched between two great East Asian powers and torn by division, the Korean peninsula provided an ideal environment for a weak power with strategic clout to make its voice heard. It is no wonder that Russian analysts underlined the strong interest their country had in the inter-Korean dialogue from 2000 to 2002 and then in the early search to resolve the nuclear standoff.[49]

In the fall of 1992, the Kremlin tried to play the "Korea card," when Yeltsin traveled to Seoul after snubbing Tokyo. He sought to show the Japanese that they could be bypassed. This did not have much effect, however, because as Russia failed to pay its debts, South Korea stopped the flow of credit more than $1 billion short of the $3 billion promised in 1991. Without more clout in Pyongyang, Moscow found that Seoul was starting to take it for granted. Not until 1999, after Moscow had started repairing relations with the North Koreans and South Korea's Kim Dae Jung began contemplating the "sunshine policy," did a genuine opportunity to become a major player in Korean affairs appear. Almost as soon, however, the nuclear crisis made it clear that Moscow's role remained peripheral as others took the lead in struggling with the problem.

After Putin met with Kim Jong Il, one mark of the upgraded relations was the increasing number of North Korean laborers in the Russian Far East. Under the supervision of labor bosses sent by Pyongyang and willing to work for wages roughly half those paid to Russians, the North Koreans became prominent in construction.[50] Meanwhile, South Korean companies also expanded in the Vladivostok area, hiring textile workers for factories that export to the United States. In short order, these companies had trouble finding and keeping adequate numbers of workers. The local media carried many articles about violations of Russian labor law due to onerous work conditions and the substitution of Chinese workers, as investors sought to take advantage of the U.S. textile quotas for Russia without using less productive Russian workers.[51] All of this ended by 2004 when the World Trade Organization replaced the old textile quotas. The marriage of South Korean capital and Russian labor was not a success. With the State Duma balking at legislation needed for South Koreans to start work on the long-planned Nakhodka industrial park, prospects for increased jobs for Russians remain uncertain. At the end of 2005 there was discussion of new plans for free economic zones, but cheap textile labor was not what Russians had in mind. The focus had turned instead to energy-intensive industries and processing natural resources for export.

When Putin took power, he acted to boost relations with North Korea. The timing proved ideal for pursuing multiple objectives. Anticipating Kim Dae Jung's initiative to Pyongyang, Putin placed himself in the position of facilitator. In July 2000, when all eyes were fixed on what Kim Jong Il would do after the June 15 inter-Korean summit, Putin stopped in Pyongyang and then proceeded to Okinawa with welcome news of a moratorium on missile tests. His report became the centerpiece of the Group of Eight summit. In that same year he thrust Russia back into planning for regionalism in Northeast Asia with a proposal to build an "iron silk road," connecting the Trans-Siberian Railroad and a newly reconstructed North Korean line that would become part of a Trans-Korean Railroad. When the Bush administration stalled in 2001 in setting a course toward North Korea, Putin did not lose hope. He hosted Kim during his three-week train odyssey across Russia and again a year later in Vladivostok. Moreover, in responding to requests by the leaders of Japan and South Korea to urge North Korea to advance talks prior to the nuclear crisis, Putin appeared as the go-between in regional geopolitics even as he kept appealing for a long-range program to meet the needs of regional economics.[52] He had to bide his time, however, as the Bush administration delayed setting a policy toward North Korea, then tried to isolate it as part of the "axis of evil." After going to war in Iraq unilaterally in March 2003, the United States focused on trilateral coordination with Japan and South Korea, while only gradually intensifying its appeal to China to bring the North Koreans to the table. Only when the limits of U.S. power became blatantly obvious, in the final months of 2003, did Bush's need for Putin's support become evident. Not only in internationalizing the reconstruction of Iraq and in pressuring Iran to abandon its nuclear weapons program but also in resolving the crisis over North Korea and in expanding oil and gas supplies for Northeast Asia as well as the United States, the Bush administration now had more reason to turn to the Russians. Putin suddenly had a stronger hand to play.

DIFFERENTIATING NATIONALISM, LOCALISM, AND GLOBALIZATION IN PURSUIT OF REGIONALISM

The classic nineteenth-century Russian struggle between Westernizers and Slavophiles was but one of repeated battles between the forces of progressive, global thinking and the stubborn defenders of one or another version of nationalist thought. Such clashes still reverberate today. Each leader who gives increased voice to reformers and accepts the value of free debate has been succeeded by leaders who revert to tight censorship and prefer strict hierarchical authority but who also enforce consensus on foreign policy priorities. Before the Bolshevik Revolution, Northeast Asia was not often a major concern and censorship was not serious. As overall controls tightened and communist causes spread to the region, this changed. Censorship became most pronounced under Joseph Stalin, when propaganda parroted continual tales of support for the inexorable advance of Soviet socialism. Anti-Japanese coverage in the 1930s not only exposed the militaristic dangers from that country in Northeast Asia but also served as the basis for spy trials alleging that Japan had infiltrated the Soviet elite. In the 1950s the image of China following in the Soviet Union's footsteps became a propaganda mainstay. Over the quarter century that followed, however, nationalism became closely associated with vehement denunciations of Chinese claims to be the true defender of the communist faith. Under the guise of communist internationalism, the heresy of Maoism was denounced in order to boost the orthodoxy of Brezhnev's "developed socialism." Ironically, communism, which had originated as an attack on nationalism, degenerated into extreme nationalism.

Reformers, however, used criticism of China as a way of discussing evils present in the history of Soviet socialism. The post-Stalin relaxation of some of the controls over society and an increased knowledge of the outside world paved the way for different types of thinking. Given the license to denounce the path China was taking, some bold writers found indirect ways to hint at the advantages of globalized ways that challenged Soviet nationalist claims.[53] Before Gorbachev's glasnost allowed increasing openness about the realities of China, then Japan, and finally the two Koreas, one of the few venues where issues of socialist identity could be explored was the literature on Chinese deviations from the "scientific" path. Soon the image of "miracle" economies helped make the case for globalization as opposed to narrow nationalism, not only in economic policies but also in strategic reasoning.[54]

Insecurity has driven Russian nationalism to a high pitch since the collapse of the Soviet Union despite the absence of direct threats apart from Chechnya separatism. In Moscow anger over U.S. power projection largely trumped fear of China's growing power.[55] Between the terrorist attacks on the United States on September 11, 2001, and the U.S. invasion of Iraq on March 20, 2003, Moscow's mood shifted. Putin, despite resistance within his own entourage, set a positive tone, suggesting that ties with Washington would take priority and China ties would not be a brake. This gave a brief boost to nationalist concerns focused on China as a long-term threat. Analysts began taking a longer-term perspective on Russia's national interests in Asia and the possible need to balance China's rise.[56] Russia's traditions, however, provided little experience in directing nationalist impulses toward a restrained balance-of-power approach. By 2004–2005, criticism again focused on the United States. Bush's assertive pressure against Russian partners riled Moscow, as did his support for regimes in the former Soviet Union that defied Moscow's control. In particular the Orange Revolution, which turned Ukraine away from Russia, rekindled nationalism targeted at the United States, raising once more China's profile as the partner of choice. Constraints on democracy inside Russia also fueled the appeal of a nationalism more sympathetic to China. Since the United States was not succeeding in projecting an image of responsible globalization, the odds of Russia setting limits on its own nationalism were reduced.

The practice of constraining localism and globalization has deep roots in Russia. In the eighteenth century, with a rise in urbanization and commercialization, both Peter I and Catherine II engaged in administrative reordering that reinforced domination from the center. Looking back, we find a foundation better suited to nineteenth-century autocracy than growing local initiative. Restrictions on local initiative, which became associated with the preservation of serfdom to the 1860s, proved excessive. The urban hierarchy revealed a new concentration of aristocrats in St. Petersburg and Moscow, strengthening the top-heavy dominance of what became essentially two capital cities. There were few regional cities of note. The more primitive means of national fairs super-seded periodic markets for large-scale exchange.[57] Even in Siberia, where great distance necessitated local improvisation, often under strong-willed governors, local society knew little of the advances in distant Europe or even of the sharp differences in nearby Asia.[58] Prospects for integration into the West and intel-lectual cross-fertilization faded under the pressure of rising nationalism, espe-cially in the 1840s and 1850s, when Russia started to push East Asian states to open their borders and recognize its increased role, and from the 1880s to the 1900s, when it advanced into the region under the flag of Western imperialism rather than of its own idealism.

The rise of Vladivostok from the 1860s and of cities along the Trans-Siberian Railway at the turn of the century challenged the old basis of Russia's presence in a region in flux. If ever there was a time for localism based on heterogeneous communities in these new cities or of leadership as a conduit of European civi-lization and of Russia's own rich culture to neighboring Asian cities, this was it. Russian literature gained an avid following in Japan. Russian political influ-ence became a balancing force in Korea. And railroad construction made Har-bin, more or less, the Russian hub for Northeast China. It was unfortunate that narrow nationalism overwhelmed forces supportive of globalist open eco-nomic tendencies or a localist acceptance of diversity. Provoking nationalism in Japan beyond what had existed and pressing for control in Korea and parts of China, Russian nationalism proved infectious. While the Russian Civil War of 1918–1919, followed by only a loose reassertion of control in the Far Eastern republic in the years immediately after, left room for renewed local initiative, this interlude did not survive Stalin's obsessive pursuit of absolute control. This time nationalism under the name of internationalism would reach such an extreme that the mere presence of foreigners or outward-looking local elites was not tolerated. It proved extremely costly to forgo globalties and local ini-tiative along a coast whose residents awakened just as Moscow authorities were going to sleep.

The costs continued to mount through the Soviet era, especially in the Bre-zhnev period, when the Russian Far East became increasingly militarized and settlements were expanded in defiance of climatic conditions and transporta-tion costs. A siege mentality insisted that national interests required extreme measures. This was predicated on assumptions about excessive nationalism in neighboring countries. While normalized relations with China from 1989 began to overcome the sharp rhetoric about its dangerous designs on Russian territory, the image of Japan was not helped by continued talk of that country's territorial pretensions. Although it appeared nonthreatening in other respects, Japan continued to be used as a symbol for beating the nationalist drums.

In the 1990s there was little debate on the importance of upgrading relations with Japan. Yeltsin sometimes made fun of Japan after he canceled his planned visit of September 1992. No vision had been conveyed of the long-term ties between the two countries that would serve Russian interests. On Japan's side, despite a seeming readiness to woo the Russians, Japanese leaders remained preoccupied with regaining the four islands rather than with finding ways of appealing to Russia's long-term interests. In January 2003 in Moscow Prime Minister Koizumi talked of developing Russia's energy resources and a pipeline to Nakhodka. Given the Russians' exaggerated perception of Tokyo's thirst for Siberian oil,[59] they took it for granted that Japan should deliver before Russia would give higher priority to the relationship. Putin had earlier sought better ties with Japan. Russian national identity was moving beyond simplifications that had left it mired in a futile search for a "Russian idea" and the dead-end embrace of Eurasianism, substituting a greater emphasis on globalization, an outlook more suited to a closer Russo-Japanese relationship. Yet, when the Iraq war led Moscow to side with Paris and Berlin while Tokyo sided with Washington, the divide between the two again widened. With Beijing also opposed to Washington, Moscow was back to seeing China as a more natural strategic partner than Japan. Koizumi failed to make a new appeal to Putin; Japan remained a symbol serving the less progressive side of Russian nationalism.

Russian territorial disputes with China and the Koreas as well as Japan fuel nationalism and give regional delegates cause to play the "nationalist card" in the State Duma. In Sakhalin the worry is over Japan's quest for the four islands or even the prospect that Moscow would return two of them. In Khabarovsk, until the agreement in October 2004, the concern was over China's ongoing claim to three river islands, two located here. In Vladivostok, where Governor Yevgenii Nazdratenko fought hard to prevent the first border demarcation, the issue was expansionism through migration and the fear that territorial ambitions would be revived.[60] Meanwhile, some in Vladivostok consider Korean migration (mostly from Central Asia, where Koreans were deported in the 1930s) to be the opening wedge for claims on the Khasan area, which, should either North or South Korea make the claim, could be considered historically part of Korean territory. If anxieties about territory survive, Russian interest in regional cooperation will be limited.

It is to be hoped, therefore, that a more secure national identity under Putin will eclipse such anxieties, given the modest scale of the territories involved. Already in 1995 some scholars had advocated a "conception" of Russian integration in the Asia-Pacific region that could overcome such narrow thinking.[61] A decade later others began thinking along similar lines. Of all those discussing the "Russian national idea" as a factor in foreign policy, Aleksei Arbatov led in charging that anti-Americanism was a sign of weakness, not strength, and that the rise of China required Japan as well as the United States for balance. Geography, he argued, is more important for the fate of the nation than extremist myths about Russia's uniqueness.[62] No matter how much Russians have tried to ignore reality, the exposed area of the Russian Far East and much of Siberia make it essential that it be integrated into Northeast Asia. For this to happen, Russia needs to magnify its presence by balancing relations intelligently and fostering its economic attractiveness. This in turn requires that Russia settle on an identity that is less of an obstacle to cooperation.

The abrupt and unsystematic nature of decentralization in Russia in the early 1990s as well as the legacy of extreme overcentralization distorts Russian thinking about localism.[63] In the Russian Far East, local initiative largely takes the form of regional governments stirring nationalist sentiments against potential dangers from outside Russia or of economic turf wars with Moscow. There is no substantial ethnic factor, except in Yakutiia, because the Far East was settled through waves of migration from European Russia beginning in the 1860s. Nor did the region contain sizable native populations. If by recalling the brief period of de facto independence during the Russian Civil War local officials hoped to wrest control of more economic assets from the central government, it did not work. Instead, the battle over a few billion dollars in annual exports unleashed when export controls were loosened refocused on criminal groups linked to these officials. The center has had limited success in registering these exports and securing its fair share or channeling the revenues into either social welfare or investment. Since the early 1990s, this sort of economic localism has actually left most of the regions in recurrent economic crisis and caught up in fights with Moscow over energy supplies. The illegal export of crabs, fish, lumber, precious metals, and other products also leaves cross-border relations in the hands of criminal networks.[64] Putin has yet to bring these irregular flows firmly under central control, but there were indications in 2005–2006 that a new development strategy for the Russian Far East accompanied by new personnel from Moscow were being put in place.

Moscow supports the regions' desire for strict control over migration into Russia. Although exaggerated media reports sometimes suggest huge numbers of illegal Chinese infiltrating the Far East, official data report that, since the visa system was tightened at the start of 1994, more Russians than Chinese have crossed the border. Indeed, the ratio of 2:1 of the late 1990s became further unbalanced in the year 2000.[65] Chinese want to entice the maximum number of shoppers to their stalls on the Chinese side of the border, having expanded the border town Suifenhe on the railway to Vladivostok into a massive bazaar. Still, the Russians fear an endless inflow of Chinese, who will use any pretext to start trading and, in some cases, set up long-term residence. They consider the current migration "uncivilized," as many young Chinese crowd together and criminal groups providing protection and demanding payoffs swell in number. In February 2003 Russia suddenly altered the visa regime, just when many Chinese had returned home for the New Year's holiday, the kind of measure that does little to build trust.

Regionalism is the missing force in Russia's struggle to balance nationalism, localism, and globalization. Left with China alone along a long border, Russians have been prone to excessive nationalism and localism, suspicious of globalization, and unable to find a balance within nationalism. If Sino-Russian relations were securely situated in a framework of regionalism, Russians could be more at ease. The first requirement is for the North Korean nuclear crisis to be resolved in a manner that stimulates regional consensus on security. Russia is counting on that. The second is for the United States to recognize that, in place of its old alliances reinvigorated to counter the rise of China, it needs a more variegated approach. It should seek to draw Russia into the processes of regional integration and give Russia a place in the regional balance of power, even if this balance remains anchored on Japan. Third, Japan's leaders must move away from their fixation on the territorial dispute and accept an interim compromise that frees their strategic thinking and allows them to raise Russia's significance in their broader regional policy. Finally, any arrangement on the gradual economic integration of North Korea should make the Russian Far East an indispensable component by integrating large-scale projects along a north-south corridor. These interrelated steps toward enhanced regionalism can serve Russia best if they are accompanied by a Russian vision of regional identity no longer focused on geopolitical struggle. Although this new identity cannot rival the EU regional identity, it may yet temper Russian nationalism and complement globalization, and at the same time steer localism in the Far East away from confrontation.

CONCLUSION

A century ago, when fateful decisions were made for a region still forming, Russia took a wrong turn. War with Japan became a precedent for a century of divisive choices. Now the best hope for a different century is a breakthrough with Japan, accepting at the same time a large regional role for the United States and the reality of globalization. In place of geopolitical glory and messianic zeal, the sources of Russia's alienation in the region, Russian leaders need to pursue an integrationist approach suitable for a new start in the region. For instance, Moscow's man in the region should represent modern economic values and transparency, rather than being better known as the friend of Kim Jong Il, as was the Far East presidential representative through 2005, Konstantin Pulikovsky. In their rush into the cities of the Far East, Moscow firms must replace shady dealings and predatory favoritism with modern, transparent business practices.

China's embrace of globalization could offer a chance to overcome the repercussions of the boom and bust character of prior Russo-Chinese relations: the "big brother" patronizing, the vilification during the "Sino-Soviet split," and more recently a cynical "strategic partnership" feigning of friendship to mask deeper fears and suspicions. Yet, locked in struggles with the United States and Japan, China is still making common cause with Russia on issues such as support for the bloody repression in Uzbekistan in May 2005 and opposition to pressuring North Korea in the six-party talks. Bolstered by a trade boom that has tripled commerce with Russia since Yeltsin left office, China is at last having some success in fostering regional interest groups inside Russia ready to lobby for closer relations. Yet, setting a goal in July 2005 of quadrupling trade to $80 billion in 2010 is more likely a matter of sending a message to others than a realistic reflection of the relationship's prospects.

History offers lessons of what should be avoided, while also leaving behind a difficult infrastructure on which Russia's reduced Far Eastern population can build anew. Manipulation by a small, fearful elite keeps alive old notions of Russian exceptionalism as a civilization alien to its region. A weaker Russia must, if it is to escape isolation, become more self-confident of its prospects realistically defined. The new focus requires joining Asia, providing natural resources, and accepting labor and capital on favorable terms. Sergey Witte, the official who devised and implemented a strategy for economic modernization in the 1890s, laid the groundwork by building up the Russian Far East and its transportation links. In the 1950s Khrushchev's massive economic assistance held the promise of drawing much of the region closer together. Gorbachev's rhetoric of the 1980s went further in accepting the goals of regional integration. Although these were temporary exceptions to the usual Russian role in the region, the opportunity is now greater than ever for setting off on a more positive course.

The vacuum left in the Russian Far East is less serious than the time bomb that has been ticking in North Korea since the 1990s, but it likewise warrants a regional approach. Three states, in succession, sought to impose their strategy on the region. During the first half of the 1990s, Japan championed regionalism, offering the Russian Far East a place in the economic circle among the states of the Sea of Japan rim. The prospect of becoming the periphery to a prosperous core raised serious doubts among Russian leaders, who worried about the loss of political influence as well as their country's place in a vertical division of labor. Then it was Beijing's turn to make a bid for leadership, hoping to use the strategic partnership created with Moscow in 1996 to boost bilateral economic integration in which proximity and population would give China a strong edge. Finally, under George W. Bush, the United States sought first to reorganize Northeast Asia to limit China's rise and then, contrary to a regional consensus, to obstruct the engagement of North Korea under the "sunshine policy." None of these three approaches has convinced the Russians to join up. Each required accepting the leadership of one country. Thus, it is not only Russia that must take regionalism more seriously if it is to overcome the vacuum on its eastern flank. The other great powers active in Northeast Asia also must adopt a more balanced approach.

Russia's historic role in Asia has not prepared it for regional integration. It has an inflated image of its own standing in the region: as the first country with Western arms to pose a continental challenge; as the revolutionary teacher to much of the region; as the victor in World War II taking control by land; and as one of two superpowers shaping the region's postwar evolution. It is not easy for Russians to accept the reality of a stranded population that is no more than 1 percent of the region's total: a few urban centers that are mere backwaters among the glitzy megalopolises in the region; economic inputs largely limited to natural resources in a region replete with industrial and entrepreneurial successes; and a fading arsenal of meager military significance in other than the context of nuclear war.

Psychologically, local Russians are prone to blame others excessively, to imagine a "yellow peril" rather than a "gold rush" from regionalism. Yet, objective conditions suggest that a region can assume a shape that offers balance to all three powers, an opportunity for the Koreas and Russia to gain influence beyond their limited means, and a strong stimulus to the local Russian economy. Only by relearning the lessons of history will Russians be prepared to accept regional cooperation that promises them a brighter future in Northeast Asia. They must recalibrate the balance of nationalism and localism at home, appreciate the necessity for a balance of globalization and regionalism, and accept economic integration as essential.

The nature of local management of regional ties has failed to instill confidence in cross-border arrangements. Many Russian officials at both central and local levels doubt that migration is being well managed.[66] They fear that economic ties work mostly to China's benefit.[67] It is doubtful that localism will regain credibility without a sharp change in the standards of governance. Here globalization should take precedence over a renewal of localism.

Extraordinarily popular in 2004 as Russia's re-elected president who had brought stability to his country, Vladimir Putin has continued his drive for centralization. While this offers a needed corrective to a region dominated by local lords who had usurped vital local resources for self-serving aims, it cannot solve the problem of an outpost bereft of vitality amid a booming region on the path to economic integration. Even if some day a Russian leader could deny local elites working with criminal groups control over the resources of the Russian Far East, it would not suffice in facilitating integration, except perhaps as a new kind of fortress linked by pipelines of natural resources but little else. The fast pace of transformation in Northeast Asia, hitched to globalization through entry into the World Trade Organization, leaves Russians still uncertain over how they should fit into a new age of regionalism. The pressure to adapt, however, has been eased by the fact that others continue to struggle over the path forward. Intensified Sino-Japanese mistrust in 2005 and further tensions over North Korean nuclear weapons left Russia with little strategic direction apart from a sense that the time was not right to act.

By the end of 2005 Putin's popularity was slipping somewhat, as was any sense that he had a plan to overcome the malaise arising from Russia's failure to meet the standards of globalization and its malingering regional strategy.

The drift left Russia's regional options under China's shadow. As a weak force in Northeast Asia, Russia waited while the United States and Japan sparred with China on the fundamental issues shaping the region. One could argue that the time had not come for Moscow to show its true colors, but in the meantime Russia slipped back toward a Soviet-era reliance on communist and authoritarian partners and an uneasy attitude toward the imperatives of globalization. Others would have to take the big steps for resolving the North Korean nuclear crisis, forging an East Asian community, and stabilizing the security relations between China and both the United States and Japan. While Putin had laid some of the groundwork for a regional strategy, Russia would need to be patient and prepared when the true test would come, allowing it to break away from its past stumbling in the region.

Putin has moved Russia in the direction of a regional strategy, but both his contradictory goals and the turmoil of a region in flux have left Russia at an impasse. Instead of advancing further toward the fundamentally new strategy that is required, Putin has allowed policies to drift back toward geopolitical balancing dependent on new post–Cold War divisions. He has not cleaned up the criminal economies of the Far East or given the green light to private investment that would integrate Russia into the rapidly expanding regional economy. Instead he is gravitating toward state controls of resources and modes of transportation dominated by government officials.

The critical question for Russia is how to balance closer ties with China as the gateway to Northeast Asia while giving greater weight to others in the region as a way of limiting China's rise before it comes to dominate the region and leaves the Russian Far East without any means of resisting its influence. Forging a special military relationship with China threatens to leave Russia dependent. Turning to Japan for balance and to the two Koreas for a major role in the integration process on the peninsula depends on a timing over which Moscow has little control. There is little indication that Putin or other Russian leaders are making the choices that would prepare their country for the long-term strategy that is needed.

Russia's identity as an Asian nation has been slow to advance over the past twenty years. After North Korea, Russia has been the least positive about regionalism. Anxieties in the Russian Far East have led to doubts about various projects that would draw Russians closer to Asia and build the trust needed for a gradual regional integration. Local leaders are obsessed with denying the realities of their geographical situation and their implications for migration and cultural interchange. National leaders still turn to countries such as China and

North Korea for leverage in the short run more than as part of a long-term strategic approach to developing both commerce and social networks suitable for a region undergoing profound change. As a weak presence with great exposure, Russia should be championing a regionalist approach fundamentally different from anything it has considered to date. Narrow notions of national identity continue to skew the Kremlin's priorities, leaving Russia as little more than a spectator to the whirlpool of regional problems, deprived of a positive role in resolving them, and unable to anticipate an appropriate agenda for the moment when matters begin to settle. If Putin has cleared away some of the barriers to a regional strategy, he has yet to face some of the most essential steps if it is to be successfully pursued.

Notes

1. Sergei N. Goncharov, John W. Lewis, and Xue Litai, *Uncertain Partners: Stalin, Mao, and the Korean War* (Stanford: Stanford University Press, 1993).

2. Odd Arne Westad, ed., *Brothers in Arms: The Rise and Fall of the Sino-Soviet Alliance, 1945–1963* (Stanford: Stanford University Press, 1998).

3. Gilbert Rozman, "Moscow's Japan-Watchers in the First Years of the Gorbachev Era: The Struggle for Realism and Respect in Foreign Affairs," *Pacific Review* 1, no. 3 (Summer 1988): 257–275; Gilbert Rozman, "Rising Soviet Expectations for the Asian-Pacific Region" (Ajia-taiheiyo chiiki e mukete takamaru Soren no kitai), *Soren no kiki to Nisso kankei* (Tokyo, 1991), pp. 86–96, 243–269; and Charles E. Ziegler, *Foreign Policy and East Asia: Learning and Adaptation in the Gorbachev Era* (Cambridge: Cambridge University Press, 1993).

4. Gennady Chufrin, "The Asia-Pacific Region in Russia's Foreign Policy," in *Russia and Asia-Pacific Security*, ed. Gennady Chufrin (Stockholm: Stockholm International Peace Research Institute, 1999), pp. 157–164.

5. Gilbert Rozman, "Sino-Russian Relations in the 1990s: A Balance Sheet," *Post-Soviet Affairs* 14, no. 2 (Spring 1998): 93–113; Elizabeth Wishnick, *Mending Fences: The Evolution of Moscow's China Policy from Brezhnev to Yeltsin* (Seattle: University of Washington Press, 2001).

6. Vl. F. Li, *Rossiya i Koreya v geopolitike evraziiskogo Vostoka* (Moscow: Nauchnaya kniga, 2000).

7. Tsuyoshi Hasegawa, *The Northern Territories Dispute and Russo-Japanese Relations*, vol. 2, *Neither War Nor Peace, 1985–1998* (Berkeley: International and Area Studies, University of California, 1998); and Gilbert Rozman, ed., *Japan and Russia: The Tortuous Path to Normalization, 1949–1999* (New York: St. Martin's Press, 2000).

8. Gilbert Rozman, "The Crisis of the Russian Far East: Who Is to Blame?" *Problems of Post-Communism* 44, no. 5 (September/October 1997): 3–12; and Judith Thornton and Charles E. Ziegler, eds., *Russia's Far East: A Region at Risk* (Seattle: University of Washington Press, 2002).

9. *Nekotorye problemy demarkatsii Rossiisko-Kitaiskoi granitsy 1991–1997 gg: Sbornik statei i dokumentov* (Moscow: Nezavisimaya gazeta, 1997); and V. L. Larin, *Kitai i Dalnii Vostok Rossii* (Vladivostok: Dal'nauka, 1998).

10. Dmitri Trenin, *The End of Eurasia: Russia on the Border Between Geopolitics and Globalization* (Washington, DC: Carnegie Endowment for International Peace, 2002).

11. V. V. Mikheev, *Globalizatsiya i Aziatskii regionalism: Vyzovy dlya Rossii* (Moscow: Institut Dalnego Vostoka, 2001); and E. P. Bazhanov, "Globalizatsiya kak obektivnyi protsess," in *Diplomaticheskii ezhegodnik 2001* (Moscow: Nauchnaya kniga, 2001).

12. Alexander Lukin, "Russia's Image of China and Russian-Chinese Relations," *East Asia: An International Quarterly* 17, no. 1 (Spring 1999): 6–7.

13. Fiona Hill and Clifford Gaddy, *The Siberian Curse: How Communist Planners Left Russia Out in the Cold* (Washington, DC: Brookings Institution Press, 2003).

14. John J. Stephan, *The Russian Far East: A History* (Stanford: Stanford University Press, 1994).

15. Victor Larin, "Poslantsy podnebesnoi na Dalnem Vostoke: otvet alarmistam," *Diaspory,* nos. 2–3 (2001): 76–112.

16. Donald S. Zagoria, ed., *Soviet Policy in East Asia* (New Haven: Yale University Press, 1982).

17. Kruglyi stol, "Sovetskii Dalnii Vostok i ATR," *Problemy Dalnego Vostoka,* no. 3 (May–June 1989): 16–34.

18. Newspapers and journals of Northeast China and the Russian Far East extensively covered the troubles associated with the leap in trade and the sharp cutbacks from 1994. See, for instance, *Yuandong jingmao xinxi,* no. 5 (1996); *Yuandong jingmao daobao,* nos. 7–8 (1996); and *Vladivostok,* July 18, 1994.

19. Gilbert Rozman, "Troubled Choices for the Russian Far East: Decentralization, Open Regionalism, and Internationalism," *Journal of East Asian Affairs* 11, no. 2 (Summer/Fall 1997): 537–569; and Gilbert Rozman, "Flawed Regionalism: Reconceptualizing Northeast Asia in the 1990s," *Pacific Review* 11, no. 1 (March 1998): 1–27.

20. V. I. Ishaev, *Mezhdunarodnoe ekonomicheskoe sotrudnichestvo: regionalnyi aspekt* (Vladivostok: Dal'nauka, 1999).

21. Gilbert Rozman, "The Geopolitics of the North Korean Nuclear Crisis," in *Strategic Asia 2003–04,* ed. Richard Ellings and Michael Wills (Seattle, WA: National Bureau of Asian Research, 2003), pp. 245–261.

22. Ilan Greenberg and Andrew Kramer, "Cheney, Visiting Kazakhstan, Wades into Energy Battle," *The New York Times,* May 6, 2006, p. A6.

23. S. C. M. Paine, *Imperial Rivals: China, Russia, and Their Disputed Frontier* (Armonk, NY: Sharpe, 1996).

24. Alexander Lukin, *The Bear Watches the Dragon: Russia's Perceptions of China and the Evolution of Russian-Chinese Relations Since the Eighteenth Century* (Armonk, NY: Sharpe, 2003), pp. 3–74.

25. Alexander Lukin, "Russian Views of Korea, China, and the Regional Order in Northeast Asia," in *Korea at the Center: Dynamics of Regionalism in Northeast Asia,* ed. Charles K. Armstrong, Gilbert Rozman, Samuel S. Kim, and Stephen Kotkin (Armonk, NY: Sharpe, 2006), pp. 15–34.

26. Tsuyoshi Hasegawa, *Racing the Enemy: Stalin, Truman, and the Surrender of Japan* (Cambridge: Harvard University Press, 2005).

27. Gilbert Rozman, "China, Japan, and the Post-Soviet Upheaval: Global Opportunities and Regional Risks," in *The International Dimension of Post-Communist Transitions in Russia and the New States of Eurasia,* ed. Karen Dawisha (Armonk, NY: Sharpe, 1997), pp. 147–176.

28. Mikhail Alexseev, "Chinese Migration in the Russian Far East: Security Threats and Incentives for Cooperation in Primorskii Krai," in *Russia's Far East: A Region at Risk,* ed. Judith Thornton and Charles E. Ziegler (Seattle, WA: National Bureau of Asian Research, 2002), pp. 319–348.

29. Gilbert Rozman, *Northeast Asia's Stunted Regionalism: Bilateral Distrust in the Shadow of Globalization* (Cambridge: Cambridge University Press, 2004).

30. Iwashita Akihiro, "The Influence of Local Russian Initiatives on Relations with China: Border Demarcation and Regional Partnership," *Acta Slavica Iaponica* 19 (2002): 1–18; and Iwashita Akihiro, "Churo kokkyo chitai: Chita to Naimongoru," *Yamaguchi kenritsu daigaku kokusai bunkagakubu kiyo,* no. 7 (2001): 25–38.

31. So Dae-suk, ed., *Hanguk goa Roshia goangye: Pyongga oa jonmang* (Seoul: Kyongnam University Institute for Far Eastern Studies, 2001).

32. Aleksander Lukin, "Nefteprovod v nikuda," *Nezavisimaya gazeta,* September 15, 2003.

33. Gilbert Rozman, "A Chance for a Breakthrough in Russo-Japanese Relations: Will the Logic of Great Power Relations Prevail?" *Pacific Review* 15, no. 3 (Summer 2002): 325–357.

34. A. D. Voskresenskii, *Rossiya i Kitai: Teoriya i istoriya mezhgosudarstvennykh otnoshenii* (Moscow: Moskovskii obshchestvennyi nauchnyi fond, 1999).

35. Kimura Akio, *Roshia, Soren no Nihonkan* (Tokyo: PHP, 1984), pp. 23–28.

36. Lukin, *The Bear Watches the Dragon.*

37. S. C. M. Paine, *Imperial Rivals,* pp. 49–71.

38. *Shahuang Eguo jinlue kuangzhang shi* (Beijing: Renminchubanshe, 1979).

39. Roshiashi kenkyukai, *Nichiro 200 nen* (Tokyo: Sairyusha, 1993).

40. Hiroshi Kimura, *Distant Neighbors,* vol. 1, *Japanese-Russian Relations Under Brezhnev and Andropov* (Armonk, NY: Sharpe, 2000).

41. The evolution of Soviet thinking on Japan can be traced in the yearbook *Iaponiya: Ezhegodnik*, for example, the chapters on Japan's economy and politics in the book for 1976 (Moscow: Nauka, 1977).

42. M. I. Ivanov, *Rost militarizma v Yaponii* (Moscow: Voenizdat, 1982).

43. Gilbert Rozman, "Chinese Studies in Russia and Their Impact, 1985–1992," *Asian Research Trends*, no. 4 (1994): 143–160.

44. Gilbert Rozman, "Moscow's China-Watchers in the Post-Mao Era: The Response to a Changing China," *China Quarterly* 94 (June 1983): 215–241; and Gilbert Rozman, "Moscow's Japan-Watchers in the First Years of the Gorbachev Era: The Struggle for Realism and Respect in Foreign Affairs," *Pacific Review* 1, no. 3 (Summer 1988): 257–275.

45. Gilbert Rozman, Mikhail G. Nosov, and Koji Watanabe, eds., *Russia and East Asia: The 21st Century Security Environment* (Armonk, NY: Sharpe, 1999).

46. *Izvestiya*, January 23, 2003, p. 6.

47. "Vladimir Mau, rector Akademii narodnogo khozyaistva: Ne nado provotsirovat krizis v Kitae," *Izvestiya*, January 21, 2003, p. 1.

48. *Rossiiskaya gazeta*, January 4, 2003, p. 5.

49. Georgii Bulychev and Aleksandr Vorontsov, "Seul i Pkhenyan nachinayut bolshuyu stroiku," *Nezavisimaya gazeta*, September 17, 2002, p. 6; and Andrei Ivanov and Aleksandr Vorontsov, "Mirovaya praktika, 'os zla,' Pkenyan bryatsaet reaktorom," *Kommersant*, December 25, 2002, p. 9.

50. Anatoly Medetski, "Koreitsy stroyat doma i druzhby," *Vladivostok*, April 5, 2002, p. 2.

51. Yuri Rogov, "Beregis, perepis," *Zolotoi rog*, October 15, 2002, p. 15.

52. Gilbert Rozman, "Russian Foreign Policy in Northeast Asia," in *The International Relations of Northeast Asia*, ed. Sam Kim (Lanham, MD: Rowman and Littlefield, 2003), pp. 201–224.

53. Gilbert Rozman, *A Mirror for Socialism: Soviet Criticisms of China* (Princeton: Princeton University Press, 1985).

54. Gilbert Rozman, "Moscow's Japan Watchers in the First Years of the Gorbachev Era: The Struggle for Realism and Respect in Foreign Affairs," *Pacific Review* 1, no. 3 (1988): 257–275.

55. Eric Shiraev and Vladislav Zubok, *Anti-Americanism in Russia: From Stalin to Putin* (New York: Palgrave, 2000).

56. V. Kuznetsova, "Sobytiya 11 sentabrya i problemy bezopasnosti v ATR," *MeiMO*, no. 12 (December 2002): 93–97.

57. Gilbert Rozman, *Urban Networks in Russia, 1750–1800, and Premodern Periodization* (Princeton: Princeton University Press, 1976).

58. Victor L. Mote, *Siberia: Worlds Apart* (Boulder, CO: Westview Press, 1998).

59. Vasily Golovnin, "Tokio zhazhdet sibirskoi nefti," *Nezavisimaya gazeta*, January 27, 2003, p. 14.

60. Iwashita Akihiro, *Churo kokkyo 4000 kiro* (Tokyo: Kakusan sensho, 2002).

61. K. Brutents, K. Sarkisov, and N. Simoniia, *O vneshnepoliticheskoi kontseptsii i Rossii v Aziatsko-Tikhookeanskom regione* (Moscow, 1995).

62. A. G. Arbatov, *Rossiiskaya natsionalnaya ideya i vneshnyaya politika: Mify i realnosti* (Moscow: Moskovskii obshchestvennyi nauchnyi fond, 1998).

63. Mikhail A. Alexseev, ed., *Center-Periphery Conflict in Post-Soviet Russia: A Federation Imperiled* (New York: St. Martin's Press, 1999).

64. Gilbert Rozman, "Turning Fortresses into Free Trade Zones," in *Rapprochement or Rivalry? Russia-China Relations in a Changing Asia,* ed. Sherman Garnett (Armonk, NY: Sharpe, 2000), pp. 177–202; and Gilbert Rozman, "Cross-Border Relations and Russo-Japanese Bilateral Ties in the 1990s," in Rozman, ed., *Japan and Russia: The Tortuous Path to Normalization, 1949–1999* (New York: St. Martin's Press, 2000), pp. 199–214.

65. "Kitaiskoe vtorzhenie v Sibir i na Dalnii Vostok: mify i real nost," *Polit.Ru,* February 14, 2003, p. 2.

66. V. G. Gel'bras, *Rossiya v usloviyakh globalnoi Kitaiskoi migratsii* (Moscow: Muravei, 2004).

67. Andrei Deviatov, *Kitaiskii put dlya Rossii?* (Moscow: Algoritm, 2004).

CHAPTER 7

Reluctant Europeans: Three Centuries of Russian Ambivalence Toward the West

Angela Stent

FOR CENTURIES, RUSSIANS AND their neighbors have grappled with the question of whether Russia is a part of Europe or apart from Europe. The crux of the puzzle lies in the relationship between geography and civilization. Russia has been both a European and an Asian country geographically for more than five hundred years. As a multinational Eurasian empire, it has developed a unique civilization that, while combining elements from a variety of cultures, belongs fully neither to Europe nor to Asia. Thus, Russia has always been a challenging partner for Europe. Indeed, Europeans have historically for the most part rejected the premise that Russia is a European country.[1] Nevertheless, Europe has been significant for Russia in three distinct yet interrelated dimensions: Europe as an idea, Europe as a model, and Europe as a geopolitical reality that has enabled Russia to become and remain a great power.

The idea of Europe involves post-Enlightenment concepts such as the importance of the individual, representative government, religious tolerance, limits on the powers of rulers, the development of a *Rechtsstaat* based on the rule of law, and later the development of capitalism and democracy. Since Russia until 1991 was ruled by tsars, commissars, and general secretaries who enjoyed few limits on their power, Europe as an idea has thus always appealed to the progressive and liberal intelligentsia, who wanted Russia to become Western, and repelled those who supported the tsarist autocracy or the communists.

Europe as a model has had a different resonance for Russians. From Peter the Great to Vladimir Putin, Russians have admired Europe as a model of modernization, advanced societies whose economic achievements were to be emulated even if their political systems were considered to be inappropriate for Russian conditions. Thus, Europe has appealed to Russian leaders who are modernizers who want Russia to become stronger and more prosperous even if they do not want it to become more democratic. Of course, Russia has always faced two Europes—the more developed Western Europe and the less developed Eastern Europe (today's original and new European Union (EU) members, respectively)—and has usually looked to Western, not Eastern, Europe as a model.

Europe as a reality has also been very important for Russia as the gateway to Russia's attainment of great-power status. Russia rose to prominence internationally through the European interstate system, whose rules it by and large had to accept but whose evolution it was able to influence. But European realities confronted Russia with a series of major decisions. What relations should Russia pursue with other European countries? How much influence can and should Russia have on the European continent and how should it exercise this influence? Would Europe accept Russia as a partner? These issues dominated Russian foreign policy in the eighteenth and nineteenth centuries and were a key element in Soviet foreign policy in the twentieth. After 1945, the United States was arguably more important in validating the USSR's achievement of superpower status; nevertheless, Europe—which today includes the western newly independent states—remains a key arena for postcommunist Russia to exercise influence on the international stage.

In the more than three centuries since Russia became a player in the European state system, only one Russian leader actively engaged all three dimensions of the Russia-Europe question—Europe as an idea, a model, and a geopolitical reality—and that leader was Mikhail Gorbachev. Gorbachev's ascent to power and introduction of perestroika represented the reappearance of Europe as model and pole of attraction for Russia. It was during the Gorbachev era (1985–1991) that for the first time the Russian political elite—or at least significant sectors of it—viewed Western Europe as a political and economic model to be emulated. Moreover, the Kremlin pursued a policy of rapprochement both with individual West European states and with the European Community as a whole. Indeed, one could argue that in his journey from conformist regional party secretary for ideology to reformist general secretary and president of the USSR, Gorbachev (and key advisers such as Aleksandr Yakovlev) increasingly recognized that Western societies had much to teach the USSR. This realization ultimately transformed their understanding of both the idea and the reality of Western Europe and convinced them to accept that "real existing socialism" in the Soviet bloc was a broken system.[2] By allowing communism in Eastern Europe to collapse and by renouncing Soviet power over half of Europe, Gorbachev opened the door for Russia to enter Europe not as an occupier but as a partner.

When Gorbachev took power, he gradually began to overturn the Brezhnevite view that the USSR represented the true socialist Europe, and sought not only a rapprochement with Western Europe but also a greater openness to European ideas. Indeed, Western ideas influenced the evolution of his thinking. Although Leonid Brezhnev had used the phrase "common European home" in 1981, Gorbachev was the first to adopt the concept in a speech to the House of Commons in December 1984, and give it new content.[3] His innovative ideas about Europe were an outgrowth of his "new political thinking," which eventually revolutionized Soviet foreign policy. The conceptual revolution preceded the behavioral revolution but had major implications for Soviet policy in Europe.[4] The "Common European Home" theme had both domestic and foreign implications: Russia was part of an all-European culture; Western and Eastern Europe were joined by a common history and destiny; and the USSR sought to promote closer ties between the two halves of Europe. There was much creative writing about the architecture of the common home, the connection between its eastern and western apartments, and the furnishings of its rooms—but the implication was clear: The longevity of the postwar division of Europe was becoming a legitimate subject of debate.[5]

Gorbachev explicitly argued that the USSR should move nearer to the mainstream of European civilization, thus providing his answer to the historical debate about Russia's place in Europe. Since Russia's first encounters with Europe, its leaders and their European partners have debated the question of Russian exceptionalism. As Russia enters the twenty-first century searching for both an identity and a role in Europe, this question is as important today as it was when Peter the Great first opened the window on Europe at the end of the seventeenth century. Do Russia's vast size, Eurasian geography, and history predispose it to a domestic political system and foreign policy that must remain outside the mainstream of the European community of nations? Can Russia become democratic enough internally and develop a post-imperial, nonmilitaristic foreign policy that might facilitate its full acceptance by and integration into Europe? Will it remain on the margins of the expanding European Union, periodically knocking at its door but unable to become truly integrated? In other words, is Russian exceptionalism, a product of straddling two continents and remaining outside the European civilizational and historical mainstream, inevitable for the foreseeable future? These questions go beyond mere academic debate: They are at the heart of Russia's future. If one agrees that Soviet

Russia squandered most of its opportunities in the twentieth century, then Russia not only has to recoup from the Soviet era but has to leapfrog into the twenty-first century under exceptionally challenging domestic and international circumstances. Europe remains the key to both Russia's democratic future and its ability to become a productive and prosperous modern state and a net contributor to Europe's security.

Postcommunist Russia once again must wrestle with the idea, the model, and the reality of Europe, and many of the current debates echo the arguments of centuries past. The difference today is that the Europe of competing nation-states and balance-of-power politics has largely been replaced by a united Europe of twenty-five countries, some of which were once occupied or dominated by Russia. These EU members have renounced both significant elements of their national sovereignty and the use of military force among themselves. As Russians debate the idea of twenty-first-century Europe, a key issue is the extent to which Russia's domestic political evolution will move toward adopting European norms as legally defined in the European Union's *acquis communautaire* and whether the economic system that Russia is now developing is consistent with the transparent and competitive capitalism of the European Union. The challenge of the reality of Europe is whether Russia can develop a viable modus vivendi with an expanded European Union, maximizing its interactions while minimizing the prospect of a new division of the continent that could once again isolate Russia from the rest of Europe.

Although Russia seeks improved ties with European states, for pragmatic reasons, the historical significance of Europe as an idea, a model, and a reality continues to have an impact on Russia's perceptions of itself and of Europe, as well as on actions taken as a result of interpreting events through this historical prism. That discussion in turn influences how the West—both Europe and the United States—interprets Russian actions and develops expectations of Russian behavior. The historical debate about Europe, therefore, is still relevant for understanding twenty-first-century Russia's internal and external faces.

It is always easier to explain the continuities in Russian history and foreign policy than it is to explain change. When discussing Russia and Europe, however, one must be wary of assuming that nothing ever changes. When the Soviet Union collapsed and the arguments about Russia's identity began, it was as if Russia had emerged from a time warp after seventy-four years of socialism, and the protagonists resumed where they had left off in 1917. But these debates are also deceptive. The experience of the Soviet era—particularly the Kremlin's military, political, and economic domination of half of Europe—has changed Russians' expectations of their role in an evolving Europe. This chapter therefore seeks answers to three questions: First, how have debates about the idea, model, and reality of Europe influenced Russia's perception of itself and European perceptions of Russia? Second, how have Russian and Soviet policies toward Europe evolved, and how have these policies shaped Russia's role in Europe? Third, what is Europe's significance for postcommunist Russia? How will Russia deal with an expanded European Union that will likely exclude it from full membership?

From Peter the Great to Vladimir Lenin: Westernizers, Slavophiles, and Russia's Emergence as a European Power

The idea of Europe as both a geographic and a cultural concept first began to influence the Russian political class under Peter the Great. Pre-Petrine Russia, according to the historian V. O. Kliuchevsky, had an "inveterate antipathy" to the Western world as a whole.[6] Once Peter assumed the throne in 1689, however, the importance of the European continent and the preeminence of the European model of development were generally accepted by his court. Thus, Europe came to symbolize economic, political, and cultural predominance and superiority. It was Russia's task to emulate this European model. Only then would it become more powerful. As the first modernizing tsar, Peter the Great imported European political and economic ideas to Russia and fashioned Russia's role as a European diplomatic player through his wars with Sweden and conquest of Estonia and Livonia. Russia thus became the predominant Baltic power. But, almost as soon as he began his reforms, the debate about Russia's relationship to Europe—both the idea and the reality—began. This argument comprised two components. The first was whether Russia could or should try to become more like Europe internally, once it had adopted and adapted Europe's economic model. The second component was how Russia should deal with other European powers and what role it should play on the European continent. These two facets of the argument about Europe involve two discrete—yet interrelated—questions about Russia's past, present, and future. Russia reached the height of its power in and over Europe from 1945 to 1989, through conquest and domination; yet during this period, it was less European internally than it had been in 1917. For Russia, exercising state power over

Europe—the reality of Europe—was arguably counterproductive to adopting the idea and model of Europe, where Europe represented democracy, rule of law, and free markets.

The Idea of Europe

Even before Peter's accession to the throne, Muscovy had interacted diplomatically with Europe for centuries but had remained largely isolated from European intellectual developments, including the Renaissance and the Reformation. Thus, the ideal of an independent, self-sufficient individual, which flourished in the Renaissance, found little echo in Russia, where earlier Christian concepts of collective responsibility and collective salvation defined the Russian autocracy and its subjects.[7] When Peter the Great ascended the throne, he was determined to modernize Russia and emulate European institutions, but not European values. He instituted lay control over the church and allowed a degree of religious tolerance, but by and large he focused on adopting European institutions, as opposed to ideas. The next great modernizing tsar, Catherine the Great, also focused more on Europe as a model than as an idea. Although she herself was a devotee of the ideas of the Enlightenment, she made sure that neither the Russian state nor its people were influenced by them. She believed that Russian society had not reached the stage of development in which Enlightenment ideas could be adopted. Catherine was one of several Russian imperial rulers who embodied a paradox: Although born and educated in Europe, once on the Russian imperial throne, they embraced the ideas of autocracy and threw themselves into the role of absolute monarchs. European ideas ultimately threatened the institution of autocracy. Nevertheless, European philosophes, such as Voltaire, considered her an enlightened monarch.[8]

In 1766 Catherine proclaimed, "Russia is a European power" (*Rossiya est evropeiskaya derzhava*). Yet she confided to her frequent correspondent and proponent of the Enlightenment, Frederick the Great of Prussia, that she acted like the raven in the fable, which adorned itself with the feathers of a peacock.[9] Russia was indeed a power in Europe, but it did not resemble a European state internally. According to one historian, "In her person, Catherine represented an extreme variation of the problem 'Russia' or 'Europe.' She, the most Western-oriented of Russian rulers, in some ways furthered most Russia's alienation from the West."[10]

Russia's unique pattern of historical development produced a great ambivalence toward the West, where Europe was admired as a model but also feared as an enemy and resented because it considered itself superior to backward Russia. Moreover, Peter and Catherine both believed that Russia could adapt the European model to Russian conditions without first adopting its ideas. By the nineteenth century, the idea of Europe had created within the Russian intelligentsia a major division into Westernizers, those who believed that Russia should emulate the idea of Europe and overcome its historical economic and political backwardness, and Slavophiles, those who believed that Russia had a unique destiny determined by both its history and its Euro-Asiatic geography.[11] The Westernizers, who believed that Russia could not adopt the European model unless it also copied European ideas, exhorted Russia to join the European mainstream. In the first half of the nineteenth century, their demands for political and social rights focused on two concrete reforms: the granting of a constitution and the emancipation of the serfs. They viewed autocracy as the enemy of liberal, European norms. After the emancipation of the serfs in 1861 and the introduction of the zemstvos (local village assemblies) in 1865, which were prompted by Russia's ignominious defeat in the Crimean War, the Westernizers took up new causes. Thereafter they split into two camps, one favoring continued liberal, constitutional reform and the other advocating socialism.

On one level, while Vladimir Lenin, Leon Trotsky, and their fellow Bolsheviks were undoubtedly Westernizers, the brand of Marxism they espoused developed a distinctly Russian character as they adapted it to Russian realities. All the leading Bolsheviks (with the notable exception of Joseph Stalin) had spent considerable time in Europe—indeed the first organized Russian Marxist group was founded there—and all spoke European languages. While denouncing the idea and model of bourgeois European industrial capitalism, they understood that Russia had to progress through this stage before it could become socialist. Nevertheless, as is clear from Lenin's *What Is to Be Done?* the future Soviet leader realized that a revolutionary party with European features, including open membership, could not develop in Russia: The country and its society were simply too backward. Lenin was probably correct that, left to their own devices, the largely peasant Russian masses would not develop a revolutionary consciousness, but the idea of organizing a tightly controlled, authoritarian group of professional revolutionaries to cajole and lead the masses was a distinctly Russian approach to creating a socialist revolution.[12]

The question of why a Europeanized, liberal intelligentsia was not able to prevail politically in nineteenth-century Russia remains. E. H. Carr's observation half a century ago about Russia's problem in the nineteenth century still applies today: "From the Russian political equation, as from the economic equation, the middle class was absent. The Russian intelligentsia was no substitute for the western middle class. Institutions and social groups, deriving directly from imitation of Western models, were quickly transformed in Russian conditions into something alien to the West and distinctively national."[13]

Opposed to the Westernizers were those intellectuals who rejected the idea of Europe. Their doctrine of Russia's national distinctiveness drew its inspiration from German Romantic thinkers.[14] By the mid-nineteenth century, Nikolai Danilvevsky's treatise, *Rossiya i Evropa*, set out what purported to be a scientific theory of the superiority of the Slavic peoples. Criticizing the Europe-imitating (*evropeinichayushtaya*) aristocracy and the radical intelligentsia, Danilvevsky proclaimed Slavdom (*slavyantsvo*) as "the highest goal, higher than freedom, higher than science, education and all material wealth." The organic unity of Slavic peoples was morally superior to Western individualism. Danilvevsky believed that Europe had rejected Russia as alien and hostile, and he argued that Europe was on the decline, while Russia was on the rise. He urged Russians to cease trying to imitate Europe, to recognize that the Orthodox Church and Slavic peoples were superior to the Europeans, and to unite Slavs in a Pan-Slavic union. "Is Russia," he inquired, "a part of Europe? Regretfully or happily, for better or worse? No, it is not— Neither honest modesty, nor honest pride can allow Russia to consider itself European."[15]

Late-nineteenth-century intellectuals who rejected the idea of Europe became known as Slavophiles. Fyodo Dostoyevsky, for instance, despite his later ambivalence toward the Pan-Slav heirs of the Slavophile tradition, attributed Russia's uniqueness to the Asian view of Russians as Europeans, as opposed to the widespread view of Russians as Asians. "We, the Russians, have two Fatherlands," he wrote, "Russia (*nasha Rus*) and Europe—even in cases where we call ourselves Slavophiles."[16] The Slavophiles split into a revolutionary wing, which considered the peasant commune (the mir) as the basis for overthrowing the autocracy, and a more conservative wing, which supported the existing ruling triad of autocracy, orthodoxy, and nationality. Both groups, however, believed that the mir embodied the uniquely Russian virtue of collective living, which rejected the individual and enabled the peasants to achieve self-realization through the community. The *narodniki* (peasant-based revolutionaries) drew many of their ideas from the Slavophiles, and the supporters of the tsar equally drew their inspiration from the same writings. But both groups, in their own ways, believed in the superiority of the Russian way of life, with its organic ties between the people and their land, and both regarded rationalist European civilization as inferior to the Russian alternative. Thus, many Slavophiles embraced a nationalism that fed into traditional Russian xenophobia, chauvinism, and anti-Semitism.

Europe the Model

Peter the Great recognized that Russia's vast size and inhospitable climate had made state building particularly difficult and slowed its political and economic development relative to that of Europe. To remedy Russia's material backwardness, Peter traveled to several European states to learn how their political and economic systems functioned. Like those modernizing leaders who succeeded him—including Vladimir Putin—he was concerned primarily with making Russia a more efficient and productive country, not with liberalizing its political system. Imitating the European model was therefore a means to the ultimate goal of becoming a great power. For this reason, Peter chose to import British techniques of shipbuilding into Russia, while rejecting the institution of the Parliament, because he believed that it curtailed the power and dignity of the royal crown.[17] He brought European manufacturing and handicraft techniques into Russia; he built St. Petersburg on a swamp as the new capital facing Europe; and he introduced military and social reforms "to bring Muscovy's universal service system to its culmination by recasting it in the European mold."[18] At the same time, however, he felt that Russia had a destiny separate from Europe, partly because he believed that Europe was fundamentally hostile to Russia.[19]

Peter's successors continued sporadically and inconsistently to adopt European institutions, often after defeat in war necessitated domestic reform. Hence, the defeat in the Crimean War in 1856 led to the abolition of serfdom, the introduction of local regional assemblies, and legal reform, while defeat by Japan in 1905 and revolution in St. Petersburg led to the creation of the first elected national legislative assembly, the Duma. The difficulty that successive tsars faced in grafting these European institutions onto the Russian triad of "autocracy, orthodoxy, and nationality" revealed the challenge of imitating the model without embracing the ideas on which the model was based.[20] By the outbreak of World War I in 1914, Russia was an autocracy, embarked on a path toward industrial capitalism, but with weak legislative institutions, an equally weak civil society, and a large, uneducated, disenfranchised peasant population.

Russia and the Reality of Europe: The Importance of State Power

Peter had ensured that Russia became an actor in the European state system, but Catherine cemented its role. During her reign Russia became a major European player by virtue of its growing military prowess and conquest of new territories. After two Turkish wars and three partitions of Poland from 1772 to 1795, the annexation of Crimea, and other military and diplomatic successes, Russia's military and political reach into Europe was unparalleled. Russia was indeed a European power, as Catherine had said, by any measure of state power and influence. Under her successors, Russia became a full member of the European concert of nations, thus ensuring its status as a great power.

The Concert of Europe, in which Russia played a leading role, embedded Russia in the European state system, which lasted from 1815 to 1914. However, the system itself was created by the other great powers and, although Russia was part of shifting alliance systems, it responded largely to an agenda devised by states that were for the most part economically and militarily stronger than Russia—a pattern that has persisted, with the exception of the years 1945–1991. Russia supported the reactionary monarchies, which opposed liberalism domestically. Thus, Alexander I sponsored the Holy Alliance with Russia, Prussia, and Austria-Hungary (1815), and Alexander II the *Dreikaiserbund* among Russia, Austria, and Germany (1872). Through successful wars and diplomacy, Alexander I was able to add Finland, the Grand Duchy of Warsaw, Bialystok, Tarnopol, Bessarabia, and Georgia to Russia's growing empire. The rapid expansion, however, caused problems in the burgeoning empire and made political reform more difficult, leading ultimately to the 1825 Decembrist uprising of discontented officers. Under Alexander II, Russia acquired a new partner—Chancellor Otto von Bismarck's Germany, which after unification altered the balance of power in Europe. Indeed, Russian policy had facilitated the realization of Bismarck's ambitions by not presenting any obstacles to German unification in 1871. Russia remained neutral during the 1870–1871 Franco-Prussian War, which enabled Germany to achieve unification after it defeated France. At the end of the war, the kaiser sent Alexander II a telegram signed, "Yours with lifelong gratitude, Wilhelm."[21]

Following unification, Russia remained a player in all the major European conflicts, particularly those in the Balkans. After Alexander II's assassination, Alexander III continued the *Dreikaiserbund*, the alliance among Russia, Germany, and Austria formed in 1872 and renewed in 1884. Thereafter, Russia concluded the secret Reinsurance Treaty with Germany in 1887 but also signed a military alliance with France in 1892, thus breaking its tradition of not supporting the more liberal states. Under Alexander III, the autocracy reinforced its control domestically under the influence of Konstantin Pobedonostev, director-general of the Holy Synod. Pobedonostev rejected European norms just as he rejected European democratic institutions. Slavophile ideas were implemented domestically and did not affect the conduct of Russian foreign policy or Russia's influence in Europe. Russia's engagement with Europe continued during periods of reform and periods of repression. The divorce between the idea of Europe as alien from Russia and the reality of diplomatic engagement with Europe persisted until the outbreak of World War I.

The era of the Concert of Europe closed with an assassin's bullet in Sarajevo in 1914, thus ending imperial Russia's European century. The Soviet Union would play only an intermittent role in the European state system until 1945, its weakness and alienation from the outside world rendering it more an object than a subject in this setting. It was drawn into World War I precisely because it was so intricately bound up in the European alliance system. After the tsar abdicated in February 1917, the provisional government, faced with the choice of remaining in the conflict or withdrawing, chose to continue fighting, despite the war's unpopularity and the government's fragile position. Lenin, on the other hand, agitated for Russia to pull out as soon as he returned from abroad in April. By keeping Russia in the war, the provisional government doomed itself to failure. Thus, imperial Russia ultimately perished in tandem with the system of European alliances in which it had actively participated throughout the nineteenth century.

While Russia was a player in the European system, many of its diplomats were not ethnically Russian, but European. For instance, of the six Russian delegates to the Congress of Vienna in 1815, only one was Russian by birth.[22] In the nineteenth century, the Baltic German nobility played a disproportionately large role in the administration of the Russian Empire and in Russian intellectual life. About 33 percent of high government officials were of German origin at a time when Germans formed about 1 percent of Russia's population. Indeed, four out of the nineteen Russian ambassadors to the court of St. James between 1812 and 1917 were Baltic Germans.[23]

Of course, the Russia-Europe relationship was not a one-way transmission belt. Europe was also influenced by Russia, although in a very different way. Russia was neither an idea nor a model for most Europeans, West and East. Europeans viewed Russia as a backward, almost barbaric society, with a repressive political system. There was, in other words, no parallel debate in Europe about whether it should emulate Russia. Western travelers to Russia, such as the Marquis de Custine recounting his experiences in *La Russie en 1839* and the elder George Kennan writing in *Siberia and the Exile System*, described a country that shocked their readers. Russia was, for much of Europe, the antimodel, the antithesis of what an enlightened society should be. As Custine wrote, "He must have sojourned in that solitude without repose, that prison without leisure that is called Russia to feel all the liberty enjoyed in other European countries, whatever form of government they may have adopted. If ever your sons should be discontented with France, try my recipe; tell them to go to Russia. It is a useful journey for every foreigner: whoever has well examined that country will be content to live anywhere else. It is always good to know that a society exists where no happiness is possible because, by a law of his nature, man cannot be happy unless he is free."[24]

THE SOVIET EXPERIENCE: STALINISM

The Bolsheviks' relationship to Europe at first appeared to represent the antithesis of imperial Russia's—a rejection of the bourgeois European state system, but a commitment to adopt one version of the idea of Europe, namely, European socialism. After all, Marxism—a European ideology—had helped to undermine the ancien régime in Russia.[25] However, this apparent reversal of images soon disappeared. In adapting Marxism to Soviet conditions, the ideology and the institutions of communism were transformed into something uniquely Russian, state-centered and authoritarian, unlike the more democratic European socialism. For most of the Soviet period, Western Europe remained the other, alien from the Soviet experiment, irrelevant to what was happening inside the USSR except as a threat to its existence. Moreover, after 1945, the Soviet Union not only became the strongest European power but, for the first time in Russian history, was no longer the subject of an international system devised by others; rather, it was its main architect, setting the agenda for the other players. When the USSR's geographic reach extended farthest into Europe, it explicitly defined itself as different from and superior to the West and imposed its own system on Eastern Europe. During the Soviet period, therefore, Europe—and the West in general—acquired a very different meaning than it did in imperial and postcommunist Russia.

The Soviet Idea of Europe and Europe's Idea of Soviet Reality

Despite the Bolsheviks' European experiences, Russian realities and their desire to hold on to power after the October 1917 coup soon lessened the appeal of European ideas and institutions. Once the civil war was over and the Bolsheviks prevailed, Lenin and his colleagues confronted the key question: Would Russia construct socialism by first building industrial capitalism? Or would it follow a distinctively Russian path that combined socialism with authoritarian rule and eschewed private property? The failure of revolutions in Europe in the immediate aftermath of the war began to answer that question, although Lenin and Trotsky may have still believed that such revolutions would succeed one day. Lenin's introduction of the New Economic Policy (NEP) in 1921 reflected a compromise between capitalism and socialism, combining private enterprise and concessions to the peasants with state control of the commanding heights of the economy. When the NEP was terminated in 1929, the last vestiges of the European economic model disappeared from Russia.

Stalin's rise to power and destruction of his rivals represented the triumph of Russian exceptionalism over traditional European norms. The idea and model of Europe were rejected and pilloried in an era when Europe was experiencing the Depression, fascism, and great political instability. The stifling of political dialogue, imposition of one-party rule, and use of secret police and purges quickly ended the brief interlude of cultural and political flexibility that postrevolutionary Russia had enjoyed. Stalin, the Georgian seminary student, always suspicious of his cosmopolitan, revolutionary colleagues, systematically eliminated the most European of his rivals—Leon Trotsky, Grigory Zinovyev, Lev Kamenev, Nikolay Bukharin, and many other Bolshevik leaders. Stalin has been seen as a modernizer because he industrialized the Soviet Union, but the way in which he implemented modernization—through forced collectivization and the five-year plans—represented the traditional Russian revolution from above. It was thus an archaizing form of modernization. Industrialization through five-year plans and collectivization from above brought economic modernization to Russia, superimposing it on the traditional autocratic Russian system. In the process the Soviet government under Stalin rapidly became the heir of the traditional Russian state.[26]

As long as the original Bolsheviks were around, Europe remained for some in Moscow an object of emulation. In 1923 Trotsky could still write, "The revolution means the final break of the people with Asianism, with the 17th century, with holy Russia, with ikons (sic) and cockroaches, not a return to the pre-Petrine period, but on the contrary an assimilation of the whole people of civilization."[27] By the time Trotsky lay dead in Mexico in August 1940 and many of the original Bolsheviks had been killed in the purges, Stalin had thoroughly Russified Soviet communism. Not only did his totalitarian style of leadership resemble the tsarist autocracy, but he explicitly appealed to nationalism to justify his policies. The most graphic example was his redefinition of an internationalist. Where Lenin and Trotsky had subscribed to Marx's credo that "the worker has no country" and believed that socialism would not survive in Russia without revolutions in Europe, Stalin enunciated the theory of socialism in one country in 1924, after it became clear that no such revolutions would happen. In a truly Orwellian redefinition of internationalism, he declared in 1927 that "an internationalist is one who without reservations, unconditionally, openly, honestly, is ready to defend and protect the USSR, because the USSR is the base of the revolutionary movement."[28] By the time Stalin replaced the slogan "Workers of the World Unite" on the masthead of *Pravda* with "Death to the German Invader," he had comprehended that the Soviet people would not fight the Nazis in the name of socialist internationalism, but they would lay down their lives for Mother Russia.

The 1917 revolution did, however, produce a sea change in European attitudes toward Russia, at least among its more left-wing elements. Whereas Europe was no longer an idea or a model for Russia, the USSR became an idea and a model for some Westerners. While Europe's remaining monarchs and aristocracy were appalled by the overthrow of the ancien régime, the wholesale expropriation of property, and the murder of the tsar and his family, European (and American) socialists were enthralled by the Bolshevik experiment, especially in the early 1920s, when social and cultural experimentation briefly flourished. Even during the worst period of Stalinism, in the 1930s, foreign socialists who visited the USSR were dazzled by what they viewed as a progressive, egalitarian society.[29] Indeed, well into the 1970s, some West European leftists were willing to give the Soviet Union the benefit of the doubt on a wide array of issues because it was, after all, the motherland of socialism and opposed the U.S.-allied, capitalist European Community. Throughout the Soviet period, therefore, Russia continued to be upheld as a model for some West Europeans and as the lesser of two evils when compared to the United States.[30]

The more controversial question is the extent to which Stalinism influenced European fascism. When Hannah Arendt, Franz Neumann, and their followers began to write about totalitarianism, analyzing the structural similarities between Nazism and Soviet communism, they were less concerned with who had influenced whom than with the impact of totalitarianism on European societies. Four decades later, when German historians began to debate whether Nazism was really qualitatively worse than Stalinism, arguing that Adolf Hitler had learned many of his techniques from Stalin, the *Historikerstreit* challenged the conventional assessment of the latter's impact on the German ruler.[31] It is now clear that both dictators observed and to some extent imitated each other's methods of maintaining power, including the use of purges and labor camps, and that Nazism and Stalinism in many ways resembled each other despite their opposing ideologies.

Soviet Power in Europe

In November 1917 the Bolsheviks announced that the new revolutionary government would withdraw Russia not only from the war but also from the bourgeois European diplomatic community. In denouncing conventional diplomacy, Trotsky, the first commissar of foreign affairs, ridiculed its "intrigues, codes, and lies" and promised the inauguration of an "honest, popular, truly democratic foreign policy."[32] For a brief period, the Bolsheviks appeared to have rejected the European state system in which imperial Russia had been a major player. Of course, Trotsky was soon forced to compromise with the reality of Europe, which included the humiliation of negotiating with the German imperial enemy at Brest-Litovsk in March 1918 and exclusion from the Versailles conference in January 1919.

Three years later, in April 1922, Trotsky's successor, Georgy Chicherin, arrived at Rapallo, Italy, wearing the top hat of bourgeois diplomacy and negotiated not only a formal treaty with Germany but also a secret treaty that enabled both Germany and Soviet Russia to evade the Versailles provisions, rearm, and train their militaries.[33] Once again, Russia had accepted the reality of Europe, although Europe sought to exclude it for many of the interwar years. The Soviets participated in Western diplomacy reluctantly, because they had no other choice if they sought trade, credits, and recognition; however, they never became full members of the European diplomatic community and they resented playing by rules that were set by the capitalist powers.[34] In 1933 an exasperated British negotiator wrote that one could never get anywhere with the Soviets because they were "completely unable to see themselves in any other light than that of an aggrieved Power struggling for their noble ideals against a world of political, financial, and commercial conspirators."[35]

However, the USSR created an entirely new dimension of interwar European reality, one in which Russia devised the rules of the game and set the agenda, namely, the Comintern. The Soviet role in the interwar European state system was highly dualistic. One the one hand, the Kremlin's official policy was to support the overthrow of bourgeois governments around the world. To this end, it created the Third Communist International, or Comintern, which established links with other communist parties—especially in Europe—and gave them logistical and financial assistance in the revolutionary struggle. Thus, from 1919 to 1934, the Comintern tried to foment revolution in Europe, supporting trade union strikes, street violence against the status quo, and other related activities. Indeed, it told communists to join the Nazis to fight socialists in Germany. After 1935 it changed tactics, exhorting communists to join socialists against fascists—until it changed sides again in 1939 with the Nazi-Soviet pact.

On the other hand, the People's Commissariat of Foreign Affairs, or Narkomindel, sought diplomatic recognition and economic ties with the same bourgeois governments that the Comintern sought to overthrow. Often this dualistic policy did not serve Soviet interests, and it earned Stalin the unending suspicion of European governments, which wanted to know the real Soviet agenda. Increasingly, it became apparent that for Stalin, the Comintern and the Narkomindel supported the same end—strengthening Soviet state power, by whatever means. Nevertheless, Stalin was a prisoner of his own ideology, inasmuch as he misinterpreted developments in Germany. He saw little difference between the Nazis and other right-wing parties, and he viewed the socialists as the major threat to the communists' power. His limited understanding of European politics proved counterproductive to longer-term Soviet goals, when the Comintern, under Soviet control, encouraged German communists to join with national socialists from 1928 to 1934 to fight the "main enemy"—the Social Democrats—thus facilitating Hitler's rise to power. The USSR did have an impact on European politics through the activities of the Comintern, which managed to persuade all of its member parties to subordinate their interests to those of the Kremlin.

Although not a key player in the shifting diplomacy of interwar Europe, the USSR was instrumental in facilitating the outbreak of World War II. Although in many ways an international pariah, it had cooperated both officially and covertly with Weimar Germany after Rapallo, an eager party to the secret military deals worked out then and later. It belatedly chose to join the League of Nations in 1934 and, when instrumentally useful, supported the European democracies in the pursuit of collective security to halt the spread of fascism. At the same time Soviet actions in other European conflicts underscored the ambivalence of Russia's view of fascism in the years leading up to Germany's 1939 invasion of Poland. The activities of the Soviet authorities during the Spanish civil war showed that the People's Commissariat of Internal Affairs was more concerned with eliminating Trotskyites and other communists who did not slavishly follow the Soviet line than it was with defeating Francisco Franco's fascists. Stalin's ultimate act of perfidy from the point of view of democratic Europe was his conclusion of a nonaggression pact with Hitler, an option he had been intermittently pursuing for more than a year. From the Soviet Union's point of view, it made perfect sense to avoid a war and gain new territory in the Baltic states, Poland (the "bastard of Versailles," as Vyacheslav Molotov called it), and Bessarabia. The return to Germany of German communists who had taken refuge in the USSR and who subsequently were exterminated by Hitler was a small price to pay for these territorial gains.[36]

Then, with the launch of Operation Barbarossa on June 22, 1941, and Stalin's decision to join a wartime alliance with Britain, France, and, later, the United States, the Soviet Union assumed the key role in defeating Hitler in Europe, losing more than twenty million Soviet citizens during the four-year struggle. The wartime alliance was a marriage of convenience with a common enemy as the unifying force, but the rout of the German army on Soviet soil and the Red Army's liberation and subsequent occupation of Eastern Europe and the eastern part of Germany ensured that Moscow would play a significant role in the postwar European state system. Nevertheless, Stalin's deep suspicions of Europe's pernicious influence continued to be felt after the war. Soviet soldiers who had been prisoners of war in Europe or who had seen extended combat were sent to the Gulag when they returned to the Soviet Union because they had seen the West. Stalin preferred to keep his population hermetically sealed from nefarious Western influences even as he extended Russian military power farther west than it had ever been.

At the end of the war, Russia had once again become a great power through its domination of half of Europe, with the United States as its only rival, as much of Europe lay in ruins. Geographically, the postwar USSR was the most "European" of any Russian state, reaching to the river Elbe, with the Baltic states, Moldova, and eastern Poland part of the expanded Soviet Union. However, control of half of Europe did not Europeanize Russia's domestic evolution. Rather, it made Eastern Europe less European. Stalin imposed the Soviet system on Eastern Europe and ensured that the USSR itself was not influenced by any suspect political ideas from the new Soviet satellites, which anyway constituted the less developed part of Europe. The political and social transmission belt went westward from the USSR, not vice versa. The brief but intense period of Stalinism in Eastern Europe extinguished—at least temporarily—what was left of European democratic political culture in a part of Europe that did not have an extensive history of democracy or the rule of law.[37]

Russia's unprecedented military power became the new reality of Europe. Moscow had more direct influence over the fate of Europe than ever before. Given the historical antipathy both to Russia and to communism of most of the countries occupied by the Red Army at the end of the war, a sphere of influence had to be a sphere of control. As Stalin told Milovan Djilas, "Every country imposes its own system as far as its army reaches. It cannot be otherwise."[38] Unlike any previous Russian ruler, Stalin was able to create European governments in the Russian image. He installed leaders in East European countries whose ruling institutions were intended as replicas of the Soviet Union, through the twin processes of satellization and Sovietization.[39] The Kremlin controlled every facet of public life, including the Communist Party leadership, secret police, army, economy, and culture. Never before had Russia's political and military reach extended so far west. For much of the Cold War, the creation of a ring of loyal buffer states, with its linchpin a divided Germany and a Sovietized German state, guaranteed the USSR's role as a major power. Once the USSR had acquired nuclear weapons, it became a superpower by dint of its military might, territorial conquests in Europe, and global reach.

When the Soviet dictator died in 1953, the USSR had created a new system of interstate relations in Europe. The takeover of half of Europe induced the United States to return militarily to Europe after the war to protect the western half from Soviet designs. The Kremlin viewed the United States and its NATO allies as the main enemy for much of the Cold War, but, unlike in previous times, Russia was the architect and not the object of this European order.

FROM KHRUSHCHEV TO GORBACHEV—EUROPE'S DIVIDED HOUSE, 1955–1985

The Revival of the European Idea

After Stalin's death and the end of wide-scale repression and purges in the Soviet Union and Eastern Europe, Soviet relations with both parts of Europe assumed new, more flexible dimensions. Once Soviet citizens were less hermetically sealed off from the outside world than they were under Stalin, Europe as an idea and as a model once again began to engage the minds of the critical intelligentsia, as it had in the nineteenth century. The Kremlin continued to attack both the idea and the model of Western Europe, but Soviet and East European intellectuals thought otherwise.

Once Brezhnev embarked on a policy of détente for political and economic reasons, Western ideas began to flow into Russia despite the Kremlin's best attempts to seal its population off from European currents. The Conference of Security and Cooperation in Europe (CSCE), which the Kremlin had sought to legitimize its hegemony over Eastern Europe, fueled the growth of dissent in Brezhnev's Russia by requiring the monitoring of human rights in member countries. The idea of Europe—Europe as the harbinger of democracy and human rights—once again inspired the disaffected Soviet intelligentsia in the 1970s. During the 1960s and 1970s, the old Westernizer/Slavophile debate had a reprise among dissident authors, even though their writings were not publicly circulated. The renowned physicist Andrei Sakharov wrote about the overriding need for peaceful coexistence with the West. He then went further to posit that the Western liberal and Soviet systems would eventually converge.[40] He argued that the USSR must emulate the example of liberal democracies if it wanted to progress economically and politically and avoid a cataclysmic war. Opposing him was Alexander Solzhenitsyn, an anticommunist Slavophile, who criticized Western liberalism and individualism and advocated a return to an organic, preindustrial Russian society ruled by an enlightened tsar.[41] As in the nineteenth century, this was primarily an argument among intellectuals and did not touch the broader Soviet populace. The debate between Sakharov and Solzhenitsyn continued even after the former was placed under house arrest in Gorky and the latter exiled to the United States. By the time of Brezhnev's death, in November 1982, the idea of Europe and its attraction as a model once again excited the imagination of educated Russians.

Managing Eastern and Western Europe: The Soviet Superpower

As the USSR progressed from being a European great power at Stalin's death to being a global superpower by Nikita Khrushchev's ouster in 1964, Russia's interactions with Europe became more complex and contradictory, involving elements of cooperation and confrontation. They ranged from outreach to all the major capitals (west and east) to the 1958–1961 Berlin crisis, yet they represented some new departures.[42] From 1953 to 1990, the Kremlin's major challenge was calibrating its policy toward both halves of Europe to enhance Soviet security on the continent. Control of Eastern Europe and influence over Western Europe were the twin goals. The USSR continued to set much of the agenda, but it also had to respond to a more active West European agenda. During this period, Western Europe renounced traditional balance-of-power politics and military force and began the process of integration. Replacing the nineteenth-century royal alliances of Europe were the North Atlantic Treaty Organization, the European Community, the Warsaw Treaty Organization, and the Council for Mutual Economic Assistance (CMEA). The latter two provided a multilateral instrument for reinforcing bilateral Soviet controls.[43] With historical hindsight, one can say that the USSR's policy toward both parts of Europe contained within itself the seeds of its own destruction. The growing economic burden of Eastern Europe induced Moscow to improve ties with Western Europe, thereby opening the Warsaw Pact countries to Western influences and ultimately undermining Soviet power. But for three decades, the twin policies of control and rapprochement appeared to be quite effective.

When Khrushchev embarked on de-Stalinization, he confronted a dilemma in Eastern Europe that continued until the collapse of communism—that between viability and stability.[44] Moscow would ideally have had allies in Eastern Europe whose governments enjoyed genuine political legitimacy and economic prosperity. But when leaders or movements arose that appeared to challenge the Soviet model or threatened loss of Soviet control, the Kremlin opted for stability over viability. The use of military force to suppress popular reform movements in Hungary in 1956 and Czechoslovakia in 1968 was the ultimate expression of this policy. As the Brezhnev era wore on, Soviet policy in Eastern Europe lost its dynamism and stagnated. Each East European country was able to formulate an implicit bargain with Moscow about how much flexibility it had to deviate from the Soviet internal model or from Soviet foreign policy. Romania, while Stalinist internally, pursued a more flexible foreign policy, dealing diplomatically with West Germany, China, and Israel when the USSR refused to let its other allies follow suit. Hungary, on the other hand, while conformist in foreign policy terms, deviated from the strict Soviet domestic economic and political model. The other Warsaw Pact states all made their own bargains. Moreover, to maintain political control, Moscow increasingly began to subsidize Eastern Europe economically. After the 1973 oil embargo and the subsequent sixfold rise in oil prices, the USSR sold oil to its East European partners for prices well below world levels, thereby forfeiting badly needed hard-currency earnings that it could have obtained from the West. Eastern Europe became an increasing economic burden to the USSR, with limited reform and political conformity. But every ruler in the Warsaw Pact, with the exception of the most repressive, Nikolae Ceaușescu, knew that he owed his continued political existence to his Kremlin masters.[45] As Brezhnev said to East German leader Erich Honecker, "We have troops in your country, Erich. I'm telling you openly, never forget this: the GDR can't exist with its power and strength without us, without the Soviet Union. Without us, there is no GDR."[46]

While trying to hold together a progressively less viable Eastern Europe, Brezhnev sought to widen contacts with Western Europe. He pursued détente for both economic and political reasons and because of the growing Soviet conflict with China. But he also sought multilateral recognition of the geographical status quo in Europe through the CSCE process. By 1975 the Kremlin appeared to have secured the endorsement of its hegemony over Eastern Europe from Western Europe and the United States. That, plus the bilateral détente with individual countries, notably West Germany, broadened the Soviet Union's access to governments and people in Western Europe.[47] Détente softened the Kremlin's image in Western Europe and gave it credibility when Moscow actively began to encourage a peace movement in Europe to oppose the deployment of U.S. Pershing II and cruise missiles in response to the deployment of Soviet SS-20 intermediate-range missiles targeted at Europe. Moscow appeared to support peace and cooperation at a time when Washington was portrayed as pursuing a hard-line policy that could lead to nuclear war. For a time in the late 1970s and 1980s, Soviet policy in Western Europe, particularly the "peace campaigns," appeared more dynamic than that in Eastern Europe, where Soviet policy was at an impasse.

Once the USSR had become a superpower, armed with nuclear weapons and extending its interests and influence well beyond Europe to Latin America, Asia, and Africa, the United States, rather than Europe, was the key to validating the Kremlin's new status. Relations with Europe acquired a new transatlantic dimension and détente created opportunities for a more coherent policy toward the alliance as a whole. While the idea of Europe appealed to some Soviets, the idea of the United States increasingly attracted the more disaffected population and had broad appeal among the youth, who began to gravitate to what they knew of American popular culture.[48] At the same time that Brezhnev sought to insulate his people from the pernicious effects of Western culture, he actively engaged the transatlantic alliance by seeking to maximize fissures in it while pursuing closer ties to both the United States and Europe. Yet, he stopped short of promoting policies that might have ultimately led to the end of the U.S. presence in Europe.[49] For instance, although the Kremlin encouraged U.S.-European disagreements over the deployment of intermediate-range missiles, it also pursued more conciliatory policies when it appeared that the United States was seriously considering withdrawing its troops from Europe. Brezhnev, like Mikhail Gorbachev, preferred a U.S. presence in Europe to restrain any potential German designs to its east. Nevertheless, the USSR also feared an Atlantic alliance that was too united, welcoming Gaullist France's distancing from the United States and the furor over the neutron bomb and the NATO two-track decision after 1979.[50] The Kremlin viewed a feuding Atlantic alliance as beneficial for Soviet national security, believing that West Europeans—especially Germans—would be inclined to take a more benign view of Soviet intentions and were more susceptible to Soviet "peace" propaganda than many Americans.

Our Common European Home: Gorbachev Embraces the Idea and Reality of Europe

When Gorbachev came to power, he realized that behind the appearance of a strong Soviet empire reaching to the Elbe River lay the reality of a stagnating system that was imposing its will at a growing economic cost on an increasingly restless East European population and a Soviet population that had become very cynical about its rulers. Glasnost and perestroika were intended to revitalize socialism in the USSR and Eastern Europe by encouraging more critical discussion and opening the system to other ideas and models. As communism began to transform itself both in Eastern Europe and in the Soviet Union, the idea of Europe and of Russia's European destiny once again became a subject of open discussion. Released from exile and leading the Inter-regional Group in the competitively elected Congress of People's Deputies, Andrei Sakharov and his followers for the first time had a public forum to debate the future of the Soviet Union. Toward the end of the Gorbachev era, it had become acceptable to advocate that Russia renounce Soviet-style communism and move toward a European democratic system with private property as its foundation. Unlike in previous times, both the Russian leadership and the intelligentsia admired aspects of the Western ideas and of the European model.

But as the Westernizers reasserted themselves, so did the Slavophiles. As in the nineteenth century, the latter group included both liberal and conservative elements. The more liberal ones argued that Russians have always "felt themselves to be of Europe, yet [they] disputed everything European—we are not a country, but a country of countries—a centaur by birth."[51] Thus, Russia should seek an identity that goes beyond Europe. The conservative, right-wing Slavophiles published a manifesto of sorts with Igor Shafarevich's essay "Russophobia." In the article Shafarevich lashed out against socialism—whose roots, he said, were not Russian—and against ecumenism, the multiparty system, cosmopolitanism, and all those trying, in his view, to undermine Russia. He took particular aim at Russia's "rootless" and Westernized Jews with their European beliefs who, as in previous times, were depicted as the enemy trying to undermine Russia from within.[52] Thus, when the question of Russia's Europeanness emerged in the public debate after decades of suppression of open discussion about Russia's identity, opponents of Russia's European vocation reverted to familiar nineteenth-century arguments.

Gorbachev essentially reversed Stalin's relations with Europe—the USSR eventually gave up military and political control of Eastern Europe, allowing Russia to become more European internally. This is not to suggest, however, that Gorbachev came into office intending to renounce either Soviet control over Eastern Europe or communism. In 1985 he believed that the economic and political problems in Eastern Europe resulted from poor performance, not a systemic crisis.[53] During Gorbachev's first three years in office, his policy toward Eastern Europe was one of benign neglect, as he hoped that eventually his socialist allies would emulate his policies of perestroika and glasnost. Even after the Berlin wall came down in 1989, he believed that there would continue to be two German states, with East Germany becoming a reform socialist country. Gorbachev made one principled decision—not to use troops to keep the East German government in power and not to use force to prevent Poland and Hungary from moving away from communism. His policies enabled communism to fall, but they were never intended to lead to the demise of the socialist system in Eastern Europe.[54] The Soviet system in Eastern Europe was politically, economically, and morally bankrupt, and it collapsed with a whimper, not a bang. By refusing to use force to maintain control over Eastern Europe, the USSR ceased to be the driver and architect of the interstate system in Europe. The fact that the Soviet system ended not as a result of defeat in a war has fueled the fantasies of those Russians who see a Western conspiracy behind the demise of communism. It remains difficult for many Russians to accept that the Kremlin could intentionally have abdicated its great-power role in Europe.

While the Soviet decision to abandon its empire in Eastern Europe was an unintended consequence of Gorbachev's liberalization policies, the successful rapprochement with Western Europe that followed was both calculated and ultimately successful. Gorbachev embraced and sought to benefit from the reality of Europe, and this was an area where the Kremlin was still able to drive its European agenda. He set out to improve bilateral ties with the major West European powers—Britain, France, and West Germany—but he also slowly began to change Soviet policy toward the European Community, which hitherto had been dismissed by Soviet officials as ephemeral and doomed to fail.[55] The overtures to Western Europe were intended to yield concrete economic results, which they began to do, and to facilitate Soviet acceptance in Western international forums, such as the Group of Seven, to which Gorbachev was invited in 1991.

Gorbachev's transatlantic policies also differed from those of Brezhnev. The rapprochement with Western Europe was linked to the rapprochement with the United States. Gorbachev realized that previous Soviet policies that aimed to drive wedges between the United States and its allies had achieved little success for Moscow. He also recognized that working with both Washington and its allies was likely to produce more favorable results. Gorbachev thus set the stage for the post-Soviet relationship with Europe by unwittingly facilitating the collapse of communism in Eastern Europe and dealing with Western Europe largely on its terms.

With the end of Soviet power in Eastern Europe, and the dismantling of the Warsaw Treaty Organization and the CMEA, Moscow's presence in and influence over the European continent was sharply reduced as Soviet troops withdrew from East Germany. The new Russia had little ideological, military, or foreign policy influence over Europe, although it continued to be closely connected in terms of economic ties, especially energy. The Kaliningrad exclave was the only place where Russia shared a border with Europe, and its European reach was reduced to that of the seventeenth century, before the incorporation of Ukraine into the Russian Empire. At the very time when Russians were most open to European ideas and models of government, the Russian state had the least influence over Europe and the smallest geographic presence there. This new reality set the stage for postcommunist Russia to grapple with how it would interact with Europe in the twenty-first century.

From Yeltsin to Putin—Russia Faces a New Europe

The collapse of the Soviet Union created a completely new context for Russia's relations with Europe. Whereas Gorbachev had hoped that Russia and Europe might grow closer through some blending of socialism and capitalism, "Yeltsin was fully prepared to accept the superiority of Western political and economic institutions and the necessity there for Russia to adopt and build them."[56] Throughout the 1990s, the Yeltsin administration and its supporters among the intelligentsia and business community accepted both the idea and the model of Europe. But, as a weak and recovering Russia tried to emulate Europe and join the major Western clubs such as the Group of Seven and the World Trade Organization, Europe was no longer as promising an arena for Russia to exercise influence as a great power. Relations with Central and Eastern Europe—which had been the focus of Russian power for forty-five years—atrophied, as former Soviet allies and the Baltic states embarked on their journey to join Europe as fast as possible.

The new Russian state, emerging out of the chaos of the USSR's demise, looked to the West for support in re-creating itself. The Kremlin viewed the European Union, and united Germany in particular, as sources of political and economic support; Europe thus possessed an unprecedented practical importance for Russia's postcommunist transition. But the new Russia was also concerned about retaining its great-power status, despite its tremendously weakened situation. For Boris Yeltsin, the United States, more than Europe, was the key to Russia's continued global relevance. Moreover, during the Yeltsin years, the U.S. free market model was favored over a European model that advocated greater state intervention in the economy. American, not European, economic advisers predominated well into the mid-1990s.[57] As Europe became more important as a source of assistance for Russia, the idea of Europe as a democratic model for the new Russia also gained greater acceptance. Thus, the end of Russian power over Europe meant that Russia could contemplate being *of* Europe since it was no longer *in* Europe.

Having renounced the communist system, Russia began a search for its postcommunist identity. This coincided with the shrinking of territory, as Russia lost the other fourteen republics of the USSR. Unlike in previous eras in Russian history, the issue of Russia's national character and exceptionalism is no longer confined to a small group of intellectuals. The debate about identity and what Russia should strive to be has reached across Russian society via the media, the Internet, and the growth of public opinion surveys. In another major change from Soviet times, many more Russians are free to travel to Europe and the United States, while the number of Westerners visiting Russia has also increased significantly. Thus, the debate about the West is better informed than it has ever been. As Russians have become more knowledgeable in a globalized world, the issue of identity is also discussed in a more sophisticated and differentiated way. Nevertheless, themes from the past three centuries have reappeared with surprising regularity. Russians have moved further toward a consensus on what their institutional relationship with Europe should be, but they remain divided over the cultural and civilizational implications of what they understand of Europe for their own society. They question whether Europe would really welcome Russia into its fold were Russia to make that choice. Moreover, they confront a transatlantic alliance that is far more fractured than it was during the Cold War, when the Soviet Union often united it against a common antagonist.

In the early 1990s, the main protagonists in the Russian debate were the Atlanticists and the Eurasianists. The Atlanticists believed that Russia should adopt the European democratic model internally and pursue close ties with both Europe and the United States. They were initially led by Yeltsin's first foreign minister, Andrei Kozyrev, a firm believer that Russia should enter Europe as a "normal, democratic power." Russia, he argued, would have a far greater chance of influencing events in Europe than did the Soviet Union, because it now sought cooperation, not military domination.[58] Kozyrev's mantra that Russia should become a "civilized" country and join the West was accepted by the emerging free market economic elite and by some foreign policy intellectuals, if not by the Foreign Ministry itself.[59] Although the pro-Western political and business groups recognized that the evolving Russian system would retain its distinctive elements, they advocated that Russia become a democratic, market society based on the rule of law. Many saw these values as Euro-Atlantic, not purely European.[60]

Early on, however, dissenting voices began to emerge. Faced with the difficulty of accepting the breakup of the Soviet Union, and conscious that Europe was not welcoming Russia with open arms, presidential adviser Sergei Stankevich and others argued that Russia should steer its own, unique Eurasian course. Opponents of Atlanticism rejected both the idea of Europe and the necessity to integrate with the reality of Europe. They advocated that Moscow establish a Russian "Monroe Doctrine," emphasizing its continuing sphere of vital interest and influence over the post-Soviet states.[61] Stankevich and others proposed a mild form of Eurasianism, recognizing that Russia should move closer to

Europe, but objecting to what they viewed as a slavish attempt to imitate the West. When Yevgeny Primakov became foreign minister in 1996, he echoed the need for a Russian multipolar policy not exclusively focused on the West. Meanwhile, communists and so-called patriotic forces, later joined by Vladimir Zhirinovsky's woefully misnamed Liberal Democratic Party, returned to more traditional Slavophile themes. "Democracy is profoundly inimical to our national culture," opined *Sovetskaya Rossiya.* "It tramples down everything it comes into contact with, in the name of some world order or another. And in general all these phenomena—democracy, globalism, Zionism, and cosmopolitanism—are identical twins."[62]

When one moves beyond questions of civilization, however, Russia's consistent pragmatic goal since 1992 has been to join Euro-Atlantic institutions. As Kozyrev said early on, "Our choice is—to progress according to generally accepted rules. They were invented by the West, and I'm a Westernizer in this respect—the West is rich, we need to be friends with it—It's the club of first-rate states Russia must rightfully belong to."[63] In the 1990s, Russia became a member of the Group of Eight and the Council of Europe; it was also a member of the Contact Group during the wars in Bosnia and Kosovo. In 1994 it signed the Partnership and Cooperation Agreement with the European Union, and in 1997 it signed the NATO-Russia Founding Act. Later, in 2002, it helped to create the NATO-Russia Council. Thus Yeltsin laid the foundation for Russia to integrate closer with, and play a greater role in, Europe; however, Russia's difficult domestic evolution, its lack of a coherent foreign policy strategy, and European questions about where Russia was headed limited the rapprochement. Although it is closer institutionally to Europe than ever before, Russia remains, literally and figuratively, at Europe's gate, unsure when it will be able to enter and, increasingly under Putin, whether it should seek to join.

Yeltsin expended considerable energy improving ties with both the United States and the major European powers. Although his government officially promoted the idea of Europe—democracy, markets, and pluralism—its controversial privatization policies and the corruption they promoted were a far cry from the market economies of either Europe or the United States.[64] Moreover, whether Yeltsin succeeded in steering Russia toward democracy in the Euro-American sense of the concept remains a subject of intense debate.[65] Yeltsin's relationship with U.S. president Bill Clinton was arguably the centerpiece of his foreign policy, although, by the end of his tenure, the relationship had deteriorated considerably because of the war in Kosovo. The Clinton administration, more than any European government, consciously tried to influence Russia's domestic political system through a variety of policies that sought to build democracy and a market system. After the controversial loans-for-shares and voucher privatization schemes, and Yeltsin's increasingly erratic domestic policies, these policies came under scrutiny both at home and in Russia.[66] The judgment on this U.S. experiment at democracy building in Russia remains a matter of sharp debate in both the United States and Europe.[67] Moscow in this period sought recognition from the United States and acknowledgment by Washington of Russia's continuing international significance, particularly at a time when it was greatly weakened both militarily and politically. In retrospect, the consensus in Russia is that it did not receive the recognition it deserved.

Russia's quest for recognition extended to Europe, even though Europe could not bestow on Russia the great-power legitimacy it craved. Yeltsin cultivated his friendship with Germany's chancellor, Helmut Kohl, which also became a key component of his diplomacy.[68] Russia's relationship with Germany, however, deteriorated during the 1999 Kosovo war, after Gerhard Schröder replaced Kohl the previous year. While Russia pursued better ties with the West European states, its relations with its former allies in Central and Eastern Europe atrophied, as the latter sought rapid integration with Europe and protection from any future resurgent Russian designs. Indeed, the greatest change in post-Soviet Russia's ties with Europe was the near absence of relations with members of the former Warsaw Pact. Despite Moscow's souring relations with Europe during the Bosnian and Kosovo wars, Russia did manage to cooperate on the ground with its NATO partners in the Contact Group.[69] Indeed, Russian troops serving under a U.S.-NATO command in the Bosnia Stabilization and Implementation Forces considered the experience a success. Yeltsin also sought to improve ties to the European Union but was disappointed by what Russians perceived as EU reticence. He also inaugurated the first Russo-French-German troika meeting, in which he called for a new dialogue among governments in Moscow, Paris, and Bonn. Some viewed this as an attempt to play a "European" card against the United States at a time when transatlantic disagreements were on the rise. More likely, however, Yeltsin was seeking to boost Russia's international standing, rather than driving wedges between different powers.

By the end of the 1990s, therefore, post-Soviet Russia was seeking closer ties with the United States and Western Europe, largely ignoring Central and Eastern Europe and increasing its economic links with all of Europe. The private sector in Russia was steadily building closer ties in Europe, irrespective of what the Kremlin did. Moreover, wealthy Russians were moving to Europe, where they bought property and sent their children to school. Russians were becoming part of European society in a way that they had never previously been. European attitudes toward Russia, however, remained cautious. While Western Europe largely supported Russia's transition toward a more pluralistic system, Central and Eastern Europe remained wary of Russia's longer-term intentions, and all of Europe was critical of Moscow's war in Chechnya.

PUTIN'S RUSSIA AND THE WEST

Since Vladimir Putin's accession to the presidency in 2000, Russia has reevaluated its relationship to the West and to the European domestic and external model. In comparison to Gorbachev and Yeltsin, Putin is a wary European. He has explicitly said that Russia will follow a path to democracy that is appropriate to Russian conditions and will not recreate a Western model. Europe's primary attraction for Putin the modernizer is the same as it was for Peter the Great (a painting of whom hangs in his office): Selective adoption of European institutions will enable Russia to become a stronger, prosperous, modern society that will participate more fully in a globalized world. But "modern" for Putin, as for Peter, does not mean that Russia will adopt all European democratic norms or seek integration with the West. The other major change from the Yeltsin era is that, with a recovered economy and high growth rates derived from soaring energy prices, the Kremlin views its energy ties to Europe as a means of reasserting Russia's role as a great power in Europe. The new source of Russian clout is no longer "hard" military power, but "soft" economic leverage.[70]

Russia's interactions with Europe revolve around six main issues. The first is Russia's domestic evolution. Can Russia move closer to Europe if its version of "managed democracy"—that is, a nontransparent political and economic system and an electoral system and society manipulated by the Kremlin— is seriously at variance with acceptable European norms? A second issue concerns Russia's ties to the expanded European Union. Is closer Russian integration with the European Union a realistic goal, and would the European Union like to see this outcome? A third aspect is Russia's relations with individual European countries, particularly the "big three"—France, Germany, and the United Kingdom—all of which are Russia's major partners, but also with its former central European and Baltic allies, with whom its relations remain brittle. How does Russia calibrate traditional bilateral ties with individual countries as opposed to ties with the European Union as a single actor? A fourth facet involves Russia's economic relationship with Europe, which now accounts for more than half of Russia's trade, and the politics of energy. Russia is Europe's major energy supplier, and its significance is likely to grow as it increasingly holds the key to Europe's future energy security. A fifth issue is Russia's view of and participation in the transatlantic relationship. How does Russia balance its relations with the United States, on the one hand, and Europe, on the other? A sixth issue, and one that is likely to grow in importance, is Russia's relationship to the western New Independent States (NIS)—Belarus, Moldova, and Ukraine—and the European Union's increasing involvement in these countries. As the European Union's newest members, particularly the Baltic states and Poland, pursue more activist policies in their new neighborhood, Russia will have to adapt to the realities of overlapping neighborhoods where EU and Russian interests often compete.

Under Putin, Russia's interactions with Europe have produced mixed results. Russia's internal political evolution has acted as a brake to further integration and development of ties between Moscow and Brussels has moved more slowly than Russia would have liked. The Kremlin has responded negatively to the enlarged European Union's more activist policies in the NIS. On the other hand, its economic growth and the increasing salience of energy exports have served to strengthen Russia's influence in Europe. It has developed strong bilateral ties to key European powers, particularly Germany, France, and Italy, and has sided with Europe in growing transatlantic differences in the wake of the Iraq war. Thus, the reality of Europe poses continuing challenges to a Russia defining its regional and global place, still pursuing a largely reactive foreign policy.

Europe as Idea and Model

Putin is the first Russian leader since Lenin to have lived in Europe—as a medium-level KGB functionary in Dresden from 1986 to 1990—and speaks German well.[71] He has said at various times that Russia is part of European civilization but, like previous Russian leaders, has also asserted that "by virtue of its geography, Russia is simultaneously a European and an Asian country."[72] Putin has sought to bring Russia closer to Europe in institutional terms and to have a seat at the EU table, but his domestic policies suggest that he believes that Russia should be *in* Europe but not *of* Europe with regard to its values and political culture. Under his leadership, the debate about Russia's identity and place in the world has evolved in a familiar historical pattern. He continues to maintain a belief first expressed in his millennial statement on assuming office that Russia was not part of traditional European civilization. As he has shed most vestiges of the chaotic—but pluralistic—Yeltsin political system, with its weak checks and balances, the ranks of those exhorting Russia to adopt Euro-Atlantic norms and become a Western-style democracy have shrunk. Since the 2003 Duma elections, only a handful of independent, democratic opposition members with no ties to the Kremlin-run United Russia Party remain in the legislature. With the de facto state takeover of the electronic media, the writings of Westernizers who are critical of Putin's policies have been relegated to the pages of small-circulation print media.[73] The shrinking democratic opposition, joined by some members of an emerging entrepreneurial class, still argues for the rule of law, a transparent economy, and European norms. It has become increasingly marginalized, however, as Putin embodies a more traditional Russian view of state power.

A significant sector of the Russian elite has proposed a new version of Russian exceptionalism: that Russia can modernize only by adopting the current "statist" model of vertical power as created by Putin. Russia should thus become a market economy with a strong, centralized state. This Russia can be a partner with the West, but only on the basis of its own unique model. It should not humiliate itself by adopting European norms and practices that are alien to its history and culture.

The Eurasian movement, aided by the Internet, also has its place in Putin's Russia. Its leader, Alexander Dugin, whom Putin took with him during a visit to Turkey in 2004, combines mystical references to the Orthodox Church with a sophisticated geopolitical argument about Russia's unique Eurasian destiny and its superiority to decadent Western culture and soulless Russian oligarchs.[74] In the words of one prominent scholar of Europe, "Existential ambivalence has marked Russia's attitudes to Europe for centuries—Russia may appear a hesitant, inconsistent or reluctant European."[75]

Indeed, the idea and model of Europe have become less popular since Putin took power.[76] The political system fashioned by Boris Yeltsin may have been chaotic, unpredictable, and inconsistently democratic and decentralized, but it promoted de facto greater pluralism, regional variation, and freedom of expression at the same time that it gave rise to the oligarchs and to a corrupt capitalist system that lacks transparency. Under Putin, "managed democracy" and "dictatorship of laws" have replaced the Yeltsin system. Putin's political system includes widespread corruption, a symbiotic and nontransparent relationship between business and political elites, state capture of private assets, restrictions on media freedom, recentralization of political power, and a more prominent role for the security services.[77] As Putin and his allies consolidate what some have termed a "corporate state," they have moved Russia further away from European norms.[78] The conduct of the 2003 Duma elections and 2004 presidential elections and uncertainties about the 2008 succession raise serious questions about the extent to which Western norms have taken root in post-communist Russia.[79] Putin remains personally popular because he is seen to have brought stability and greater prosperity to a Russian population reeling from the chaos and unpredictability of the 1990s, many of whom associate this period of insecurity with the "democratizing" policies of the Yeltsin government. Thus, Russia is unlikely to embrace either the idea or the model of Europe as long as the current regime—and possibly its successor—prevail.

Individual European views of Russia's domestic evolution under Putin embody considerable diversity. In response to the question "Is Putin a flawless democrat?" former chancellor Gerhard Schröder in 2004 replied, "Yes, that's exactly what he is."[80] These sentiments have been echoed by some other European leaders such as former Italian prime minister Silvio Berlusconi. Other officials have been more critical, particularly the farther east one travels in Europe, which is to be expected. Nevertheless, most European governments, including the German coalition under Chancellor Angela Merkel, understand that Russia's domestic evolution toward greater democracy and the rule of law will take a matter of decades, not years, and hence advocate consistent and long-term engagement with the Kremlin and with Russian society in order to promote European norms.[81]

Energy: Russia's New Path to Great-Power Status in Europe?

One of Putin's major goals when he took office was to restore Russia's role as a player in the European state system. In 1999, he admitted that, while he understood that the fall of the Berlin Wall was inevitable, "I only regretted that the Soviet Union had lost its place in Europe, although intellectually I understood that a position based on walls and dividers cannot last. But I wanted something different to rise in its place. And nothing different was proposed. That's what hurt."[82] The challenge has been to craft a new role for Russia, one that is no longer based on military and political domination of half the continent.

It appeared that, by 2005, Russia had created a new role for itself in Europe based on economics and energy. The European Union is Russia's largest trading partner—50 percent of Russia's trade is with EU countries—although Europe is more important economically to Russia than Russia is to Europe, and Europe is Russia's largest export market. With Russia's economic recovery from the 1998 ruble collapse and rising energy prices, the country has enjoyed growth rates of 7 percent per year, making European investors increasingly bullish about the Russian stock market and about the huge domestic consumer market that is evolving. Moreover, Russia has used its windfall energy revenues to pay early many of its debts to Europe incurred both in the Soviet and post-Soviet eras. Despite the imprisonment of Mikhail Khodorkovsky, the former chief executive officer of the giant energy concern Yukos, and the destruction of his company, which was the most profitable Russian oil company, and despite uncertainties about the security of foreign investments, European investment in Russia continues to grow.

Russia's major economic significance for Europe—one that will grow over the next decade—is as an energy provider. Russia is the European Union's biggest single source of oil and gas imports. It will soon supply 50 percent of the gas needs of some European countries, including Germany and Italy; new EU members, including Poland and Lithuania, are particularly dependent on Russian hydrocarbon imports. Finland also imports 70 percent of its gas, and 70 percent of these imports come from Russia. In September 2005 President Putin and German chancellor Schröder signed a $6 billion agreement to build a gas pipeline under the Baltic Sea, bypassing Ukraine and Poland (thus not providing central Europe with gas), that will deliver more natural gas to Germany and other West European countries. Schröder, who is chairman of the pipeline's supervisory board, has said that it is "foolish" to believe that Europe can reduce its dependence on Russian oil and gas, while emphasizing that Russia is a "reliable supplier."[83]

This last remark has raised some controversy in Europe. Although Russia has never used Europe's energy dependence as a political or economic lever in the thirty years it has been exporting gas to Western Europe, it has used energy as a form of political leverage in the post-Soviet space, including with Belarus, its only ally. But the incident that caused the most concern in Europe was the gas cutoff to Ukraine on January 1, 2006, after the breakdown of negotiations with Kyiv on raising the price paid to Gazprom, Russia's giant gas monopoly with close ties to the Kremlin. Eighty percent of Russia's gas reaches Europe through Ukraine, and Europe was affected by the gas cutoff, causing some countries to question Russia's reliability as a future supplier. The gas cutoff also provoked a discussion in Russia and Europe about whether Russia had now become an "energy superpower," seeking to use its energy resources as a form of political leverage and achieve with oil and gas what it sought to achieve with nuclear weapons during the Cold War, namely, political intimidation of Europe. While the concept of an "energy superpower" is ill defined and exaggerated, the European Union has criticized Russia for refusing to ratify the European Union's Energy Charter, because that would give European companies access to the Russian energy infrastructure. Meanwhile, Gazprom is actively buying into the downstream business in several European countries, playing one company against another in negotiating deals.

As Russia grows in importance as an energy supplier to Europe, the question of where business stops and politics begins will become more complicated. The Ukrainian gas cutoff and subsequent renegotiation of terms with Kyiv has both political and economic dimensions, since Ukraine pays significantly less for its Russian gas than does Germany, for instance. Thus, Gazprom could legitimately claim that it deserved to charge higher prices for its gas. However, it is also true that, since the Orange Revolution, Russian-Ukrainian relations have deteriorated and, given Gazprom's closeness to the Kremlin (Gazprom chairman Dmitry Medvedev is the first deputy prime minister and former head of the presidential administration), there is clearly a political element in these gas negotiations. Energy remains the centerpiece of Russia's relationship with Europe, and the major theme of Russia's 2006 Group of Eight presidency was energy security. By virtue of its vast reserves of oil and natural gas, Russia under Putin has become a significant European player at a time when Europe has few alternative sources of energy.

Russia's European Diplomacy

In his approach to Europe, Putin has preferred the traditional policy of cultivating bilateral ties with selected European leaders as opposed to dealing with the European Union as an institution. He has succeeded, through his European diplomacy, in restoring Russia as a regional player. The most important relationship is with Germany, for historical and economic reasons. France and Italy also have become key partners, as has Britain, although this relationship has deteriorated since London's decision to grant asylum to Chechen rebel leader Akhmed Zakayev. By developing close bilateral ties with Europe's major powers, Russia has been able to evade some of the European Union's criticism of its domestic policies because EU remonstrations about Chechnya or democratic deficits have not been echoed in individual European capitals.

Putin's European diplomacy has also developed a transatlantic dimension. With U.S.-Russian relations in the last year of the Clinton administration at a low point because of the Kosovo war, Putin initially focused on strengthening ties with Western Europe. After the terrorist attacks of September 11, 2001, and the U.S.-Russian rapprochement that followed, speculation that Putin would choose the United States over Europe increased, because only America can bestow on Russia the recognition of great-power status that it still seeks. Putin's quick support of Washington after 9/11 was an example of Moscow taking the initiative and altering the course of relations. In the lead-up to the 2003 Iraq war, when Russia sided with France and Germany against the United States, commentators argued that Russia had decided to support Europe, because France and Germany, like Russia, view the United Nations Security Council—the only international body in which Russia has an equal voice with the United States—as the key arbiter regarding the legitimacy of the use of military force. This kind of speculation advances a false dichotomy—that if Russia joins European countries on a particular policy issue, it is trying to drive a wedge in the transatlantic alliance. Putin clearly played a weak hand with skill in the lead-up to the Iraq war, but he has been less critical publicly of U.S. policy in Iraq since the war than have other European leaders who opposed the war. He has cultivated relations with the United States, France, and Germany, as well as with European countries that supported the U.S. war, namely, Britain and Italy, demonstrating that he does not have to choose between them. Indeed, Putin alone among major world figures has enjoyed cordial relations with the leaders of the United States and all the major European countries.

Russia's relations with the United States and Europe under President Putin improved after 9/11, when Russia became an important partner in the war on terror and began to cooperate more closely with the United States on efforts to stop the proliferation of weapons of mass destruction (WMD) in Iran and North Korea.[84] Indeed, it appeared that Putin would have preferred to deal with a more united Western alliance than he has faced thus far. In contrast to the pre-Gorbachev era, when leaders tended to encourage fissures in the alliance, thus weakening the common anti-Soviet front, in the postcommunist era, the calculus changed. Shortly after the September 11 terrorist attacks and the U.S. invasion of Afghanistan two months later, Russia and the United States appeared to agree on the necessity to use military force against terrorism, whereas many European countries rejected even the notion of a "war on terror" and the legitimacy of the use of military force in these circumstances.[85] In response to the war in Iraq, on the other hand, Russia allied itself with "old" Europe (i.e., France and Germany), which opposed the invasion. The public quarreling between the United States and both Germany and France did not, in the eyes of many Russia officials, bring Russia concrete gains. Thus, the Cold War calculus appeared to have changed; Russia would prefer to deal with a more, as opposed to less, united transatlantic community. As former foreign minister Igor Ivanov said, "The preservation of a unified Euro-Atlantic community, with Russia now part of it, is of immense importance."[86]

By the end of 2004, however, the Kremlin's views appeared to have changed. Moscow believed that the "colored" revolutions in Georgia, Kyrgyzstan, and Ukraine were engineered primarily by the United States and secondarily by Europe and viewed these as a threat to its own stability. Increasingly it saw the United States as unwilling to recognize that it has legitimate interests in its neighborhood, creating obstacles to Russia's efforts to play a role on the global stage. Although it does not view Europe as an equivalent obstacle to its foreign policy goals, it nevertheless has become more wary of its relationship with Europe, prompting one Russian scholar to announce "Russia Leaves the West."[87]

The European Union

As part of this changing view, the political elite in Russia has become more critical of the European Union's reticence in offering Russia the European role they feel it deserves. Since 2004 Europe has moved closer to Russia geographically, though not politically. EU enlargement has meant that Russia's near abroad and Europe's near abroad now overlap. Not only has Russia lost the Baltic states and Eastern Europe, but these former communist countries currently have tangible interests in the western NIS and the Caucasus, which the Kremlin views as a potential threat to Russian security, as was evident during Ukraine's Orange Revolution in December 2004. EU enlargement has challenged the Kremlin to craft a policy that maximizes economic ties while minimizing the attraction of Europe for Russia's western neighbors in what the Kremlin still refers to as the post-Soviet space—Belarus, Moldova, and Ukraine. Russia's interactions with the European Union raise anew the old Pobedonostev question: Can Russia enjoy closer relations with the European Union on an economic and foreign policy level without having the European Union impinge on Russia's domestic developments?

With the European Union now at twenty-five members, including the Baltic states and their significant Russian-speaking minority, Brussels, not Moscow, sets the agenda and largely controls the evolution of these relations, which the Kremlin often finds unpalatable. The European Union's primary goal vis-à-vis Moscow is to promote policies that maximize Russia's stability and development as an effective state and minimize Russia's ability to disrupt European security and stability. As the 2000–2006 *Country Strategy Paper* declares, "Soft security threats from Russia are a serious concern for the EU and require continued engagement—nuclear safety, the fight against crime, including drug trafficking and illegal immigration, the spread of disease and environmental pollution."[88] Brussels fears that Russia's inability to tackle these security threats could have a spillover effect, potentially harming neighboring states. What happens inside Russia is therefore of direct concern to the European Union. It officially pursues a dual-track policy: engagement to raise concerns about domestic developments, including Chechnya, and promotion of Russia's European integration and advancement of "shared values."[89]

Although Russian officials used to be much more sanguine about the implications of EU enlargement than they were about NATO enlargement, their position has changed significantly since the European Union expanded in 2004.[90] Russia's changing attitude became evident in the lead-up to enlargement with the difficult negotiations over the Kaliningrad exclave. With Poland and Lithuania in the European Union, Russian inhabitants of Kaliningrad are subject to the European Union's Schengen regime, which has created a visa-free travel zone for EU members but applies restrictive criteria for non-EU members. Wary of Russians migrating illegally into EU territory, Brussels insisted that the 1.5 million inhabitants of the exclave must obtain visas if they want to travel to the Russian mainland across Lithuania. For the Kremlin and Russian citizens, the reality that Brussels has decided whether or not a Russian in Kaliningrad can visit a cousin in Pskov is another reminder of Russia's territorial losses in the postcommunist era and the humiliation of having to submit these decisions to Brussels. In November 2002, the European Union reached a compromise whereby residents of Kaliningrad receive a "facilitated transit document" for multiple entries into Russia. Nevertheless, this issue remains a festering source of resentment between Moscow and Brussels.[91] Moreover, it symbolizes the deeper question of Russia's future place in Europe, which is being divided into those "have" countries that are in the European Union and those "have-nots" such as Russia and the other post-Soviet states that are not and may never become members.[92]

Publicly the Russian government maintains a dual attitude toward the European Union. Putin has stated that Russia does not seek to join the European Union, but it does want closer association with it. On the level of pragmatic cooperation, Moscow enjoys a multifaceted relationship with Brussels. The May 2005 EU-Russia summit in Moscow produced a new agreement that supersedes the common strategy. It lays out a road map for future relations focusing on "four spaces." The first space is economic, encompassing measures aimed at increasing trade ties through boosting investments, promoting economic integration, facilitating regulatory convergence, and investing in infrastructure development. The second involves justice, freedom, and security, as well as measures to tackle "soft" security issues such as HIV/AIDS and environmental concerns. The third concerns external security, covering regional conflict and crisis management, WMD proliferation, and response to natural disasters. The fourth is focused on research, education, and culture, aiming to reinforce people-to-people contacts through exchanges and the mutual adoption of best practices. This road map represents a means of advancing the EU-Russia relationship on a pragmatic level, and, if it were fully implemented, would indeed bring Russia and the European Union much closer together. But it also represents an acknowledgment that true integration is not likely in the next decades.[93] This document will likely determine the contours of the EU-Russian relationship until the Partnership and Cooperation Agreement expires in 2007. It is unclear what will replace that agreement.

The European Union has several component parts, however, not all of which follow the same policy toward Russia. The European Parliament (like the parliamentary assembly of the Council of Europe) has irked Moscow by taking a much more critical stance on Russia's domestic situation than has, for example, the commission, emphasizing that Russia falls far short of European norms. "The gulf between words and truth has widened—the situation has now become intolerable," concluded a European Parliament report, sharply criticizing the Putin administration for its backsliding on human rights, particularly in the North Caucasus, and on democratic freedoms.[94] Thus, European parliamentarians agree that the values gap between Russia and the European Union has widened under Putin.[95]

A few independent Duma members and liberal foreign policy experts continue to advocate Russia's EU membership, partly because they believe that this would ensure that Russia becomes European in a normative sense.[96] This sentiment finds little support in the European Union. Despite occasional European murmurings to the contrary (e.g., Italian prime minister Silvio Berlusconi's backing of Russia's eventual EU membership in November 2003), Brussels has made it clear that this is highly unlikely. As the commission has said, "Russia's conformity with generally valid and European values will largely determine the nature and quality of our partnership."[97] The European Union's view is in part based on the classic European attitude toward Russia: The country is simply too large, too backward economically, and not democratic or postimperial enough to be a full partner with Europe.

For the foreseeable future, therefore, the best that Russia can hope for from the European Union is a gradual rapprochement along current lines; enlargement of the energy dialogue; more cooperation on "soft" security issues, particularly; more discussion about "hard" security cooperation within the framework of the European Security and Defense Policy; and discussions about creating a broader free-trade area in Europe. But Russia's ability to integrate more fully with Europe will be constrained by its uneven domestic development. Although its more robust economic performance and energy output in recent years have made it more attractive to Europe, the continuing war in the North Caucasus, the weakness of the rule of law, and restrictions on the media reinforce Russia's separateness from European norms.

Challenges of the "New" Europeans

The enlargement of the European Union to include former communist countries and former parts of the USSR has exacerbated official Russia's criticism of the European Union and sharpened differences between Moscow and Brussels. Simply put, the Baltic states and Poland, together with other central European states, having recently emerged from decades—even centuries—of Russian and Soviet domination and living in Russia's neighborhood, have an agenda toward Russia that differs from that of states that have been EU members for a longer period. They are determined to remain independent of Russian influence and to ensure that Russia does not try to reestablish its dominance over what has become the European Union's new neighborhood— Belarus, Moldova, and Ukraine—which is also Russia's neighborhood. Indeed, the European Union's New Neighborhood policy is designed to encourage the western NIS countries and the Transcaucasian states to develop in stable, democratic, and transparent ways. The Kremlin views the European Union— together with the United States—as a competitor in Eurasia, challenging what many Russian officials consider to be Russia's sphere of influence. As Putin told a group of Western experts, "We are not trying to restore an empire. But we want the West to take our interests into account in the post-Soviet space."[98]

The reality of EU enlargement was driven home during Ukraine's Orange Revolution in December 2004. Russia had backed Viktor Yanukovych in an election that was deemed fraudulent by the Ukrainian population. His opponent, Viktor Yushchenko, had the support of large crowds of people who gathered in Kyiv's Maidan Square to demand new elections. While Russia continued to back the pro-Moscow Yanukovych, Polish president Aleksander Kwasniewski and Lithuanian president Valdas Adamkus persuaded the foreign policy commissioner of the European Union, Javier Solana, to convene a roundtable with the feuding parties to seek to resolve the situation peacefully. A few weeks later, a third round of elections took place, and Yushchenko was installed as president. The specter of Polish and Lithuanian leaders helping to bring to power a candidate that Moscow had explicitly opposed provoked the Kremlin's ire. As Sergei Yastrzhembsky, Russia's special envoy to the European Union, said of the new EU members, "There's a kind of pushy, pestering drive to impose their view on the EU as a whole."[99] Vladimir Chizhov, Russia's ambassador to the European Union, was somewhat more diplomatic, hoping that the "beneficial impact of old European traditions" will "positively influence our former co-nationals."[100]

The relationship between Russia and the Baltic states has deteriorated since the latter joined the European Union and NATO. For example, following the entry of these states into NATO, aircraft from other member states have begun to police the border between Lithuania and Russia, raising objections from Russia regarding what it views as potential violations of its airspace. It has rejected border treaties with Estonia and Latvia, and the Kremlin was furious with both countries for boycotting the May 9, 2005, ceremonies in Moscow commemorating the sixtieth anniversary of the end of World War II. Both refused to attend because Russia would not admit to having occupied them after the war. Russian officials constantly complain that the European Union has double standards on human rights because it does not criticize Estonia and Latvia for violating the rights of Russian speakers in these two countries. This EU enlargement has complicated Moscow's pragmatic partnership with Brussels.

Beyond the Baltic states, Russia views EU (particularly Polish and Lithuanian) attempts to promote democracy in Belarus and Transcaucasia with suspicion and has criticized the European Union for not supporting its Kozak plan for resolving Moldova's Transnistria problem—a plan that would retain

Russian influence in the breakaway republic. Thus, EU enlargement has raised the specter of competition for influence in the post-Soviet space where the Russian-managed democracy model competes with the European democratic model. It is therefore possible that EU enlargement could act as a brake on the development of ties between Moscow and Brussels.

RUSSIA AND THE NEW REALITY OF EUROPE IN THE TWENTY-FIRST CENTURY

Could this potential reconsideration of the idea, model, and reality of Europe represent a return to Russia's historical pattern of reaching out to Europe and then retreating into isolation or focusing on its Asian side? Since the Gorbachev era, skepticism about whether Russia wants to be *of* Europe has continued to grow. Putin's Russia represents a rejection—at least for now—of Western values of the rule of law, democracy, and a transparent market economy. However, although its military power in Europe has largely evaporated under Putin, Russia has strengthened its role in Europe through the strategic use of energy resources. Thus, Russia has once again become a European player. However much the European Union may question its domestic political evolution, it accepts that Russia and Europe are interconnected and that it is dependent on Russian energy supplies. This model of Russia as a European player without adopting European norms has precedents in Russian and Soviet history, as this chapter shows. Europe's dependence on Russian energy supplies implies that Russia and Europe will continue to be partners irrespective of what happens inside Russia.

Two possible scenarios await Russia and Europe. In the best scenario, the EU and NATO enlargements, by creating a zone of stability, security, and prosperity on Russia's borders, could have a positive influence on both Russia and its CIS neighbors that are not in either organization. In this case, the idea and model of Europe would eventually begin to take hold within Russia more firmly than they have until now, and Russia's economy and society would gain advantages from proximity to the European Union. Similarly, Russia's more active participation in EU institutions would enable it to deal with the reality of European structures that could gradually have an impact on how Russia develops internally.

Another scenario is possible, however. The enlargement of the European Union to include poorer, postcommunist states is a tremendous challenge for

Brussels, considerably greater than NATO enlargement because it involves a wide range of domestic as well as foreign policy adaptations by the new member states. This, plus the European Union's continuing internal debates over constitutional reform and further enlargement, including to Turkey, might absorb so much of the European Union's energies that it inevitably turns inward and is unable to give much attention to its new neighbors to the east. Russia, meanwhile, as it seeks to restore its great-power status, continues to increase its influence over its neighbors, especially those that are not part of this new, prosperous European reality. The weakness of these states renders them particularly susceptible to Russian pressure both at a state-to-state level and through the role of Russian businesses, especially energy companies. The logical conclusion of this scenario is a Europe that is again divided, but the dividing line is farther east, as Russia begins to lead the states that have been excluded from either NATO or EU membership. This situation need not be static—there could be further enlargements at some later point—but this could be the reality of the first decades of this century.

A Russia that succeeds in reestablishing a dominant role in Eurasia is likely to be a Russia that is less European internally than one that continues to pursue closer ties with the European Union. Similarly, the Russia in this scenario is more likely to come into conflict with the United States if it believes that Washington has too great a presence in its traditional sphere of influence, be it central Asia, Georgia, or Ukraine. While these questions involve primarily foreign policy, they also have domestic implications for a Russia pursuing pragmatic ties with the West but trying to contain Euro-Atlantic influences at home.

Over the next few years, the Kremlin will make choices that will determine whether Russia can become a European power, both *of* and *in* Europe.[101] The experience of the last three centuries has shown that, when Russia played a major diplomatic and military role in Europe, it was un-European domestically. Indeed, at the height of Russian power in Europe, during the Soviet period, Russia was the least European internally. Today Russia has limited political power in Europe, but considerable economic power. It interacts with a European Union that has deliberately eschewed many of the traditional forms of diplomacy and sovereignty, which Russia itself has not given up. Europe's major importance for Russia is economic, and this situation is unlikely to change as long as Russian-European trade patterns remain the exchange of Russian raw materials for European manufactured goods and technology.

Russia has alternatives to Europe, but none are substitutes for what Europe can offer Russia. The United States is a significant political and security partner, but it is a far less important economic partner than is Europe. China is a significant economic and security partner, representing an alternative to Russia's Western integration. The Eurasian states are also increasingly important partners, but they offer Russia different benefits than does the European Union. In other words, Russia has alternative interlocutors, but, given its geographic situation and the attraction of the European Union's prosperity, Russia will seek closer ties with Europe if it wants to pursue economic modernization and integration into the global economy, as Putin does.

Nevertheless, it is not clear that the current or future Russian leadership will make the choice for a European Russia. For the past three centuries, Russia has viewed Europe with ambivalence. The idea of Europe, which has challenged, attracted, and repelled the Russian elite, has historically been embraced by only a small group of Russian liberal intellectuals, enlarged today by some within Russia's rising new middle class. The model has at times been embraced by a larger group of pragmatic officials and businessmen, only to be replaced by more traditional Russian statism and the "power vertical." The reality of Europe has had far more attraction for the ruling class, which has viewed it as a means to greatpower status. Debates about Europe today suggest that post-Soviet Russia has yet to decide where it belongs. Its leaders and population face the choice of overcoming their ambivalence or continuing to exist in a gray zone suspended between Europe and Eurasia. By following the Eurasian route, Russia could restore its regional clout and reinforce its traditional identity as a great power. This could bring prosperity, but it will bring neither democracy nor the rule of law. Europe and the United States can continue to offer Russia the wherewithal to take the European path. Ultimately, though, the Kremlin and the Russian people themselves will have to decide whether to become European, a choice that has preoccupied and divided them for three hundred years.

Notes

1. See Martin Malia, *Russia Under Western Eyes: From the Bronze Horseman to the Lenin Mausoleum* (Cambridge: Harvard University Press, 1999), for a provocative account of changing European views of Russia.

2. Mikhail Gorbachev, *Zhizn i Reformy* (Moscow: Novosti, 1995).

3. The address can be found in *Pravda*, December 19, 1984, p. 2.

4. Robert Legvold, "The Revolution in Soviet Policy," *Foreign Affairs: America and the World* 68, no. 1 (Winter 1998–99): 821–898.

5. For a representative discussion, see Vladimir Baranovsky, "Stroitelstvo 'obshchego evropeiskogo doma': politicheskie i ekonomicheskie aspekty," mimeograph (Moscow: Institute of World Economy and International Relations, 1987).

6. V. O. Kliuchevsky, *Kurs russkoi istorii*, cited in Mark Bassin, "Russia Between Europe and Asia: The Ideological Construction of Geographical Space," *Slavic Review* 50, no. 1 (Spring 1991): 4.

7. On April 11, 2006, the Russian Orthodox Church, warning that the world "is facing a threat of conflict between the civilizations with their different understanding of the human being," criticized Western concepts of human rights and proclaimed a "unique Russian civilization." Russian Orthodox Church, Official Web site of the Russian Orthodox Church, "Tserkov na zashchite prav cheloveka," http://www.mospat.ru/index.php?page=30830.

8. Malia, in *Russia Under Western Eyes,* argues that European perceptions of Russia had more to do with Europe's own domestic preoccupations than with what was actually happening in Russia.

9. Quoted in Reinhard Wittram, *Russia and Europe* (New York: Harcourt Brace Jovanovich, 1973), p. 61.

10. Ibid., p. 64; see also Isabel de Madariaga, "Catherine and the *Philosophes*," in *Russia and the West in the Eighteenth Century*, ed., A. G. Cross (Newtonville, MA: Oriental Research Partners, 1983), pp. 30–52.

11. For an extensive discussion of the relationship between geography and the ideologies of different groups, see Mark Bassin, "Russia Between Europe and Asia: The Ideological Construction of Geographical Space," *Slavic Review* 50, no. 1 (Spring 1991), pp. 1–17.

12. V. I. Lenin, *What Is to Be Done?* in *Essential Works of Lenin,* ed. Henry Christman (New York: Bantam, 1966), pp. 53–175. In the *Communist Manifesto,* Marx had discussed the need for a vanguard party, but Lenin was more explicit in describing its organizational structure.

13. E. H. Carr, "Russia and Europe as a Theme of Russian History," in *Essays Presented to Sir Lewis Namier,* ed. Richard Pares and A. J. P. Taylor (London: St. Martin's Press, 1956), p. 385.

14. Nicholas Riasanovsky, *Russia and the West in the Teaching of the Slavophiles* (Cambridge: Harvard University Press, 1952).

15. Nikolai Danilvevsky, *Rossiia i Evropa* (New York: Slavic Series, 1966).

16. Fyodor M. Dostoyevsky, *The Diary of a Writer, 1881* (New York: George Braziller, 1954), p. 342, cited in Iver B. Neumann, *Russia and the Idea of Europe* (New York: Routledge, 1966), p. 65.

17. Wittram, *Russia and Europe,* p. 49.

18. Malia, *Russia Under Western Eyes,* p. 31.

19. Vasily Kliuchevsky, *Peter the Great* (New York: Vintage Books, 1961), p. 262.

20. For an illuminating discussion of these themes by a contemporary observer, see Sir Donald Mackenzie Wallace, *Russia on the Eve of War and Revolution,* 1912 ed. (New York: Random House, 1961).

21. Cited in Wittram, *Russia and Europe,* p. 108.

22. Hajo Holborn, "Russia and the European Political System," in *Russian Foreign Policy,* ed. Ivo J. Lederer (New Haven: Yale University Press, 1962), p. 382.

23. Walter Laqueur, *Russia and Germany* (New Brunswick, NJ: Transaction Publishers, 1990), p. 53.

24. Marquis de Custine, *Empire of the Tsar: A Journal Through Eternal Russia* (New York: Doubleday, 1989), p. 619.

25. According to Malia, Marx accorded Russia "a grudging admiration for her unexpected revolutionary potential, but on the other hand he hated her as the worst enemy of progress in Europe because of her still barbaric autocracy." Malia, *Russia Under Western Eyes,* p. 184.

26. Some have argued that Russia was able to escape colonial conquest precisely because it sustained centralized, autocratic rule that enabled it eventually to modernize. See Marshall Poe, *The Russian Moment in History* (New York: Norton, 2003).

27. Quoted in Neumann, *Russia and the Idea of Europe,* p. 118. For a discussion of Eurasianism in exile, see ibid., pp. 110–114.

28. Quoted in ibid., p. 121.

29. For an extensive discussion of this phenomenon, see Paul Hollander, *Political Pilgrims: Travels of Western Intellectuals to the Soviet Union, China, and Cuba, 1928–1978* (Cambridge: Harvard University Press, 1981).

30. Of course, by the 1970s several European communist parties—in particular, those in Italy and Spain—had explicitly rejected the Soviet model as inappropriate for their societies.

31. See Hannah Arendt, *The Origins of Totalitarianism* (New York: Harcourt, 1951); and Franz Neumann, *Behemoth: The Structure and Practice of National Socialism, 1933–1944* (New York: Oxford University Press, 1942). For the *Historikerstreit,* see Jeffrey Herf, *Divided Memory: The Nazi Past and the Two Germanys* (Cambridge: Harvard University Press, 1997).

32. Cited in Gordon A. Craig, "Techniques of Negotiation," in Lederer, *Russian Foreign Policy,* p. 361.

33. Aleksandr Nekrich, *Pariahs, Partners, Predators: German-Soviet Relations, 1922–1941,* ed. and trans. Gregory Freeze (New York: Columbia University Press, 1997).

34. George Kennan, *Russia and the West Under Lenin and Stalin* (Boston: Little, Brown, 1960).

35. Cited in Craig, "Techniques of Negotiation," p. 365.

36. Dimitri Vokogonov, *Stalin: Triumph and Tragedy* (Rocklin, CA: Prima Publishing, 1995), p. 352.

37. Of course, Germany and Czechoslovakia had experience of democracy, however flawed, in the interwar years. The other countries' understanding of democracy, however, was far more limited. See Joseph Rothchild, *Return to Diversity: A Political History of East-Central Europe Since World War Two* (New York: Oxford University Press, 1989).

38. Quoted in Milovan Djilas, *Conversations with Stalin* (New York: Harcourt, 1962).

39. Charles Gati, *The Bloc That Failed* (Bloomington: Indiana University Press, 1990).

40. Andrei Sakharov, *Progress, Coexistence and Intellectual Freedom* (New York: Norton, 1968); and Andrei Sakharov, *My Country and the World* (New York: Vintage, 1975).

41. Solzhenitsyn has expressed these views in many places, but a succinct summary is to be found in his commencement address at Harvard University, June 8, 1978, in Alexander Solzhenitsyn, *East and West* (New York: Harper and Row, 1980), pp. 39–71.

42. For an insightful, comprehensive discussion of these policies, see William Taubman, *Khrushchev: The Man and His Era* (New York: Norton, 2003), chaps. 14–17. On the Berlin crisis, see Hope Harrison, *Driving the Soviets Up the Wall* (Princeton: Princeton University Press, 2003).

43. Zbigniew Brzezinski, *The Soviet Bloc: Unity and Conflict* (Cambridge: Harvard University Press, 1967).

44. Gati, *The Bloc That Failed*, pp. 32–35.

45. For a discussion of these bargains, see Sarah Meiklejohn Terry, ed., *Soviet Policy in Eastern Europe* (New Haven: Yale University Press, 1984).

46. Conversation between Brezhnev and Honecker, July 28, 1980, quoted in Jochen Stadt, ed., *Auf hoechster Stufe: Gespraeche mit Erich Honecker* (Berlin: Transit, 1994), p. 13.

47. For a discussion of Soviet–West German détente, see Angela Stent, *Russia and Germany Reborn: Unification, the Soviet Collapse and the New Europe* (Princeton: Princeton University Press, 1999), chap. 2.

48. For details, see Robert Kaiser, *Russia: The People and the Power* (New York: Atheneum, 1976); and Hedrick Smith, *The Russians* (New York: Quadrangle, 1976).

49. See Angela Stent, "Western Europe and the USSR" in *Areas of Challenge for Soviet Foreign Policy in the 1980s*, by Gerritt W. Gong, Angela Stent, and Rebecca V. Strode (Bloomington: Indiana University Press, 1983), pp. 1–52.

50. See Raymond Garthoff, *Détente and Confrontation* (Washington, DC: Brookings Institution, 1985), chaps. 14, 25, 28.

51. Liberal historian Mikhail Gefter, in a conversation with Gleb Pavlovsky, quoted in Neumann, *Russia and the Idea of Europe*, p. 169.

52. Igor Shafarevich, "Rusofobiya," *Nash Sovremennik*, no. 57 (June 1989), 167–192.

53. Gati, *The Block That Failed,* p. 66.

54. See Stent, *Russia and Germany Reborn,* chaps. 3, 4, 5.

55. See Angela Stent, *From Embargo to Ostpolitik: The Political Economy of West German–Soviet Relations, 1955–1980* (Cambridge: Cambridge University Press, 1980), p. 66.

56. Michael McFaul, "Drifting Away? Russia and the West," *Current History,* October 2005, p. 307.

57. See Angela Stent, "America and Russia: Paradoxes of Partnership," in *Russia's Engagement with the West,* ed. Alexander J. Motyl, Blair A. Ruble, and Lilia Shevtsova (Armonk, NY: Sharpe, 2005), pp. 260–280.

58. Andrei Kozyrev, *Preobrazhenie* (Moscow: Mezhdunarodnye Otnosheniya, 1995), p. 203.

59. See the reports by the Council on Foreign and Defense Policy, chaired by Sergei Karaganov: "Strategiya dlya Rossii," *Nezavisimaya gazeta,* August 19, 1992; and "Strategiia dlia Rossii II," *Nezavisimaya gazeta,* May 14, 1994.

60. For a more differentiated analysis of the prevailing debate, see Ted Hopf, *Social Construction of International Politics* (Ithaca: Cornell University Press, 2002), chap. 4.

61. Sergei Stankevich in *Nezavisimaya gazeta,* March 28, 1992.

62. *Sovetskaya Rossiya,* July 4, 1992.

63. Interview with Andrei Kozyrev, "Of Course We Can Return Former Russian Lands. Only Count Me Out," *Moscow News,* June 7–14, 1992, p. 2.

64. For contrasting views, see Peter Reddaway and Dmitri Glinsky, *The Tragedy of Russian Reform* (Washington, DC: United States Institute of Peace, 2001); and Leon Aron, *Yeltsin: A Revolutionary Life* (New York: St. Martin's Press, 2000).

65. See Lilia Shevtsova, *Yeltsin's Russia: Myths and Realities* (Washington, DC: Carnegie Endowment for International Peace, 1999).

66. The voucher privatization scheme involved dissolving large, state-owned companies by issuing vouchers for their shares to the companies' workforces. Most vouchers were quickly bought by a few men who became very rich from the privatizations. Loans for shares involved a few oligarchs lending money to the 1996 Yeltsin re-election campaign in return for highly lucrative assets. For a comprehensive discussion of the U.S.-Russian relationship, see James Goldgeier and Michael McFaul, *Power and Purpose: U.S. Policy Toward Russia After the Cold War* (Washington, DC: Brookings Institution Press, 2003).

67. See Angela Stent, "Russia and America: How Close an Embrace?" *World Policy Journal* 20, no. 4 (Winter 2003–2004): 75–84.

68. Stent, *Russia and Germany Reborn,* chap. 6.

69. For a detailed discussion, see Strobe Talbott, *The Russia Hand* (New York: Random House, 2002).

70. Although political scientists make the distinction between hard and soft power, if one examines closely the way in which Russia used gas supplies to Ukraine

in January 2006 to achieve its economic goals, one might conclude that energy can also be a form—albeit a nonlethal one—of hard power.

71. For a discussion of Putin's time in East Germany, see Alexander Rahr, *Wladimir Putin: Der "Deutsche" Im Kreml* (Munich: Universität Verlag, 2000).

72. Cited in Andrew Jake and Stefan Wagstyl, "Four More Years: But Will Putin's Desire for a Strong State Hamper Economic Reform?" *Financial Times*, March 17, 2004, p. 17.

73. There are several high-profile defenders of democracies, such as Grigory Yavlinsky, Vladimir Ryzhkov, Irina Khakhamada, and writers Lilia Shevtsova, Andrei Piontkovsky, and Alexander Golts.

74. Alexander Dugin, "Evraziya Prevyshe Vsego: Manifest evraziiskogo dvizhenniia," *Zavtra*, February 2, 2001, p. 8.

75. Vladimir Baranovsky, "Russia: A Part of Europe or Apart from Europe?" *International Affairs* (London) 76, no. 3 (July 2000): 445.

76. See Alexander Pumpyansky, "Do Russians Want to Join Europe?" *New Times*, September 30, 2003, pp. 36–39.

77. For different views on Putin, see Lilia Shevtsova, *Putin's Russia* (Washington, DC: Carnegie Endowment for International Peace, 2003); Andrew Jack, *Inside Putin's Russia: Can There Be Reform Without Democracy?* (Oxford: Oxford University Press, 2004); and Peter Baker and Susan Glasser, *Kremlin Rising* (New York: Scribner, 2005).

78. See *Financial Times*, June 19, 2006.

79. In the Duma elections, the pro-Putin United Russia Party, whose sole ideology is support of the Kremlin, ran virtually unopposed. In the 2004 presidential election, Putin also faced no serious opponents. The Organization for Security and Cooperation in Europe characterized both elections as not conforming to generally accepted democratic norms.

80. Schröder, speaking to the ARD television channel, cited in "Putin ist lupenreiner Demokrat," *Hamburger Abendblatt*, November 23, 2004, p. 2.

81. Author's conversations in the Federal Chancellery and Foreign Ministry, Berlin, June 2006.

82. Vladimir Putin, *First Person* (New York: Public Affairs, 2000), p. 80.

83. Schröder quoted in Stephen Boykewich, "Schroder Tells Europe to Trust Gazprom," The *Moscow Times*, June 20, 2006, p. 1.

84. For a discussion of the U.S.-Russian relationship, see Robert Legvold, "All the Way: Crafting a U.S.-Russian Alliance," *National Interest*, no. 70 (Winter 2002–2003): 21–31.

85. For a discussion of the triangular U.S.-Russian-European relationship, see Angela Stent and Lilia Shevtsova, "America, Russia and Europe: A Realignment?" *Survival* 44, no. 4 (Winter 2002–2003): 121–134.

86. Foreign Minister Igor Ivanov, interview, *Financial Times*, February 14, 2003.

87. Dmitri Trenin, "Russia Leaves the West," *Foreign Affairs* 85, no. 4 (July–August 2006): 87–96.

88. *Country Strategy Paper, 2000–2006, National Indicative Program, 2002–2003, Russian Federation* (Brussels: European Commission, December 27, 2001).

89. For a fuller discussion of these issues, see Dov Lynch, *Russia Faces Europe,* Chaillot Papers, no. 60 (Paris: European Union Institute for Security Studies, May 2003).

90. For a discussion of these issues, see Timofei Bordachev, "Russia's European Problem: Eastward Enlargement of the EU and Moscow's Policy 1993–2003," in *Russia and the European Union,* ed. Oksana Antonenko and Kathyrn Pinnick (Oxford: Routledge, 2005), pp. 51–66.

91. See Paul Holtom and Fabrizio Tassinari, eds., *Russian Participation in Baltic Sea Region-Building: A Case Study of Kaliningrad* (Gdansk: BaltSeaNet, 2002). For the agreement, see "Joint Statement on Transit Between the Kaliningrad Region and the Rest of the Russian Federation," Tenth EU-Russia Summit, Brussels, November 11, 2002, http://europa.eu.int/comm/external_relations/russia/summit_11_02/js_kalin.htm.

92. Margot Light, Stephen White, and John Lowenhardt, "A Wider Europe: The View from Moscow and Kyiv," *International Affairs* 76, no. 1 (2000): 77–88.

93. For a critical discussion of the four spaces and the road map, see Sergei Karaganov, "Russia's European Strategy: A New Start," *Russia in Global Affairs* 3, no. 3 (July–September 2005): 72–85.

94. *Report with a Proposal for a European Parliament Recommendation to the Council on EU-Russia Relations,* document A5–0053/2004, European Parliament, Brussels, February 2, 2004.

95. For an extensive discussion of EU views and the Russian response, see Hannes Adomeit, *Putin's Westpolitik: Ein Schritt vorwaerts, zwei Schritte Zurueck* (Berlin: Stiftung Wissenschaft und Politik, April 2005); and Karaganov, "Russia's European Strategy."

96. See, for example, Arkady Moshes, "Reaffirming the Benefits of Russia's European Choice," *Russia in Global Affairs* 3, no. 3 (July–September 2005): 86–97.

97. "Communication from the Commission to the Council and the European Parliament on Relations with Russia," document COM (2004) 106 09/02/04, European Parliament, Brussels, September 2, 2004.

98. Putin speaking in the Kremlin to the Valdai Club (of which the author is a member), September 5, 2005.

99. Quoted in Stefan Wagstyl, "Putin Glosses Over Tensions Between EU and Russia," *Financial Times,* October 4, 2005, p. 10.

100. Cited in *Eurasia Daily Monitor* 2, no. 147, July 29, 2005.

101. For a discussion of a broad range of views on Europe by Russia's Foreign Policy and Defense Council, see *Rossiya i Evropa: K Novoi Povestke Dnya* (Theses of the Council on Foreign and Defense Policy), Moscow, 2005.

CHAPTER 8

Global Challenges and Russian Foreign Policy

Celeste A. Wallander

T HE CONVENTIONAL IMAGE OF Russia is of a country that has only fitfully and recently emerged from the isolation imposed by its geography,
culture, and political system. Russia's diplomatic relations, foreign policy, and
place in the international system, however, have been shaped by global challenges throughout its history. Russia has never been among the most globalized countries in any given era: In 2004, it ranked forty-fourth in an index
composed of measures of economic, personal, technological, and political globalization.[1] Indeed, Russia has encountered economic, military, social, and
global challenges to varying degrees for centuries, from the earliest trading
routes that brought new influences and people to eastern Europe to the effects
of the twenty-first century's global energy markets. That Russia has faced periods of global challenge for centuries is indisputable. The question is whether
Russia's foreign policy and role on the international stage have been affected in
a systematic way that helps to facilitate an understanding of Russian foreign
policy in the twenty-first century.

In this chapter I examine the relationship of global challenges to Russian
foreign policy. I frame these challenges in terms of the concepts of globalism
and globalization. Globalization is a poorly defined and controversial concept
in academic debates, and using it as a premise or independent variable risks
opening a Pandora's box of unresolved definitional and epistemological disputes. Whatever the merit of doubts about the concept, there is nonetheless
some value to the argument that at certain points in history, connections
between states and societies change qualitatively in their scope, depth, and
reach. ·

Globalism is a condition of international relations in which networks of interdependence connecting states and societies transmit effects in one part of

the globe to others that are not in direct proximity. It is the flow of information and ideas, economic exchange, and threats not merely between states that may be neighbors, but among states not thought of as connected in a classic geopolitical sense. During centuries of international history, globalism has increased, but it also has decreased. "Globalization" refers to periods of increased globalism; "deglobalization" is the term for periods of decreased globalism.

Globalization has posed challenges and opportunities that have influenced Russian foreign policy in roughly two ways at different points over twelve centuries. The first is straightforward: The pressures and opportunities created by increases and decreases in globalism shaped the goals of Russian leaders in their foreign relations as well as the conditions under which they pursued those goals. Most important, globalism influenced Russian power, either by challenging it or by creating opportunities for resource expansion. Globalism, therefore, reordered Russia's relative power relations with important international allies and adversaries.

Second, increases in globalism created changes in Russian society that inevitably stressed the existing order. The stresses of change almost always inspired a state response and attempts by the political elite to control their effects—to reinforce imaginary state boundaries revealed as permeable by globalism—while pursuing their potential benefits. The attempt usually succeeded in increasing internal political control through adaptation of domestic political institutional arrangements, but not in a way that positioned Russia to benefit from globalism's new opportunities. The result was the reinforcement of a Russian tendency to fall back on a foreign policy strategy of catching up, of managing weakness and second-class status among the great powers. In particular, Russia's tendency to fall behind in achieving the economic, scientific, and technological benefits of globalization revealed its weaknesses, which Russia's leaders then sought to redress primarily through military and political means in its foreign policy.

Globalism and Globalization: Definitions and Conceptualizations

Popular conceptions associate globalization with modern international economic integration and have sparked debates about whether it is a positive or negative phenomenon.[2] In this vein, globalization connotes a unidirectional process, in which the world is increasingly enmeshed in a web of global contact and exchange.[3] In addition to being factually incorrect—there have been periods of deglobalization as well—such conceptions carry the implication that globalization is an inexorable phenomenon that countries may as well accept. States and societies, however, have a choice: They can encourage and embrace globalization; they can work to manage it; or they can even resist it. And far from being an unmitigated good, modern globalization also brings a host of challenges, including terrorism, instability in global monetary markets, and the spread of HIV/AIDS. Even generally positive networks of interdependence, such as multinational trade, can have destabilizing effects on states and societies. Contemporary globalization may be a given, but openness to its effects can be a matter of national choice and international governance.[4]

Globalism is a condition that involves "networks of interdependence at multicontinental distances."[5] It can be economic, environmental, sociocultural, or military. Economic globalism concerns flows of goods, services, and capital. Environmental globalism entails atmospheric phenomena such as pollution or diseases such as HIV/AIDS that are transported or transmitted across continental distances. Social and cultural globalism involves the movement of ideas, information, knowledge, and beliefs. This can entail simple or discrete bits of knowledge—such as instant global access to images of the terrorist attacks on the World Trade Center and the Pentagon on September 11, 2001—to systems of belief—such as the transnational networks of belief and commitment created by Al-Qaeda. Military globalism is perhaps the most difficult dimension to accept as qualitatively different from mere political-military affairs between states. However, as with the trade among neighboring countries of nationally produced goods versus commercial relations with production and sales involving countries across the globe, there is a qualitative difference between disputes and conflicts between neighboring countries over territory or power and military threats with global reach and impact such as imperialism, nuclear proliferation, and a range of other transnational security concerns.

Globalization and deglobalization are themselves consequences of changes in technology and costs. Global security and military threats in the twentieth century resulted from the invention of long-range aircraft and ballistic missiles. Contemporary globalization is the product of advances in information technology, primarily the Internet. Future deglobalization may well be the result of the rising costs of fossil fuels and the increase in economic and transaction costs that could cause contraction of global markets. The fracturing of economic networks during World War I most directly caused deglobalization, but it was sustained after the war by the high costs of international financial exchange and international trade.

Globalization occurs when any of the following four aspects of globalism increase (and deglobalization occurs with a decrease in any of the four): (1) extensity (the extensiveness of the networks of interdependence), (2) intensity (the number of networked and interdependent relationships), (3) velocity (the speed with which these networks transmit the effects of interdependence), and (4) impact (the degree to which the interdependencies extend into the cultures, states, or societies networked through globalism).[6]

Modern globalism is clearly of a different scale in extensity, intensity, velocity, and impact than earlier periods of globalization. Analysts have coined the term "thick" globalism to denote a form of globalization that involves multiple relationships along several dimensions that has a deep impact on states and societies. An example of "thin" globalization is the Silk Road. The economic and cultural relationships along the Silk Road linking Europe with the Far East signaled a period of increased globalism. They did not, however, involve large numbers of people, nor did they deeply influence economic and social relationships within the societies. In comparing the impact of globalization over time, therefore, it may be useful to determine whether it is thick or thin.[7]

In assessing whether the rise of globalism affects a country's foreign policies, however, it may not be as important to know whether the globalism in question is thick or thin, because the relevant points of comparison may be the periods preceding and following the increase or decrease in globalism. Thus, if one is interested in understanding the effects on Russian foreign policy of rising globalism, the points of comparison are before and after changes in globalism. Therefore, one should not ignore early periods of globalism for their potential impact on foreign policy, even if by comparison they were thin. The relevant issue is whether increases in economic, military, environmental, or sociocultural globalism—through increases in extensity, intensity, velocity, or impact—have influenced Russian foreign policy, and if so, how.

GLOBALIZATION, GLOBALISM, AND FOREIGN POLICY

Globalization can affect a country's foreign policy in several ways. First, it can bring new resources to the state or society; it can increase trade, spur innovation, and create efficiencies—in short, it can lead to economic growth and development. In a recent study, the World Bank notes that countries that

participate in globalization tend to experience growth, whereas nonpartici-
pants suffer from lower levels of development and slower reductions in poverty.[8] Access to ideas and information can also stimulate economic development
by supporting innovation, or at least emulation of new technologies and practices, enabling less advanced economies to lower costs or incorporate efficient
practices that encourage growth. The spread of railroads in the late nineteenth
century, for example, not only was a cause of the economic globalization that
marked the period 1850–1914 (by reducing transportation costs for trade), but
was itself a result of the globalization of knowledge and information about this
new technology, as it diffused from Britain and the United States to other European countries, and ultimately to European colonies in Africa and Asia. Military globalization has allowed strategically located, innovative, or simply lucky
countries to increase their national power for defense and security, or for expansion and conquest.[9]

Globalization as a source of resources to enhance wealth and power thus
potentially influences a country's foreign policy in two ways. First, it can increase the resources and power available to a state either directly (by expanding the state's military capabilities or the assets available to it, such as colonial
possessions) or indirectly (through taxation of successful economic activities
or its citizens). Second, the prospect of such resources and power may come to
define a state's national interests or objectives. That is, while a country may not
naturally benefit from the opportunities of globalization, the ambition to gain
from globalization shapes the definition and pursuit of its foreign policy.

Globalism, however, is not only about opportunities; it is also about challenges. This is the second main causal path by which globalism affects foreign
policy. Increases in the extensity, intensity, velocity, or impact of networks of
economic, environmental, military, or sociocultural interdependencies challenge states' social and political institutions, especially their ability to regulate
and control the lives and behavior of their citizens. States are, after all, human
constructs. They may or may not match well with their geography, indigenous
cultures and languages, commercial potential, or flows of environmental effects (e.g., acid rain) that transcend state boundaries. Throughout history,
increases in globalism have challenged states by creating transnational relationships and opportunities that do not fit well with existing state structures,
by creating transnational problems that they may not be well equipped to han-
dle, and by creating conditions that may challenge the legitimacy or authority
of existing states. Changes in globalism challenge states simply by bringing
changes in information, ideas, resources, wealth, disease, and external threats.

If a state's claim to legitimacy lies in its role to protect the lives and property of its citizens, what becomes of that legitimacy in an era of global conquest, for example, the assault of the Mongols against the early Russian state? Or, if one of the primary functions of the modern state is to manage macroeconomic and monetary policy to maintain stable conditions so that individuals and firms can make long-term investment decisions, what legitimacy does that state have if it cannot prevent a monetary crisis that results in the devaluation of the national currency and the consequent disappearance of the value of the savings of millions of its citizens? The greater degree to which capital can move freely in a highly globalized world has undermined a key mechanism by which the state has historically been able to exercise control over its economy.[10]

That is, globalization can challenge the state's role as a state. A state, or rather the political leadership that controls it, can respond by adapting well to new challenges. It can develop new capacities for dealing with new areas of economic policy, for example, by establishing a ministry for industry or perhaps a ministry for agriculture. It can build defenses appropriate to the new military challenges it faces. It can cooperate with the governments of other countries to create international institutions to manage transnational global challenges, such as unregulated financial flows or criminal networks.

Although no government can prevent globalism as a general phenomenon, states can often erect barriers to its networks of interdependence. A state can make its national currency nonconvertible and can tax, or even prohibit, imports. It can require foreign importers to buy and sell only with state agencies as a means to control economic activity within the country and the value of its currency. Although preventing globalism or globalization is impossible, a state can take actions that to some degree can insulate it from their effects. In doing so, however, the state may forgo the opportunities of globalization. Barriers to trade maximize control and minimize foreign influence over the state and its society, but they limit the efficiency effects of free trade. A nonconvertible currency immunizes a country against imported inflation or instability in global financial markets, but it increases the costs of commerce. State control of foreign trade either adds costs to transactions (because the state is acting as an intermediary for private and domestic private entrepreneurs) or undermines market efficiencies (if the state itself is deciding what to buy and sell rather than the private sector responding to market mechanisms).

Globalism, therefore, challenges states to craft foreign policies that manage the negative effects arising from their vulnerability to its destabilizing influences, while taking advantage of its positive effects. In the contemporary world, this could entail, for example, whether and under what conditions a state should join the World Trade Organization. In earlier eras, it could have meant whether a state should join alliances for common defense that could have also led the country into war. Or, in a period of military globalism, it might mean the choice of a foreign policy of expansionism to extend national borders away from core economic and political regions of the country, or retrenchment to retreat from confrontation.

The third causal relationship between globalism and foreign policy lies in the effects of globalism on states and societies themselves. Changes in globalism can alter the balance of social, economic, and political power and interests within states. Economic globalization can give rise to new economic winners, who might seek to change the political conditions under which they engage in commercial activities. For example, globalization that brings industrialization can create new successful economic players in a formerly agrarian society. Increasing transnational financial flows may undermine a state's control of its monetary policy in favor of private investors who have their own objectives, while changes in trading partners may challenge the importance of old allies. The availability of information about events abroad may confound the ability of governments to remain impervious to societal pressures in foreign policy, as the Russian state learned in the early twentieth century with the rise of Slavicist sentiment focusing attention on Russian policy in the Balkans. Globalization thus forces states to deal with shifting configurations of power and interest within their societies. In this way, globalism potentially influences foreign policy by affecting the array of domestic interests and actors, which in turn shape foreign policy interests, capabilities, and priorities.

As in the case of responding to new challenges, states can react in a variety of ways to how globalism alters their internal politics, economics, and societies. They can adapt through constitutional or legislative means, through peaceful and legal changes of regime, or through mechanisms that involve new economic and social interests in political decision making and governance. Political systems can adapt to cope with the destabilizing effects of global change. For example, changes in economic opportunities that create unemployment in some sectors can be managed through social welfare programs, education, and retraining programs. Changes in the ideas and interests of new economic or social actors can be peacefully incorporated into policy through representative political institutions such as legislatures.

States can also respond, however, by raising barriers to globalism. Ideas that do not align with national cultural or political norms can be filtered, censored, or prosecuted. Foreign investors can be banned or simply deterred by creating a prohibitive or unwelcoming domestic legal environment. In preventing or limiting globalism's effect on its society, however, the state is choosing to forgo the opportunities, resources, and efficiencies that can be realized in larger markets of economic, social, and political exchange. The state may be able to prevent, or at least minimize, changes that networks of interdependence introduce to its society, but in so doing, it forfeits the benefits as well as the costs of change.

Thus, a key factor in the relationship of globalism and foreign policy is whether and how a country's government and society choose to accept or reject globalization. The ability to make a cup of coffee from beans grown in Kenya in a coffee machine manufactured in Germany while reading about U.S. casualties in Iraq on the Internet via a computer manufactured with parts from several different Asian countries is an example of the penetration of modern globalization into one's daily life. That all of this happens, however, is a result of the policy choices of the government, and likely of society. The state could have chosen to protect local coffee growers and domestic consumer goods manufacturers by raising tariffs or prohibiting trade, and to declare information about wars a threat to national security. The choice is shaped by the country's situation and experience. How vulnerable is it to external attack? How diversified is its economy? How stable is the national culture? How functional and adaptive are its basic political institutions?

For Russia, globalism is both a challenge and an opportunity in the context of substantial geopolitical vulnerability and temptation, great natural wealth but lagging economic development, a multilayered identity and national culture, and a state tradition of leading society rather than responding to it. As a result, Russia has usually reacted to global challenges by seeking greater state control and management of the opportunities and challenges they present. This approach has almost never worked, however, and has instead weakened Russia's position internationally. This in turn has contributed to Russia's pattern of falling behind and having to catch up.

Understood from this perspective, the question of Russia's foreign policy response to globalism becomes richer and more in need of significant historical analysis. It is as legitimate to analyze the foreign policy responses of states and cultures to the globalization of Alexander the Great's empire, or of the Roman Empire, as to the globalization of today.

In the Russian case, globalism first occurred with the exploration by Viking traders through the lakes and river systems of East Central Europe in the ninth century, and the East-West trading globalization that linked Europe with Central Asia and China. Russia's second encounter with globalization occurred in a military form, with the Mongol invasions of the thirteenth century. This period partly caused and partly gave way to a long period of deglobalization in the European and Eurasian regions. For Europe, globalism increased with the Age of Exploration of the sixteenth and seventeenth centuries and the development of European global empires, a process that largely bypassed Russia. Russia's isolation and backwardness as a result of its peripheral position led to a form of globalization manufactured by Peter the Great in the early eighteenth century. For the most part, however, the rise of trade, global travel, and commerce, as well as the exploration of the Western Hemisphere, did not engage or involve Russia. The foreign policy of Russia during this period is instructive, therefore, because the country did not face the challenges and opportunities of rising globalism. It is also instructive because this was the period of the great expansion of the Russian Empire under Peter and his successors and of the emergence of the empire as a European great power.

This situation changed at the beginning of the nineteenth century, with the Napoleonic wars. Once again, Russia's main encounter with a global challenge proved to be military. By midcentury the subsequent instabilities and social changes in Europe that sparked reform and revolution brought a new form of cultural and ideational globalism to a conservative, monarchist, and imperial Russia. As a result of its achievement of great-power status, Russia would increasingly experience the same waves of rising globalism as other European and western Eurasian countries. But even though its experience with industrial, trade, communications, technological, and cultural globalization during the period 1870–1914 differed in many respects from that of other European countries (and from that of the United States), it was no less multidimensional or comprehensive. And like the other European great powers, Russia, too, experienced the deglobalization that began with World War I and lasted through the economic dislocations of the 1920s and 1930s. Even when it embraced economic and social isolation, the Soviet Union learned, as had Russia before it, that it was not as easy to avoid military globalization when confronted with the threat of a second world war.

In contrast, the Soviet Union's isolation went against the tide of rising economic and cultural globalization in the period 1950–1970, which was based on the liberalization of trade and the global spread of American ideas and culture—especially through the media. At the same time, the Soviet Union was fully a part of the growth of military globalism because, through its policies, technology, and industry, it drove global military challenges as much as the United States did. With its embrace of détente in the 1970s, the Soviet Union began to seek some of the same economic, trade, and technology benefits that other participants in globalizing commerce were pursuing; this had profound effects on Soviet foreign policy and ultimately on the Soviet Union itself. The seeds of the Soviet Union's failure were sown with its opening to the West in the 1970s, not in its confrontation with the United States in the 1980s. Economic, social, and cultural globalization were at least as much the causes of Mikhail Gorbachev's "new thinking" as was the Soviet Union's inability to keep pace in military spending and competition. It might be an overstatement, but it is still interesting to contemplate that, at least in part, globalization won the Cold War.

Finally, there is the current period of globalization, driven primarily by the liberalization of financial markets and advances in information technology. Globalization since the 1980s has been "thick": It has economic, military, cultural, and environmental forms; it reaches deeply into the states and societies it touches; and the velocity of its effects is measured in minutes, days, and weeks, not decades or even years as in previous periods of globalization. Because contemporary globalism is so different from that of earlier periods in its reach and impact, it is not surprising that globalization is having an effect on Russian foreign policy. What is somewhat unexpected is the degree to which many aspects of the relationship between globalism and Russian foreign policy at the beginning of the twenty-first century are familiar in Russia's history.

Contemporary Russian Foreign Policy

Russia's first post-Soviet leadership sought out and embraced globalism's opportunities. Ultimately, however, it was defeated in part by both the reality and fear of globalism's challenges. President Boris Yeltsin's domestic political and economic priorities were to change fundamentally the Soviet political and economic system, with two immediate objectives. The first was straightforward, well articulated, and perhaps somewhat idealistic: to establish a democratic political system and a market economy with private ownership. The second was more political, strategic, and unspoken: to shatter the institutions and resources of Soviet power, create new powerful classes of interests in Russia that would oppose a return to the Soviet past, and make the changes irreversible.[11]

These were internal goals that could have been accomplished with a strictly domestic political strategy. In the context of a globalized world at the beginning of the 1990s, however, the Yeltsin government's internal reform policies involved global mechanisms as well, and therefore fundamentally enmeshed Russian domestic and foreign policy. The effect was in part deliberate but in large measure a feature of how reducing barriers to global forces is difficult to accomplish selectively.

The Yeltsin government deliberately sought global forces to leverage resources, expertise, and even power for its reform programs. It sought resources in the form of foreign investment, official government assistance, and loans and credits from international organizations. It accepted technical assistance from both Europe (TACIS, the European Union-funded program) and the United States (primarily in the form of U.S. Agency for International Development programs). Russia was flooded with foreign advisers expert in elections, constitutions, government budgets, monetary policy, privatization, media campaigns, and social programs. These advisers and programs were by and large welcomed by the Russian government in the early 1990s, often given space to operate in official Russian government buildings.[12] International experts and expertise included World Bank and International Monetary Fund officials and delegations, technical assistance programs funded bilaterally by the European Union and the United States, and private programs such as the Strengthening Democratic Institutions project, housed within the John F. Kennedy School of Government at Harvard University and funded by Western private foundations. Western consultants performed a variety of official and nonofficial roles in decisions to free prices, to pursue and implement voucher privatization, and to emphasize certain economic policy goals (e.g., sustaining the value of the ruble) over others (e.g., encouraging investment by maintaining low interest rates). Although ultimately the responsibility for the policy choices was the Yeltsin leadership's, ideas and certain models of economic reform—"shock therapy" among them—were imported from abroad.[13] Policy responsibility was the government's, but with regard to causal pathways, the impact of highly influential globalized networks of policy ideas was paramount.

As much as the ideas and the resources themselves, opening Russia to foreign delegations, projects, and experts afforded the Yeltsin government—or was meant to afford it—leverage against domestic opponents of the policies. What better way to rule out alternative proposals for privatization, or slower approaches to freeing prices, or government spending priorities, than to point to the conditionality and expectations of international private and official actors? Yeltsin government officials welcomed Western conditionality in the first few years because it allowed them to push through programs opposed in the legislature. The government's programs could be justified as being part of International Monetary Fund programs, required to obtain credits and resources to support reform.[14]

Because the leadership's basic strategy was to secure Western support for Russia's internal reforms via resources, expertise, and leverage, the need to engage with and accommodate Europe and the United States became a driving force in the Yeltsin government's foreign policy.[15] This is not to argue, however, that there were not other reasons for an integrationist, Western-oriented foreign policy. Foreign Minister Andrei Kozyrev was not merely being instrumental when he laid out a foreign policy that called for Russia to become part of the "civilized" West—there was an ideational motivation behind his commitment as well. Still, the instrumental value of the strategy within Yeltsin leadership circles accounted for its broad support. Russian leaders understood that if Europe and the United States were to be receptive to their country's economic and trade policies, they needed to send signals that Russia was truly post-Soviet in its political and security realms as well.

This context of leverage encouraged Russian cooperation with regard to many important security and military issues. It facilitated the ultimate withdrawal of Russia's military forces from the newly independent Baltic states; a negotiated and balanced agreement on revising the Conventional Forces in Europe Treaty on terms to which the newly independent countries could agree; Russian acceptance that Ukraine, Kazakhstan, and Belarus would be involved in updating and implementing the START I treaty; and a measure of restraint in some of the conflicts that emerged in the post-Soviet states in which Russia was suspected of playing a neo-imperial role.[16]

Contemporary globalization influenced Russian foreign policy in its first years by facilitating linkage with the West. This was not an inexorable effect, however; it happened as a matter of choice—constrained choice to be sure, but choice nonetheless. To achieve certain domestic goals, the Yeltsin leadership opted for a strategy made possible by the existing context of global networks of interdependence, which in turn required a foreign policy of engagement and accommodation. Russia sought membership in numerous international organizations, particularly Euro-Atlantic institutions that bind it to follow their rules, at least in theory.[17]

Two problems crippled Yeltsin's strategy. First, although the Soviet Union had passed into history, the state had not been transformed overnight into a modern, Western, liberal democratic structure well adapted to the extensity, intensity, velocity, and impact of contemporary globalism. The controlling force of the Communist Party was gone, but the enormous bureaucracies, ministries, agencies, layers of governments at the regional and local levels, and practices of patrimonialism and corruption remained.[18] New social and economic actors encountered a kind of hybrid Soviet state with freewheeling elections and a newly liberated media, all unconstrained by a legitimate legal or regulatory system. Wealth could be accumulated by exercising new freedoms, but mostly it was made by knowing how to play the structures of the Soviet state through patron-client relations and insider deals. The media could report on any issue its editors and journalists sought to pursue, but often important media outlets were the tools of those who owned them.[19]

At least two consequences flowed from the creation of a new Russian state that combined inefficient features of the Soviet political system with one that embraced many of the liberating aspects of democratic political systems—but without their stabilizing features. First, much of the technical expertise either went to waste (as the overwhelming majority of bureaucrats simply ignored new methods and concepts) or was imposed by undemocratic means on a state and society that neither understood nor embraced its requirements or implications. For many Russians, globalization in the 1990s came to mean costly policies forced on the country by their leaders, who turned out to be unaccountable to their citizens. And because reforms took place in the context of a strategy of using globalization and the international community to motivate and sustain painful change, Russians blamed not only their leaders but also those global forces.[20] Second, Russia in the 1990s benefited little from the opportunities and advantages of opening to the international economy because its economic system remained highly corrupt, concentrated, politicized, unaccountable, and opaque. Opening to global financial markets did not attract investment and capital; instead, it facilitated capital flight. Privatization did not promote entrepreneurship; it encouraged asset stripping, created large and unproductive business holdings, and discouraged foreign direct investment. Shifting to a market economy did not subject Russian businesses and the Russian state to the disciplining constraints of the market; rather, it enabled them to amass wealth without the threat of bankruptcy and spend

state funds without balancing the budget, largely by attracting foreign investors willing to enter the new Russian stock market and purchase Russian government securities bearing favorable interest rates.[21]

The second problem of Yeltsin's strategy was the challenge of globalization for
an unstable society and unprepared political system expected to incorporate decades of political, economic, and social evolution in only a few years.
Globalization is always disruptive: For a Russia emerging from decades of effective isolation undergoing political, economic, social, and cultural revolution,
globalization strained an already unstable country. And although structures of
the Soviet state and economy remained, they were incapable of managing the
forces and effects of change in ways that contributed to the long-term well-being
and development of the country. True, by the mid-1990s an individual could buy
any consumer good he or she wanted (if that consumer was in Moscow and had
the resources). Because of both the lure of the new and the effects of policies to
keep the value of the ruble low, however, globalization fueled growth in imports
and failed to stimulate Russian industry and enterprises. True, Russians could
invest in newly privatized companies or use their government vouchers to join
investment funds. But the lack of transparency, regulation, and most of all a legal
system for protecting the rights of average investors left millions cheated by industry or political insiders and unscrupulous pyramid schemes. True, Russia
held elections in the 1990s, with competing candidates. But biased media owned
by newly wealthy interests prevented genuine debate and criticism of the Yeltsin
leadership's policies in, for example, the 1996 elections. And true, the repressive
machinery of the Soviet state no longer intruded on the lives of Russians. At the
same time, however, Russians' insecurity grew in other ways, including a war in
Chechnya in 1994–1996, rising murder rates, and NATO's use of force against
Serbia in Kosovo in 1999, which to Russians meant that the West was neither a
benevolent nor a reliable security partner.[22]

Even before the Russian financial crash of August 1998 and the series of
bombings attributed to Chechen separatists in September 1999,[23] Russia's society and leadership had begun to question whether embracing globalization
would ever make them prosperous. Opening to the world economy increased
Russia's vulnerability to the effects of the Asian financial crisis.[24] Openness to
international trade had created balance-of-payments deficits (oil prices were
low in this period, as low as $15 per barrel) and contributed to deindustrializa-
tion. Most of all, from the Russian perspective the West's advice on "shock
therapy" had given rise to an economic system that produced little and benefited a handful of oligarchs. What was to like?

From the Russian perspective, the experiment with embracing globalization (primarily by opening Russia to the international financial and economic system and decreasing state regulation of domestic and international market exchanges) to create synergy in foreign and domestic policy was discredited.[25] The Russian economy actually shrank 50 percent in the 1990s; Russia's acceptance of international loans and assistance left it deeply in debt and burdened with policies that did not provide the basis for future growth and prosperity, instead enriching a small group of Russians who either broke the rules or manipulated them to win. In the security realm, Russia's weakened state increased its vulnerability to new types of conflict, including regional instability on its borders and domestic terrorism. This new insecurity, moreover, was not mitigated by a strong cooperative partnership with the United States. Instead it was exacerbated by the enlargement of NATO's membership and mission, which at least some influential Russian leaders believed could be used to dominate their country.

With the election of Vladimir Putin in 2000, the realities of globalization did not change, although Russia's internal and foreign policy responses to it did. During President Putin's first term, it became clear what the leadership believed the problem to be: not globalism per se, but how the Russian state managed the flow of opportunities and challenges.

The basic strategy of growth through international trade was preserved. As Robert Legvold notes in his contribution to this volume (chapter 2, "Russian Foreign Policy During Periods of Great State Transformation,") Putin's focus has been on the domestic economy, but for Putin that also means the global economy and Russian participation in it. The 1998 financial crisis produced enormous loss and a fall in living standards, but it also cut imports (by causing a devaluation of the ruble), reduced debt (because of defaults), and lowered interest rates (because the government was not borrowing money). More important, the conditions for an economic and financial restructuring coincided with a rise in global oil prices—from $15 per barrel in 1998 to $70 per barrel in 2006. This fueled growth not only in Russia's gross national product but also in the government's revenues and the country's trade surpluses. The increase in oil prices helped Russia to restore its production capacity, which had fallen to 6 million barrels per day by the mid-1990s from highs in the Soviet period. The lure of higher prices and greater investment in the oil sector resulted in the production of 9.5 million barrels per day in 2006. Furthermore, because of the decline of the Russian economy in the 1990s, there was less domestic demand for Russian oil, so instead of exporting less than one-quarter of its production, today's Russia exports two-thirds of its production, 6.5 million barrels per day.[26]

This means, at least in the short to medium term, that the Putin government does not need the United States as much, or in the same way, as did the Yeltsin government. No longer desperate for International Monetary Fund credits or leverage to implement reforms, the Putin leadership does not need to pursue a foreign policy of accommodation in the political and security spheres to win financial support. Economic growth and international integration as means to improving Russian development, national security, and overall well-being remain at the core of Russia's foreign policy, but the government is no longer as vulnerable as it once was. Trade increased; international investors and businesses returned to Russia; computer ownership and Internet usage grew; and Russians used their new prosperity to purchase foreign as well as domestically produced consumer goods and to travel abroad.[27]

Economic interests do not stand alone, however, in defining Russian foreign and security policy: They stand alongside strategic interests in how Russia defines its security and status—that is, Russia as an influential, autonomous, and legitimate great power. The enmeshing of these core economic and strategic national interests was summarized in Putin's "state of the union" address to the Russian Federal Assembly on May 26, 2004: "Now, for the first time in a long time, Russia is politically and economically stable. It is also independent, both financially and in international affairs, and this is a good result in itself." He goes on, "We want high living standards and a safe, free, and comfortable life for the country. . . . We want to strengthen Russia's place in the world." Moreover, "we must grow faster than the rest of the world if we want to take the lead within today's complex rules of global competition. We must be ahead of other countries in our growth rate, in the quality of our goods and services and level of our education, science, and culture. This is a question of our economic survival. It is a question of ensuring that Russia takes its deserved place in these changing international conditions."[28]

Therefore, Russia's is not a foreign policy driven by economic growth for economic growth's sake. It is one driven by economic growth for the sake of power, autonomy, and global position.[29] Economic interests do not drive Russia's foreign policy, although they are extremely important to it. Russian interests in expanding its energy exports explain its relations with Europe, its increasing interest in the Commonwealth of Independent States, its growing attention to Japan and China, its commercial relations with Iran, and its concerted efforts to increase foreign arms sales (which amounted to more than

$6.1 billion in 2005). Foreign trade, particularly in the energy sector, is very much in the commercial and economic interests of Russia's businesspeople and, through overall growth in the economy, its citizens.

For foreign policy, this meant a change in tone, direction, and tactics. The United States remains important, but it is not all encompassing. More important, U.S. preferences and criticism matter far less to a Putin government that can pay its bills and count on domestic support. The reduced focus on the United States and the increased appreciation of the power and economic value of Russia's energy assets and transit corridors have contributed to a greater, more strategic focus on Europe, Asia, and the newly independent countries on Russia's borders. Russia's interest in internal trade and business is not limited to interest and activity in the West, but applies as much to relations with the countries of what Russia continues to conceptualize as the Commonwealth of Independent States.

The impact of globalization on Russian foreign policy is mediated by the leadership's determination to control and manage globalization's challenges while pursuing its opportunities. Rising trade is fine, but foreign ownership of Russian oil or gas is not, because the globalization of international business brings transparency and the primacy of commercial interests to policy. International summits and modern global media technologies are useful benefits of the globalization of technology and communication, but only if their message is controlled by the Russian state. Opportunities for great power partnership to address global security and political challenges such as transnational terrorism, proliferation, and trafficking are part of Russia's proper status as a great-power member of the United Nations Security Council and the Group of Eight, but the international community is not welcome either to offer its views on whether Russia's elections are free and fair or to play any role in the resolution of conflicts in the countries of the former Soviet Union. High-profile international conferences involving leading Western scholars and policy figures are welcome in Russia, but Russian nongovernmental organizations and civil society groups are suspect if they receive funding from international foundations.

Putin's foreign policy is one of recognizing both the advantages and the dangers of globalization for his goal of increasing Russia's power, stature, and wealth. The result is a foreign policy that is active but not expansionist, sensitive to asserting prerogatives but cautious in exerting Russia's still-limited power. Most important, it is a foreign policy based on a strategy of growth through international trade, as well as the increasing role of the state in controlling the economy, society, and globalization's influences. It is an internationalist foreign policy, but not a liberal one, and in that regard, Putin's policy has a long pedigree in Russian history.

Kyivan Rus and Russia's Global Origins

Russia owes its origins to the pressures and flows of globalization. With established khanates to the southeast, Byzantium to the southwest, and Franks to the west, Slavic tribes occupied the lands of East Central Europe. It was territory difficult to hold and easy to traverse, both because it is relatively flat and because it is a basin of great western Eurasian rivers: the Volga River, flowing from the southern Baltic region to the Caspian Sea; the Don River, flowing from south of the Volga's headwaters into the Sea of Azov; and the network of rivers originating in the Gulf of Finland and linking up with the Dnieper before it flows into the Black Sea.

While ranging far into Western Europe and even into the North Atlantic, Viking traders in the eighth and ninth centuries looked east and were attracted to the region of agricultural Slavic tribes for the trading and commercial networks made possible by this north-south network of rivers linking the Baltic Sea with the Black and Caspian seas. Furthermore, these river trading routes intersected the western reaches of the great Eurasian Silk Road. Controlling the western Eurasian rivers meant accessing trade with Byzantium, South and Central Asia, and China. By traveling these river routes, traders could buy the hides, fur, wax, and honey produced in northern forests and sell or trade them for gold, silver, wine, silk, and other advanced goods produced in the Near East and Asia.[30]

The growing transport and global commercial opportunities drew the Varangians (as the Slavs called the Vikings) to the region. Merely participating in the trade, however, was not enough. First, the Vikings were not just traders and sailors; they were also warriors seeking to extend their rule as well as their restless search for wealth. Second, rivers are vulnerable commercial transit routes because they lack the broad expanse of oceans or seas, and ships can be easily attacked from their banks. Securing regular and profitable trade through these extensive river systems also required defenses and control of the surrounding land.

Therefore, the Rus (the name the Varangians called themselves) established fortified settlements along the trade routes from Scandinavia to the Black Sea. A major settlement was founded on the Dnieper in the mid-ninth century where defenses against eastern steppe warrior states were necessary to secure the trade; the settlement became known as Kiev (or Kyiv, in Ukrainian). Having established its position and with growing wealth and power, Kyivan Rus began to push back weaker neighboring political communities and to negotiate with the more powerful ones. Having failed to defeat or occupy Byzantium, the Russian rulers concluded commercial agreements with its leaders. They battled and held at bay steppe nomads, although they failed to hold the territory between the Black and Caspian seas for long. Kyivan Rus developed a foreign policy of military defense against the khanates on its southeastern borders, relative subordination but commercial cooperation with Byzantium (the power to its south), and encouragement of trade in its towns and on its rivers. Globalism affected the foreign policy of Kyivan Rus primarily in its economic and commercial relations, while the proto-Russian state's geopolitical position required a security policy that emphasized territorial defense, as it would to varying degrees throughout Russia's history.

Russia's surprising character as primarily a commercial player in the foreign affairs of this period resulted from the impact of commercial globalism. This shaped, to some extent, Russia's early forms of political organization. The desire to trade had brought the Varangians to Slavic lands. The need to consolidate, defend against, and negotiate with the neighboring political forces created the basis for the political organization of their rule over Slavic peoples and leaders. Economic activity at the level of the Slavic communities was primarily agricultural. As the Kyivan prince developed relationships with primary supporters and local leaders, he granted them the right to collect tribute from their communities, with obligations to pay him a tribute. Over time, the Kyivan prince would send sons or brothers to rule towns and communities in his name, a system that worked when it fostered loyalty and did not when it fostered rivalry.

The Kyivan state (such as it was) was based on concepts of relationships and obligation, based in turn on family lineage for authority but also on the relationship and obligations of the community to local leaders, and local leaders to princes.[31] Clearly, this was a potentially fragile method of political organization. Over time, claims to legitimacy through blood ties became weakened by equally credible claims by other lines of the ruling family. In this, Rus was a typical European medieval state "where the sinews of sovereign statehood were simply not strong enough to operate over great distances or to contain the pressures generated by ambitious subordinate princes and their families."[32] Interestingly, however, while the system of relational and dynastic rule developed by the Kyivan princes was internally fragile, it did not prove vulnerable to external interference or king making by foreign powers. Although the feuding rulers of Kyivan Rus often were not particularly united against external threats (a weakness that would prove fatal against the Mongols), they did not fall prey to the tendency common in other parts of Europe to seek foreign sponsors in their internal rivalries. As a result, early Russian foreign policy remained focused on sustaining commercial relations and rights and holding core territory against periodic attacks by neighbors. Globalism in this period did not penetrate or challenge Russia; it for the most part enriched it. Commerce, trade, and constant raids and warfare were the primary features of globalization in this vulnerable but successful borderland between Europe and Eurasia. Russia was responding chiefly to the opportunities globalism posed, rather than to its challenges or stresses.

Globalized ideas also had an important effect on Russia's foreign relations in this period, in the form of the globalized sweep of religion and its impact on Russian politics and policy. The Kyivan prince Vladimir's choice of Orthodox Christianity over Roman Catholicism and Islam in 988 is by tradition explained by his attraction to the beauty of the ceremonies of the Eastern Orthodox faith compared with those of Rome, and by Islam's proscription against drinking alcohol. Whatever the reason, the mere choice illustrates how the transnational forces of religion shaped Russia's development and its foreign relations. As a result of Vladimir's embrace of Orthodox Christianity, Kyivan Rus developed stronger relations with Byzantium, and in contrast dealt with rival powers to the southeast and, increasingly, northwest through policies of strength rather than engagement. Russia adopted the Cyrillic script, further cementing relations of its leaders with Greek, Balkan, and Byzantine leaders and elites. In the early centuries, this choice drew Russia into profitable relations with the world's major power. It linked Russia with a leading artistic, architectural, spiritual, and scholarly culture of its time. As Byzantium declined and Roman Catholic Europe rose, however, the choice would come to instead distance Russia from future waves of European cultural globalism. And with the fall of Constantinople in 1453, Russia was left as the only remaining major power embracing Orthodox religion and culture, with important effects on its internal sources of political legitimacy and state authority. All this ultimately would serve to isolate Russia—or at least to create greater obstacles in the form of differences to be overcome—from Europe's rise as a global center. Russia's cultural distancing reinforced its leaders' autonomy, as well as the hierarchical social and political relationships supported by the state's relationship to the Orthodox Church that came to form the basis of tsarist rule.

By the reign of Kyivan prince Yaroslav the Wise in the first half of the eleventh century, Kyivan Rus extended north and south from the Gulf of Finland and Lake Ladoga to the Black Sea, and east and west encompassing the upper reaches of the Don and Volga to those of the Bug River. It was in this period that Kyivan Rus reached its height as a medieval state, finding an equilibrium in armed relations and trade with neighbors and even more distant markets, which in turn created the need for building domestic political institutions for governing this now large central European Christian state. The "state" was a supra-authority of the Kyivan prince, ruling a set of principalities (or in the case of Novgorod, a city-state), which were themselves usually ruled by sons or male relatives of the prince. From the ninth to the eleventh century, power and security rested on a selective combination of trade and armed might both to build a strong defense and to ensure that trade.

As the towns of Kyivan Rus developed and became more secure, they relied less on global trade for wealth and more on manufacture and agriculture. Maintenance of trade routes and trade relations mattered less for power. Control and ownership of land grew more important. The network of relations among Kyivan princes and families, which had centered on Kyiv, became less valuable, and local leaders became less inclined to accede to its power in pursuit of their own. By the eleventh century, the main story of the domestic politics of Kyivan Rus became that of rivalries, competition, struggle, and fragmentation. Hints of the internal challenges are clear as early as the transition from Vladimir, who had secured his rule in part by sending his sons to various subject cities to rule in his name, to his son Yaroslav, who had to fight his brothers to secure his claim.

At the same time, the forces that had made the region valuable as the epicenter of river-borne trade between Northern Europe and Eurasia diminished with the shift in trade patterns. Kyivan Rus's main trading partner was Byzantium, and by the twelfth century, it was in decline. European trade with the Near East and Eurasia could be conducted more directly as Europe occupied the Holy Land, and as European traders began to set out on the oceans and seas rather than relying on the river trading systems of western Eurasia. Battling steppe nomads and kingdoms focused Kyivan Rus on building armies even as other European countries began to develop shipping capable of ocean travel. In addition, ocean routes and ports began to flourish, as in the rise of the Hanseatic League in the twelfth and thirteenth centuries. Kyivan Rus's lack of major ocean ports was a further disincentive for investing in oceangoing ships. The economy of Kyivan Rus came to rely more on internal production and trade (agriculture and small-goods manufacture) than on global trade.[33]

By the early thirteenth century, therefore, Russia was already experiencing deglobalization. The effects on its foreign policy were indirect, primarily by re-inforcing already existing patterns of fragmentation and competition in its internal politics. A weakly institutionalized Russia was lucky that its potential competitors in Europe and Byzantium either had lost interest in it because of shifting trade patterns or were experiencing the localizing effects of feudalism themselves.

Instead of a comprehensive retreat from global opportunities and challenges, however, the thirteenth century brought probably the most fundamental global challenge that Russia has experienced in its history, when in 1223 the forces of Genghis Khan arrived north of the Black Sea. Russia's second encounter with globalization was as important for shaping its state and society—and thus foreign policy—as its first experience with commercial and trade globalization. Thirteenth-century military globalization in the form of Mongol imperialism, however, brought primarily challenges.

The Mongols brought steppe-raiding warfare to new heights through political organization that in turn enabled an aggregation and organization of military forces above the tribal level. This made possible the creation of larger formations (the largest Mongol formation comprised ten thousand fighters), and coordination of operations, because military leaders owed allegiance to the khan, not to their tribes. The combination of greater numbers and more integrated operations unleashed the potential of horseback steppe warfare beyond border raids to a truly global scale. The Mongols first defeated and acquired much of northern China, before overwhelming Central Asia, Persia, and the steppe khanates that had stood on the southeastern borders of Kyivan Rus.

When the Mongol forces turned toward Europe under the command of Genghis Khan's grandson, their superior organization simply rolled through town after town. It did not help that the fragmentation and rivalry among Russian principalities meant that no united effort was made to come to the aid of the first victim, Ryazan, in 1237. Whether a united Russian state could have defended against the onslaught is far from clear. But a united Russian state might have had the credibility and authority to negotiate with the invaders. Instead, over the next several years, Russian cities and principalities were attacked, destroyed, and occupied one by one. The forces defeated the disunited principalities and towns of Rus, getting as far as southern Poland and Hungary before falling back to consolidate control. Although some cities, such as Novgorod, were never defeated, the majority of the unoccupied principalities had to recognize subjugation to the Mongol Empire, providing tribute, army recruits, and other forms of labor. The Mongol invasion also brought the bubonic plague—the first global epidemic—to Europe, with catastrophic effects on economies and societies from Russia to England.

Trade continued under the Mongols, but Russia was no longer at its core, and consequently its cities, rulers, and merchants did not profit from it to the same degree as Kyivan Rus had. Novgorod benefited from its negotiated subservience to the Mongol Empire and its proximity to Baltic trade routes. Interior Russian cities were able to trade with Central Asia and even China through the trade routes maintained by the Mongol Empire. But in either direction, Russia was the last station on the trade routes, not their crossroads. And as clients of the political and commercial powers that ran the routes, Russian cities were unable to accrue wealth in the same way. Having to pay tribute and demonstrate fealty to the Mongol Empire limited Russia's scope for power and growth. And of course, the loss of central political organization to cities and principalities that individually negotiated terms and relations with the Mongol Empire further prevented any aggregation of wealth or power. The foreign policies of Russia's principalities and cities in this period were those of managing weakness and dependence, and seeking to preserve a measure of physical security and the space to conduct local economic activities and participate in trade networks controlled by others.

In addition to changing trade and production, the Mongol invasion reinforced aspects of Russian state-society relations. The destruction of cities undermined the city assembly (*veche*). The subordinate relationship of the prince to the khan liberated the prince from obligation to aristocratic or merchant classes. When Mongol rule was overthrown by Muscovy in the fifteenth century, tribute, obligations, and state service were now owed to the prince (or grand duke), with no reciprocal obligation or restraint on state power.[34]

Russia's responses to these two very different periods of globalization illustrate the importance of understanding the role of the state in shaping Russia's foreign policy response. To be sure, Russia's experience with commercial globalization in its first few hundred years of existence was a matter of responding to opportunities more than threats or challenges; thus, it is not surprising that the experience was more positive and constructive. But it is also the case that there was not an existing Russian state with its own interests and power that had to cope with the new opportunities. In this first period,

Russia's political leaders could and did seek out the opportunities that trade globalization presented them. They used foreign policy to manage the challenges of dealing with other countries—some more powerful, such as Byzantium, some less, such as the various steppe nomad political communities—primarily to ensure that they could engage in and profit from the enormous advantages of being at the crossroads of European and Eurasian trade. It was a foreign policy neither of strength nor of weakness, but rather of negotiation, management, balance, and engagement.

By the time Russia was challenged by the military globalization of the Mongols in the thirteenth century, its state and society had already turned inward. That it did so without the benefit of at least consolidating and strengthening the state so as to be prepared to manage its defense and security, as well as to pursue wealth and well-being, is a useful point of comparison for later periods.

Muscovy, the Time of Troubles, and Establishment of the Eurasian Empire

The emergence of Muscovy as a leading force among fragmented Russian towns amid the waning powers of Mongol rule had little to do with the larger world around it, being rooted in Moscow's relative political, economic, and cultural advantages compared with its rival Russian principalities. In the context of an analysis of the impact of globalization on Russian foreign policy, what is important about the rise of Muscovy is how the absence of globalism (largely the result of the disintegration of the Mongol Empire and the retreat to smaller political entities and reduced trade among far-flung local political entities) enabled a newly confident and powerful Russia under Muscovite rule to exploit the opportunities for broadening its power and economic presence, and to launch its expansion in Eastern Europe across the Urals and into Siberia.

Moscow's expansionism began at home. Ivan III absorbed nearby towns before annexing Novgorod in 1478. His successors acquired Pskov in 1510 and Smolensk in 1514. In the same period, Moscow's rulers defended its southern borders against the various political entities that were remnants of Mongol khanates. Moscow did not, however, expand to the west or the south so far as to battle or threaten the more powerful states that surrounded it: Sweden, Denmark, Poland, and Lithuania, in addition to the Ottoman Empire. When

Ivan IV was tempted to press against Russia's more powerful western neighbors in pursuit of Baltic territories and the international trade they would make possible, he failed. Instead, Moscow expanded eastward, which (after the fall of Kazan in 1552) was easily occupied and contained a wealth of natural resources in demand in Europe. As a result, despite its isolation relative to the broader sweep of global exploration and empire building by Western European countries, Russia expanded its trade in the fifteenth and sixteenth centuries as a provider of raw materials such as timber and fur.

It was thus as a result of the lack of globalism that Russia grew in territory, power, and wealth. It was an extensive, rather than intensive, period of growth: Russia increased the valuable resources under its territorial control for sale abroad. This was made possible by a happy coincidence of Muscovy's consolidation and the availability of a vast expanse of territory rich in resources populated by smaller and weaker political entities. Both of these factors, however, were in part a result of the deglobalized environment the new Russia found itself in as a result of the disintegration of Mongol rule. The lack of globalizing pressures allowed its leaders to embark on a state-building process based on patrilineal rule and a growing class of state servitors who obtained their positions not by independent ownership of land (as, for example, in feudal Europe) but as a result of service to the tsar.[35] Pressures on Russia's rulers in this period (and there were pressures, from discontented boyars, rival claimants to Kyivan Rus's legacy, peasant leaders seeking to restore traditions of egalitarian rule) came from within.

The result was a period of territorial expansion and a foreign policy characterized by confidence and little need for compromise. Moscow absorbed Novgorod and Pskov, gaining as a result a Baltic Sea shore. It took Smolensk and, though not gaining Kyiv, extended its rule to most of the eastern cradle of Rus. It did so through a combination of negotiation and appeal to its rightful place as successor to historic Rus against Lithuanian and Polish power, but it also did so backed by power and military dominance. When confronted by a greater opposing force, particularly Poland and Sweden during the seventeenth century, Russia was circumspect and limited its expansion and challenge.

Internally, the growing expanse of the empire risked an attenuation of existing forms of political rule and strained existing state capacities. But territorial expansion also brought the Russian state enormous resources, enabling it to expand the ranks of nobility and other servants of the tsar. Moscow's expansion, however, increased its vulnerability and the scope of territory that needed to be defended. As a result, Russian expansion under Moscow in the sixteenth and seventeenth centuries broadened the size and scope of its political and military establishments. It was in this period that Moscow first negotiated the service of the Cossacks to secure Russian territory against the perennial insecurity of its southern steppe borderlands.[36]

The period of the rise of Muscovy and the Time of Troubles that followed illustrates how the relative lack of global challenges facilitated Russia's empire building despite its relative weakness. During the Time of Troubles, when competing tsarist claimants came and went, Russia's relative weakness resulted in Polish and Swedish intervention in support of rival claimants and in significant occupation of Russian territory. These influences do not meet the definition of "globalism" or "globalization" used here precisely, because Poland and Sweden were neighboring powers with regional scope. They did threaten, destabilize, and challenge Russia, but they were not global challenges.

Once the country was able to settle on a legitimate claimant to Russian rule, the new tsar, Mikhail Romanov, could reconstitute essentially the elements of Ivan IV's success in much the same context (i.e., the absence of globalism) and with much the same results. Russia was beleaguered by weakness, but not by globalization. Mikhail was able to end foreign occupation, but he had to make territorial concessions to achieve a secure border in the west. He took up again Russia's eastern expansion, with Russian forces and settlers founding Krasnoyarsk and Yakutsk, and reaching the Pacific coast by the middle of the seventeenth century. As in the west, Russia's tsars expanded until they met a more powerful state—in this case, China. Mikhail went on to complete Ivan IV's work to create a taxation system for the raising of permanent armies in the service of the state, rather than having them contributed through feudal systems of obligation.[37]

Although the fourteenth through the seventeenth centuries were a period of deglobalization for Russia, trade and commerce continued, and external military threats and challenges abounded. The period was very different from that of the height of Russia's origins as the nexus of overland European-Eurasian trade routes, however, and unlike the period of Mongol political-military globalization. Trade during the rise of Muscovy and in the Time of Troubles was local or cross-regional, not transregional, in scope. To the extent that Russian trade ranged internationally, it was through export and import networks in which Russian merchants and producers dealt with foreign traders, who themselves moved the goods abroad. That is, to the extent that there was international trade in Russian goods, Russian merchants and producers were not the ones trading them abroad. Thus, Russia itself was not exposed to the larger world even through trade. Needless to say, this method of foreign trade meant that Russian merchants did not reap the profits they would have had they ranged abroad themselves.[38]

Similarly, although military threats to Russia by no means disappeared during this period, increasingly Russia's military encounters were not with globally ranging military forces sweeping to or through its lands. They were engagements for control over territories claimed by Russia along its own borders. These engagements occurred when Russia faced local resistance to incorporation or, more often, when Russian expansion bumped up against equal or greater powers, primarily in Europe, but also in Asia (i.e., in its encounter with China and the limits of Russian expansion in the region).[39]

The absence of globalism meant that a fragile and internally conflicted Russian political system did not face external challenges. Russia also greatly benefited from the draw of globalism among the larger European powers to the world's oceans and new, non-European territories. Russia missed the Age of Exploration and the Europeanization of the Americas, Africa, and Asia. But the Age of Exploration missed Russia, and that allowed its political elites to engage in struggles among themselves without being threatened on a large scale from abroad. The consolidation of the system of tsarist rule in this period was more indigenously Russian than Kyivan Rus or those that followed, and it is this period—when its leadership enjoyed the latitude of deglobalization—that popular conceptions associate with Russian autocracy, set apart as distinct from European culture and political systems.

MANUFACTURED GLOBALIZATION AND THE RUSSIAN EMPIRE

The late seventeenth century began a period of Russian pursuit of international influences and experience to strengthen the country and establish Russia as a European great power. This process is most closely associated with Peter the Great, exemplified by his creation of a European capital for Russia in St. Petersburg, but its roots were in the half century before when, under Tsar Alexei, Russia adopted European-style administrative reforms and encouraged European traders to take up business in Moscow. Tsar Alexei invited European military advisers to train the Russian army and impart lessons learned by European militaries in the Thirty Years' War. His advisers studied and practiced the emerging European art of diplomacy, including training and posting permanent representatives in foreign capitals. The tsar's government passed laws to establish rules governing international trade.[40]

Peter took up and further developed these beginnings. He required the Russian elite to be educated and trained in European ways, including speaking French, so that Russia's representatives abroad could participate in European balance-of-power diplomacy. He famously required his elite to shed outward markings of eastern barbarism, such as the wearing of beards. His travels to Europe convinced Peter that for Russia to become a European great power, it would have to adopt European science, technology, and economics. The conviction was as instrumental as it was cultural: Peter may have wanted Russia to be European, but he wanted Russia to be European so that it would be powerful. He sought to expand at Sweden's expense; after his first defeat against Charles XII at Narva, he developed a modern navy in large measure to challenge Sweden on the sea as well as on land. Sweden was defeated by Peter's reformed army at Poltava in 1709 and invaded by Russian forces in 1721, forcing the Treaty of Nystad, which gained Russia the Baltic territories and ports Peter sought.[41]

In addition, Peter's Europeanization of Russia's military, administration, economy, technology, and mission altered the balance of power in Northern Europe by limiting the Swedish empire. But this was not the result of the inexorable influences of globalization. It was a deliberate policy of Russian leaders seeking to import methods for bolstering Russia's power, and using Russia's power and geopolitical advantages to gain on Europe's diplomatic and military stages. European global culture, science, commerce, and influence did not flow to Russia in the late seventeenth and eighteenth centuries; ambitious leaders pursuing modernization selectively drew it there.

Russia's eighteenth-century rulers were keenly aware of the advantages of reaching out for the benefits of globalism arising from increasing trade, advanced technology, and knowledge and education in building state power; however, because Russia was not subject to globalization, they were able to reach out selectively and control the process. The more authentic dimensions of globalization continued, in fact, to be directed away from the Eurasian landmass. The Age of Exploration was followed by the first age of European empire in the Americas, East Indies, Asia, and Africa. Russia remained potentially threatened by bordering states or empires, but it did not experience waves of economic, financial, political, cultural, or ideational globalism.

As in the time of Muscovy's rise, Russia's relative insulation from globalization pressures and opportunities coincided with a period of imperial expansion.[42] Marginal expansion at the expense of Sweden was followed by a more significant and deliberate expansion into European regions to Russia's west that had been under Polish-Lithuanian control, ultimately resulting in the partition of Poland itself. Russia had successfully learned and executed the European terms of balance of power, but it was an opportunity afforded by the lack of globalization pressures and distractions on its state and society. Peter's successors were Europhile and even European (Catherine, for example, was German), and therefore the goal was to compete with European countries as a European power—with the additional assets of Eurasian resources and geopolitical space in the bargain. Elizabeth joined France and Austria in the Seven Years' War against Prussia out of ambition to play a European role, not because of insecurity or foreign invasion. Under Peter, Elizabeth, and Catherine, Russia stood up against and defeated European great powers that had limited its security and claims to historic (if also mythic) Russian lands, extending the Russian Empire by 1796 to encompass modern Belarus, Lithuania, and Ukraine. In addition to whittling away and ultimately partitioning Poland, Russia's eighteenth-century Europhiles defeated the Ottoman Empire on the northern shores of the Black Sea, sending the Russian Baltic navy through the Atlantic and Mediterranean to destroy the Ottoman navy. By the late eighteenth century, the Persian Empire was in retreat as well, creating an opportunity for the Russian Empire to move into the steppes north of the Caucasus Mountains, encouraged at first by the kingdoms of Armenia and Georgia, which welcomed a Christian patron against Muslim rule.

Russia became a modern European power in size, power, scope, and diplomacy even as its rulers reinforced nonmodern political and social institutions at home. The tsars wanted a modern Russian state that would also be a European great power, but it was a selective modernity that combined enhanced administrative capacities, taxation, and military modernization with serfdom, absolutism, and a contingent form of property ownership that preserved dependence on the tsar. Europeanization did not mean internal modernization precisely because the Russian state controlled the terms of its manufactured globalization in the eighteenth century. Globalization was not a force to which Russia could or had to respond; it was a force selectively invited in for its usefulness to enhance Russian power.

Peter and Catherine made Russia a European power as well as a Eurasian empire, but they achieved this largely by choice and on their own terms, out of ambition and from the general comfort of a vast heartland that provided the resources to support the expanding extension of control over weaker border-lands, particularly where other great powers were weakening or for reasons of their own (such as Prussia and Austria) chose not to challenge Russia on its own turf. They certainly did not win every battle, nor was every expansionist desire met (the Balkans, the Ottoman Empire, and the Caucasus remained only partially achieved ambitions), but Russian foreign policy of the eighteenth century was not that of a country under siege. Peter's and Catherine's success-ful enhancement of Russia's internal and foreign power enabled them to achieve an objective that their sixteenth- and seventeenth-century predeces-sors could not: to seize the offensive for expanding and consolidating control even against powerful neighbors to the west and south. They were able to profit from a period in which Russia was not beset by the multiple opportunities and challenges of globalization to sustain relatively secure control at home and fo-cus on empire consolidation. The eighteenth century also saw the expansion of Russian control to its farthest eastern reaches, in Central Asia and in the Pa-cific, including Alaska.

Precisely because Russia became a European great power while maintain-ing and even increasing the state's role in society and the economy, its society and economy did not transform as well. Russia continued to trade, but it con-tinued to rely to a great degree on licensed foreign traders.[43] Russian goods were still in demand on newly global markets, but they continued to be raw materials and natural resources extracted from the vast imperial territory or agricultural products grown in fertile regions. Much of Russia's trade was fu-eled by Britain's early industrial revolution, but because the state and state-licensed foreign traders controlled the trade, it did not have the effect of opening Russia's society or economy to global influences.[44] In a period in which European global traders began to develop great banking houses and develop systems of private finance and credit, even Russia's banks remained closely tied to the state.

As the two rulers of the beginning and end of the eighteenth century, Peter and Catherine pulled Russia out of its relative isolation imposed by geography and the Mongol invasion. They sought modern European advan-tages, which were controlled by the state both to enhance Russia's power and to enable it to play on the stage of the European great powers. This pe-riod demonstrates how global influences do not necessarily lead to the liber-alization of political institutions. The agent of manufactured globalization was the state, and the state was strengthened in the process. The period also demonstrates how the Russian state and globalization do not, in the end, coexist amicably.

The Nineteenth Century: Globalization and Russia's Strengths and Weaknesses

Americans associate globalization primarily with technology and economics, but Russians know that it has political and military dimensions as well. The nineteenth century began with a surge of political-military globalization: Revolution and imperialism that began in the United States and ultimately shook the European balance-of-power system continued in the revolutions of 1848 and the Crimean War. It was only in the last decades of the century that commercial, economic, and technological globalization dominated globalism, with the growth of international trade, development of transport (particularly railroads), and huge strides in technology that shrank communication distances and changed industry (e.g., telegraph, steam engine, and electricity).

Thus, the nineteenth century was on all fronts a globalization challenge to Russian power, stability, security, prosperity, and social cohesion. Globalization in its multiple forms revealed Russia's strengths and weaknesses and elicited foreign policy responses in a pattern similar to that of the Varangians toward commercial globalization, and the Mongols toward military globalization: negotiation and compromise, retrenchment of territory, and strain on existing internal institutions and capacities. Most important was Russia's failure to meet external challenges by adapting internally, with the state's main response ultimately to try to block and manage the opportunities and challenges of globalization, thereby reinforcing elements of premodernity in Russian politics and society.

Russia under Tsar Alexander I attempted a period of distant alliance with France, but Napoléon's plan for Europe included a version of the modern nation-state incompatible with Russia's domestic political system and its imperial rule in Eastern Europe. In the end, Russia allied with the monarchies of Europe that saw Napoléon as not merely a foreign military threat, but a challenge to their traditional internal political power.

Coping with the Napoleonic threat required not only extraordinary military choices—allowing Napoléon's forces to take Moscow so that they would be destroyed in retreat given the futility of holding it through the winter—but also defeating the French Revolution's ideas of liberty and equality. Russia's rulers were threatened in 1812 not only by the presence of Napoléon's armies but also by the idea of emancipation of the serfs and the ideals of the Enlightenment, which appealed to many discontented with Russia's autocratic system of rule. As would again be the case in the 1940s when Germany's armies were at first welcomed in parts of the Soviet Union, in the end even Russian peasants rallied to the state to fight off the foreign invader.

Safe from Napoléon's armies with their complete defeat and triumphant Russian occupation of Paris in 1814,[45] and with the reassertion of conservative monarchical rule in the Congress of Vienna in 1815, Russian imperial rule continued to be challenged by revolutionary ideas nonetheless. The defense of Russia had awakened a genuine nationalism, and the counterinvasion into Western Europe had exposed Russian military officers to concepts of political order in support of the nation that were not limited to autocratic rule and denial of citizen rights. Officers, members of the nobility, and intellectuals formed secret societies that developed plans for federal, constitutionally based government. They were repressed by Alexander, but with his death in December 1825, they sought to take power in the confusion over which of his brothers would succeed him.[46] In 1825 the Decembrists briefly held part of St. Petersburg, but they were quickly defeated and their leaders executed or exiled to Siberia. Alexander's attempts to entertain measures for political reform were abandoned by Nicholas I, who instituted limited reforms in the legal system and explored the possibility of freeing Russia's serfs, but who otherwise reverted to autocratic rule and control.

The global impact of revolutionary ideas in Europe did not fade, however, and revolution again dominated Europe and its foreign relations in 1848–1849. Russia intervened against revolution in Hungary in defense of imperial-monarchical Austria and broke with France under Napoléon III. Nicholas also sought an alternative Pan-European basis for foreign policy in pursuing the liberation of Slavic and Orthodox nations in the Balkans and Southeastern Europe from the Ottoman Empire. It was also during this period that the long-standing debate between Slavophiles and Westerners originated. One way to understand the development of a Slavophile alternative concept of Russia was as a reaction against the global influences that had attracted the ambitions of its leaders from Peter I to Alexander I.[47] Of most lasting impact, the clash of ideas in this period also entailed competing conceptions of socialism: a European idea grounded in progressive constitutionalism and a Slavophile version grounded in the communal ethic of Russian workers and peasants.

Nicholas I's ambitions to play a role as Europe's defender of Slavic people and Orthodox belief threatened the Concert of Europe system that Alexander I had helped to create in 1815, leading Britain and France to join in alliance against Russia to defend the Ottomans.[48] Russia suffered an enormous defeat in the Crimean War: it lost territory and ports in southeastern Europe, as well as the right to maintain a fleet in the Black Sea, nullifying the strategic gains of the eighteenth and early nineteenth centuries.

Even more important, the Crimean War demonstrated the fragility of Russian power. For a century and a half, Russia had successfully played the role of a European great power. Russia's vast resources fueled its trade; its geopolitical advantages made it a force in European diplomacy; and its strategic depth enabled it to defeat smaller states on its borders while remaining relatively safe from competing great powers. But this had worked primarily because Russia was not challenged by globalism. It worked in a period when Russia fought border wars and intervened in conflicts of its choosing, but not in a period when foreign powers struck deep into Russian territory. It worked when foreign influences touched Russian society but did not overwhelm it beyond the control of its rulers.

By the mid-nineteenth century, the new wave of globalization had changed those terms. Russia's success in defeating Napoléon had brought it to the center of great-power diplomacy and therefore made it a threat to other great powers. Furthermore, the mechanisms of balance of power were not those that had served Russia so well in earlier periods of imperial expansion, when it could exploit gains in territorial control in regions uncontested by other great powers or by declining powers such as Sweden. As long as Russia had expanded against the Ottoman Empire into the steppes and northern shores of the Black Sea, it retained the advantages of relative geographic and political distance from Europe's dynamic great powers. But in extending Russia's reach to the western Black Sea and by asserting rights in Ottoman affairs, Nicholas I effectively created a soft underbelly for the Russian Empire, which France and Britain as maritime powers were well equipped to strike against.

In addition, the very success of Russia's economic imperial expansion during this period had laid the foundations for what would become one of its enduring potential weaknesses: the success of extensive development—acquiring new territories and wealth that could be exploited through trade—obviated incentives for intensive development. In a period when Western European states were developing technology, industry, and innovation as sources of modern growth in their economies, Russia was able to fuel growth and power by increasing its territory and control over agricultural, fishing, and natural resources. The result was a wealthy empire, but not a modern one, at precisely the time when decisive military power would depend more on industrial might and new technology than on human and natural resources, as would become apparent in the victory of the industrial North over the agrarian South in the American Civil War in the decade following Russia's Crimean defeat. During the Crimean War, Russia's poor supply lines and inadequate railroad system hobbled its ability to supply armies even on its own territory.

Even more, however, Russia's defeat in the Crimean War demonstrated that the country's political system left it ill equipped both to profit from the economic growth opportunities of globalism and to manage its challenges. Alexander II and Russia's political elite were virtually united in identifying Russia's political system as a major source of the humiliating defeat.[49] Serfdom was abolished in 1861; mechanisms for local assemblies were created; an independent judiciary and the profession of lawyer were established; and a professional military with universal service was formed. The reforms, however, were for the most part ineffective. The abolition of serfdom left most land in the possession of the nobles or in the ultimate control of the state. Local governments were established, but with peasants vastly underrepresented. The nobility reclaimed its privileges and resources as sources of the officer corps.

Most important, the problem of half measures in reform created expectations, discontent, and reaction. The Polish rebellion of 1863 and repeated assassination attempts against Alexander II seemed to demonstrate that efforts to make Russia a modern European nation-state in political terms risked instability and disorder rather than creating power and effectiveness. The discontent that developed in the wake of the introduction of European ideas facilitated not only the formation of radical socialist and anarchist groups but also radicalization of their revolutionary means to include terrorism. One such movement, the Narodnaya Volya, succeeded in assassinating Alexander II in 1881. The Russian reaction was to reassert state control and try to restrict participation in political life. The government was empowered to declare emergency rule, enabling officials to govern outside of legal procedures and without being subject to representative institutions. The government relied increasingly on repression and secret police to contain violent, but also peaceful, opposition.

As a result, Russia remained weak in foreign affairs. In addition, the reforms the regime adopted failed to create the conditions necessary for Russia to enjoy the industrial and technological advances that dominated late-nineteenth-century globalization. At the same time, the Russian leadership did not shed or suspend its ambition in foreign affairs. In part, it followed the more successful and lower-risk path of seeking expansion where it did not challenge the European great powers—in the Caucasus, Central Asia, and the Far East.

Refusing to give up its European great power role, the Russian leadership also pursued a new and dangerous form of foreign policy rooted in the globalization pressures and ambitions of the late nineteenth century: a foreign policy driven by nationalism, ideology, and the hope of achieving legitimacy and domestic support when such legitimacy and support could not be achieved in the face of discontent with Russia's internal conditions.[50] Slavic nationalist ideas played a role in Russia's Turkish war of 1877–1878, as did the geopolitical ambition of re-establishing a Russian presence in the Black Sea. Despite military success, Russia was defeated diplomatically at the Congress of Berlin and constrained by European great powers (including a united Germany) determined to contain Russia, particularly in the Balkans. Frustrated in both its strategic objectives and its need to justify to smaller Slavic nations its normative claims to a role in their foreign affairs, Russia embarked on a forty-year period of ineffective entanglement in the region, which brought it into conflict with Germany and Austria and ultimately ended in war and revolution.

The most important impact of this period of globalization, however, starts with its influence on the Russian economy and how that affected Russia's political institutions and foreign policy. As David McDonald notes, Russia's pursuit of late-nineteenth-century industrialization was driven by a desire to maintain its great-power status in Europe.[51] Railroads were necessary both to pull together the vast expanse of the Russian Empire and to enable the state to deploy military forces to defend Russian territory and back up diplomacy with power. In particular, Russia's growing interest in managing its relations with a rising Japan and foreign powers in China justified the expense and effort of building the Trans-Siberian Railroad in 1891–1903, but this period also brought the development of railways in European Russia and the Caucasus. Foreign investment was necessary to support the building of railroads, first from German banks and in the last decade of the century from French financial institutions. With the railways, Russia could more fully exploit and develop its production and trade in metals and industrial goods, which grew by around 5 percent per year from 1883 to 1913.[52] Russia's industrialization increased the role of the state in the economy. After experimenting with an emphasis on private initiative for industrial development and growth, the Russian government reversed itself, setting tariffs, controlling the railroads, expanding the role of the state bank, and fueling industrial growth through state orders.[53]

Russia's rapid involvement in global industrialization had a deep impact on its state and society. Industrialization fueled migration to cities, with all the social dislocations that accompany modern urbanization, but in a time frame shorter than that in Western Europe and with greater disruptive effects on traditional peasant and village life. This urbanization coincided with the political retreat from Alexander II's reform experiment, with the result that Russia's new working class had no recourse to address its needs. Further adding to this combustible mix, the underground socialist and anarchist movements created in the mid-nineteenth century began to find supporters, including those willing to join violent terrorist cells focused on political assassination. The connection between Russia's newly urbanized millions and revolutionary political movement was cemented in the revolution of 1905–1907, with the emergence of workers' soviets and the establishment of the Duma as a representative institution.

What was Russian foreign policy in the context of this wave of economic globalization and its effect on Russia's social and political order?[54] In the Far East, Russia's traditional advantage of being stronger in a weak environment came up against a rising Japan, resulting in the disastrous war of 1904–1905. Seeking to secure its control over Eurasian wealth and resources through expansion in the Far East, the Russian Empire instead faced the limits of extensive development in Asia. Similarly, while consolidating the empire's control over Central Asia, Russia also had to come to an accommodation with a new regional power—the British Empire in Afghanistan and Persia—although this it managed to do peacefully.

In Europe, Russia's interests in the Balkans and the Ottoman Empire were at risk because Austria had begun to enjoy Germany as a new powerful supporter of its efforts to reassert its imperial ambitions in the region. Russia, too, had an interest in German support, demonstrated in the series of public and secret diplomatic efforts to forge a variety of alliances to cope with numerous contingencies and counteralliances that characterized this period of European history. Yet although Russia played an important role in the balance-of-power calculations that exemplified European great-power diplomacy, it was conducting a foreign policy of relative weakness meant to minimize its exposure and vulnerability. The Russian Empire was at its zenith after two hundred years of expansion. Russia's rulers had exploited the opportunities of its relative isolation in the eighteenth century to gain territory and wealth as well as strategic advantage in portions of Europe, given the advantage of not being beset by global challenges or influences. Russia also gained from opportunities created by military, political, and economic globalization in the nineteenth century, expanding the empire even farther and launching its own period of industrial growth and modernization. But in the end, the stresses and challenges of nineteenth-century globalization fundamentally damaged the Russian Empire primarily because Russia's political system was ill suited to consolidate and manage the country's extensive power resources while channeling the energies of its people to cope with the challenges of new influences, new ideas, and the dislocations that come with global military threats, revolutionary ideas, and the emergence of new social classes.

Russia was thus a powerful country, but always a weak player. It could throw resources at a foreign policy objective or problem and often as a result defend itself. But it could not initiate a strategic foreign policy that would address in the long term its vulnerabilities of economic backwardness and political fragility, because the state had to be ready to fight the multitude of challenges that arose from its weakness.

The era of nineteenth-century globalization ends, of course, with World War I and the Russian Revolution. Communication, commerce, global empire, and intricate alliances led all of Europe's great powers to pursue the commercial and political prizes of globalization and the power they promised; but they also unleashed forces—for example, rapid communication and advanced industrial technology in the service of military forces—that none of the players, including Russia, were ready politically to manage. The interweaving of complex and carefully balanced alliances, which were themselves a feature of the nature of the networks of economic, political, and ideational interdependence of the European great powers in the late nineteenth century, drew them into a war that their industrialized economies and militaries could and did fight to extreme devastation. World War I exposed Russia's weakness and fragility and led to the instability and internal vulnerability that resulted in the 1917 February and October revolutions.[55]

The multiple challenges of nineteenth-century globalism sharpened in historical perspective the paradox of Russia's place in the international system: a powerful country with vast resources and wealth that could absorb enormous costs and losses yet was never able to accept a secondary role commensurate with how its political system could translate that power into influence. Geoffrey Hosking points out that the Russian Empire entered World War I to prove that it was a European great power.[56] It lost, and disappeared as an international actor, because in truth it was not one: Globalism had exposed all its weaknesses and afforded it few of the benefits, especially a modernized political system, that the handful of successful European powers had evolved in the nineteenth century. Globalization gave Russia the opportunity and reason to become a modern great power, but in the end that same phenomenon destroyed the Russian Empire because its political institutions could not adapt to exploit the opportunities and manage the challenges.

SOVIET FOREIGN POLICY

Lenin was a theorist and scholar before he was a party organizer, revolutionary, and the Soviet Union's first leader. *Imperialism, the Highest Stage of Capitalism,* his most important work on international affairs, was his thesis on the relationship of capitalism to globalism and the foreign relations consequences. In one of his many departures from strict Marxist theory, Lenin argued that the result of the capitalist system's internal contradictions and falling productivity was not necessarily a workers' revolution, because national governments could seek new resources and new markets in overseas colonies. As long as capitalist economies could expand internationally, they could avoid the contradictions that would otherwise produce revolution at home.

Therefore, nineteenth- and twentieth-century imperialism was the highest stage of capitalism, according to Lenin, because it was the logical and even necessary consequence of capitalism in Europe. To secure new markets and new resources, European states developed the political system of global imperialism to support the economic system of global capitalism. Furthermore, global capitalism was also the source of war—most notably, the Great War engulfing Europe's imperial metropoles at the time Lenin wrote. When the European great powers first sought and achieved control of colonial lands abroad, there were plenty to go around. But as territories were claimed and controlled, the great powers eventually faced zero-sum competition for the global empires that would enable them to survive as capitalist imperial centers.[57] The result was World War I.

No single source is more important for understanding nearly seventy-five years of Soviet foreign policy responses to global challenges. Soviet foreign policy would be shaped by geopolitics, military ambition and necessity, national economic development, leadership styles and changes, and even individual personalities. But until Mikhail Gorbachev declared in 1988 that the defining feature of international politics would no longer be understood as the zero-sum confrontation between international socialism and international capitalism, the basic Leninist conception of the fundamental challenge that the international system posed to the Soviet Union defined Soviet choices, strategies, and objectives. There could be periods of isolation, coexistence, or even détente to provide a hard-headed Soviet leadership with the breathing space it needed to build the Soviet Union's military capability or to avoid nuclear confrontation. But in the end, the Soviet Union could not be integrated into an international system with which it was incompatible. Either the system of global capitalism would be challenged by Soviet power, or the Soviet system would be undermined. And as the end of the Cold War would show, Lenin was not entirely wrong.

The Bolshevik leadership's first foreign policy decision in November 1917 was to issue the Decree on Peace, calling on the European great powers to end the war and on the workers of those countries to rise against their governments, which had led them into this unjust war in defense of capitalism and imperialism. The Bolsheviks recognized that Russia was an unlikely vanguard of world socialist revolution, and they believed that workers' revolts in the most developed European capitalist countries would likely follow in reaction to the war and with the Russian Revolution as their example. They also believed that further revolutions would be necessary for their own survival. Russia was among the least developed and weakest European countries, so it would need resources and know-how from the advanced economies and their workers. Furthermore, any concerted effort by the allies, or by Germany, to overthrow the Bolshevik regime had a good chance of success, so the Bolsheviks counted on revolutions in Europe to bring to power socialist regimes that would not pose a threat.

Neither the European powers nor workers followed the Bolshevik call, and in early 1918 it was left to the new commissar for foreign affairs, Leon Trotsky, to negotiate peace with Germany. When he could not do so without accepting German annexation of Poland and the Baltics, as well as the independence of Ukraine, he simply stated that the Bolshevik regime declared peace and expected that Europe's working-class combatants would revolt.[58] The policy failed when Germany instead launched a new offensive into Bolshevik-held territory, and Lenin convinced the leadership to negotiate for peace, resulting in the Treaty of Brest-Litovsk, in which the new regime lost more Russian imperial territory than it would have had Trotsky agreed to German demands just a month earlier.

Nevertheless, the new leadership had not learned the lesson that the forces of global revolution would not work in their favor. They created the Communist

International in 1919 in an attempt to support foreign socialist revolutions but came up empty. After battling White Russian forces in the civil war as well as European intervention in their support, the new Soviet regime had to mount a defense against the new Polish government for control of Ukraine. Having defeated Polish forces in Ukraine, the Soviet regime replaced national defense with a renewed goal to spread European revolution westward, and invaded Poland. Soviet forces were defeated and a peace treaty signed in October 1920.

The defeat in Poland was a turning point in the Soviet response to globalism. The new regime defeated both internal and external enemies that had intervened in its civil war, but its economy produced a fraction of what it had before the war, and discontent and opposition within the country were growing. The Bolsheviks faced food shortages and noncompliant peasants who hoarded agricultural surpluses or did not bother to produce surpluses in the face of low prices and the expropriation they experienced during civil war. It was time to get serious about economic reconstruction.

Facing hostility in a still-capitalist Europe and growing instability within, the Soviet leadership adapted Lenin's international thesis to the reality they faced: The way to advance socialism under these conditions was to develop and defend "socialism in one country"—that is, the Soviet Union. Soviet socialism would need to be protected and insulated, not internationalized. Deglobalization was a political as well as an economic choice of the leadership, but it was one that followed the general trend in the European and broader international economy of the 1920s. The war had disrupted international trade, weakened European currencies, and destroyed industry and resources in many European countries, leading to protectionism. Already weakened, European trade and production were undercut by periodic inflation and then suffered again in 1929 with the American Depression when U.S. loans and investment dried up.[59]

It would be difficult to argue, therefore, that the policy of socialism in one country and deliberate turning away from the stresses of global challenges forced the Soviet Union to sacrifice opportunities of any importance in the 1920s. From the Soviet point of view, global effects were all negative. The leading countries were hostile and more powerful; their economies, weakened and unstable. A national policy of political and economic protectionism went with the trend of the times, while a foreign policy that deferred world socialist revolution had the dual advantage of being more realistic and not further antagonizing the regime's enemies. Soviet foreign policy was one of managing weakness by maintaining distance, with selective engagement for specific objectives. The regime negotiated a variety of cooperative agreements with postwar Germany to selectively import technology and permit German development prohibited by the 1919 Treaty of Versailles. In a concession to the international rules of the game, the Soviet regime sought diplomatic recognition and representation in the capitalist countries, even as it sought to maintain international socialist leadership through the Comintern, which was directed to support the strategy of socialism in one country.

The more important effect of the Soviet Union's self-imposed deglobalization was in the consolidation of the domestic economic and political system under Joseph Stalin. In the 1920s, differing views on economic and political development could be expressed within the Communist Party and involved limited policy experimentation in the degree and methods of political control over the economy.[60] By the end of the decade, options had narrowed to heavy industrialization and the most rapid increase in industrial and agricultural development possible through collectivization of agriculture and the migration of millions from villages to urban centers. The role of the Communist Party in motivating, monitoring, and imposing discipline strengthened the party's domination of the political system. Social change, dislocation, and resistance fueled the search for opponents of the new system and methods to remove obstacles, including imprisonment. The tsarist systems of prison camps and exile were adopted by the regime to punish real and imagined dissent, but also as sources of forced labor, particularly in remote and inhospitable regions where free labor would be difficult to attract.[61] The Gulag was a brutal system of political repression and control, but it also was a product of Stalinist industrialization and the drive for socialism in one country. While prisoners labored under harsh conditions to build roads, dig canals, mine minerals, and build industrial cities where no market economy or free labor would have, free labor was driven by a watchful and increasingly intrusive political system in which the Communist Party paralleled and monitored state enterprises.

Stalinist development continued despite the threat of foreign hostility and warnings of capitalist encirclement. The purges of the 1930s destroyed any opposition to Stalin or to independent Communist leaders, as those accused and found guilty were forced to confess to a conspiracy conducted from abroad. Even socialism in one country, it turned out, was not enough to protect the Soviet Union from hostile foreign forces. Even foreign communists who had immigrated to the Soviet Union to support the first socialist revolution came under suspicion and were sent to the camps.[62]

Yet Soviet foreign policy in the 1930s was primarily occupied with diplomacy, seeking both nonaggression pacts and (after the Nazi electoral victory in

1933) alliances against the growing threat of Germany. The new Soviet army proved strong and well led enough to defend the country from Japan, but the Soviet Union would need allies or at least neutral countries on the sidelines to withstand a newly powerful Germany. For all the talk of a capitalist threat at home, Soviet foreign policy in the 1930s was traditional in its efforts to seek partners in a balance of power—even with class enemies—against the primary threat. The response to weakness in a period of isolation and lagging globalism was a foreign policy of managing and balancing weakness while maintaining isolation, exemplified by the Nazi-Soviet Pact of 1939 and Stalin's steadfast strategy of placating and not provoking Hitler.

Like the Kyivan princes and Alexander I before him, Stalin sought negotiation and compromise, first with other European powers and then, when that failed, with Hitler. As with the Mongols and Napoléon, in the end diplomacy could not succeed, and only prevailing power combined with the artful use of Russia's vast resources and territory would. Because of what the repressive Soviet regime had achieved for itself in the 1930s, however, the Soviet Union was able to exploit its industry and political system to produce the armaments and commitment needed to mount a robust defense. The Soviet Union did crack its isolation to welcome U.S. assistance through Lend-Lease and to cooperate to some extent in Allied military planning and wartime intelligence,[63] but by this point the system's political, social, and economic functioning required insulation from outside forces, and the experience of military globalization reinforced the message.

Like previous Russian leaders, Stalin (and the Communist Party) emerged from the near-death experience of military globalism determined to build Soviet power without exposing the Soviet Union to global influences or challenges. Where Peter and his successors sought to selectively import European methods and resources to modernize the economy while limiting political change, Stalin expropriated large portions of East European industry and human capital and raised an Iron Curtain to keep out influences the Soviet system could not control. By expanding Soviet territory and by extending Soviet control into Eastern Europe through dependent socialist regimes, Stalin achieved both a territorial buffer against traditional sources of military global challenges and exploitation of human and economic resources in a larger territory. Although by the 1980s Soviet–East European economic relations were a net drain on the Soviet Union,[64] in the immediate postwar period the Soviet economy benefited from the trade, the expropriation of assets, and the transfer of knowledge. Stalin, however, refused to import resources and technology without maintaining control. The Soviet Union declined to join the Marshall Plan and prevented its new socialist allies from doing so. As a consequence, the Soviet Union would not participate in the trade and multiple business and financial linkages that developed between the United States and Western Europe, which would more fully develop during the rise of the global economy in the 1950s and 1960s.[65]

Indeed, the Soviet response to the Western international system in the 1940s came to define the Cold War. The Soviet Union reaffirmed its policy of isolation and autarky to increase its overall power, while using its relatively great diplomatic and military power to build a quasi empire on the borders with its Western rivals. It thus did its part in creating a bipolar structure that was based not only on bipolar power but also on rivalry between two different domestic and international systems. This was new in the history of Russian responses to globalism, where the response had been to accommodate and engage although remain isolated, and to participate when Russia was relatively more secure and powerful. Because the Soviet Union was no longer on the periphery of a new period of globalism, and because it was not merely one among several great powers, its response to the challenge was different. It was still a foreign policy based on autarky and control against external influences, but it was a response that created a global challenge for its major rival, the United States.[66]

The Soviet Union had achieved a level of economic development, political control, and military power that enabled it to match any potential renewed conventional military challenge in Europe, and as the Korean War would show, in Asia as well. But military technology had changed, and with it the nature of the global military challenge. Now it was not a cavalry horde or mechanized army, but the dual challenge of intercontinental flight and nuclear weapons. Of course, retreating from the challenge was not an option, nor was reliance on political control or isolation. But the Soviet response was different (it matched the United States in building nuclear weapons and intercontinental aircraft, and it beat the United States in developing ballistic missile technology), not only because it had to be given the circumstances, but also because it could be. Stalin's brutally effective political-economic system had dragged the Soviet Union from backwardness and had created the capacity for advanced military capabilities on a par with the United States. It enabled the Soviet leadership to focus its resources and achieve its objectives, whatever the cost. If entire cities had to be built to isolate leading scientists so they could produce weapons, then they would be. If multiple prototypes of weapons had to be developed in parallel to ensure that one would meet requirements, then redundancy in military production would be paid for, whatever the costs. If stealth and silence were to win the battle of evasion in submarine warfare, the Soviet navy would build virtually silent titanium-hulled submarines.[67]

The challenge was met, but there was a problem. By the 1960s and 1970s, not only were the costs of meeting the global military challenge high—consuming possibly more than one-third of Soviet gross domestic product—but the system itself, which had made the Soviet Union a modern powerful country, was incapable of achieving the next stages in modern development. After Stalin, Nikita Khrushchev experimented with political and economic reforms in an effort to spur growth and new development in the economy, but the reforms failed. His criticism of Stalin's repression, and the brief period of political reform in Eastern Europe, led to a near invasion of Poland and resulted in the Soviet occupation of Hungary in 1956. The political-economic and internal-international logic of the Soviet response to global challenges was tightly linked, and a loosening in one area risked a shaking of the edifice. Khrushchev's attempts to modify the system from within required a foreign policy of challenge, defiance, and maintenance of the barriers against economic and political influences from the West.[68] The building of the Berlin Wall in 1961 became a symbol of Soviet repression of East European nations, but it was also a visible sign of how the Soviet Union had come to deal with global military and developmental challenges: It was an equilibrium of power built on isolation and political control.

It was not as if the brittleness of the Soviet equilibrium was apparent at the time. Soviet foreign policy experienced extraordinary success in developing new allies in the period of nationalist and socialist liberation movements with the retreat of colonialism in Africa, Asia, and even Latin America. With the Russian homeland now powerful and secure, and with global influences managed and held at bay by a strong state, Soviet leaders, like Peter and Catherine, could operate from a position of strength to support sympathetic leaders. Socialism in one country had not been operative after World War II, given Soviet client regimes in Eastern Europe, but now the implications of its passing became global. The original Leninist conception of security—that the global system could be secure for socialist countries only with the disappearance of capitalist states—was revived and became a key feature of Soviet foreign policy. Given the reality of nuclear stalemate, active Soviet military intervention or confrontation with the United States was avoided, but Soviet military assistance and advisers were sent globally to support challenges to the United States and to extend Soviet influence.[69] The Soviet Union could participate in the political and military dimensions of globalization in the 1960s and 1970s because, instead of being the object of global forces, it had become an agent of them. By the 1970s the Soviet Union had achieved global strategic nuclear parity with the United States and was challenging it for influence around the world. It was even challenging the United States for influence in Europe, where the post-Vietnam generation of European leaders questioned U.S. leadership and Cold War confrontation.

The global stage, however, hid Soviet weakness, and it was also where the Soviet leadership would turn in another attempt to mitigate that weakness. As Alfred Rieber argues in his contribution to this volume (chapter 4, "How Persistent Are Persistent Factors?"), détente was at least in part a foreign policy strategy to cope with falling growth and stagnation in the Soviet economy. If the Soviet leadership directed financial and political resources to high-priority sectors, they could and did grow and develop. But the focus on a limited number of high-priority sectors, primarily defense and space, was leaving the rest of the economy far behind. In the context of this chapter, détente involved a limited globalization of the Soviet economy. The Soviet leadership bought grain and technology, and it began to sell energy to finance its imports, but without political change. It was yet another attempt to exploit the opportunities of globalization without facing the challenges.

The formula would not work. In the nineteenth century, the tsar might have been able to control ideas by controlling newspapers and other printed media. In the second half of the twentieth century, however, even the Soviet state could not entirely prevent many Soviet citizens from receiving international broadcasts.[70] In the nineteenth century, large printing presses could be destroyed; in the late twentieth century, samizdat could be produced on small copying apparatuses that could more successfully be hidden from the authorities.

More important, the old international system of billiard ball politics, in which states interacted leader to leader and only in the sphere of foreign affairs, had been replaced by an international political system increasingly bound together by transnational political, social, and economic ties in which matters within countries were seen as legitimate issues of foreign relations.[71] The human rights movement of the 1970s was a major challenge for a Soviet leadership seeking better relations with Europe. European countries were interested in reducing Cold War tensions but also in advancing the cause of political and social rights in the Soviet republics. The result was the Helsinki Final Act of 1975, which conceded legitimacy to the post–World War II borders of Europe but also obligated the Soviet and East European leaderships

to allow the exercise of certain political rights. This created the space for political movements not only in Eastern Europe but also in the Soviet republics, which would prove vital to the erosion of authoritarian rule in the late
1980s.[72]

The détente compromise failed because, in the end, neither the Soviet nor
U.S. leadership was satisfied with its cost-benefit trade-offs. Détente reduced
tension and stabilized the arms race, but it enabled the Soviet leadership to
continue to pursue political influence abroad and military parity while maintaining the fundamentals of its socialist political and economic system. From
the Soviet point of view, détente exposed the Soviet Union to Western influence and revealed its political and economic vulnerabilities, without gaining
the Soviet leadership the recognized right to compete in the political and military spheres it thought it had earned.

The result was a return to the confrontation that began in the late 1970s
and reached its height over the Soviet invasion of Afghanistan and Ronald
Reagan's extension of the arms race in pursuit of strategic defense.[73] The
confrontation was far from one-sided, as leaderships in both countries for
whom the defining feature of the Cold War international system was zero-
sum conflict between incompatible social systems pursued it. The problem
for the Soviet leadership was that a return to confrontation could not, this
time, squeeze resources or growth out of the economy. More fundamentally,
the Soviet Union's ability to meet global military and political challenges
during the Cold War had rested on its military power, and little else.[74] Military power, in turn, rested on economic performance, which was lagging.
The idea that economic growth could be found in limited international trade
and acquisition of technology might have created not only resources for
growth and military power, but also the impetus to adapt the economic system to enable it to shed socialist dogma, an experiment toward which Communist China inched. But the experiment with opening to global economic
factors exposed the political system as well, and the Soviet leadership was not
ready to risk political change. The Soviet Union was stuck between a rock
and a hard place: the hard place of global Cold War competition and the rock
of its inflexible political economic system.

When change came, for all his revolutionary image and effect, Gorbachev
was initially not all that different from the Russian leaders who had preceded
him over the centuries. He began with half measures to motivate the existing
system without fundamentally changing it. He fostered greater discussion
and criticism, but within the existing system of party control. He encouraged

experiments to free private initiative in the economy, but within a system of state ownership and control.

Gorbachev's primary response to the multiple challenges of "thick" globalism in the 1980s was to use Soviet foreign and security policy to reduce global military and political challenges. He sought to restart U.S.-Soviet arms control, arguing that militarized confrontation was making the Soviet Union less secure. He called for a "common European home" where the Soviet Union would be seen as a neighbor instead of as a threat, pursuing, as Hosking observes, "a thoroughly Russian tradition of peacemaking tsars and foreign ministers, conscious of their country's poverty and vulnerability, trying to build pan-European structures of peace."[75] He pulled Soviet advisers out of countries in the developing world, reduced Soviet financial support for client states, and began the Soviet withdrawal from Afghanistan. Gorbachev's "new thinking" was a welcome retreat from confrontation and global competition. But it was also an instrument to relieve pressure on a Soviet system that needed to adapt to survive. The goal was in part to reduce the burden of defense spending on the Soviet economy, but it was also to create the political space necessary for reform of the system.

Until late 1988, this was tinkering with the system without fundamentally changing it. In December 1988, Gorbachev's speech to the United Nations fundamentally changed Soviet foreign policy by renouncing class struggle. Without capitalist-socialist incompatibility at the core of Soviet foreign policy, there was no justification for Soviet military forces to back compliant regimes in Eastern Europe. With freedom of choice in Eastern Europe, political leaders in the Soviet republics who had been exposed to movements for human and political rights during détente began to press for reforms, autonomy, and even the right to choose national independence.[76] Gorbachev was increasingly faced with opposition from a newly open Soviet society suffering from experiments that had disrupted the system without replacing it. A political backlash within the Soviet political leadership that opposed the erosion of the Communist Party's power, combined with the growing separatist movement within the Soviet Union itself, resulted in the attempted coup of August 1991 and the demise of the Soviet Union on December 26, 1991.

A cooperative foreign policy could not save the Soviet Union in an era of thick globalization, because it was not enough to allow the new Soviet leadership to benefit from the opportunities created by networks of economic, cultural, and political interdependence. It did reduce the military challenges, much as Russia's ability to play as a European great power in the eighteenth and nineteenth centuries had enabled its leaders to manage potential external threats and challenges. But to benefit from the opportunities of international trade and investment, technological advance and innovation, and membership in the international institutions that make economic transactions effective, the Soviet Union required a different domestic policy as well. It needed private ownership, a convertible currency, transparent corporate governance, rule of law, and a stable political system that was not corrupt.[77] Gorbachev could not have achieved these objectives overnight, even if he had been ready in 1985 for the fundamental political changes that he came to late in 1990. But in failing to see control of politics and the economy as a central obstacle to managing global challenges and opportunities, the Soviet leadership at the end of the twentieth century was carrying on a long Russian tradition.

CONCLUSION

Since 2000 it has become increasingly clear that the current Russian leadership is responding to the multiple challenges and opportunities of contemporary thick globalism by seeking a greater role for the Russian state in the economy and society. Access to international media cannot be limited, but independent media are limited to print and regional sources: The national outlets that most Russians rely on for information are under direct state control or strong state influence. Russia actively pursues opportunities to increase its international trade, particularly in the energy sector, but international investors such as ChevronTexaco and ExxonMobil have had contracts for development revoked, and the most lucrative parts of Russia's most internationalized energy company, Yukos, have been seized by the state to meet demands for immediate payment of questionable back taxes. Russian and foreign nongovernmental organizations, especially those with agendas relating to human or political rights, have been the target of closer scrutiny by the security services and other state agencies.

Most important, Russia's political system has lost the mechanisms of checks and balances central to a well-functioning democracy. Regional politicians largely subservient to the president appoint legislators in the upper house of parliament. The lower house is dominated by United Russia, a political party created by the Kremlin. The presidential administration is able to control politics and policy to a degree not seen in the country for twenty years. It is neither accountable, nor transparent, nor answerable in any meaningful way to Russian citizens. In foreign policy, the Putin leadership increasingly emphasizes Russia's status as a great power, the importance of using foreign policy relationships to create conditions for building the Russian economy, selective cooperation with the United States and Europe within the context of friendly relations, and greater integration with the newly independent states of the former Soviet Union. It is a foreign policy of coping with Russia's current weaknesses by using important sources of leverage: its energy wealth, its geopolitical importance for stability and counterterrorism in Eurasia, and its arsenal of nuclear weapons.

The Putin leadership argues that this is necessary if Russia is to deal with the challenges of globalism. There is no doubt that terrorism is a major problem and that Russians are far less secure in their daily lives than they were two decades ago.[78] There is no question that the lack of stable government oversight in the 1990s led to irresponsible and greedy behavior that in turn led to economic dislocation and unpredictability in the 1990s. And it is certainly the case that Russia's new openness created new interest groups, new social actors, and new forces that were disruptive and did not always contribute constructively to Russia's post-Soviet development.

Will Russia succeed? Will it be able to benefit from the opportunities of globalization to expand its trade, develop its economy, advance technologically, and become a modern twenty-first-century great power by expanding the role of the state in the economy and society and by increasing the scope and powers of the state to control domestic forces and international networks of interdependence? Both its historical record and comparison to contemporary countries suggest that it is unlikely. Effective government is necessary to manage the strains of global opportunities and challenges, but a domineering state is not necessarily an effective one. By increasing control of the economy, the Russian state risks deterring foreign investors and leaving too much of the Russian economy impervious to competition and the sources of innovation. By limiting oversight of its military and security forces, it risks the inertia that left Russia unreformed and ill equipped to meet global military challenges in 1853 and 1917. By controlling information and intimidating independent thinkers, Russia again risks having to import technology and expertise, a choice that relegates it to an expensive process of constantly mitigating backwardness.

As a result, twenty-first-century globalization is most likely to result in a Russian foreign policy that is not expansionist but that is aimed at keeping challenges at a distance rather than addressing them. Russia is likely to be a friendly partner of the United States, Europe, and possibly a rising China. But it is unlikely to deeply engage with them to tackle global challenges such as nuclear proliferation. It will seek to participate in the global economy, but not to become deeply integrated with it, because integration would require relinquishing autonomy in the external world and control within the country.[79] Russia's security policy will recognize global threats, but it will focus on avoiding entangling alliances, choosing instead a largely self-reliant strategy of deterring major threats while eliminating, if possible, specific threats to Russian territory. In short, Russian foreign policy will return to the tradition of meeting global challenges by seeking time and space to consolidate and rebuild. In doing so, Russia will likely be as secure and prosperous as it needs to be, but never quite the great power that it has always sought to be.

NOTES

1. A. T. Kearney, "Measuring Globalization: Economic Reversals, Foreign Momentum," *Foreign Policy*, no. 2 (March–April 2004): 54–69.

2. For a positive assessment, see Thomas Friedman, *The Lexus and the Olive Tree: Understanding Globalization* (New York: Doubleday, 2000). For skeptical assessments, see Joseph E. Stiglitz, *Globalization and Its Discontents* (New York: Norton, 2002); and George Soros, *George Soros on Globalization* (New York: PublicAffairs, 2002).

3. Thomas Friedman's *The Lexus and the Olive Tree* is a well-known example of this set of assumptions.

4. For analyses and proposals on transnational governance, see Amitai Etzioni, *From Empire to Community: A New Approach to International Relations* (New York: Palgrave Macmillan, 2004); David Held and Anthony McGrew, eds., *Governing Globalization: Power, Authority, and Global Governance* (Malden, MA: Blackwell, 2002); John D. Steinbruner, *Principles of Global Security* (Washington, DC: Brookings Institution Press, 2000); Joseph S. Nye and John D. Donahue, eds., *Governance in a Globalizing World* (Washington, DC: Brookings Institution Press, 2000); and Georgy Derluguian, "Natsionalnoye gosudarstvo I ocherednaya globalizatsiya," in *Rossiya v tsentro-perifericheskom miroustroystve*, ed. Dmitri Glinsky (Moscow: Friedrich Ebert Foundation Moscow Office, 2003), pp. 61–78.

5. Robert O. Keohane and Joseph S. Nye Jr., "Governance in a Globalizing World," in *Power and Governance in a Partially Globalized World*, ed. Robert O. Keohane (New York: Routledge, 2002), pp. 193–218, quotation at p. 193.

6. Held and McGrew, *Governing Globalization*, p. 16, drawing from Keohane and Nye, "Governance in a Globalizing World," p. 15.

7. Keohane and Nye, "Governance in a Globalizing World," p. 198.

8. World Bank, *Globalization, Growth, and Poverty: Building an Inclusive World Economy* (New York: Oxford University Press, 2002), pp. 4–5.

9. Colin Elman, "Horses for Courses: Why Not a Realist Theory of Foreign Policy?" *Security Studies* 6, no. 1 (Autumn 1996): 7–53.

10. Soros, *George Soros on Globalization*, p. 3.

11. For accounts of the strategies, see Chrystia Freeland, *Sale of the Century: The Inside Story of the Second Russian Revolution* (New York: Little, Brown, 2000); Joel Hellman, "Breaking the Bank: Bureaucrats and the Creation of Markets in a Transition Economy" (PhD diss., Columbia University, 1993); Boris Yeltsin, *Midnight Diaries*, trans. Catherine A. Fitzpatrick (New York: PublicAffairs, 2000); Strobe Talbott, *The Russia Hand: A Memoir of Presidential Diplomacy* (New York: Random House, 2002); and Edward A. Hewett with Clifford Gaddy, *Open for Business: Russia's Return to the Global Economy* (Washington, DC: Brookings Institution Press, 1992).

12. These conclusions are based on my visits to Moscow in 1992, 1993, and 1994 and meetings attended there.

13. Jeffrey Sachs, *Poland's Jump to the Market Economy* (Cambridge: MIT Press, 1993); Jeffrey Sachs, "Privatization in Russia: Some Lessons from Eastern Europe," in *Development Policy*, ed. Soumitra Sharma (London: St. Martin's Press, 1992); Maxim Boycko, Andrei Schleifer, and Robert Vishny, *Privatizing Russia* (Cambridge: MIT Press, 1997).

14. Russian officials, interviews with the author, in Moscow 1992, 1994. For details, see Celeste A. Wallander, *Mortal Friends, Best Enemies: German-Russian Cooperation After the Cold War* (Ithaca: Cornell University Press, 1999), especially chaps. 3, 7.

15. Talbott, *The Russia Hand*, chap. 2.

16. Wallander, *Mortal Friends, Best Enemies*, chaps. 4–6.

17. See chapter 7, by Angela Stent, in this volume: "Reluctant Europeans: Three Centuries of Russian Ambivalence Toward the West."

18. Steven L. Solnick, *Stealing the State: Control and Collapse in Soviet Institutions* (Cambridge: Harvard University Press, 1998); and David E. Hoffman, *The Oligarchs: Wealth and Power in the New Russia* (New York: PublicAffairs, 2002).

19. Peter Reddaway and Dmitri Glinsky, *The Tragedy of Russia's Reforms: Market Bolshevism Against Democracy* (Washington, DC: United States Institute of Peace Press, 2001); and David Woodruff, *Money Unmade: Barter and the Fate of Russian Capitalism* (Ithaca: Cornell University Press, 1999).

20. Theodore P. Gerber and Sarah E. Mendelson, "Young, Educated, Urban—and Anti-American: Recent Survey Data from Russia" (PONARS Policy Memo Series, no. 267, Center for Strategic and International Studies, Washington, DC, 2002).

21. Reddaway and Glinsky, *The Tragedy of Russia's Reforms*, chap. 9.

22. Ted Hopf, *Social Construction of International Politics: Identities and Foreign Policies, Moscow, 1955 and 1999* (Ithaca: Cornell University Press, 2002).

23. Sarah E. Mendelson, "Russians' Rights Imperiled: Has Anybody Noticed?" *International Security* 26, no. 4 (Spring 2002): 49–50.

24. Abbigail J. Chiodo and Michael T. Owyang, "A Case Study of a Currency Crisis: The Russian Default of 1998," *Federal Reserve Bank of St. Louis Review* 84, no. 6 (November–December 2002): 7–17; and Homi Kharas, Brian Pinto, Sergei Ulatov, Lawrence Summers, and John Williamsson, "An Analysis of Russia's 1998 Meltdown: Fundamentals and Market Signals," in *Brookings Papers on Economic Activity,* ed. William C. Brainard and George C. Perry (Washington, DC: Brookings Institution Press, 2001), pp. 1–68.

25. Yuri Fedorov, "Democratization and Globalization: The Case of Russia" (working paper, no. 13, Democracy and Rule of Law Project, Global Policy Program, Carnegie Endowment for International Peace, Washington, DC, May 2000).

26. Clifford G. Gaddy and Barry W. Ickes, "Resource Rents and the Russian Economy," *Eurasian Geography and Economics* 46, no. 8 (2005): 559–583, details at 572–573.

27. Keith Bush, *Net Assessment of the Russian Economy* (Washington, DC: Center for Strategic and International Studies, 2003), and the World Bank, *Russian Economic Report: June 2004* (Washington, DC: World Bank, 2004).

28. Vladimir Putin, "Address to the Federal Assembly of the Russian Federation," May 26, 2004, President of Russian Web site, http://www.kremlin.ru/eng/sdocs/speeches.shtml?type=70029.

29. Robert Legvold, "The Three Russias: Decline, Revolution, and Reconstruction," in *A Century's Journey: How the Great Powers Shape the World,* ed. Robert A. Pastor (New York: Basic Books, 1999), pp. 139–190, especially pp. 183–184; Stephen E. Hanson, "Russia: Evil Empire or Strategic Partner?" in *Strategic Asia, 2004–05: Confronting Terrorism in the Pursuit of Power,* ed. Ashley J. Tellis and Michael Wells (Seattle, WA: National Bureau of Asian Research, 2004); Yury E. Fedorov, "Strategic Thinking in Putin's Russia," in *Russian Military Reform and Russia's New Security Environment,* ed. Yury E. Fedorov and Bertil Nygren (Stockholm: Swedish National Defense College, 2003), pp. 157–170, detail at p. 163.

30. I draw this description of the origins of Kyivan Rus primarily from Geoffrey Hosking, *Russia and the Russians: A History* (Cambridge, MA: Belknap, 2001), as older, established histories of Russia did not have access to the most recent scholarship, which clarifies the factual basis for mythic competing ideas about the original Rus.

31. Michael T. Florinsky, *Russia: A History and an Interpretation,* vol. 1 (New York: Macmillan, 1953), pp. 18–22, 29–31.

32. Hosking, *Russia and the Russians,* p. 47.

33. Ibid.

34. George Vernadsky, *A History of Russia,* 6th ed. (New Haven: Yale University Press, 1969), pp. 79–80.

35. Richard Pipes, *Russia Under the Old Regime,* 2d ed. (London: Penguin, 1993), p. 73.

36. Vernadsky, *A History of Russia*, p. 95.

37. Hosking, *Russia and the Russians*, p. 175.

38. Ibid., p. 150.

39. Ibid., p. 148.

40. Ibid., pp. 178–180.

41. Lindsey Hughes, *Russia in the Age of Peter the Great* (New Haven: Yale University Press, 1998), chap. 2.

42. John P. LeDonne, *The Russian Empire and the World, 1700–1917: The Geopolitics of Expansion and Containment* (Oxford: Oxford University Press, 1997), pp. 347–354.

43. Pipes, *Russia Under the Old Regime*, pp. 194–195.

44. See Alfred Rieber, *Merchants and Entrepreneurs in Imperial Russia* (Chapel Hill: University of North Carolina Press, 1982), especially pp. xx–xxii.

45. For an example of globalization transcending time as well as space, consider the French word *bistro*, whose origins are attributed to Russian soldiers occupying Paris in 1814, calling out in cafés for service *"buystro"* (quickly)! A visitor to Moscow or St. Petersburg today will find the reverse manifestation of twenty-first-century globalization: I recently walked past a café advertised as a bistro on Nevsky Prospekt, transliterating back into Cyrillic the French pronunciation, and thereby producing a new Russian word.

46. As George Vernadsky notes, the lack of telegraphs or railroads contributed to the poor communication and confusion. Vernadsky, *A History of Russia*, p. 209.

47. On this debate, see chapter 7, by Angela Stent, "Reluctant Europeans: Three Centuries of Russian Ambivalence Toward the West," in this volume.

48. LeDonne, *The Russian Empire and the World*, pp. 124–129.

49. Michael T. Florinsky, *Russia: A History and an Interpretation*, vol. 2 (New York: Macmillan, 1953), pp. 879–881.

50. Astrid Tuminez, *Russian Nationalism Since 1856: Ideology and the Making of Foreign Policy* (Lanham, MD: Rowman and Littlefield, 2000), chap. 3.

51. David McDonald, chap. 3, "Domestic Conjunctures, the Russian State, and the World Outside, 1700–2006," in this volume.

52. Hosking, *Russia and the Russians*, p. 356.

53. Vernadsky, *A History of Russia*, p. 246.

54. On this period in Asia and Europe, see Dietrich Geyer, *Russian Imperialism: The Interaction of Domestic and Foreign Policy, 1860–1914*, trans. Bruce Little (New York: Berg, 1987), especially chap. 6.

55. Stephen M. Walt, *Revolution and War* (Ithaca: Cornell University Press, 1996), chap. 4; and Peter Holquist, *Making War, Forging Revolution: Russia's Continuum of Crisis, 1914–1921* (Cambridge: Harvard University Press, 2002), especially chap. 2.

56. Hosking, *Russia and the Russians*, p. 388.

57. V. I. Lenin, *Imperialism, the Highest Stage of Capitalism* (Moscow: International Publishing Company, 1969).

58. Adam B. Ulam, *Expansion and Coexistence: Soviet Foreign Policy, 1917–73*, 2d ed. (Fort Worth, TX: Holt, Rinehart, and Winston, 1974).

59. Charles P. Kindleberger, *The World in Depression, 1929–1939*, rev. ed. (Berkeley: University of California Press, 1986).

60. For the classic argument that Stalinism was not the only potential result of the Bolshevik Revolution, see Stephen F. Cohen, *Bukharin and the Bolshevik Revolution: A Political Biography, 1888–1938* (Oxford: Oxford University Press, 1971).

61. Anne Applebaum, *Gulag: A History* (New York: Doubleday, 2003), chap. 3.

62. Ibid., pp. 122–124.

63. Bradley F. Smith, *Sharing Secrets with Stalin: How the Allies Traded Intelligence, 1941–1945* (Lawrence: University of Kansas Press, 1996).

64. Valerie Bunce, "The Empire Strikes Back: The Evolution of the Eastern Bloc from a Soviet Asset to a Soviet Liability," *International Organization* 39, no. 1 (Winter 1985): 1–46; and Randall W. Stone, *Satellites and Commissars: Strategy and Conflict in the Politics of Soviet-Bloc Trade* (Princeton: Princeton University Press, 1995).

65. Gaddy, *Open for Business*, pp. 10–24.

66. Marshall D. Shulman, *Stalin's Foreign Policy Reappraised* (New York: Atheneum, 1969), chap. 2.

67. Peter Almquist, *Red Forge: The Soviet Defense Industry Since 1965* (New York: Columbia University Press, 1990); and Clifford Gaddy, *The Price of the Past: Russia's Struggle with the Legacy of a Militarized Society* (Washington, DC: Brookings Institution Press, 1996).

68. James Richter, *Khrushchev's Double Bind: International Pressures and Domestic Coalition Politics* (Baltimore: Johns Hopkins University Press, 1994); and James Goldgeier, *Leadership Style and Soviet Foreign Policy: Stalin, Khrushchev, Brezhnev, and Gorbachev* (Baltimore: Johns Hopkins University Press, 1994).

69. Bruce D. Porter, *The U.S.S.R. in Third World Conflicts: Soviet Arms and Diplomacy in Local Wars, 1945–1980* (Cambridge: Cambridge University Press, 1986).

70. Michael Nelson, *War of the Black Heavens: The Battles of Western Broadcasting in the Cold War* (Syracuse, NY: Syracuse University Press, 1997), especially chap. 8.

71. Matthew Evangelista documents that this was true not only because of Gorbachev's political liberalizations; it extended back to the 1950s. Evangelista, *Unarmed Forces: The Transnational Movement to End the Cold War* (Ithaca: Cornell University Press, 1999).

72. Renée de Nevers, *Comrades No More: The Seeds of Change in Eastern Europe* (Cambridge: MIT Press, 2002); and Jeffrey T. Checkel, *Ideas and International Political Change: Soviet/Russian Behavior and the End of the Cold War* (New Haven: Yale University Press, 1997), chap. 5.

73. Raymond L. Garthoff, *Détente and Confrontation: American-Soviet Relations from Nixon to Reagan*, rev. ed. (Washington, DC: Brookings Institution Press, 1994).

74. Robert Legvold, "The Nature of Soviet Power," *Foreign Affairs* 56, no. 1 (October 1977): 49–71.

75. Hosking, *Russia and the Russians,* p. 573.

76. Mark Kramer, "The Collapse of East European Communism and the Repercussions Within the Soviet Union (Part I)," *Journal of Cold War Studies* 5, no. 4 (Fall 2003): 178–256; and Astrid S. Tuminez, "Nationalism, Ethnic Pressures, and the Breakup of the Soviet Union," *Journal of Cold War Studies* 5, no. 4 (Fall 2003): 81–136.

77. For a comprehensive and astonishingly accurate contemporaneous analysis of the weaknesses of Gorbachev's policies, see Ed A. Hewett and Victor H. Winston, eds., *Milestones in Glasnost and Perestroyka: Politics and People* (Washington, DC: Brookings Institution Press, 1991); and Ed A. Hewett and Victor H. Winston, eds., *Milestones in Glasnost and Perestroyka: The Economy* (Washington, DC: Brookings Institution Press, 1991).

78. On globalization and Russian insecurity, see Alexander Cooley, "Globalization and National Security After Empire: The Former Soviet Space," paper prepared for the Olin Institute Workshop on Globalization and National Security, Harvard University, June 11–12, 2004.

79. As one of Russia's leading political economists and experts on the World Trade Organization writes, World Trade Organization membership "is able to generate nonmonopolistic, competitive mechanisms of economic development. It is these mechanisms, which are able to foster economic development of Russia better than any decision of national government." Stanislav Tkachenko, "Russia's Membership in WTO: Implications for Economic Security of Post-Soviet Countries," in *Post-Communist Countries in the Globalizing World,* ed. Konstantin Khudoley (St. Petersburg: St. Petersburg State University Press, 2004), pp. 170–199, quotation at p. 195.

CONTRIBUTORS

Lawrence T. Caldwell

Lawrence T. Caldwell is the Cecil H. and Louise Gamble Professor of Politics at Occidental College. He has served as research associate at the International Institute of Strategic Studies in London; as a visiting professor and director of European Studies at the National War College in Washington, D.C.; as a scholar in residence in the Office of Soviet Analysis at the CIA from 1981 to 1983; and as a staff member and consultant at the Jet Propulsion Laboratory from 1983 to 1985 and at the Rand Corporation from 1985 to 1989. He taught in the Rand–UCLA Center for Soviet Studies graduate program from 1987–1993. His current projects include a study of the letters of Sir Ivor Heron-Maxwell, a British military intelligence officer during the Russian Revolution, and the intelligence issues arising from the "lies and leaks" in American policy on Iraq.

Robert Legvold

Robert Legvold is the Marshall D. Shulman Professor of Political Science at Columbia University and former director of the Harriman Institute (1984–1990). His most recent books comprise (with Bruno Coppieters) *Statehood and Security: Georgia after the Rose Revolution* (2005); (with Celeste Wallander) *Swords and Sustenance: The Economics of Security in Belarus and Ukraine* (2003); *Thinking Strategically: The Major Powers, Kazakhstan and the Central Asian Nexus* (2002); and (with Sherman Garnett) *Belarus at the Crossroads* (1999).

David McDonald

David McDonald is the Mortenson-Petrovich Professor of History at the University of Wisconsin–Madison, where he specializes in the history of the Russian Empire. He has written on Russian intellectual, political, and international history, including the book *United Government and Russian Foreign Policy, 1900–1914* (1992).

Alfred J. Rieber

Alfred J. Rieber is professor of history at the Central European University and emeritus at the University of Pennsylvania. He has divided his research between the social and political history of imperial Russia and Soviet foreign policy. Among his major works are *The Politics of Autocracy (1966)*; *Merchants and Entrepreneurs in Imperial Russia* (1982); *Stalin and the French Communist Party, 1941–1947* (1962); and "Stalin: Man of the Borderlands" *The American Historical Review* (December 1991).

Gilbert Rozman

Gilbert Rozman is Musgrave Professor of Sociology at Princeton University. His latest monograph is *Northeast Asia's Stunted Regionalism: Bilateral Distrust in the Shadow of Globalization* (2004). Recent coedited books include: *Korea at the Center: Dynamics of Regionalism in Northeast Asia* (2006), *Russian Strategic Thought Toward Asia* (2006), and *Japanese Strategic Thought Toward Asia* (2007).

Angela Stent

Angela Stent is professor of government and director of the Center for Eurasian, Russian, and East European Studies at Georgetown University. She previously served as national intelligence officer for Russia and Eurasia at the National Intelligence Council and in the State Department's Office of Policy Planning. She has published widely on Russian-German and Russian-European relations, including *Russia and Germany Reborn: Unification, The Soviet Collapse, and the New Europe.*

Ronald Grigor Suny

Ronald Grigor Suny is the Charles Tilly Collegiate Professor of Social and Political History at the University of Michigan and Professor Emeritus of Political Science and History at the University of Chicago. He is the author of *The Revenge of the Past: Nationalism, Revolution, and the Collapse of the Soviet Union* (1993), and *The Soviet Experiment: Russia, the Soviet Union, and the Successor States* (1998) and the editor of the *Cambridge History of Russia: The Twentieth Century* (2006).

Celeste A. Wallander

Celeste A. Wallander is visiting associate professor in the School of Foreign Service at Georgetown University. Previously, she was director and senior fellow of the Russia and Eurasia Program at the Center for Strategic and International Studies (2001–2006); senior fellow at the Council on Foreign Relations in Washington, D.C. (2000–2001); and associate professor of government at Harvard University (1989–2000). She is the founder and executive director of the Program on New Approaches to Russian Security. She is the author of over seventy scholarly and public interest publications, including *Swords and Sustenance: The Economics of Security in Belarus and Ukraine* (2003), coedited with Robert Legvold; *Mortal Friends, Best Enemies: German-Russian Cooperation After the Cold War* (1999); and *The Sources of Russian Foreign Policy After the Cold War* (1996). She is currently writing Global Russia: Economics, Politics, and Security and The Geopolitics of Energy in Eurasia.

Abkzian diversion, 326
ABM Treaty. *See* Antiballistic Missile (ABM) Treaty
absolutism. *See* Stalin, Joseph; totalitarianism
absolutist tradition, 147–148, 157–159; postabsolutism, 182–187; reforms based in, 160–161, 163–164, 168–169, 171–173. *See also* strong state model
Aehrenthal, A., 173–174, 200n.120
Afghanistan, 57–58, 223, 226; Bolshevik diplomatic relations with, 226; People's Democratic Party of, 57–58
Afghanistan-U. S. conflict, 7, 99, 122, 258, 323, 346
Afghan war, 22, 57, 57–58, 103, 231, 364; ending of Soviet intervention, 96, 99, 103, 170, 177, 190n.27, 489; Russia's tensions with China over, 364; U. S. involvement in under Reagan, 488
Africa, Soviet Union interest in, 21
Age of Exploration, 451, 469, 470
Akayev, Askar, 64
Albright, Madeleine, 128
Alexander I, 167, 287, 307, 402, 473, 475
Alexander II, 45, 100, 101, 106, 127; assassination of, 127, 241, 307, 402, 476; defeat in the Crimean War, 89, 94–95, 97, 114, 117, 126, 476; domestic and foreign policy interactions, 153, 155, 169; Emancipation Edict, 88–89, 90, 94, 399, 401, 474, 476; Great Reforms under, 89–91, 155, 158, 167, 168; great state transformation in reign of, 77, 85, 86, 88–91, 101, 106–107, 125–126, 284; military conscription under, 45; Pan-Slavism in reign of, 20, 110, 167, 400
Alexander III, 44, 94, 294, 402–403
Alexeev, Nikolai, 110
Alexei, N. Romanov, Tsar, 281, 469–470
alliances, 7, 57, 124, 248, 473; against terror, 5, 27, 445, 478, 491; in Northeast Asia, 360–365; strategic and short-term rather than long-term, 18, 123–128; uncertainty in, 125–127; under Stalinist regime, 22, 126, 127–128, 229–230, 484. *See also* North American Treaty Alliance (NATO)
Allied Forces, 484
Al-Qaeda, 445. *See also* terrorism
American popular culture, 413
Amin, Hafizullah, 58
ancien régime. See tsarist Russia
Anderson, Benedict, 43–44, 46, 155
Anglo-Russian Treaty of 1907, 208
Anisimov, Evgeny, 107
Antiballistic Missile (ABM) Treaty, 7, 62, 97, 119, 129, 318, 319

anticolonial revolutions, 214
anti-imperial ideology, 48–50, 56
anti-Russian coalitions, 100
anti-Semitism, 415
anti-Soviet organizations abroad, 227
anti-U. S. alliance, 6
arable land, 23, 207
Arbatov, Georgy, 303
armaments: arms sales, 184, 222,
    458–459; flow of arms, 5, 234;
    technology and, 167, 221
armed forces. *See* military personnel
Armenia, 64, 258
arms control. *See* nuclear arms control
arms race. *See* nuclear arms
arms sales, 184, 222, 458–459
Asia: communist parties in, 242–254;
    perception of Russia, 25, 26; U. S.
    geopolitical role in, 346. *See also*
    China; Japan; Northeast Asia
Asian investment, 28
Asia-Pacific Cooperation, 368
Astrakhan, Khanate of, 93, 209, 210
Atlanticists, 62, 111, 418. *See also* Kozyrev,
    Andrei; Westernizers
August 1991 coup, 54, 58, 175, 176, 178, 181, 489
Austria, 126, 474
Austria-Hungary, 48, 172, 173, 295, 402;
    1849 rebellion, 22, 47. *See also* Hungary
Austro-German alliance, 289
authoritarianism: bureaucratic
    authoritarianism, 31–32, 131–132, 455;
    rejection or erosion of, 75n.59, 84,
    158–159, 488. *See also* autocracy;
    censorship
autocracy, 19–20, 24, 35, 44, 59, 73n.35,
    81, 148, 153, 292, 399; as autarky, 215,
    220, 225, 266n.44, 485; economic
    backwardness and, 23–24, 46; idealized
    as part of Russian greatness, 77, 82–85,
    92, 114–116, 148, 162, 174, 185, 398; recast
    in great state transformations, 78–80,

82; and regime type, 47; in the Soviet
    era, 82–83, 86, 89, 100, 115, 128, 160,
    254–255, 331, 404–405; in the tsarist era,
    82–83, 89, 115, 160, 331, 476. *See also*
    authoritarianism; national security;
    state power
autonomy, 23, 27, 193–194n.54, 458
Azerbaijan, 63–64, 259; NATO ties
    with, 6

Baikal-Amur Railroad, 353
Balkans, 153, 173, 180, 316–317
Baltic region, 7, 17, 118, 233, 403, 467;
    contemporary Russian relations with,
    432–433; Protestant roots, 209; Russian
    expansion into, 17, 20. *See also* East
    Germany
Baltic republics, 217, 244, 429, 454
banking system, 472, 477
Bashkirs, 209
Belarus, 28, 240, 314, 454, 471;
    authoritarian turn in, 32; current
    Russian policy towards, 32, 121, 122,
    258, 326, 422, 425
Belinsky, Visarion, 82–83
Berezovsky, Boris, 121–122, 182
Beria, Lavrenti, 243
Berlin insurrection of 1953, 22, 251–252
Berlin Wall, 232, 270n.80, 308, 309, 486;
    fall of, 415, 424
Berlusconi, Sylvio, 424, 431
Beslan school massacre, 120, 146, 187n.3,
    279, 315
Bessarabia. *See* Moldova
Bhaghdad Pact, 300
bilateral détente, 414
bilateralism, 414, 426–427
bilateral negotiations, 347–348
billiard ball construction of states, 38,
    185, 487
bipolar world, 212, 298, 326. *See also* Cold
    War

Bismarck, Otto von, 106, 118, 127, 151, 165, 288–289; close relationship with tsarist rulership, 288–289, 402–403; on imperial unification, 165–166

Black, Cyril, 21, 28; *The Pattern of Russian Objectives*, 16–18

Black Sea, 14, 127, 475

Blagoveshchensk-Vladivostok corridor, 365–366

Bolshevik Revolution, 86, 136n.56, 217, 406; World War I leading to, 85, 95, 106

Bolsheviks, 164, 214; foreign policy of, 217, 286, 296; ideology of, 48–50, 56, 290; initial peace orientation of, 56, 481; seeking a federation of sovereign states, 24–25, 238–239; "war communism" under, 85, 215. *See also* Lenin-Stalin communist transformation

Bolshevik treaties of 1920–1921, 226

border crossings, 257

borderlands, 4, 21, 208, 229, 326; colonization of, 21, 207, 208, 209; deportation of population in, 242–244; loss of, 255; nationalist sentiment in, 64–65, 209–210, 245; resistance and uprisings in, 22, 44, 234–235, 245, 252, 291, 412; Russian-speaking populations in, 255–256, 314; as "shatter zones," 21, 209; southern tier states, 63–65. *See also* multinational society; neighboring countries; periphery

border sealing, 226; construction of the Berlin Wall, 232, 270n.80, 308, 309, 486; "Iron Curtain" sealing off Eastern Europe, 26, 484

border security, 208, 211–212, 216, 218, 223, 228, 257–258; eastern border security interests, 365–366, 368, 370, 376

Bosnia Stabilization and Implementation Forces, 420. *See also* Kosovo War

boyar class, 79–80, 159, 467

brain drain, 225

Brest-Litovsk treaty, 216–217, 291, 293, 407, 481

Brezhnev, Leonid, 22, 153, 166, 412; Asian foreign policy, 364, 372; foreign policy toward the West, 395, 412–414. *See also* Afghan war; Brezhnev Doctrine; détente; ethnicity principle (*korenizatsiya*)

Brezhnev Doctrine, 146, 152, 213, 235

British Broadcasting Corporation (BBC), 237

British workers, Soviet aid to, 240

Brodie, Bernard, *The Absolute Weapon*, 303

Brodsky, Josif, 254

Brubaker, Rogers, 64

Buckle, Henry Thomas, 12, 33n.7

Budapest summit, Conference on Security and Cooperation, 119

Bukharin, Nikolay, 220, 291, 406

Bulgarian populations, 243

bureaucracy, 79, 88, 134n.22, 159, 223; corruption in, 160, 181; effect of centralizing state power, 50; enlightened bureaucrats, 160, 161, 236; reform and, 265n.35, 312, 455

bureaucratic absolutism, 149, 192n.41

bureaucratic authoritarianism, 31–32, 128, 131, 131–132, 455

Bush, George W.: abrogating the ABM Treaty, 7, 62, 97, 119, 129, 318, 319; Afghanistan intervention, 7, 99, 122, 258, 323, 346; Northeast Asian foreign policy, 259–260; preemptive war doctrine of 2002, 35, 333; Putin joining with him in the war on terror, 5, 9, 27, 124, 146, 427, 445, 478, 491; Putin's relationship with, 70, 146–147, 184, 330, 378; unilateral actions, 97, 327, 330, 347; war on terror, 5, 9, 27, 124, 146, 427, 445, 478, 491. *See also* Iraq War; war on terror

Butterfield, Herbert, 14

Byzantium, 113, 210, 462, 463. *See also* Orthodox Christian Church

Caldwell, Lawrence T., 21, 24, 279

Cambodia, 364

"campaign mentality," 223

Cam Ranh Bay airbase, 119

capital, 223; absence of, 207

capital flight, 455

capital flows, 225

capital investment, 91

capitalism: industrialization under, 23, 46, 449; Lenin's analysis of, 96, 480–481; Soviet analysis of, 25, 300–301; and Soviet socialism, 118–119, 218–219; state capitalism, 85–86

Carillo, Santiago, 252

Carr, Edward H., 11, 12–13, 399–400

Catherine II (the Great), 157, 210, 307, 379–380, 402; absolutist model of the state, 157; border security concerns, 287; Europeanization under, 393, 398–399, 471–472; the "Greek project," 307

Caucasus, 69, 121; Caucasian republics, 217, 233; Russian expansion into, 17, 107

Ceaușescu, Nikolae, 413

censorship, 9, 378; of foreign ideas and culture, 226–227, 450; jamming of long-range radio broadcasts, 237

Central Asia, 18, 117–118, 161, 258–259; Russian expansion into, 17; terrorism and, 347; U. S. bases in, 122–123; Yeltsin supporting U. S. war in

Central Committee of the Communist Party, 49, 175, 177, 254, 299–301

Central Committee Report to the Twentieth Party Congress, 299–300, 301

Central Europe, 4–5, 172, 244, 288, 288–289, 425, 460. *See also* Baltic republics; Eastern Europe; Europe; Poland; Warsaw Pact

centralized authority, 80–81, 82–84, 86–88, 153; erosion or weakness of, 25, 47, 54, 175; localism and, 343, 378, 379, 379–381, 384; Putin's orientation toward, 386; Soviet goal to control world communism, 217, 228, 236, 250, 251–252. *See also* metropole; state structure

Central Powers, 216. *See also* Germany; Hungary; Poland

Chaadaev, Peter, 160

Charles XII, 136, 150, 156, 166, 184, 286–287. *See also* Sweden

Charter for American-Russian Friendship and Cooperation, 4

Chechen wars, 7, 27, 29, 100–101, 147, 315, 326, 328, 421, 456; Chechen rebellion (19th c.), 244; post-Soviet era Muslim states and, 256–257; Putin's pursuit of, 69–70, 100–101, 184; second rebellion, 256–257

Chechnya, 36, 61, 67, 186, 379, 429

Cheney, Dick, 318, 360

Chernigov, 18

Chicherin, Georgii, 56, 218, 248, 407

China, 20, 28, 212, 361, 362, 372; as a potential threat, 358–359; ascendancy of, 104, 112, 352–353, 375, 387; Confucian heritage, 28, 30, 349–350; international diplomacy and, 115, 129, 352–353; rise of Chinese communism, 212, 230; Russian bilateral trade with, 355, 365; Russian trade with, 374–375; Soviet military and arms support of, 229, 234; Three Gorges dam project, 373. *See also* Sino-Japanese relations; Sino-Russian relations; Sino-Soviet conflict; Sino-U. S. relations

Chinese communism, 252–253

Chinese Eastern Railway, 370

Chizhov, Vladimir, 432

Chubais, Ivor, 60

CIS. *See* Commonwealth of Independent States

city government. *See* local civil government

civil society, 128, 151, 179, 182, 186, 401, 439; local civil government, 53–54, 95, 117, 379–380, 399, 465, 476; "local nationalism," 53–54, 95

civil war of 1918–1922, 161, 198n.91, 199, 210, 215–217; communist era taking shape from, 48, 95, 164, 223, 239, 482

class struggle, 4, 45, 47, 57, 302, 371, 489

Clausewitz, Carl von, 36

Clinton, William J. (Bill), U. S.-Russian relations during, 5, 6, 128–129, 318, 419–420

coastlands, 20

Cold War, 230–233, 281, 352, 413, 428, 486–487; contemporary resonances, 67–69, 129, 318, 360, 368, 428; ending of under Gorbachev, 58, 170, 177, 452; mentality of, 56, 145, 146, 326, 481, 485; secrecy during, 311–312; specter of nuclear confrontation, 62, 96, 303. *See also* bipolar world; détente

collective security, 56, 169. *See also* League of Nations

Collective Security Treaty, 314

collectivization, 85, 241, 400, 405; the commune, 160, 207, 400, 474

colonialism, 59

colonization of borderlands, 21, 207, 208, 209

Cominform (1948–1955), 217, 253

Comintern (1919–1943), 56, 58, 246, 481–482; Second Comintern Congress, 250; Stalin and, 118, 228–229, 233; Third Communist International, 217, 247, 408

command economy, 89, 216; of the Soviet era, 60, 216, 272, 344; unraveling of, 63, 81, 266n.38

commodities and consumer goods, 91, 115, 132, 219, 221, 354–355, 425, 450, 456, 458

"Common European Home" (Gorbachev), 4, 235, 395, 414–416, 489

Commonwealth of Independent States (CIS), 225, 238, 256, 257, 260, 313–314

Commonwealth of European States, 4

Commonwealth of Independent States, 238–239

commune, 160, 207, 400, 474

communications technologies, 236, 237, 444, 452, 487

communism. *See* Communist Party (CPSU); world communism

Communist Party (CPSU), 251, 254, 312, 483; antiparty groups, 298, 306; Central Committee of the Communist Party, 49, 175, 177, 254, 301; conservative attack on Gorbachev, 54, 58, 175, 176, 178, 181, 489; disintegration of, 170, 175, 245; Fifteenth Party Congress, 220; interparty conflict, 159, 177–178; Nineteenth Party Congress, 90; Tenth Party Congress, 297; Twentieth Party Congress, 297–303, 305, 331. *See also* Cominform 1948–1955; Comintern, 1919–1943

Concert of Europe system, 13, 402–403, 475

Conference on Security and Cooperation, 119, 411

Confucian heritage in China, 28, 30, 349–350

Congress of Berlin, 118

Congress of People's Deputies, 414; Inter-regional Group, 414

Congress of Vienna, 167

conjunctural factors for change, 211–212

conservativism, 54, 58–59, 62, 175, 176, 178, 181, 332–333, 489

constituencies, 40

constructivist approach to international relations, 35, 38–40; social constructivism, 38–40

consumer goods. *See* commodities and consumer goods

contemporary Russia. *See* Russian Federation

contraband, 27

Conventional Forces in Europe Treaty, 454

core state. *See* metropole; Russian core territory

corporate estates (*soslovie*), 207

corporate state, 424

corruption, 358, 424, 490; historically embedded, 60, 66, 168; under Putin, 32, 160, 374, 424; under Yeltsin and privatization, 62, 91, 178, 181, 355, 419, 455. *See also* oligarchs

Cossack brotherhood, 208, 209

Cossacks, 468

Council for Mutual Economic Assistance, 250, 412

crime, 91

Crimean War, 126, 208, 248, 351, 474; Russia's defeat in, 23, 89, 94–95, 97, 114, 117, 126, 169, 399, 401, 475–476

criminality, along eastern border, 348, 354, 356, 359, 373, 374, 382, 383, 386, 387

crisis of 1998, 225

Cuban Missile Crisis

cultural alienation, 27, 206, 210, 247; as a barrier to globalization, 450, 451; Bolshevick goals alienating Western powers, 246; Soviet political culture and, 254–255, 257, 259; Soviet rhetoric increasing, 246–247; in tsarist Russia, 113–114, 140n.101. *See also* border sealing; censorship; isolation; Western powers' relationship with Russia

culturally distinct peoples of Russia. *See* multinational society

cultural/religious rebellions, 209. *See also* ethnic cleansing and relocations; military interventions

Cultural Revolution, 372. *See also* China

Custine, Marquis de, 210; *La Russie en 1839*, 404

Customs Union, 314

Cyrillic script, 462

Czheckoslovakia, 22, 56, 169, 228, 248; Prague Spring rebellion and Soviet intervention, 152, 167, 234–235, 251, 412

Czech Republic, entry into NATO, 5, 69, 313, 326

Daniel, Yury, 254

Danilvevsky, Nikolai, *Rosiya i Evropa*, 400–401

debt repayment, 10

Decembrists, 474

decentralization, 382–383

decolonization: of Russian borderlands, 212; of third world, 212, 235

Decree on Peace, 481

defeat in war or foreign policy, 40, 46, 172; restructuring in periods of decline, 163. *See also* Cold War; Crimean War; Russo-Japanese War

defense spending, cuts in, 4

defensive realist theory, 37, 38, 57

deglobalization: defined, 444–446; during Soviet era, 483–484; in Russian history, 451, 464, 468–469, 482

deindustrialization, 215, 225, 366, 456. *See also* industrial development

democracy, 65, 438n.37; as emergent within Soviet rule, 60; Putin's "managed democracy" concept, 32, 84, 421, 423, 433; Russian and Western conceptions of, 27, 131, 436n.7

democratic failings, 27

democratic zone of trust, 4

demography: demographic descent in
contemporary Russia, 102; demographic
disasters, 215, 221; of the USSR, 238. *See
also* depopulation;
deportations; emigration; migration
Deng Xiaoping, 254
Denmark, Russian wars with, 93, 107
depopulation, 221, 366; current decline in,
27, 102, 349, 359; outflow of labor, 223;
under Ivan IV, 81. *See also* demography
deportations, 210, 241, 242–244, 243
depopulation. *See also* emigration
derzhavnost (great "powerness"), 92, 114,
115, 116, 148, 185. *See also* great power
identity; state power
détente, 222, 236, 237, 245, 253–254,
302–303; European-Soviet relations
softened during, 413, 414; failure of,
488–489; a step toward economic
globalization, 452, 487; under Brezhnev,
411, 413
deterrence, 305–306, 325
Deutsche Welle, 237
diplomacy, 246, 283, 478; diplomatic
creativity in security policy, 226, 246,
283, 288, 299, 301, 307, 309, 321, 325–326,
327–328. *See also* alliances
"dirigiste" practice, 32, 147. *See also* state
power
disease epidemics, 445, 447, 465
dissenters, 254
Djilas, Milovan, *The New Class*, 160
domestic and foreign policy interactions,
domestic imperatives constraining
foreign policy, 128, 129–132, 169–170,
179–181; foreign policy ignoring domestic
imperatives, 147, 149–150, 154–155, 165,
199n.99; integration of foreign and
domestic policies, 147–149, 150, 155, 156,
167–168. *See also* national security
domestic conjunctures. *See* domestic and
foreign policy interactions

domestic economy. *See* economy
domestic policy, 27, 29, 145, 490; and
internal development, 128, 129–132;
national evolution and, 3, 17, 31,
62n.35, 129–130, 421, 424; rulers as
reformers, 160–161, 163–164, 168–169,
171–173; self-reliance orientation, 23,
40, 220, 398. *See also* autocracy;
economy
Donskoi, Dmitri
Dostoevsky, Fyodor, 113–114
drugs, flow of, 5
dualistic concepts of Russian identity,
108–109, 111, 197n.86, 254, 399, 418
Dugin, Alexander, 109–111, 112, 423
dukhovnost (spirituality), 115
Duma, 132, 145, 171–172, 173, 181, 201n.125,
330, 430; 2003 elections, 423, 440n.79;
reacting against reforms, 332–333

East Asian foreign policy, 28
East Asian summit of 2005, 350
East Central Europe, 460
eastern border: Asian migration viewed as
a threat, 353, 355, 358, 370, 386;
balancing multiple objectives along,
350, 382–383; criminal elements along,
348, 354, 356, 359, 373, 374, 382, 383, 386,
387; geopolitics, 344–345, 377; historical factors, 351–355, 362; security
interests along, 365–366, 368, 370, 376.
See also Northeast Asia; Russian Far
East
Eastern Europe, 269n.68, 415; economic
relations with Soviets, 412–413,
484–485; insurrections against Soviets,
234; loss of empire in, 103–104;
Russian expansion and expropriation
in, 17, 25–26; Soviet power over,
396–397, 407–410, 412. *See also*
Czechoslovakia; East Germany;
Hungary; Poland

East Germany, 221, 232, 301, 309, 415;
mass exodus from, 232–233; Soviet
expropriation of human and industrial
capital, 25–26; USSR intervention in
1953 rebellion, 22, 234, 251–252; USSR
withdrawal from, 416
East-West divide, 4
economic backwardness, 20, 23, 24, 27,
206–207; and autocracy, 23–24, 46;
collectivization and, 241; during the
1920s, 218–225; and identity, 46;
military might paradoxically existing
with, 165–166; of peripheral states, 239;
possible amelioration of, 31; view of
challenged as oversimplified, 282–283
economic crises, 6, 90, 451, 456, 457, 491;
economic collapse under Yeltsin,
101–102, 259, 453–454, 455; following
great state transformations, 81, 87–88
economic deficits, 23
economic exchange, 444
economic globalization, 225; vs. security
interests, 7. *See also* expansionism;
globalization
economic growth, 27, 60, 145, 329, 457;
in periods of Soviet era, 60, 241, 300,
483, 485
economic localism, 365–366, 382, 382–383
economic models, 259
economic protectionism, 482–483; trade
restrictions, 22, 24, 448, 477. *See also*
trade
economy, 24, 27, 132, 225; balance of
payments deficit, 456; banking system,
472, 477; economic oligarchy (*see also*
oligarchs), 356, 439n.66, 456; exports
(*see also* oil and gas exports), 218, 219,
225, 457–458, 487; foreign policy
interacting with, 8, 17–18, 220; GDP
and income, 90–91, 294t., 324, 457;
growth and development periods in
Soviet era, 60, 241, 300, 483, 485;

modernization of, 5, 8, 23, 89, 109, 128;
premodern aspects of, 83, 473, 475–476;
in Soviet era, 90–91, 153, 215, 264n.22
and 24; tradition of state control over,
81, 214, 225; of the USSR, 90–91, 153,
215, 264n.22 and 24. *See also* economic
backwardness; economic crises;
market reforms; trade
Ehrenburg, Ilya, 226
Eisenhower, Dwight, 306
Elbe River, 18
Elizaveta Petrovna, Empress, 229, 287, 471
emancipation of the serfs, 88–89, 90, 94,
399, 401, 474, 476
Embassy to Europe of 1697, 100
emigration, 64, 223, 244–245, 254–255;
efforts to stem, 226. *See also*
depopulation
Emmons, Terence, 95
empire, 35, 50; as a regime type, structure
of, 40–43; autocracy intrinsic to, 47;
metropole (core) of, 42–43, 47–48;
periphery of, 42–43; political hierarchy
in, 43; rulership differing from that of
a nation-state, 43; the Soviet Union as
an empire state, 47–55
empiricism, 13
Empress Elizabeth, 229, 287, 471
encirclement, 21, 166, 226; capitalist
encirclement in Soviet era, 75, 227, 231,
235, 249, 261, 483
energy markets, 9–10, 457
energy policy: cost to USSR of cheap oil
within the Warsaw pact, 412–413; gas
cutoff to Ukraine incident, 10,
425–426; gas subsidies, 225; global
economy and, 9–10, 224–225, 329–330,
422, 457; megaprojects, 344, 356–357,
366; oil exports as foreign policy
leverage, 98, 101, 103, 205, 321, 349, 374,
378, 426, 435, 458, 462. *See also* oil and
gas resources

Enlightenment ideals, 393, 398, 474

Entente Cordiale, 48, 172, 218

epidemics, global, 445, 447, 465

eras of great state transformation. *See* great state transformations

European and American socialists, 406

Esenin, Sergei, 218

Estonia, 226, 239, 432; entry into NATO, 313

ethnic cleansing and relocations, 242–244, 249. *See also* cultural/religious rebellions

ethnic discrimination, 45

ethnicity principle (*korenizatsiya*), 50, 51, 72–73n.23, 208, 240–242; concept of indigenous ethnicities, 50–51, 240–241; failure of, 53. *See also* Brezhnev Doctrine

Eurasianist movements: democratic or moderate Eurasianists, 110–111; during the Imperial era, 110, 139n.87; new Eurasianism, 259–260, 418–419, 423; postimperial identity and, 108, 109–111, 139n.91, 381. *See also* Pan-Slavism

Eurasian "special position," 27–28, 67, 108, 210, 320–324; Asia as part of Russian core territory, 18–19, 110, 362, 393; Asian aspects of Russian identity, 387–388, 431; the Eurasian empire, 466–469. *See also* Eurasianist movements; Northeast Asia

Euro-Atlantic foreign alliances, 7. *See also* Western powers' relationship with Russia

Eurocentrism in Russian policy, 349, 369

"Euro-communisim," 252

Europe, 410, 482; Age of Exploration, 451, 469, 470; the New Europeans, 431–433; penetrating Soviet airwaves, 237; perceptions of Russia, 17, 210. *See also* Central Europe; Eastern Europe; Europe and Russian identity

European Bank for Reconstruction and Development, 10

Europe and Russian identity, 393; Europe as a geopolitical reality, 394, 402–404, 433–435; Europe as a model, 23, 25, 393–394, 397–398, 417, 422–424, 435; Europe as an idea, 398–401, 410–411, 422–424, 435; periods of Europeanization in tsarist Russia, 397–399, 401–402, 470, 471–473; rejection of European political institutions, 401; Soviet experience and, 395, 396–397, 404–407

Europeanization, under Catherine II (the Great), 393, 398–399, 471–472

European Parliament, 430

European socialism, 404

European Union (EU), 8, 212, 453; *2000–2006 Country Strategy Paper,* 429; enlargement, 428–429, 433; national sovereignty and, 396; New Neighborhood policy, 431; Russian ties with, 97, 125, 421, 422, 425; unresolved issues of Russia's relationship with, 430–431

Europe-Russian relations, 8, 25, 32, 393, 414, 454; during Imperial era, 25, 403–404, 474; European intervention in the Russian civil war, 217, 238, 482; European marginalization of Russia, 25, 393, 404, 407; future possibilities, 433–435; post-Soviet era, 420–421; pre-Petrine antipathy, 397; Russian autocracy and, 80–81; under Putin, 146–147, 325–326, 327, 421–428. *See also* western border; Western powers' relationship with Russia

Europe-Soviet relations, 407–410; in the post-Vietnam generation, 487; pro-Europe shift under Gorbachev, 4, 235, 394–395, 395, 414–416, 489

exceptionalism. *See* Russian exceptionalism

exile populations, 27
expansionism, 17, 205; link to autocracy, 20; not eliminating risks, 244; porous frontiers leading to, 229–230, 232, 234–235, 281; Russian expansion as a myth, 205; of tsarist Russia, 100, 107–108, 471–473, 475–476; "unification" of former territories, 18
exports, 218, 219, 225, 457–458, 487; arms exports, 184, 222, 458–459; energy exports, 98, 101, 103, 205, 321, 329–330, 349, 374, 378, 426, 435, 462; untaxed resource exports, 356

fascism, 409. *See also* Hitler, Adolph; Third Reich; World War I
famine or food shortages, 81, 88, 101, 215, 482
Far East. *See* Russian Far East
Farkhutdinov, Igor, 348
fascism, victory over securing USSR superpower status, 52, 121, 166, 178
federalism, 238–239, 273
Fifteenth Party Congress, 220
Figes, Orlando, 114
Final Act, 5
Finland: Bolshevik diplomatic relations with, 226; Bolshevik mutual assistance pact with, 226; post-WW-I independence of, 217; Protestant roots, 209; Soviet attack on, 243, 247; Soviet bases in, 230
First World War. *See* World War I
Five Year Plans, 88, 220, 221, 228, 405
forced labor, 483. *See also* Gulag
foreign alliances. *See* alliances
foreign debt, 225, 457
foreign intervention, 49, 215, 217, 239, 241, 255, 258
foreign investment, 375, 425, 453, 459, 477
foreign loans, 207, 218, 221
foreign trade. *See* trade
former Soviet Union. *See* post-Soviet space

Founding Act on Russia-NATO relations, 317. *See also* North American Treaty Alliance (NATO)
Fradkov, Mikhail, 321
France: French revolution, 18; Russia's relations with, 126, 325–326, 327, 421, 473, 474; Soviet relations with, 248
Frankov, Mikhail, 321
Freedman, Lawrence, 102
freedom of choice policy, 4
free-market measures. *See* market reforms
frontier communities. *See* borderlands
frontier defenses. *See* border security
future directions and possibilities, 17, 26, 26–27, 29–30, 131–133; conjunctural factors for change, 210–212; for Europe-Russian relations, 433–435; for post-Soviet space, 65–70; potential in Northeast Asia, 357, 384–388; prospects for a post-Putin Russia, 184–187; regarding globalism and Russia, 31, 491–492

Gaidar, Yegor, 86
gas subsidies, 225
Gazprom, 425–426
Geertz, Clifford, 57
General Winter, 21, 166
geopolitics, 28, 29, 98–99, 179–181, 239; ascendancy of China (*see also* China), 104, 112, 352–353, 368–369, 375, 387; influence of geography (*See also* Eurasian "special position" of Russian land; porous frontiers), 21, 99, 283, 320–321, 443, 451; of Russia and the West (*See* Western powers' relationship with Russia); Russia's great power identity and (*see also* great power identity), 103–104, 108, 393, 451, 458. *See also* international institutions; international system; national interest

Georgia, 63–64, 67–68, 258, 259; color revolutions in, 9, 32; current Russian policy towards, 10, 32; NATO ties with, 6, 313; Rose Revolution, 9, 63, 122; Russian boycott of wines, 225, 313, 315; Russia's reach into, 64–68; to Stalin part of historical patrimony, 239, 240

German minorities in Russia, 241

German reunification, 177; fall of the Berlin Wall, 415, 424

Germans in Russia, deportation of, 210, 243

Germany: Brest-Litovsk treaty with, 216–217; rise and expansion of in the 20th c., 208–209, 212; Russia's relations with, 325–326, 327, 421. *See also* Bismarck, Otto von; Hitler, Adolph; Third Reich

Germany, Wilhelmine, 187

Gerschenkron, Alexander, 150, 216

Geyer, Dietrich, 88, 101, 110, 117–118

Giers, Nikolai K., 294

glasnost, 58, 224, 245, 354, 379, 414, 415

global hegemony. *See* unipolar hegemony

globalization: 19th c. wave of, 475–480; authoritarianism inhibiting, 23, 472, 479, 490–491; balancing with national- ism and localism, 343, 379–383; debate over Russian strategy of, 418–419; defined and conceptualized, 443–446; during tsarist era, 469–473; global belief networks, 445; index of, 443; internationalism under Putin, 458–460; military globalism, 445, 447, 449, 452, 473, 484; and national security, 444; and Russian foreign policy, 28, 104–105, 185, 443, 444, 446, 450; social and cultural globalism, 445; "thick" globalism, 446, 452, 489; time- space dimensions, 495n.45. *See also* economic globalization

global monetary markets, 218, 445, 452

global origins of Russia, 460–466

Gomułka, Władysław, 239

Gorbachev, Mikhail, 4, 5, 25, 105, 176–177, 250, 488–490; as a liberal internationalist, 4, 88–91, 109; ceasing interventions in the Soviet empire, 96, 103, 170, 177, 190n.27, 233, 415, 416; economic reforms, 222–233, 224; ending jammed airwaves, 237; ending the Cold War, 480–481, 489; foreign policy toward Europe, 235, 395, 414–416, 489; integrating foreign and domestic policy, 177–178; military and arms treaties, 4; renouncing Soviet-style communism, 58, 235, 414–415; stopping military interventions within the USSR, 96, 103, 170, 177, 190n.27, 233, 415, 416; unintended consequences of his reforms, 54, 79, 274n.117, 489–490. *See also glasnost*; "new thinking"; *perestroika*

Gorbachev-Yeltsin post-Soviet transformation, 77, 81, 86, 88–91, 96–97, 119, 121; adapting to revised international environment, 152; as distinct from prior regime changes, 150–151. *See also* post-Soviet transition

Gorchakov, A.M., 117, 127, 154, 244

gosudarstvennost, 147, 150, 185, 200n.124. *See also* statehood

grain expropriation, 86, 90, 219, 220, 482

grain harvest, 91

grain imports, 223

Great Britain, 20, 208, 220; Anglo-Russian Treaty of 1907, 208; the Entente Cordiale, 48, 172, 218; relations with Russia, 117–118, 119, 173; relations with Soviet Union, 240–241; Russian relations with, 421

great power identity: actual status and
fluctuations in, 69, 75n.53, 180,
199n.105, 294t., 409, 416, 444; autocracy
associated with, 77, 92, 114, 115, 116, 148,
174, 185, 398; defeat of Napoleon
ensuring, 473–474, 475; desire for
parity with the West, 23, 114–115, 207,
222, 259; foreign policy and, 69, 71n.5,
115, 186, 259, 293, 371, 459–460;
geopolitics and, 65–66, 103–104, 108,
393, 451, 458; influencing contemporary
Russian policy, 424–426, 458–460, 491;
interacting with state transformations,
101, 103, 105, 108, 109, 113–114, 115–117
Great Reforms, 88–91, 158, 167, 168;
Emancipation Edict, 88–89, 90, 94,
399, 401, 474, 476
Great Russians, 61, 238, 241
great state transformations, 10, 52–53, 77,
78, 83; Gorbachev-Yeltsin post-Soviet
transformation, 77, 81, 86, 88–91,
96–97, 119, 121; Lenin-Stalin communist
transformation, 77, 85, 86–88, 118–119,
121; under Alexander II in the 19th c.,
77, 86, 88–91, 94, 101, 106–107, 125–126;
under Ivan IV in the 16th c., 77, 79–82,
86, 92–94, 100, 107–108, 126; under
Peter the Great in the 18th c., 77, 82–83,
84–85, 94, 100, 107, 113–114, 126–127,
134n.22. *See also* political crises and
collapse of statist regimes
Greek populations, 243
Gromyko, Andrei, 249
gross domestic project (GDP), 90–91,
294t., 324, 457
Group of Eight, 184, 279, 320, 327–328, 459;
2006 summit, 8
Gulag system, 88, 254, 409, 483
Gulf War, 170

Hapsburg empire, 18, 20
Hashimoto-Yeltsin plan, 355

Heartland. *See* Eurasian "Heartland"
Hegel, G.W.F., 164
hegemony. *See* unipolar hegemony
Heilongjiang Province, 366
Helsinki Final Act (1975), 5, 487–488
Herder, Johann Gottfried von, 11
Hi Jintao, 368
Hirsch, Francine, 42
historical narrative, 14, 52
history, 31, 33n.12, 130; political science
compared to, 12–14; relation of past to
present, 1, 11, 14–15
Hitler, Adolph, 219, 241, 247, 406–407
Hobbes, Thomas, *Leviathan*, 157
Hobbesian worldview, 10
Ho Chi Minh, 252
Hohenzollern dynasty, 18
Holy Alliance, 126, 307, 402
Holy Synod, 403
"homeland myths," 61–62, 64–65
Honecker, Erich, 413
Hopf, Ted, 38, 60
Hosking, Geoffrey, 47, 83, 113, 489
Hughes, Lindsay, 82
Hu Jintao, 115, 327
human resources, 80, 259, 366;
expropriation of, 26, 147
human rights, 255, 260, 411, 430, 432,
436n.7, 487–488
human trafficking, 5
Hungary: deportations and refugee crisis,
234, 244; entry into NATO, 5, 69, 313, 326;
intervention in 1956 revolution, 22, 232,
234, 235, 251, 252, 301, 412, 415, 474, 486
identity. *See* Russian national identity
Ideological Commissions of the Central
Committee, 254, 277n.139
ideology, 155–156; heterogeneity, 190n.27,
284; national interest and, 36–38, 309;
shifts in, 283–284
ideology—themes and movements:
Atlanticists, 111, 418; Bolshevik period,

48–50, 56, 290; dualistic concepts of
Russian identity, 108–109, 111, 197n.86,
254, 399, 418; liberal vs. conservative
views, 175, 176, 393, 399, 411, 425; Marxist
revisionism, 234, 252; "realists," 112–114;
Russian intelligentsia, 47, 108, 164, 221,
254, 352, 393, 400, 404, 411, 415; Soviet
(*see also* Marxist-Lenism), 47–50, 236;
Westernizers, 111, 112, 378, 474. *See also*
intelligentsia; Marxist-Leninism;
Slavophiles
immigration. *See* migration
Imperial era. *See* tsarist Russia
imperialism: autocracy and, 20;
Bolshevik anti-imperial ideology,
48–50, 56, 290; delegitimazation of,
47–48; vs. modern state forms, 20;
Western imperialism, 55
imperial unification, 18, 165–166
imports, 223, 456, 487
index of globalization, 443. *See also*
globalization
India, 6, 28; cryogenic technology sale to
halted, 5
industrial development, 47, 52, 60, 220, 300,
405, 457; capitalist industrialization, 23,
46, 449; effects of (*See also* resource
extraction), 225, 477–478; globalization
and, 449, 483; Gulag system and, 405,
483, 485–486; proindustrial worldview,
216; slow progress of, 165, 207; state
efforts toward, 49, 85, 88, 101, 158, 160,
163, 174, 187; state power increased by,
477. *See also* deindustrialization
information flow and technologies, 236,
237, 444, 452, 487
Institute of the USA, 303
intelligentsia, 47, 108, 164, 221, 254, 302,
352, 393, 400, 404, 411, 415. *See also*
ideology—themes and movements
intercontinental ballistic missiles
(ICBMs), 304, 306

interdependence of states, 4. *See also*
globalization
international system, bipolar politics, 212,
298, 326
internal security forces, 227
international institutions, 320
international aid, 179, 453, 457
International Eurasianist Movement, 109
international institutions, 448; relations
of states (*see* geopolitics; international
system); Russia generally supporting,
18. *See also* International Monetary
Fund; North American Treaty Alliance
(NATO); United Nations Security
Council; World Bank; World Trade
Organization (WTO)
international law, 237, 319–320; maritime
rights of neutrals, 18
International Monetary Fund, 10, 261, 320,
453, 454
international relations theory, 35–41,
37–38. *See also* international
system
international system, 17, 41, 104, 211–213,
444; billiard ball construction of
states, 38, 185, 487; Bolsheviks excluded
from, 214–215; collapse of 1917–1918,
105, 214; debates over Russia's role in,
179–180; globalization impacting,
487–488; Russia as an international
actor, 10–11, 16–17, 29, 79, 98, 118–119;
Russia tending to support status quo,
18, 28, 123. *See also* geopolitics
international trade, 490
interwar period, 55, 199n.105, 407,
408–409
investment fraud, 456
Iran, 226, 368; nuclear energy program, 5,
9, 147, 427; partitioning of in Imperial
era, 208; Safavid (Iranian) Empire, 208
Iranian people in Russia, 242
Iranian revolution, 231

Iraq war, 8, 258; reconstruction efforts, 378; Russian relations with U. S. and Europe regarding, 9, 125, 183, 317, 427

Iron Curtain, 26, 484

"iron silk road," 356, 377

Ishaev, Viktor, 348

Islamic Fundamentalism, 69, 256, 346–347

isolation, 93, 154, 215, 360, 373, 384, 396, 398, 496; from dynamic Asian economies, 364; European marginalization of Russia, 25, 393, 404, 407; foreign policies and, 122, 160, 228, 248, 372, 433, 484, 485–486; geographic, 443, 472; from globalization pressures during Imperial era, 467–468, 469, 471; global participation affected by, 451–452, 456, 478; harsh rhetoric increasing, 119–120, 246–247, 249–250; by other nations, 107, 351, 462, 466–467; the self-isolating state and, 160, 168–169, 173. *See also* cultural alienation; Eurasian special position

Israel, 217, 244

Isvolskii, A.P., 172, 175

Ivan III, 18, 24, 92, 466

Ivan IV (the Terrible), 22, 92, 93, 113; conquests, 22, 107–108, 210; great state transformations in reign of, 77, 79–82, 86, 92–94, 100, 107–108, 126; modernization under, 284; Stalin compared to, 87–88

Ivanov, Igor, 428

Ivanov, Sergei, Ivanov doctrine, 310–311, 318, 325

Izvolsky, Alexander, 173–174, 200n.120

Jackson-Vannik Amendment, 245

Jahn, Hubertus, 46

Japan, 20; "economic miracle," 372; expansionism of, 208–209, 212, 228; Russian trade with, 374–375. *See also* Koizumi Junichiro; Sino-Japanese relations

Japanese-Russian relations, 10, 343, 365; contemporary diplomacy, 330, 344, 348, 366–368; disputed islands, 347, 367–368. *See also* Russo-Japanese War

Jewish population, 209, 217; anti-Semitism, 415; deportation of, 210, 244; emigration, 64, 223, 244–245

John, Dewey, 15

Kadets, 172

KAL 007, shooting down of, 237

Kalingrad exclave negotiations, 429

Karimov, Islam, 368

Karmal, Babrak, 58

Kazakhstan, 63–64, 256, 258, 314, 454

Kazan, Khanate of, 209, 210, 467

Kennan, George, 36, 210, 334n.2; *Siberia and the Exile System*, 404

Kennedy, John F., 249, 307

Kersten Amendment, 232

Khabarovsk, 242, 348, 357, 374, 381

Khanabad air base, 368

Khanates, Muslim, 117, 209, 210

Khasan area, 381–382

Khodorkovsky, Mikhail, 182, 329, 425

Khrushchev, Nikita, 21, 299–300; de-Stalinization campaign, 84; flexibility of foreign policy, 308–309; goal of surpassing the U. S., 23; his rhetoric alienating the West, 246–247, 249–250; nuclear weapons program, 24; political and policy reforms of, 161, 298–303; pullbacks in Manchuria and Xinjiang, 234; virgin soil program, 223. *See also* détente

Kievan Rus. *See* Kyivan Rus

Kim Dae Jung, 376

Kim Jong Il, 347, 359–360. *See also* North Korea

Kissinger, Henry, *Nuclear Weapons and Foreign Policy*, 303

Kliuchevsky, Vasily, 80, 84, 127, 397

Kocharian, Robert, 64

Koizumi Junichiro, 348, 359–360, 368, 381. *See also* Japan

Kokovstov, V.N., 175

Korea: Russian relations with, 362–363. *See also* North Korea; South Korea

"Korean card," 355, 376

Korean War, 485

korenizatsiya. See ethnicity principle (*korenizatsiya*)

Kosovo War: Bosnia Stabilization and Implementation Forces, 420; diplomacy regarding, 346, 419; Russia's defense of Serbia, 120, 129, 326; straining U. S.-Russian relations, 5, 119, 318, 419, 420, 456

Kozak plan, 432–433

Kozyrev, Andrei: affirming need for a powerful state, 67, 202–203n.154; proposing a new "Marshall Plan," 259; pro-Western position, 4–5, 111, 454; Putin modifying policies of, 310

kulaks, 217, 242

"kulaks," expulsion of, 223

Kurbsky, Andrei, 93

Kuropatkin, A.N., 288

Kyiv, 18, 467

Kyivan Rus, 460, 461–464; state structure, 461–462, 465

Kyrgyzstan, 123, 258, 259, 314; color revolutions in, 32

Lake Baikal, 18

Lamzdorf, V.N., 172

Latvia, 226, 239, 432; entry into NATO, 313

Law of USSR state borders, 237

leadership: constraints on, 40; the leadership myth, 205; sacralization of, 80, 82, 83–84; strategies and styles of, 211, 213, 264–265n.25

League of Nations, 56, 228

LeDonne, John, 18–19

legality. *See* rule of law

legitimacy, 47, 53, 63, 162, 245–246, 447–448; of the ruling elite, 84, 213; of Russia as a great power, 292, 420; sources of in the early Russian state, 461, 462, 477

Legvold, Robert, 3, 31, 77, 252, 280, 285–286, 331, 457

Lend-Lease, 221

Lenin, Vladimir Ilyich, 85–86, 196n.83, 251, 275n.125, 422; authoritarianism increasing over time, 291–292, 297; border guard under, 227; New Economic Policy, 291, 405; peaceful coexistence doctrine, 249, 298, 332; pragmatic foreign policy, 216, 218, 276–277, 291–293; state capitalism and, 85–86

— theories of, 49, 239; analysis of capitalist expansionism, 96, 480–481; necessity of a class-conscious vanguard, 159, 161; "state capitalism," 85–86; theory of Asiatic mode of production, 253

Lenin, Vladimir Ilyich—works cited: *State and Revolution,* 164; *What Is to Be Done?,* 159

Lenin-Stalin communist transformation, 77, 85, 86–88, 118–119, 121; domestic and foreign policy interactions of, 155–156. *See also* Bolshevik Revolution; Bolsheviks; Soviet Union

Liaodong Peninsula, 370

liberal humanism, 55, 62

liberal internationalism, 4, 38, 149, 452

liberal modernization, 5, 8, 23, 89, 109, 128

Lieven, Dominic, 89, 89–90

life expectancy, 91

Ligachev, Yegor, 159, 176

Limonov, Eduard, 109

Lincoln, W. Bruce, 149

linguistic Russification, 209

List, Frederich, 165

Lithuania, 239, 471; entry into NATO, 313; EU membership, 429; resistance movement, 244; tsarist Russia warring against, 94, 108

Lithuania-Poland, wars with, 92–93

Litvinov, Maxim, 232, 248–249

Litvinovtsy movement, 249

Livonia, 22, 94, 108

local civil government, 53–54, 95, 117, 379–380, 399, 465, 476. *See also* civil society

localism: balancing with globalization, 343, 379–383; economic localism in Northeast Asia, 365–366, 382, 382–383; Northeast Asia and, 343, 378, 379, 379–381, 384

"local nationalism," 53–54, 95

Lotman, Yuri, 80

Lovejoy, Arthur O., 14

Lukyanov, Anatole, 197n.86

Machiavelli, Noccolò, 36

Machpolitik, 25. *See also* state power

Mackinder, Halford, 18, 112

Madariaga, Isabel de, 81–82

Mahan, Alfred, 18

Malenkov, Georgy, 302

Malinovsky, R. Ya., 306

"managed democracy" concept, 32, 84, 421, 423, 433

Manchuria, 230, 371; Khrushchev's pullback from, 234

manned space flight

Mao Zedong, 233–234, 252–253, 345, 361

market reforms, 255; failure of post-Soviet, 91, 259, 453, 455–457, 456; loans-for-shares, 420; privatization, 62, 63, 145, 181, 259, 419, 455; resistance to, 24; voucher privatization plan, 420, 439n.66, 453; vs. authoritarian statism, 23, 27, 224–225

Marshall Plan, 221, 230, 485

Marshall Plan for Russia proposal, 259

Marxist and post-Marxist historians, 152–153

Marxist-Leninism, 4, 20, 57–58, 290, 296–297; European influence on, 399, 405

Marxist parties, pre-Soviet, 172

Marxist revisionism, 234, 252

mass culture, 60

McDonald, David, 21, 23, 27, 29, 32, 145, 477; positive perspective on contemporary Russia, 30

McFaul, Michael, 90

Mearsheimer, John, 36, 37–38, 68–69, 71n.5; *The Tragedy of Great Power Politics*, 293

Mediterranean Sea, commercial outlets, 17

Mendselson, Sarah, 190n.27, 196n.80

Merkel, Angela, 424

metropole: of an empire, 42–43, 47–48; collapse of the core state, 25, 47, 54, 59–60, 177–178; as the *vnutrennie guberniya*, 44; weakness of the core causing state collapse, 25, 47, 54, 59–60, 177–178

Metropolitan Ioann, 115

Metternich, Klemens W.N.L.F. von, 167

Michelet, Jules, 11

micromanagement of globalized trade, 31

Middle East: Soviet Union interest in, 21; turbulence in, 10

migration, 227; from Asia viewed as a threat, 353, 355, 358, 370, 382, 386

military: military-industrial complex, 177, 219, 306; modernization of, 10, 322–326, 324t., 328; relationship with the communist party, 306; vs. civilian goods, 216, 224

military conscription, 45, 79–80, 82

military demobilization, 219

military globalism, 445, 447, 449, 452, 473, 484

military interventions, 7, 67, 118, 151, 210, 226, 228, 247, 251, 301, 315, 496; in Hungary 1956, 22, 232, 234, 235, 251, 252, 301, 412, 415, 474, 486; Prague Spring rebellion, 22, 167, 234–235, 251, 412. *See also* war

military personnel, 209, 221, 262n.7, 357; Red Army, 219, 229, 243, 244, 292; *streltsy* (tsarist musketeers), 24, 282. *See also* Red Army

military power, 198n.93, 287, 294t., 295, 410, 451; defense intellectuals, 303; diminution of in post-Soviet era, 96–97, 102, 105, 349; great state transformations impacting, 81, 82; mobilization of the military, 23, 24, 80, 93, 120, 147, 157, 162–163, 173, 245, 294t.; of the Muscovites and tsarist Russia, 467, 470; political leverage from, 305; Russian military style, 285, 309–310; Russian mobilization in World War I, 292–296, 328; use of no longer feasible in Northeast Asia, 343–344, 345–346; vs. civilian progress, 24. *See also* Red Army; war

military technology: advances despite economic backwardness, 165–166, 282; industrialization linked to, 220–221; production of, 264n.22, 484–486; Russian advances in, 24, 476; sales of, 184, 458–459. *See also* nuclear arms

Miliukov, P., 80, 133n.9

Milyutin, Dmitri, 118

mir, 400. *See also* collectivization

models of statehood, 9, 29; Byzantine model, 259; corporate state, 424; European model, 23, 25, 393–394, 397–398, 417, 422–424, 435; Russia as its own model, 423–424; Western and Asian models, 259. *See also* absolutist tradition; statehood; strong state model

modernization, 5, 8, 23, 89, 109, 128, 284; of the military, 10, 322–326, 324t., 328; passage of the Great Reforms (*see also* Alexander II), 165–166

modernizing empire, 41

Molatov, Vyacheslav M., 230, 248, 249, 275n.123, 409

Moldava, ties with NATO, 313

Moldavian Autonomous Soviet Socialist Republic, 240

Moldova, 10, 239, 256, 409, 422, 432–433

"monarchical principle," 172

monarchy, 157, 398

monetary policy, 449, 453, 490

Mongol conquest and rule, 210, 448, 464–465; tribute system, 465

Mongolia: Bolshevik diplomatic relations with, 226; Outer Mongolia, 234

Morgantheau, Hans, 36

Moscow, 466. *See also* Muscovite core state; Russia; Soviet Union

multilateralism, 29–30, 320, 322, 327, 346

multinational society, 27, 162, 206, 209–210, 255–256; as a weakened multinational state, 41, 64; culturally distinct peoples, 21, 113; fragmentation of Russian identity, 24, 36, 45, 70, 162; Russia as, 24; Soviet Union as multinational empire, 55–59, 214. *See also* ethnicity principle (*korenizatsiia*)

Munich Pact of 1938, 56, 228

Muscovite core state, 17, 23, 206–207, 465, 466–468, 469

Muscovite-Ming period, 233

Muscovite state, 92; transformation of in the 16th c., 77, 79–82, 86, 92–94, 100, 107–108, 126

Muslim populations, 27, 209, 256

Muslim separatism, 261. *See also* Islamic fundamentalism

mutual dependency, 23

Mutual Security Act, 232

1991 coup attempt against Gorbachev, 54, 58–59, 175, 176, 178, 181, 489

911 terrorist attacks, 6, 7, 8, 97, 146, 445

1917 revolution. *See* Bolshevik revolution

Napoléonic wars, 106, 229, 451; defeat of Napoléon, 287, 473–474, 475

Narodnaya Volya movement, 476

narodniki, 400–401

"national Communists," 53–54

national evolution, 3, 17, 31, 73n.35, 129–130, 421

national interest, 25, 36–38, 49

nationalism, 49, 106–107, 234; nationalist protest movements in the Soviet bloc, 59, 106–107, 209–210, 239, 245; self-determination intrinsic to, 47–48. *See also* Russian nationalism

nationalizing empire, 41, 44–45

national missile defense (NMD), 5, 316, 318, 319, 322

national security, 7, 38–39, 97, 130–131, 279–286, 284, 331–334; authoritarianism and, 100, 158; Bolshevik foreign policy and, 290, 296–297; collective security arrangements, 56, 95, 169, 228, 248, 409; concerns affecting leadership decisions, 95–96, 123, 186, 286–290, 296; contemporary flexible strategy, 30; diplomatic creativity in seeking, 226, 246, 283, 288, 299, 301, 307, 309, 321, 325–326, 327–328; domestic constraints on, 229–280, 284, 286–292, 293, 309, 448, 449, 469; economic globalization and, 444; economic growth vs., 8, 17, 23, 28; internal security forces, 227; internationalism vs., 31, 98, 227; nonmilitary defense thinking, 303; rethinking of, 130–131; "soft" vs. "hard" issues, 430, 431; Sokolovsky Doctrine, 297, 303–306, 309, 333; strategic distance as part of, 296–297, 307–310, 326–332;

U. S.-Russian shared intelligence, 146. *See also* border security; Putin, Vladimir—security policy

nation-state, 41, 43–44; whether to define Russia as a, 45–47. *See also* statehood

NATO. *See* North American Treaty Alliance (NATO)

NATO-Russia Council, 8, 124, 146, 317, 328

natural resources, 32, 65, 220, 229, 259, 315, 320, 374; arable land, 23, 207; in Central Asia, 258, 372, 385; extraction and depletion of, 102, 117, 168, 215–216; spurring expansionism, 353. *See also* oil and gas resources

Nazarbaev, Nursultan, 63

Nazdratenko, Evgenii, 348

Nazism, 406–407

Nazi-Soviet nonaggression pact of 1939, 22, 229–230, 333, 484

neighboring countries, 9, 10, 11, 27, 205, 216, 241, 255, 380

Nesselrode, Karl, 154

New Economic Policy (NEP), 291, 405

New Eurasianism, 259–260

New Independent States. *See also* Belarus; Moldova; Ukraine

New Independent States (NIS), 422, 428

"new Soviet Man," 25

"new thinking," 56, 170, 177, 395; improving Sino-Russian relations, 345–346. *See also* Gorbachev, Mikhail; *perestroika*

Nicholas I, 167, 171, 235, 474; foreign and domestic policy links under, 149, 153; Slavophile goals, 115, 166–167, 474; travel restrictions under, 22, 267n.47. *See also* Stolypin, Pyotr I.

Nicholas II: abdication of, 290; Asian policy, 175, 370; conservatives in reign of, 176; foreign and security policy, 287–288, 289, 296, 331

Nikitenko, A. V., 90
NIS. *See* New Independent States (NIS)
nobility, 45
nomenklatura, 86
nonaggression pacts, 22, 228, 241, 409,
 483–484
nongovernmental organizations (NGOs), 9
Nonproliferation Treaty, 320
North American Treaty Alliance (NATO),
 28, 412; attack on Serbia, 120; Contact
 Group, 419, 420; expansion into
 post-Soviet nations, 4–5, 7, 36, 69, 212,
 314, 433; expansion perceived as a threat
 by Russia, 68, 97, 98, 112, 119–120, 230;
 Helsinki Final Act (1975), 5, 487–488;
 Partnership for Peace, 6, 340n.48. *See
 also* Kosovo War; NATO-Russia
 Council
North Caucasus, 28; tensions, 27
Northeast Asia: Blagoveshchensk-
 Vladivostok corridor, 365–366;
 economic dynamism of the region, 364,
 386; economic localism, 365–366, 382;
 labor issues, 376–377; localism and
 constraints on, 343, 378, 379, 379–381,
 384; militarization under Soviets,
 372–373; military options no longer
 feasible in, 343–344, 345–346, 349–350;
 past Russian policy marked by
 misjudgments, 351, 372–373, 384;
 Seoul-Pyongyang-Vladivostok corridor,
 366; Sino-centric tribute system, 353. *See
 also* China; eastern border; Japan;
 North Korea; Russian Far East; South
 Korea
Northeast Asian regional strategy: diplomatic possibilities, 350–351, 356–358, 379,
 382–388; elements involved in, 346–350,
 358–359, 366–368, 375, 377–378; goal of
 economic integration, 353–356, 384–388;
 search for, 343–344, 373–374, 386–388
Northern War, 94

North Korea, 29–30; cultural alienation a
 challenge to communist union with,
 26; nuclear standoff, 9, 347, 356, 357,
 358, 427; occupation of, 230; Russian
 relations with, 343, 366–367, 375–378;
 Russian territorial disputes with,
 381–382; six-party talks, 343, 350, 357,
 368; Soviet alliance with, 363–364. *See
 also* Kim Jong Il
North Korean-Russian relations,
 contemporary diplomacy, 344
North Vietnam, cultural alienation a
 challenge to communist union with,
 26
Novgorod, 463, 465, 467
nuclear arms, 236, 245; arms race, 153, 303,
 305t.; first strike, 285, 295, 304;
 invention and existence of, 212; recent
 "nuclearization" of Russian foreign
 policy, 280, 322, 324, 328, 332, 333;
 Russia's arsenal, 5, 24, 96, 120, 205, 323;
 specter of confrontation, 62, 96, 303;
 strike threshold, 322; U. S. arsenal and
 program, 7, 413; weapons testing, 219.
 See also military technology; weapons
 of mass destruction (WMD)
nuclear arms control, 253, 259, 283,
 304; Antiballistic Missile (ABM)
 Treaty, 7, 62, 97, 119, 129, 318, 319;
 parity issues, 236, 486, 487; treaties, 4,
 7, 97, 320
nuclear "truants," 9, 47, 120. *See also* Iran;
 North Korea

Obruchev, Vladimir, 294–295
October Manifesto, 290
October Revolution, 51, 292, 297, 371, 479
Octobrists, 172
offensive realist theory, 37, 38. *See also*
 Mearsheimer, John; Waltz, Kenneth
"official nationalism," 43–44; "official
 nationality," 49–50

oil and gas pipelines, 68, 225, 256; Baltic Sea gas pipeline agreement, 425; in Central Asia and Caucasia, 258; the "iron silk road," 356, 377; routes in Northeast Asia, 344, 348, 358, 366–368, 374, 381, 386

oil and gas resources: gaining political leverage with, 10–11, 17, 27, 67, 103, 185, 223, 225, 329–330, 344, 358, 368, 381, 425; Russian Far East rich in, 364, 372, 386

oil price increases (2004–2006), 9–10, 346, 457

oligarchs, 356, 423, 439n.66, 456; Putin's stand against, 145, 181, 182, 185, 225, 259–260, 330, 423

Operation Barbarossa, 409

Orange Revolution, 122, 184, 258, 426, 428

Organization for Security and Cooperation in Europe (OSCE), 316–317

Orthodox Christian Church, 18, 79, 82, 93, 159, 284, 423; abolition of the patriarchate by Peter the Great, 82–83; cultural isolation and, 436n.7, 462; Metropolitan Ioann, 115; Russian identity and, 61, 109–110, 113, 115, 162, 205, 475; Soviet repression of, 86. *See also* Third Rome

Ottoman Empire, 17, 20, 107, 208, 471, 472, 478. *See also* Crimean war

Palmerston, Lord, 36

Pan-Slavism, 20, 110, 167, 400. *See also* Alexander II

Paris Treaty, 117, 127, 288

parity with the West, 23, 114, 207, 222, 259. *See also* great power identity

Partnership for Peace, 6, 340n.48

Partnership with the West, accepted by Russian public opinion, 27

Pasternak, Boris, 238

patriotism, 45–47

patterns in Russian foreign policy. *See* persistent historical factors

patterns. *See* Foreign policy patterns

Pavlovsky, Gleb, 115

peace concerns and diplomacy, 6, 413; Decree on Peace, 481; in early Bolshevik period, 56, 481; Partnership for Peace, 6, 340n.48; Peace Conference of 1919, 247; peaceful coexistence doctrine, 249, 298, 332; "zone of peace," 300–301, 302–303, 331

peasantry, 73n.35, 90, 219, 474, 476, 482; the commune, 160, 207, 400, 474; disenchantment, dissent, and emigration of, 159, 160, 161, 168, 208, 223; early Slavic agricultural communities, 45, 460, 461, 467; emancipation of the serfs, 88–89, 94, 399, 401, 474; *narodniki* (peasant-basedrevolutionaries), 401; peasant roots of Stalin, 299; reforms to obtain support, 173, 174, 405; revolutionary thought in respect to, 251, 253, 276n.132, 399; taxation and grain expropriation of, 86, 90, 219, 220, 482; tied to the land, 79. *See also* serfs

perestroika, 58, 84, 88, 148, 153, 170, 415; conditions enabling, 96, 105

periphery: of an empire, 42–43, 72n.22; military withdrawal from, 453; non-Russian populations in, 27, 44, 50, 209; vs. center or metropole, 21, 25, 42, 50. *See also* borderlands; empire

Permanent Joint Council, 5, 8

Persia, decline in power in 16th c., 19

Persian empires, 20

persistent historical factors, 11, 16–21, 23, 25–28, 132, 205, 206. *See also* cultural alienation; economic backwardness; multinational society; porous frontiers

Peter I (the Great), 23, 25, 207, 210, 219, 229, 281; absolutist model of the state, 157–158; centralization under, 379–380; domestic and foreign policy interactions under, 149, 155; effort to industrialize, 85, 88; Europeanization of Russia under, 397–398, 401, 402, 470, 471–473; great power ambitions influencing his policies, 401–402, 477, 479; modernization under, 284

Petrine empire, 41

petroleum. *See* oil and gas resources

Petrovna, Elizaveta, 229

Piedmont principle, 240

Piedmont-Savoy, 240

Piłsudski, Józef, 56

pipelines. *See* oil and gas pipelines

Pipes, Richard, 336n.12

Poe, Marshall, 80–81, 198n.92

poets, 52, 53, 137

Poland: 1863 rebellion, 22, 106, 106–107, 169, 476; 1920 Soviet invasion resulting in Soviet defeat, 55, 56, 481; 1956 rebellion, 22; Bolshevik treaty with, 226; border villages, 241, 467; current Russian policy towards, 258; defeat of the Soviet invasion in 1920, 482; entry into NATO, 5, 69, 313, 326; the "fourth Polish partition" (1939), 229–230, 409, 484; as part of New Europe, 429, 431–432; the Polish empire, 19, 20; Solidarity movement, 234; Soviet ambassador assassinated in, 241; tsarist conquests and partitions of, 18, 22, 94, 108, 209, 231, 471

Polish-Lithuanian Commonwealth, 208

Polish population, deportation and resettlement of, 241, 242, 244

political backlash, 107, 223, 287, 306, 309, 489; reaction against reforms, 332–333, 478

political constituencies, 40, 162, 170–171

political crises and collapse of statist regimes, 148, 279; collapse of the USSR, 3, 25, 54, 59, 64, 101, 148, 170, 255, 297, 313, 325t., 415, 416–417; collapse of tsarist Russia, 47, 48, 198n.91, 332; comparison of Soviet with late Imperial state collapse, 169–178; conservative coup against Gorbachev, 54, 58–59, 175, 176, 178, 181, 489; weakness of the core state in, 25, 47, 54, 59–60, 177–178. *See also* economic crises

political culture, 254

political discourse, 246, 254

political economy discourse, 156–157

political globalism. *See* unipolar hegemony

political ideas, censorship of foreign, 226–227

political parties, 48, 291, 415, 419, 423; antiparty groups, 298, 306, 336n.12; one-party rule, 50, 84, 405. *See also* Communist Party (CPSU)

political science, compared to history, 12–14

Polotsk, 18; incorporation of, 18

pomestie system, 79–80, 81–82

popular concessions, 170–171

popular fronts, 245

popular sovereignty, 43, 72n.23, 156, 162

popular uprisings in the Soviet bloc, 44, 234–235, 252, 291, 412; nationalist protest movements, 59, 209–210, 239, 245

porous frontiers, 20–21, 99, 257–258; as an enduring vulnerability, 27, 100, 206, 208–209, 226, 281; ideological as well as physical, 238; leading to expansionism, 229–230, 232, 234–235, 281; of modern and tsarist Russia, 20–21; modern technologies increasing vulnerability, 236–237; possible amelioration of, 31; weak borders driving foreign policy, 21–22, 28–29. *See also* borderlands; border security; eastern border; encirclement; periphery; southern border; western border

Portsmouth Treaty, 289–290

post-Cold War. *See* post-Soviet space;
    Russian Federation

postcolonial national liberation move-
    ments, 222, 298–299

post-Soviet space, 6, 8, 30, 216, 315,
    421–422; authoritarianism in, 28, 32;
    commitment toward Russian influence
    in, 4–6, 10, 65, 111, 112, 120, 121–122;
    common spaces concept, 8; former
    Warsaw Pact countries, 313, 314, 420,
    431–432; future directions for, 65–70;
    Western penetration into, 104, 258,
    428–429, 431–433

post-Soviet transition, 255; economic
    collapse under Yeltsin, 101–102, 259,
    453–454, 455; relation to Muslim states,
    256–257; search for postcommunist
    identity, 417–418. *See also* Gorbachev,
    Mikhail; Yeltsin, Boris

post-Vietnam generation, 487

post-World War II period, 221, 245, 251, 301

Pozdnyakov, Elgiz, 109

Prague Spring rebellion, 22, 152, 167,
    234–235, 251, 412. *See also*
    Czechoslovakia

preemptive war, 35, 333; first strike
    (nuclear), 285, 295, 304. *See also* war

pre-Petrine and post-Petrine Russia, 83

Primakov, Yevgeny, 5, 67, 121, 180, 220, 321

Prisítina, 120

private property, 23

privatization, 62, 63, 145, 181, 259, 419, 455;
    voucher privatization, 420, 439n.66, 453

proletarian internationalism. *See* world
    communism

pro-Russian movements, 205

pro-Soviet discourse, 62

Prussia, annexation of, 230

public discourse, 9

public health, 91

public opinion

Pushkov, Aleksei, 115

Putin, Vladimir, 28, 119, 224–225, 387, 457;
    Asian foreign policy, 6, 344, 347, 348,
    366, 369, 377–378, 381; attacking wealth
    of the oligarchs, 145, 181, 182, 185, 225,
    259–260, 330, 423; belief in a strong state
    (*see* strong state model); border
    problems of, 257, 258; compared with
    Stolypin, 163, 182; criticism of
    authoritarian trends in government of,
    9, 103, 111, 129, 145–146, 148, 152;
    economy under, 60, 145, 329–330, 457;
    efforts to assert influence in post-Soviet
    space, 120–122, 313–316; Europe-Russian
    relations under, 146–147, 325–326, 327,
    421–428; foreign policy directions of,
    10–11, 23, 27, 65, 97–99, 121–123, 321–322,
    458; goal of restoring great power status,
    163, 424–426; and G.W. Bush, 9, 70, 147,
    184, 311, 330, 378; integrating foreign and
    domestic policy, 29, 84, 183, 316, 457;
    internationalism under, 131–132,
    458–460; joining with the U. S. against
    terror, 5, 9, 27, 124, 146, 427, 445, 478,
    491; "managed democracy" concept of,
    32, 84, 421, 423, 433; personal attributes,
    69–70, 110–111, 183; popular support for,
    19, 145, 386–387, 424; relations with
    U. S. under, 5, 27, 142n.126, 346, 445, 478,
    491; self-confidence of foreign policy,
    32, 125, 132–133; stability of the state
    under, 145, 152, 155–156, 178, 182–184,
    386, 424; strong state ideal (*see* strong
    state model); support for the U. S.
    following 911 terrorist attacks, 6, 7, 8, 97,
    146, 445

— Putin's security policy, 326–334; "Basic
    Provisions of Military Power," 322–323;
    cautions in interpretation of documents,
    311–313; focus on deterrence, 305–306,
    325; "Foreign Policy Concept," 16–17, 310,
    314, 317–319; "Military Doctrine" (draft

and emendation)-11, 310, 323–324; "National Security Concept," 322; pragmatism in power relations, 25, 29, 69–70, 329, 330–331; regarding the U. S., 317–319

Pyongyang. *See* North Korea

Qing empires, 208

radio broadcasts across borders, 237, 487

Radio Free Europe, 237

Radio Liberation, 237

Rajk, Lázslé, 239

Ranke, Leopold von, 11, 152–153

Reagan, Ronald, 96

"realists," 112–114

realist theory, 37, 38, 57

Red Army, 219, 229, 243, 244, 292. *See also* military personnel

reforms, 109; based in the absolutist tradition, 160–161, 163–164, 168–169, 171–173; and bureaucracy, 265n.35, 312, 455; reaction against, 107, 223, 287, 306, 309, 332–333, 478, 489; resistance to, 284–285; of state structure, 178–179, 181, 185–186

regime types, 40–41; Russian history of, 41. *See also* empire; nation-state; state structure

regionalism, 343, 351, 383; neighboring countries, 9, 11, 27, 205, 216, 241, 255, 380; Northeast Asian regional strategy; regional stability, 315, 348; Russia seeking regional hegemony, 4–6, 10, 65, 111, 112, 120, 121–122. *See also* Northeast Asian regional strategy

religion, 462. *See also* Orthodox Christian Church

repression in Soviet Era: under Lenin, 291–292; under Stalin, 60–87, 86, 100, 128, 251, 254–255, 404–405

republic of Russian speakers, 61

resource extraction, 102, 117, 168, 215–216. *See also* natural resources

Revolution of 1905, 151, 154, 160, 166, 170, 171, 172, 209–210, 250–251, 289–290

rhetoric: of globalization, 28; increasing isolation, 246–247, 249–250

Rice, Condoleezza, 318

Rieber, Alfred J., 20–21, 21, 22, 23, 25, 27, 148, 205

Right Opposition, 241

river trading routes, 18, 460, 463–464, 465

Romania, 127, 412

Romanovs, 24, 150, 468. *See also* tsarist Russia

Roosevelt, Franklin, 283

Roosevelt, Theodore, 289

Roosevelt-Litvinov agreements, 232

Rossyanin, 162. *See also* Russian Federation

Rozman, Gilbert, 21, 26, 28, 29–30, 30, 321, 343

rule of law, 23, 89, 145, 156, 186, 303, 398, 424; advocates of, 151, 418, 423; market economy must be based in, 431, 433, 435, 490; political economy discourse of, 156–157; as *zakonnost*, 245

rulership, 37, 43, 83, 154; or an empire vs. a nation-state, 43; rulers as reformers, 160–161, 163–164, 168–169, 171–173

rules of the game, 160, 164

ruling elite, 19, 37, 43, 45, 79, 213, 435, 476

Rus, 460, 467. *See also* Kyivan Rus; Varangians

Russia. *See* great state transformations; Kyivan Rus; post-Soviet transition; Russian Federation; Soviet Union; tsarist Russia

Russia as an international actor, 10–11, 16–17, 29, 79, 98, 118–119; during great state transformations, 31, 77–78, 103–108, 121–125, 130, 131

Russian civil war. *See* civil war of 1918–1922

Russian core territory: Asia as part of, 18–19, 110, 362; Kyivan Rus, 460–465; Muscovite core state, 17, 23, 44–45, 206–207, 466–468, 469

Russian culture, 5, 54, 380

Russian exceptionalism, 27, 165–168, 205, 210, 384, 393, 423. *See also* cultural alienation; Eurasian "special position"

Russian Far East, 18, 20, 101, 343, 348, 354, 355, 365, 385–386; 19th c. expansion, 17, 21; corridor(s) to Korean peninsula, 366–367; criminal elements, 348, 356, 359, 373, 374, 382, 383, 386, 387; during Soviet era, 380–381; economic corruption, 354–355; economic growth and energy development in, 30, 344, 356–357, 366, 374–375, 381, 383; new cities in, 370; oil resources in, 364, 372, 386; security interests in, 365–366, 368. *See also* eastern border; Northeast Asia; oil and gas pipelines

Russian Federation, 9, 20, 41, 70; borders similar to those 1650, 27, 104; contemporary expression of statehood, 32, 147; desire for autonomy, 23, 27, 193–194n.54, 458; desire for parity, 207, 259; domestic economy emphasis, 27, 434; international role, 179–180, 434; military power, w10, 322–326, 324t., 328; multilateralism in foreign policy, 29–30, 320, 322, 327, 346; post-Soviet debates over statehood, 61–63; seeking regional hegemony, 4–6, 10, 65, 111, 112, 120, 121–122; seeking status as an energy superpower (*see* energy policy); ties with the EU, 97, 125, 421, 422, 425. *See also* domestic policy; future directions; Putin, Vladimir; Russian national identity; Yeltsin, Boris

Russian foreign policy: and Asia (*see* China; Northeast Asia; Eurasian "special position" of Russian land); of the communist era (*See* Bolsheviks; Soviet Union foreign policy); of contemporary Russia (*See* contemporary Russian foreign policy); and domestic policy (*see* domestic constraints on foreign policy; economy); during great transitions (*see* great state transformations); foreign alliances (*see* alliances); international aspects (*See* geopolitics; globalization; international system); persistent historical factors in (*see* persistent historical factors); security issues (*See* military power; national security); of tsarist Russia (*see* tsarist era Russian foreign policy); and the West (*see* Western powers' relationship with Russia)

Russian national identity, 20, 46, 47, 54, 65, 110, 132, 381–382, 388; Asian aspects, 387–388; diverging traditions of (*see also* ideology—themes and movements), 28, 111–113, 254, 399; dualistic concepts of, 108–109, 111, 197n.86, 254, 399, 418; fragmentation of (*see also* multinational society), 24, 36, 45, 70, 162; great state transformations and, 101, 103, 105, 108, 109, 113–114, 115–117; post-Soviet "identity crisis," 28, 59–63, 65–66; *Rossianin* (supra-ethnic term), 162; search for a postcommunist identity, 417–418; search for great power status (*see also* great-power identity), 25, 108, 259, 293, 352, 371, 459–460; sense of vulnerability (*see also* vulnerability and weaknesses), 21, 36, 113–114, 281–282, 382; Soviet socialist identity, 57–58. *See also* Eurasian "special position"; Europe and Russian identity; great power identity; traditional values of Russia

Russian nationalism, 162, 209–210, 287, 296, 474; balancing with globalization,

343, 379–383; as "official nationalism," 43–44, 45–50; Pan-Slavism, 20, 110, 167, 400. *See also* Slavophiles

Russian parliament. *See* Duma

Russian Revolution of 1905, as the October Revolution, 51, 292, 297, 371, 479

Russian foreign policy, 27, 28, 443; imprint of historic anxieties on, 120–125; lacking a clear strategy, 125–128; persistent factors in, 255, 260–261; youthful reformers in, 109

Russian United Party, 423

Russification, 22, 44, 45

Russo-Turkish War, 127

Russo-Chinese relations. *See* Sino-Russian relations

Russo-Japanese War, 21, 151, 210, 292, 363, 371, 478

Russo-Turkish war. *See* Turkish war (1877–1878)

Ryzhkov, Nikolai, 90, 176, 177

Saakashvili, Mikhail, 68

sacredness of state and rulership, 80, 82–84

Safavid (Iranian) Empire, 208

Sakhakunskaya, 348

Sakhalin to Khabarovsk gas pipeline, 374

Sakharov, Andrei, 411, 414

Sanborn, Joshua, 46

Sarajevo, 403

Sarajevo crisis. *See* Kosovo War

Sasonov, S.D., 175

satellite surveillance, 236, 237

Savitsky, Petr, 110

Saxony, Russian wars with, 107

sblizhenie, drawing together, 241–242

Schelling, Thomas, *The strategy of Conflict*, 303

Schengen Agreement, 429. *See also* European Union (EU)

Schröder, Gerhard, 424, 425

Schroeder, Paul, 11, 14

Sealing of borders, 22

search for a postcommunist identity, Russian national identity, 417–418

Second Chechen war. *See* Chechen war

Second Comintern Congress, 250

Second World War. *See* World War II

secrecy, 311

secret police, USSR, 243

security threats. *See* national security

self-confidence, 32, 125, 384–385; of Putin 2nd-term government, 32, 125, 132–133

self-isolating state, 160, 168, 173; desire for autonomy, 23, 27, 193–194n.54, 458

self-reliance orientation: of Russian domestic policy, 23, 40, 220, 398; vs. foreign capital, 220

Seoul. *See* South Korea

Seoul-Pyongyang axis, 356–357. *See also* Northeast Asia

Seoul-Pyongyang-Vladivostok corridor, 366

separatist movements, 205

September 11th. *See* 911 terrorist attacks

Serbia, 118, 175, 326. *See also* Kosovo War

serfs: emancipation of, 88–89, 90, 94, 399, 401, 474, 476; *pomestie* system, 79–80, 81–82. *See also* peasantry

Sergunin, Alexander, 112

Seton-Watson, Hugh, 43

Shanghai Cooperation Organization (SCO), 99, 123, 258, 368–369

"shatter zones". *See also* borderlands

"shatter zones," peripheral states as, 21, 209

Shevardnadze, Eduard, 58, 63

Shevtsova, Lilia, 84

"shock therapy," 91, 259, 453, 455–457, 456

Siberia, 93, 207, 288, 367, 382; development problems, 352, 354; energy resources and projects, 356, 372, 381; land route connecting, 370; Trans-Siberian Railway, 288, 345, 377, 380, 477

Silk Road, 446, 451, 460

Siniavsky, Andrei, 254

Sino-centric tribute system, 353

Sino-Japanese relations, 321, 350–351, 362–363, 369, 371–374

Sino-Russian relations, 5–6, 6, 10, 332, 368, 384; as a focus of Russia foreign policy, 345, 347, 364; Gorbachev's "new thinking" opening up, 345–346; historic, 112, 236, 245, 360–362, 373–374; Putin focusing on economic mutuality, 327, 330, 349; Soviet era alliances and tensions, 18, 26, 252–253, 353–355, 363–364, 370, 372–373, 378–381; territorial disputes, 381–382. *See also* Sino-Soviet conflict

Sino-Soviet conflict, 26, 105, 252, 253–254, 345, 371–372

Sino-U. S. relations, 357. *See also* China; United States (U. S.)

six-party talks, 343, 350, 357, 368. *See also* North Korea

Six Weeks War, 244

Slavic agricultural communities, 45, 460, 461

Slavophiles, 61, 160, 287, 369, 411, 449; liberal adherents, 411, 415, 425; philosophical tradition of, 108–109, 378; Russian nationalism and, 403, 477; socialist adherents, 474

Slavs, 18. *See also* Slavism

Smith, Adam, *Wealth of Nations*, 156

Smith, S.A., 46

Smolensk, 18, 467

sobornost (community), 115

social and cultural globalism, 445

social constructivism, 38–40. *See also* Hopf, Ted; Wendt, Alexander

social dislocation, 478

social forms endangering autocracy, 23

social groups, 40

socialism, 474

socialist revolutions, 214

social resources, 102

sociocultural factors, 23

Sokolovsky, V.D., 295; *Military Strategy*, 303–304, 305, 306, 309

Sokolovsky Doctrine, 297, 303–307, 309, 333

soldiers. *See* military personnel

Solidarity theme, 234. *See also* Poland

Solovev, S.M., 163–164

Solzhenitsyn, Alexander, 61, 411; *Gulag Archipelago*, 254; *One Day in the Life of Ivan Denisovich*, 309

Southeast Asian Treaty Organization, 300

southern border, 208, 216, 230, 260, 296, 352, 466

southern tier states, 63–65. *See also* borderlands

South Korea, 355; contemporary Russia's relations with, 343, 366–367, 375–378; Russian territorial disputes with, 381–382

South-Korean-Russian relations, contemporary diplomacy, 344

"sovereign democracy," 31–32

Soviet-American relations. *See* U. S.-Soviet relations

Soviet American Trade Treaty (1973), Jackson-Vannik Amendment, 245

Soviet bloc, republics in-40, 239

Soviet economy, 90–91, 153, 215, 264n.22 and 24; periods of growth and development, 60, 241, 300, 483, 485

Soviet news broadcasting, 237–238

Soviet Union, 410; authoritarianism and repression in, 60–87, 86, 100, 128, 251, 254–255, 404–405; collapse of, 25, 238; deification of Stalin, 83–84; demise of, 480–481, 489; demographic characteristics, 238; Five Year Plans, 88, 220, 221, 228, 405; former Warsaw Pact members, 301, 412, 413; interwar period, 55, 199n.105, 407, 408–409; *korenizatsiya*, principle of ethnicity, 50, 51, 240–241; political cultures in, 254; power over

Eastern Europe, 17, 396–397, 407–410. *See also* Bolsheviks; Brezhnev, Leonid; Khrushchev, Nikita; post-Soviet space; Red Army; Stalin, Joseph; world communism

Soviet Union as a nationalizing empire, 47–55, 411–413; attempt to create a "Soviet people," 51–52, 54–55; interventions within Soviet bloc (*see also* Afghan war; Czheckoslovakia; Hungary; Poland; Chechen war), 231; modernizing processes, 52–53, 54; national incubation within, 48, 51, 52–53, 64; "official nationalism," 43–44, 49–50; providing cheap oil to Warsaw Pact nations, 412–413; regional elite recruitment, 53–54; Soviet ideology, 47–50, 236. *See also* empire; regime types

Soviet Union foreign policy, 1, 35, 55, 212, 408; armistice agreements, 230; desire for parity (*see* parity with the West); as an empire in denial, 55–59; goal of parity with the U. S., 23, 222; ignoring domestic imperatives, 149; joining the League of Nations, 56, 228, 247, 248, 408; managerial state as a goal of, 27; nonaggression pacts, 22, 228, 241, 409, 483–484; suspicious of globalism, 482–483; unification as expansionism, 18–19; world communism and imperative of, 290–291. *See also* Nazi-Soviet nonaggression pact of 1939

Sovnarkom decree, 242

Spain, 250; USSR's military assistance to, 229

Spanish Civil War, 247, 251, 409

spatial concepts, 206

"spillover effect," 234–235, 429

stability of the state, 154, 209, 411–413, 428; under Putin, 145, 152, 155–156, 178, 182–184, 386, 424

Stalin, Joseph, 85, 86, 87, 101, 136–137n.59, 248; dissolving the Comintern, 233; Ivan IV compared to, 87–88; peasant roots of, 299; Peter the Great compared to, 25; policies regarding peripheral states, 25–26, 234, 269n.68; policy for independence of Outer Mongolia, 234; sacralization of, 83–84

— Stalinist regime: as a totalitarian regime, 38, 86, 158, 182, 284, 483; Gulag system, 88, 254, 409, 483; mass deportations under, 22, 242–244, 253; uncertain alliances, 22, 126, 127–128, 229–230, 484

standing army. *See* military conscription

Stankevich. Sergei, 418–419

START I Treaty, 454

state budget, 456

state capitalism, 85–86

statehood, 46; discourse on, 28, 61–63, 149, 151–152, 155, 175; eclectic theory of, 40–41; *gosudarstvennost*, 147, 150, 185, 200n.124; reforming of, 185–186; the state as historic transformer, 163–164; whether Russia is a nation-state, 45–47. *See also* models of statehood

state-managed corporations, 225

state power, 151, 202–203n.154; collapse of, 3, 148, 178, 279; in contemporary Russia, 147, 168, 178, 181–184, 261; *derzhavnost* (great "powerness"), 92, 114, 115, 116, 148, 185; "dirigiste" practice, 32, 147; historic development and use of, 87, 150, 151, 155–160, 164, 184–187; mobilizing resources while retaining control, 161–162; pragmatism in power relations, 25, 29, 69–70; Putin's model of, 32, 84, 146, 421, 423, 433; soft vs. hard power, 421, 429, 439–440n.70. *See also* autocracy; rulership; totalitarianism state structure and processes, 83, 145, 239, 447–448; reformed under Yeltsin, 178–179, 181; regimes types and, 40–41; restructured in periods of decline, 163; structure of the nation-state, 41, 43–44; of the USSR, 52–53. *See also* centralized authority

state terror: under Ivan the Terrible, 135n.31; under Stalin, 86, 87, 101, 123, 233, 241, 254–255, 410

state transformation. *See* great state transformations

status quo, Russia tending to support, 18, 28, 123, 146

Stent, Angela, 23, 25, 27, 30, 393

steppe warfare, 64–65, 208, 464

Stettin-Trieste line, 232

Stolypin, Pyotr I.: annexation of the Balkan provinces and, 173–174, 200n.120; assassination of, 151, 174, 183; crisis and challenges facing, 164, 169, 170–171, 175–178, 183, 215; integrating foreign and domestic policy, 154, 163, 170–171; personality, 172–173; reforms of, 161, 163, 177, 183, 200–201n.124, 215

Strategic Arms Limitation Talks, 304; strategic arms treaty of 2002, 8

strategic distance, 22, 283, 286, 288; national security style and, 296–297, 307–310, 326–332

streltsy (tsarist musketeers), 24, 282

strong state model, 84, 116, 133n.9, 158–159, 160, 181–182; as a postabsolutist tradition, 182–187; autocracy the Russian path to greatness, 82–85, 92, 114, 115, 116, 148, 185, 398; Kozyrev affirming, 67, 202–203n.154. *See also* absolutist tradition

Sukhomlinov, V. A., 295

Suny, Ronald Grigor, 3, 21, 23, 24, 25, 28–29

superpower status of the Soviet Union, 75n.53, 95, 385, 394, 409, 411–414, 420; loss of, 66, 68, 101–103, 104, 148, 373; U. S. validating, 394; victory over fascism securing, 52, 121, 166, 178. *See also* great state transformations

supersonic aircraft, 236

surveillance, 118, 236–237

Suslov, Mikhail, 254

Sweden: Charles XII, 136, 150, 156, 166, 184; Swedish empire, 19, 208, 467, 470; wars of tsarist Russia against, 81, 92, 93, 94, 107, 108, 126, 281, 282, 286, 287, 397, 470–471

Swedish empire, 20

Szamuely, Tibor, 80, 93

Taishet, Siberia, 367

Tajik intervention, 326

Tajikistan, 259, 314

Talbott, Strobe, 121

tariffs, 477. *See also* trade

Tatar tribes, 92

Tators. *See* Mongols

taxation, 93

taxation system, 468

technological development, 5, 23, 245. *See also* military technology

technology transfer, 23, 223–224, 227, 264n.19, 483

territorial integrity, 18, 40, 71n.6, 381–382, 461, 462

terrorism: Beslan school massacre, 120, 146, 187n.3, 279, 315; war on, 5, 9, 27, 124, 146, 427, 445, 478, 491. *See also* 911 terrorist attacks

"thick" globalism, 446, 452, 489. *See also* globalization

Third Communist International of 1919, 217, 247, 408. *See also* Comintern (1919–1943)

Third Reich, 219, 228. *See also* Hitler, Adolph

Third Rome, 20, 36, 113, 148, 284, 320. *See also* Orthodox Christian Church

third world: decolonization of, 212, 235;
    USSR supporting national liberation
    movements in, 236
three-part nationalities policy, 238
Tilly, Charles, 92, 94
Time of Troubles, 19, 82, 215, 286, 466–469
Tito, Josip Broz, 231, 233, 239
Tolz, Vera, 61–62
totalitarianism, 38, 86, 158, 182, 284, 483;
    theory of, 197n.89, 275n.124, 406–407.
    See also Stalin, Joseph
trade, 219, 223, 458, 459; arms sales,
    458–459; with China, 374–375; increase
    under Putin, 458; multinational trade
    and institutions, 445; restrictions on,
    22, 24, 448, 477; through foreign
    traders during Imperial era, 467,
    468–469
trade routes, 93, 443, 460, 463, 465, 468
traditional Russian values, 4, 80–81, 115,
    162, 188n.11, 236; sacredness of the state
    and rulership (*see also* autocracy; state
    power), 80, 82–84. *See also* Slavophiles
Transcaucasian republics, 233
transformation. *See* future directions;
    great state transformations
transitory empire, 41
Trans-Korean Railroad project, 377–378
transnationalism, 487–488
transparant corporate governance, 490
transportation, 447
Trans-Siberian Railway, 288, 345, 377, 380,
    477
travel restrictions, 22, 226–227, 267n.47
Treaty of Goodneighborliness, Friendship
    and Cooperation, 6
Sino-Russian relations, 6
Treaty of Paris, 117, 127, 288
Treaty of San Stefano, 118
Treaty of Westphalia, 210
Treaty of Nerchinsk, 369
Trenin, Dmitri, 30, 132

Trotsky, Leon, 160, 220, 290, 405–406, 407,
    481
Trubetskoy, Nilolai, 110
tsarist Russia, 18, 44–45, 468; as a
    modernizing empire, 35, 44–45, 47–55;
    autocracy in, 82–83, 89, 115, 160, 331,
    476; cultural alienation in, 113–114,
    140n.101; destruction of (*see also*
    Bolshevik revolution), 85, 95;
    expansionism of, 100, 107–108, 471–473,
    475–476; foreign policy of, 18, 154–155;
    globalizing influences on, 469–473;
    periods of Europeanization, 397–399,
    401–402, 470, 471–473; permanent
    armies under, 24, 93, 468; rule based in
    Orthodox Church, 83, 462; the tsar
    sacralized as the embodied state, 80,
    82, 83–84; wars of, 92–95, 207. *See also*
    empire
Tukhashevsky, M. N., 282
Turkey, 19, 94, 175, 226
Turkic tribes, 92
Turkish war (1877–1878), 127, 477
Turkmenistan, 63–64
two2008 political succession, 10
tyranny. *See* totalitarianism

U-2 spy plane, shooting down of, 237, 306,
    307, 331–332
Ukraine, 230, 235, 240, 258, 454, 471; 2004
    color revolution in, 9, 32; current
    Russian policy towards, 10, 32, 422,
    425–426; elections of 2004 and 2006,
    315; left-bank, 207; need for Russian
    energy resources, 10; Orange Revolu-
    tion, 122, 184, 258, 426, 428; post-WW-I
    independence of, 217; Russian
    populations in, 256
Ukrainian Liberation Movement, 241
Ulam, Adam, 95, 118
Ulbricht, Walter, 232
UN. *See* United Nations (UN)

"unconsolidated autocracy," 131–132

unilateralism: of the U. S., 97, 327, 330, 347; of the USSR, 364

unipolar hegemony, 142n.126, 318, 473; UN Security Council as an alternative to, 319–320; the U. S. as sole hegemonic power, 5–6, 35, 104, 121, 142n.126, 261, 318

United Kingdom. *See* Great Britain

United Nations Security Council, 4, 327, 427, 459; as an alternative to U. S. hegemony, 28, 319–320

United Nations (UN), UNDP Human Indicators Report, 101–102

United Russian Party, 423

United States (U. S.), 9, 28; Afghan war involvement under Reagan, 488; Asian foreign policy, 258, 357, 385; cultural exports, 261; emergence as a world power, 212; Lend-Lease Act, 221; 911 terrorist attacks on, 6, 7, 8, 97, 146, 445; nuclear weapons program, 7, 413; penetrating Soviet airspace, 236–237, 306–307; post 911 Afghanistan conflict, 7, 99, 122, 258, 346; presidential election problems of 2004, 9; as the sole superpower (*see* unipolar hegemony). *See also* American popular culture; Iraq war; Sino-U. S. relations; unipolar hegemony

urban migration, 478

U. S. relations with the Russian Federation, 32, 98–99, 221–222, 279; advice and aid to Yeltsin, 4–6, 453; partnership against terrorism, 5, 9, 27, 124, 146, 427, 445, 478, 491; reduction in Russian focus on, 459; under Putin, 124–125, 146–147, 379

U. S.-Soviet relations: direct bilateral disengagement, 5–6, 10; energy issues and, 358; Lend-Lease assistance, 221. *See also* nuclear arms control

USSR (Union of Soviet Socialist Republics). *See* Soviet Union

Uvarov, S.S., 162

Uzbekistan, 63–64; authoritarian turn in, 32, 384; NATO ties with, 6; U. S. presence in, 123, 258, 259

Varangians, 460–461

Vasily III, 92

Vernadsky, George, 94, 110

Versailles Treaty, 56, 199n.105, 219, 407

Vietnam, 364

Viking traders, 460–461

Vladimir I

Vladivostok, 353, 354, 355; maritime zone, 369–370

Vladivostok-Khabarovsk corridor, 366

Voice of America, 237

Volkdeutsch, German minorities in Russia, 241

Voltaire, René, 157, 398

voucher privatization, 420, 439n.66, 453

vozhd (leader), 87

vulnerabilities and weaknesses, 20, 78, 92, 130–133, 169, 230, 243; affecting national identity, 36, 113–114, 281–282, 382; aggressive foreign policies and, 24, 69, 95, 107, 118–119, 240, 295; Alexander II's policies related to, 101; cautious intentions in foreign policy and, 56; of civil structures, 293; contemporary Russia and, 101–105, 116–117, 119–130, 280; globalization and, 448–449, 450; as opportunities, 21; penetration of Soviet airspace during the Cold War, 236–237; Soviet policies affected by, 21–22, 101, 106, 118–119, 127–128; technological, 295, 333; tsarist era policies related to, 100, 106–108, 113–115, 117–118, 126–127. *See also* porous frontiers

Vyshinsky, Andrei, 23, 249

Wallander, Celeste A., 24, 25, 27, 31, 443; on future directions in Russian policy, 31

Waltz, Kenneth, 36, 37

war, 92–96, 104, 105, 130; affecting identity and economy, 81, 92–99, 110, 113, 130–131; globalization and, 105; preemptive war, 35; Russian civil war (*see* civil war of 1918–1922). *See also* Afghan war; Chechen war; Cold War; Crimean War; Napoleonic wars; World War I; World War II

war communism, 85, 215

warm-water ports, 20, 281–282

war on terror, 5, 9, 27, 124, 146, 427, 445, 478, 491

Warsaw Pact, 146, 167, 177, 231, 250; former members of, 313, 314, 420, 431–432; members of, 301, 412, 413; opening to Western influences, 412–413

waterways and warm-water ports, 20, 281–282

weaknesses. *See* vulnerabilities

weapons of mass destruction (WMD), 427, 430. *See also* nuclear arms

weapons technology and production, 207, 219. *See also* nuclear arms

Wendt, Alexander, 38

western border, 100, 166, 227–228, 233, 248, 295; as a Mitteleuropa, 209; historic permeability of, 81, 229, 232, 258, 326

Western intelligence agencies, 9

Westernizers, 111, 112, 160, 378, 474. *See also* Atlanticists and *zapadniki*

Western powers' relationship with Russia, 7, 28, 247; autocratic policies causing alienation, 9; failed efforts to ally, 123–125, 128; partnership possibilities, 6, 111; and post-Soviet space, 121–122; Russian ambivalence toward the West (*see also* Europe and Russian identity), 25, 393; Soviet communist agenda alienating the West, 250, 251–252; Soviet rhetoric increasing isolation, 246–247, 249–250; Western advisors post-Soviet era, 453. *See also* Europe-Russian relations; North American Treaty Alliance (NATO); parity with the West; U. S. relations with the Russian Federation

West European Union, 300

White governments, 215

White Russians, 61, 481, 482

William II, 287. *See also* Germany

Wilson, Woodrow, 48

Winter War, 243

Witte, Sergei Iu, Count, 151–152, 158, 160, 163, 174, 187, 215, 288, 363; Portsmouth Treaty, 289–290

World Bank, 10, 261, 320, 446

world communism, 56, 227, 290; centralized control of a goal of the USSR, 217, 228, 236, 250, 251–252; and the culture of the USSR, 26; deemed necessary for Soviet survival, 290–291, 481; Marxist revisionism challenging Soviet hegemony, 234, 252. *See also* Comintern (1919–1943)

world oil price increases of 2004–2006, 9–10, 346, 457

World Trade Center, 445; 911 terrorist attack on, 6, 7, 8, 97, 146, 445

World Trade Organization (WTO), 8, 449; China supporting Russia's membership, 348; Japan supporting Russia's membership, 368; Russia's desire for entry into, 8, 97, 225, 386, 497n.79

World War I, 207, 209, 210, 283, 286, 289, 291–296, 297, 305, 335n.6; Brest-Litovsk treaty, 216–217, 291, 293, 407, 481; disarray of the *ancien régime* following, 85, 95, 106, 164; European alliance system and, 403; Mobilization

World War I (*Continued*)
Schedule 19, 295–296; question of whether
    Russia was a nation-state during,
    45–47; Russian mobilization in,
    292–295; victory of Central Powers,
    293
World War II, 18, 22, 216, 217, 219, 229,
    267n.54, 281, 304; Russia as part of the
    Allied Forces, 283, 484; sixtieth
    anniversary commemoration, 432;
    Soviet role in, 408–409
WTO. *See* World Trade Organization
    (WTO)

Xinjiang, Khrushchev's pullback from, 234
Xinjiang Province, 261

Yaroslav the Wise, 463
Yastrzhembsky, Sergei, 432

Yeltsin, Boris, 4–6, 67, 175; Asian foreign
    policy, 355; foreign policy constrained
    by domestic crisis, 179–181; liquidating
    autocratic structures, 84; military
    and strategic policies, 96–97;
    pro-globalization strategy, 452–455;
    "shock therapy" reforms under, 91, 259,
    453, 455–457, 456; U. S.-Russian relations
    under, 347, 419. *See also* Kozyrev,
    Andrei; post-Soviet transition
Yugoslav-Soviet break, 233
Yushchenko, Viktor, 184

Zakayev, Akhmed, 426
zakonnost, rule of law, 245
zapadniki. See Westernizers
Zedong (Mao). *See* Mao Zedong
"zones of foreign intervention and
    occupation," 22